Essentials of
Psychological Testing

Essentials of Psychological Testing

Fifth Edition

Lee J. Cronbach
Stanford University

HarperCollins*Publishers*

Sponsoring Editor: Laura Pearson
Project Editor: Thomas R. Farrell
Design and Cover Coordinator: Heather A. Ziegler
Cover Design: Delgado Design, Inc.
Production: Willie Lane

ESSENTIALS OF PSYCHOLOGICAL TESTING, Fifth Edition

Library of Congress Cataloging-in-Publication Data
Cronbach, Lee J. (Lee Joseph), (date)–
    Essentials of psychological testing / Lee J. Cronbach. — 5th ed.
        p.   cm.
    ISBN 0-06-041418-9
    1. Psychological tests.   I. Title.
BF173.C76   1990
150′.28′7—dc20   89-27772
                                                            CIP

97 98   9 8

Contents

List of Figures

List of Tables

Preface

This book is about current and emerging practices, some of them radically new. But it is also a book about a mature discipline, one whose basic principles have stood firm under the pressures of new social demands and the emergence of new technology.

After 40 years in print this book is, I believe, the oldest psychology textbook that is still being kept up to date. To be sure, a revision of Guilford's *Fundamental Statistics for Psychology and Education* (1942; sixth edition, with Fruchter, 1977) could recapture the crown any day it comes along. Good company, as is the Anastasi-Foley *Differential Psychology* (1937; last revised 1958), still found in *Books in Print*.

My aim in teaching, now as it was 40 years ago, has been to communicate general concepts and principles of interpretation and criticism that can apply to most psychological assessment—including the tests and suggested meanings *that will appear long after the course is over*. Beyond that, I want to prepare students to evaluate the broad views about human affairs that are continually being derived, logically and illogically, from test data—views about race differences, for example, or a suspected decline in educational standards.

When I started to teach "Mental Measurements" regularly in 1946, I was distressed by the textbooks available. Earlier there had been reflective texts on mental testing, notably one by Frank N. Freeman (one of my teachers at Chicago), but these were left behind by the emergence of the Wechsler-Bellevue, wartime experiences in personnel testing and in evaluation of neuropsychiatric casualties, and the appearance of many clinical tests (including MMPI) and of multiple-aptitude batteries. Most texts of those days were primarily descriptions of one test after another— number of minutes allowed per section, number and sources of cases in the norm group, encyclopedic facts on reliability and (sometimes) external correlates. Having stripped such forgettable detail from my text (save as needed to make examples concrete), I titled the book *Essentials*. I would have more pointedly expressed my aim with the title *How to Think About Psychological Tests and Test Findings*. That is still my concern.

Over time, the tone of *Essentials* has changed somewhat, pursuing in increasing depth such central issues as "test bias" and the limitations of profile interpretation. But, mindful of the student for whom the book is a first introduction, I subordinate subtleties. I expect readers to get the big picture if they choose merely to scan some page that goes deeper into a subtopic than they would wish.

Testing was once taught as a technology of assessing individuals and programs. As long ago as 1960 attention began to shift toward policy and ethics. Each successive edition of this book has given more attention to conflicts among the rights, needs, and purposes of tester and tested. The 1984 edition stressed social justice as the proper aim of test use, and this edition extends that discussion. Surely few contemporary policymakers notice books like this, but the policymakers of the future are sitting in our classes, and the courses should prepare them to see many angles in each slogan-driven policy dispute that arises in the future.

The big ideas of the 1984 edition remain here, with little change. The 1984 edition took advantage of an intensive study of policy issues by the National Research Council's Committee on Testing, and of the deliberations of the committee revising the *Testing standards*. (I was a member of the first committee and a consultant to the second.) The views those reports advanced have now been extended by a study of test user qualifications, by a code of fair testing practice, and by guidelines for computer-based test interpretations.

The old issues continue to take new twists, of course. This edition looks at the following controversial matters, among others: the Golden Rule, the Lake Wobegon effect, the Department of Education "wall charts," and a race-conscious selection rule proposed by the U.S. Employment Service (USES). New principles are not needed to think about the current controversies; rather, these are occasions to apply thinking that matured in the previous decade.

Test descriptions in this book are vehicles for large ideas, not themselves the primary content. It is ironic, therefore, that need to update descriptions is what motivated me to revise the 1984 edition for a 1990 copyright (a 6-year cycle, compared with an average interval of 12 years previously). I did not want to leave instructors with the burden of describing the prominent, but much-changed Stanford-Binet of 1986 (or of conveying specifics of the 1985 *Testing standards*). After I started revising, much else happened, hence this edition covers much that is new in the testing field.

The Test of Mechanical Comprehension now has a computer-adaptive version (which makes it even more suitable as a basic example for Part One). The Strong Interest Blank has gone through a metamorphosis. The revisers made a fresh start with Strong's methodology, and for interpretative purposes meshed the many new keys with Campbell's and Holland's conceptualizations of interests. The USES, pressed to extend minority opportunity and to recognize Jack Hunter's recommendations on validity generalization, has proposed radically altered rules for translating its aptitude profiles into decisions. My 1984 edition described the Kaufmans' then-new ability test, but evaluation was superficial because the technical manual became available only while the book was in production. Now I take into account the Kaufmans' research and that reported by others.

The computer is changing most aspects of testing, bringing benefits and costs. Automation of test administration and interpretation is gaining ground, although it tends to reduce interaction between assessor and examinee—with consequent impoverishment of information on both sides. Supplying computer-generated "self-interpreting" reports to clients seems likely to invite misunderstanding, and to encourage overreliance on the test as authority. Persons not qualified as test interpreters are writing software for start-up companies in the field; the risks are obvious. On the positive side, if the computer is kept in an adjunct role it reduces testing costs, and its reports stimulate thought in the professional interpreter. Adaptive testing is paying off, and we are beginning to see new test tasks, resembling video arcade displays, which have obvious potential. The computer, then, comes in for extensive discussion in every section of this book.

"Dynamic assessment" is developing along many lines. One of several approaches that link continuing assessment closely with instruction, it challenges psychometric traditions in order to provide more help for individuals in difficulty.

Ideas about personality appraisal are changing notably. Twenty years ago, psychologists measuring personality traits were thrown onto the defensive by Mischel's famous book and other attacks on the trait concept. That controversy has dropped to a murmur. Mischel acknowledges that there is appreciable stability and consistency in a person's style of behavior. And trait theorists now recognize more explicitly that traits do not shape actions without regard to the situation. Clinicians who for a time refused to consider any evidence except for overt "behaviors" now seek information on the client's feelings and self-concept, as well as on acts. Today's balanced outlook is producing better theory and better experimentation.

Simultaneously, personnel testers are returning enthusiastically to development *(and validation)* of personality inventories for employees. As always, the published literature is mostly a mishmash of small and noncumulative studies, with isolated positive and negative results. Much more substantial studies, with large samples and careful collection of criteria, are appearing in current technical reports, especially from the Army's mammoth Project A. The optimism of the latest reports may not persist; but self-reports on personality *are* coming back into personnel decisions.

Movement on other fronts continues. I have added to the previous edition's treatment of cognitive psychology, validity generalization, cross-validation, item response theory and tailored testing, learning disability, and several other topics.

In revising, I of course took the opportunity to clarify here and there, to tighten the organization, and to remove whatever errors my friends and I have caught. I paid attention also to book reviewers. They generally treated the content respectfully, but on one matter of style several reviewers were so forcefully negative that I have bowed to them. In the 1984 edition I eliminated as many formulas as possible. Students often shy off from algebra, and I believe that the concepts they need can be explained without formulas. In deference to the reviews, quite a few formulas are offered this time, though not enough to make this a book on mathematical psychometrics, which was never its mission. Still, I try to write so that even students who are slow readers of algebra will understand what the formula accomplishes.

As usual, many informed persons have helped me, and I thank them. In particular, I thank the following reviewers: Winifred Arthur, Texas A&M University; Donald Bubenzer, Kansas State University; John Cornell, Baylor University; Joseph Gorczynski, Trenton State University; John Poggio, University of Kansas; Peter J. Rowe, College of Charleston; Samuel Seaman, Baylor University; and Allen Shue, California State University, Hayward. I also offer special thanks to those who went beyond my requests and suggested further material—in particular, Susan Barnes, David Bartram, Wayne Camara, Marvin Dunnette, Kevin Moreland, Jerry Murphy, Robert Most, Gary Robertson, Richard Snow, and Alexandra Wigdor.

LEE J. CRONBACH

Notes to Students

A few features designed to assist students (and other users) require comment.

Superquestions.   The five questions at the start of each chapter have several purposes. They give an initial impression of the content to come, pointing out some main concerns of the chapter. They suggest connections to be made during reading across the subdivisions of the chapter. Some readers will want to jot down, as they proceed, points to consider in answering this or that question. And, obviously, a student would be wise to return to the questions after reaching the end of the chapter. The superquestions are appropriate for essay examinations; a reader who can write sensible, meaty paragraphs on one of them must have a grasp of that main theme. I emphasize, however, that the superquestions do not exhaust the significant ideas of any chapter.

Orientation.   It is a good idea to examine a chapter's Table of Contents before starting to read its text. The titles of the subdivisions seen all together indicate how ideas progress; and the number of pages in a section usually hints at its complexity and importance.

That is not always a good basis for distinguishing big ideas from small ones, however. Sometimes a longish section merely presents an example not deserving close study, and sometimes a brief section is vital. Therefore, paragraphs headed *Orientation* appear in most chapters. These paragraphs suggest what is most worth studying in the chapter, and what is presented chiefly by way of illustration or as material for future reference. Obviously your interests, or the emphasis in your training program, may cause you to depart from my suggestions.

Discussion questions. A second kind of question is scattered through each chapter. Typically, these are invitations to think realistically about problems of test developers and users of tests. Usually, several principles and values can be brought to bear on a question. To a question about testing practice or decisions based on tests, the best answer will usually be "Yes and no" (or the like), followed by remarks about circumstances that affect the decision. Not many questions have a single "right" answer that applies everywhere. That is the case with questions that arise in practice.

Abbreviations.   Test titles are long, and some tests are referred to often. Therefore, initials are much used in talking about tests. Abbreviations are listed in Appendix B; but to provide even quicker retrieval a footnote at the start of each chapter lists abbreviations appearing in it. Certain exceptions help to keep the lists short. I do not list an abbreviation introduced in a subsection of the chapter and used only in the two or three next pages, nor do I list common statistical abbreviations (s.d. for standard deviation and r for correlation).

Glossary and index.   Following the appendices is a glossary that reviews briefly the meaning of most of the technical terms used in the text. These short and simple statements are less formal than a dictionary definition, but they should be easy to hold in mind.

The text discussion of a term is usually more complete, and to locate the discussion you should turn to the Subject Index. Often, the discussion is divided, appearing at two or more places. This reflects the policy by which this book is organized. Most topics are treated in more than one place. That permits a comparatively simple introduction, followed at a later point by greater detail or by a presentation that ties the idea to a new context. Such division of material should help in learning, because it provides for review of ideas presented early.

PART
One

BASIC CONCEPTS

Chapter
1

Who Uses Tests?
And for What Purposes?

1A. "Testing of abilities has always been intended as an impartial way to perform a political function." Explain.

1B. Test production is largely centralized nowadays. What are the good and bad consequences of centralization?

1C. What information about a test is found in a catalog? Where can more complete information by obtained?

1D. An inadequately qualified tester may misuse a test. Whose responsibility is it to make that less likely?

1E. Illustrate each of these uses of tests: classification; promoting self-understanding; program evaluation; scientific inquiry.

Assessment of personal characteristics plays a large role in modern life, shaping individuals' schooling, careers, and treatment by institutions and caregivers. Tests make many kinds of assessment more dependable. They can survey a student body to identify the talented and those who should have special help. They can check out the effectiveness of social programs and generate hints regarding better policies. In guidance and clinical work, tests evaluate each person's assets and needs.

Almost never should a test score by itself determine what will be done by or for the person. In examining an adult, for example, the clinical psychologist is likely to consider—alongside the test scores—the past and present family history, the educational and employment history, the medical record, feelings expressed in an interview, and opinions elicited from the person's acquaintances, as well as the resources for help that the community can offer.

Tests have been much criticized because misconceptions and misapplications have led to unfortunate decisions. Professional leaders have bad ideas as well as good ones. Some of today's "best" ideas will surely be rejected by our successors. It is this corrective process that sets testing apart from other sources of information about persons and institutions. *Tests are almost unique in being reproducible and explicit.* Because the validity of interpretations and decision rules can be checked out, information from tests is more likely to be steadily improved than is appraisal of other kinds.

In this book, the concept of "test" encompasses Socratic questioning of a student, use of an apparatus in which a pigeon obtains a grain of rice by pecking at the brighter of two light spots, and a round-robin chess tournament. The book will concentrate, however, on tasks designed to be presented in the same way to many persons in many places. These "standardized" tests are important in themselves, and they are especially suitable for textbook treatment because research on them accumulates. Most of the concepts used to analyze these tests apply also to unstandardized tests.

One main topic is ability tests. The book also takes up systematic observation of behavior, questions about beliefs and feelings, and probes that search out motives of which the examinee may be unaware.

Test interpretation will receive more attention here than test construction, and particular tests will be described primarily as illustrations. The book will discuss the kinds of tests used in schools, treatment centers, industry, and military settings.

Use of tests in research will also be considered. How does a certain new drug affect mood and alertness? How does the makeup of a group affect its teamwork? At what age is a child able to "see things through the eyes of another person"? In a developing country, how do new attitudes about work styles and social institutions spread? Each such inquiry requires its own form of test.

TESTING AND SOCIAL POLICY

I shall discuss public policy and public debates, as well as test technique and scientific findings. Month after month, disputes about tests and test results make headlines. You may recall some of the controversies: Does compensatory education work? Do services that coach for the Law School Admission Test give an unfair advantage to applicants who can afford time and money for the coaching? Can a medical school properly put an applicant of minority origin ahead of a nonminority applicant with a higher test score? Although specific disputes fade into history, the basic conflicts recur. Recent debates have echoed others dating back to the beginnings of modern testing (Cronbach, 1975; Haney, 1984). The same misunderstandings about tests and the same value conflicts surface again and again.

There are two sides to most of the issues. For example, many critics oppose using tests to judge whether a child is "retarded." The truth is that some children have profited from being placed in a class for the "educable mentally retarded" (EMR)[1] and some have not. At times unsound testing or bad interpretations of tests have assigned children to the retarded category who did not belong there. On the other hand, *the majority* of children whose failure in schoolwork leads teachers to suspect retardation are saved from the EMR class by the positive evidence of the psychological examination (Lambert, in Glaser & Bond, 1981).

Public controversy deals in stereotypes, never in subtleties. Although it is easy for Luddites to smash up a device, to improve a system requires calm study. So, following the advice of a professional study committee, the same California legislature that voted to outlaw group mental testing by local districts instituted a new, carefully safeguarded, statewide test of mental ability for first-graders, these data being needed as a baseline in evaluations of reading instruction that the legislature desired. On the advice of the same committee, a statewide mental test in Grades 6 and 10 that had no proper function was canceled. Sound policy is not *for* tests or *against* tests; what matters is how tests are used. Unfortunately, the public is most often exposed to angry clamor from extremists who either see no good in any test or see no evil.

Reformers' Hopes for Tests

"Testing has been politicized in recent years," some professionals complain. They can point to biased treatment of testing issues, even in respected newspapers (Herrnstein, 1982). Although the bias of journalists is objectionable, the passionate interest of citizens is not. Testing of abilities has always been *intended* as an impartial way to perform a political

---

[1]On abbreviations, see "Notes to Students" (p. xxv).

function—that of determining who gets what. Some positions in society inevitably carry more responsibility and influence than others; ambitious individuals seek those posts, and each subcommunity with a special interest seeks to increase its share.

Power and privilege, responsibility and reward are allocated by formal and informal processes. Broadly speaking, it is through connections or through competence that individuals move into rewarding roles. Inheritance of a family firm, an uncle's influence at city hall, the acquaintances a poor youth makes at a rich kids' university—these are forms of advancement-through-connections. Coming up with a slogan that captures customers, handling a football well enough to attract professional scouts, listening carefully enough to citizens that one's next campaign speech addresses their concerns—*that* is moving ahead through competence. A society can give great scope to connections or little. Shifting that balance is the aim of many a political movement.

Those who want to match responsibility to competence often advocate testing as a superior way to distribute opportunities. Proposing reforms for education in Virginia, Thomas Jefferson said that the state should start everyone off with a few years of education close to home. Then a traveling examiner should choose, each year, "the boy of best genius"; if his parents were poor, he would be sent forward to a regional grammar school at state expense.[2] After his 2 years there, another test would select who should continue. Ultimately half of these would be subsidized to study at college, the less excellent being left to find posts (very likely as schoolmasters). Since children of wealthier parents could attend these same schools at their own expense, Jefferson was not erasing privilege. But his intent was to bring forward a "natural aristocracy" of virtue and talent, to displace a "tinsel aristocracy" founded on wealth and birth (quoted from a letter to John Adams, October 28, 1813). In this spirit, civil service systems introduced after 1830 were intended to place public business in the hands of qualified workers rather than of applicants with powerful patrons. (The history of this kind of testing can be traced back to at least 1000 B.C., in China.)

Perhaps the high point among meritocratic proposals was one from John Stuart Mill. Although Mill wanted to extend voting rights from property owners to all ranks of British society, he placed a premium on competence. The first necessity, as he saw it, was universal education. For the sake of what we would now call pluralism, Mill wanted numer-

---

[2]The gender here is Jefferson's. In the remainder of this book, I adopt a convention that will annoy some readers until they come to appreciate its virtues. Such gender-equalizing devices as "he or she" and speaking only in plurals are awkward, and in psychology they can blur meanings. Therefore, I arbitrarily shall use female nouns and pronouns when referring to a tester or investigator (other than an identified male). Except where special emphasis on both sexes is required or where I identify a female by name, I assign males to all other roles—test taker, a person who engages the tester's services, and so forth. At times I change pronouns within a quotation to conform to the style.

ous private local schools rather than a state system. State funds would help poor parents pay for tuition, however. Achievement tests should be given annually to make certain that every child was being properly schooled; if the child failed the test, the parent (!) would be fined (Mill, 1859/1977, vol. 20, pp. 302ff.). In elections, every adult male was to have one vote; but, to qualify, he would have to pass a test of reading, writing, and arithmetic. Mill also favored giving extra votes to those whose opinions deserved greater weight, so he proposed giving the banker more votes than the tradesman. For equity, he proposed to offer a harder, optional test by which the tradesman might prove himself the mental equal of the banker and gain a banker's number of votes (Mill, 1859/1977, vol. 19, pp. 323ff.).

Tests have helped to extend educational opportunity. The prestigious eastern U.S. colleges had little need for entrance examinations in the days when they drew their applicants mostly from nearby academies. Knowing the curricula and standards of those schools, the colleges could judge the credentials supplied by the academies. When in the 1920s they sought applicants from the entire nation, the colleges found transcripts from distant high schools hard to interpret. Tests in school subjects, they felt, would be a poor basis for comparing students when course content differed from school to school. To permit fairer comparisons, they established the Scholastic Aptitude Test.

Ability pretests came into the lower schools for a similar reason. Prior to 1900 the schools were Procrustean. Students kept up with their class or repeated the grade; those with poor records left school early. Once the schools accepted the challenge of providing 12 years of education to as many youngsters as possible and of keeping children with classmates of their own age, it became necessary to propose a level and pace of instruction to fit each student. Ability grouping, assignment of some children to "special" education, and allocation of high school students into precollege, commercial, and technical courses were all part of this attempt. Tests were a favored basis for such decisions because they seemed blind to sex, to color, and to family origins. John Gardner's comment (1961, p. 48) recaptures some of the thinking of those times:

> An acquaintance of mine who recently visited a provincial school in France reported, "The teacher seemed to find it impossible to separate his judgment of a pupil's intelligence from his judgment of the pupil's cleanliness, good manners, neatness of dress and precision of speech. Needless to say, his students from the upper and upper middle social classes excelled in these qualities." Before the rise of objective tests American teachers were susceptible—at least in some degree—to the same social distortion of judgment. Against this background, modern methods of mental measurement hit the educational system like a fresh breeze. The tests couldn't see whether the youngster was in rags or in tweeds, and they couldn't hear the accents of the slum. The tests revealed intellectual gifts at every level of the population.

Competence is the key to productivity. Tests for workers pay their way by bringing greater skills and greater talent into a firm, and by helping to fit the assignment to the employee. Tests in the military reduce costs by shortening training time, reducing failures, and making sure that those who complete training can do the job.

Employers, the armed services, schools, and mental hospitals all employ tests to keep institutions running smoothly. But do not be misled by the fact that the largest sales of tests are for such essentially conservative, stabilizing purposes. Tests also serve—indeed, are sometimes of great value to—the reformer. The pioneering tests of Galton, a hundred years ago, advanced the idea that one's place should depend on competence and not on family position. The same hope animates today's pioneers who devise educational activities for children who do not prosper under the usual instruction (Scarr, in Glaser & Bond, 1981). Tests call administrators' attention to schools where children from impoverished homes do less well than similar children elsewhere. When a school's approach works, tests can provide convincing evidence of the achievement and can encourage other schools to adopt similar practices. A private practice is not "an institution," but tests pay off there also—by contributing to the client's insight, by directing the professional's effort, and by assessing progress.

Over and over, evidence from tests has challenged familiar practices and ideas. The very first use of behavioral measures to study character (see p. 618) found that traditional "character-building" programs did not immunize youngsters against temptation to cheat and steal. By this standard, both the Boy Scout organization and the Sunday school failed. A little later, the origins of hostility, distrust, and bigotry were studied. It turned out that many of the bigots were prosperous citizens, respected and chosen for responsibility in social organizations. The tests disclosed inner fears and feelings of inadequacy in many persons whom acquaintances thought of as secure and trustworthy adults (Adorno et al., 1950).

Critics' Discontents

Responsibility and opportunity are not distributed as critics of society would wish. Evaluating the criticisms fits properly into later chapters, but here I note three main complaints.

Matching opportunity to competence, some say, is exaggerated into winner-take-all competition. Everyone agrees that persons who are assigned responsibilities should be competent to carry them. Above the level of adequacy, however, should small differences in apparent competence determine who gets the opportunity?

Second, it is said that evidence of competence or adjustment collected at one age is allowed to determine the person's remote future. How heavily should one's past performance determine future prospects?

Third, there is discontent that youngsters born into favorable circumstances tend to do better in the educational system and to reach higher-level occupations. They also score higher on ability tests. One humanist (Barzun, 1959, p. 142) explained the connection this way:

> There is no mystery about it: the child who is familiar with books, ideas, conversation—the ways and means of the intellectual life—before he begins school, indeed, before he begins consciously to think, has a marked advantage. He is at home in the House of Intellect just as the stableboy is at home among horses, or the child of actors on the stage.

If less educated parents or those from a certain subculture are not equipping the child with the competence the school builds on, then matching opportunity to competence may be perpetuating a social hierarchy. And yet: Should evidence of competence be discounted if the performer was given advantages by his family?

A society must sort. Specialized roles have to be filled. So individuals *should* follow somewhat different paths in order to accumulate training and experience relevant to this or that role. But for which roles should sorting replace open access? At what ages should selection and self-selection into lines of concentration (and levels of intellectual demand) take place? What evidence about individuals should enter these routing decisions? And, once the evidence is in hand, what policies should govern the sorting?

No policy applying to all opportunities can be found. Even with regard to a single specialty, there is bound to be disagreement. Among those shaping policy for admission to pediatrics, for example, some will emphasize scientific competence; others will give priority to skill in developing positive emotional relationships.

Each generation has to think afresh about basic principles—about the meaning of "equal opportunity," for example. Members of the new generation may differ from their elders because fresh knowledge has emerged or priorities have shifted. To understand and evaluate old practices and new proposals, we will have to give some attention to legal decisions about testing practice, to the laws that impose tests on schools and students in the name of "accountability," and even to moth-eaten arguments about the inheritance of abilities (Glaser & Bond, 1981; Heller et al., 1982).

Beyond the three complaints listed a few paragraphs back, there is another type of discontent. Predicting a person's fate is seen to be a less worthy accomplishment than helping the person to a better fate. Tests sometimes do help in career guidance, for example, or in guiding day-to-day microadjustment of speech therapy. But the use of tests to shape educational or clinical services for a particular person on a particular day is much less advanced than their use for prediction and after-the-fact evaluation (Linn, 1989a, p. 9).

A reader might reasonably ask about my biases. I am critical of many practices in testing; on the other hand, I could not write this book if I opposed testing. Individuals ought to develop understanding of themselves, and institutions have to reach decisions; tests, I think, can help. So I shall be pointing out how suitable tests can be helpful and warning against questionable practices.

One further preliminary remark: The words "bias" and "fairness" score points in debate, but make poor terms for scholarly analysis. "Bias" can refer to a deliberate effort to harm an individual or group, to a completely honest misinterpretation, or to a sound interpretation that the speaker dislikes. The meaning of "fairness" changes from year to year in legal circles, and in reviewing testing practice even the Supreme Court occasionally splits down the middle. I shall avoid the words "fairness" and "bias" where I can, but I take up the pertinent research and value questions in connection with specific uses and interpretations.

1. *What do these terms mean to you?*
   a. *equality among citizens*
   b. *equality of opportunity*
   c. *elitism*
   d. *merit system*
2. *Some courts have screened prospective jurors by testing their verbal comprehension and reasoning. What can be said for and against such a procedure?*
3. *The licensing examination for drivers is applied mechanically without taking facts about the person's background and past opportunities into account. Is it proper to be so "objective" when the applicant's quality of life and earning power are at stake?*
4. *It is conceivable that by the year 2040 women, blacks, and other identifiable groups in the United States will have the same range of education and occupational responsibility as any other group and will have wage rates to match. Assume that the sorting processes (not necessarily based on "tests") are appropriate to the various responsibilities. What objections to that society would be likely to come from an egalitarian?*

HOW THE TESTING ENTERPRISE HAS EVOLVED

Testing had informal, even casual beginnings. A psychologist or physician wanted to observe some type of motor, intellectual, or emotional response and set up a situation that gave a good opportunity for observation. As she mentioned her findings to others, they copied the technique in their own clinics and laboratories. Soon there was a small market for equipment (tachistoscopes for studying flash perception, formboards for testing perception and reasoning, etc.). Before and after 1900 a few books were written, each describing one investigator's procedures.

The 1920s saw the publication of tests in editions of hundreds of thousands of copies. This bespoke the enthusiasm for testing in schools that followed the publicity given to mass testing of recruits in World War I. To psychologists of those days, the great advantage of published tests was the norms they provided. Until norms were available, the clinician's basis for identifying especially strong and weak performance was limited to her own experience. The school administrator likewise found it advantageous to give a test that other school systems were using; then the local averages could be compared with experience elsewhere (D. Resnick, in Wigdor & Garner, vol. 2, 1982).

Independent Test Authorship   Test publishing was publishing and nothing more in those days. After a psychologist had prepared a test, copies were printed for general sale, perhaps through a firm selling apparatus to psychology laboratories. As the demand for tests grew, some textbook publishers began to handle tests, and some firms specializing in school tests or industrial tests were established. Until about 1945, the typical test was developed by an author or team of authors who completed the test and offered it to the publisher. The publisher assisted in the final stages of research and in editing the test manual, but the author had the main responsibility for designing the test, preparing items, and suggesting how to interpret results.

Testing was largely decentralized. Every institution—college, business, clinic, or whatever—planned and administered its own program. Each school system was free to adopt tests or not and to choose the ones used. Counseling agencies purchased different tests, and sometimes each psychologist within the agency chose the tests she preferred. This decentralization encouraged publication of a great variety of tests. With published tests available, the industrial psychologist no longer thought it necessary to make up new tests for her own factory. Even a great national agency such as the Veterans Administration relies on published tests in its clinical and counseling services.

Centralized Test Development   Centralization began slowly. Specialists at the state university might develop an "every-pupil" test to be given in the lower grades throughout the state, so that local officials could compare the local score range with that of other schools teaching much the same curriculum. In the 1920s a national association of colleges commissioned L. L. Thurstone to test linguistic and quantitative aptitudes of high school seniors. The aim was guidance rather than selection; a secondary use was to tell college officials and faculties how student intake varied from college to college. Likewise, the College Board introduced its Scholastic Aptitude Test. To assist employers, the U.S. Employment Service developed entry tests for many occupations.

A wave of expansion occurred after 1945—in clinical psychology, in vocational guidance, in selection for schools and jobs, and ultimately in policy-oriented surveys. Centralization proceeded apace. The Educational Testing Service, formed in 1948, became a facility for developing tests for college admission, for testing of student accomplishment at all levels, and for policy research—for example, research on the effect of "Sesame Street" on children's development. Commercial publishers of tests merged, and some became subsidiaries of giant corporations (Holmen & Docter, 1972). Testing programs were more often centralized; nowadays we have some industry-wide personnel testing, for example, and statewide tests for high school graduation.

Development of technically refined tests requires concentrated effort and large resources, especially when a test must be prepared for just one season of use. The Law School Admission Test, for example, must be given several times per year to accommodate applicants, and there must be a new form for each testing. The effort is enormous: item writing; tryout of items and review of the resulting data; assembly, printing, delivery, and administration of the final test; scoring; reporting of scores to those tested and to the schools of their choice; plus follow-up research to profit from the year's experience.

For popular types of tests, the market is large and competitive. The publisher of an established test fights to keep it prominent and to dominate the auxiliary market for scoring services; the sponsors of a new test or a competing service must make a major effort to break in. The increasingly numerous software packages that permit a user to administer, score, or interpret a test on her own microcomputer have raised competition to a higher power.

"Test publishers" evolved into test developers. A developer's staff of professionals identifies a kind of instrument that can serve a client agency or be marketed more broadly, designs and constructs the instrument (perhaps with help from teachers, clinicians, or other experts), carries out research before and after releasing the test, and organizes a scoring-and-reporting service. Other staff members advertise the test and arrange seminars to train interpreters. Development of software for psychologists' microcomputers has emerged as a separate craft.

Centralized testing brings benefits. Qualified staffs produce steady technical improvement. A central organization can enlist qualified subject-matter consultants. A large data-processing facility provides prompt and extensive score reports and permits elaborate, instructive analyses of data. Information accumulating in the central file of a developer provides an increasingly rich base for interpretation and for making next year's test comparable to earlier editions.

Centralization is an enemy of diversity. Some tests become prominent while worthy competitors go out of print. Large firms are understandably reluctant to invest in a test that will have a small market, and a small firm cannot afford to develop an extensive research base. The surest way to find a large market is to bring out a test that resembles the popular ones. An industry with a large investment cannot move far ahead

of its customers. Only if the next generation of test purchasers appreci-
ates the possibilities in uncommon types of tests will someone be enterprising enough to keep them available.

Along with centralization of test production has come an increasing
influence of central authorities on test use. Some tests are imposed on
schools to obtain information for state or national planners and perhaps
to press schools to focus on curriculum areas or types of students that
concern the central authority. The National Collegiate Athletic Association, in the late 1980s, has imposed on member colleges a uniform eligibility rule that factors in scores from the SAT (and similar tests). The
tests were not intended for such use and are only tangentially relevant.
Charged with enforcing civil rights laws, the Equal Employment Opportunity Commission has filed complaints against many employers, charg-
ing bias in selection. As one consequence, fewer employers test nowadays than did in the 1970s. There is lively debate about whether the
tests imposed on schools are elbowing worthwhile topics out of the instruction, and whether the reliance on less-controlled information in
place of tests for hiring is holding back productivity.

Computerized Testing   The nature of tests and testing is changing rapidly
as new possibilities of the computer are developed. It is now possible
for the computer to give complicated tests and to score responses as they
are made. Moments after the test ends, a report can be printed out for
the test taker or for the tester's file. The computer may supplement the
scores with a verbal interpretation that is similar to what a psychologist
would write after viewing the same record. The computer's precision
makes it a major resource for laboratory studies of memory, perception,
and brain functioning, and these measurements are beginning to spill
over into clinical examinations. For checking on effects of glaucoma, for
example, there is now an automated psychophysical test that maps pe-
ripheral vision.

With auxiliary equipment, the computer can present lifelike tasks of
many kinds. Physicians' skill in diagnosis, for example, can be tested
with simulated patients (Melnick & Clyman, 1988). After reading a brief
account of symptoms, the physician being tested requests specific information such as blood pressure or an X ray. That prerecorded information
is displayed, and the physician recommends a next step in treatment.
Further information on the patient's progress and further proposals for
action alternate. The events of several days are simulated in 30 minutes
or so. At present, this procedure is used as a self-test during medical
training, but there are plans to use it in licensing.

The Role of Professional Associations   There is rather little governmental
regulation of test publication and use. A few pieces of federal legislation
have been significant—notably those having to do with education of

handicapped children and with equitable employment testing—and there are scattered state laws including those that license psychologists. Court decisions, actions by administrative agencies, and governmental investigations have left some marks on testing practice and I shall come to them. (One example that falls outside the scope of this book is a Labor Department ruling in 1988 that largely prohibits the use of lie detectors by private employers.)

Mostly, however, it is professional associations that have studied the adequacy of tests and testing and have distributed guidelines for sound practice. The greatest influence has come from three organizations: the American Psychological Association (APA), the American Educational Research Association (AERA), and the National Council on Measurement in Education (NCME). Important statements have also come from divisions of APA, from organizations chiefly concerned with client interests, and from others. Associations direct their activities toward educating professionals, administrators, and the public. (An official APA statement criticizing the inadequate scientific basis for lie detectors encouraged the Labor Department ban.)

The Ethical Standards that APA issues from time to time (American Psychological Association, 1981) are a statement for study by members of the profession, persons in training, and employers of psychologists. "Enforcement" is minimal. Gross unethical violations may, to be sure, be grounds for canceling a person's membership in APA, or for a state's canceling a practitioner's license.

The most influential of the many reports related to testing is *Standards for educational and psychological testing* (often referred to as the *Testing standards* or the *Standards*). APA, AERA, and NCME collaborated on the original version in the early 1950s and on three revisions, the latest adopted in 1985 (American Educational Research Association et al., 1985; cited as "*Standards* 1985" hereafter in this book). This again is an educational document, not an enforceable regulation. Publishers have taken the *Testing standards* into account in the materials they produce and in their advertising, and courts have cited the *Standards* as a basis for judging test use (Bersoff, in Glaser & Bond, 1981; Novick, in Wigdor & Garner, vol. 2, 1982). I shall draw upon the *Standards* in connection with particular topics as we proceed and shall say more about their function early in Chapter 5. For specimen standards, see p. 90.

Figure 1.1 serves both to illustrate such recommendations and to preview the topic of the next section. The *Code* from which the figure comes is a presentation of ideas from the *Standards* for the benefit of test takers and the interested public (see also p. 5.8). The message is, "This is the level of practice you should expect from persons and agencies that give tests." (Single copies of the full document are available without charge from NCME, 1230 17th St., Washington, DC 20036.)

Selecting Appropriate Tests

Test users should select tests that meet the purpose for which they are to be used and that are appropriate for the intended test-taking populations.

Test Users Should:

1. First define the purpose for testing and the population to be tested. Then, select a test for that purpose and that population based on a thorough review of the available information.

2. Investigate potentially useful sources of information, in addition to test scores, to corroborate the information provided by tests.

3. Read the materials provided by test developers and avoid using tests for which unclear or incomplete information is provided.

4. Become familiar with how and when the test was developed and tried out.

5. Read independent evaluations of a test and of possible alternative measures. Look for evidence required to support the claims of test developers.

6. Examine specimen sets, disclosed tests or samples of questions, directions, answer sheets, manuals, and score reports before selecting a test.

7. Ascertain whether the test content and norms group(s) or comparison group(s) are appropriate for the intended test takers.

8. Select and use only those tests for which the skills needed to administer the test and interpret scores correctly are available.

Figure 1.1. **Selecting appropriate tests: responsibility of test users.** (*Source: Code of Fair Testing Practices in Education*, 1988.)

PURCHASING TESTS

Sources of Information

Someone who thinks that testing could serve one of her purposes must first survey the tests available. Books such as this cannot list the many tests in each category; even a specialized book on, for example, disorders of speech is unlikely to be exhaustive.

Persons choosing tests should consult the *Mental Measurements Yearbooks (MMY; BI)* and the *Test Critiques (TCA)* (see p. 147), both of which carry test reviews. Reference listings appear in *Tests in Print (BI)* and *Tests (TCA)*. One further resource from *TCA* is *Psychware,* a listing of software for administering and scoring tests by microcomputer. The Educational Testing Service provides significant services: *News on Tests* covers recent offerings of publishers; *Tests on Microfiche* reproduces specialized tests that are not commercially distributed; the *Test Collection* maintains a file of tests, manuals, and technical reports (and publishes bibliographies on testing topics). Increasingly, services such as those listed in this paragraph are available in central data bases that can be called up via computer. Those data bases can be kept up to the minute. Catalogs of test publishers (free on request) are another source of up-to-date detail. An exhaustive list of publishers appears in the *MMY*. Appendix A lists some publishers that persons who do much testing should know about. Also, this appendix identifies the publishers who are referred to in the text by shortened names or initials.

To illustrate catalog content I present, in Figure 1.2, one publisher's listing for the embedded figures task (EFT) shown in Figure 1.3). This task, also called hidden figures, has been prominent in research.

Publishers generally offer a "sample set" or "specimen set," as seen in the entry for the Group EFT. This set includes a copy of the test and the scoring key. The manual (here priced separately) is often part of a specimen set. Professionals using many tests collect specimen sets and supplementary technical manuals. Most universities maintain collections that can be examined by persons with a professional need-to-know.

Before deciding to adopt a test for some use, one should study its manual and any relevant research summary. Whereas the catalog description is a few paragraphs long, the manual offers several pages of information on purposes, methods, and limitations. Sometimes a separate book provides the research summary. That is the case with EFT. A bibliography of 2800 references can also be purchased.

The research summary is entitled *Cognitive styles* (Witkin & Goodenough, 1981). Witkin investigated for many years the idea, suggested by Gestalt psychology, that some people are dominated by any strong frame of reference or pattern in a stimulus field, to such an extent that they have trouble in perceiving elements that cut across the pattern. Research ultimately pushed aside Witkin's suggestion that EFT measures

Embedded Figures Test (b)

Herman A. Witkin

The *Embedded Figures Test* (EFT), designed originally for research in cognitive functioning and cognitive styles, has been used extensively in assessment studies relating performance on the EFT to analytic ability in other tasks, social behavior, body concept, preferred defense mechanisms, and problem solving style.

The EFT is available in alternate forms. Each requires subjects to find simple geometric figures in each of 12 complex colored designs. For individual administration to older children, adolescents, and adults.

Time: No limit. 10 to 45 minutes.

CODE	DESCRIPTION	PRICE/UNIT
3009	**EFT Kit** Card Sets, Stylus. 50 Recording Sheets	$26.50
3001	**Manual**	$7.50
3004	**Card Sets: Forms A & B** with Simple Figures & Practice Items	$18.00
3061	**Stylus**	$2.50
3024	**Recording Sheets** 1 pad of 50	$7.00/pad
	5 of more pads of 50	$6.50/pad

Manual for the Embedded Figures Tests (b)

Herman A. Witkin, et al

This 32-Manual contains directions for administration and scoring, plus normative, reliability, and validity data for three tests in the series—the EFT, CEFT, and GEFT. 131 references. 1971

3001	**EFT Manual**	$7.50

Children's Embedded Figures Test (b)

Stephen A. Karp
Norma Konstadt

The *Children's Embedded Figures Test* (CEFT) is an individually administered figures test for children aged 5 to 12. It is used to assess field dependence in developmental studies of psychological differentiation. The test series contains 25 items, preceded by 13 practice items.

Time limit. Testing stops after several failures.

CODE	DESCRIPTION	PRICE/UNIT
3309	**Test Kit** simple cardboard forms, 38 color plates, clear plastic envelopes, Star Rubber Stamp, & pad of Recording Sheets	$26.00
3324	**Recording Sheets** 1 pad of 50	$7.50/pad
	10 of more pads of 50	$7.00/pad

Group Embedded Figures Test (b)

Philip K. Oltman
Evelyn Raskin
Herman A. Witkin

A 25-item embedded figures test in a 32-page booklet, the *Group Embedded Figures Test* (GEFT) is designed for group administration. Subjects find one of 8 simple figures in the 18 complex designs and mark them.

Time limit: No limit. 20 minutes.

CODE	DESCRIPTION	PRICE/UNIT
3100	**Sample Set** Scoring Key, Test Booklet	$2.50
3001	**Manual**	$7.50
3105	**Scoring Key**	$1.50
3113	**Test Booklets** (expendable) 1 pkg of 25	$18.50/pkg
	10 or more pkgs of 25	$16.75/pkg

Figure 1.2. **Illustrative catalog entries.** The code (b) indicates that the purchaser must have completed courses in testing or have equivalent training. (*Source:* Reproduced with minor modifications from the 1989 catalog of Consulting Psychologists Press.)

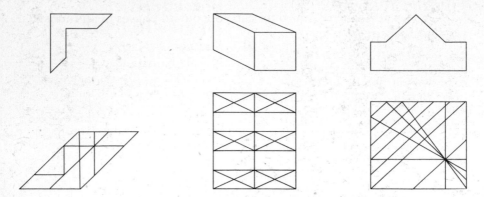

Figure 1.2. Embedded figures.

a "style of field independence" requiring a theory of its own, separate from ability theory. On page 183 I shall say a bit about this issue. EFT is interpreted in this book as one of many measures of general mental ability, but the publisher lists it under "Personality." Many times in this book it will be pointed out that personality and ability are not truly separable.

Who May Obtain Tests?

In the hands of persons with inadequate training, tests can do harm. Untrained users may administer a test incorrectly. They may rely too much on inaccurate measurements, and they may misunderstand what the test measures and so reach unsound conclusions. Therefore, the user should confine herself to tests that she can handle properly and that are known to be relevant for her purposes.

To see the implications of this remark, consider industrial personnel testing. To a manager, it may appear simple to give a printed reasoning test, score it with a punched-out key, tabulate the scores, and hire applicants with top scores. A personnel psychologist, however, knows that applicants of middling ability are better bets for some routine jobs than applicants who score very high but are likely to become bored and quit. She knows that a general mental test may not measure the abilities most important in a factory job and that even experts make errors when they try to guess which tests will predict success in a given job.

Levels of Qualification   Let us pursue this example. Industrial personnel workers in the United States are qualified at various levels:

- Diploma in industrial-organizational psychology. A diploma is awarded by the American Board of Professional Psychology to an applicant who possesses (among other qualifications) the training

and experience required for carrying out all phases of an industrial testing program.[3]
- Doctoral degree in personnel psychology. A psychologist at this level (who may have been trained in a university department of psychology, education, or business management) should be able to plan a selection procedure and verify its soundness by research. If she has limited experience, she may need to consult a better-qualified person, especially in planning the program. Numerous consulting firms provide assistance in planning.
- Limited specialized training. Workers who have training in personnel methods equivalent to a master's degree can carry out specialized functions within a general plan. They can administer complicated tests, collect data on the performance of employees, and make some decisions about individuals. A psychologist can train an intelligent assistant to perform such functions under supervision.
- Intelligent workers without psychological training. A person without psychological training can learn to administer many group tests, take charge of the scoring of objective tests, and apply clearly stated rules for reducing the list of applicants to a list of finalists.
- Ordinary clerical workers. These workers should be used only for routine scoring under competent supervision and for assisting in test administration.

When tests are used in a vocational counseling service, a school testing program, or a diagnostic service in a mental hospital, we would observe similarly varied roles are to be played. There is need for some routine handling of tests and test data, for responsible supervision, and for high-level framing of policies and programs.

Being a trained psychologist does not automatically qualify one to handle all types of psychological tests. Being expert in personnel selection or in the analysis of poor readers does not necessarily qualify one for other test applications. Being a psychiatrist, social worker, teacher, or school administrator does not by itself imply readiness to use personality tests or even to make sound use of standardized achievement tests. Persons other than the tester come into the picture. If an excellent procedure is hard to explain to nonprofessionals, the psychologist may be wise to select a simpler test that is less informative.

Some tests can be administered and interpreted by responsible persons who have no specialized training. Other tests serving the same general purpose can be used only by well-qualified psychologists. For example, two tests that might have some value in selecting prospects for

---

[3]The board also grants diplomas in clinical psychology, in school psychology, in counseling, and in other specialties.

training as junior executives are the Concept Mastery Test and the Thematic Apperception Test (TAT). The former is a difficult test of word knowledge. The directions for administering and scoring are simple enough for a high school graduate to follow. An employer with no psychological training can easily understand the results. To administer and interpret the TAT, a person must have graduate training in the psychology of personality and should have supervised experience with the TAT itself. It is used to investigate the motives of the test taker and his feelings about other persons. Serious errors would result if the test were interpreted by anyone save a cautious psychologist who is acquainted with the logic of its interpretation and the misinterpretations that experts on the test have warned against.

Final decisions about hiring or promotion or treatment ought not, in general, be left to psychologists. Other members of the organization bring needed perspectives. *After* discussion in a broad group, a policy can sometimes be reduced to rules whose administration is properly left to the testing team.

Test Distribution   Misuse of tests is to be discouraged by every feasible means, and restricting a test to qualified users would be desirable. Restricting tests to psychologists will not do. That would be a disservice to persons served by, for example, speech therapists and primary teachers. Moreover, a trained psychologist is not a qualified user of all tests in all circumstances; and no credential—not even board certification—is a guarantee against misuse.

Because it is impractical for a publisher or other central agency to check on each user's practices, the ultimate safeguard has to be self-regulation. It is inevitably the purchaser's responsibility to judge which test records she can interpret soundly and where she is out of her depth. A school psychologist may need to make such judgments about the members of the school staff, and help them recognize and overcome their limitations. Self-regulation is the key idea behind the *Testing standards.* The *Standards* call more specifically for the test user to match her own qualifications to those required for proper administration and interpretation of the test and to make a similar check before delegating any testing responsibility to another.

Here is part of a statement about who may properly use a test:[4]

> The test user, in selecting or interpreting a test, should know the purposes of the testing and the probable consequences. The user should know the procedures necessary to facilitate effectiveness and to reduce bias in test use. Although the test developer and publisher should provide information on the strengths and weaknesses of the test, the ultimate responsibility for appropriate test use lies with the test user. The user should become knowl-

---

[4]From *Standards for educational and psychological testing,* p. 41. Copyright © 1985 by the American Psychological Association. Reprinted by permission.

edgeable about the test and its appropriate uses and also communicate this information, as appropriate, to others.

This point of view is elaborated in the *Code* quoted in Figure 1.1.

Most publishers have tried to screen orders to keep tests out of the hands of unsuitable purchasers. Any industry-wide roster of approved purchasers, however, would very likely be regarded as unfair restraint of trade. Indeed, a system of screening purchasers that was in place in the late 1960s was overturned after an investigation by the Federal Trade Commission (Holmen & Docter, 1972). The investigation apparently was triggered by complaints of business consultants who wanted to provide a mail-order testing service to help their clients screen job applicants, and whose purchase orders were rejected. (Professionals disapprove of attempts to offer opinions on persons the analyst has not interacted with.)

A new system is emerging from the efforts of a "Test User Qualification Working Group," a collaboration of test publishers and professional associations (Eyde et al., 1988). The group has conducted research to identify the most troublesome misuses of each major type of test. Prominent misuses include inappropriate choice of tests, faulty administration, interpretations that are insensitive to the limitations of scores, and poor communication of test findings. These concerns will reappear at many places in this book.

Here it is worthwhile to cite five "principles of effective test use."

Sound, professional use of educational and psychological tests means that all test users must:

1. maintain the security of testing materials before and after testing.
2. avoid labeling students based on a single test score.
3. adhere strictly to the copyright law and under no circumstances photocopy or otherwise reproduce answer forms, test books, or manuals.
4. administer and score tests exactly as specified in the manual.
5. release results only to authorized persons and in a form in keeping with accepted principles of test interpretation.

(This wording is appended to the form in Figure 1.4. These topics, all included in the *Standards*, are highlighted in the form because comparatively inexperienced testers need these basic reminders.)

The Working Group tried several types of questionnaires to be filled out by would-be purchasers, and then it produced suggestions that each firm will apply in its own way in deciding which orders to fill. There is no standard qualification form, both to avoid antitrust complaints and because firms distributing different kinds of tests or serving different types of purchasers probably should emphasize different questions. Still, all publishers are likely to collect much the same kind of information.

One firm that produces ability tests, primarily for school psychologists to use, developed the form in Figure 1.4 in the light of the Working

Test Purchaser Qualification Form

1. Your purpose for using tests (check as many as apply)

☐ Educational diagnosis/remediation ☐ Clinical diagnosis/classification ☐ Counseling ☐ Therapy ☐ Personnel selection ☐ Research
☐ Learning disabilities screening ☐ Other _____

2. Your level of training (check as many as apply)

☐ Bachelor's Degree: Year _____ Institution _____ Major field of study _____
☐ Master's Degree: Year _____ Institution _____ Major field of study _____
☐ Doctorate: Year _____ Institution _____ Major field of study _____

3. Your professional credentials (check as many as apply)

☐ Licensed in: Area _____ State _____ License # _____
☐ Member of professional organization(s): (AACD, AERA, APA, ASHA, CEC, NASP, etc.) _____
☐ Formally recognized professional competence (fellow, diplomate, special certificate): ☐ fellow ☐ diplomate ☐ other certification
Organization _____

4. Your educational background (courses and other study)

a. Courses (check each course completed and circle level at which course was completed.)
U = Undergraduate, G = Graduate, O = Other (special course you have completed, workshop, in-service training, etc.)

	(circle)		(circle)
☐ Basic tests and measurements	U G O	☐ Use of tests in counseling	U G O
☐ Descriptive statistics	U G O	☐ Career assessment	U G O
☐ Intelligence testing	U G O	☐ Neuropsychological assessment	U G O
☐ Speech, hearing, language assessment	U G O	☐ Other (list below)	
☐ Educational diagnostics	U G O	_____	U G O
☐ Assessment course in major field:	U G O	_____	U G O
		_____	U G O

b. Other Study (check each type of program completed)

☐ Practicum in test administration and interpretation
☐ Internship (school psychology, counseling, etc.) type: _____

5. Your updating of professional knowledge and skills (check activities below and give an example)

☐ Attending workshops, seminars, conferences: _____
☐ Reading professional publications (journals, test manuals, etc.): _____

6. Your special competence

(List one test which you use regularly that best illustrates your skill in test administration and interpretation.)
_____

Figure 1.4. **Information requested from individuals seeking to purchase tests.** This Test Purchaser Qualification Form is being used by the American Guidance Service (Robertson, 1988). Several introductory lines ask about the applicant's position, address, and supervisor's name.

Table 1.1   PART OF A SCORING PLAN FOR THE FORM IN FIGURE 1.4

Qualification	Credits
Element 1. Level of training	
a. Advanced degree (master's, doctorate) in field relevant to individual intellectual assessment	4
b. Bachelor's degree only	0
Element 2. Professional credentials	
a. State licensing in area relevant to individual intellectual assessment	2
(no state certification)	0
b. Professional membership in organization relevant to individual intellectual assessment	2
Other organizations	0
c. Professional competence	
Fellow or diplomate in relevant organization	2
Recognition of competence in other organization not relevant to individual intellectual assessment	0
Element 3. Educational background	
Courses	
a. Intelligence testing	5
b. Neuropsychological assessment	4
c. Educational diagnosis	3
d. Basic tests and measurements, descriptive statistics	2
e. Use of tests in counseling; career assessment	1
Other study	
a. Internship in relevant professional field	5
b. Practicum in test use and interpretation	4
c. Relevant supervised experience	3

The credits listed are intended to evaluate would-be users of individual intelligence tests (Robertson, 1988). The complete table of credits (which is at the tryout stage) also includes sections that assign up to 6 points for study of and experience with intelligence tests.

Group's findings. The complete form asks the applicant to pledge that she will adhere to the principles quoted above and to the *Testing standards*.

Instead of reaching a decision after inspecting the form, the publisher intends to apply a scoring key. The tentative key, partially illustrated in Table 1.1, must be tried further before the number of credits needed for approval of a purchase order is finally settled. It will be possible to develop one scoring formula and cutting score for comparatively simple tests and other rules for tests that require substantial professional judgment.

5. *An employer without psychological training decides to buy personality tests and use them on applicants. What is gained by refusing to sell the tests, in*

*view of the fact that without them the employer will base judgments en-
tirely on superficial impressions gained through an interview?*

6. *Psychologists do not favor distributing tests to people who wish to assess
their own (or their children's) aptitudes or personality characteristics. Why?*

7. *Five "principles of effective test use" are quoted above. Explain how violating principles 1, 2, 4, and 5 could reduce effectiveness of testing, for the
present examinee(s) or in the future. (With regard to principle 3: Copyright
should be respected, but photocopying interferes with testing only if imperfect copying alters the test or causes inaccurate scoring.)*

8. *How might the credits in Table 1.1 be modified for purchasers of a group
test of word recognition skills of primary-grade children?*

9. *After 100 or more purchase requests for individual intelligence tests have
been collected, it will be possible for the publisher to collect data on the
scoring system of Table 1.1. Consider, for example, the question of whether
individuals with scores of 18–19 are good risks. Assuming that investigation
cannot go beyond telephone calls to the applicant and her professional acquaintances, what questions would help to evaluate a proposal to accept or
reject, hereafter, would-be purchasers with this score?*

DECISIONS FOR WHICH TESTS ARE USED

A personnel manager decides whom to hire; a teacher decides whether a
pupil is ready to take up long division; a physician decides how a patient
should be treated. For every such decision made about the person by
others, he makes dozens about himself. He decides to try for an A in
chemistry or to settle for a B, to go to the community college or to take
a job, to seek work as a salesperson or as a taxi driver. Even 10-year-olds
are making significant decisions. The child who sees himself as capable
of excellence will spend long hours at the workbench or the piano
bench; the child who expects little of himself turns to pastimes.

Reaching decisions or conclusions or policies is a broader process
than "testing." Even when matters are so routinized that a test is allowed
to dictate action (as when a person who gives too many incorrect answers
on a driver's test is denied a license), the decision rule reflects much
reasoning and judgment. Terms such as "assessment" and "evaluation"
properly suggest a combination of information with value judgments that
go far beyond testing.

Every decision rests on a forecast. A test tells about performance at
this moment. That information would not be worth knowing if one could
not then predict something about later performance.

Consider a test of visual recognition. We flash a row of letters on the
screen for an instant, and the person reports what he has seen. Some
people recognize four letters; others grasp seven in the same brief interval. This difference is intriguing, but it is unimportant until it can be
related to other behavior. The applied psychologist sees that this task

possibly has something in common with perception in reading. She investigates whether the flash recognition test will predict success in learning to read. If so, it can help the primary-grade teacher to plan reading instruction.

A clinician might use the flash technique to see whether a person has special difficulty in perceiving emotionally toned words like "guilt" and "failure," that being a possible indicator of emotional conflict. Such a test is useful only if the unusual score indicates probable deviant behavior or serious emotional upset at some time in the future. The significance of the clinical test is that it predicts behavior that should be forestalled or forecasts that a certain treatment method will bring improvement. Also, if perception of emotionally toned words is a sensitive indicator, it may serve as a way to check on the person's progress.

The scientific investigator may not care about practical applications, but she too must have tests that predict. Flashing letters on the screen is a good laboratory procedure because, if conditions are not altered, today's test predicts tomorrow's score. If the score changes when the experimenter changes the illumination, we know that the change resulted from the illumination and not from chance variation. The experimenter, therefore, can study systematically how flash perception is related to illumination.

It is convenient to distinguish four uses of tests:

Classification.

Promoting self-understanding.

Evaluation and modification of treatments or programs.

Scientific inquiry.

The first and second uses have to do primarily with decisions about the particular persons tested. The first and third are most often a part of the operations of an institution. Enhancing self-understanding, on the other hand, serves the individual first and institutions only incidentally. The diversity of test functions implies that no one test or type of test is likely to serve the several purposes equally well.

10. *Demonstrate that prediction is intended in each of the following situations:*
    a. *A teacher gives James a grade of C in algebra and Harry a grade of A.*
    b. *Airlines require a periodic physical examination of pilots.*
    c. *A psychologist investigates whether students are more "liberal" in their attitudes toward arms control after two years of college study.*

Classification

Classification takes place whenever a person is assigned to one category rather than another (and treated accordingly). The assignment may have long-term consequences or may be for the short term, easily reversible.

The choice may be between two categories or among ten, or there may be a unique prescription for each individual. Many terms refer to varieties of classification: selection, licensing or certification, screening, placement, and diagnosis.

Selection is a go/no-go decision. The term is most often applied to admission of students, hiring of employees, and picking individuals for an advanced responsibility. *Screening* ordinarily refers to a quick survey to locate individuals who may need or merit special treatment. Screening pupils to locate possible hearing disorders is an example; so is a "talent search." A closer case study follows the screening.

The licensing test for drivers also has an in/out character. *Licensing* (mandatory) is sometimes distinguished from *certification* (voluntary). Every physician must pass a test to be licensed for practice; applying for certification in a medical specialty, however, is optional. *Placement* is a sorting of persons to receive different levels of service—e.g., inpatient versus outpatient status, advanced English versus remedial English.

Diagnosis usually refers to explanation. The conceptualization of a person's problem strongly influences the treatment plan. The succinct label—"learning disability," for example—has a certain place in summary statistics for administrative purposes and for certain kinds of research. Also, it sometimes provides a clever bypass of bureaucratic regulations that take the form "No label, no funds for treatment." But a proper psychological diagnosis is concerned with recognizing how the situations the learner copes with differ from those where he has trouble. (A decision to administer drugs or other physical intervention considers physiological functioning in addition.)

Diagnosis takes many sophisticated forms, requiring expertise in a relevant specialty. On one front is diagnosis of organic brain damage (Dean, in Plake & Witt, 1986); on another, diagnosis of speech pathology (p. 404); on another, diagnosis of schoolchildren's errors in arithmetic. Only those trained in the theory related to these disabilities can appreciate the subtleties on which each kind of reasoning turns; yet all are to be evaluated by the principles applied to less specialized measurements.

Selection, diagnosis, and the other terms all refer to categorization, and hence logically they are classification decisions. But psychologists most often use the term *classification* to refer to the process of sorting recruits into military specialties or picking assignments for particular employees. That is how the term will be used in my later chapters.

Figure 1.5 brings out a fundamental difference between classification and simple selection. Suppose we are filling two kinds of jobs and that the average applicant is marginally acceptable in each job. If Test A is equally relevant to both jobs, we can accept applicants who score average and above, but Test A gives no basis for deciding which job is better for an applicant. If Test B is relevant to Job 1 and Test C is relevant to Job 2, we can divide the applicant pool as shown in panel ii. The tests are providing information on a difference within the person as well

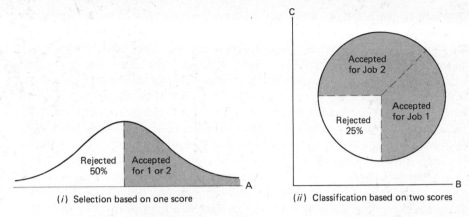

(i) Selection based on one score   *(ii)* Classification based on two scores

Figure 1.4. Expansion of opportunity through classification.

as on differences among persons. This permits use of a larger fraction of an applicant pool (which lowers recruiting costs) or a higher standard of acceptance (Brogden, 1951). Predictors that are relevant to one assignment and not another have been hard to find, however.

11. *What determines how many persons pass*
    a. *in selection for employment?*
    b. *in screening for learning disabilities?*
    c. *in licensing foreign-trained physicians?*
    d. *in certifying elevator inspectors?*

12. *Is there any logical difference between selection and screening? between military classification and diagnosis?*

13. *Is there any occasion for "diagnosis" of persons who are functioning adequately?*

Promoting Self-Understanding

There may have been a day when the counselor saw herself as an authority who sorted out the facts about the client and told him what career lines he should follow. As the profession matured, counselors realized that decisions of this kind are for the client to make. The counselor acts as a teacher, helping the person to perceive his full range of options, to anticipate probable outcomes, and to judge how satisfied he would be with each choice.

A similar emphasis on self-determination has come into college admissions. Entrance into a college is now seen as a reciprocal process (Boyer, 1987). Both student and college are making choices. The student needs to know what colleges to consider, what each one offers for his abilities and interests, and how strong the competition will be. Admission tests are installed because institutions must make decisions, but the process is lopsided unless the prospective student is well informed when he takes up one offer of admission rather than another.

One's self-impression affects actions year after year. From early years a person develops impressions of his competence, interests, and traits. There is a generalized self-concept—"I'm OK"—and an endless string of differentiated perceptions—"My oral reports get by without criticism if I keep them short and simple." Tests are only one among the many sources that contribute to these impressions, but tests often take on special weight because the scores are definite. Significance is added by such reference points as the "perfect" score, the "passing" score, and the group average.

A descriptive portrait gives more help with the person's ever-changing questions than does a score or a simple categorization. For instance, a test battery plus other facts might classify Tasha as a promising engineer and this would lead her to enroll in engineering. A description would report in addition the assets and liabilities that distinguish Tasha from other prospective engineers. She is especially interested in aviation; she has a rather immature and uncooperative attitude toward superiors; she works energetically in short bursts with no long-range scheduling. All these facts, brought to consciousness, help Tasha to choose situations where she is likely to perform well, to regulate her conduct, and, in time, to overcome some limitations.

Program Evaluation

Modern educational testing is ordinarily dated from the efforts of the reformer Joseph Mayer Rice, who in the 1890s was attacking "the spelling grind" and other traditional teaching practices. Rice persuaded schools in many communities to administer the same spelling test. Schools spending more time on spelling drills did not finish with higher average scores; the time, said Rice, could be better spent on more enriching lessons. Rice's purpose in testing was to evaluate a school policy, not to judge individual students, teachers, or even school districts.

In discussions of program evaluation, "program" ordinarily refers to a plan for rendering service of a particular kind. Thus, there are evaluations of job training, of welfare programs, and of campaigns to encourage behavior that reduces the likelihood of a heart attack. The scale is large when a federal agency commissions an evaluator to determine how well day-care programs around the nation function and what effects seem to follow from differences in the child-to-staff ratio and other features. The scale is small when a chemistry teacher's end-of-year test indicates which topics should be given extra attention next time round. Evaluation ought to advance the thinking of the entire policy-shaping community and not merely of those who head the program (Cronbach et al., 1980). The evaluation supplies facts, but the facts mean different things to per-

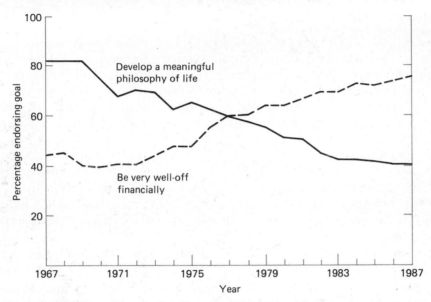

Figure 1.6. **Changes in goals of college freshmen over twenty years.** Percentages indicate the proportion of freshmen who respond "Essential" or "Very important." (*Source:* Astin et al., 1987, p. 8.)

sons holding different social values and having different interests at stake. Some citizens, for example, would be enthusiastic about any training program that reduces the ranks of the unemployed; but if graduates mostly enter dead-end jobs a critic is likely to call the program a near failure. This illustrates the importance of appraising the full range of outcomes.

Evaluation of specific programs shades off into the evaluation of institutions, communities, and whole social systems. Figure 1.6 comes from repeated surveys of college students by means of attitude questionnaires. The result highlights a social problem with which policy makers must be concerned. Unlike other psychological measurement, evaluations are concerned with results for groups and subgroups. Often the instrument is designed to produce only a group statistic and not an individual score.

Some evaluations are close to pure science, but nothing value-laden can be purely scientific. A controlled experiment can establish whether a tranquilizer elevates mood and can identify physiological or behavioral side effects. If the findings are positive, how freely to administer the drug remains an issue. *One Flew over the Cuckoo's Nest,* you will recall, attacked the mental hospital's reliance on tranquilizers just because the tranquilizers succeeded so well in making patients "manageable."

Scientific Inquiry

The functions of testing considered so far bear immediately on practical affairs. Tests also play a large role in science—for example, in checking on such a hypothesis as "The change of perceptual span with change in illumination is greater when a person is under stress." Tests provide a more objective and dependable basis for evaluating hypotheses than rough impressions do, and measurement is essential to arriving at a numerical relationship.

Sometimes a scientific investigator uses tests published for practical purposes, but a test invented to fit the experiment will often work better. In one study, for example, the experimenter played sound recordings of words backward in order to study how people learn to recognize strange stimuli. Such a task, just because it is novel, makes a good experimental test.

14. *Show that a college-level reading test might be used for any of the four functions listed in this section.*

15. *Rice found that schools providing more drill did not have better average scores in spelling. Can his finding be explained in any way except by the conclusion that drill does not work?*

16. *A program aimed to reduce teenage pregnancies will surely be the subject of political controversy. Does this political sensitivity influence the conduct of its evaluation? Or can the evaluator view her task as straightforward factual inquiry down to the point where the results are released? (This example is relevant to testers because an evaluator would want to assess concepts and attitudes, not merely count pregnancies.)*

17. *Classify each of the following with respect to the four categories of test use. More than one use may be pertinent.*
    a. *An instructor rides with a pilot at the end of his training, and fills out a checklist to show which maneuvers he performed correctly.*
    b. *A psychologist compares the average vocabulary size of only children with that of children from larger families of similar social background.*
    c. *Students sign up for a series of "behavior modification" sessions intended to increase their assertiveness. They keep a log of incidents in which they hear a statement (in class or in conversation) with which they disagree, and they record in the log whether they responded and how. The log is kept during the first week and the last week of the training.*
    d. *A representative sample of high school seniors in Colorado are tested on their understanding of the Bill of Rights.*
    e. *A medical clinic places a device in its lobby that enables visitors to take their own blood pressure. A booklet explaining the readings is provided.*

Chapter
2

Varieties of Tests and Test Interpretations

2A. Some tests are standardized, some are objective, some have norms. How do these features differ? Why are they valuable?

2B. What are the potential advantages and risks in impressionistic assessment?

2C. How can one recognize whether a test measures maximum performance or typical response?

2D. How can the computer extend the range and accuracy of testing?

2E. Sometimes the kind of behavior sampled in a test is of direct interest; sometimes it is only a basis for inference to other characteristics. What measurement objectives lead to each kind of interpretation?

Abbreviations in this chapter: ASVAB for Armed Services Vocational Aptitude Battery; EFT for Embedded Figures Test.

WHAT IS A TEST?

The word "test" usually calls to mind a standard series of questions to which the examinee gives written or oral answers. But the road test for a driver's license has neither questions nor answers, and the procedure varies from one examiner to the next. The task set for the driver cannot be standardized, as the traffic through which drivers are asked to maneuver will vary from one hour to another.

Perhaps the following definition is broad enough to cover the procedures with which this book will be concerned: A *test* is a systematic procedure for observing behavior and describing it with the aid of numerical scales or fixed categories. "20/100" locates visual acuity on a numerical scale; "red/green colorblind" refers to a category. By "systematic" I mean that the tester collects information by questioning or observing one person after another in the same manner, in the same situation or comparable situations. This definition embraces questionnaires for obtaining reports on personality, procedures for observing social behavior, apparatus tests measuring coordination, and even records of output on a production line.

As was said in Chapter 1, "assessment" is a broader word than "testing" when (as is usual) it connotes integrating and evaluating information. An assessment of an individual will ordinarily consider tests along with a case history and interviews. But the term has also been applied to statistical surveys based solely on tests ("National Assessment of Educational Progress") and to narrow experimental measures ("assessment of fear of snakes").

A test may be all of one piece, scores for questions or parts being ignored once the total is obtained. In other tests part scores are carried forward for interpretation. When several part scores are charted side by side on comparable scales, the chart is called a "profile." (The parts are sometimes referred to as "subtests." Sometimes the parts are called "tests" and the whole is called a "battery." These differences in terminology are unimportant.)

The meanings of *pencil-and-paper test, apparatus test, oral test*, and so on should be obvious. Although all behavioral data reflect performance of some sort, *performance test* usually refers to a task requiring a physical response. Among performance tests that have been used are repairing a piece of electronic apparatus, drawing a picture of a man, stringing beads, and "inventing" a hatrack when given two long sticks and a C-clamp. Verbal though the task is, responding to an interview in French is also a performance test.

Group tests permit testing many persons at once. *Individual tests* allow observation of reactions and permit follow-up on an indefinite answer. Many tests have both individual and group versions. Computer administration blurs this time-honored distinction in that administration is individual, but the exercises are usually similar to those in a group test.

Standardization of test procedures became a concern about 1900. In that day every psychology laboratory had its own method of measuring memory span, reaction time, and so on. Therefore, it was difficult to compare research findings. Likewise, when every teacher used a different test, it was difficult for school officials to judge how well pupils were learning to spell.

A test is considered to be *standardized* when the tester's words and acts, the apparatus, and the scoring rules have been fixed so that the scores collected at different times and places are fully comparable. If the standardization is fully effective, every tester "gives the same test." As we shall see later in this chapter, this statement does not necessarily mean that everyone faces the same questions.

If a procedure is *objective,* every observer of a performance arrives at the same report. To achieve objectivity each one must pay attention to the same aspects of the performance, record observations to eliminate errors of recall, and score the record by the same rules. Objectivity may be judged by comparing the scores that independent observers assign. The more subjective the observing and scoring, the less the judges agree. Tests in which the respondent selects the best answer (e.g., true-false or multiple-choice tests) have objective scoring. In contrast, an ordinary essay test allows room for great disagreement among scorers. By the use of careful instructions to the observer or scorer, however, the numbers assigned to essay responses and to observations can be made fairly objective. Objectivity and standardization often go together, but a test with loose procedures may be scored by a definite rule, and a standardized procedure may have judgmental scoring.

A table of norms tells how scores are distributed in some relevant population. Tests having norms are sometimes called "standardized tests." I am not using the word in that sense, because I wish to emphasize standardization *of procedure.* A test whose procedures are not standardized may have a table of norms, but the norms do not mean much. (The terms "norm-referenced" and "criterion-referenced" do not designate types of tests; they refer to interpretations, as Chapter 4 will explain.)

1. *Judge each of these statements true or false and defend your answer:*
   a. *Batting averages are* objectively *determined.*
   b. *The 220-yard low hurdle race is a* standardized *test.*
   c. *A teacher has each member of the class read the same article in a current magazine. Time is called at the end of 3 minutes, and each pupil marks the place where he is reading. He then counts the number of words read and computes his reading rate in words per minute. This score is compared with a table of average reading speeds for typical magazine articles. This test is highly* objective.
   d. *The test described in* c *is* standardized.

2. *Psychological tests often start from crude procedures. Dr. Glass thinks that she obtains useful information by laying a sheet of paper on the table at arm's length from the test taker and asking him to touch with his pencil exactly in the center of a circle printed on the paper. The person is told to*

withdraw his hand and repeat the movement, as rapidly and accurately as possible, until told to stop. Dr. Glass assigns a mark from 1 to 10 on each of the following qualities: speed, carefulness, and persistence. What aspects of the procedure would need to be taken into account in standardizing the test?

3. *Industrial morale surveys can use questions made up by the plant personnel office or its consultants. What advantages and disadvantages would there be in using the same questions in many companies?*

4. *The block design task (see Figure 3.1, p. 58) is one of the most popular testing procedures. The person constructs a pattern from colored blocks to match a printed sample. The test is chiefly used in child guidance, clinical diagnosis, and measuring general ability of persons who do poorly on verbal tests. It is also used for research on frustration and on cultural differences. Many versions of the test (different items, different scoring rules, etc.) are used in different clinics and different countries. What are possible advantages and disadvantages of this diversity?*

5. *Members of a faculty teaching sections of the same college course prepare a multiple-choice examination to be used in all sections. Is that exam "standardized," as the term is used here? If just one professor prepares and uses the exam for all sections, is it "standardized"?*

6. *Can an essay test be a standardized test?*

Psychometric and Impressionistic Styles of Testing

Methods of collecting information range from a psychometric extreme to an impressionistic extreme. The chief contrast is the emphasis placed on standardization and objectivity, which is greatest at the psychometric extreme. There is a difference also in interpretation; some testers aim to "measure" the individual, some to "characterize" him.

Psychometric testing sums up performance in numbers. Its ideal is expressed in two famous old pronouncements:

If a thing exists, it exists in some amount.

If it exists in some amount, it can be measured.

Note the assumption that the psychologist is concerned with "things," with elements or traits that somehow "exist." All people are considered to possess the same traits (e.g., assertiveness or mechanical comprehension), but in different amounts. This view of psychological investigation takes its cue from physical science, which identifies common aspects of dissimilar objects. Numbers representing abstract dimensions—weight, velocity, and intensity of energy of a certain wavelength—serve to describe rocks and rockets, candles and fireflies.

A psychometric approach is most profitable when a well-defined question is to be answered, and where the interpreter has sufficient experience to translate the measurement into an estimate of the probable outcome of each available course of action.

An impressionistic style of assessment strives for individualized description. The psychologist tries to be a sensitive observer who picks up cues by any available means and generates an integrated interpretation. For such a tester, even a focused test is an opportunity to study the person as a whole. The impressionist is not satisfied with a numerical estimate of level of ability. She asks how the person expresses his ability, what kinds of errors he makes, and why.

To evaluate a person's background, a psychometric tester would present a checklist covering experiences that many people have (for example, "Were you a Boy Scout or Girl Scout patrol leader?"). She would count the items checked to get scores for, say, "interest in sports" and "leadership experience." The impressionist, on the other hand, would perhaps set no more definite task than "Please write your life story in 2500 words." She would note what the individual considers important to report and also his emotional tone. The free response gives unsystematic information but covers matters the checklist ignores.

The psychometric style is marked by definiteness of task, objectivity of recording, rigor in scoring and combining data, and stress on validation. In pointing out these features of the psychometric style, I do not imply that psychometric testing necessarily has all these features at once.

Most test applications are psychometric in some respects and impressionistic in others. The measurer must fall back on judgment when she applies score information in teaching, therapy, or supervision of employees. And the portraitist should attend to the facts from measurement. The more exceptional the person under study or the more unprecedented the decision to be made, the greater the need to frame questions and procedures to fit the case. This book is primarily a presentation of ideas and methods from the psychometric tradition; but the impressionistic tester must understand these, if only as a point of departure.

Let us examine the contrasts in more detail, beginning with task structure. The examinee may be set a definite task or a vague one. The writer of a biographical essay is free to employ any style and bring in any content. Not so when he is asked to check activities on a printed list.

A task is said to be *structured* when everyone interprets it in much the same way. Structuring obtains a definite answer to a question formulated in advance.

The test developer may ask the examinee to construct his own response, or may offer a choice among fixed response alternatives. We may speak, then, of *choice-response* and *constructed-response* ("free-response") tests. Psychometric testers commonly opt for choice response in order to make the test more structured.

An interviewer might ask, "Are you at ease in social gatherings?" A more psychometric tester provides alternatives such as ALWAYS, OFTEN, SOMETIMES, NEVER. A series-completion item (7 5 8 6 9 . . .) may be open-ended or supplied with answer choices.

The choice format makes scoring easy, but the behavior displayed is less rich. Even on a number-series item, differences can appear. One person says "Seven" directly; another hesitantly says, "Well, it might be seven. I guess that's right." Psychologists who prefer open-ended response value the supplementary observations. The English teacher prefers to judge a student from a sample of free writing rather than from tests in which he merely identifies errors. The mathematics teacher wants students to solve problems, not merely to select the best of several alternatives. I leave to Chapter 9 the evidence on the degree to which the two types of test overlap, as well as the considerations in choosing between them.

Psychometric testing concerns itself more with product than with process. The product is unambiguously observable—the answer given, the block tower constructed, or the essay written. When a psychometric tester does pay attention to the process, she arms herself with a record sheet for tabulating what she sees. And she selects in advance the particular aspects of response style she will record. Listing the variables in advance is a restriction unacceptable to the impressionistic psychologist. She prefers to look for what is significant in each examinee's behavior as she watches him at work. Consequently, she favors tasks that people approach differently.

When a decision is to be made, one can combine the recorded facts by a formal rule or can combine them impressionistically. For example, one teacher assigns course marks by averaging the tests. Another relies on overall impressions: This student is "doing B work even if he did slump at the end" whereas that one is "not really as good as his tests suggest." The psychometric tester prefers a uniform, impersonal method, whereas the impressionist prefers flexibility.

Finally, we come to validation. Psychometric testers place their trust in interpretations made by a rule derived statistically from previous groups; they distrust more subjective, individualized interpretations. A psychometric tester accompanies every numerical score with a warning regarding the error of measurement and would like to attach an index of uncertainty to every prediction. The impressionist is less concerned with formal validation. If no two cases are alike, interpretations are not repeated, and experience tables cannot be cumulated. Validating "portraits" is much more difficult than validating numerical predictions. In effect, it requires validating the interpreter.

The impressionistic interpreter aspires to be an artist, sensitive in observing and skillful in conveying impressions. Some psychologists are presumably better judges of personality than others. The psychometric method seeks procedures that everyone can use equally well. The objective test is a camera pointed in a fixed direction; every competent photographer should get the same picture with it. Thus, psychometric testing aims to reduce measurement to a technical procedure. To the extent that it succeeds, it reduces the need for a "wise" professional psychologist.

The psychometric and impressionistic approaches differ most sharply on the issue of confidence in the psychologist. Advocates of rigor

regard the tester as an erratic instrument whose unregulated interpretations entangle truth with speculation. Impressionists view the observer
as a sensitive and even indispensable instrument. The impressionist
does not deny the danger of bias and error. She, however, is unwilling
to ignore the person's background and present situation—and the meanings he gives to them.

7. *"Psychometric testing trusts the judgment of the test constructor, where it
is unwilling to trust the tester as observer." Is this a defensible statement?*

8. *Distinguish between* structured *and* standardized.

9. *In what respects are the following procedures unstructured?*
   a. *In the Ayres handwriting test, pupils are told to write the Gettysburg
   Address neatly, doing as much as they can in a fixed time.*
   b. *In a test of mental development, the child is told to "draw the best man
   you can."*
   c. *In a recorded pitch-discrimination test, the subject hears two tones and
   responds* H, L, *or* N, *accordingly as the second tone appears higher than,
   lower than, or no different from the first.*

CLASSIFICATION OF PROCEDURES

For convenience this book sorts procedures into two broad classes: those
that seek to measure maximum performance and those seeking to measure typical response.

How well a cooperative person performs when asked to do his best
indicates "ability." Maximum performance is a convenient fiction. The
concept helps in organizing my discussion, but observing the maximum
is no easier than locating the end of the rainbow. A person's best time
in the mile is only his best to date; he may break that record tomorrow.
Ericsson (1987) tells about a person whose maximum ability to hold
number strings in mind tested out at seven digits. After 6 weeks of practice with a special technique, he was able to remember 80 digits! He
improved his "capacity" by capitalizing on his familiarity with times in
track events. He could assign meanings to *groups* of digits, leaving fewer
"items" to keep in mind. Given a string containing 3-4-9-2, for example,
he might think of three minutes, 49.2 seconds—a magnificent performance in the mile run (Posner, in Chi et al., 1988, p. xxx).

Second, there are procedures to find out what the person most often
does or feels, in a recurring situation or class of situations. Measures
of typical response cover aspects of personality, habits, interests, and
character.[1] Here, "response" may refer to overt actions such as taking

---

[1] In previous editions of this book, I referred to the second category as "tests of typical
behavior." That was consistent with the tendency to speak of a person as typically cautious,
or responsible, or anxious. But modern personality theory emphasizes the role of the situation in determining the person's actions and feelings, and the terminology "typical response" is intended to suggest the question "response to what?"

the lead (or remaining silent) in a social group, or to statements the person makes, or to hidden thoughts and feelings. Martin typically *acts* as if interested in his spouse's anecdotes about her day at the office and might typically *say* that he is interested, even though he is not. Both are within the realm of typical responses. (But to make her believe—*that* is ability!)

Typical response and ability are not truly separable. A person's record on typing tests establishes that his ability has reached some level, but the score also reflects his willingness to push himself in that kind of situation. That is to say, my distinction does not take purposes into account. Purposes are important, but they have been given little consideration in the psychology of individual differences (Snow & Farr, 1987).

Psychologists engaged in behavior modification make a distinction much like mine. With regard to some desirable behavior they ask first whether the response (e.g., a social skill) "is in the person's repertoire." When satisfied that the ability is present, they go on to investigate how often the person responds that way in various recurring situations.

Test directions almost never tell the examinee how to approach the task. Theoretically, style of performance falls under the head of typical response; but variations in style affect "ability" scores. The Porteus maze (Figure 2.1) is an observation technique in which the tester looks for evidence of planning and foresight, as well as being an ability test scored for speed and correctness.

10. *"An ability test is one on which the person cannot earn a better score than he deserves; on measures of emotional adjustment and social attitudes the person can give responses that make a good impression even if the responses are false." Does this distinction match the distinction between maximum performance and typical response?*

Tests of Maximum Performance

The distinguishing feature of a test of ability is that the test taker is encouraged to earn the best score he can. The goal of the tester should be to bring out the person's best possible performance (within the rules), and this means that the examinee must want to do well and must understand what is considered a good performance. If he is to show at his best, directions need to be clear and explicit, even to the extent of explaining how various sorts of errors will be penalized.

Some ability tests pose familiar tasks; others require the person to do something unfamiliar. In the Complex Coordination Test (Figure 2.2), a person who has never flown a plane operates a "stick" and "rudder bar." Flashing lights signal for certain movements; prompt, coordinated responses earn a high score.

One large group of tests includes EFT and mazes, and also tests of verbal reasoning; I refer to these as measures of "general mental ability." This term refers to a set of abilities valuable in almost any type of

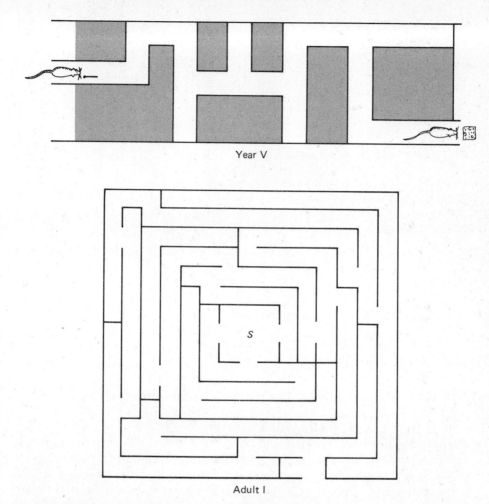

Year V

Adult I

Figure 2.1. **Two of the Porteus mazes.** The test taker is to trace the shortest path through the maze. A trial is scored as a failure whenever his pencil enters a blind alley. He is then given further trials on the same maze. When he gets one maze correct, he goes on to a more difficult one, continuing until he fails several trials on a maze. *(Source:* These mazes are copyright © 1933, 1953, 1955 The Psychological Corporation and reproduced by permission.)

thinking. Tests of this sort are often called "intelligence tests," but test interpretation is sounder if we avoid the myths that cling to the word "intelligence." Alongside general abilities are those pertinent to a limited range of tasks: mechanical comprehension, sense of pitch, finger dexterity, and so on.

Performance on a task important in its own right gives evidence of proficiency or competence. One can measure proficiency in speaking

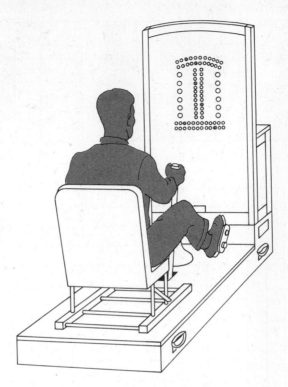

Figure 2.2. **Complex coordination test.**

French, in "hot-line" counseling, in fixing a faucet. The narrower term *achievement test* refers to a test covering something that the school presumably has taught directly—reading, for example, or knowledge of the solar system. A "mastery test" is an achievement test on a limited topic or skill, designed to establish whether a student has command of that material. The term "minimum competency" came into use in the 1970s. Critics of the schools had complained that many high school graduates were not adequately literate and employable. A test used to identify such students (either as an early warning or as a last hurdle) came to be known as a minimum competency test (Jaeger, in Linn, 1989a).

An *aptitude* test is one intended to predict success—there are tests of engineering aptitude, musical aptitude, aptitude for algebra, and so on. These tests are not distinct in form. A test of engineering aptitude may include sections measuring general mental ability, mechanical and spatial reasoning, and proficiency in mathematics.

The achievement/aptitude contrast is one of point of view, more than of test content (see p. 298). Any test is an achievement test inasmuch as it is a report on development and learning to date; and it is an aptitude test inasmuch as it says something about the future. Flaugher (1978) suggests that many of those who ask for "aptitude" testing look on individual differences in abilities as fixed and count on selection or classification to match persons to responsibilities. Those who ask for "achievement" testing, he says, think of individual differences as reflecting past experience and hope that training can equip the low scorer for future responsibility.

Measures of Typical Response

To most questions about feelings and habits, no particular response can be singled out as "good." There is nothing good or bad about interest in engineering. Likewise, we cannot say that a certain degree of dominance is best; the world offers roles congenial to persons all along the scale. Those hiring an executive whose past success guarantees ability wish also to know *how* he usually operates. Does he supervise closely, down to the last detail? Or does he outline a general task and turn his subordinates loose? Is he equally concerned with production, human problems, and finances? Does he prefer long-range planning or quick adaptation? Knowing his pattern helps to place him properly in the organization.

Information on habits has predictive value; what a person does once he is likely to do again. Most psychologists would deny, however, that a person's observed habits *are* his personality. A person does not always act as he did on past occasions. We do not wish to regard exceptional reactions as capricious and unexplainable. Therefore, we assume that the responses are generated by a consistent personality structure or belief system that is sensitive to situational differences. The structure has to be inferred from observations of behavior and reports on acts, opinions, and fantasies.

In the weeks before Prince Charles's wedding, the British press pursued every last scrap of information on the princess-to-be. She had taught kindergarten, and a reporter tracked down one of her pupils to ask, "What was she like?" Said the tot, "I don't know. She never told me." Most psychologists are in the position of the child—90 per cent of the information collected on personality, interests, and attitudes comes from subjects' reports. Nearly all the other psychologists are in the position of the reporter, relying on second-hand impressions. Direct and systematic observation by the psychologist and her aides is comparatively uncommon—but potentially a superior source of data.

Observation   Standardized observation requires that each person be placed in essentially the same situation. Personality may be observed during a mental test, during a group discussion, or when the person is challenged to walk along a two-by-four while blindfolded. Special tasks—performance tests of personality—have been devised to provide a good opportunity for observation.

The standardized observation enables us to compare persons who are not normally seen in similar circumstances. Moreover, it elicits responses that could be seen only occasionally in everyday life. For example, to examine reactions to frustration, the person is started on an activity and then prevented in some way from attaining the goal. In one study, preschool children were given the opportunity to play with ordinary, reasonably interesting toys. Then they were allowed into an adjoining room with highly attractive toys. After a period of play in this room, they were herded back into the first room, and a wire screen was placed between them and the attractive toys. The children reacted in many ways: pounding on the fence, regressing to simple play with rocks, trying to pry under the fence, or going off to take a pretended nap. In general, games after frustration were less mature and less constructive than before.

If typical behavior is wanted, the subject must not know what is being observed. The observer may be concealed, or the person may be led to believe that he is being tested on one characteristic while something else is observed. When reaction to frustration is being studied, the test taker may be told that his mental ability is being tested. When he is frustrated by difficult questions, his responses are little disguised.

Typical behavior may also be observed in samples taken "in the field." Children on the playground reveal a good deal about their habits and personality; so do noncoms leading platoons and workers in the office. The baseball batting average summarizes systematically recorded field observations. The industrial supervisor's merit ratings are also based on observation, but they are almost always unsystematic.

The situations referred to in the preceding paragraph are standardized only to a limited extent. On the playground, each child is reacting to playmates' unstandardized acts. On the diamond, the pitches offered change from one at-bat to the next.

When the tester proposes to disguise her purpose or to observe without the target's knowledge, ethical questions arise. Ethical principles worked out for the conduct of research have implications also for testing (American Psychological Association, 1973; in brief, 1981).

"Invasion of privacy" is being more and more strictly interpreted; practices considered normal in one decade are judged inadvisable in the next. Every psychology laboratory has a half-silvered mirror that enables an observer to look into the interview room or playroom without herself being seen. In times past, the subject would not have been told about the observer. Today a common practice is to show the subject (or the parent if the subject is a young child) the observer's station and the view through the mirror, explaining casually that the arrangement is intended to eliminate distraction. Once absorbed in a task and especially on repeat visits, the subject is not likely to remain mindful of the mirror. Another fair practice is to give a generalized indication: "We'll be observing how you interact with your child from time to time when you are at the center, even when we do not tell you that we are keeping a record. Sometimes the observations will help us to make suggestions to you. Of course, if you do not wish to be observed, you should tell us. And if, on a particular day, something happens that you don't want in the file, you can ask us to tear up any record and we will."

Candor ought not be pressed beyond the limits of common sense. The speech clinician does not say, "I'm going to count how many times you stammer"; the child psychologist does not tell the mother, "I'm going to count the times when you seem uncertain of yourself."

Self-report   A person knows a great deal about his own behavior. Questionnaires—often called "inventories"—are used to obtain self-descriptions. There are study habit inventories, interest inventories, social-attitude inventories, and so on. The biographical inventory may touch on anything from marital history to feelings about one's father to past and present recreations. A questionnaire title should avoid the word "test" in order to avoid suggesting that (say) dominance is directly measured.

Whereas the traditional inventory asks generalized questions—"Are you a heavy drinker?"—another approach asks the person to observe his own behavior at a particular time. The person can be asked to record *each evening* his alcohol intake for the day, perhaps along with a note on the circumstances under which he took each drink. The virtue of self-observation is the definiteness of the information. The procedure is intrusive and is likely to alter the behavior itself—an advantage when the recording reinforces a therapeutic process, but a disadvantage when one is trying to investigate typical behavior.

Direct self-observation of actions should tell us pretty much what a second observer would report. Direct self-observation of thoughts and feelings, however, captures information not otherwise available. A structured measurement procedure—the Experience Sampling Method—was devised by Csikszentmihalyi and Larson (1984) for research on adolescence. The respondents, enlisted as junior coinvestigators, understood that information collected was not going to affect them in any way.

Each participant wore a pager and carried a pad of the forms illustrated in Figure 2.3. Signals—about 80 in all—were sent at spaced, irregular intervals during the week of data collection, at hours from 7:30 A.M. to 10:30 P.M. (later on Friday and Saturday). The participant was to fill out the form immediately when the pager signaled, but perfect compliance was not demanded. The response rate of 69 per cent was held down mostly by failure of the pagers; there seems to have been little censorship. Many responses, including the one in Figure 2.3, were obviously spontaneous. (Incidentally, the mother appeared to the investigator to be sensitive and reasonable; R. Larson, personal communication, 1989.)

A principal virtue of the technique was the standard report form that seemed to fit every person and event. This permitted statistical comparisons across individuals and across kinds of settings. The data show some striking associations; for example, a clear rise in excitement as weekend evenings grew later, matched to a self-conscious decrease in self-control.

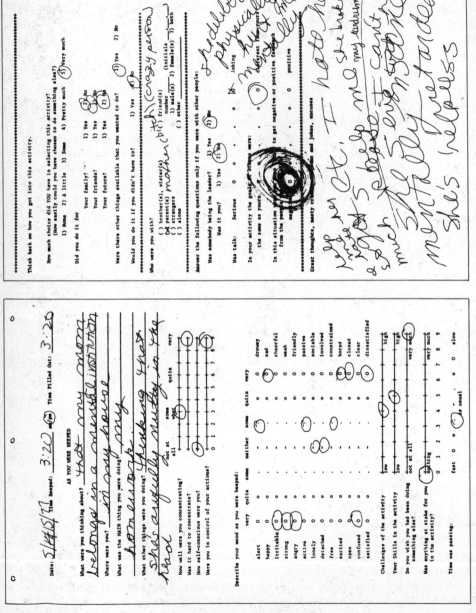

Figure 2.3. **A self-report of mood and behavior at a sampled moment.** (*Source:* From *Being Adolescent: Conflict and Growth in the Teenage Years* by Mihaly Csikszentmihalyi and Reed Larson. Copyright © 1984 by Basic Books, Inc. Reprinted by permission of the publisher.)

11. *Classify each of the following as a test of ability, a self-report, an observation in a standardized situation, or an observation in an unstandardized situation:*
    a. *An interviewer from the Gallup poll asks a citizen how he will vote in a coming election.*
    b. *A television producer wishes to know what program features appeal to different types of listeners. She presents a show to a small audience, who press signal buttons to indicate whether they enjoy or dislike what they are seeing at each moment.*
    c. *A test of "vocational aptitude" asks how well the counselee likes such activities as selling, woodworking, and chess.*
    d. *A spelling test is given to applicants for a clerical job.*
    e. *Inspectors in plain clothes ride buses to determine whether operators are obeying the company rules.*
    f. *During a maze test, the examiner watches for evidence of self-confidence or its absence.*
    g. *Students are told about a proposal to limit population growth in a suburb by giving few permits for new sewer connections. They are asked to say what the town council should do and to give reasons to support the choice.*
    h. *An inspector in a stocking factory is supposed to detect all stockings with knitting faults. As a check on efficiency, at certain times a number of faulty stockings that have been marked with fluorescent dye are mixed into the batch for inspection. The dye is invisible to the worker, but by turning an ultraviolet lamp onto the stockings after inspection the supervisor can readily locate any faulty stockings the inspector missed.*
12. *Classify each of the following tests, using as many of the descriptive terms discussed in the text as are clearly applicable.*
    a. *The Study of Values consists of printed questions, such as*

    In your opinion, can a man who works in business all week best spend Sunday in
    1. trying to educate himself by reading serious books?
    2. trying to win at golf, or racing?
    3. going to an orchestral concert?
    4. hearing a really good sermon?

    The respondent checks whichever answer he prefers. A numerical key counts up how important "aesthetic," "religious," and other values are for him.
    b. *In a certain "mechanical aptitude" test, the person marks illustrations of tools and other objects to show which go together (e.g., hammer and anvil).*
    c. *A Picture Arrangement item presents four pictures that, arranged in the correct order, tell a story in the manner of a cartoon strip (see Figure 7.2, p. 246). Each picture is on a separate card. The cards are presented in a random arrangement and the test taker arranges them to make an intelligible story.*
    d. *The Short Imaginal Processes Inventory consists of 45 items such as these:*

I tend to be easily bored.
My daydreams are often stimulating and rewarding.
In my dreams I show anger toward my enemies.

*The person responds on a 5-point scale, ranging from "strongly charac-
teristic of me" to the opposite. Three scores are reported: Positive-Con-
structive Daydreaming, Guilt and Fear-of-Failure Daydreaming, and
Attentional Control.*

TESTING IN THE COMPUTER AGE

The computer plays many roles behind the testing scene and can do a
star turn as tester. The topic is introduced here because the computer is
changing ideas of what tests can and should be (Roid, in Plake & Witt,
1986). Because of its consistency, the computer carries standardization
to an extreme; yet it can achieve standardized measurement while presenting different questions (and personalized feedback) to every test
taker.

Feedback can be remarkably complex, almost like a personal conference. In career guidance, for example, the computer can ask questions
that help the person reflect on his interests and work experience, and
can suggest where to obtain information about suitable occupations.

Item Banks

The most familiar kind of test is a printed booklet filled with questions.
Nowadays, a well-printed test to fit particular local requirements can be
produced quickly by drawing on an "item bank"—a file of items classified by content and difficulty level. A school system can ask a supplier
for a social studies test whose mix of topics matches its curriculum. It is
now practical to store item banks locally and to assemble tests with a
microcomputer (F. Baker, in Linn, 1989a). Any number of equivalent
tests can be made up by selecting every set of items according to the
same plan.

The federal government once planned to place much of civil service
testing on computers (Urry, 1977). The plans were shelved before completion—not, apparently, because feasibility and cost were in question.
The fact that the computer can generate a fresh test for every person is
its prime attraction for the civil service. Month after month, applicants
for the same kind of job come in for testing, and questions leak when a
test is used over and over. A human staff can assemble no more than a
few test forms for each job. With numerous items on a computer tape,
the computer can assemble a fresh form for each applicant and yet transform all scores to a common scale.

The advantage becomes considerably greater when the test covers
problems a computer can solve. Would-be customs officers might be
asked to compute the duty to be paid on a shipment of assorted imports,

using a complex rate schedule. That task can be framed in a general way. For each examinee, the computer can arbitrarily alter the rates, rules, or makeup of the shipment. Facing that kind of test, the candidate has no option but to learn to apply rate schedules. He gains nothing from finding out which rules a friend had to apply last week.

The desire to maintain test security motivated the Department of Defense to spend five years redesigning for computer administration the qualification test (ASVAB) it gives to potential recruits. The services do not want to encourage applicants of limited ability, but the recruiters who round up prospects are eager to enlist all possible warm bodies. Knowing the test items, some recruiters coach weak applicants who would otherwise fail the test (or at least that is suspected). With the infinitely variable computerized test, such coaching would become impossible. In the end, designs for the computerized ASVAB were shelved without use, because someone with a sharp pencil calculated the cost of installing the necessary hardware nationwide (Bunderson, Inouye, & Olsen, in Linn, 1989a, p. 383).

Automated Administration

Computers are good at presenting tests directly to individuals—an audiometric test, for example. In diagnosing hearing disorders and in fitting hearing aids, the tester adjusts pure tones upward and downward in volume to determine the lowest volume the person can hear. A human tester would direct the examinee to press a key when he hears the tone in his headset. She would set the frequency dial at (say) 800 hertz (cycles per second), set the volume dial at a middling level (say, 5), and press for 0.5 second the key that delivers the tone. After the response, the tester would mark a record sheet. More trials at the same frequency—without further audible directions but with a "ready" light—might use settings 4 (eliciting a positive response coded $+$), 3 ($+$), 0 ($-$; a trial to test for false claims), 2 ($-$), 3 ($-$), 2 ($-$), 3 ($+$), and so on. At some point the tester would settle on an estimate (somewhere near 3 in this case) of the person's hearing threshold at 800 hertz, then shift to another pitch.

The computer can do the same things, saving the costly time of the professional. The computer delivers directions visually or through earphones. resets the signal without error, and times signals precisely. Unlike a knob turner, it can set signal values at 3.1 or 3.05. The computer can locate the threshold faster and, seconds after the last response, can immediately print out a profile of success as a function of pitch. Satellite transmission makes it possible to send the information instantly to a specialist halfway around the world.

Among the talents of the computer seen in this example are the following:

Precise adherence to schedules and plans.

Delicate control of stimuli.

Choice of successive test items in the light of performance to date ("adaptive testing").

Immunity to fatigue, boredom, lapse of attention, and inadvertent scoring error.

Instant and accurate scoring.

Legible records, with multiple copies and distant transmission.

Naturally, computerizing a test loses something, particularly in eliminating the unstandardized observations that a skilled clinician makes during a traditional individual test.

Interacting with the computer fascinates test takers (at least in these days when the experience is still novel). When reasoning problems were presented to college students either by a computer or by a human tester, this was the report:

> [C]omputer-run subjects are more apt to pause for long periods of time without typing anything into the computer. Human-run subjects may feel under some pressure to keep behaving even at the risk of doing something wrong. Computer-run subjects have been heard (through the semi-soundproofed walls of their cubicles) to shout for joy, curse, bang the walls, and sing, certainly modes of expression which a typical subject avoids in the presence of an experimenter. (Johnson & R. Baker, 1972, p. 31; for a formal report, see Johnson & Baker, 1973).

You might think that the computer is adapted only to literate and emotionally stable subjects. But preschool children and mental patients respond well to automated displays. The computer's patience is inexhaustible. If the deteriorated schizophrenic does not make a move for 4 hours, the display simply waits. If the distractible child can be captured for testing only after four preliminary sessions with animated cartoons, the computer provides them without fidgeting.

Many tests and inventories have versions for on-line testing by means of a microcomputer in a school or a psychologist's office. The software not only can administer the test with no human tester in the room, but will prepare a score report for immediate printout. The computer-administered version of a test first developed in printed or oral form is usually a close match to the original version.

It seems that the conventional and computer versions of a test do usually measure the same variables, but difficulty or reliability can easily change. Whether the computer version is "the same test" must be questioned with each instrument in turn psychologically. Diagrams may be harder to read from the terminal than from the printed page. Test takers unfamiliar with the keyboard may have trouble if the actions required (for example, to review an item and change the answer) are at all complicated. Even when the test itself is unchanged, interacting with a machine may be psychologically different from responding to a human tester. When computer technology permits a change in the task—introducing time-controlled displays, for example—what the test measures will change. The computer test of patient-management skills (p. 13) ranks candidates for certification quite differently than they rank on a paper-and-pencil test that was designed for the same purpose (Melnick, 1988).

Adaptive Testing   A most valuable feature is the computer's ability to choose test items in the light of the examinee's previous successes and failures. This is called sequential or adaptive or tailored testing. Audio-metric testers have always chosen test stimuli in the light of previous responses. In the example given above, it was sensible to present signals at levels 2 and 3 once the respondent had detected signals of strength 4; if a person made errors at 4, slightly louder signals would be appropriate.

"Branching" techniques are especially useful in testing complex intellectual skills, the test for physicians described on page 13 being an example. After the test taker responds to an initial display of information about the patient, further information is provided. Step-by-step, the test taker proposes an action or requests further specific information and is told what the laboratory finds or the nurse observes or the like.

Adjusting difficulty so that the examinee works mostly on items that are neither too hard nor too easy for him should improve motivation. Also it is easy for the computer to indicate instantly whether an answer is right or wrong, and that can heighten motivation (although this is not a usual feature of adaptive tests used in assessment). An illustrative finding: Without instant feedback, blacks in an inner-city high school omitted many items and got lower scores than white classmates. When the computer provided feedback after each item, blacks omitted few items and overtook the white students (Betz, 1975; for other studies, see Betz & Weiss, 1976a, 1976b; Prestwood & Weiss, 1978). A general statement would be risky, however; what encourages one person disturbs another.

Computer-assisted instruction embodies many features of adaptive testing. When the student logs onto the terminal today, the computer recalls not only yesterday's level of performance but the tasks on which the student was least adequate; today's exercises are chosen accordingly. The exercises themselves serve as a test. Hence the computer's record becomes an up-to-the-minute multidimensional description of the individual, more differentiated than an ordinary test and more accurate than a teacher's perceptions. There are similar possibilities in speech therapy, career exploration, and other developmental activities.

Computer-generated Displays   New technology is greatly increasing the possible variety of test stimuli. For testing physicians, a display called up from videodisk presents photographs for interpretation (an X ray or a microscope slide, for example). Simulators for astronauts have realistic stimulus arrays, realistic equipment to manipulate, and continuous feedback of the results of actions. Although designed for training, the devices measure the trainee's progress and so they *are* tests.

The Micropat equipment in Figure 2.4 presents a modern complex coordination test (cf. p. 40) that the British armed services are investigating. The foot pedals are somewhat like the old ones, but the realistic joystick has been replaced by a small one. Today, handling of information is regarded as far more significant than large-muscle coordination. The important part of this test, of course, is the software that generates an ever-changing display. The old test was inflexible. The new one— with stimuli that can be endlessly altered, and controlled in speed— permits thousands of variations. Much research will be needed to determine what patterning of stimuli provides the best predictive information. (For an example of such "parametric" research, which is a step toward "engineering" of psychological tests, see Bartram et al., 1985.)

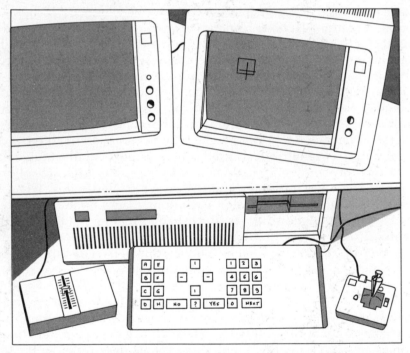

Figure 2.4. **Micropat system for delivering perceptual and motor tests.** The small "stick" at the right controls up-and-down movement. Foot pedals not seen here control tilt, and the slide at the left hand controls size or, in some tasks, speed. In the coordination task shown, the square wanders about irregularly and the examinee tries to keep the cross centered in the square and matched to it in size and tilt. The second display can present information or instructions. The keyboard has ten letters, ten digits, four arrows, plus YES and NO. (*Source:* D. Bartram. Reproduced by permission. The Micropat test designs, software, documentation, and screen displays are all U. K. Crown copyright © 1985, 1987, 1988. Micropat is distributed by the U. K. Ministry of Defence approved licencees: Bartdale (Human Factors Specialists) Ltd. Applegarth, Leconfield, Beverley, N. Humberside, HU17 7NQ, UK.)

Micropat is a delivery system rather than a "test." Many functions—reaction time, control of motor speed, spatial reasoning, and so on—can be programmed for assessment with the same equipment.

13. *It would be possible to put an audiometric test on a sound tape. The tape would, let us say, speak the item number, then present a tone or a silent period; the respondent would check items during which he hears a tone in his headset. What are the advantages and disadvantages of this procedure? Compare with the procedures described in the text for*
    a. *the human tester*
    b. *the computer*

INFERENCES, SHORT AND LONG

Some interpreters are willing—and some reluctant—to make inferences regarding future circumstances. For some purposes, the tester need scarcely look beyond the time and place of observation. She observes that a child makes no errors such as "The cows is" in today's composition; this fact might be extended no further than "This week he is handling singular-plural constructions correctly." Bold long-reach inference is illustrated when a fond mother, noting that her child often sings a tune correctly upon first hearing it, says, "He has a real aptitude for music." That generalizes over a broad class of tasks, over many years to come.

The most conservative approach to inference is to assume that the person will in the future be what he has been in the past (or, allowing for growth, will hold his relative position among his fellows). An assessment of competence in a practical task or role is likely to be valid for a long time to come (McClelland, 1973; Wernimont & Campbell, 1968). In the absence of physical decline, even competence that fades through disuse can be recaptured with renewed practice. Habits also are more likely to persist than to change. A driver's record of accidents and traffic citations is a sound basis for inference by the insurance company.

The chief business of the helping professions, however, is to bring about change. For the persons they serve, conservative predictions are inherently pessimistic or limiting. The professional must make longer inferences to help the person set goals for change and to judge what assistance will benefit him most.

Long inference is usual in impressionistic interpretation; it tries to suggest how the person will respond to changing conditions. Some psychometric interpretations also have a long reach, as when certain errors made in copying geometric drawings are identified (probabilistically) with a particular kind of brain damage or when earthbound tests are used to select persons for training as astronauts.

An observation states a time-bound fact (or the observer's impression that she considers factual). For example: "Today Sam took $4\frac{1}{2}$ minutes to type 200 words." But facts are recorded with broader questions in view.

As a minimum, that performance is regarded as representing Sam at this point in training. It is a sample of this day's, or this week's, work. If the tester is conducting research on fatigue, and this score comes on the fifth piece of copy Sam typed during a single session, the score sums up performance at this moment; the investigator does not regard the score as representative even of the session. Still, the investigator is assuming that the decline in performance that accompanied fatigue today represents what would be found on other days. All tests, then, are samples.

Sometimes the behavior sampled is of no direct interest; rather, it is taken as a sign or indicator of other behavior or inner states. The maze test is of interest as a sign, not as a sample. No animal or person ever runs a maze except as a psychological test. The number of trials required to learn the maze is taken as an indicator of a broader ability. It is far more difficult to study learning in the natural ecology than in the test situation, and rates of learning something with which some learners are already partly familiar would be harder to interpret than rates on the unfamiliar, artificial task. Inferring brain damage from errors in copying diagrams is another example of reasoning from a sign.

Traits, States, and Acts Psychologists investigate both "traits" and "states." With regard to anxiety, for example, the intensity of anxious feelings (the person's present state) shifts from day to day. The person's trait level is usually conceived of as an average or typical state; if so, it reflects not only his characteristics but also the stresses usually present in his environment. "Ability" almost always is thought of as a moderately stable trait, but performance level is transient. A runner can be "up" for a track meet, or "off his form." These are states.

Concepts such as "anxiety" and "ability" are constructs ("*constructs*"). They describe not one action but the characteristic organization or efficiency of thoughts or actions. Construct interpretations evolve. One old-time hypothesis was that the maze score indicates "intelligence pure and simple." That idea has had to be replaced with more specific descriptions. A carefully bred strain of rats that did well on mazes did not give other evidence of superior "intelligence." As research proceeded, the narrower construct "aptitude for maze learning" also broke down. Trying a variety of test conditions led to a restricted conclusion: "This strain has aptitude for learning elevated mazes when kept hungry and given food at the goal box" (p. 322). This conclusion is still a generalization, but one with a short reach.

A formal construct is invoked when inference reaches out to diverse situations. "Musical talent" is a more convenient dimension than "talent for stringed instruments." That, in turn, is handier but less definitive than "dexterity in rapid finger movements" and "pitch discrimination." The broad construct is neither true nor false; it is adequate for some purposes and inadequate for others.

Constructs that go deeper into the psyche are obviously bolder hypotheses. (Compare "Is unable to accept his own hostile impulses" with "Response to challenging questions is cool, formal, polite.") The deeper interpretation rests on a complex theory about the wellsprings of behavior, and few such theories have been well substantiated. How appropriate it is to offer a somewhat speculative, somewhat artistic analysis-in-depth is much disputed. Only two morals need be drawn at this point. Those who stick to literal reports of acts leave to others the burden of interpretation; those others might (or might not) be better served if the psychologist had offered an interpretation. Those who offer imaginative hypotheses as if they were scientific reports lead their clients into quicksand.

Since the days when phrenology was exposed as fallacious, psychologists have been trying to get away from the notion that traits are objects, comparable to the pituitary gland and the X chromosome. We find it natural to speak of "shyness." But shyness is not an entity; the word is a summary of responses. To say that a person is shy means only that, in many situations, the person has exhibited actions associated with that construct.

Placing a person on a scale or tallying up actions merges diverse acts, and so glosses over the texture of behavior. A person may be shy at parties and not in debate, with strangers and not with acquaintances, with females and not with males. The shyness may be wholly internal; the person confides feelings of social unease to a counselor that everyday associates know nothing of. Another person's inhibition and withdrawal may be apparent to everyone.

Behavior Analysis   The behavioral tradition minimizes reference to mental states, categories of disorder, and global traits of personality. The behaviorist, however, still has to categorize situations and acts. In assessing how messages regarding heart disease affect eating, she could ask each subject to record daily food intake on a checklist. One entry would be "eggs." Would it not be better to ask whether the eggs are boiled or fried? And, if fried, in lard or safflower oil? The finer categories fit the information more closely to the problem. Even so concrete a measurement, then, is framed by constructs ("high cholesterol," "polyunsaturated"). The fineness of categories will depend on the purpose of an inquiry, but categories there must be.

Those engaged in behavior modification and other situation-oriented applications sharply distinguish short-inference description from assigning labels, summing up responses in "trait" scores, or explaining in terms of inferred motives. In the book that inspired the neobehaviorist school of thought Walter Mischel (1968, p. 10) stated the motif: "In behavioral analysis the emphasis is on what a person *does* rather than on inferences about what attributes he *has* more globally." What the person does in a defined situation can be described in a simple count of actions on several occasions. To say "what the person is like" would require the psychologist to go beyond counts of actions to descriptive language and, beyond that, to imaginative construction of an explanation.

In planning treatment, in evaluating progress, and in assessing alternative treatment methods, behaviorists have as much occasion to test as other applied psychologists. Indeed, tests play a special monitoring role in their work because the client learns to regulate himself by keeping track of his responses. He is taught, for example, to note whether he does speak up each time he is at odds with something his spouse says. Behaviorists are particularly concerned with the frequency of significant acts in context and with changes in the pattern. Just as schoolteachers keep an eye on a pupil's progress and confusions from lesson to lesson or week to week, psychologists attempting to reshape behavior monitor the process and change their tactics as needed.

Behaviorists feel no need to probe into the origins of a response pattern; they search out current circumstances that trigger the response. When a person with emotional distress seeks assistance, a psychologist of this school tries to pin down the *kinds* of situation the client typically has trouble coping with or that arouse unpleasant feelings.

Behaviorists minimize inference. The data they use are closely matched to the client's difficulties—no inkblot tests for them. Behavioral treatment bears directly on the acts that are to be retrained (and not on attempts to develop the client's "insight" or to resolve his internal conflicts). When one is trying to increase self-assertion, the repeated tallying-up of acts of self-assertion is a test that matches the "lessons."

Behaviorists continue to prefer short inferences, but what was once a generalized opposition to "testing" has abated. Behaviorists recognize that their focused procedures have to be judged by the same psychometric standards as conventional tests. Also, they are finding conventional tests valuable in their work (Hersen, in Goldstein & Hersen, 1984; Strohsahl & Linehan, in Ciminero et al., 1986; Turkat, 1985).

14. *In which of these respects would you expect behavior analysts to follow the tradition of psychometric measurement?*
   a. *Expressing numerically the strength of a response tendency.*
   b. *Grouping within one category or score two kinds of behavior, such as submissiveness and shyness, that tend to be found together.*
   c. *Specifying a definite kind of task or situation in which to collect data on many persons.*
   d. *Use of norms in evaluating frequency of problem behavior.*

15. *What testing, if any, would play a part in a behavior analyst's approach to a 10-year-old who has made poor progress in learning to read?*

16. *"Comprehends what he reads" is a broad construct. What narrower constructs might describe distinct types of comprehension?*

17. *Anastasi (1988, p. 510) notes that the behaviorist uses constructs when speaking even of something as definite as "fear of dogs." She says that the boundaries of the construct have to be checked so that generalization is not too broad. How would one check the boundaries? Would they be similar for all persons distressed by dogs?*

Chapter
3

Administering Tests

3A. What should be covered in the standard directions to examinees for an aptitude test to be used in guidance of adolescents?

3B. How does the role of the person giving an individual test differ from that of a medical technician collecting a blood sample for analysis?

3C. What principles should guide the person who, for purposes of legal procedures, is assigned to administer an individual test to an uncooperative adult?

3D. Those who prepare students to take ability tests (and testers themselves) can do many things that tend to improve scores. What actions would tend to make the students' scores less valid?

3E. How may restrictions intended to protect test takers impede collection or use of information that would be helpful in decision making or research?

Abbreviations in this chapter: DAT for Differential Aptitude Tests; MCT for Mechanical Comprehension Test; SAT for Scholastic Aptitude Test.

The tester's first responsibility is to choose a test that fits the test taker. It is gross malpractice to give an ability test on which the person is likely to do poorly for irrelevant reasons. The maze test, for example, should be given only to persons possessing normal control of their hand movements. Similarly, 14-year-olds in a nonacademic program should not be invited to fill out a vocational-interest questionnaire designed for college students—at least not without verifying that they understand the questions.

A misleading score is worse than none at all; if a suitable test cannot be found, the proper report is "no score could be obtained." Even when someone engages the tester to give a specific test, the tester ought to judge independently whether the test is suitable. The same is to be said of the research assistant told to collect data on a group of uncooperative drug users. Choking off the flow of bad data is no small part of the job.

If data are to be interpreted in the light of norms, the tester must follow the standard procedures. But in administering an ability test the tester is obligated to give the examinee a full chance to display his competence and standard procedures may not fit. The tester will not necessarily realize in advance that a test is unsuitable, but she should remain alert to indications of invalid response. When standard procedure will lead to invalid conclusions, she probably should change the procedure. Her report must emphasize that the test was nonstandard.

Some tests are sufficiently simple for any adult to give; a few are so subtle that extensive supervised practice is recommended. Considerable skill is required when the tester is to question the examinee orally and to use follow-up questions whenever the first answer is unclear.

1. *In testing a group of college freshmen to obtain information for use in guidance, the examiner finds that a student newly arrived from Latin America is having great difficulty following directions because of unfamiliarity with English. The student asks many questions, requests repetitions, and seems unable to comprehend what is desired. What should the examiner do?*

ORIENTATION

The main message in this chapter—the tester's responsibility to collect good information—is easy to grasp. Doing the job right is not so easy; I provide as concrete a guide to practice as possible in the central portion of the chapter (pp. 63–78). Preceding that important material, I introduce two specimen tests. The description is for background. The Block Design test and the Test of Mechanical Comprehension will reappear later to provide concrete instances of norms, errors of measurement, and so on. Merely reading the descriptions will provide the image of the tests you will need to flesh out the later examples. The extended quotations from test directions also demonstrate that many details must be given attention to standardize test procedure (but there is no point in remembering particular bits of these directions).

Short sections on two subtopics—"guessing" and "coaching"—deserve close attention so that you will remember the policy recommendations and understand the reasons behind them. Attached to the material on coaching is a note on "dynamic" testing procedure, which I shall discuss more thoroughly in Chapter 9. (I mention it in Chapter 3 just to show that rigorous "standardization" is not always the ideal way to test.)

A comparatively simple but highly important section outlines rights of test takers. You ought to fix all the recommendations in your mind and think about the difficulties in applying them. Much of the advice departs from past practices. Try to make up your own examples of situations where there is danger that a rule will be violated because of institutional tradition or a tester's insensitivity.

TWO SPECIMEN TESTS

To illustrate this chapter and several later ones two tests are described in some detail. These tests are important in themselves, but serve in this book primarily to illustrate general principles.

Block Design

In Block Design, the examinee is to construct prescribed designs out of colored 1-inch cubes. The Block Design test, developed by S. C. Kohs, was one of many mental tests invented during the 1920s, when applied psychology first came into prominence. As schools began to hire psychologists to examine children, demand arose for standardized collections of tests. A psychologist acting as editor collected tests by various authors; improved the directions, materials, and scoring procedures; and applied the whole set to many children to obtain norms for each age. The block design task was chosen for many of these collections inasmuch as it measures nonverbal reasoning over a wide range of difficulty. Revision and restandardization have continued down to the present day. The modification may alter the items or the directions or change the procedure radically (pp. 95, 308, 329).

I shall describe the version used in WISC-R, the Wechsler Intelligence Scale for Children—Revised (Wechsler, 1974, pp. 84–88). I am told that only a few details of the procedure will change in the forthcoming WISC-II. Red-and-white blocks and cards (Figure 3.1) are used. Designs 1 and 2 are presented as block models to be copied; for Designs 3 to 11, the child is to match the pattern on a card.

The directions are detailed. For example, the examiner is told to make sure that the child is seated squarely before the table and is told to place the model slightly to the child's left if the child is right-handed—to the right otherwise. The blocks are laid out irregularly before the child, but the rules specify, for example, that when four blocks are used, only one of them is to have its red-and-white surface facing up.

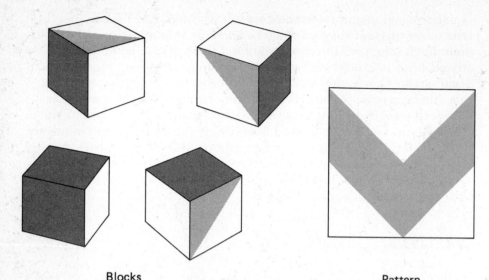

Blocks   Pattern

Figure 3.1. Block Design materials. *(Source:* Pattern copyright © 1940, 1955, 1976, 1981 by The Psychological Corporation and reproduced by permission.)

The general procedure is to lay out the pattern and the required number of blocks, time the performance, and allow credit if a correct copy is made in the specified time. If the child does not perform adequately on Design 3 (where children 8 years old and older start), he is allowed a second trial before moving back to Design 1. On Designs 4 to 11, only one trial is allowed, and a quick success earns a bonus. The specific directions to the tester are as follows, when the test begins with Design 3:[1]

> Design 3. Take four blocks in hand and say, **See these blocks? They are all alike. On some sides they are all red; on some, all white; and on some, half red and half white.** Turn the blocks to show the different sides. Then say, **They can be put together to make a design like the one you see on the card. Watch me.** Construct the design slowly. Then scramble the blocks, give them to the child, and say, **Now you make one like the card. Go ahead.** Start timing, and allow 45 seconds.

If the child fails, the demonstration and the scrambling are repeated for the second trial. When the child passes, he goes directly to Design 4. The directions continue in part as follows:

> DESIGNS 4–. Be sure the child has four blocks; scramble the blocks. Place the card with Design 4 before the child and say, **Now make one like this. Try to work as quickly as you can. Tell me when you have finished.** Start timing, and allow 45 seconds.

---

[1]Copyright © 1974 by The Psychological Corporation. Reprinted by permission.

(Designs 9–11 require all nine blocks.) The test stops when the child fails on two consecutive designs. In addition to noting time and errors, including errors the child spontaneously corrects, the tester watches for any revealing remark, any emotional reaction or blocking, and any unusual method of attacking the task. Some children deal with the pattern as a whole, and some consider each tiny section in turn. Some give up when they face difficulty, some become erratic, and others show increased interest under the greater challenge.

2. *What techniques are used in Block Design to give the child a full opportunity to understand what is wanted?*

3. *What style of work will earn the highest score on Block Design as Wechsler scores it? Is it appropriate to reward that style?*

4. *The manual is not regarded as sufficient to prepare one to give the Wechsler test. The tester learns by observing an experienced tester and discussing procedures with her. What do you think you could learn about giving Block Design that the manual did not specify?*

Mechanical Comprehension

The Bennett Mechanical Comprehension Test (MCT) is widely used for employee selection. The Mechanical Reasoning section of the Differential Aptitude Test (DAT) battery for high school guidance is a near twin. Illustrative data and research findings will be drawn from the DAT and from current and past editions of the Bennett test. I shall let MCT refer to any forms of these. According to the manual,[2]

> Forms S and T of the *Bennett Mechanical Comprehension Test* . . . measure the ability to perceive and understand the relationship of physical forces and mechanical elements in practical situations. This type of aptitude is important for a wide variety of jobs and for engineering training, as well as for many trade school courses.
>
> . . .
>
> Mechanical comprehension may be regarded as one aspect of intelligence, if intelligence is broadly defined. The person who scores high in this trait tends to learn readily the principles of operation and repair of complex devices. . . . Care has been taken to present items in terms of simple, frequently encountered mechanisms that do not resemble textbook illustrations or require special knowledge.

Two items are presented to orient the person before the test proper begins. (The DAT version has an orientation booklet that includes specimen items to which the directions are tied—of which X in Figure 3.2 is one—and five practice items similar to the test proper. Item 5 in the figure is a moderately difficult practice item.)

---

[2]Quoted material in this section is reproduced by permission of The Psychological Corporation. Typography has been altered for consistency with other selections.

Example X.

Which person has the heavier load?
(If equal, mark C.)

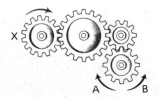

5.

When gear "X" turns in the direction
shown, which way does the bottom
gear turn?
(If either, Mark C.)

Figure 3.2. **Mechanical Comprehension items.** (*Source:* Both items appear in the orientation booklet for the DAT. Copyright © 1972, 1973, 1975, 1980, 1982 by The Psychological Corporation. Reproduced by permission.)

More than 17 aspects of machines appear in items of Forms S and T; each form has 8 items on hydraulics, 5 on pulleys, 3 on electricity, and so forth. The distribution of content reflects not only the authors' judgments about importance but also their success in devising challenging items. Suitable items depend more on reasoning than on specific technical knowledge.

The Bennett manual says this to the examiner:

Seat the examinees in a well-lighted, adequately ventilated room. There should be enough desk or table space to accommodate a test booklet and answer sheet for each person. Chairs with tablet arms should be avoided if possible. Each examinee should have two well-sharpened pencils, and the examiner or proctors should have a spare supply.

Distribute answer sheets first and then the test booklets. Speaking clearly and loudly enough for everyone to hear, say:

Please do not open the test booklet until I tell you to. You will do all your writing on the answer sheet only. (Examiner holds up answer sheet.) **Now look at your answer sheet.**

[Instructions to fill in name and other information follow.]

Open your test booklet to Page 2 and fold back the rest of the booklet. Read silently the directions at the top of Page 2 while I read them aloud. Look at Example X on this page.

Example X shows a picture of two people carrying a typewriter on a board and asks, "Which person has the heavier load? (If equal, mark C.)" Person B has the heavier load because the weight is closer to him than to person A. Therefore, the circle for B has been filled in on line X of your answer sheet.

Now do the next one, Example Y, yourself. Mark the correct space on line Y of your answer sheet.

[After a time, this answer is discussed. The examiner continues:]

Now read silently the instructions at the bottom of Page 2 while I read them aloud. On the following pages there are more pictures and questions. Read each question carefully, look at the picture, and fill in the circle under the best answer on the answer sheet. Make sure that your marks are heavy and black. Erase completely any answer you wish to change. Do not make any marks in this booklet.

After the instructions have been read, say:

You will have thirty minutes for the entire test. . . . Are there any questions? If you have any questions, you must ask them now because we cannot allow questions after the test has begun.

During the ensuing thirty minutes walk about quietly, checking whether the examinees are marking the answer sheets properly. If any of the examinees finish before the end of the test period, collect their answer sheets and test booklets and dismiss them quietly. At the end of thirty minutes, say:

This is the end of the test. Please give me your answer sheets and test booklets.

The Computer Version   Another form of MCT is administered on a personal computer (usually as part of the whole DAT battery). The test is essentially self-administering; ordinarily a school obtains the materials and invites students to come in one by one for the test. When it ordered test materials, the school was supplied with orientation booklets. The test taker should have been given one to study in advance so that he comes to the test familiar with the directions and the kind of items he will face. Even though the disk is intended to be complete in itself, an informed person should be standing by for the test taker to call upon if he needs help.

The student signs out the diskette, slides it into the computer, and follows instructions that appear on the screen. The session starts with prompts requesting the student to type in his name, the date of testing, and a few other facts. A warm-up exercise follows, and then there are several very easy items to make the response routine familiar. Next, the disk presents the specimen items and directions for MCT (which the orientation booklet had already presented).

Although MCT originated as a multiple-choice test, the computer version calls for YES/NO responses. The picture appears on the screen along with the choices and "Is A correct?" If the student presses N for NO, the dialogue might run on as follows:

"Is B correct?" Y; "Are you sure?" N;

"Is C correct?" Y; "Are you sure?" N;

"Is A correct?" N;

"Is B correct?" N;

"Is C correct?" Y; "Are you sure?" Y;

"The right answer is B."

Then the next item appears. Note that responding YES to "Are you sure?" does not mean that the test taker *is* sure; it only means that he has made his final choice. (The initial directions told him to make a best guess if in doubt.)

The computer administration differs from the booklet administration in several ways:

The student is forced to answer every item in turn. Omissions are not allowed.

The student is unable to return to earlier items. However, before he makes the "sure" response, he can run through alternatives as many times as he wishes.

The test is not timed. The student is told that there will be 35 items and that he is to work as rapidly as possible. (The conventional version has 70.)

Perhaps no orientation booklet with practice items will be supplied prior to booklet administration.

The computer version is adaptive (in the sense of p. 49).

To start the adaptive process, the test begins with items of middling difficulty. If the test taker does well, the computer begins to feed him harder items. When the test taker makes errors, easier items are chosen for him. Even when no two persons face the same items, the computer can calculate a score for every person on the same scale. The procedure permits shortening the test without loss in accuracy. I say more about the technique at the end of Chapter 4.

5. *If MCT were administered individually, could profitable observations be made?*

6. *Can you think of any questions a test taker might ask that the directions do not cover?*

7. *An orientation booklet for the DAT pencil-and-paper MCT is essentially like that for the computer version, save that it does not discuss responding on the computer. It is sold separately, the price being about one-fourth that of the answer sheet. Should a school using the printed test spend the extra amount for the orientation material?*

8. *The cost per student of the complete (eight-test) DAT-Adaptive battery is about 50 per cent greater than the cost of the booklet version, with scoring and reporting from a mail-in service prepaid. (This comparison disregards start-up costs.) What benefits does the school or the test taker get for the added cost?*

PROCEDURE FOR TEST ADMINISTRATION

The importance of uniform procedure is especially obvious in the great competitive testing programs for scholarship awards and college admissions. On seven weekends, forms of the Scholastic Aptitude Test are given in more than 1000 centers. At 9 A.M. on a particular Saturday in January, the seal is broken on the test package in each center: in Bronxville and Berkeley and Kodiak, in Berne and Beirut and Kodaikanal. The completed papers pour into the scoring center, and reports go out to the candidates and the colleges they are applying to. A test taker in Beirut may be in competition with one in Berkeley for admission to the same college, and the selection procedure is unfair unless the two are tested in an identical manner.

To obtain meaningful results, the tester must become thoroughly familiar with the test. Even a simple test presents stumbling blocks; most will be avoided if the tester studies the manual in advance. But carelessness can produce spectacular errors. At a time when the adequacy of an all-volunteer army was a focus of public debate, the Pentagon asked its staff to find out how many recruits fell below borderline ability. The staff defined the borderline by testing a sample of qualified soldiers; scores toward the lower end of that group were accepted as a standard of adequacy. Unfortunately, whoever tested these soldiers cut the testing time short by mistake. Recruits who reached the same score level in the full working time were far less able than the soldiers who had reached it under time pressure. The Pentagon report said that few recruits were below the borderline score; if its logic had been applied with a proper, less generous borderline, six times as many recruits would have been counted as substandard. (Whether standards should be set on the basis of score distributions is another issue. See p. 108.)

When to Test   Occasionally, it is necessary to test a person at an unfavorable time—for example, when psychological examinations must be given to an accused person prior to a trial. College freshmen may be tested in the midst of a hectic week of establishing new friends and living arrangements. Military classification tests have been given to soldiers just after induction when they lack sleep, are recovering from a farewell party, or feel ill from inoculations. In one study soldiers who took a second form of such a test after becoming stabilized in army routines raised their scores, on the average, by the amount that separated prospective noncoms from prospective officers (Duncan, 1947).

There is no point in adhering to a testing schedule if that schedule will give false information. Emergencies arise that prevent uniform testing. Thus, if an examinee becomes ill, it should be possible to provide for a makeup test later.

Results can often be improved by spacing tests. Alert examinees are more likely to give their best than examinees who are weary. But equally good results *can* be produced at any hour of the day if the examinees want to do well. Fatigue (within reasonable limits) apparently affects effort rather than the ability one can summon up.

With school beginners and other young children it is necessary to be especially mindful of readiness for testing. The setting for the test, the persons present, and the task demands may all be strange. Not surprisingly, then, scores collected in the first week of school experience can run quite a bit lower than those obtained 2 weeks later. In evaluation of early education, the gains from the program are overestimated if pretests are given before children are accustomed to the setting.

Testing a Group

The physical setting for a group test matters: Does the examinee have a convenient place to write? Sufficient space to spread out materials? A position from which directions can be heard and demonstrations seen? Very large rooms are bad for group testing unless proctors are provided. In the large room, a person may hesitate to ask a question about unclear directions that he would raise before a smaller audience. A proctor can come to his seat and answer his question.

With reasonably mature and cooperative examinees who expect to do as the tester requests, group testing is essentially a problem of command. One person should be in charge, standing in front of the group where she can see all members. She will find helpful the adage "Never give an order unless you expect it to be obeyed." False starts, preliminary attempts to call the group to order while latecomers are finding seats, and ineffectual rapping for attention are counterproductive. The tester should have full attention before she starts to explain.

Directions should be given simply, clearly, and singly. A complex instruction such as "Take your booklet, turn it face down, and then write your name on the answer sheet" will lead to confusion. Much better: "Take your booklet." (Hold up a sample. Check to be sure everyone has his booklet.) "Turn it face down." (Demonstrate. Wait until everyone has done so.) "Now take your answer sheet." (Exhibit a sample, and wait for compliance.) "Write your name on the first line, last name first."

The person who proceeds coldly and "scientifically" to administer the test, without convincing the test taker that she regards him as important, will get only limited cooperation. Evidence of poor rapport includes inattention during directions, giving up before time is called, restlessness, or complaining about the test items. Both control and rapport can be achieved if the examiner is friendly and patient, and is informal when formal control is not called for. After establishing control, for example, she may relax her "command manner" and make informal comments about the test and its purpose; this practice does not interfere with resuming formal control for the test proper.

The purpose of standardizing is to obtain a measurement comparable with measurements made at other times. Administering tests by tape recorder has advantages for many tests. The tape says the right words, and it times the test accurately. Taped administration can present the same test in many languages and dialects. See also pages 47–49 on computerized testing.

Directions should be complete and free from ambiguity (except where—for the sake of observing the examinee's preferred style—a test is deliberately left unstructured). A test for aviators illustrates the crucial importance of defining the task. In making a check on ability to execute a maneuver, testers found it necessary to tell the pilot exactly how the performance would be scored. When they did not, one pilot kept attention on maintaining altitude perfectly; a pilot of equal ability who concentrated on the plane's heading earned a different score.

The directions are part of the test situation; in some tests the way the examinee follows the fixed directions is intended to influence the score. The standard directions usually invite the examinee to ask questions after the directions have been read. In answering these questions, sometimes the tester will decide to supplement the directions; when she does so, she is in effect creating a new test, and the norms no longer apply.

Most psychological tests are designed to extract one purified variable from the total life activity. In setting the stage for a test, the psychologist tries to bring all examinees to a "standard state" of motivation, expectation, and interpretation of the task. The psychometric tester tries to eliminate the influence of every characteristic save whatever the test seeks to measure. To clarify this, consider the physiological measure of basal metabolism rate (BMR). A doctor who wants a BMR measure requires the patient to fast for 8 hours before the test because the digestive process uses oxygen. For the test itself, a measure of oxygen intake and carbon dioxide exhaled, it is necessary to reduce bodily activity to a minimum by putting the person into bed. Every examinee is, in effect, reduced to an artificial "standard condition." The person's everyday metabolism rate is not much like his BMR since the former is raised by his eating and movement.

No matter how standardized and long-established a task, the test taker may give it a meaning wholly his own. Pour water from one jar to a narrower one; the water level is now higher. Has the amount changed? Children around the world have answered this Piagetian question, correctly or incorrectly. When a Pakistani 5-year-old said, "Yes"—an "immature" response—the tester was not surprised. The tester *was* surprised when the child amplified by touching a dusty finger to the bottom of the original jar and bringing up a droplet the pouring had left behind (Berland, 1981). Only the individual tester has a good chance to learn what question the test taker is really considering.

9. *An employment office gives all applicants a reasoning test when their applications are filed. One man takes the test, together with several friends, and*

the group leave together. Ten minutes later he returns, greatly agitated: "Was I supposed to turn over the last page? I thought I had finished when I got to the bottom of page 9, so I looked back over my answers. I had plenty of time, and I'm sure I could have done well on the last page—my friends say the questions there were easy." What should be done in this case, if at the bottom of page 9 the booklet carried the printed statement, "Go on to the next page"?

10. *In the Hand-Tool Dexterity Test, nuts and bolts are to be mounted in a frame as fast as possible, with the aid of two wrenches. Somewhat more than 200 words of directions tell how to do the task. Before stating the directions, the manual says this to the examiner: "The essence of the examination procedure is to measure the ability of the examinee to perform the manual tasks required; ability to understand directions is not part of the intended measurement. Accordingly, the examiner should feel free to supplement the following directions in any reasonable way to improve the examinee's understanding of the task."*
    a. *What can be said for and against this departure from standardization?*
    b. *What would be an "unreasonable" way to supplement the directions?*

11. *MCT (DAT printed version) can be given with or without supplying students the orientation booklet in advance. Its norms were obtained before the orientation material was available. Comment in the light of the remark in the text above: ". . . creating a new test, and the norms no longer apply."*

12. *A journalist critical of SAT (Owen, 1985) says that he saw a test administrator in New York City depart from approved procedure. The violations included inaccurate timing and failure to read directions aloud. Worse, perhaps, the tester started the first timed section of the test while some examinees were still filling in face sheets, then continued to talk distractingly about the face sheet as some students worked on the first section. Some of the malpractice suggests misunderstanding of the rules, some suggests carelessness. Can you suggest precautions the central test sponsor could take—at acceptable cost—to determine how widespread faulty administration is and to make it less likely?*

Policies regarding Guessing

Over and over the tester is asked, "Should I guess when I am not sure?" "How much is taken off for a wrong answer?" "If I find a hard question, should I skip it and go on, or should I answer every question as I go?" The published directions were evidently not adequate if they ignored these topics. When the tester refuses to add advice on guessing, some examinees will guess and some will not. Whatever advice the test directions give, room for judgment remains. The discussion that follows is intended to clarify the guessing problem for the tester and the test developer. It should not influence procedure in giving a standard test, because supplementary advice is against the rules.

For the moment, suppose that questions fall into two categories: those whose answer the respondent knows and those he cannot answer. Choice response gives the ignorant person a chance to pick the correct response. On true-false items, guesses will succeed about half the time by chance alone. One common scoring formula assumes that every wrong choice represents an unlucky guess. The number of lucky guesses is supposed to be proportional to the number of wrong responses, and credit is subtracted accordingly. The final score on a true-false test is then "number of items right minus number marked wrong." The penalty is the number of items thought to have been marked correctly by guessing.

With n choices per item, the probability of a correct guess is $1/n$ and that of an unlucky guess is $(n - 1)/n$. For every $n - 1$ incorrect guesses, there will be one correct guess, on the average. Hence the usual formula is "*rights* minus *wrongs*/$(n - 1)$." On a 50-item test with 3 choices per item, a person who gets 36 right and 10 wrong receives a score of 31 ($= 36 - 10/2$). The formula attempts to wipe out the advantage of those who take more chances. (An alternative computation for the same purpose has recently been introduced; see p. 139. The message of the next two paragraphs applies to that procedure also.)

Unfortunately, the formula does not neutralize all of the risk taker's advantage. Items do not divide into those the respondent knows perfectly and those he does not know at all. There are items he knows fairly well but is not positive of, and others where he has hazy knowledge. Perhaps he can eliminate one or two choices as implausible. A person who "guesses" intelligently on 10 five-choice items can expect to get perhaps 4 items right, not 2. Four right answers would give a formula score of $2\frac{1}{2}$ points. Since he would score zero on those items if he did not guess, the score is raised by willingness to gamble. The opposite is often true for the test taker who knows almost nothing. A clever item writer can make incorrect answers so appealing to an uninformed examinee that he guesses wrong at a greater-than-chance rate (Lord, 1974).

From the point of view of the tester, tendency to guess is an uncontrolled variable that interferes with measurement. The systematic advantage of the guesser is eliminated if everyone is directed to guess, but guessing increases chance variation. It is usual now to warn only against wild guessing, for example:

> Students often ask whether they should guess when they are uncertain about the answer to a question. Your test scores will be based on the number of questions you answer correctly minus a fraction of the number you answer incorrectly. Therefore, it is improbable that random or haphazard guessing will change your scores significantly. If you have some knowledge of a question, you may be able to eliminate one or more of the answer choices as wrong. It is generally to your advantage to guess which of the remaining choices is correct.[3]

---

[3]From the cover of the Scholastic Aptitude Test, 1988; reproduced by permission. The 1988 orientation booklet, *Taking the SAT*, which is supplied well in advance of the test, spells out the same advice more simply and illustrates the scoring formula.

Techniques have been invented in which the test taker bets on his degree of certainty. The simplest method is to ask the person to mark, not the right answer, but every choice he can rule out. Consider:

The capital of Chile is A. Valparaiso B. Buenos Aires C. Santiago.

The child who knows a little about Latin America gains some credit by rejecting B, without having to guess between A and C. This sensible procedure has had little use.

An alternative that irons out differences in confidence and willingness to take a chance is an "answer until correct" rule. With computer administration the respondent can be told at once that the choice is right or wrong. If it is wrong he makes further choices until he succeeds. The same instant feedback can be provided by a chemically treated answer sheet that changes color when the right choice is marked.

Let me return to the false assumption that a person knows an answer or does not, and draw some morals that will apply in many later contexts. All numerical analyses of test scores rest on assumptions. The assumptions generally are false to some degree, because they treat the world as simpler than it is. "Violation of assumptions" sounds bad, but we live with violations much of the time. We plan a trip, for example, with a map that assumes the world to be flat. That could cause trouble on a long voyage, but not otherwise. The assumptions common in psychometrics work well enough most of the time. The more one knows of the assumptions, the more aware she will be of the circumstances where they lead to seriously wrong conclusions. Almost always, for such a circumstance there is a complex alternative analysis that avoids the assumption.

13. *Compute scores for each of the following persons by the correction formula:*

Test 1, true-false.	*A has 20 right, 6 wrong, 7 omitted.*
	B has 22 right, 8 wrong, 3 omitted.
Test 2, 3-choice	*C has 15 right, 6 wrong, 4 omitted.*
	D has 18 right, 3 wrong, 4 omitted.
Test 3, 5-choice.	*E has 20 right, 6 wrong, 9 omitted.*
	F has 6 right, 6 wrong, 23 omitted.

14. *Earlier forms of MCT were scored by a correction formula; in Forms S and T, the score is the count of right answers. What kinds of evidence would justify this simplified scoring?*

15. *When scores are "corrected for guessing," some person may receive a negative score. What does this mean? Is he less able than a person scoring zero?*

16. *Some instructors advocate scoring achievement tests by formulas that penalize "bluffing" heavily, such as "number right minus twice number wrong." What is the probable effect on validity of measurement?*

17. *In the Metropolitan Achievement test for elementary grades, the pupil has the option of checking* DON'T KNOW *rather than an answer option. This response, of course, receives no credit. The test developer argues that this option encourages an honest attitude in test taking.*

a. *Why is the practice open to question?*
b. *Not uncommonly, teachers giving this test warn their classes against marking* DON'T KNOW *(because it cannot improve their scores; Horne & Garty, 1981). Who, if anyone, suffers from this violation of standard procedure?*

Establishing Rapport in Testing an Individual

Personal rapport is much more important in individual testing than in group testing. The tester who has become acquainted with a child over several sessions of non–test activities is likely to elicit higher scores than a strange tester (Fuchs & Fuchs, 1986). The recommendations are obvious: wait until the child is at ease; retest when a low score would have important consequences.

The following advice, applicable to most individual tests of ability, grew out of the experience of the pioneer tester Lewis Terman. (Reprinted here from the latest manual for the Stanford-Binet scale; Thorndike et al., 1986, pp. 13, 16–17. For more detailed advice see Sattler, 1988, Ch. 5.)

Limit changes in the order in which you administer tests to those necessary for the practical requirements of testing. For example, if a certain test arouses resistance, try shifting to another test. When the examinee is once more at ease, try the troublesome test again. . . . Under no circumstances should you alter the order in which the items appear within each test. This order is based upon the relative difficulty of the items and must not be changed.

. . .

Eliciting the examinee's best efforts and maintaining both high motivation and optimal performance level throughout the testing session are the *sine qua non* of good testing, but the means by which these ends are accomplished are so varied as to defy specific description. The form of address that puts one examinee at ease with a strange adult may not work with another. You must be able to sense the needs of the examinee so that you can help the examinee to accept and adjust to the testing situation. . . .

. . .

Children are accustomed to accepting the decisions of adult authority figures. The confident assumption on your part that the child will come willingly to the testing room is usually enough to ensure that that happens. It is better not to ask whether or not the child wants to come with you since this invites indecision, if not refusal. Of course, the problems of handling emotionally disturbed children are much more complicated. . . .

Encouraging the examinee . . . can be accomplished in many subtle, friendly ways: by an understanding smile, a spontaneous exclamation of approval, an appreciative comment, or just a quiet understanding between you and the examinee that carries assurance and appreciation. In general it is effective to praise frequently and generously, but if this is done in too lavish and stilted a fashion it is likely to defeat its own purpose. Expressions of commendation should be varied and should fit naturally into the conversation. *Remember that you are giving approval for effort rather than for success on a particular response.* To praise only the successful responses may negatively influence efforts in the succeeding tests.

Under no circumstances should you show dissatisfaction with a response, though you may smilingly refuse to accept a flippant answer that is obviously intended to "test the limits." With younger children especially, praise should not be limited to tests on which the child has done well. Young children are characteristically uncritical and are often enormously pleased with responses that are in fact inferior. In praising poor responses of older examinees, remember that the purpose of commendation is to ensure confidence and not to reconcile the examinee to an inferior level of response.

In the case of a failure that is embarrassingly evident to the examinee, point out that you do not expect the examinee to be able to do all of these things, or you may interject, "That was a good try!" The difficulty of the items may be commented upon, especially as an examinee is nearing his or her ceiling level. Such comments as "That was a hard one," "You haven't had that one yet in school, have you?" or "I don't expect you to know all of these, but I do want to see how many of them you can do," serve to keep examinees from getting discouraged. . . .

. . . .

. . . .[A]void the practice of dragging out responses by too much urging and cross-questioning. To do so robs responses of significance and discourages spontaneous effort. Guard against mistaking exceptional timidity for inability to respond. Learn also to distinguish the silence of incapability from the "I don't know" of an examinee who really does know without realizing it.[4]

Sometimes credit is allowed only when a task is done in (say) 2 minutes, but the directions do not tell the examiner whether to let the person work beyond that time. Art comes into such a decision; no rules can prescribe how to minimize the frustration that attends an unsuccessful trial. Success on one problem has an encouraging effect during the next, but the effect of failure depends on the tester. In the tester's eyes, the person failed when he did not complete the task within the time limit. Allowed to continue without interruption, he may finish the task and be encouraged by that. Another examinee, even with extra time, may not solve the problem. If he is becoming confused and upset, to let him continue might leave him more discouraged. The tester should observe carefully and choose whatever course seems likely to have the best effect.

It is the duty of the tester to obtain the best record the examinee can produce by his own efforts—without aid. The tester must learn to suppress direct and indirect hints. Unintended help can be given by facial expression. The person taking a test is always concerned to know how well he is doing and watches the examiner for indications that he is doing right. Suppose the task is this: "Repeat backward, 2–7–5–1–4." He may begin "4–1–7 . . ."; if the examiner, on hearing the "7," permits her

---

[4]Reprinted by permission of the Riverside Publishing Company.

expression to change, the test taker may take the hint and catch the mistake. The examiner must maintain a completely unrevealing expression while at the same time silently assuring the examinee of her interest in what he says.

For exceptional cases the tester has no alternative but to throw away the rule book. Palmer (1983, pp. 214ff.) describes half a dozen "games children play" when they find an assessment stressful. One example is Shapiro's (1957) story of a resistant 7-year-old who at times was aggressive toward the tester. The first session was wasted; the girl simply would not do the test. The second session started equally unhappily. Finally the psychologist slammed one of the playroom toys against the wall. Said the child, smiling at last, "Do it again." After a bit of routine cooperation—child fetching toy and psychologist smashing it against the wall—they were pals; in due time, the girl settled down to take the test and scored in the normal range.

Not only in exceptional cases but also in routine testing, the tester ought to write down a brief account of the procedures. Even when all goes smoothly, the tester should record an impression of the apparent confidence, cooperation, and level of tension of the person or persons tested. Such a record may shed light on discrepancies among data collected at different times.

18. *In the course of a clinical analysis of a preschool child who is believed to be poorly adjusted, tests are requested. The psychometrist finds the child negativistic. After cooperating reluctantly on two tests, the child becomes inattentive and careless on the third. Assuming that the test results are needed as soon as possible, what should the tester do?*

19. *In a court case (Larry P.), psychologist W was engaged to support the contention that a certain disadvantaged child should not be classed as retarded. Several testings by school psychologists had yielded IQs around 70. Here is the account, based on the court record, of W's effort (Elliott, 1987, pp. 32–33, slightly edited here).*

   W went to his home, chatted with him for an hour and a half or so, and left, writing his reports a few days later. The test [Wechsler] produced a Full Scale score of 94.

   W's departures from standard administration and scoring provide the explanation of the discrepancy, at least in part. For example, when he asked Darryl how scissors and a copper pan are alike, he accepted the answer "They are both iron" as fully creditable because it had the idea of metal; he accepted "acting bad" as a definition of nonsense. When W asked Darryl why criminals should be locked up, Darryl seemed not to understand the question, so W rephrased it, identifying criminals as people who sometimes break the law.

   W's view of standardized testing was this: "If the purpose of psychological testing is to tap psychological functions and if by asking a child a question different from the way it is posed in the manual affords me the chance to tap the function, then that appears to be much more important than to be compulsive and concretistic in mentioning every word that is listed in the manual."

What can be said for and against W's policy and practices?

TESTING AS A SOCIAL RELATIONSHIP

Testers have been accustomed to thinking of themselves as unemotional, impartial task setters. The traditional language suggests that the psychologist, like an engineer, is "measuring an object" with a technical tool. But the tester's "object" is a person. The traditional recommendations that the tester be encouraging and help the person to understand the value of the test barely touch the sociopsychological complexities of testing.

What Schafer (1954, p. 6) has said about clinical testing applies in some degree to every test that may affect the person's opportunities or self-esteem:

> The clinical testing situation has a complex psychological structure. It is not an impersonal getting-together of two people in order that one, with the help of a little "rapport," may obtain some "objective" test responses from the other. The [disturbed] . . . patient is in some acute or chronic life crisis. He cannot but bring many hopes, fears, assumptions, demands and expectations into the test situation. He cannot but respond intensely to certain real as well as fantasied attributes of that situation. Being human and having to make a living—facts often ignored—the tester too brings hopes, fears, assumptions, demands and expectations into the test situation. She too responds personally and often intensely to what goes on—in reality and in fantasy—in that situation, however well she may conceal her personal response from the patient, from herself, and from her colleagues.

The person coming for an individual test is almost invariably in difficulties. He may have been referred by some authority who has control over his fate; if so, the tester may be simply another authority to fear or rebel against. One might expect cooperation when the client is self-referred, but his objectives can conflict with the tester's. The test taker may have doubts, which he is attempting to suppress, regarding his adequacy. It is commonplace to discover, behind a college student's self-referral for remedial reading or vocational counseling, a problem of sexual adjustment or conflict with parents. The student, focusing his attention and that of the psychologist on a lesser problem, is using unconscious sleight of hand to conceal the problem he does not want to face. None of us is willing to expose himself completely or to learn the whole truth about himself, yet the tester is commissioned to penetrate. Often the clinical examiner must try to learn about sexual attitudes, hostilities, feelings of inadequacy, or wishes the patient is ashamed of. Even when the testing has a limited aim, the patient may believe that the test will expose intimate desires and anxieties. Conversely, a patient concerned about himself may believe that the test is too insensitive to bring his difficulties fully to the attention of the therapist; then the clinician must try to allow for exaggeration of symptoms.

Giving a test individually, one establishes a relationship that can bring emotions close to the surface. Joseph Matarazzo (1972, pp. 494ff.) tells what happened in his assessment of a 41-year-old male who had applied for a post as executive vice president. The man had a record of vigor, productivity, and success; he had taken over as head of the family business when his father died 2 years earlier. Although the man spoke confidently and cheerfully in the intake interview, the tests suggested serious disturbance (see p. 306).

Matarazzo continues, speaking of himself in the third person:

> [T]he psychologist, having established the element of mutual trust and respect so critical and necessary in executive assessment . . . shared with this young executive his findings of numerous assets but also his concern that all was not as well with him currently as it had been in the past. This was the stimulus for a flood of tears and the shared statement, *in confidence,* that he had not recovered from his father's unexpected and precipitous death two years earlier. In view of the immediate clinical demand, various elements of this frank, depressive episode were explored in this initial session; and the suggestion was offered that psychotherapy might provide some relief for his by now openly discussed personal suffering. He accepted the idea and arrangements were made. Discussion then returned to his candidacy for the position of Executive Vice President and the client volunteered that he had entertained this idea more as "flight" from his current, unendurable situation than in terms of any effectiveness he might bring to the challenge.

The man asked what report would be made to the hiring firm. The answer was that if the client thought himself unready for the stress of the position, he should withdraw, which would make it inappropriate for the psychologist to report. The client was referred to therapy and continued in it, but the story ends with his suicide 2 years later.

Schafer recommends that the social situation itself be considered an important way of understanding the person and that his strategies, demands, and resistances be taken into account in the interpretation. Schafer's view is summarized in this paragraph (1954, pp. 72–73):

> The ideal of objectivity requires that we recognize as much as possible what is going on in the situation we are studying. It requires in particular that we remember the tester and her patient are both human and alive and therefore inevitably interacting in the test situation. True, the further we move away from mechanized interpretation or comparison of formal scores and averages, the more subjective variables we may introduce into the interpretive process. . . . But while we thereby increase the likelihood of personalized interpretation and variation among testers, we are at the same time in a position to enrich our understanding and our test reports significantly.

Schafer calls for impressionistic interpretation. Those who reject Schafer's recommendation must find their own solution to the problems of interpersonal dynamics. Even a strictly poker-faced administration of an individual mental test can be an hour-long stress situation, every moment of which involves emotional interaction between tester and test taker.

20. *Does a formal and impersonal attitude toward all test takers standardize the testing relationship?*

21. *In an "agility" test used by the British Armed Forces at one time, each soldier was tested separately while his squad of perhaps 20 others watched. The task called for running back and forth along a cross-shaped pattern, transferring rings from one post to another.*

    a. *What effect on score would be expected from being tested in a group rather than without an audience?*

    b. *What effect would be expected as a result of announcing each person's score at the end of his trial—to be applauded if good?*

    c. *What advantage or disadvantage would a person have who came last in the group?*

22. *An anthropologist doing cross-cultural research wanted to test representative Eskimos in villages where she had no acquaintances. She therefore asked some non-Eskimo member of the community to obtain volunteers. In one village the community nurse "simply stepped outside her house and waited in ambush, so to speak, for some prospect as the Eskimos walked down the path . . . beside her house. Such subjects were told in a kindly, but peremptory, fashion that he or she was to do whatever I asked" (Preston, 1964).*

    a. *Does this method of recruiting have any effect on the interpretation of Preston's Eskimo records on mental tests and personality measures?*

    b. *Is your answer to question a modified by learning that two of the Eskimos thought the study was intended to locate persons who should be locked up in a mental hospital?*

Characteristics of the Tester

Many investigators have tried to find out which styles or tester characteristics raise scores on ability tests and by how much. Does it matter if the tester is familiar to the child? Does frequent encouragement help? What about the sex of the tester? Warmth and chattiness? Age? Her anxiety? And so on. (For bibliographies, see Lutey & Copeland, in Reynolds & Gutkin, 1982; and Sattler, 1974, pp. 31, 60ff., and 1981, pp. 93, 361ff.)

Studies typically report that the variable under study neither raised nor lowered scores by much on the average, and successive reports of average differences contradict each other. One reason that studies add up to no rules or generalizations is that averages are beside the point. Test takers react to what the examiner does and to immediate circumstances.

The recurrent question about the match of tester to test taker in ethnicity or race is a serious one. I shall not dwell on the obvious—if one person does not fully understand the other's speech, the testing will be invalid. But Western psychologists, turning to pantomime, have had considerable success in giving maze tests and the like in isolated tribes whose language they could not speak. Language is not an impassable barrier.

No doubt, children having better command of Spanish than English should be tested in Spanish (unless the intent is to measure, specifically, performance in English). Testers must remember, however, that many schoolchildren from Hispanic homes in the United States speak English better than Spanish. For testing urban blacks, it has been suggested that Black English be used. The evidence, however, is that blacks are not handicapped by testing in Standard English (Quay, 1974). Sometimes they are handicapped when the tester uses Black English, perhaps because of local variation. On average, black children do not score higher when the tester is black rather than white; here again, the differences found in controlled studies are inconsistent and usually small (Jensen, 1980, pp. 596ff.; Sattler & Gwynne, 1987).

Let us put aside the pessimistic (and racist!) hypothesis that you cannot relate to another person unless your skins have the same color. And let us put aside attempts to generalize as if blacks (or Hispanics or any such category of persons) are uniform. A social relationship is constructed by the parties. The conventional style of testing may elicit little response from a test taker who considers the tester an alien and a threat. The tester, of whatever social and family origins, must discover a style that reaches persons from a different background or disqualify herself.

Labov's memorable story (1970) carries its own moral. Interviewers collected speech samples from Harlem 8-year-olds in school, using a friendly but dignified technique. Rarely did the boys produce full sentences or elaborate their ideas; one-word responses were the norm. Formal interviews in a boy's home sometimes did no better, so an informal approach was tried. The interviewer brought in one of the boy's friends, got down on the floor with the two youngsters, dumped out a bag of potato chips, and started a conversation. A few taboo words were tossed in as an "Anything goes" signal. The boy whose speech was rated immature on the basis of the formal interviews now burst into expansive, fluent speech.

One experimenter, by changing conditions, reportedly improved the comparative performance of minority examinees (Bernal, in Reynolds & Brown, 1984). Bernal gave letter-series and number-series tests (both speeded measures of reasoning) to eighth-graders in Texas. The pupil was tested under one of two conditions. In the first, a white examiner followed the usual routine directions, testing a mixed group of 10 or more pupils. The second method ("facilitating") had all these features: groups of 5 or less with uniform ethnic composition, an examiner from that background, a friendly and informal practice session with much of the conversation in black dialect for black groups and in Spanish for bilingual Hispanics (not for those who spoke English only). The aim was to encourage a positive attitude more than to coach. Following this interaction, the test was given in the normal formal way. Bernal analyzed subgroups matched on social class. I have reduced all averages to a scale on which the 96 standard-condition students have mean 50 and s.d. 10. The means of the subgroups were as follows:

	White	Hispanic	Black
Standard condition	55	48	48
Facilitating condition	55	55	52

The changes are large and would be impressive if the samples were larger. Bernal's approach deserves further study.

23. *A readiness test for kindergartners is designed to be administered by the child's parent (partly to initiate parent-school collaboration and partly in the hope that the parent's testing will be more valid than testing by the school). Parent and child come to the school some months before the child will move to Grade 1. The child waits in a playroom while the parent receives 30 minutes of instruction in testing procedure. (The tasks include counting, letter matching, and memory.) The parent then tests the child, in whatever language is usual at home. A member of the staff looks on and offers help if necessary. What risks of invalidity are there in this process? How could they be minimized? (The matter is discussed in Mitchell, 1985, vol. 1, pp. 45–48.)*

How Testers Distort Results

Self-delusion by trained observers has been reported often in the history of science. Many of the errors are self-serving—slanted not to gain material rewards but to satisfy needs of the observer or to confirm her beliefs or desires.

Testers seek emotional satisfactions. A tester chooses the profession because it satisfies her needs. The tester, for example, may be one who, feeling inadequate in social relations, can obtain reassurance from seemingly objective instruments. The overly "objective" tester may be quick to detect difficulties that can be treated unemotionally (limited vocabulary, for example), but may overlook emotional needs. The tester who seeks emotional response may be too lenient. The competitive tester may be too eager to find weaknesses. A prison psychologist (Wilson, 1951) trained selected convicts to test new inmates; he had to supervise constantly to prevent their making procedural errors that would reduce the examinee's score and so magnify their own superiority.

"Motivated error" can be unintentional. Standard procedure cannot prevent subtle influences on scores when the tester expects the pretty little girl in the starched dress to do well or when the tester's social conscience demands that her black examinees show up well. The more the tester knows of her own personality, of her preferences for different types of test taker, and of the biases she brings to test interpretation, the greater the chance that she can meet each situation properly.

Palmer (1983, pp. 182–183) emphasizes that in examining a child the assessor should set aside her identification with the school system, the legal system, or other such parties: *"The primary and single motivation of the assessor must be the welfare of the individual child."* He advises differentiating the assessor's role from that of persons controlling the child, by means of opening lines such as these: "Judge _____ asked me to talk to you. He and your attorney thought because my job is understanding boys and girls that I might be able to explain things to them for you." Or, in another case, "Your teacher and the school are very dissatisfied with your behavior. I'm supposed to find out what is really wrong and advise them. But I am most interested in how I might help *you* so that you would be more happy."

Bias may arise from preconceptions; here are examples from Rosenthal (1966):

- In studies of telepathy a respondent attempts to guess what symbol a "transmitter" is concentrating on at a given moment. A recorder writes down the guesses alongside the true signal. Recording errors made by those who believe in telepathy run 2 to 1 in the direction favoring telepathy; errors made by disbelievers tilt the other way.
- Laboratory technicians counting blood cells through a microscope take check readings on the same slide. They agree more closely than they would if proper (necessarily fallible) procedure were followed. Evidently discrepant readings are suppressed.
- Student experimenters are told (untruthfully) that the rats they are to run have been genetically selected for brightness. These rats learn a maze faster than those run by experimenters who are told that they are running a dull strain. (Is it possible that teachers who are told that certain of their students are bright teach them more? See page 353.
- Student testers are led to think that college students normally give a sizable number of responses to an inkblot. They get about 50 per cent more responses than other testers led to expect few responses.

Distortion of test results is a danger in program evaluation. Suppose that *you* have designed a new method of teaching mechanical comprehension and want to prove its excellence. To an experimental set of trainees you give Form S of the Bennett as a pretest and Form T as a posttest. You can almost guarantee a positive finding if, when pretesting, you tell the trainees that the scores "don't count," run through the directions fast, and perhaps misread your watch, shortening the working time. The opposite tactic can raise the pretest scores of a control group or the posttest scores of the experimentals.

Biased testing is especially likely when the scores will bring benefit or blame to the person collecting the data. Teachers whose futures depend on the test scores their classes earn are quite likely to help the children in illegitimate ways (Horne & Garty, 1981). It is easy to nudge children toward the keyed responses. ("Are you *sure* you want to erase that?") The California Assessment Program reports publicly the standings of schools on its annual achievement test. Papers from certain schools show so many erasures as to suggest that the principal and teachers are "fixing up" bad performances to escape unpleasant publicity. Indeed, a few principals have confessed to this cheating (*San Francisco Chronicle*, October 8, 1988).

In recent years some legislators have desired to provide extra money to schools where the educational need is greatest. When they propose to define "need" by average start-of-year test scores of student bodies, the lawmakers come close to inviting fraud. In one city, teachers were told that *they* should fill out the answer sheet for any student whose native language was not English, making enough errors to produce a failing score. "We need a zero score to satisfy federal and state funding requirements," said the director of the school testing department (*San Francisco Examiner*, October 19, 1980). It is impractical to have government agents give the tests. On the other hand, it is unrealistic to expect the school staff to elicit a student's best performance when his *worst* performance will bring funds to the school. (A proposal to base financial aid on an end-of-year test would have another fault. If two schools with equal budgets take in equally unprepared students, the one that produces higher posttest scores will be judged less "needy," will get no extra funds next year, and so will be penalized for having done a superior job.)

Medical research adopts the double-blind technique to guard against self-delusion. Half the patients are given a neutral substance (placebo); half are given the drug under investigation. All doses are coded and look the same. Neither doctor nor patient nor laboratory technician knows which patients are receiving the drug. Psychologists and educators cannot arrange complete blinding. But tests can be given by outsiders who do not know which persons have been receiving treatment. And all papers—from pretests, posttests, experimentals, and controls—can be intermixed randomly before scoring begins.

24. *In what way could sympathy and love for children bias a tester? What parts of the testing process would be affected by this bias?*
25. *What acts or judgments of the tester—short of gross error—might modify the scores earned*
   a. *in an individually administered vocabulary test?*
   b. *in a group-administered vocabulary test?*
   c. *in an individual story-completion test in which the responses are tape-recorded and later scored, by persons other than the tester, for aggression and hostility themes.*

MOTIVATION OF THE TEST TAKER

When a truckload of wheat is weighed, motivation is not a concern. Likewise, in weighing a person, when we put him on the scale we get a good measure no matter how he feels about the operation. In a psychological test the examinee places himself on the scale; and unless he cares about the result, he cannot be measured.

Effort and productivity depend on the reward the person foresees. The most direct reward for good test performance is being hired for a job or being given a desirable assignment. Equally powerful and more universally available as a source of motivation is the desire to maintain self-respect and the respect of others. Effort is stimulated also by sheer interest in the task, by the habit of obeying authority, and by the friendliness of the tester. Scores tend to improve when the test task is convincingly presented as important.

Providing immediate knowledge that each answer is right or wrong improves scores, making the person more careful to check his response as he makes it (see also p. 49). On the other hand, simple incentives—prizes, pep talks, or a monetary payment after the test to reward a good score—rarely make a difference (Lutey & Copeland, in Reynolds & Gutkin, 1982).

Not every examinee wants to do well. The accident victim seeking compensation or the worker applying for a disability pension may deliberately exaggerate his difficulties or, for example, attempt to mimic the test performance of an aphasic. The tester may recognize such malingering because fakers do not mimic disorders accurately, but she is left with an uninterpretable test record (Heaton & Heaton, McMahon & Satz, both in Filskov & Boll, 1982).

Test Anxiety   Maximum motivation may not be optimum motivation. The very desire to do well may interfere. A tense performer overlooks errors that he would correct otherwise. In psychomotor tests, tension leads to poor coordination and erratic movements. In a verbal test, the respondent may guard against criticisms of his answers by saying too little. In clinical tests, anxious patients find fault with their own answers, and in elaborating spoil some answers that would have received credit.

Wiener (1957) showed how anxious and defensive reactions interfere. Student nurses were classified as "trustful" and "distrustful" by means of a questionnaire. Each nurse took the Wechsler Picture Completion test, which asks what is missing in a picture (e.g., one eyebrow in a sketch of a face). Distrustful subjects were inclined to deny that anything was missing when the answer did not come to mind immediately. Likewise, on Similarities ("How are 'praise' and 'punishment' alike?") the distrustful students were more inclined to deny that the words were alike. Distrustful students averaged three times as many suspicious comments as the trustful students. In Wiener's words: "People who say, 'There is nothing missing in that picture!' are responding to internal needs rather than to the testing situation."

A questionnaire may focus either on persistent "trait" anxiety or on temporary "state" anxiety. A trait measure refers to typical or average behavior—for example, "I freeze up on intelligence tests."

Adjective checklist responses of student nurses provided illustrative data on state anxiety. The nurses, who were taking the same courses and exams, filled out the checklist every evening for 11 weeks. As Figure 3.3 shows, anxiety built up as crucial examinations approached, tending to peak on the evenings after examinations.

Items on trait anxiety fall into two groups. There are "emotionality" items such as "I have an upset, uneasy feeling before taking a final examination." And there are "worry" items, such as "Thinking about the grade I may get in a course interferes with my thinking and my performance on tests" (Spielberger et al., 1978). The worry component is the one that correlates with low grades.

One cannot be sure about the direction of causation. Poor learning may be the source of weak test performance, from which anxiety follows.

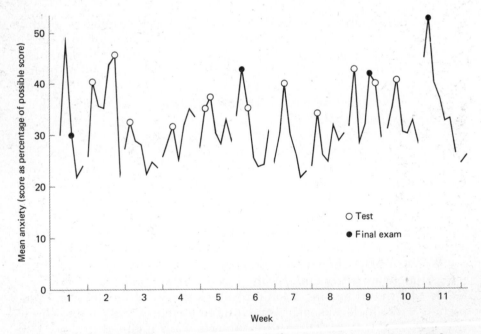

Figure 3.3. **Student anxiety on examination days.** On 77 evenings, students checked a list of adjectives to describe "how you feel now—today." Open dots represent the average score on the evening of the testing day (i.e., after the test). In each week save Week 1, the first point is for Sunday evening. (*Source:* Based on a figure in the manual for the Multiple Affect Adjective Check List and data supplied by M. Zuckerman. See Zuckerman, 1976.)

Worry about tests seems much like "learned helplessness." The scheduled test reminds the underconfident person of unpleasant events in the
past, and he exaggerates the difficulties to be faced. Case studies led
Topman and Jansen (1984, p. 245) to the view that

> test-anxious students often do not have the slightest idea what kind of behav-
> ior might lead to the desirable result; and have wrong ideas . . . like: "One
> should know absolutely everything"; "One should be 100% at ease"; . . .
> and so on.

A research program that we shall consider in another context (p. 562)
interprets test anxiety as "fear of failure," which causes the person to
choose safe, limited goals that are far below what an all-out effort could
reach.

The tester cannot, here and now, overcome long-standing habits, but
she should be aware that her words may relieve or intensify the test
taker's immediate anxiety. Unfortunately, the stimulus that brings out
the best in one examinee panics another. Yale freshmen were given a
maze test (S. Sarason et al., 1952). Half the students were told that this
"intelligence test" would be used in interpreting entrance tests they had
taken. These "ego-involving" (EI) instructions resemble many commonplace testing situations. In contrast, an "NEI" group was told that no
attention would be paid to individual scores, that the aim was merely to
norm the test. High-anxiety (HA) and low-anxiety (LA) subgroups were
defined by Sarason's questionnaire on trait test anxiety. The LAs did a
little better than the HAs under NEI instructions (Figure 3.4). The tension aroused by EI instructions nearly doubled the error rate of anxious
students—and it improved the scores of the LAs by a small amount.

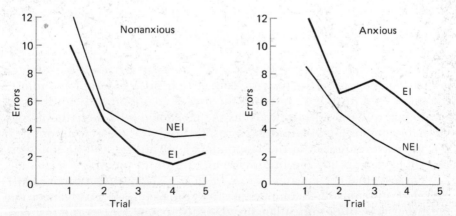

Figure 3.4. **Maze performance with and without ego involvement.** *(Source:* S.
Sarason et al., 1952. Copyright © 1952 by the American Psychological Association. Adapted by permission.)

A striking example of the effect of anxiety is the case of the young reserve officer, eager to serve in time of war, who failed his physical examination twice. The importance of passing made him emotional—and the emotion brought his blood pressure over the acceptable limit. "Reconditioning" treatments made it possible for him to take the test calmly.

The accumulated research on counseling and reconditioning procedures (Benjamin et al., 1981; I. Sarason, 1980; Spielberger et al., 1976; Tryon, 1980) indicates that it is easy enough to change *reported* anxiety—mere suggestion will do that much. Training in relaxation and reconditioning appear to go further in reducing emotionality, but academic performance seems to improve only when the therapy is combined with training in study skills. Tryon recommends reducing the "worry" component by training the student to focus on the task and to push self-oriented, distracting thoughts about consequences of failure out of his mind. Topman and Jansen (1984) see greater promise in a still more strongly cognitive approach that develops test-wiseness (see next page).

26. *Professional test developers almost always arrange items of an ability test from easiest to hardest (as determined in a tryout). What is to be said for and against this practice, assuming that the whole set of items is presented to every examinee?*

27. *Sarason's EI directions were intended to put some stress on the freshman test takers, and they were false. Acknowledging the possible benefit from the research, is this deception justifiable? (Issues of this character were not recognized when Sarason did the study.)*

28. *Hebb and Williams (1946) devised a test to measure the learning ability of rats. The test consists of a set of mazes to be run, the performance being called a success when a direct path to the food box is taken on the second trial on each maze. What problems of motivation would need to be considered in administering this test?*

ADVANCE PREPARATION AND COACHING

Even where test scores are to guide decisions by others, the examinee can be made a part of the tester's team. The tester can honestly indicate the purpose of testing and portray the test as an opportunity for the person to find out about himself just as the physician tells the patient what medicine is being given and what results are to be expected from it. If sound measurement is to the respondent's advantage and he knows it, he will have little motive to provide an untruthful picture.

For tests that act as gatekeepers, such as tests for selection or certification, it is increasingly common to orient the examinee in advance. The publisher may offer an explanatory booklet that describes the test content, displays representative items, and advises on efficient work procedures. The armed services, for example, offer a test through high schools.

Chiefly, the test collects information for recruiters, but it also assists school counseling. A movie that dramatizes the importance of test information in career choice is available for the school to show. Students and parents must sign a consent form in advance of the test; the movie encourages them to agree, and it should increase students' readiness for the tests.

Sophisticated test takers bring both skills and special tricks to bear (cataloged by Millman et al., 1965). In general, it is sensible to work through a test rapidly, making a quick judgment or even a guess, then returning to reconsider answers in the time that remains. That is far better than methodically finishing each question in turn. Paying careful attention to directions—for example, to what is said about the scoring rule—is advisable. Responding when not completely certain of the answer choice is advisable. And so on.

Another set of techniques depends on "psyching out" the test constructor or capitalizing on her mistakes (Table 3.1). When two closely similar alternatives appear in a choice-response item, the test-wise student knows that both are probably incorrect. He also has observed that, in a true-false test, "always" appears mostly in false statements. Allowing test-wiseness to operate lowers test validity because the wise students rank higher than they would on the basis of content knowledge alone. By providing sound directions and editing carefully, the test maker can reduce this influence.

As they go through school, all students should gradually be informed about effective test-taking strategies. (But teachers probably give as much bad advice as good: "Take your time, and don't guess.") Sarnacki (1979) reviews much research on test-wiseness—even reporting on a test of test-wiseness.

29. *Regarding "tricks" taught by coaching schools,* Taking the SAT *(see footnote 6) warns the prospective examinee: "On the rare occasions that a useful*

Table 3.1 TRICKS OF THE SAT-TAKING TRADE

1. Become thoroughly acquainted with a "Hit Parade" of 100 words or so —*apathy, enigma, indifferent*, . . .; these terms show up frequently in SAT Verbal items.

2. Leave the Reading Comprehension section until last, because more points can be earned per minute of time on other Verbal sections.

3. Because items are presented in order of difficulty, an item late in the Quantitative Comparison section that *looks* easy probably has a catch in it.

4. In geometric items where the length of a line is to be calculated, estimate the length from the scale drawing that accompanies the item. This estimate can rule out many — sometimes all — of the wrong choices, so that less mathematical reasoning is needed.

Source: Adapted from Owen, 1985, pp. 126–133. These suggestions are among those given to prospective SAT takers by certain coaching schools that, according to Owen, produce large gains. (But SAT may already have been changed to make some of these suggestions useless; see question 29.)

trick has surfaced, the test developers who write the SAT immediately have changed the test so that the trick would no longer help. It is a risky business to rely on tricks. . . ." How might the test developers prevent the techniques listed in Table 3.1 from working?

Pros and Cons of Coaching

Bulletin boards on every campus are papered over with ads for coaching schools serving applicants for business school, law school, medical school, you name it. High school juniors aspiring to selective colleges crowd into coaching schools, and some high schools allocate class time to preparing for college aptitude tests. Your nearest drugstore may have a rack of do-it-yourself coaching guides for civil service tests as well as for admissions tests.

Similarly, when administrators impose achievement tests to judge how well particular schools or teachers are doing, it is not uncommon for teachers to set the regular course of study aside while preparing students specifically for the test. One group of educational innovators, distressed because experimental teaching methods they had confidence in were not raising standard test scores, added lessons in test taking to the experimental treatment, so that any actual gains in reading would be sure to show. Various aids have been marketed to prepare classes to show up well on the next standard achievement test given for administrative purposes.

After much dispute regarding the effectiveness of coaching, a consensus has emerged about the facts—if not about the propriety of coaching (Anastasi, in Glaser & Bond, 1981). The controversy and the research have centered on the Scholastic Aptitude Test. Prior to 1980, the College Entrance Examination Board advised students that coaching is a poor investment; experimental comparisons of coached and uncoached groups were said to show little advantage for those coached. The Federal Trade Commission (FTC) took the reasoning a step further: if this is true, it said, coaching schools defraud the consumer and should be prosecuted. When it collected evidence, the FTC was surprised to discover that one school was producing notable score increases (and two were not). The comparison was ambiguous because self-selection accounted for some of the superiority of coached applicants. The combined evidence, however, including studies with equated groups, has generated the following conclusions (Kulik, Bangert-Drowns, & Kulik, 1984; Messick, 1980; Powers, 1986; Slack & Porter, 1980).

- Coaching programs differ in character, and their effects depend on the student's prior preparation and motivation. The mere opportunity to take a test twice will have some effect, especially if the students originally had little idea what the test would be like.
- Coaching is especially beneficial for item forms that have complicated directions.

- Average gains of around 10 points in the SAT total are to be expected from a few hours of orientation, hints about test taking, and practice.[5] (That average includes some persons whose scores rose 20 points or more and some whose scores declined a bit; luck plays a part.)

The 20-point gains begin to seem important when we learn that, in the typical selective college, just 30 points separate the average accepted applicant from the best of the applicants told to go elsewhere. This question remains: Does the 20-point benefit for a few students, or the more usual 10-point benefit, warrant the time investment?

The payoff mounts as the coaching changes from a quick brushup to an intensive course. When they truly taught mathematics—21 hours of classwork and 21 hours of homework—Evans and Pike (1973) produced an average gain of 16 points in the SAT Mathematics score. In the FTC study, a 40-hour course plus homework produced gains of 20 to 30 points on both the Verbal and Mathematics tests. So instruction in the abilities crucial to test performance and presumably to much college work has an appreciable effect. On the other hand, Messick and Jungeblut (1981) warn of diminishing returns. Their estimate of the hours of student effort required to produce specified score increases is as follows:

For a gain of	10	20	30	40	points
in the Verbal score:	12	57	260	1185	hours
in the Mathematics score:	8	19	45	107	hours

The current College Board advice reviews these facts and takes this position:[6]

> Some students may improve their scores by taking these courses, while others may not. Unfortunately, despite decades of research, it is still not possible to predict ahead of time who will improve, and by how much—and who will not. For that reason, the College Board cannot recommend coaching courses, especially if they cost a lot or require a lot of time and effort that could be spent on schoolwork or other worthwhile activities. . . .
>
> If you decide to consider a course, investigate it carefully. Examine carefully and ask for verification of all claims of results. Weigh the investment—both in time and in money.

---

[5]Owen (1985, pp. 89–140) argues that the power of coaching is seriously underestimated by the averages cited in this section because they take into account results from poor (even detrimental) coaching as well as results from well-conceived courses in SAT-wiseness. He illustrates programs of both kinds.

[6]From *Taking the SAT*, 1988, pp. 6–7; reproduced by permission of the College Board.

The major complaint about coaching has to do with inequity. Students with time and money for a substantial coaching course are more likely to get into the colleges they prefer than students who get no coaching.

The fair procedure, some people say, is to make coaching available to every student in high school who wants to attend a selective college. But then the tail of testing wags the instructional dog: what is pushed out of the student's school schedule may be more significant than the test-oriented instruction. A national policy committee said this: "[T]here may be considerable advantage to explicitly preparing students for an examination *if the examination tests abilities and knowledge that are educationally worthwhile*" (Wigdor & Garner, 1982).

If coaching specific to a test is prevalent, something is wrong with the system. In a society in which life at the top is much better than the life of the majority *and* one make-or-break decision takes away a young person's chance for high status, the tests that influence the decision take on an all-too-rational importance. It is the system that is irrational. There are many kinds of talent and these talents emerge over the years; so there is no one right age at which to sort people out. In some nations a young man has to complete the academic course to escape a life as hoe wielder. Parents become abnormally sensitive to news that certain high schools come out ahead in college admissions, that certain lower schools get the most graduates past an earlier test hurdle and into these prestige high schools, and even that certain kindergartens increase the child's chances in life. Coaching for the kindergarten entrance examination follows! Since private tutoring is costly, the overselective system gives an advantage to children of the prosperous.

30. *In some college residence halls, students build up files of the examinations they have taken. From the point of view of the professor teaching the course year after year, do these files increase or decrease the validity of measurement?*

31. *Do the suggestions in Table 3.1 have any value for the prospective college student besides a possible gain in SAT points?*

32. *What changes in insight and motivation are likely to take place during a 5-hour coaching course?*

33. *What implications do the investigations of coaching have for those who use mental tests to select scholarship winners?*

34. *In Japan a young person's career opportunities depend very much on capturing one of the limited number of openings in a good university. Vacancies are filled on the basis of entrance examinations and school records. Magazines bearing such titles as* Student Days, Examiners' Circle, *and* Period of Diligent Study *have large circulations. These magazines deal with topics of interest to candidates including information about typical test materials (though the actual test questions are of course guarded). Would such magazines increase or decrease the validity of the tests?*

Dynamic Assessment

A practice commonly referred to as "testing the limits" has been useful in clinical testing. The informal procedure is very much like coaching save that it is done *after* all or part of the test has been given in the usual manner. The examiner then presents again the items where performance was poor (or comparable items), supplying whatever guidance seems likely to elicit fuller or better responses. Such an inquiry is especially suitable when the poor performance is inconsistent with other parts of the record. (Another way to test limits is to suggest answers, good and bad, to see whether the examinee can judge them.)

Here is one approach. Suppose that most of a child's scores are in the low-to-normal range, but he does much more poorly on Block Design. After completing the standard examination, the tester may go back to one of the failed designs, or another of comparable difficulty, and work with the child. She might, for example, place a finger on one corner of the card and ask, "What block do we need here?" The child is likely to succeed, although he may need the further prompt: "Is it turned the right way?" Proceeding block by block, the child assembles the design with the examiner's limited help. After two such trials, the examiner might check whether the child can now construct a third pattern unaided. The clinician considers these observations in deciding what the original low score means, but of course does not revise the score itself. At most, the original score might be flagged as questionable because of the positive evidence the guided trials elicited.

This clinical prompting or tutoring is now to some degree formalized in "dynamic assessment." Many of the approaches are described by their designers or users in Lidz (1987). Lidz's authors call the conventional test "static"—usually with a disapproving tone. In particular, it is believed that children (or adults) who score far below normal in conventional individual testing differ considerably in their ability to respond to instruction. If so, some of them will approach normal levels in a "dynamic" procedure.

It is usual to focus on one test task at a time. Following standard administration, an interactive session of perhaps 30 minutes follows. Some testers interpret the first performance impressionistically and shape their suggestions accordingly. A more psychometric version consists of a series of standard prompts, from minimal to highly directive. The series of prompts is sometimes computerized.

A count of prompts can be made on each item. The count tends to go down as the session moves from problem to problem. Instead of counting prompts, the tester may end the interactive session and return to a conventional posttest to see how well the child does on his own after being "tuned" to his best performance. Equally important is whether, after practice on one task, the child shows improved efficiency on related ("transfer") tasks where he received no direct help. This improvement does occur with the majority of children (Ferrara et al., 1986).

Advocates of dynamic assessment, particularly for children having or expected to have educational difficulties, do not propose to discard the "static" scores and their rich interpretative base. Nor would they consider it ethical or scientific to call the score from the dynamic procedure the "correct" measure of ability. It is a different score, from a different measuring operation. The dynamic performance is telling in its own right, however.

Dynamic assessors want those making educational decisions to view the child in as positive a light as can be justified, because then they are likely to give the child more help. Videotapes of good performance in the testing room convey a more powerful message than the score report. Seeing a static test and then a dynamic test, teachers took from them different messages (Delclos et al., 1987). Whereas the static test led teachers to see the child as mediocre or worse (X's in Figure 3.5), the dynamic test (solid circles) gave a strongly positive impression of the children's competence. Frank, a 6-year-old with an estimated mental age near 3 was classed as mentally retarded and physically handicapped (poor muscle tone, delayed walking). His response to dynamic testing made a strong impression. Gary, 9 months younger, had a similar mental age and was classed as mentally retarded and emotionally disturbed.

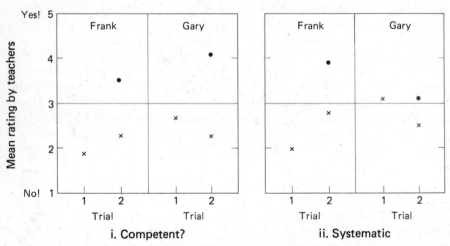

× Rating immediately after viewing static test
● Rating immediately after viewing dynamic test

Figure 3.5. Teachers' impressions from conventional testing and dynamic testing. Three videotapes of testing sessions were made, for Frank and for Gary. All teachers saw tapes of the first "static" testing and rated the child on two multi-item 5-point scales. One scale asked for ratings of understanding, competence, and the child's ability to recognize his own successes and failures. The other scale asked how attentive and systematic the child was. After the first rating period, the teachers saw a second test of the same child, but for half the teachers the second test was administered with feedback and coaching. (*Source:* Vye et al., in Lidz, 1987, pp. 351–353; for details of the rating scale see Delclos et al., 1987.)

Perhaps because of his emotionality, the dynamic session did not bring out better organized work.

35. *In the interests of standardization and objectivity, traditional psychometrics reduces the report of a test to a score. Teachers viewing videotapes (or a live testing session) will make a subjective evaluation, directing their attention idiosyncratically and perhaps being swayed emotionally. Are better educational decisions likely to result when teachers observe the performance or when they are given only a score based on standard procedure?*

36. *One may standardize dynamic testing by preparing a script. For example, the script might dictate what to say if a child pulls together five blocks to make a four-block pattern. The alternative is to leave the tester to use her own judgment about how to assist the child. What is to be said for and against standardizing the prompts?*

RIGHTS OF THE TEST TAKER

Members of all professions are expected today to be far more open in their relations with those served than was usual in times past. Our codes have always avowed that the professional acts to advance the interests of the client and the public; the new theme is that people can judge what serves their interests better than the professional can. Consequently, professional standards are changing. Testing practice is affected by laws and recommendations on such themes as privacy, informed consent, limits of experimentation on humans, and freedom of information. Details of the changing regulations are less important than principles.

The tester enters into a contract with the person tested. In former days the understanding was left vague. The tester is now expected to be frank and explicit in her agreement with the client (or, in the case of a young child or disturbed adult, with the client's representative). The tester is often a go-between—between a college and an applicant or between a court and a prisoner, for example. The tester has responsibilities in both directions, and should try to make sure that these opposite numbers have mutually consistent expectations. If the tester promises that persons in certain specific responsible posts—and no one else—will see the client's scores, the tester ought to assure herself that the institution to which she reports will maintain that degree of confidentiality.

Figure 3.6 reproduces leading paragraphs of the latest full statement on examinee rights, addressed to and written by psychologists and educational testers. It amplifies points made below.[7] Opinion has not stabi-

---

[7]The principles in this section are derived also from policy statements of the American Personnel and Guidance Association (1978) and the American Psychological Association (1981); and from the discussions of a national committee on ability testing (Wigdor & Garner, 1982). See also London and Bray (1980), and Korchin & Cowan, in Kendall and Butcher (1982). The sources do not cover precisely the same points, but they are in harmony. In addition to principles listed here, issues particularly pertinent to personality tests (such as concealing the purpose of the test) were touched on earlier on page 42 and will be discussed further on pages 524–527.

16. Protecting the Rights of Test Takers

Standard 16.1   Informed consent should be obtained from test takers or their legal representatives before testing is done except (a) when testing without consent is mandated by law or governmental regulation (e.g., statewide testing programs); (b) when testing is conducted as a regular part of school activities (e.g., schoolwide testing programs and participation by schools in norming and research studies); or (c) when consent is clearly implied (e.g., application for employment or educational admissions). When consent is not required, test takers should be informed concerning the testing process. *(Primary)*

Comment:

Informed consent implies that the test takers or representatives are made aware, in language that they can understand, of the reasons for testing, the type of tests to be used, the intended use and the range of material consequences of the intended use, and what testing information will be released and to whom. When law mandates testing but does not require informed consent, test users should exercise discretion in obtaining informed consent, but test takers should always be given relevant information about a test when it is in their interest to be informed.

Young test takers should receive an explanation of the reasons for testing. Even a child as young as two or three and many mentally retarded test takers can understand a simple explanation as to why they are being tested. For example, an explanation such as "I'm going to ask you to try to do some

Figure 3.6. Recommendations for protection of test takers. (*Source:* Excerpted from pages 85–87 of *Standards for Educational and Psychological Testing.* Copyright © 1985 by the American Psychological Association and reproduced by permission.)

lized regarding these rights. Representatives of client interests press for ever-increasing restraints on testing. Professionals accept many of the restraints but believe that the trend can go too far. They point to risks of inhibiting research, impairing the quality of decisions, and increasing their cost.

- The record of test performance is the property of the person tested. Individual scores should not be supplied to any person or agency without the examinee's authorization except where it is necessary to warn someone of physical danger or where an authority with acknowledged jurisdiction commissioned the testing. An initial authorization is established when the tester—in obtaining consent for the testing—explains why the test is given. The examinee should be told what will be done with the test results: who will things so that I can see what you know how to do and what things you could use some more help with" would be understandable to such test takers.

Standard 16.2   In school, clinical, and counseling applications, test users should provide test takers or their legal representative with an appropriate explanation of test results and recommendations made on the basis of test results in a form that they can understand. *(Primary)*

Comment:

This standard requires both the use of the appropriate language with non-English speaking test takers and the use of conceptually understandable explanations with all types of test takers. Even children and many mentally retarded test takers can understand a simple explanation of test results.

Standard 16.4   In educational, clinical, and counseling applications, when test scores are used to make decisions about individuals, the affected person or legal representative should be able to obtain transmittal of this test score and its interpretation for any appropriate use. *(Secondary)*

Figure 3.6. *Continued.*

see them, what decisions may be affected by them, and how long they will be kept on file. (See also p. 523 on threats to privacy.)

- Scores and score interpretations that will have an important effect on the person's future should be reported to him in understandable form. Exceptions are warranted where the person is immature, or disclosure would be unsettling, or special training is required to understand the report (Standard 16.2).
- A procedure for challenging a test report should be available to the test taker and he should be informed of it. A score found to be seriously invalid should be removed from the record. (Standard 16.4; see also p. 149.)
- When examinees are suspected of misconduct, investigators should be sensitive to the risks of distressing and damaging the suspects. (In the early 1980s there was much concern about scattered instances of possible cheating in high-stakes testing programs such as the SAT. Computers have been programmed to recognize when two candidates tested at the same session have given suspiciously similar responses. When a questionable pattern is turned up, the inevitable follow-up questions are highly threatening.)
- In educational and employment testing, a score from 2 years back is out of date. It is useful—if at all—only as a benchmark against

which to judge current performance. Old scores should not be retained except in research files. This principle would not apply in some clinical practice, where a long-term history of ups and downs in test performance is likely to shed light on a current decision. But the clinician should be mindful that evidence on emotional adjustment can go out of date quickly.

Such principles are not easily put into practice; and costs of a well-intentioned procedure have to be weighed against benefits.

Take scoring errors as an example. When a person's opportunity hinges on a score, he should have a way to question its accuracy even though the likelihood of error is small. The principle of openness has its limits, though. When two members of a union were passed over for promotion, the union sued on their behalf. It claimed for itself the right to rescore the promotion tests of these workers and the ones who were promoted in order to confirm whether its clients had done as poorly as the company said. The company objected particularly to releasing test papers of successful candidates without their consent, but security of the test was also a concern. The risk that the questions and answers might be leaked to future candidates outweighs the risk of a scoring error, said the U.S. Supreme Court—by a vote of 5 to 4 (*Detroit Edison Co. v. N.L.R.B.*, 99 S. Ct 1123, 1979; Roskind, 1980).

Disclosure   This example is part of a larger concern about release of test items. In 1979, New York State mandated public release ("disclosure") of the questions from college entrance tests after they have been administered. Test developers objected to having to assemble entirely new questions each time the test is offered. This process is costly, and for some kinds of tests fresh items are hard to invent. One consequence of the law is that candidates in New York State have fewer testing dates to choose from than are scheduled in states without disclosure (Donlon, 1984, p. 7).

Two justifications for disclosure were offered: releasing the tests has educational value because students will study the items missed; second, release enables students to verify the scoring and the answer key itself (Bersoff, in Glaser & Bond, 1981). (For a fee, students can obtain their answer sheets to check against released tests. This is true for persons anywhere who take an SAT form that is scheduled for disclosure in New York.)

The opportunity to study items seems not to have raised subsequent scores (Stricker, 1984). But recurring news stories demonstrate that among hundreds of thousands of college applicants, one of them at a certain moment can reason more subtly than the test developers and can defend a response originally keyed as unacceptable. Releasing items seems to invite wrangles over items that call for subtle judgment. Such threats tend to drive out tasks where judgment enters, shifting test questions toward recall of indisputable facts.

What tests are given and how they are reported is likely to change as more reports are opened to examinees. Test records will avoid words having strong emotional connotations, such as "mental retardation" and "neurotic." Testers will be tempted to muffle a serious finding in phrases to which no one could object. "Face valid" tests (transparently related to the decision under consideration) will become more popular. On the one hand, the quality and richness of test information can be expected to decline; on the other hand, the emerging policies will reduce misuse, misunderstanding, and harmful labeling.

Security of Test Findings   Citizens are rightly uneasy about files containing information that could someday be dragged out by an adversary. Research files can be subpoenaed. For example, social scientists who had interviewed recipients of public welfare were unable to deny access to supposedly confidential files when a prosecutor suspected some recipients of fraud. Similar conflict could arise in a suit alleging medical or educational malpractice. The Public Health Service Act provides some hope for relief; an investigator studying behavior problems, drugs, and many other topics can apply for a certificate of confidentiality to protect files from subpoena. But few certificates have been issued, and as of early 1989 none has been tested in court.

Two principles can be added to the earlier list:

- Files should be secured so that no one sees a case record without specific authorization from the responsible professional.
- Identities of individuals should be removed from a test record when they are not essential.

In particular, records in research files should be coded so that users of the files cannot identify scores with individuals. When individual identification is erased, the files no longer can serve a prosecutor. But there is a hidden cost. Sometimes, 10 or 20 years later it may be scientifically important to trace the subsequent development of individuals. Conversely, it could be important to look back at the early history of those who, at age 30, display some unusual excellence or defect. A number of devices for protecting research values without endangering privacy have been suggested (Boruch & Cecil, 1979; see p. 526 for one device).

Policies for testing by employers and schools have received more attention than policies for clinical testers. Clinical psychologists have generally seen their responsibility to persons they treat as requiring confidentiality similar to that between physician and patient. But the psychologist who finds a client hostile to a family member and fears he may do harm is advised to warn the potential victim, or at least to seek the advice of colleagues on the matter. A court may reject the "privacy" defense if, following a violent act, the psychologist is sued (Fulero, 1988; Korchin & Cowan, in Kendall & Butcher, 1982, p. 79). Even medical confidentiality is now questioned, as institutions seek access to clinical records to guard against false insurance claims, to trace the spread and causes of diseases, and to defend in suits arising from various hazards.

37. *When two persons are flagged as having given similar responses, one possible resolution of the suspicion of cheating is to offer each candidate the opportunity to take the test again without charge, with no report of the first test and the attendant suspicion going outside the testing organization. Why is this not always wholly satisfactory to the examinee?*

38. *One member of Congress pressed (unsuccessfully) for the rule that a patient's file could be examined only with his explicit consent. Those familiar with health research said that this would make the files available for research on the effectiveness of treatment so unrepresentative as to be worthless (Holden, 1977). What rights and values are in conflict here? Consider particularly files of persons treated for behavioral or emotional disturbances.*

39. *On a mathematical reasoning test, a student planning to go to graduate school earns a score that is about average for seniors in scientific fields. He does much better on another form of the test 6 months later, ranking in the upper quarter. Should he have the right to specify that only the second score be transmitted when he applies to graduate schools? (Would you give the same answer if his first score had been the higher one?)*

40. *What explanation would you give the test taker in each of the following cases?*
    a. *College freshmen are to be tested to determine which ones may fail because of reading deficiency.*
    b. *At the end of a course in industrial relations for supervisors, an examination on judgment in grievance cases is to be given.*

41. *How could a "cooperative" point of view in testing be adopted:*
    a. *By a school principal who wishes to find out how well each eighth-grade class is mastering written English?*
    b. *By a veteran's counselor who must approve the plan of a handicapped veteran to go to college and prepare for dentistry?*
    c. *By a consulting psychologist who is asked by a social agency to diagnose and report on a potential delinquent?*

42. *The first principle listed earlier—"the record is the property of the person tested"—is stated strongly enough to be debatable. Consider these applications:*
    a. *Should a law school supply, to the prospective employer of a graduate, the person's score on a test given at the time of admission? The student's grade record?*
    b. *A school psychologist evaluating an emotionally disturbed child employs a sentence-completion test with items such as*

    When I can't answer a question the teacher asks, I. . . .
    My parents. . . .

    When the psychologist recommends that the child be placed in a residential school, should the parents be allowed to see the child's responses?
    c. *A teacher in Grade 9 asks students, midway in the year, to write autobiographical essays. Should copies of those essays be available to other teachers?*

d. *Should the advanced calculus teacher have access to a student's grades in lower-level math courses?*

Providing for Physical Handicaps

Conventional testing can only be a barrier to the physically handicapped. In a selection situation, low scores resulting from limited vision or poor coordination underestimate competence. Clinical testers allow for disability by altering procedures (recognizing that, with nonstandard procedures, the scores do not have their ordinary significance). A number of tests are specially adapted to one or another handicap: for example, a block-design test for the blind in which surface textures replace the usual colors (Dauterman & Suinn, 1966). Also, programs such as the SAT regularly make special provision for the handicapped. Testing time is usually extended where there is a language or motor handicap. Print can be enlarged, tests can be printed in Braille, or questions can be read aloud. The person with a motor handicap can dictate answers. For the deaf, directions in sign language can be filmed.

It is pointless to try to equate handicapped test takers with others. To develop norms for each category of handicapped examinees would be impracticable and probably equally pointless (Willingham et al., 1988). A person who is average within his category may be a better or worse candidate than the person who is average in the general population. To study just what each altered test measures and how well it predicts success in various training programs (themselves suitable only when adapted to each handicap) is an inexhaustible task. Often the best solution is to exempt the handicapped person from the usual test and rely on evidence from school records or a job tryout. For recommendations on appropriate testing and test interpretation for the handicapped, see Sherman and Robinson (1982).

Although the professional *Testing standards* endorse the practice of modifying tests and testing procedures when the test taker with a disability would otherwise encounter inappropriate difficulty, serious problems remain. Test manuals should warn against placing confidence in interpretation of results from an altered test unless the changed test has been validated for persons whose type and severity of handicap matches the present case. Considerable clinical judgment is required when there has been no such direct validation. Interpretation is particularly difficult when the handicap affects cognitive functioning. A person who became deaf in infancy, for example, does not process language as others do. Theory pertinent to verbal abilities of the hearing person does not apply to this deaf examinee.

A common practice is to "flag" the score report from a test administered under nonstandard conditions. Flagging seems entirely sensible, as the scores are not open to the "regular" interpretation; but the writers of the *Standards* did not recommend flagging. They backed off because handicapped persons protested that "to identify their scores as resulting from nonstandard administrations and in so doing to identify them as handicapped is [in a selection situation] to deny them the opportunity to compete on the same grounds as nonhandicapped test takers, that is, to treat them inequitably."[8]

43. *If sighted persons take the textured version of Block Design, will they rank as they did on the version with colored patterns? Do the two tests measure the same thing?*

---

[8]From the *Standards for Educational and Psychological Testing*, p. 78. Copyright © 1985 by the American Psychological Association. Reprinted by permission.

Chapter
4

Scores and Score Conversions

4A. What characteristics should a test have if its total score is to be given a domain-referenced interpretation?

4B. Tell how standard scores and percentile equivalents are obtained from a raw-score distribution. What are the main practical differences between the two kinds of conversion?

4C. What testing purposes make good national norms particularly important? not very important?

4D. What is the equipercentile method? For what is it used?

4E. How do procedures based on item-response theory contribute to constructing comparable forms of tests? to adaptive testing?

Abbreviations in this chapter: ABIC for Adaptive Behavior Inventory for Children (Mercer); DAT for Differential Aptitude Tests; DRP for Degrees of Reading Power; IRT for item response theory; KABC for Kaufman Assessment Battery for Children; MCT for Mechanical Comprehension Test; SAT for Scholastic Aptitude Test, with V and M for the Verbal and Mathematical sections; SOMPA for Mercer's System of Multicultural Pluralistic Assessment.

ORIENTATION

This chapter describes the kinds of scores used in reporting test results and tells how scores are interpreted in case work and in statistical studies. These topics have to be developed further in later chapters, and you will probably want to return to this chapter many times. In a sense, the chapter is about "statistics." Computational procedures are introduced for reference, however, rather than as the focal point. Your main task is to learn what is meant by the numbers used in test reports.

The opening section, on raw scores, describes a few devices that improve scoring; the devices are illustrative, not important to study. More important here is to see why raw scores can rarely be interpreted by themselves. The rest of the chapter explains how raw scores are supplemented and modified.

The three contrasting methods of developing meanings for scores are important to distinguish because they answer different questions about examinees. I describe at some length a reading test that was scaled by complex procedures. Your goal should be to understand what the scale tries to accomplish. The type of scaling is new and likely to be increasingly important. But the research procedures and the final scale will take different forms with other tests, so—beyond the main idea— you need not remember how the reading test was scaled. From the short section on setting standards, try to understand why standards must be set by negotiation rather than solely by technical analysis.

For score conversion we have two main systems. Percentiles are a kind of ranking. Standard scores use the standard deviation as a yardstick. Your aim should be to learn to "read" statements such as "Francis scored at the 40th percentile in mechanical comprehension and had a standard score of 40 on manual dexterity." And also, to read statistical summaries such as "Scores in this class had a mean of 72 and a standard deviation of 6." All the material on definition and calculation of statistics is presented as a base for developing this understanding. You can always look up the procedures when you need them later. (Unfortunately, there are many standard-score scales. Concentrate on the one I label "50 ± 10." Once you grasp that, the rest will fall into place.)

Pay close attention to the numbers in Figure 4.5; they are the key to whether, for example, Francis stood higher in mechanical comprehension or in dexterity. Many later statements in this book will rely on these numbers.

Inadequate norms, or norms that do not fit the cases in hand, lead to bad decisions. Therefore, you need to be able to ask the right questions before relying on the norms for a test. The long section on norms tells you what to look for and illustrates ways in which norms generate misleading conclusions. Take both aspects seriously.

On page 136 we turn to a powerful new system of score conversion, foreshadowed in the example of the reading test. In a sense, this section stands by itself, because nearly all the evidence on test scores and their meaning to be found in this book was collected before the technique came into use. You need to understand the material as a basis for keeping up with the field. It is the key procedure behind the emerging computer-adaptive tests. I pack a tremendous amount into a few pages. Depending on your level of training and experience, you may want to grasp just the main ideas or to get the most out of every paragraph. Mainly, you should understand what the approach can and cannot do, not how it works. That is a topic for more specialized books.

OBTAINING RAW SCORES

Scoring Procedures

It is difficult to define a good answer and to assign suitable credit for less-excellent answers. Long ago, Starch and Elliott (1912, 1913) provided famous evidence. They asked teachers attending a convention to grade a pupil's English composition on a percentage scale. The grades ranged from 50 to 98. *This* disagreement could perhaps be tolerated, because judging a composition is inherently subjective. To drive home their point, Starch and Elliott had teachers grade a geometry paper; those scores ranged from 28 to 92. Some scorers gave credit for neatness and some did not. And some assigned more credit to an incomplete solution than others did.

To systematize scoring of constructed responses one must set uniform rules for judgment. A classic example is the Ayres guide for rating pupil handwriting (Figure 4.1). The guide displays specimens that judges agreed on as representing evenly spaced levels of quality. To determine the score, the teacher locates the sample most similar to the pupil's writing.

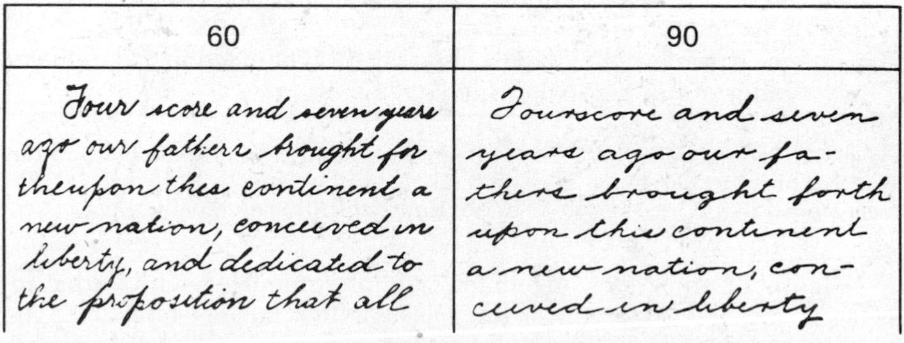

60	90
Four score and seven years ago our fathers brought for theupon this continent a new nation, conceived in liberty, and dedicated to the proposition that all	Fourscore and seven years ago our fathers brought forth upon this continent a new nation, conceived in liberty

Figure 4.1. **Part of the Ayres scale for scoring handwriting.** (Reproduced by permission of the present publisher, the University of Iowa Press.)

SCORING CRITERIA

All the answers given in the examples following this section are complete—it will be apparent that with a more extended response they could merit a higher score, but in these cases this was not forthcoming.

Conversely, a few responses are over-extended; having completed a response the child has produced irrelevancies subsequently, but should not be penalized for this. . . .

Score 0—Pre-reasoning

The child is unable to comprehend what is required, or to provide a relevant response. . . .

Score 1—Immediate Consequences

The child now responds relevantly, but only in terms of **immediate reactions or consequences,** often talking about the punishment or reward which one person in the item will get, or how he will feel. This may be shown by references to getting into trouble, being punished, being good or naughty, without further elaboration, being injured or breaking things. . . .

Score 2—Partial Evaluation

The child has now progressed to a broader grasp of **one side of the problem only.**
This may be expressed either as value judgements about stealing, keeping promises etc., statements of simple rules about behaviour, or practical solutions for solving the problem from one angle only. What is **not** apparent is a real view of both sides of the problem; one person is seen as being in the right or as being wrong. . . .

Score 3—Full Evaluation

An attempt is made to find reasons and explanations for the actions of **both parties.**
Some stereotyped judgements may be given, but unlike the Stage 2 response, an attempt is made to see both or all sides of the problem. However, the Stage 3 child is still immersed in the rights and wrongs of the particular problem. . . .

Figure 4.2. **Scoring rules for a Social Reasoning item.** (*Source*: Manual 3 of the British Ability Scales by C. D. Elliott, D. J. Murray, and L. S. Pearson, 1978. Reproduced by permission of NFER-Nelson Publishing Company, Ltd.)

Figure 4.2 illustrates a common type of guide used with verbal responses; we see a fraction of the scoring rules for one question. The rules (derived from the theories of Piaget and Kohlberg) give greater credit for more mature thought. Maturing children become increasingly able to see a situation through the eyes of others. Following the material

Joe did not have many toys, but he had a teddy bear he loved very much. One day some older children took his teddy bear and burned it. They said it didn't matter. What do you think? . . . .
Why? . . . .

Note for scoring:
Most responses focus either on Joe's having no more toys—a one-point score unless further elaborated; or on Joe having loved his teddy—usually a two-point score.

Score 0   That's a good story.

He cried—my dad's name is Joe.

Score 1   If he likes his teddy so much he shouldn't make friends with other children.

His mum smacked him—because he lost his teddy bear.

Did matter—they'll get into trouble.

Does matter—the boys will get told off and Joe will be sad.

Score 2   It did matter—they are thieves.

They shouldn't have burned it—they are naughty for taking other people's things.

It did matter—Joe loved it very much and did not have other toys.

Score 3   If he was a baby it did matter, but if he was a grown up boy it didn't matter—grown-up boys don't have teddy bears.

It did matter to Joe because he cared for it—it didn't matter to the boys because they were cruel.

It mattered to him—perhaps they didn't know how much it meant to him.

Figure 4.2. *Continued.*

in the figure, the directions continue with illustrations of response at the level of a general principle.

For choice-response items one specifies the answer key and a rule for counting up scores. Scoring of choice responses by machine is rapid, accurate, and economical. A device can translate each mark on the answer sheet into an electrical impulse that can be matched against the key. Some scanners use photocells; another type relies on the fact that pencil marks conduct electricity. The examinee who erases carelessly or who makes stray marks sends false signals. Therefore, clerks should inspect papers and make some erasures. The test giver should emphasize filling the printed spaces with solid black marks.

Scoring can be built directly into the testing procedure. Both the old and new versions of the complex coordination test (pp. 40, 50) allow automatic recording of response times and errors, ready for summary by computer. In fact, every computer-administered test has automated scoring.

1. *The question "Why should people wash their clothing?" is used to test adults' comprehension of common situations. Prepare a set of standards for judging correctness of answers. Make your rules so clear that scorers would be able to agree in scoring new answers. Try to base credit on quality of thought rather than fluency of expression.*

2. *Use Figure 4.2 to score the following responses to Item 2 of the Social Reasoning Test. (These are taken from the BAS manual.)*
   a. *They wanted one because they are selfish—so they took his to be mean.*
   b. *It was a new teddy.*
   c. *John feels sorry he ain't got no toy to play with. He will tell his mum and she'll come back and tell them to get another one.*

Limitations of Raw-Score Scales

The direct count or measure of performance is called the *raw score*. This may be the number of questions the person answered, the time he required, a count of right answers plus bonuses for fast work and minus penalties for errors, or perhaps a rating of overall quality.

Raw scores can easily be misinterpreted. Willie's report card shows a 75 in arithmetic and a 90 in spelling. His parents can be counted on to praise the latter and disapprove the former. Willie might quite properly protest, "But you should see what the other kids get in arithmetic. Lots of them get 60 and 65." The parents, who know a good grade when they see one, refuse to be sidetracked by such irrelevance. But what do Willie's grades mean? It might appear that he has mastered three-fourths of the course work in arithmetic, and nine-tenths in spelling. Willie objects to that, too. "I learned all my combinations, but the teacher doesn't ask much about those. The tests are full of word problems, and we only studied them a little." Willie evidently gives correct answers to 75 per cent of the questions asked, but since the questions may be easy or hard, the percentage itself is meaningless to his parents. We cannot compare Willie with his sister Sue, whose teacher in another grade gives easier tests. It could be, too, that Willie's shining 90 in spelling is misleading if the spelling tests are restricted to the words assigned for study.

Physical measuring scales generally have a true or absolute zero and equal units along the scale. This permits us to say, for example, that one boy is twice as tall as another or has attained 60 per cent of his probable adult height. We cannot make statements like those about psychological measures. Suppose that Willie scored 10 per cent in spelling. Would this mean that he knows only one-tenth of the words he should? No, for the teacher probably did not ask about easy words that Willie was sure to know. A zero on the test would not mean zero ability to spell.

The same argument applies to tests of reasoning. A raw score of 80 may appear to represent ability twice as great as a raw score of 40. The test does not include the problems everyone can solve, however; if the test included every suitable problem, the true ratio might be 140 to 180 or 1040 to 1080. Even an infant, looking toward the door when he hears a parent's footstep, gives evidence of reasoning. Absolute zero in any ability is "just no ability at all."

Differences in raw scores do not ordinarily represent "true" distances between individuals. Suppose that, on a 68-point mechanical reasoning test, Adam gets 46 points, Brenda gets 56, and Charles gets 66. The raw-score differences are equal. Is Charles truly as different from Brenda as Brenda is from Adam? We cannot be sure, because the score difference depends on the items used. Adding difficult items to the test would give Charles a chance to lengthen his lead. "Equal differences" is a meaningful phrase only after some practical criterion pins down a scale of values. Different standards lead to different comparisons. The three raw scores are equally spaced. The corresponding probabilities of passing a college engineering course almost certainly are not equally spaced; they might be something like 0.3, 0.4, and 0.6. The students' most likely freshman grade averages may be D, C+, and B−. And their respective probabilities of later success in a demanding engineering firm may be 0.0001, 0.1, and 0.5. "Equal intervals" on one scale are unequal by another standard.

3. *Decide whether an absolute zero exists for each of the following variables and, where possible, define it. (Where the zero level cannot be defined, it is sometimes possible to define the opposite extreme, the upper limit. That would be an absolute zero for the error score. In defining a zero level of an ability, assume that the person understands the task directions.)*
   a. *Height of a person.*
   b. *Ability to discriminate between the pitches of tones.*
   c. *Speed of tapping.*
   d. *Gregariousness, seeking the companionship of others.*
   e. *Rifle aiming.*

4. *Amelia, a college freshman, seeking counseling on her academic plans, takes four tests of ability. Scores could be presented in four ways. Interpret separately each row of scores.*

	Vocabulary	Verbal reasoning	Nonverbal reasoning	Mechanical comprehension
Raw score	116	32	44	48
Percent of possible points	77	73	80	71
Points above average	24	10	20	0
Rank among 260 freshman	104	113	161	136

5. *Is it sensible for a school to fix percentage requirements for course marks based on test averages? (For example: 93–100 = A, 85–92 = B, etc.)*

6. *Some instructors "grade on the curve," assigning A's to a fixed proportion of the class, B's to another proportion, and so on. Is there any logical basis for fixing these percentages?*

7. *Two runners train for the mile. One, between his junior and senior years, reduces his time from 4 minutes 56 seconds to 4 minutes 44 seconds. The other starts with a time of 5 minutes 56 seconds. What time must he achieve for us to say that he has made as much improvement as the first runner?*

DOMAIN-REFERENCED INTERPRETATIONS AND THE ALTERNATIVES

To understand a score, we must bring in information about the task or the performance of other persons or both. This section is most concerned with consideration of task content, but as a preliminary it is necessary to distinguish types of interpretation.

Three Kinds of Interpretation

Three labels for interpretations are popular; I introduce them by means of an example. Here are three interpretations of the same score:

- Norm reference. "Janet did better in solving these linear equations than 80 per cent of representative algebra students tested at this stage of training."
- Domain reference. "The score indicates that Janet can be expected to solve about two-thirds of all one-variable linear equations."
- Criterion reference. "Students who have reached Janet's level on linear equations usually succeed in the subsequent unit on simultaneous equations without special help or extra time." (That is, Janet is ready to move ahead.)

Almost any test could be given all three types of interpretation. Arguing for or against one kind of interpretation is pointless. The question is: Which kind is relevant to a particular use?

An interpretation is said to be *norm-referenced* if it compares test takers; thus, the teacher who "grades on the curve" is making a norm-referenced interpretation. (Norm-referenced interpretations do not necessarily rest on *external* norms.)

A *domain-referenced* report tells how well a person copes with the kind of task found in the test, or how likely he is in everyday life to make a kind of response that a tester has observed.

A *criterion-referenced* report tells how the person is expected to perform in a situation (or response class) unlike the test—usually, how likely the person is to satisfy some practical requirement.

Criterion reference is a kind of "sign" interpretation (p. 51). An expectancy statement refers to behavior in a statement *unlike* the test. For example, "A student with this score on numerical ability has a 4-to-1 chance of completing a community college course in accounting." A "criterion" is an outcome to be predicted (pp. 160, 413).

A domain-referenced interpretation emphasizes level of performance on the tasks or situations sampled by the test. The interpretation may also be called "content-referenced." The interpretation is meaningful only when the domain of tasks is identified clearly (Nitko, in Berk, 1984).

The chosen domain may be homogeneous ("unidimensional"), all the items measuring essentially the same attribute. Technically, an ability domain is *homogeneous* if a person who passes one item is very likely to pass all items that are easier (judged by the average of other persons). Ability to detect differences in musical pitch near middle C is an example. The domain may instead be heterogeneous: knowledge of current events, for example.

(Associating "domain reference" with anticipated performance on further samples of the same kind, and "criterion reference" with anticipated performance of a kind that the test did not directly sample, is consistent with the *Testing standards.* But in writings on tests "domain-referenced" and "criterion-referenced" are given many other meanings; Berk, 1984.)

Recent enthusiasm for criterion reference and domain reference is chiefly a reaction against a competitive, comparative emphasis in education. The pupil who improves in reading during the school year, for example, receives little encouragement if a teacher's norm-referenced test interpretation focuses on the fact that he is somewhat below average at the end of the year, just as he was at the beginning.

Pioneer psychological testers thought that their main task was to highlight individual differences. Therefore, they rarely worked out criterion-referenced or domain-referenced interpretations. Published achievement tests have emphasized norms, in part because local, teacher-made tests lack this feature. Many of today's achievement tests are designed to indicate *which* skills a pupil or class has mastered within a subject such as arithmetic, rather than how they rank on a composite score.

Enthusiasm for norm reference remains high in much testing for guidance. I would say, however, that there is little point in telling a student that (for example) many people have greater interest in science than he does; the question ought to be, does he like scientific activities well enough to find such a career satisfying? Chapter 12 will explain why many colleagues disagree with me and call for norm-referenced interest profiles. Criterion reference fits best into Chapter 5 and we return to it there. This chapter will return to norm reference after the statistics used in norms are introduced. At this point, there is more to be said about domain reference.

8. *Which of the following reports is (are) referenced against a criterion? Against a domain? Against a norm group?*
   a. *A vision test is reported in such terms as "at a 12-inch distance, can read 10-point, or larger, type."*
   b. *A measure of "dental age" is obtained by comparing a child's teeth with a chart showing what teeth are ordinarily present at age 5, at age 6, and so on.*
   c. *Six children out of 30 name Barbara as "a good person to play with."*

9. *Which of these domains is (are) close to unidimensional?*
   a. *ability in baseball*
   b. *high-jumping ability*
   c. *ability to spell*
   d. *warmth in interpersonal relations*

10. *For each of these decisions, would you prefer a report that is criterion-referenced, domain-referenced, or norm-referenced?*
    a. *Susana's teacher wants to know the maturity of Susana's interests as a basis for selecting literature for her to read.*
    b. *A student reports many symptoms of anxiety, and the counselor wishes to decide whether this degree of anxiety is unusual.*
    c. *A school wants to provide intensive exercise for every student whose physical fitness is poor.*
    d. *Ruby transfers from another high school. The counselor wants to know whether her proficiency is good enough for her to enroll in third-year Spanish?*
    e. *The school wishes to make a report to parents of students whose spelling is poor enough to be of concern.*

Reading Power: Illustration of a Content Scale

Interpretation of a content scale is not sensible unless the content is significant in its own right. When the content is significant, an established standard may apply. The teacher may say, for example, that no one will be allowed to take up the study of shorthand until his typing speed reaches 50 words per minute.

Content interpretation requires well-defined levels of difficulty. To say only "reads 280 words per minute" means very little until we know something about the text read, and the level of comprehension the tester demanded. The most direct way to give meaning to a raw score is to display the content of the test, but a summary report cannot do this. Nor can a long test readily be inspected. A reasonable substitute is to illustrate tasks within reach of a person at this-or-that score level.

Degrees of Reading Power (DRP) is a reading sample interpreted on a content scale. (Norms are also provided.) The test has the form known as "cloze." A test booklet presents eight essays of about 300 words. From each, a few significant words have been deleted, and the test taker decides which of five options best fills each blank. Success shows comprehension. Selections vary in difficulty, so it is easy to see what levels are within the pupil's grasp. (The word "cloze" comes from *closure,* a term from Gestalt psychology. It refers to perceiving the pattern in an incomplete display.)

DRP interpretation is enhanced by the *Readability report,* a book that lists difficulty values of school readers, science texts, and other instructional materials. The values were produced by a formula. To develop it, varied passages were selected, every fifth word was blanked out, and representative pupils tried to supply the missing words. Features that made passages harder to complete were identified. The most important ones—sentence length, number of words per sentence, and frequency of unusual words—are combined in a "readability formula."

To rate readability of any book, the formula is applied to representative passages. A readability level near 30 indicates primer level, whereas selections in the 80s are harder than most college texts. Newspapers generally fall near 70, although sports pages are usually easier. (Computer software enables a school district to calculate DRP values for publications not included in the published *Readability report.*)

The student's raw test score is translated into his "reading power" on the readability scale. One sixth-grader has these DRP scores: Independent, 40; Instructional, 51; Frustration, 62. This student is expected to handle selections at DRP level 40 with little trouble, to find selections around level 51 challenging, and to grasp only about half the paragraphs at level 62.[1] The teacher can reasonably assign materials at level 45–55 to advance the pupil's basic reading skill. Materials near 40 would be suitable for his free reading on wide-ranging supplementary topics, and for practice on such subtle skills as comparing two writers' accounts of lumbering in the Northwest. The potential importance of this individualization is indicated by the fact that 10 per cent of sixth-graders have Independent scores below 25 while the highest 10 per cent exceed 60. (The pupil described here is at the 60th percentile for Grade 6.)

Setting Standards

In some applications of tests, decision rules can be highly flexible. Whether a student should enter a course where he has one chance in three of a poor grade is usually regarded as something for him to decide. Candidates for admission to a college may be rejected outright if the odds against survival are high, and those who seem certain to do well may be admitted without hesitation. In midscale, the admissions committee will take into account not only facts unique to the individual but also a preference for diversity in the student body. At the classroom level, a decision that Janet is ready to go on to simultaneous equations

---

[1]Because several steps of inference come between the DRP sample and this expectation, interpretation has criterion-referenced as well as domain-referenced features.

and Jerry is not will be based on a rule this teacher has worked out by experience. If the standard is too lenient, no harm is done because Janet can be sent back to review the basics when and if the decision proves to have been too optimistic.

It is in certification and licensing that the setting of standards is critical. In these applications it is usual to apply cutoff scores "blindly" (because individualized judgment would invite charges of favoritism). The safeguard for the individual is the opportunity to take the test again, without prejudice. The number of candidates allowed to pass the bar exam is not constrained by a quota of places to be filled (whereas places are limited in admitting students and hiring workers). Likewise, those in authority are free (within the limits of political acceptability) to raise or lower the score requirement for high school graduation.

Determination of standards has three aspects: empirical (i.e., based on experience), political, and judgmental. One might, over time, trace the success of young persons in getting and holding jobs, for example, and prepare an experience table relating that success to scores on the test for graduation. This table would indicate the region of the score scale where the risk of unemployability is substantial. However, such a follow-up study with respect to lawyers or drivers or any other certified group uses an incomplete criterion, so it should not be the sole basis for the decision rule.

There are political pressures for higher standards and for lower standards. Employers would like schools to set tough standards; then graduates could be hired with confidence. With regard to professional certification, persons already certified have many motives for raising standards—some high-minded and some selfish.

To candidates, an increase in standards reduces opportunity. Furthermore, high standards entail social costs. The cost of remedial work for students who do not meet the standard for graduation rises with the number failed. There is a subtler cost if the resources put into reading and arithmetic squeeze civics, art, or economics from the student's course of study. Also, the handicap faced by the student who leaves school without a diploma must be considered, for raising standards increases the number of dropouts. Obviously, weighing up benefits, costs, risks, and political palatability comes down to an exercise of judgment.

Technical procedures improve content-referenced judgments (Shepard, in Berk, 1984; Mills & Melican, 1988). If a committee is asked to pinpoint a passing threshold on the score scale the decision is bound to be an arbitrary compromise. Only political judgment can defend a norm-referenced cutoff—"Let's set it so that 10 per cent fail." To say "70 out of 100 is a passing mark" leaves the candidate at the mercy of the item writers. Requesting judgments at the item level makes better use of reviewers' expertise. Committees of judges and lawyers can review a bar exam. Teachers, employers, parents, and recent graduates can review a high school proficiency test. The instructions given reviewers are subtle, but they come down to this: "Should *nearly every* high school graduate in our state pass this item?" This process, repeated with all the items, identifies items that the great majority of borderline performers should pass and also the complicated or unimportant items on which an error is not serious.

Such information can be used in two ways. First, it can be used to eliminate items judged to be unreasonably hard or unimportant. Second, statistical procedures can determine what score on the total test implies that students tested in the future have reached the level defined by the judges.

Calibration methods described later in this chapter can reduce or eliminate the need for fresh judgments when further item sets are developed. Procedures of this kind are still undergoing development. The various procedures that seem logical do not necessarily reach a common conclusion (Jaeger, in Linn, 1989a, pp. 497–500). Andrews and Hecht (1976) applied two well-regarded techniques to the same test. Technique 1 put the cut score at 46 per cent correct; Technique 2, at 69 per cent. Thirty-seven per cent of typical candidates would fail by the first standard, 93 per cent (!) by the second. See also page 571 on "policy-capturing" research.

11. *One state administers a form of Degrees of Reading Power to all high-school seniors and (for graduation) requires them to handle passages of readability 65 with no more than 30 per cent errors. (This is close to the "Instructional" level of comprehension.) How can a standard of 65 rather than 55 or 75 be defended?*

12. *If judges of items are told that many students are likely to fall short of a standard they have proposed, they usually change to a more lenient standard. Assuming that their original judgment was conscientious, what is to be said for and against allowing this stage of revision?*

13. *One device is to set the diploma requirement by giving the test to "successful" adults living in the school district and choosing the cut score that would pass (say) 90 per cent of them. What is to be said for and against this plan?*

CONVERSIONS OF RAW SCORES

Percentiles

It is difficult to compare scores from tests of different lengths unless a common scale is introduced. The easiest form of comparison is ranking: "Tony stands third out of 40 on Test A, tenth on Test B." Because ranks depend on the number of persons in the group, we have difficulty when group size changes. Therefore, ranks are changed to percentile scores. A *percentile score* is the rank from the bottom expressed in percentage terms. Writers use various terms: percentile score, percentile rank, percentile, centile—all have the same meaning.

A percentile rank tells what proportion of the group falls below this

1. Begin with the raw scores. (These are scores of 75 job applicants on Bennett Form S).	54	42	35	51	50	66	36	47	21	40	58

1. Begin with the raw scores. (These are scores of 75 job applicants on Bennett Form S).

54	42	35	51	50	66	36	47	21	40	58
32	48	66	35	25	45	41	49	46	40	51
48	57	31	53	50	38	53	52	58	28	45
51	49	42	41	45	60	24	46	50	56	38
48	38	41	44	57	41	37	17	49	64	41
47	28	49	22	55	52	43	59	43	25	25
33	51	54	61	26	43	56	43	40		

Highest score = 66; lowest score = 17; range = 49.

2. Identify the highest score and the lowest score. Choose a class interval of 1, 2, 5, 10, 20, etc., and divide the range into classes of equal width. Fifteen or more classes are desirable. This table stops at 68, the highest possible score.

A class interval of 5 will be used. (A smaller interval, perhaps 2, would be preferable but would be inconvenient in this computing guide.)

3. Tally the number of cases having each score.

4. Write the number of tallies in the Frequency (f) column. Add this column to get N, the number of cases.

Scores	Tallies	Frequency (f)	Cumulative frequency	Cumulative per cent
65–68	//	2	75	100
60–64	///	3	73	97
55–59	//// ///	8	70	93
50–54	//// //// ///	13	62	83
45–49	//// //// ////	14	49	65
40–44	//// //// //// /	16	35	47
35–39	//// /	6	19	25
30–34	///	3	13	17
25–29	//// /	6	10[a]	13
20–24	///	3	4	5[b]
15–19	/	1	1	1
		N = 75		

[a] 10 cases fall below 29.5; 13 below 34.5; etc.

[b] 5 per cent of the cases fall below 24.5; 5 is the cumulative percentage corresponding to a raw score of 24.5.

5. Begin at the bottom of the column and add frequencies one at a time to determine the cumulative frequency, the number of cases below each division point.

6. Divide the cumulative frequencies by N to determine cumulative percentages.

Figure 4.3. **Determining percentile equivalents.**

person. Tony ranks third; below him are 37 persons. We arbitrarily divide Tony (and all persons tied with him) between the "above" and "below" groups. Assuming no ties, $2\frac{1}{2}$ cases are above Tony and $37\frac{1}{2}$ below. Since 94 per cent of 40 is $37\frac{1}{2}$ the percentile score is 94. Notice that the highest ranking person is not at "the 100th percentile." If two persons out of 40 tie for the top score, we count as if one is just above that score and one just below, making the percentile equivalent 97.5 ($= 100 \times 39/40$). With just one person in the top rank, we also split, reaching 98.7 as the conversion.

7. Plot cumulative percentage against score (chart below). (In practice, a large sheet of graph paper would be used. Panel 8 assumes that ordinary graph paper is used; a special "probability paper" makes it easier to fit this kind of curve.) The first point is at 19.5, 1; the last point is at 68.5, 100 (above the highest possible score).

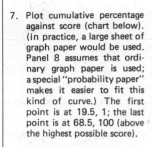

8. Draw the smooth curve that best fits the points plotted.

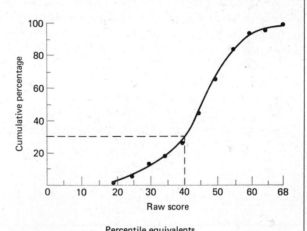

Percentile equivalents

Raw	%ile	Raw	%ile	Raw	%ile
20	1+	35	18	50	66
21	2	36	20	51	70
22	2	37	23	52	73
23	3	38	25	53	77
24	5	39	28	54	80
25	5	40	30	55	83

9. Determine the percentile equivalent of a score by reading from the curve. (The lines on the chart show how one finds that the percentile equivalent of a raw score of 40 is 30).

Figure 4.3. *Continued.*

By this method of computation, the person exactly in the middle of the group is at the 50th percentile; "at the median," we say. The *median* can be thought of as the performance of a "typical" person.

A graphic procedure is advantageous. It smooths out irregularities in the sample and so gives a better estimate of what may be expected when further groups are tested. Figure 4.3 demonstrates this method, using MCT scores of 75 job applicants.

Raw scores and percentiles are distributed differently. In Figure 4.4 the distribution of raw scores is high at the center and tapers away at each end. To prepare the lower part of Figure 4.4, I changed each raw score to its percentile equivalent and tallied the number of persons in each part of the percentile scale. This distribution is nearly rectangular. The percentile conversion spreads apart persons near the middle of the raw-score distribution. Thus a large percentile difference near the median can arise from a small difference in performance. Persons with extreme raw scores are squeezed together by the percentile scale. The difference between the 90th and the 99th percentiles may be as great as the difference between a 5-minute and a 4-minute mile. To take this into account, profile forms space out the 95, 90, and 80 percentile points, crowd 60, 50, and 40 together, and spread out 20, 10, and 5. For an example, see Figure 4.6 on page 122.

Norms are a kind of census figure, and as such they provide a frame of reference. If the median ability of applicants coming to the firm is much below that of the general norm group, the employer should reexamine his or her recruiting procedures. It appears that the firm is not attracting a full share of able applicants. If, among students entering a course, the median score in reading is much below that of the norm group, that becomes important in planning instruction.

Norms are basic to comparisons across tests. Norms on a test battery enable one to say that a student is at the median in mechanical compre-

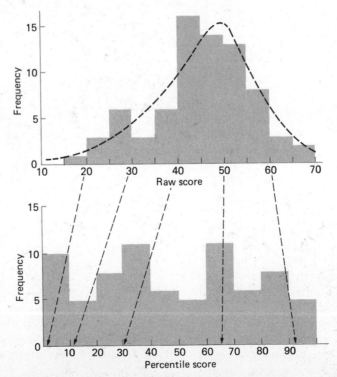

Figure 4.4. **Distributions of raw scores and percentile equivalents.**

hension, around the 80th percentile in verbal abilities, and at the 20th percentile in numerical ability. Interpretations across tests are treacherous, however (see pp. 123, 399).

Percentile scores from two tests cannot be compared unless the groups on which the conversions are based are similar. One test may base norms on students or job applicants, another on workers actually hired. A test taker whose MCT score stands at the 70th percentile among applicants to a union training program for apprentices in the construction trades is at the 5th percentile among applicants for mechanical jobs in an aviation company. Whenever norms are used, the group they represent must be kept in mind.

The 1980 Bennett norms provide percentile conversions for reference groups in a dozen industrial settings. (Two were mentioned in the preceding paragraph.) Some norm tables separate cases by sex or minority status. The DAT version of MCT is provided with norms for fall and spring testing in Grades 8 through 12; Table 4.1 reproduces a fraction of the information. When norms for several subtests appear on the same page, this format is more convenient than that at the end of Figure 4.3.

14. *Estimate Amelia's percentile score in each of the four tests she took (question 4, p. 103).*

15. *Interpret the following record of ability test scores for one person, where all scores are percentile scores based on a random sample of adults: Verbal, 54; Number, 46; Spatial, 87; Reasoning, 40.*

16. *Why is a perfect score not converted to the 100th percentile?*

17. *Scores usually change when a test is repeated because of chance errors of measurement. If each of the following persons changes 2 points up or down in raw score on MCT, how much would the percentile score change?*
    a. *a tenth-grade boy with a percentile score of 55 on the first test*
    b. *a tenth-grade boy at the 10th percentile on the first test*

18. *The norms on the Abstract Reasoning test of DAT are almost identical for boys and girls in Grade 10. The median is close to 32 for each sex. Suppose that both Ralph and Rosemary score 34 on Abstract Reasoning and 45 on Mechanical Reasoning. The norms suggest that Rosemary is "better" on Mechanical Reasoning than on Abstract Reasoning, and that Ralph is "worse." Explain the contradiction.*

19. *The following scores are the times, in seconds, required by a group of persons to construct a block design. Prepare a table of percentile equivalents for this group:*

52	34	41	42	46	45	27	48	35	35	38	29
48	39	44	36	36	34	51	40	30	33	37	41
37	28	28	45	31	39	31	27	35	36	34	42
39	28	36	33	37	36	34	54	34	32	33	38
54	36	33	30	56	32	48	35	38	33	33	31

20. *According to the table prepared in question 19, how much difference in seconds does a difference of 10 percentile points represent?*

Table 4.1   PERCENTILE NORMS FOR DAT
            MECHANICAL REASONING

| | Corresponding raw score | |
| | Males | Females |
Percentile	(N = 6150+)	(N = 6250+)
99	66–70	61–70
97	64–65	58–60
95	62–63	56–57
90	61	53–55
85	59–60	51–52
80	58	49–50
75	56–57	48
70	55	46–47
65	54	45
60	53	43–44
55	51–52	42
50	50	40–41
45	48–49	39
40	47	38
35	45–46	36–37
30	43–44	35
25	41–42	33–34
20	39–40	31–32
15	36–38	29–30
10	31–35	26–28
5	27–30	23–25
3	24–26	20–22
1	0–23	0–19
Mean	48.7	40.9
s.d.	10.8	10.1

Source: Administrator's Handbook for the Differential Aptitude Tests (DAT), 1982, p. 21. Reprinted by permission of The Psychological Corporation.

Standard Scores

Mean and Standard Deviation   The second common way to summarize performance of a group is to use the mean and standard deviation. The mean ($\overline{X}$) is the arithmetical average obtained when we add all scores and divide by the number of scores. The *standard deviation* (s.d., or *s*) describes the spread of scores.

The standard deviation is a kind of average of the departures of scores from the group mean. We might determine how far each person is from the mean and then average these values (ignoring the direction of deviation). Instead of doing this, we square each deviation and average the squares. This average is called the *variance* of the set of scores. The standard deviation is the square root of the variance.

The procedure can be illustrated simply. Consider five scores whose sum is 50 (mean = 10). We have

Score	9	16	4	10	11	
Deviation	−1	6	−6	0	1	Sum = 0
Square	1	36	36	0	1	Sum = 74

Dividing 74 by 5 gives a variance of 14.8 and a standard deviation of 3.85.[2] The larger the range of scores, the larger the s.d. tends to be. Here the range is 4 to 16—12 points—and the s.d. equals about one-third of the range. But the range is most often 5 or 6 times the s.d. (see Table 4.1). The s.d. rather than the range is used to describe the spread of scores because it is more stable from one sample to another.

In interpreting score statistics, the standard deviation serves as a kind of yardstick. Suppose, for example, that the average difference between two groups taught reading by different methods is 4 points. That difference may be important or negligible; only someone who is quite familiar with the test can evaluate the figure as it stands. If the standard deviation is 8 points, the difference is 0.5 s.d. This ratio of mean difference to s.d. is called the *effect size*. If the s.d. were 2, the effect size would be 2.0. Ordinarily, a solidly established mean difference as large as 0.5 s.d. is of practical value (unless greater effectiveness is accompanied by excessive cost). The s.d. yardstick is also used to state how exceptional is an individual's score: "0.8 s.d. below the mean," for example.

Variance can be interpreted as "amount of information." It is not a topic in this chapter, but the term will turn up later, especially in Chapter 6. Score variance can be divided into components. We can ask, for example, whether a complex coordination test "is accounted for by" (i.e., is predictable from) abilities that pencil-and-paper intellectual tests measure. The score variance reflects all sources of individual differences among the persons studied. Research might find that 35 per cent of the variance is predicted by printed mental tests and that 20 per cent arises from error of measurement, leaving a 45 per cent remainder. Nearly half the information, then, comes from some genuine ability that the coordination test measures and the printed tests do not. For an example of another kind, see Figure 13.2 (p. 502).

---

[2]In modern statistical practice, it is usual to divide by $N-1$, not N, although this makes little difference when N is large. An explanation of the preference for $N-1$ can be found in texts on statistics.

$74 \div 4 = 18.5$ (variance) $\sqrt{18.5} = 4.3$ (s.d.)

Conversion Scales   A standard-score scale serves the same purpose as the percentile scale. A *standard score* reports how many standard deviations above or below the mean the person is. Changing from raw scores to standard scores of this kind does not alter the form of the distribution.

The scores introduced in Figure 4.3 had a mean of approximately 44 and a standard deviation near 11. Then a raw score of 55 is one s.d. above the mean and the standard score is +1. A standard score of −1.8 would be 1.8 s.d. below the mean. The corresponding raw score is 44 minus (1.8)11 or approximately 24.

Table 4.2 shows how to convert raw scores to a scale with a mean of zero and with each s.d. above the mean counted as one unit. I speak of this as a "zero ± one" scale, referring to the numbers assigned the mean and s.d. respectively. This z conversion, important in statistical work, is not often used in test reports.

Test scores are more often placed on a 50 ± 10 scale—one with the mean at 50 and the s.d. equal to 10 points. That makes it possible to express every score as a positive whole number. As Table 4.2 indicates, converted scores are derived from the 0 ± 1 scale.

Wechsler Block Design norms are in standard-score form, as Table 4.3 illustrates. The range of converted scores is from 1 to 19, because Wechsler chose a 10 ± 3 scale. That is, he set the mean equal to a standard score of 10 and counted each s.d. above or below the mean as 3 standard-score points. (The manual refers to these standard scores as "scaled scores.")

Other values for converting the mean and s.d. are also in use. Table 4.4 provides a reference list of the standard-score scales you are most likely to encounter in reading about tests. For several other scales, and· comments on their virtues and limitations, see Petersen et al. (in Linn, 1989a, esp. pp. 226–228).

The inventor probably had a reason at the time she devised an unusual scale, but the reasons rarely hold up today. The stanine, for exam-

Table 4.2   DETERMINING STANDARD SCORES

1. Begin with the raw scores to be converted.	Assume mean = 44, s.d. = 11
2. To obtain z scores, express each raw score as a deviation from the mean. Divide by the s.d. $z \text{ score} = \dfrac{\text{raw score} - \text{mean}}{\text{standard deviation}}$	For raw score 60: $z = \dfrac{60 - 44}{11} = \dfrac{16}{11} = 1.5$ For raw score 25: $z = \dfrac{25 - 44}{11} = \dfrac{-19}{11} = -1.7$
3. To obtain scores on 50 ± 10 scale, multiply each z score by 10 and add to 50: $50 + \dfrac{10(\text{raw score} - \text{mean})}{\text{standard deviation}}$	For raw score 60, $z = 1.5$. $50 + 10(1.5) = 65$ For raw score 25, $z = -1.7$. $50 + 10(-1.7) = 33$

Table 4.3   A TABLE OF STANDARD-SCORE NORMS

Scaled score		1	2	3	4	5	6	7	8	9
Raw score		0	1	2	3–8	9–15	16–20	21–23	24–27	28–31

Scaled score	10	11	12	13	14	15	16	17	18	19
Raw score	32–35	36–38	39–41	42–44	45	46–48	49	—	50	51

NOTE: Standard-score equivalents of raw scores for the Block Design test, ages 20–24; a 10 ± 3 scale is used.

Source: Manual for the Wechsler Adult Intelligence Scale—Revised, p. 144. Copyright © 1981 by The Psychological Corporation, New York, N.Y. All rights reserved. Reproduced by permission.

ple, was invented back when it was economical to put as much information as possible in one column of a punch card. The conversion makes the information coarse, however, and with modern computers there is no need to compress information in that way.

Score reports would be better understood if most of the offbeat standard-score scales disappeared. In my opinion, test developers should use the system with mean 50 and s.d. 10 unless there are strong reasons for adopting a less familiar scale. (Scores with a 100 ± 15 scale, which simulate IQs, are especially open to misinterpretation; see pp. 240–242).

The scale used for the Scholastic Aptitude Test is so often encountered that its peculiarities need to be explained. The scale began as a 500 ± 100 scale, based on the distribution of college applicants in 1941. In theory, today's conversion table assigns the score of 500 to whatever score on today's test would have been earned by the average 1941 applicant, as estimated by special calibration methods (Donlon, 1984). A college that has learned to expect good performance from applicants with an SAT-V score of 600 can make that same interpretation year after year because the level of ability required to earn that score does not shift with the changing distribution of applicant ability. The scale does *not* represent standard scores for today's applicants. Because the SAT is now used in less select colleges and because a larger segment of the population is now applying to college, recent averages have been below 500— around 430 for V and around 480 for M. In some recent periods, declines in student effort during high school and less demanding courses may have lowered the performance of applicants; see College Entrance Examination Board (1977). In the 1980s, however, the trend has been slightly upward.

Age Scales and Grade Scales   This is as good a place as any to mention— and condemn—the popular but fallacious conversions known as "age equivalents" and "grade equivalents." Whatever score the average 7-year-old earns is converted to an "age-equivalent" score of 7; thus a 5-year-old or a 10-year-old may have a converted score of 7.0. Whatever score the average fifth-grader earns at the start of the school year is converted to 5.0 on the "grade-equivalent" scale; an eighth-grader who makes the same score is said to be performing at the fifth-grade level. Whereas

Table 4.4 STANDARD-SCORE SCALES

Mean set equal to	s.d. set equal to	Standard score corresponding to 1 s.d. above mean	Standard score corresponding to 2 s.d. below mean	Name of system, remarks
0	1	1	-2	z scores, prominent in mathematical theory of testing
5	2	7	1	Stanine ("stay-nine") scores
10	3	13	4	Scaled scores for Wechsler and KABC subtests
50	10	60	30	Most widely used system; when scores have been transformed to the normal distribution, may be called a T-score
50	21.06	71	8	Normal-curve equivalent (NCE); mandated for certain evaluation reports from schools to the Federal government
100	15 or 16	115 or 116	70 or 68	The usual scale for IQ; used also for overall scores on certain mental tests that have dropped the term "IQ".
100	20	120	60	Used for aptitude tests of U.S. Employment Service

the standard score compares the pupil with a group of which he is a member, these scales compare him with groups he may not belong to.

Petersen et al. (in Linn, 1989a, pp. 231–236) explain the several methods used to produce such scales. (Their evaluation of the conversions is sympathetic; even so, their section on "limitations" is longer than mine!)

Grade equivalents generate such misleading statements as "The average Hispanic child entering the seventh grade here is two grades behind the Anglo children in performance." The child's test performance may not have been far below that of the Anglos in his class. Perhaps a third of the seventh-graders of Anglo parentage are also "2 years behind." The progress made in a year varies from one school subject to another. According to national norms for the Iowa Test of Basic Skills (ITBS), the middle two-thirds of entering seventh-graders range from 5.2 to 9.0 in language usage, that is, from fifth-grade to ninth-grade level. The reason is not that the ablest seventh-graders have mastered the curriculum in language for the next two grades. They "equal" average entering ninth-graders because the average pupil, ordinarily coming from a home where elegant usage is not prized, is still making many commonplace errors at the start of Grade 9. The seventh-graders whose usage is good would not do so well if tested specifically on rules of usage studied in Grade 8.

Too often, laypersons expect every class or even every individual to be "at grade level" and to advance one grade-equivalent unit each year. Because abler classes make greater progress, a low-scoring class would have to progress *faster* than average classes in order to show "one year of gain" on the test norms; that goal places an unfair demand on weaker pupils and their teacher. (Age conversions are also likely to be misinterpreted; see pp. 241–242).

21. a. *Compute the mean and standard deviation for the Block Design scores given in question 19.*
    b. *How does the mean compare with the median computed previously?*
    c. *What is the approximate percentile rank for a score 2 s.d. above the mean in this distribution?*

22. *Wechsler fixes the mean IQ at 100 and the s.d. at 15. Express on a 50 ± 10 scale the following IQs: 100, 85, 130, 140.*

23. *Show the relation between raw scores and standard scores in Table 4.3 in the manner of Figure 4.4.*

24. *The middle two-thirds of entering seventh-graders range from 5.8 to 8.5 on the grade-equivalent scale of ITBS mathematics. This range is less than that for language. Suggest an explanation.*

The Normal Distribution

The frequency distribution shown at the top of Figure 4.4 is jagged, but if many more cases were added and smaller class intervals were used, it would become relatively smooth. A likely shape for that smooth distribution is the curve shown in the top portion of Figure 4.4; the curve was obtained by smoothing, as in Step 8 in Figure 4.3. This distribution is not perfectly symmetrical, but it tails off on both sides. Most score distributions have this general character. It is sometimes advantageous to convert the score scale so that the test has the distribution form of the normal probability curve.

The normal curve (Figure 4.5) is symmetric; the distance from the mean to the point on the shoulder that separates the convex, hill-like portion from the concave tail equals the s.d. Unbalanced distributions, for example those of Tests A and B in Figure 6.2 (p. 212), are said to be "skewed."

Many biological measures such as heights of American men fall into a nearly normal distribution, perhaps because chance combinations of chromosomes determine much of the variation. Score distributions of many psychological tests are also approximately normal. Early investigators thought it a natural law that abilities are normally distributed. But the test developer can change the shape of the score distribution by selecting many extreme items, or few. Also, some variables typically have nonnormal distributions. (Consider Americans' ability to speak French, or frequency of boys' fighting on the playground, or times of 20-year-olds running 400 meters.)

The normal curve does not describe score distributions accurately, but test interpreters keep it in mind because in most circumstances it provides a good approximation. If the normal distribution is sliced into bands of equal width, a fixed percentage of the cases falls in each band. As Figure 4.5 shows, about two-thirds of the cases fall between −1 s.d. and +1 s.d. Since 99.6 per cent of the cases fall between +3 s.d. and −3 s.d., the range of test scores is somewhere near 6 standard deviations. These facts enable us to reconstruct roughly the score distribution from its mean and s.d.

Assuming a normal distribution, one can quickly convert standard scores to percentiles and vice versa. Below the mean are 50 per cent of the cases. Below +1 s.d. are 50 + 34 or 84 per cent of the cases; hence

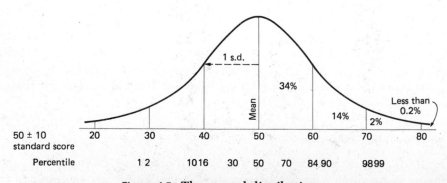

Figure 4.5. **The normal distribution.**

a standard score of 60 (on the 50 ± 10 scale) corresponds to the 84th percentile. When the raw-score distribution is not normal, the normal curve may be used to create normally distributed standard scores. The "normalizing" procedure is essentially to *assign* a standard score of 40 to the 16th percentile, and to make similar assignments consistent with the other areas in Figure 4.5.

Most test specialists would say that the use of normal curves in test scaling is a convenience. It does not assume any "normal distribution of behavior" in nature. Jensen (1980, p. 93) expressed a minority view in saying that "mental ability is normally distributed in the population." Horn (in Sternberg, 1986, p. 40) criticized Jensen's position.

25. *What percentile rank corresponds to a score 2 s.d. above the mean? To a score 1 s.d. below the mean?*

26. *Translate the following percentile scores into approximate standard scores on a 50 ± 10 scale: 5, 40, 85. (Assume that the distribution is like Figure 4.5.)*

27. *Are the male and female distributions for Mechanical Reasoning (Table 4.1) close to normal?*

28. *Scores on the Law School Admission Test are reported on a 30.5 ± 8 scale; only whole numbers are reported. Assuming a normal distribution, what is the likely range of scores in the applicant population? What score would fall nearest to the 80th percentile?*

Comparison of Score Conversions

If norms are to be used, which system of scores is preferable?

The percentile score has these advantages: it is readily understood, which makes it especially satisfactory for reporting to persons without statistical training; it is easily computed; it can be interpreted exactly regardless of the distribution shape. The disadvantages of the percentile score are these: it magnifies differences near the mean that may not be important, and it reduces the apparent size of large and practically important differences in the tails of the distribution. Also, some statistical analyses embody assumptions that percentile scores do not satisfy.

The advantages of standard scores are these: differences in standard score are proportional to differences in raw score; use of standard scores in correlations and many other calculations gives the same result as would come from use of the raw scores. The disadvantages: standard scores cannot be interpreted readily when distributions are skewed, and they are unfamiliar to untrained persons. Nonspecialists can learn to interpret standard-score scales. High school teachers and parents quite comfortably discuss Pete's SAT-V of 550 alongside his 66 on a 50 ± 10 scale from the other test.

Normalized scores, obtained by stretching a distribution to make it nearly normal, are a compromise. They spread out cases in both tails of the distribution and yet can be readily translated into percentiles. The

DAT profile form shown in Figure 4.6 illustrates typical current practice. Percentiles are plotted, but the spacing corresponds to normalized scores.

29. *A teacher wishes to convert scores on class examinations so that the record book will show at a glance how well a person is doing and she can average all tests equally in the final grade. Should she use raw, percentile, or standard scores?*

30. *A high school gives a reading test to all ninth-graders. The results are to be listed and supplied to all teachers for their use in planning instruction.*

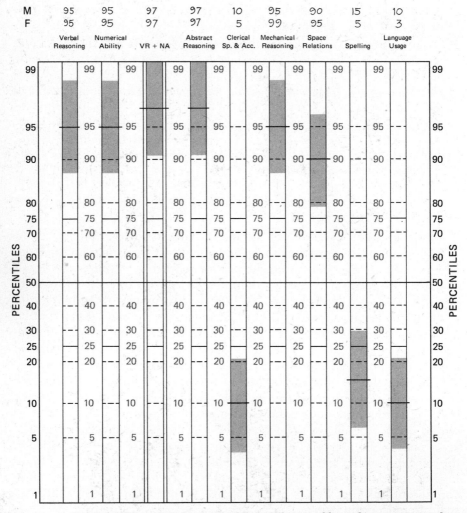

Figure 4.6. **DAT profile of Robert Finchley.** (The profile information is taken from *Counseling from Profiles*, Copyright 1951, © 1977. The report form is copyright © 1972, 1973, 1982 by The Psychological Corporation. All rights reserved. Reproduced by permission.)

Should the report be in terms of raw scores, standard scores, percentiles, or a content-referenced scale (perhaps that of DRP)?

31. *What disadvantage might normalized standard scores have? (Consider, as an example, a measure of reaction time that will be used in clinical diagnosis.)*

Profiles

Derived scores make it possible to compare standing on one test with standing on another, but profile interpretation must be circumspect. Equal percentiles do not mean equally good performance. If almost everyone can count, the 50th percentile means good performance—perhaps an error rate of 2 per cent. If almost no one can carry a tune, the singer at the 50th percentile is poor; he hits many wrong notes. *It is logically impossible to "equate" scales for distinct variables.* Failure to recognize this leads to errors that will be discussed in Chapter 10.

Profiles play a large role in guidance. The Differential Aptitude battery contains eight tests including MCT. After raw scores are changed to percentiles (or normalized standard scores), a profile charts standings in all fields. Robert, whose profile appears in Figure 4.6, is almost equally outstanding on all the reasoning tests, but on three nonreasoning tests he ranks low.

The profile displays scores as bands rather than as points, thereby recognizing errors of measurement (see p. 193). Looking only at the percentiles of 95 and 90, one might think that Robert is definitely better in mechanical comprehension than in spatial reasoning. The band suggests the possibility that the spatial score might be the higher one if Robert were tested again. Both scores are expected to remain high.

A bit more information about Robert will be of interest. Robert was regarded as bright until he reached high school. In the ninth grade he did badly on a reading test and on a test of scholastic aptitude that required a good deal of reading. His teachers and Robert himself came to think of him as not very able. The DAT profile showed superiority on all but the tests of language skills and the speeded clerical test. Once the profile was available, the teachers "were talking . . . of his several abilities and his identified handicaps," says the report.

32. *Rearrange the DAT subtests of Figure 4.6 in random order, and sketch a new profile for Robert Finchley. Do you get the same impression regarding the consistency of his performance and the location of his peak abilities? For profiling, is any one ordering of subtests better than another?*

33. *The following information about Walter Zordaky is taken from* Counseling from Profiles, *1977, pp. 92–93. All the tests mentioned would be classified as general-ability or academic-aptitude tests, except for the California Achievement Tests. Do the tests present a consistent picture? What is a reasonable summary of Walter's scores?*
    a. *Grade 12. Cooperative School and College Ability Tests. Percentiles. Verbal, 8; Quantitative, 55.*

Differential Aptitude Tests. Percentile bands. Verbal Reasoning, 6–29
Numerical Ability, 6–29.

b. Grade 10. California Test of Mental Maturity. IQs. Language, 104; Non-
Language, 96.

c. Grade 8. California Achievement Tests. Grade equivalents. Reading Vocabulary, 5.9; Reading Comprehension, 7.9; Mathematics Computation, 8.8; Mathematics Concepts and Problems, 7.1.

34. Figure 4.7 displays a portion of the profile for an interest questionnaire. A
person scores high on Dominant Leadership, for example, by saying he
would like a job where he gives orders. Describe his characteristics in
words. You need to know that the raw score is the number of positive responses out of a possible 17 in each scale, that percentiles are based on
students and young adults, and that Jackson chose a 30 ± 10 standard-score
scale based on the two sexes together. The respondent is a 25-year-old male
artist (unsuccessful) who had dropped out of engineering school.

35. Would this profile look the same if the male percentiles were converted to
standard scores and plotted? What can be said for or against Jackson's use
of a mixed-sex group as the basis for the profile?

36. Would it mean anything to say, "John is as heavy as he is tall"?

37. Which of these can be given meaning without reference to how other persons perform?
a. Belle is better at the backstroke than the crawl.
b. Max speaks Italian better than French.
c. Math is easier for Perry than foreign languages.
d. John is better in Basic Arithmetic than in Vocabulary.

38. A test intended for Grade 1 provides norms by age, in the form of a "School
Ability Index" (SAI), a standard score on a 100 ± 16 scale. A perfect score
on the test is converted to an SAI of 150 if the child's age is 5 years 10
months and to an SAI of 137 if the age is 7 years 10 months. Is it reasonable
to suppose that the upper limit of ability drops in this period? Can you
explain the anomaly? (Hint: The manual says that a child reaching a top
score should be given the next, more difficult test in the series.)

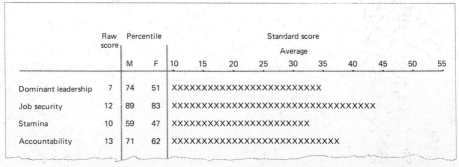

Dominant leadership	7	74	51	XXXXXXXXXXXXXXXXXXXXXXXXXXX
Job security	12	89	83	XXXXXXXXXXXXXXXXXXXXXXXXXXXXXXXXXXXXXX
Stamina	10	59	47	XXXXXXXXXXXXXXXXXXXXXX
Accountability	13	71	62	XXXXXXXXXXXXXXXXXXXXXXXXXXXXX

Figure 4.7. **Report on four variables from a self-report inventory.** For explanation
see question 34. (*Source*: From the manual of the Jackson Vocational Interest
Survey, 1977, p. 27.)

39. *Primary teachers who have given and scored Level I of the Metropolitan Readiness Test are advised to lay out several types of scores on the record sheet shown in Figure 4.8. (Norms tables convert the raw scores.) The teacher's intent is to appraise how well the pupils can use skills needed in learning to read.*
    a. *Sketch norm-referenced profiles of Kaveh, one using percentiles and one using stanines. Do they tell the same story? (Is this answer true for the other four children?)*
    b. *Do the norm-referenced profiles tell the same story as the −/+ code used with the left columns?*

NORMS

Characteristics Desired in Norms

When the distribution of scores in some population of persons has been compiled, a test is said to be "normed." It must be emphasized that norms are not standards of good performance. A common mistake is to assume that all ninth-graders should reach the ninth-grade norm. This reading is, of course, a fallacy; 50 per cent of the standardizing sample

METROPOLITAN READINESS TESTS	CLASS RECORD LEVEL 1					METROPOLITAN READINESS ASSESSMENT PROGRAM						

CONTENT-REFERENCED SCORES						NORM-REFERENCED SCORES*			
Skill Area	Auditory		Visual		Language	Auditory	Visual	Language	Composite
Number Possible	12	14	11	14	15	11	26	25	26	77

							A B C	A B C	A B C	A B C
Emily C.	8 ✓	6 ✓	10 +	2 –	15 +	5 ✓	14 36 4	12 11 3	20 52 5	46 26 4
Kaveh D.	9 ✓	5 ✓	9 ✓	14 +	14 +	9 ✓	14 36 4	23 72 6	23 79 7	60 56 5
Joshua F.	10 –	4 –	4 ✓	9 ✓	9 ✓	6 ✓	14 36 4	13 13 3	15 21 3	42 20 3
Carrie F.	9 ✓	5 ✓	4 –	9 ✓	14 +	6 ✓	14 36 4	13 13 3	20 52 5	47 28 4
Peter H.	5 ✓	5 ✓	6 –	12 ✓	14 +	6 ✓	10 19 3	18 32 4	20 52 5	48 29 4

Figure 4.8. **Score reports used to plan reading instruction.** A, B, and C refer to raw scores, percentiles, and stanines. The raw score is the sum of two subtest raw scores listed at left. The subtests, in order, are Auditory Memory, Beginning Consonants, Letter Recognition, Visual Matching, School Language and Listening, and Quantitative Language. Minor changes in the layout have been made to make the chart readable after reduction in size. In the actual form, information I have dropped to the note appears at a slant above the score columns. I have omitted age and sex columns; these five children are near age 5 years, 7 months. (*Source:* Reproduced and adapted from the record form of the Metropolitan Readiness Tests, 5th ed., Level 1. Copyright © 1987 by Harcourt Brace Jovanovich, Inc. All rights reserved.)

fell below the norm. It is equally wrong to be complacent if one's class or school reaches the average. The norms show what schools are doing at present. It is highly unlikely that schools are doing so well that the national average represents what could be attained with the best of teaching.

A given interpreter may or may not find the norms of a test useful. Norms are not important to someone examining individual differences *within* a group or determining whether examinees meet an absolute standard of performance. Thus norms say little to the employment manager who has to hire the ten most promising applicants or who knows from actual trial that most persons with scores of 72 or better on Test A make satisfactory punch-press operators. On the other hand, an individual clinician rarely has enough personal experience to be sure which high and low scores are rare. So clinicians can benefit greatly from tabulations of experience in the broad population and in particular categories of patients or persons in difficulty. Matarazzo and Herman (in Wolman, 1985, p. 913) point out that norms are particularly useful in justifying a clinical judgment in court—for example, where the psychologist is a witness in a personal-injury suit.

National norms mean less to many test interpreters than norms for a local group. A teacher can reasonably ask how the ability range in a new class compares with the usual range in that school. A high school counselor could profitably use information about the score distribution for all students in her high school, for males in the shop curriculum, for students who later attend the local college, and for workers in certain large local industries.

Norms play a prominent role when educational programs are evaluated with standardized tests. The school officials and the public may be content if the end-of-year performance of the pupils matches the national average and will be dissatisfied if the local pupils fall short.

Press releases—or the statistics behind them—are often misleading (Frechtling, in Linn, 1989a). We see this in the following example and also at pages 78 and 268. In 1988 an interested citizen, John Cannell, collected reports on standardized tests from state and city school officials. The reports took many forms, but by his compilation the average performance in every one of the 50 states was said to exceed the national norms. That would be impossible, and the press ridiculed the schools' reports as a "Lake Wobegon effect." (In Garrison Keillor's mythical town of that name, "the women are strong, the men are good looking, and all the children are above average.")

If school officials advertise that their students in 1988 are above the national average, but the average was compiled in 1980, we could accuse them of deception. Or, ignoring the costs, we could complain that publishers do not renorm these tests each year. One publisher of achievement tests now draws from its files an annual trend report, based on whichever schools use a certain test in successive years. If schools used that reasonable interim substitute for updated norms, there would be less room for complaint.

Further bases for criticizing school reports and Cannell's conclusions can be seen in comments made by Cannell (1988) and his supporters, or by his critics (in the same source). Possibly the "Lake Wobegon effect" is not as large as Cannell thinks; his statistical reasoning is inaccurate. On his side, it is suspected that schools under pressure to look good in the annual assessment send weaker pupils home on the day of the survey; also, some exclude special classes, whereas these were counted in the norms. When higher authority chooses whichever test fits the authorized curriculum, results are likely to look better than the results a broader test would report. The fit with the curriculum is artificially heightened when schools "teach to the test."

Even excellent norms honestly used would not give a good basis for judging a school or a group of schools. States and communities differ demographically, and no allowance for those differences is completely satisfactory. That statement applies to norms for categories of schools—Catholic, for example, or urban. A school using the California Achievement Tests has the option of describing the makeup of its student body. When scoring the papers from this student body, the computer then uses information from the publisher's national standardization sample to say how the local average on each subtest compares with that of the schools having similar student bodies. This is, at best, a partial and approximate adjustment, but much better than none.

Norms in the test manual should refer to defined, clearly described populations. Then the user can judge the norms by these questions:

- Does the norm group consist of the sort of persons with whom my examinee(s) should be compared?
- Is the sample (as weighted) representative of this population?
- Does the sample include enough cases?
- Is the sample appropriately subdivided?

The manual should indicate how relevant background variables affect the level and spread of scores. There is no call for within-sex norms, for example, if it is known that the sexes have similar distributions.

Sample Selection   The norms for the DAT version of MCT come from a systematic national sample of students. The manual devotes about 3000 words plus two tables to describing the sample and its selection. The following paragraphs give some impression of the care that goes into modern sampling.

The starting place was a directory of all public school districts enrolling 300 or more students. Sorting by size and by socioeconomic level gave 32 categories of public schools; a list of Roman Catholic school systems was added. Districts chosen at random from the 33 lists were invited to give the tests. Any district that declined to participate was replaced from the same list. (Refusals were comparatively frequent among wealthy school districts and urban school districts.)

In small districts, every student in Grades 8 through 12 was tested; in districts of intermediate size, a sample from every school was drawn; in very large districts testing was carried out in a sample of schools. The scores were weighted to adjust for departures of the actual sample from the sampling plan and for new census data that became available as the study proceeded. A separate table for Catholic schools was prepared. Further tables were compiled for less systematic samples of students in vocational high schools and in a few institutions of higher education.

What matters in norming a test is the match of the sample to an appropriate population. Applicant pools, clinic intakes, and school districts can differ markedly. It was wise, in norming DAT, to test a fraction of each student body in order to cover more student bodies within about the same budget.

When the sample is properly distributed, a larger sample gives better norms. Saying that a test was normed on 2039 cases may make norms look better than they are. There should be enough cases *and sites* to produce a stable distribution for every subpopulation on which norms are reported. If the 2039 scores have been split up to yield norms for two sexes within four grade groups, the number of cases per tabulation is about 250. This suffices for a crude description of each subpopulation, *if* the spread of communities is adequate.

It is not essential that the norm group have the same makeup as the population. Suppose that socioeconomic status (SES) has the distribution shown in the first column here:

	Population	Sample	Weight
High SES	20	30	.67
Middle SES	40	50	.80
Low SES	40	20	2.00

Too large a fraction of the sample is from the higher levels. The score distribution can be adjusted with the weights shown in the third column. In this example, every lower-class person would be counted twice, and others counted only fractionally. The estimates of population characteristics will be unbiased, though less accurate than an ideally balanced sample of the same size would give.

Even with substantial effort and a sampling plan that looks good on paper, things go awry. When two standardized tests are given side by side in several fifth-grade classes, the percentile scores (and standard scores) may run higher on one test than the other. This can occur when the sampling plans differed, or a plan was not followed strictly, or the tests were normed in different decades. Among achievement tests, at least, the test whose converted scores "run high" has a certain market advantage. Teachers prefer a test that makes their students look good.

Developers of most ability tests have gone to great trouble to obtain credible norms. I have been told that it cost about a million dollars to norm one recent wide-range individual mental test. Such investment is made because quality of norms is one thing buyers have learned to look for in making their choices among such tests. Interest inventories are often treated equally seriously.

Although current norms for widely sold tests are much better than those of 1950, the following complaints from that date are of more than historical interest; they apply to tests recently published.

Legitimate and illegitimate general norms abound in current test manuals. People-in-general norms are legitimate only if they are based upon careful field studies with appropriate controls of regional, socioeconomic, educational, and other factors—and even then only if the sampling is carefully described so that the test user may be fully aware of its inevitable limitations and deficiencies. . . . [M]any alleged general norms reported in test manuals are not backed even by an honest effort to secure representative samples of people-in-general. Even tens or hundreds of thousands of cases can fall woefully short of defining people-in-general. . . . Many such massed norms are merely collections of all the scores that opportunity has permitted the author or publisher to gather easily. Lumping together all the samples secured more by chance than by plan makes for impressively large numbers; but while seeming to simplify interpretation, the norms may dim or actually distort the counseling, employment, or diagnostic significance of a score.

With or without a plan, everyone of course obtains data where and how [she] can. Since the standardization of a test is always dependent on the cooperation of educators, psychologists and personnel [specialists], the foregoing comments are not a plea for the rejection of available samples but for their correct labeling. If a manual shows "general" norms for a vocabulary test based on a sample two-thirds of which consists of women office workers, one can properly raise [her] test-wise eyebrows. There is no reason to accept such norms as a good generalization of adult—or even of employed-adult—vocabulary. It is better to set up norms on the occupationally homogeneous two-thirds of the group and frankly call them norms on female office workers. Adding a few more miscellaneous cases does not make the sample a truly general one [Seashore & Ricks, 1950].

Reliance on the cases that come to hand is illustrated in the manual of a modern questionnaire on stress, intended for research and for clinical appraisals. The norms are based on "2588 males in middle- or upper-echelon jobs who were employed in ten large corporations in the San Francisco Bay and Burbank areas of California and ranged in age from 48 to 65." The occupational level is also described (e.g., 1195 of the cases were "managerial"). In addition to the general group, score statistics are reported for 35 samples as exotic as "Faculty of private university in Oklahoma" and "Random sample of the male European population of

Auckland, New Zealand." This is not an isolated example. Norms for personality inventories are notoriously inadequate, and this inadequacy is all the more troublesome because interpretations are generally based on a norm-referenced profile.

The Piers-Harris self-concept scale will be described in Chapter 14 as a superior example of instruments intended for use in schools. But the norms for the total score were collected 20 years ago from 1183 school children from a public school system in a Pennsylvania town. Later, the scale was subdivided; subscale norms were collected in the 1980s from a "United States sample." This consisted of 279, 55, and 151 children in elementary, junior high, and senior high schools, respectively. The sample is not described in the manual, and the publisher has been unable to supply me with a description. Making matters worse, total scores are still converted with the old Pennsylvania norms. The user who reads every line in the 100-page text of the manual will encounter the warning that "the two samples are not exactly comparable, further underscoring the need for caution in interpreting these scores." The discrepancy seems not to be trivial, but the user has no way to allow for it.

Updating   The "Lake Wobegon" controversy (p. 126) dramatized how norms go out of date. Changes in population distributions alter the meanings of "average" and "subnormal" on any kind of test. Flynn (1987) has compiled data showing substantial increases, over three decades, of score averages in many countries. Such changes presumably arise from increased amounts of schooling and other social trends. In the United States (Flynn, 1984), the increase in the adult ability of cohorts born since 1920 has been a steady one-sixth s.d. per decade; such cumulative change quickly renders norms obsolete. Schaie, who documented the trend in greater detail (p. 283), arranged for automatic updating of norms for his tests published in 1985 (see p. 383). After providing age norms describing the persons he tested in 1977, Schaie used past trends to project the norms (for ages 50 and above) in 1984, 1991, 1998, and 2005!

Changes in a test obviously call for revision of the norms or at least for a check on their continued applicability. For a "structural visualization" test, a circular disk was cut into pieces of irregular shape for the test taker to reassemble. Originally, this test was made of heavy aluminum. Then the manufacturer changed to wood. Persons who averaged 140 seconds on the metal version averaged 182 with wooden pieces. The norms collected on the metal version did not apply (Wilson & Carpenter, 1948). Even superficial changes of format can matter.

Marking in a test booklet may give a score range different from that obtained with a separate answer sheet or at a computer terminal. Experience summarized by Roid (in Plake & Witt, 1986) indicates that—with *most* tests—computerized administration does not change scores enough to make inappropriate the norms obtained with the printed form.

40. *The suggestion that the counselor develop norms for males in the shop curriculum is made because few females enroll in shop. When the counselor has records for 200 males and 10 females in auto shop, is it better to prepare within-sex norms for both sexes, to mix the two in one set of norms, or to prepare male norms only?*

41. *Suppose that you wish to collect norms for the stress questionnaire to assist clinical users. You believe that you can obtain a grant from the National Institutes of Health, but you recognize that the larger the budget, the less chance there is of getting the grant. What population or populations would you try to represent? Would you pay the persons you solicit to fill out the questionnaire? How many cases? How would you locate them and win their consent?*

42. *The U.S. Employment Service has a test for statistical typists. It desired norms for employed statistical typists so as to compare persons considering such work against employees in the field. To obtain norms, state employment services in a large number of the states were asked to test employed typists. Consider the following aspects of the sampling plan.*
    a. *Would you take an equal number of cases from each cooperating state, take whatever number each one could conveniently provide, or what?*
    b. *What restrictions would you place on the work experience of persons admitted to the sample?*
    c. *Would you prevent the agencies from overweighting the sample with government typists, whom they can locate relatively easily?*

Differentiated Norms

A truly perplexing question, for test maker and test user alike, is whether to focus on a broad or a narrow comparison group. The obvious function of specialized norm groups is to compare a person with others "of his kind." But when the person will compete with a certain range of others, *that* defines the relevant comparison group.

Consider the role of sex in DAT interpretation. Although the computer plots the profile with own-sex norms, values based on *opposite*-sex norms are also printed out (Figure 4.6). Here is part of the publisher's reasoning:

> Larry . . . obtained a raw score of 50 in Mechanical Reasoning. . . . [A]ccording to . . . percentile norms combining males and females, a score of 50 would place him at the 65th percentile. On such evidence, a counselor might be inclined to suggest that Larry consider a career requiring mechanical aptitude. This suggestion could be misleading, however, since . . . a raw score of 50 falls at the 50th percentile [for males in Larry's grade]. This 50th percentile is a more realistic estimate of Larry's success than is the combined 65th percentile since most of the applicants to programs requiring mechanical aptitude in the 1980s are male—not half male and half female.

... [U]sing combined-sex norms may result in an unduly discouraging picture of a female's ability on this test. ... Linda, ... who wants to become an engineer and who obtained a raw score of 50 on Mechanical Reasoning, ... would fall at the 65th percentile if combined-sex norms were used, but compared with other females at the same grade level, Linda is at the 80th percentile. Since many programs requiring mechanical aptitude are looking for qualified females in order to achieve a better balance in male-dominated professions, Linda has a good chance of getting into such a program based on her same-sex, 80th percentile ranking. However, in order to get a realistic picture of her chances in the program, she must also consider the opposite-sex norms, based on the scores of the male competition she will meet in the classroom. (Psychological Corporation, 1982, p. 2)

Many background factors correlate with scores and could be used in differentiating norms. Tests of comprehension of English and Spanish among Hispanics in the United States will serve as an example. Performance could be judged without reference to other persons or with reference to scores in the child's own schoolroom. But comparison with norms is sometimes inescapable, for example, in establishing that a child is eligible for special services or that a research sample is representative of the relevant school population. What norms would be helpful? Should children of Puerto Rican background be kept separate from Cubans? Should Florida norms be used in Florida? or national norms? Should a Texas community use general norms for children of Mexican background—or should it separate those whose families have lived in Texas for years from those who just crossed the border?

Asking sufficiently complex questions is hard enough. Answering all of them is nearly impossible. But a tester ought to recognize the need for compromises and trade-offs. A parable may make the dilemma clearer. Henry Crumpet tells Dr. Good that he isn't sleeping well—4 hours a night, on average, Henry complains. She would like to give Henry reassurance or, if his sleep is abnormal, to work on his problem. Dr. Good's computer console can call up norms for any broad or narrow population she defines. (Too good to be true, but in a parable anything goes.) Henry is remarkably short on sleep, compared with norms for Americans, for 40-year-old males, for 40-year-old American executives. He is "below normal." Why stop there? The interview puts Henry in a more specific category: His wife is threatening to leave him; he suspects that his boss will soon fire him; he is drinking quite a lot. When Dr. Good asks the computer about hard-drinking 40-year-old males threatened with divorce and unemployment, the message changes. Four hours of sleep *is* their norm. If Dr. Good took norms seriously, her message would be something like, "I'm sad about your nonmedical problems, Henry, but fortunately you can be contented with your sleeping performance. It exactly fits a person like you." Scores that seem "normal" in a population that is in trouble are symptoms of present trouble and indicators of greater future trouble. (If nothing else, Henry will drink more to get to sleep.)

Overadjustment can erase the message of the test. If schools in some region are coping miserably with newly arrived immigrants, to compare a child with the performance of that region's recent immigrants only papers over the defect. If adolescent females in midwestern schools know vastly less about gears and levers than male classmates, only an ostrich would dismiss the fact as "normal."

SOMPA The most elaborate scheme of differentiated norms is that for Mercer's System of Multicultural Pluralistic Assessment (SOMPA). As part of the case workup, the child's background is summed up in indices for family size, family structure, socioeconomic status (SES), and urban acculturation. The child's ability test is interpreted in the light of what children of the same background and ethnic origin do. As Mercer's manual says, "We have as many norms as there are various combinations of the sociocultural scores, and the child's performance is compared only with the performance that would be expected from the same sociocultural background. Thus, we have an assessment model based on pluralistic norms."

Mercer accomplishes this statistically. Test scores and indices from a sample are fed into the computer. Out comes a formula such as this one developed on 520 Hispanic children: Add together

—0.38 times the family size index

0.27 times the SES index

0.30 times the Urban Acculturation index

That (plus a constant) predicts the Wechsler Verbal IQ of the Hispanic child. (Family structure did not enter this formula because, among Hispanics, that index did not correlate with the test.) The numbers in the formula do *not* imply nearly equal emphasis on the three predictors. The respective *z*-score weights, which do indicate relative emphasis, are close to -2, 1, and 8!

If a predicted IQ is less than 100, Mercer subtracts that value from the score the child earned. A table transforms this difference into a 100 ± 15 standard score, which she labels "Estimated Learning Potential" (ELP). For example, if a child earns IQ 85 and has a predicted IQ of 85, the zero difference translates into an ELP of 100—"exactly normal." (The procedure takes a subtly different form if the predicted IQ is over 100.)

Mercer's procedure is daring, and the assumptions behind it are dubious (Reschly, in Reynolds & Gutkin, 1982; see also reviews in Mitchell, 1985, pp. 1516–1525.) Mercer's transformation puts the average of *any* socially defined subgroup very close to 100. A superior ELP, then, reports that the child is outdoing others *in similar circumstances.*

If 50-year-olds were given a medical examination, converting the evidence relevant to life expectancy by Mercer's technique would produce an "Estimated Living Potential." The urban poor would average out at 100, and so would the well-to-do, who on average are in much better physical condition. If insurance companies were willing to scale life insurance premiums according to this ELP, the urban poor could afford more insurance than when premiums are matched to risk. That is the sort of equity Mercer seeks to attain by judging children against their own group. "Pluralistic" norms are a two-edged sword. A Living Potential score of 100 ("just average") implies "no need to be concerned"; reporting it has bad consequences when the person belongs to a group whose typical health habits are detrimental. Chapter 7 says more about SOMPA.

Mercer's idea of using norms from persons of similar background has a counterpart in one prominent program of employment testing. That will be discussed (somewhat favorably!) on page 453.

43. *An interest inventory is used with adolescents who are acquainting themselves with career options and (usually in state employment offices) with adult workers seeking new positions. The norms were collected by asking employment services in 28 states (unnamed) to collect specified quotas of cases proportional to the state's population. The aggregate 6530 cases divided evenly between in-school and out; included 2876 males; and included 231 Orientals, 92 American Indians, 999 Hispanics, 1788 blacks, and 3420 "nonminority." All cases were combined in the norms except that some norms are split along sex lines.*
    a. *What further information would help the user judge the adequacy of the norms?*
    b. *How well does the norm group seem to fit the population on whom the test will be used?*
    c. *Would norms for subpopulations other than the two sexes be useful?*

Norms by Calibration

Instead of collecting a fresh representative sample for a new test, developers nowadays are likely to tie the new test to a test for which recent norms are already compiled. The calibration process is like the procedure makers of aneroid barometers use when they mark each dial to agree with an accurate mercury barometer. Such a technique has been used with the Scholastic Aptitude Test from 1941 to date, by the device of trying items (without counting them in the score) in a test administration prior to the year in which they "count." As was explained earlier, holding to the same score scale when test forms change from year to year enables a faculty to use past experience with students who score 600 on SAT-V.

A reasonably simple explanation of practical considerations in calibration is given by R. L. Thorndike (1982, pp. 116–123, 133–142). Explaining just one procedure, the "equipercentile" method, will suffice here to demonstrate the main idea.

Suppose that high school norms for the Bennett MCT are wanted, and it is accepted that the DAT norms for *its* MCT are adequately representative of current students. A few hundred persons would be given both tests; it is not essential that they be a representative norm group, but they ought to come from several schools. They should include males and females and the pertinent range of grade levels. Raw scores can be expressed as percentiles within this group; inasmuch as the maximum score on DAT is 70 points and the maximum on the Bennett is 68, the two could not match perfectly. Suppose we have these numbers:

Percentile in equating sample	10	25	50	75	90
DAT raw score	30	41	50	56	64
Bennett raw score	28	38	47	53	61

A Bennett score of 61 is just as exceptional as a DAT score of 64. All along the scale we can map Bennett raw scores onto the DAT scale and look up percentiles in the DAT norm table.

Calibration methods are comparatively inexpensive, and can piggyback new tests on old ones (until the population changes so much that the original norms are unacceptable). Another increasingly popular method of scaling is the topic of the next section.

Calibration is often spoken of as "equating." The *Standards*, however, limit the word "equated" to tests that are equally accurate measures of the same variable. (See also Petersen et al., in Linn, 1989a, pp. 241ff.) Consider a short-form Wechsler IQ determined by giving just a few subtests. The IQ scale remains the same as for the full test, but the tests are not "equated" because the short form is less accurate and requires more cautious interpretation.

A noteworthy application of calibration was the Anchor Test Study of seven prominent reading tests (Jaeger, 1973; Loret et al., 1974). Part of the Metropolitan Achievement Test was chosen as anchor, and fresh norms for it were established. A sample of children took the tests under investigation, no child taking more than two tests; the sample was carefully constructed and the subsamples were counterbalanced. The calibration of other tests against the Metropolitan scale enabled federal officials to compare evaluation reports from schools that had administered different tests. This scaling project, which provided a common scale for tests at the same level, was a "horizontal" comparison.

Much the same technique can put elementary and advanced levels of a test onto a common scale ("vertical" comparison). Achievement tests are, of course, geared to the grades in which they are given, but schools would like to compare a student's performance in Grade 4 with his performance when he took an easier test in Grade 3. It is necessary to test a sample for whom both forms are reasonably appropriate—classes tested early in Grade 4, for example. A score of 20 out of 30 on the easy test falls at the same percentile point as a score of, say, 12 on the harder test.

These matched points can be converted to some arbitrary common scale. If such a scale is built up over the range from the primary-grade test to the test for Grade 9, the school or the research worker can trace the development of each student even though the difficulty of the test changes with each administration. (Publishers do not all follow the same procedure; the several alternatives are evaluated by Petersen et al., in Linn, 1989a.)

The fact that easier and harder tests are chained together by a common scale does not reduce the importance of matching difficulty level to the ability of the test taker. When Chicago schoolchildren were given whatever level of an achievement battery matched their year in school, as high as 85 per cent in some schools scored at the chance level. When, in another year, teachers chose the test form whose reading difficulty corresponded to the children's reading level (on average), the scores were better than chance—but further behind the norms than the scores of the previous year's group. When the test was too hard, the "floor effect" obscured the facts (Wick, 1983).

UNIDIMENSIONAL SCALING

In a "pure" scale, tasks or questions varying in difficulty measure the same dimension. One way to find out how many grams object X weighs is to put it on the left pan of a balance and put objects of known weight— 200 g, 250 g, and so on—on the right pan. Each of these is like a test item. Object X "passes" the item when the left pan goes down; the test continues until we reach a weight great enough to pull down the right side of the balance. The test is unidimensional because the items all measure weight. Familiar though such an example is, "measure the same thing" is a subtle notion.

A set of tasks is strictly "unidimensional" if the order of difficulty is the same for everyone in a population of interest. Memory for digits has the property: If you can remember strings of eight random digits, you can also remember shorter strings. (Some irregularity has to be accepted. You won't be consistent on successive trials.)

I spoke, above, of item difficulty and shall speak also in this section about ability and proportion passing. With some rewording, the discussion applies to measures of typical response. Thus, regarding an interest measure we would speak of appeal of item, strength of interest, and proportion endorsing. Likewise, situations can be ordered from most to least stressful, for example. If the situations are nearly unidimensional, the ordering is much the same for everyone in the group studied.

The scaling procedure first checks a pool of items for coherence, discarding misfits if necessary. Next, it creates a scale having certain mathematical properties. Then, after an examinee has responded to a number of the items, it locates him on the dimension that runs through the pool.

Persons who respond to different subsets of the item pool (easy or hard items, few or many items) can be assigned comparable scores. All the subsets are calibrated to the same scale (Lord, 1980).

Basic Arithmetic as Example   I illustrate the flexibility this scaling introduces into testing before describing the method itself. The Basic Arithmetic scale of the British Ability Scales is a set of 28 items; items are individually administered. The average 8-year-old passes about half the items at this level:

$$
\begin{array}{ccc}
14 & 5 & 33 \\
+87 & -2 & -15
\end{array}
$$

The average 10-year-old passes about half of a set like these:

$$
3\overline{)9} \qquad \begin{array}{c} 87 \\ \times 14 \end{array} \qquad 12\overline{)72}
$$

We could give the full test and count up the child's correct answers. But with the ordered set a subset of the items gives nearly as good a measurement. A 10-year-old might take subset C (items 1 through 20) and a 12-year-old might take D (13 through 28). A raw score of 6 on C is translated to a scale value close to 40. On the harder scale (D), passing 6 items converts to a scaled score of 77.

Stretching the Score Scale

Unidimensional scaling is referred to by several names including item response theory (IRT) and latent trait theory.[3] The basic idea is to arrange items in order of difficulty and then to stretch the scale to satisfy mathematical assumptions. We have already seen scale stretching in Figure 4.4; IRT stretching follows a different rule.

The scaling can be thought of as a curve-fitting procedure. The starting point is a record of who passed each test item. Records are grouped by score level and proportions of success are calculated. Panel i of Figure 4.9 depicts simplified data; a real analysis has many items and many groups. The dots show what proportion of the persons at each score level passed each of the four items. Item a is easier than item b all along the scale, b easier than c, and c easier than d.

In a free-response item, 50 per cent is the halfway mark between ignorance and excellence, so I have placed a cross ($+$) where each line crosses that level. These so-called characteristic curves or response functions have a slanted S shape (not always complete). If choice-response

---

[3]Extensions of the theory to multidimensional item sets have not yet reached practical application.

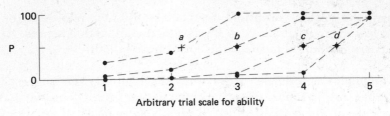

(*i*) Proportions passing four items at each score level

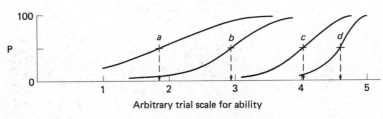

(*ii*) Smoothed item characteristic curves

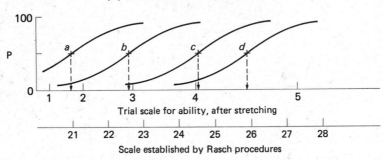

(*iii*) Characteristic curves with uniform slope

Figure 4.9. **Stages in scaling test items.**

items were plotted, the curves would level off above zero at the left. The irregular curves are smoothed, much as in Figure 4.3. This produces panel ii.

Each curve can be described in terms of three numbers ("parameters"):

Location. The left-to-right position where the curve attains half its full height. This "scale value" corresponds to item difficulty.

Slope. Steepness of the curve. The steeper the curve, the stronger the relation of the item to the central dimension.

Base level. An estimated probability that a person at the extreme low end of the ability scale will answer correctly.

One-Parameter Model   A procedure that considers only the location parameter is often referred to as the Rasch model, crediting the Danish biostatistician Gunnar Rasch. (Rasch assigned constant values to the slope and chance parameters. Making the slope constant in effect assumes that all items measure the central variable equally well. Followers of Rasch set the third parameter at zero. With choice response, however, a better constant is the success rate expected with blind guessing.)

Next, the scale is stretched horizontally wherever the slopes tend to be steep. In panel ii, the rightmost curves are steeper. Stretching pulls apart points 4 and 5 of the original scale; the other spans are stretched somewhat less. The last stage of the fitting process produces curves of uniform shape, as in panel iii. A series of numbers (starting with any convenient value) are now spaced equally along the horizontal scale. The final step is to obtain a scale value for the item; the scale position corresponds to the 50 per cent marker. Thus, the scale position of a is just above 21.

Fred's position on the scale is the difficulty level where his probability of passing items is 50 out of 100. When Fred takes the four items represented in the figure and passes just the easiest one, his ability is estimated to lie between 21.1 and 22.6. After he has responded to more items, his scale score will be estimated more precisely. The adaptive-testing example of Figure 4.10 will illustrate this.

Two- and Three-Parameter Models   The two- and three-parameter models avoid the assumption that items measure the underlying dimension equally well. They require more data, however, and run up computing costs.

Under these models, the stretching of the score scale attempts to equalize only the *average* slope in various regions of the scale. An item strongly related to the total scale retains a steeper slope than its companions and is given more weight in placing individuals, and thus measurement becomes more accurate.

The three-parameter model is superior for multiple-choice items. The one- and two-parameter analyses can at best embody the ordinary correction for guessing (p. 67). The three-parameter model considers where the passing rate of an item levels off at the low end. A three-choice item can have a "chance" pass rate of 0.50 (rather than 0.33) if one of the suggested answers is transparently wrong. And the success rate of guessers can drop to 0.10 if some item writer's trick fools most of them. Recognizing these possibilities, the three-parameter model provides a sounder correction for guessing than the traditional formula. (Because something other than chance is operating, the base value is called a "pseudochance" parameter.)

Many books on test theory explain and illustrate the various procedures based on IRT (Crocker & Algina, 1986, among others). The comments that follow are not specific to any system of analysis. Remarks on the value of the methods must be balanced with cautions; enthusiasts have claimed almost magical virtues for tests constructed in this way.

Applications

Building and Using Item Banks   Once a set of items has been scaled, it is stored in an item bank along with the parameters. Further items can be added to the bank. A simple tryout of new items alongside some previously scaled items estimates their parameters.

Drawing on the bank, a test form can be constructed that will measure, at any desired level of difficulty and precision, the dimension the bank represents. Publishers have assembled banks of items on fractions, decimals, long division, and so on. A school system can order custom-made tests having content matched to its curriculum, with forms suited to advanced and less advanced classes. All the scores are reported on the same scale.

The scaling methods are especially compatible with domain-referenced interpretations. Policymakers can specify the scale position (difficulty level) where an adequate performer would pass 70 per cent of the items. This standard can be applied in the future without fresh judgments on new items and test forms.

If norms representing some population are compiled for one set of items from the pool, a conversion table can be calculated that allows norm-referenced interpretation of any new form. Questionable assumptions, however, enter the inference from a test normed nationally to a local customized test (Yen et al., 1987).

Adaptive Testing   A scaled item bank is essential for fully adaptive testing (pp. 49, 61), in which items are chosen uniquely for the examinee.

Figure 4.10 carries two students through five items of an adaptive test, more or less as would happen with the adaptive MCT. Testing should start with an item of middling difficulty. Let us suppose we have a scale on which the average ability level of persons like those to be tested is near 1.3; then items m, n, and o are suitable entry points. Here, m (scale position 1.4) was the first item given. When the person passes m, his scale position (symbolized by the Greek theta, θ) is more likely to be above 1.4 than below.

After student A passes, he gets a harder second item. The computer determines, here and at other steps, which item (from a to l) would give the most information. The calculation might select i; when A fails i, the information tentatively locates him between 1.4 and 2.2. (The computer works out an exact best-fit value at each step; I suppose that value to be 1.8.) One of the three items nearest the estimated θ is chosen; say j. When A passes again, the ability estimate goes up. A is given k next and

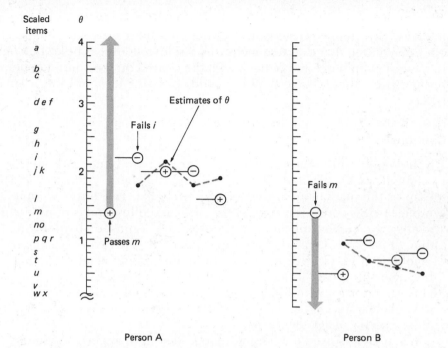

Figure 4.10. **Progress of two students through five items of an adaptive test.** All information is made up for purposes of the example. The pool of items has been scaled; item *a* is the most difficult item. Only the 24 items with values above 0.1 are shown. The short bars indicate the successive items selected. The dotted line connects successive estimates of the person's scale position. (A shaded band indicates the initial uncertainty). For further discussion, see the text.

fails, so the estimate of his θ now slips down. Passing item *l* raises the estimate a little. The computer would next administer *h,* and so on.

The uncertainty attached to the estimate decreases as more responses are taken into account. In DAT, every student takes 35 MCT items. Some other computer programs end an adaptive test as soon as the individual's θ is established accurately enough for the purpose of the testing. Under that procedure, one student might take only 20 MCT items and another might have to take 45.

Comparing Items across Groups   One further use of IRT is to detect items that are disproportionately easy or difficult for some subgroup. Scaling can be carried out separately on males and females, for example. Ordinarily most items will be ordered the same way in both groups, even if the group means differ on the ability measured. Suppose that the males do worse than the females on nearly all the items. Then, if item 17 is equally easy for males and females, some peculiarity of item 17 is making it comparatively easy for males. It is not a clean measure of what the rest of the pool measures. Some would call item 17 "biased against females." An item so flagged may or may not be discarded. The developer may judge that the item measures a relevant element that belongs in the test even if it does not track with the central dimension. Judgment, not statistics, should have the final word (Cole & Moss, in Linn, 1989a, p. 211).

Cautions

Psychologists' "unidimensional" scales are generally not truly uniform in content, as the Basic Arithmetic subtest illustrates. A beam balance measures the mass of an object, and nothing else. The Basic Arithmetic score measures competence in arithmetic—and effort and carefulness. It stretches over many subskills. A child can be confused about decimals although he has command of improper fractions; the reverse can be true of another child. Growth in arithmetic is not simply acquiring more of "the same thing." As a matter of fact, tasks from entirely different domains can come out "unidimensional" in the usual scaling procedure if one kind of task is easy and the other is so hard that the *order* of difficulty is the same for nearly everyone.

When IRT is used for calibrating one test form against another, it is advisable to check the solution with a second method; not infrequently, the two solutions disagree. The knowledge presently available does not indicate a clear basis for resolving such conflicts (Skaggs & Lissitz, 1986). Hambleton (in Linn, 1989a, p. 172–182), in a comprehensive review of IRT methods, warns that assumptions are not always valid, that the usual statistical checks on model fit are inadequate, and that false conclusions can result. These risks should not be a source of great concern unless scores are being used for a major decision that will be hard to reverse when more facts come in.

The scales depend on a reference group (even though they are not norms). They describe a population of persons having particular histories. In the Basic Arithmetic scale, subtraction is easier than multiplication. But the order would be reversed if schools taught multiplication ahead of subtraction, as they logically could. It is incorrect to suggest, as some writers have, that scale values are independent of culture, education, and age. How much the setting or population can change before the initial scale gives bad results is hard to judge. (But experience with transfers has generally been good.)

Finally, the numerical scale has "equal units" in only a limited sense. In making the curves equally steep all along the scale, the scalers apply an approach that goes back a century and a half. Gustav Fechner, one of the first experimenters in psychology, wanted to measure the *apparent* loudness of sounds—the psychological dimension as distinct from the physical energy. Let us assume, he said, that judgments equally hard to make represent equal differences in loudness. So he presented tone pairs X/Y and Y/Z. If signal X is called louder than signal Y on 80 per cent of the X/Y trials, and Y is called louder than Z on 60 per cent of the Y/Z trials, then on the psychological scale Y must be closer to Z than to X. Scales based on this principle are not like the scales for variables having an additive property (e.g., length or weight). Suppose that, during Grade 3, Gina moves from 40 on a Rasch scale to 50, and then to 57 during Grade 4. There is no justification for saying that Gina "grew faster" during Grade 3. (L. V. Jones, in R. L. Thorndike, 1971, explains why psychological scales have this limitation.)

45. *Describe the progress of Person B in Figure 4.10, and the successive choices of items, as the text did for Person A.*

46. *What might cause the scale values of fixed items to change from one generation to another? Of the following tests, which would be most likely to change in this respect: Block Design, Porteus maze, or MCT?*

Chapter
5

How to Judge Tests: Validation

5A. On validity, the *Testing standards* indicate characteristics desired in investigators' reports. They do not say what degree of validity tests should have. Why not?

5B. What information carried in an experience table is lost when the report is reduced to a correlation?

5C. A test that predicts grades in freshman English composition ($r = 0.7$) may not be suitable for routing some students into regular sections and others into remedial sections. Why?

5D. For a test on knowledge about U.S. government, a topical outline (with the specified number of items for each topic) is prepared. If the final distribution of items fits that description, what additional inquiries would contribute to content validation?

5E. Construct validation of a single test is an "endless" process. Why?

Abbreviations in this chapter: ASVAB for Armed Services Vocational Aptitude Battery; LSAT for Law School Admission Test; MCT for Mechanical Comprehension Test; SAT for Scholastic Aptitude Test, with V and M for the Verbal and Mathematical sections.

ORIENTATION

All chapters in this book should contribute to ability to judge tests, but Chapters 5 and 6 raise the most crucial questions. (Although I speak of tests, the logic of choosing a procedure applies also to any measure or source of information: interviews, ratings, informal observations, and so on.) Some pages of simple information and stage setting come before the large topic of validation. In the introduction, note especially what the *Standards* try to do and why they do not specify the form tests should take.

Put simply, *validation* is inquiry into the soundness of the interpretations proposed for scores from a test. Three somewhat different styles of investigation are needed, the three being integrated in evaluating the test. The chapter runs quickly over the three kinds of inquiry on pages 150–160. Even though these pages are intended as an overview, almost every sentence (apart from the concrete examples) is saying something you should remember. Some of the pithy statements will become much clearer as the chapter develops; so mark the section for review at the end.

The large section on criterion-oriented studies introduces topics that enter many interpretations coming later in the book. Do find out how to ask critical questions about criteria, how to give meaning to "The correlation of the variables was 0.6" and similar statements, and why many uses of tests can be justified only by evidence of interaction.

Again in the section on content, learn what questions to ask. Content that looks reasonable to the nonexpert sometimes is much less pleasing to the trained eye. Figure 5.8 deserves study; and it is simpler than it will seem at first glance. Curves more or less like these (first seen at the end of Chapter 4) are important in test development.

Construct validation is harder to describe than the other approaches because it goes in so many directions. In fact, the main thing to see here is why many kinds of evidence are required. Note especially the reasoning about "convergence and divergence"; it will be applied in many later evaluations of particular tests. The other crucial idea is "plausible rival hypotheses"; these set priorities among possible lines of inquiry.

The final, much easier section restates some key ideas and explains why validation goes beyond science to argumentation.

THE NEED FOR CRITICAL SCRUTINY

"What is the best measure of general mental ability? of reading comprehension? of anxiety?" Industrial, clinical, and school psychologists ask questions in that form; so do classroom teachers, sociologists, and evaluators. When questioners ask about the same variable, the test that best serves one of them will almost surely not be the best for most of the others. Not even a narrow question—"What is the best measure of mechanical comprehension for selecting industrial trainees?"—has a universal answer.

No test maker can put all desirable qualities into one test. A design feature that improves the test in one respect generally sacrifices some other quality. Some tests measure good readers validly but not poor readers; some give precise answers but require much time; some estimate overall ability well enough, but do little to analyze strengths and weaknesses.

A test is selected for a particular situation and purpose. What tests are pertinent for a psychological examination of a child entering first grade? That depends on what alternative instructional plans the school is prepared to follow. Which test of skill in English usage is suitable for a high school class? Those teachers for whom clarity of expression is important will be discontented with a test requiring only that the student identify grammatical errors.

Many persons who are not professional testers need to know what questions to ask about tests and testing practices. In arriving at recommendations regarding a juvenile offender, for example, the clinical psychologist may be overenthusiastic about the procedures in which she is expert and may draw too forceful a conclusion. The youth advocate should be ready to ask pointed questions, and so should the judge.

Sometimes it makes sense not to act as the psychologist recommends. A counselee may, for example, be able to consider facts not available to a tester. Yet giving great weight to supplementary impressions, and little weight to observations that are objective and relevant, spoils more decisions than it helps. The user of test information who knows how to judge a test can also judge which other impressions are substantial enough to deserve comparable weight.

Reputation is not an adequate indicator of merit. New tests are produced, new uses of tests are discovered, and some old uses are discredited. Modern test development is usually self-critical, and the quality of tests and test information has improved. Nonetheless, there are bad tests and bad testing practices. Moreover, test titles, advertising, and manuals can mislead. Consumers and those affected by tests have to remain alert.

In the 1970s, for example, the armed services persuaded high schools throughout the nation to give their vocational aptitude test (ASVAB) to a million students a year. The test scores helped recruiters locate talented prospects and were also valuable in the school's guidance efforts—at least that was the plan. When in 1977 the test came under professional review, it was seen to be badly constructed. Worse, it offered wildly inappropriate suggestions regarding the careers students with certain score patterns should consider. In this instance, because members of Congress showed concern, the test promoters quickly corrected the gravest faults in the interpretative materials. Still, the test supplied to schools was left unchanged for nearly 10 years. In contrast, the

counterpart test used *within* the armed services was overhauled to discard certain subtests their measurement specialists considered invalid.
(For a fuller story, see Cronbach, 1979.)

1. *Improving a test in one way weakens it in another. What advantage and
   what disadvantage come from each of the following changes?*
   a. *Lengthening a test.*
   b. *Making it interesting to children.*
   c. *Making it more diagnostic of strong and weak points.*
   d. *Giving it as an individual test instead of as a group test.*

2. *This is from a letter received by a psychologist from an industrial personnel
   manager hiring office and factory workers. How would you answer it on the
   basis of the preceding paragraphs, knowing that the tests mentioned are
   representative of their types? We are planning to use the following tests:
   Wonderlic intelligence and Minnesota Multiphasic Personality Inventory
   and aptitude tests related to our openings, such as the Bennett test. Does
   this seem to be a well-balanced testing schedule for industry? Are there tests
   that you think would be preferable to these?*

3. *It was once suggested that the American Psychological Association award
   a seal of approval to all well-prepared psychological tests. Discuss the advantages and disadvantages of such a system. Would this plan eliminate the
   need for critical judgment by users?*

4. *Would your answer to question 3 be the same if it referred to the National
   Council on Measurement in Education and to tests of school learning?*

Sources of Information and Criticism

Some limitations of tests reflect only the fact that no one test can do
everything, but some reflect insufficient self-criticism by the developer
or user. Fortunately, a great deal of information is available on most published tests, which provides a basis for evaluation by qualified professionals. The manual, together perhaps with a technical handbook, is ordinarily the principal source of information. A firm or a public authority
making a test for its own use rarely distributes a manual, but the agency
ought to assemble the kinds of data that would go into a manual for such
a test. The data can aid in quality control and in examining the fairness
of decisions based on the test. That information should be open to a
concerned outsider.

It is not easy to make a report clear and comprehensive. The more
research there is, the harder the task of summary. A test manual should
be clear enough that any qualified user can comprehend it—and clear
enough that the reader who is not qualified will realize that fact.

Test construction and reporting were much improved by the efforts
of the late O. K. Buros, who began to release critical reviews of tests in
1934. Nearly all tests currently marketed in English-speaking countries
are reviewed in the yearbook series he founded (Buros, 1941/1978).
Each test is examined by two or more specialists; they suggest proper

uses of the test and draw attention to any questionable claims in the manual. In 1985 *The Ninth Mental Measurements Yearbook (MMY)* appeared (Mitchell, 1985). A paperback *MMY Supplement* was issued in 1988, and as further reviews come in they are being placed on an immediately accessible computer data base. Hardcover compilations will appear from time to time.

Another reviewing service is *Test Critiques*, from Test Corporation of America; six volumes have appeared. Whereas *MMY* reviews are primarily evaluative, *Test Critiques* summarizes information from publishers and adds brief evaluative comment. Test reviews also appear in *Journal of Educational Measurement, Journal of Psychoeducational Assessment, Measurement and Evaluation in Counseling and Development,* and other journals. In the industrial field, the first issue of a *Test Validity Yearbook* should be available when this book appears (Landy, in press). It is planning to report original validation research rather than judgmental reviews.

It remains for the purchaser to exercise considerable judgment, especially when reviewers disagree. A test that has faults is not necessarily a bad choice. Appropriateness depends on the particular purpose to be served. Often that purpose will be served better by making cautious use of scores than by relying wholly on nontest information.

The *Testing Standards*

Codes of practice are prepared by study groups, exposed for criticism, and ultimately endorsed by the governing body of a professional association.

For a discussion of the origins of *Standards for educational and psychological testing* see p. 14. The *Standards* cover psychological and educational tests in general use. They are not geared to tests having only a local use, such as those a teacher prepares, nor to informal, unstructured interviews and observations. Specialists in industrial psychology prepared a supplementary statement. *Principles for the validation and use of personnel selection procedures* (Society for Industrial and Organizational Psychology, 1987). Test reports prepared by computers are the subject of a third document (American Psychological Association, 1986).

None of these documents demands that test quality reach a specified level. The level of quality needed depends on the function a test is to serve. The *Standards* call for information and evidence. It is sensible to request, for example, that the size and composition of any norm group be reported. The user who wants norms has to judge whether the norm sample is relevant to her situation. Appropriately, the *Standards* do not say that every test should have norms or that every norming sample should reach a specified size. To impose a fixed demand on every test developer would increase the cost of tests and would discourage development of special-purpose tests whose market is likely to be small. The

Standards consider an economical shortcut acceptable when the departure from ideal procedures probably will do no serious harm or injustice to those tested.

Although the *Standards* have had considerable influence during their 35-year history, and although the latest version is highly regarded, it is indefinite in places. Because testing impinges on political and commercial interests, drafts of the revision came under criticism and the working committee felt impelled to make compromises (Haney & Madaus, 1988). Everyone agreed that universal, hard-and-fast rules would not fit all kinds of tests and test applications. Increasing the latitude for professional judgment in applying the *Standards* did tend to make them less demanding and less "enforceable" than some critics of common testing practices would like.

Standards identified with test construction and evaluation include 25 on validity, 25 on test development, and shorter sections on norming and other topics. A second part has general standards on test use, plus standards pointed toward such settings as employment testing, plus others on testing of linguistic minorities and the handicapped. Finally, there are standards on broad matters including the rights of test takers (see Figure 3.6, p. 90).

Each standard is classed as primary or secondary or conditional. The first two standards in Figure 3.6 are "primary." Primary standards are to be followed whenever a test is used for practical purposes. It may be necessary in some particular case to depart from the recommended practice, but the professional is expected to have a sound justification for the departure.

A "secondary" standard is a suggestion rather than a mandate. Sometimes the recommendation is too costly for many developers to comply with. Sometimes the suggestion goes too far beyond usual present practice to be made the standard.

Other secondary standards deal with topics about which professional opinion is divided. An example is Standard 16.4 in Figure 3.6, which says that any interpretation should be available to the person concerned or to his representative. Parents who are discontented with a school's plan for their educationally laggard child are entitled to a second opinion from a suitable specialist, and that specialist should have access to objective scores that influenced the school's plan. On the other hand, release of a clinical tester's interpretation of an individual mental test (which relies on subtle observations and judgments) could invite unjust criticism and even a malpractice suit. Where such a report is at issue, the best safeguard for child and parents (and perhaps the best support for the clinician) is likely to be a second evaluation independent of the original report.

A "conditional" standard is primary for some tests or uses, and not others. Thus Standard 5.5 calls for revising the test manual as time passes. Keeping up-to-date is a proper demand when a test is used on a large scale and new data flow in. But to demand periodic reports (and continual research) on a special-purpose test that is not widely used would be a heavy imposition. If the demand were to lead publishers to withdraw a low-use test from circulation, that would be a disservice to the professionals who use it responsibly.

It is important to note the following cautionary sentences:[1]

Individual standards should not be considered in isolation. Therefore, evaluating acceptability involves the following: professional judgment that is based on a knowledge of behavioral science, psychometrics, and the professional field to which the tests apply; the degree to which the intent of this document has been satisfied by the test developer and user; the alternatives that are readily available; and research and experimental evidence regarding feasibility.

The use of the standards in litigation is inevitable; it should be emphasized, however, that in legal proceedings and elsewhere professional judgment based on the accepted corpus of knowledge always plays an essential role in determining the relevance of particular standards in particular situations.

Following completion of the *Standards* in 1985, the associations responsible for the *Standards* and two others prepared a companion *Code of fair testing practices in education* (*Code*, 1988). Major test publishers have announced their intention to abide by the *Code*. This is a succinct and simple statement for the general public, including mature test takers and parents of younger ones. The four-page *Code* presents selected themes from the *Standards* under four headings: Developing/Selecting appropriate tests; Interpreting scores; Striving for fairness; and Informing test takers. Parallel columns explain what developers should do to help professional users, and what schools, counselors, and others who give or interpret tests should be expected to do to make the testing beneficial. The "user" half of one section is shown in Figure 1.1 on page 15.

METHODS OF VALIDATION INQUIRY

Validation looks into the soundness and relevance of a proposed interpretation. A test may be excellent in other respects, but if it is wrongly interpreted it is worthless in that time and place. Only as a form of shorthand is it legitimate to speak of "the validity of a test"; a test relevant to one decision may have no value for another. So users must ask, "How valid is this test for the decision to be made?" or "How valid are the several interpretations I am making?"

Note this important point: Validation is *inquiry* into the soundness

---

[1]From the *Standards for Educational and Psychological Testing*, p. 2. Copyright © 1985 by the American Psychological Association. Reprinted by permission.

of an interpretation. Challenge is at least as appropriate as compilation of supporting evidence.

Three key terms, referring to types of inquiry, dominate discussions of validation: criterion-oriented, content, and construct validity. The *Standards* have been organized around the three terms for 35 years. In that time, unfortunately, they came to be seen as *distinct* lines of inquiry, becoming separate "roads to psychometric salvation," as Guion (1980, p. 386) put it. Validation ought to integrate all pertinent arguments (Cronbach, in Wainer & Braun, 1988). On the history of the concept of validity, see Messick (in Linn, 1989a, pp. 18ff).

I begin with examples of the separate usage of the three terms, though the chapter will provide many reminders that they are not truly separable.

- Criterion emphasis. When the navy is assigning sailors to a course on ships' engines, it seeks those who will succeed in the course. Personnel psychologists try out MCT, comparing the sailors' scores against a *criterion*, a measure of success in the course.
- Content emphasis. When a school system is testing how well its high school seniors understand U.S. government, the test ought to cover the *content* that district officials consider important. The testing officer has to satisfy herself that the items are relevant, clear, and soundly keyed, and that as a set the items distribute emphasis suitably over the relevant facts and concepts.
- Construct emphasis. An "introversion" score claims to describe an aspect of behavior or feelings. To evaluate the truthfulness of a description, we must first understand its intended meaning. How (according to the interpreter's theory) do "introverts" act in this or that situation? What incentives do they respond to? How do they handle emotional stress? Once meanings have been spelled out in this way, we can check out whether persons who score high on the test act as the theory says they will. Terms entering explanations—such as "introversion"—are constructs; hence this is *construct* validation.

Do not jump to the conclusion that criterion validation is for aptitude tests, content validation for educational tests, and construct validation for personality tests. The *Standards* list all the following as examples of constructs used in test interpretation: Spatial visualization, reading comprehension, sociability, endurance (in athletics), and consideration for subordinates (in leadership). One other side comment: The first two aspects of validity to some extent echo criterion reference and domain reference in interpretation (p. 104). The correspondence is not hard and fast, and construct interpretation does not match any of the terms from Chapter 4. Rather, it applies primarily to explanation of test performance.

With almost any test it makes sense to join several kinds of inquiry.

The three famous terms do no more than spotlight aspects of the reasoning. To emphasize this point the latest *Standards* speak not of "content validity," for example, but of "content-related evidence of validity." The end goal of validation being explanation and understanding, construct validation is of greatest long-run importance (Cronbach in Linn, 1989b; Messick, 1980; for a dissent, see Ebel, in Reynolds & Gutkin, 1982).

A complete inquiry will bring in value considerations: What are the social and personal consequences, good and bad, of using the test? (See articles by Cronbach and by Messick, in Wainer & Braun, 1988; and by Messick, in Linn, 1989a.) Recent debates about mandatory testing for drug use and for AIDS have centered on this kind of functional question.

5. *Illustrate that a criterion-oriented study could be relevant to an educational test. To a personality test.*

6. *Illustrate that critical review of content could be pertinent for a measure of typical behavior.*

7. *Some early writers said, "A test is valid if it measures what it purports to measure." What aspects of today's conception, as sketched in the preceding paragraphs, does this phrasing neglect?*

Introduction to Criterion-oriented Inquiries

A criterion-referenced interpretation translates a score into a statement about some other variable. The statement is a prediction about what could be expected if the second variable were observed; such expectations follow from experience. The suitable prediction for a test taker who scores 25 is inferred from the experience of similar test takers who previously scored at that level.

Experience Tables and Charts.   Table 5.1 is an experience table based on test scores and grades in 25 widely scattered high schools. It was prepared to assist counselors in interpreting scores from a measure of several aptitudes. Two subtests, covering arithmetic and form perception,

Table 5.1   EXPERIENCE TABLE FOR DRAFTING COURSES

Aptitude score[a]	Probability of earning a grade at least as high as			
	D	C	B	A
41–50	99	92	62	21
31–40	98	82	42	10
21–30	94	66	25	4
11–20	85	47	12	1
1–10	71	29	5	<1

[a]Composite of Arithmetic Reasoning and Space Perception scores from ASVAB.

Source: Adapted from G. L. Bower and J. R. Lewis, 1975, p. 9.

related to success in drafting. The counselor advising a student would add those two subtest scores and direct the student's attention to the row of the table that corresponds to his total. If his score is 25, the table indicates that he has two chances out of three of earning at least a C. Such a table gives a more complete, more definite picture than any other system of norms can offer, especially when tables are available for many of the courses the student is considering.

The word *actuarial* is often used in connection with forecasts based on tabulations like these; the term comes from the actuarial tables of the life insurance industry, which indicate risks associated with age and other predictors.

An experience chart, though less precise than a table, displays trends dramatically. Figure 5.1 presents charts for three tests; the dexterity test is a much less accurate predictor than the other two. Figure 5.1 carries the title "Expectancy chart." The term *expectancy* is used when the chart comes not from a direct count of cases in the file but from a statistical process that smooths out the data. That estimates the proportions in the population the file cases represent.

Follow-up Studies   Validity of predictions is checked by follow-up, which compares test scores with another measure. A measure is a "criterion" only when an audience accepts it as important. Before an investigator adopts a criterion she should take a hard look at its relevance, completeness, and freedom from bias. Some studies check on multiple criteria.

Table 5.2 is a summary-in-advance of later pages. The left column lists what the investigator looks at. She has to look into a certain situation. She seeks an adequate criterion. And so on. An actual plan falls short of the ideal, as the examples will show. Departures from the ideal force the investigator back to indirect reasoning.

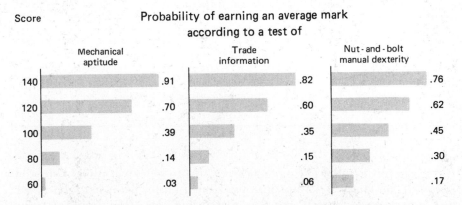

Figure 5.1. **Expectancy charts for aircraft-armorer trainees.** These three charts represent validity coefficients of 0.5, 0.45, and 0.25, respectively. Such coefficients will be explained in later in this chapter. (*Source: Personnel Classification Tests*, 1946.)

Table 5.2   ELEMENTS IN A STUDY OF TEST-CRITERION RELATIONS

Element (in ideal study)	Examples of realistic practice	
	Example 1. Law-school admissions	Example 2. Certifying proficiency of graduates
Situation that concerns the test user	Law school A has an established curriculum. Applicants outnumber places. Faculty desires to admit students likely to do well.	Manufacturer Z trains workers to maintain equipment. After training, they work out of local offices, repairing most breakdowns but calling experts from headquarters when necessary. It is costly to send out an underqualified worker.
Criterion; accepted as adequate by client and investigator	Course grades received during the first year of law school are averaged.	Regional supervisor rates employees in the field after examining a log of service rendered and related information.
Elapsed time; accepted as adequate	Confining attention to the first year produces an early report.	Ratings at end of first 6 months are to be used.
Sample; accepted as representative of those about whom decisions will be made hereafter	The aptitude test under investigation is given to all entering students in 1988. They are not actually representative of 1988 applicants.	The proficiency test is given to all persons completing the course in January through June of 1988. The workers—no matter what their scores—are sent to the field unless the instructor has rated them seriously deficient in performance.
Test; data are collected as they will be when predictions are made "for keeps."	Testing is conducted during the first week of school; student attitude may not match that of applicants.	The test is given at the end of training. Each trainee's errors are discussed with him.

Example 1 in the table considers a test to screen applicants to a law school. The study develops an experience table. After conferring with the investigator about it, the committee that sets admission policy will decide whether to require future applicants to take the test and how much weight to put on the score.

The experience table summarizes the history in this school in this year. The rather typical study described in Example 1 does not provide a final answer. The reported relations may not hold in this school next year if the curriculum or grading standards change. The direct evidence is on the first-year grade average, not on "success in law school" or "performance as a lawyer." Moreover, the experience table is not based on representative *applicants*. No one knows how many applicants not admitted in the year studied would have done creditably in this school.

Example 2 outlines a follow-up study for an achievement test. If this test works well, the investigator should be able to suggest a passing standard for certifying workers expected to be adequate or better on the job. Workers below the standard could be retrained and retested. Again we have an unrepresentative sample, because the firm cannot afford to send a badly qualified employee to serve customers. Note the suggestion that only workers the instructor considers adequate should be sent to the field. Ruling out some workers with good test scores prevents the investigator from following up repairmen about whom instructor and test disagree.

Concurrent Studies   The follow-up in Example 1 spanned one year. Sometimes, instead, the test and criterion measurements are separated by a short interval or none. Strictly speaking, this is "concurrent" evidence, but in most contexts it does no harm to stretch the term "predictive" to cover such data.

A concurrent study is fully logical when a test is proposed as a substitute for a more expensive procedure. The developer hopes that the test indicates what the expensive procedure would say about the person at this time. The soundest way to survey mental health in a community would be to have an experienced clinician interview every member of the sample and rate the degree of adjustment of each one. It is far more practicable to print up a list of questions, have members of the sample respond YES or NO, and score the responses. Do these scores tell the story the professional ratings would? To check this out, one would apply both procedures to perhaps 30 persons, perhaps in the same week. Cross-tabulation would show the degree of agreement.

Sometimes the concurrent study is a preliminary to a long-term follow-up, and sometimes it is a substitute. Thus Z Company might give its proposed proficiency test to workers already in the field. If performance ratings on these workers are in line with their test scores, that encourages the use of the test at the end of training. But the argument is indirect. Possibly superior test scores reflect what the more alert workers learned on the job. If so, some high-rated workers probably would have seemed inadequate if tested as they left school. The concurrent study leaves more uncertainty than a predictive study.

When E. K. Strong produced his interest questionnaire to help adolescents choose careers, concurrent studies were appropriate. To find out if the score profile of a 20-year-old really predicts what work he will enjoy as an adult, Strong would have had to collect the profiles and then put himself on hold for 20 years while the criterion ripened. Strong, therefore, offered as evidence of validity the fact that questionnaires answered in middle age distinguished men or women in one occupation from those in another. For example, the scores of doctors on Strong's Physician scale averaged much higher than those of nondoctors. The purpose of the test, however, is not to find out which middle-aged person is a doctor; it is to find out if a young person will in later years be satisfied with that career. If the direction of interest at 40 is usually the same as at 20, then the concurrent validation on older persons is indirect evidence that the test predicts. Until follow-up evidence came in, users of the Strong questionnaire had to assume that a person's interests remain much the same from age 20 to age 40. Strong did accumulate evidence by following some persons for 20 years or more and ultimately verified his long-term predictions. True follow-up studies usually—but not always—confirm findings from concurrent validation (p. 413).

Illustrative Reports for MCT   The 1980 manual for MCT gave 14 examples of relations with criteria. The manual aimed to illustrate typical findings, not to answer users' questions about particular applications. Table 5.3 presents five of the results to show what a manual offers. For the moment, simply regard the values of r as numbers on a 0-to-1 scale that show how well the test forecasts the criterion.

Earlier reports had generally taken ratings as criteria, but in this re-

Table 5.3   MCT CORRELATIONS WITH CRITERIA

Group (with mean and s.d. on *MCT*)	N	Criterion	r
Coal producer; inexperienced miners (50.9; 8.1)	178	Combined rating and ranking	0.23
Southern chemical plant; operators (45.1; 7.0)	87	Rating on reaction to emergency	0.36
		Rating on safety rules	0.21
		Rating on job knowledge	0.39
Southern chemical plant; operators (48.0; 7.5)	136	Test on job knowledge	0.63
Steel producer; apprentice millwrights and mechanics (50.0; 6.8)	30	Average course grades	0.54
Utility company; technician trainees (39.6; 9.7)	83	Time needed to complete training modules	−0.52

Source: Manual supplement for Forms S and T of the Bennett Mechanical Comprehension Test, 1980, pp. 6–7.

port the criteria are diverse. Note in particular that in the chemical plant a test of job knowledge was predicted much more accurately than a rating of knowledge.

As is the case with many manuals, the report has limitations. Samples are as small as 30 cases, and hence the evidence is thin. We do not know how much time (and how much training) came between test and criterion measurement. Nor are we told how much more select the group providing data was than the original applicant pool. Why that is important will be explained later.

Despite the departures from ideal design and reporting, the information warrants the conclusion that, in many kinds of technical work, MCT has a worthwhile relation to success.

8. *Prior to training, a prospective aircraft armorer earns these scores: Mechanical Aptitude, 120; Trade Information, 140; Nut-and-Bolt Test, 100. Interpret, using Figure 5.1.*

9. *Experience tables prepared for local use are clearly meaningful. In view of the fact that probability of success in a job or in a course of study depends on local conditions, can experience tables profitably be included in test manuals?*

10. *Four MCT coefficients for operators in a chemical plant are reported. What reasons can you suggest for the variation among them?*

Introduction to Content-related Inquiries

Scrutiny of content is especially important in a test that certifies competence or that is used to evaluate an educational or therapeutic service. Those delivering a service try to develop competence of a certain kind or to encourage certain attitudes or to cause people to act in a certain way. A final test, then, ought to assess *those* characteristics, not something else. Table 5.4 outlines examples of two kinds. Example 1 illustrates how careful task definition and sampling support the content validity of a measure of typical behavior. This argument is direct.

Example 2 returns to the test of maintenance skills of Table 5.2. If the examination is a good "work sample," then the graduate of the maintenance course demonstrates that he can do the job when he passes the test. To judge content validity, the investigator compares the test content with job duties. There will be some mismatch; how much this impairs the usefulness of the test is a matter for judgment. Identification of the pertinent domain and obtaining agreement on it are as critical in content validation as the choice of criterion is in predictive validation.

11. *The pencil-and-paper portion of the licensing examination for drivers has a different mix of content in different states. What questions would you raise in order to decide which of the examinations have superior content validity?*

12. *What questions would you raise in order to evaluate the content validity of the behind-the-wheel portion of the test for drivers?*

Table 5.4   ELEMENTS IN ENSURING OR INVESTIGATING ADEQUACY IN A CONTENT SAMPLE

Element and investigator's role	Examples of realistic practice	
	Example 1. Observing teachers	Example 2. Certifying proficiency of graduates
Situation that concerns the test user	A workshop for teachers encourages them to use certain kinds of reinforcement. The success of the workshop is to be judged from follow-up observations of teaching.	Manufacturer Z trains workers to maintain equipment. After training they work out of local offices, repairing most breakdowns but calling experts from headquarters when necessary. It is costly to send out an underqualified worker.
Domain of content; specified by investigator, accepted by client	Workshop director tells investigator what actions he is encouraging. Investigator defines categories and prepares a guide so observers can classify each classroom episode. She also prepares a briefer version to serve as record sheet.	Psychologist obtains record of all service calls encountered by the newly trained workers and summarizes the types of malfunction they have dealt with over a 3-month period. Supervisors and experienced workers indicate what action they would recommend in the situation described.
Domain of occasions; specified by investigator, accepted by client	Investigator suggests, and workshop director agrees, that behavior is to be observed only during classwork in reading and arithmetic and that the data will be collected during a 4-week period, 2 months after the workshop.	
Sampling of observations: Investigator's plan guarantees adequate sample; *or* sampling is unsystematic and the distribution of content, occasions, etc., is judged against the domain.	Investigator lays out schedule so that each teacher is visited on randomly chosen days and so that at scheduled moments the teacher's next act of reinforcement is recorded.	The psychologist classifies the tasks of the proficiency test and points out how the emphasis on various tasks or the responses given credit differ from practice in the field.

Construct Validation: Explaining Scores and Their Relations

The test developer and test user seek to understand why some persons score high and some score low, and why performance on a test does (or does not) correspond to everyday behavior. Explanations have practical consequences: improvement in the test, change in the way it is used, modification of the requirements of a job or an instructional program, and hints for designing new tests. For example, evidence that vocabulary and reading ability predict how much fire fighters learn during training should prompt the question: "Did the training program make unnecessary verbal demands?" If so, perhaps the training can be modified so that aspirants with limited verbal ability can master the job. This would benefit them, would benefit the service by increasing the supply of suitable applicants, and would benefit society by reducing the number of "unemployables."

Sooner or later every tester has to go behind the experience table and behind the test content, to say what processes seem to account for the responses observed. Every test is to some degree impure and unlikely to measure exactly what its name implies. Identifying impurities is one part of the process of explanation.

Explaining test scores is much like any scientific reasoning—a back-and-forth exchange between curiosity, speculation, collection of evidence, and critical review of possible interpretations of the evidence. A theory is built out of constructs, each one a category invented to describe apparently similar events, objects, situations, or persons. *Construct* comes from *construe;* a construct is a way of construing—organizing—what has been observed.

The theory used in explaining test scores, though sometimes close to everyday thinking, is hard-won knowledge going well beyond the obvious. It was and is obvious that "memory" counts in college work, and memory for strings of numbers is a traditional test of memory. Yet grade averages have almost no correlation with memory for digit strings. Today's interpretation of memory emphasizes how ideas are organized. The fact that digit strings are unorganized explains the lack of correlation with college learning.

To speak of "aptitude for sales jobs" implies that the several jobs given this label have similar requirements. This kind of interpretation is likely to be only partly correct; research has to determine just which jobs belong in the category. If sales jobs prove to be diverse, the research will have to suggest finer job categories.

The originator of a test sets out to measure a loosely defined trait. The tentative conception suggests a kind of item to try. The inventor's working hypotheses are challenged, first when surprises come up in the data and later when other investigators disagree with her interpretations. Sometimes additional studies can settle the disagreement. Sometimes two or more alternatives are retained as possibilities to keep in mind.

This lengthy—indeed, endless—process of revising hypotheses is referred to succinctly as construct validation. As the preceding examples show, it is a matter of asking tough questions about the test content and its correlates. For such a free-ranging program of analysis there is no simple or ideal design.

VALIDATION AGAINST A CRITERION: A CLOSER LOOK

The Criterion

To consider predictive studies in more detail, I turn to another example. A wholesale hardware firm hires salespersons. Test scores can be put on file as persons apply for jobs, during a period of several months. Ideally, these scores will not be allowed to influence hiring. That gives us a chance to examine the job performance of persons all along the score scale.

The hardest part of predictive validation is getting satisfactory criterion data. The outcome that interests the firm is how much each employee sells. Perhaps "amount sold during the first 6 months" will be suggested as a numerical index of success. If the 6-month record does not really represent "selling success," the test has not been given a fair trial. Look at the weaknesses of the suggested criterion. Although "amount sold" appears to be a fair basis for judging success, some of the salespersons were assigned more desirable territory than others. Suppose we control this by comparing the sales record with the average sales in past years in the same territory. We still have not allowed, for example, for poor crops in one region that make business bad this year. Another limitation is that sales alone may not be what is wanted from the firm's representative. High-pressure selling may build up sales on a first trip, but overselling can eventually harm the firm's business.

Note that the study is limited to the wholesale hardware business. Additional predictive studies will be wanted if the test is considered for hiring sellers of insurance or machine tools. (Some psychologists believe that a test valid in one situation can be counted on to work in another. Chapter 11 will pursue this question of "validity generalization.")

13. *Criticize each of the following criteria:*
    a. *Number of accidents a driver has per year, as an index of driver safety.*
    b. *Number of accidents a driver has per thousand miles, as an index of driver safety.*
14. *A study habits inventory asks such questions as "Do you daydream when you should be studying?" What criterion would you use to determine how well the inventory evaluates study habits?*
15. *Criticize the procedure indicated in the following report of a study of success of students who graduated from a teachers' college:*

The correlation between all thirty of the predictor variables and the school superintendents' ratings was only 0.17, but that between the variables and marks earned during four years of college was 0.79. Since college marks were predictable on the basis of the thirty variables and the superintendents' ratings were not, the marks were substituted for the ratings as a criterion of success.

16. *How long a time should elapse between test and criterion measurement when*
    a. *the U.S. Employment Service wishes to determine which job seekers have had enough experience to be referred to contractors listing vacancies for electricians?*
    b. *a pencil-and-paper test is proposed for identifying students entering junior high school who have emotional difficulties and should be singled out for counseling?*

17. *Which of the following examine concurrent relations and which examine predictive relations? In which instances would some other time interval between measurement and collection of criterion data be more informative?*
    a. *A new employment test is found to correlate 0.9 with a clerical test that has been satisfactorily used for some time as a predictor of job success.*
    b. *A manual for a test of mental ability reports correlations of scores with high school course marks assigned 1 month later.*
    c. *A correlation is calculated to determine how well a certain test distinguishes patients who have been diagnosed as schizophrenic from those diagnosed as brain-damaged.*
    d. *School records of delinquents and nondelinquents in high school are searched to learn what data recorded during the elementary grades correlate with present delinquent status.*

Correlation and Regression Coefficients

Correlation coefficients and *regression coefficients* tell how closely two variables correspond. A correlation of a test score with a criterion measure is called a *validity coefficient*. This chapter introduces the topic of interpreting correlations; more will be said in many later chapters. Correlations are not restricted to test-criterion relations. They are also used to answer questions such as the following: Do the ranks of these persons today agree with their ranks a year ago? Are people who become anxious over tests also more anxious in social situations?

Let us work through an artificial illustration. Ten salespersons took tests when they came on the job; criterion information was obtained later. Table 5.5 records the criterion in units of $10,000; so 25 implies sales of $250,000.

Inspection tells something about relations among variables. Because raw scores are hard to scan, the data have been translated into ranks— not a necessary part of the analysis. Man E, the poorest salesman, ranked low on Test 1, high on Test 2, and middling on 3. Woman I, middling on the criterion, ranked high on Test 2 and low on Tests 1 and 3. Before reading ahead, study the ranks to form an impression of the validity of each test for the purpose of this firm.

It is always advisable to look at a plot. Figure 5.2 is called a "scatter diagram." The predictor is placed on the horizontal scale. Woman A is

Table 5.5   DATA ON TEN SALESPERSONS

Salesperson	Sex	Test score 1	Test score 2	Test score 3	Criterion measure C	Criterion rank	Test rank 1	Test rank 2	Test rank 3
A	F	30	45	34	25	6	4	7	7
B	M	34	64	35	38	2	2	3	5½
C	M	32	32	35	30	4	3	9	5½
D	F	42	52	31	40	1	1	5	9
E	M	20	74	36	7	10	9	1	4
F	M	24	50	40	10	9	7	6	1
G	F	27	53	37	22	7	5	4	3
H	F	25	36	30	35	3	6	8	10
I	F	22	71	32	28	5	8	2	8
J	M	16	28	39	12	8	10	10	2

plotted above 30 on that scale and opposite 25 on the vertical scale. The trend is easily seen: as Score 1 rises, criterion C tends to rise.

If high test scores go with high criterion scores, the correlation coefficient is positive. For Test 1 and criterion C, the correlation r_{1C} is 0.77. The two variables correspond imperfectly. Correlations in research reports are usually reported to two decimal places; in this book, to avoid

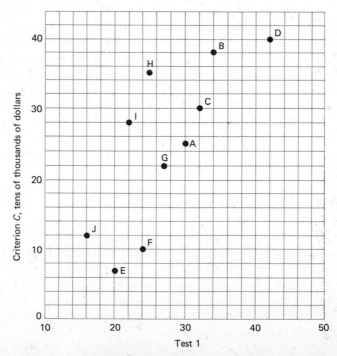

Figure 5.2. Scatter diagram for Test 1 and Criterion C.

a false appearance of precision, I shall generally round to the nearest 0.05.

The correlation coefficient relating Test 1 to Test 2 is defined as the average of z_1z_2, the product of the z scores for each person. (This is a "product moment" coefficient; psychologists use it far more often than other kinds of coefficient.) You will recall from Chapter 4 that z scores have an s.d. of 1. This means that the sum of z_1z_1 is 1, and a score correlates perfectly "with itself." Table 5.6 spells out a calculating procedure that will provide insight into the buildup of a correlation. Steps 1–3 apply methods from Chapter 4 (pp. 115 and 116 to obtain z scores on the test and the criterion for all persons. Then the product is formed. (But note that the direct formula at the bottom of the table would be used in practice.) Persons with large products are exceptionally good or poor on both test and criterion, and they raise the correlation. Note where D, E, and J, whose z-score products are largest, fall in Figure 5.2. Anyone whose product is negative—as is the case with H and I—brings down the correlation. In Figure 5.2 you can see that H and I are out of line

Table 5.6   COMPUTING THE PRODUCT-MOMENT CORRELATION

1. Begin with the pairs of scores to be studied. Here, consider Test 1 and Criterion C from Table 5.5. Relabel the test scores X.
2. Find the means, deviation scores, and standard deviations. For X we have

	A	B	C	D	E	F	G	H	I	J	Mean
X	30	34	32	42	20	24	27	25	22	16	27.2
x	2.8	6.8	4.8	14.8	−7.2	−3.2	−0.2	−2.2	−5.2	−11.2	0.0
x^2	7.7	46.2	23.0	219.0	51.8	10.2	0.0	4.8	27.0	125.4	51.5[a]

$$s_X = \sqrt{51.5} = 7.18$$

A similar calculation gives $M_C = 2.7$ (in thousands of dollars) and $s_C = 11.2$.

3. Divide x by s_X to get z_X. Convert C to z_C similarly. Form products z_Xz_C. Average.

	A	B	C	D	E	F	G	H	I	J	Mean
z_X	0.39	0.95	0.67	2.06	−1.00	−0.45	−0.03	−0.31	−0.72	−1.56	0.0
z_C	0.03	1.19	0.47	1.37	−1.58	−1.31	−0.24	0.92	0.29	−1.13	0.0
z_Xz_C	0.01	1.13	0.31	2.82	1.58	0.59	0.01	−0.29	−0.20	1.76	**0.77**

Note: In practical calculation steps 2 and 3 are compressed as follows: For each person, form X^2, C^2, and XC. Sum these across persons, along with X and C. Enter in this formula, where Σ stands for "sum of":

$$r_{XC} = \frac{N\Sigma XC - \Sigma X \Sigma C}{\sqrt{(N\Sigma X^2 - (\Sigma X)^2)(N\Sigma C^2 - (\Sigma C)^2)}}$$

$$r_{xc} = \text{Mean } z_xz_c = 0.77$$

---

[a] The choice of N or $N - 1$ as divisor in obtaining s does not affect the final value of r.

with the general trend. They performed better than their subaverage test scores promised.

A correlation close to zero says that the test does not predict the criterion. The value of -0.05 for r_{2C} implies that Test 2 does not predict. If high test scores go with low criterion scores, the coefficient is negative. When $r_{3C} = -0.75$, you may wonder how it happens that a low score on Test 3 goes with good job performance. This is most likely when a good score on the test is a low number (a time score, or an error count).

Tests 1 and 3 are good predictors for this firm; Test 2 is not. There is only a moderate relation between Tests 1 and 3: $r = 0.45$. Evidently these two tests look at somewhat distinct aspects of performance, so both together might be useful in picking employees.

The artificially regular scatter diagrams in Figure 5.3 give a sense of the meaning of coefficients of various sizes. When $r = 1.0$, one variable is predicted perfectly from the other. With $r = 0.6$, prediction is approximate; in Figure 5.3, people who stand at 8 on X average near 7 on Y, but they spread from 4 to 9.

The trend line in each diagram is known as the Y-on-X regression. When there are many data points, we can slice up the X scale and find the average Y at each X level. When plotted, these averages ordinarily fall along a straight line or a curve. The line that best fits the points is the regression line. The stronger the relation of outcome to test score, the steeper its slope. The higher the correlation, the closer the individual data points cling to the line. (A similar line, through the midpoints of the *rows*, is the X-on-Y regression.)

The regression coefficient tells how steep the trend line is. The correlation coefficient is actually the regression coefficient calculated from standard scores. The raw-score regression, which describes the trend in practical terms, is also useful. Recognizing that the criterion in Table 5.5 is in tens of thousands of dollars, we see that expected sales go up by about $10,000 for each additional score point on Test 1.

The usual formulas assume a straight-line trend. That assumption is sometimes violated in a spectacular way—look at the U-shaped trend pictured on page 211. Departures from linearity cause trouble so rarely, however, that more than 99 per cent of correlations and regressions are calculated under the linear assumption.

Interpreting Correlations   When r_{AB} is high, it does not follow that one variable "causes" the other. A may cause or influence the size of B, B may cause A, or A and B may depend on other variables. Vocabulary scores correlate with reading scores. Does good vocabulary cause one to read more easily? Does good reading lead to a larger vocabulary? Common sense says yes to both questions. Beyond that, both reading skill and vocabulary result from superior mental functioning, a home in which books and serious conversation abound, and superior teaching in

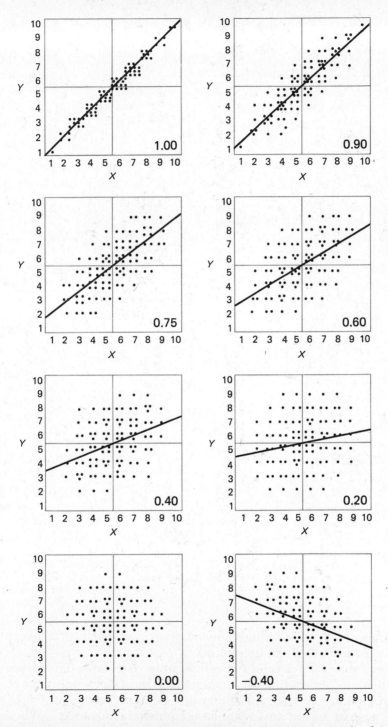

Figure 5.3. Scatter diagrams yielding large and small coefficients. The decimal in the corner is the correlation coefficient.

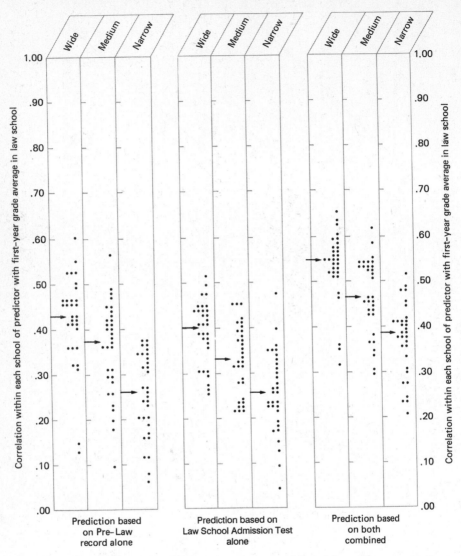

Figure 5.4. **Predictive correlations in groups with wide and narrow range.** (*Source*: Adapted from Schrader & Pitcher, 1969.)

the first years of school. Almost always, more than one plausible explanation for a correlation can be offered.

It is unusual for a validity coefficient to rise above 0.6. Because social situations are continually changing and because people change, perfect prediction is a false ideal. Long ago, William James warned psychologists against trying to "write biographies in advance." Whether a validity coefficient is large enough to warrant prediction from the test depends on the benefit obtained by making predictions, the cost of testing, and the cost *and validity* of alternative selection methods. To the question, "What is a good validity coefficient?", the only sensible answer is, "The best you can get." Predicting with validity 0.2 sometimes makes an appreciable practical contribution. A greater contribution is required to justify an expensive, inconvenient procedure than an inexpensive one.

Other things being equal, a correlation is larger in a wide-range group. Figure 5.4 presents validity coefficients from 94 law schools whose students had taken the same aptitude test. The schools were classified according to the spread of aptitude scores among entrants. Validity coefficients are considerably higher in the schools with a wide ability range (large s.d.). Note also the variation among coefficients in each column. Some of this variation is statistical noise ("sampling error"), and some arises from systematic differences among the colleges. (For more on effects of range, see pp. 206–207 and 432.)

18. *Would the correlation between Test 1 and Criterion C be increased or decreased if J had sold twice as much? (Think it through with the aid of Figure 5.2.)*

19. *How large a correlation would you anticipate between the following pairs of variables?*
    a. *age and annual income (men aged 20 to 50)*
    b. *age in January 1980 and age in March 1990 (adults in a community)*
    c. *scores on two block design tests given the same week (children randomly chosen from a third-grade class)*
    d. *annual income and number of children (married urban men)*
    e. *maximum and minimum temperature in Wichita (days within a year)*

20. *Prepare a scatter diagram relating Test 3 to the criterion.*

21. *Beginning with the information in Figure 5.3, prepare an "experience table" similar to Table 5.1, corresponding to each of the following values of r: 0.9, 0.4, 0.2.*

22. *What causal relations might underlie the following correlations?*
    a. *Between amount of education and annual income of adults (assume that r is positive).*
    b. *Between average intelligence of children and size of family (assume that r is negative).*
    c. *Between Sunday-school attendance and honesty of behavior (assume that r is positive).*

23. *Interpret this difference in correlations reported by Osterlund and Cheney (1978). The Test of Standard Written English, given at the start of a college English course, correlated 0.4 with course marks and 0.6 with a grade on essays. Instructors in four sections had graded students in their usual manner. Two short essays written at the end of the course were assigned grades by judges who did not know the students.*

Validity in Classification

Diagnosis is designed to guide choice of therapeutic or educational treatment. Every such classification implies a prediction of the form "Treatment A will work out better for this individual than Treatment B."

Extending the word "treatment" slightly, we can speak of guidance into career lines and assignment to military specialties as choices of treatment. Sometimes the number of alternative treatments is large, as in working out an individualized educational plan. In effect, a prediction has to be made for each treatment, and the predictions have to be compared. For comparison, outcomes from the treatments must somehow be mapped onto a common criterion scale.

An example of the effect of circumstances on success is Forehand's (1968) comparison of "group-centered" and "rule-centered" organizations. He sorted agencies into the two categories after asking, for example, whether friendship between a superior and a subordinate was considered normal or was avoided for the sake of impartiality. He asked the staff in each agency to rate the innovativeness of the agency manager. Also, he gave the managers several tests; Table 5.7 presents the most interesting correlations. (Names of variables are simplified here, and some personality scores that showed negligible correlations are omitted.) With only 60 cases in each group, Forehand's data are limited; supporting findings come from Andrews (1967) and Schneider (1978).

The data show an interaction between personality and organization type. In the group-centered organizations, the managers rated highest tended to be intellectually superior and to be discontented when constrained by rules. In the rigid organizations, managers indifferent to others' feelings more often generated change. Bright and autonomous persons, then, should be encouraged to go into group-centered organizations. Dull, conforming persons tend to do no worse than average (by Forehand's criterion) in a rule-centered agency and are better off there. This information, obviously, is relevant to vocational guidance and to making job assignments, and to self-understanding in career planning.

Table 5.7   RATED INNOVATIVENESS CORRELATED WITH ABILITY AND PERSONALITY MEASURES

Predictor	Group-centered organizations	Rule-centered organizations
General mental ability	0.45	0
Fluency of ideas	0.3	−0.15
Willingness to defer to others[a]	−0.4	−0.1
Preference for ordered, predictable situations[a]	−0.35	0
Desire to respond to other's feelings[a]	0.2	−0.35
Desire for close personal relationships[a]	0	−0.1

[a]Self-report, on the Edwards Personal Preference Schedule.

Source: Forehand, 1968, p. 71.

Attempts to match individuals to treatments or settings call for a study of interaction. So do attempts to explain why a treatment works better for some persons (or in some settings) than for others. When the outcome-on-predictor regression slope differs from treatment to treatment, we speak of an *aptitude-treatment interaction*. Although questions about interaction are central to psychological theory and testing practice and although some provocative findings are summarized in this book, it is well to say here that findings to support use of tests in classification, diagnosis, placement, and so on, are limited and inconsistent. With regard to instruction, Cronbach and Snow (1977, pp. vii, 492) had this to say:

> No aptitude-treatment interactions [ATI] are so well confirmed that they can be used directly as guides to instruction. . . . Aptitude-treatment interactions exist. To assert the opposite is to assert that whichever educational procedure is best for Johnny is best for everyone else in Johnny's school. Even the most commonplace adaptation of instruction, such as choosing different books for more and less capable readers of a given age, rests on an assumption of ATI that it seems foolish to challenge. It becomes clear that the problem of characterizing, understanding, and using . . . interactions poses the major challenge to educational and psychological science today.

Snow (1989) repeats this message and stresses the complexity of recent positive findings that he reviews.

Frederiksen et al. (1972) and Dance and Neufeld (1988) say almost exactly the same thing in the contexts of organizational psychology and clinical treatment, respectively; and the perplexities of personality research are exhibited by dozens of authors in Magnusson and Endler (1977) and in Pervin and Lewis (1978).

To carry out adequate research is exceedingly difficult. Most studies such as Forehand's try to make sense of relations in existing groups. A strict experiment with controlled assignment is required to produce directly interpretable results, however, and experimental trials encounter many difficulties (Cronbach, 1982).

How might we validate a school's classification policy? Here, again, it is useful to describe an ideal design. Suppose—to oversimplify what teachers do—that entering first-graders are sorted on the basis of Test X. Pupils whose scores imply "readiness" are started immediately on instruction in reading (Treatment A). The others are given developmental experiences and are started on actual reading only when the teacher considers them ready (Treatment B). In due time outcomes are assessed, and regression lines are determined. The logic of the research would lead us to send equivalent groups into the two treatments, but it would be unethical to send excellent students into a "slow" treatment and vice versa. A sound compromise is to put low scorers into B and high scorers into A, but to divide those near the borderline strictly at random. (In the figure, dotted lines extend the regression lines into the region where no observations were made.)

The school's assignment is justified if the regressions resemble those in panel i of Figure 5.5. The crossing of the lines indicates a "disordinal" interaction. (In this chart it appears that the trial borderline was set a bit low.)

When the regressions do not cross (panel ii of Figure 5.5), the same treatment averages out best for children at every score level. Lines of unlike slope that do not cross indicate "ordinal" interaction. An ordinal interaction is of theoretical interest and can be practically important. Where the A regression is above the B regression at all levels of the test, yet the gap between the lines changes with the score level, differential assignment may still be justified. Examples:

- Treatment B is superior to A on some second criterion, such as emotional tension.
- Treatment A is more expensive than B.
- Facilities for giving Treatment A are limited.

Demonstrating a test-criterion correlation is not enough to validate use of the test for classification. Test X″ predicts outcome, yet it is useless for classification. No interaction appears in panel iii.

24. *"Figure 3.4, on test anxiety, describes an interaction." Defend that statement.*

25. *In Figure 1.5, the outcome variable is not displayed graphically. Sketch a three-dimensional figure to show the regression of outcome on aptitude. What predictor shows the strongest interaction (largest difference in regression slopes)?*

26. *Consider the hypothesis that sex of examiner interacts with the confidence of a child to affect the score on Block Design. Sketch panels like those in Figure 5.5 (with confidence as the horizontal axis and Block Design as the vertical axis and one line for each sex). What testing practice would be recommended if evidence on the question took the form of panel i? panel ii? panel iii?*

27. *In the Larry P. v. Riles decision, the judge ruled against the use of mental tests on the ground that no one had demonstrated the validity of low scores for placement in special classes. If a psychologist were to try to demonstrate criterion-related validity of such a test for special-class placement, how should the study be designed? (Court opinions on pupil classification are divided at this time; see p. 350. The issues are too complex to be settled by purely statistical findings.)*

CHECKING OUT TEST CONTENT

Selection of Content

The validity of content—that is, its relevance—is improved when the test is carefully planned. Making a sound plan requires a clear vision as to what the test is intended to measure. Ideally, the test developer de-

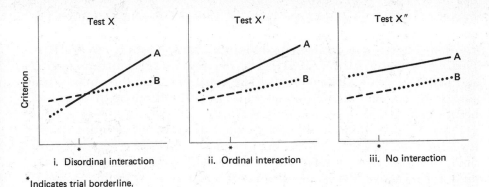

*Indicates trial borderline.

Figure 5.5. **Possible findings in an experiment on pupil classification.**

fines the domain appropriately and represents it fairly in the test. The definition ought to cover the following:

The appropriate range of tasks, stimuli, or situations.

The kinds of response the observer or scorer is to count.

The statement that tells the test taker what he is to do.

Altering any of these can change the test significantly. In measuring reading for some purposes, one would confine the selections to text material; for other purposes, one would want the selections to range over fiction, newspapers, or instruction manuals or a combination of these. The examinee may be asked to read for detail or to read for the main idea. Once the definition is made clear, the prospective user can decide whether the test aims at the target she has in mind.

Validity of content plays an important role in judging the soundness of a school examination. In general, the test should cover what some evaluating authority *wanted* the school to teach. Decision makers are likely to have different ideas as to what content is important. A test on, say, geography distributes its content over particular topics and skills. A teacher might be satisfied to judge its validity by comparing the test outline with the outline of the course he or she has been giving. The State Board of Education might have in mind a substantially different domain—maybe a broader one, maybe a more conventional one. The test that has a high degree of content validity in the eyes of the teacher will not be so satisfactory to the board and vice versa. One resolution of the difficulty is to prepare a broad test that covers what any of the parties regards as important and to report the achievement on each subset of the content separately.

A test that affects the fate of individuals encounters objections—no matter how worthwhile the content—if the teacher did not devote time to that content. Reviewing a Florida examination required for high school graduation, a court approved the content as such, but refused to allow enforcement of the requirement until the state could prove that all the items were covered in each student's course of study (*Debra P. v. Turlington,* 644 F.2d. 397 [1981]; for discussion by specialists on testing and instruction see Madaus, 1983.) The court held that the diploma is a constitutional right of any student who has faithfully done the work set before him or her.

The ideal of limiting the test to what the school has indeed been teaching the student ("instructional validity") has since been watered down, because it is impractical to document what each student was taught. Nowadays, the demand is that graduation tests fit the course of study that the school authority has prescribed as basic. (The confusion between "instructional," "content," and similarly named concepts of validity is discussed by Jaeger, in Linn, 1989a, pp. 500ff.)

The best guarantee of representativeness is to map out subdivisions of the domain and collect the desired number of items for each subdivision. In a reading test, for example, this technique prevents such faults as overemphasis on content from economics or selection of a set of passages that is too easy.

To sample content from a clearly defined domain is a pleasing and logical ideal, but test construction is rarely so simple. Most often the test constructor has some general idea of the behavior to be observed but cannot give a neat definition. Can an investigator measuring sociability of preschool children catalog the situations in which sociable behavior arises? Can another investigator characterize unambiguously the whole set of human relations problems a supervisor should be able to deal with? Can a third test developer truly define the domain of situations in which scientific reasoning is to be shown by a science student? Obviously not.

Reviewing content, therefore, requires judging whether each item bears on what the tester wants to measure. Two further judgments are required: Did the test items overemphasize any subtopic? Did any feature of the test that was not part of the intended "content" have much effect on scores? (Examples are pictures that are hard to read, pressure for rapid work, and obscure directions.) The test *user* has to make these judgments though it is, of course, desirable for the test author to tell how the content was chosen. In the end, it is the user's intent that counts.

The reviewing guide in Figure 5.6 illustrates how carefully a professional test constructor scrutinizes details of items. The questions are equally helpful for teachers and others who make up achievement tests. The reviewer is to consider each question for every item. (Judgments of many items can be put on the same sheet if columns are laid out.) Questions 1 and 2 call for judging the item with respect to a particular element of the instruction. It would be possible to consider a whole list of objectives at once by recording, at Question 1, the number of the objective to which the item seems most relevant.

Some experts see rather little value in content validation. Anastasi

Mark √ for "yes," × for "no," and ? for "unsure."

1. Is the content of the item closely matched to the goal statement, objective, or task? ____

2. Are the answer choices free of irrelevant material? ____

3. Is the readability level of the test item stem and answer choices suitable for the examinees being tested? ____

4. Does the item stem describe a single problem for an examinee? ____

5. Is the item stem free from ambiguities and/or irrelevant material? ____

6. Are all negatives underlined? ____

7. Do the item stem and answer choices follow standard rules of punctuation, capitalization, and grammar? ____

8. Is there *one* correct or *clearly best* answer? ____

9. Is any material provided in another test item that will provide a clue to the correct answer?* ____

10. When pictorials, tables, or figures are used, are they printed clearly and labeled correctly? ____

11. Can the test item be answered by simple logic or common sense?* ____

12. Have words that give verbal clues to the correct answer such as "always," "may," "none," "never," "all," "sometimes," "usually," "generally," "typically," etc., been avoided? ____

13. Have repetitious words or expressions been removed from the answer choices? ____

14. Will the distractors be plausible and appealing to examinees who do not know the correct answer? ____

15. Are the answer choices of approximately the same length? ____

16. Is the correct answer stated at the same level of detail as the other answer choices? ____

*Entry where "no" is the favorable answer.

Figure 5.6. Checklist for reviewing multiple-choice items in editing an achievement test. (*Source*: Adapted from Hambledon, in Berk, 1984, p. 227.)

(1988) acknowledges the importance of task specification in educational tests and "job sample" measures of occupational competence, but goes on to say (p. 144):

> For aptitude and personality tests, on the other hand, content validation is usually inappropriate and may, in fact, be misleading.... [T]he content of aptitude and personality tests can do little more than reveal the hypotheses

that led the test constructor to choose a certain type of content for measuring a specified trait. Such hypotheses need to be empirically confirmed to establish the validity of the test.

Anastasi has put a sound point too strongly, I think. To obtain evidence on nonverbal problem solving, Block Design presents a convenient type of stimulus. No user thinks of block patterns as intrinsically important, so content validation is not a primary concern. Still it was the recognition of an irrelevant difficulty that led to a change from color to texture in the version for the blind, so it did pay to examine "content."

Likewise, Anastasi probably does not mean to say that examining content is irrelevant to judging the mathematics section of the Scholastic Aptitude Test. My evaluation of it as a measure of mathematical *reasoning* (Cronbach, in Mitchell, 1985, p. 363) became more favorable when I found that only elementary mathematics entered the problems. Familiar mathematical forms are presented in novel combinations to make this a reasoning test.

Sound choice of content does help justify interpretation. Evidence of plausible content is "misleading" only if it is taken as *sufficient* and seems to make unnecessary further inquiries—into the various processes that can lead to a low score, for example, or into predictive power (Messick, in Linn, 1989a, pp. 40–42).

28. *In the checklist for reviewing multiple-choice items (Figure 5.6), why are the features in entries 6, 11, and 15 considered beneficial?*

29. *With regard to an inventory on test anxiety, what questions about the content domain could reasonably be considered in designing the instrument or deciding how to interpret it?*

30. *Skill in the use of library reference materials is to be measured at the end of a how-to-study course for first-year college students. Try to specify the domain of tasks from which the test should be drawn.*

31. *A test is carefully balanced to cover the kinds of knowledge and skill in physics that the college physics course expects of entering freshmen. A high school teacher's course distributes effort quite differently. Is the test a proper basis for grading her students? For judging the adequacy of her course?*

32. *The bar exam given by a state ought to have content validity. But few practicing lawyers work in all areas of the law, and law schools not only have different sets of courses but cover the same area differently. What is an appropriate basis for choosing the domain for the exam content?*

Format

The form of a task can be as important as its substance in determining what is measured. A U.S. Navy test of mechanical knowledge contained four types of items: mechanical facts, tested verbally; mechanical facts, tested pictorially; electrical facts, tested verbally, and electrical facts, tested pictorially. Similar content produced lower correlations than similar form (Table 5.8). In other words, the form of the items strongly influenced the score. (See also p. 329.)

Speed is relevant and important in tests of typing attainment or arithmetic for cashiers. Speed is irrelevant when we wish to know how large a pupil's vocabulary is, how much science he knows, or how penetrating his reasoning can be.

Many popular testing techniques allow superficial response styles to affect scores. A *response style* (or *set*) is a habit (or a momentary attitude) causing the examinee to earn a score different from the one he would earn if the same questions were posed in a different form. In true-false tests particularly, some people tend to mark TRUE when in doubt; some others are characteristically suspicious and tend to mark FALSE when uncertain. If three-fourths of a test's items are keyed TRUE, the acquiescent student will earn a fairly good score even if his knowledge is limited. Other response styles include leaving items unanswered when in doubt (caution), sacrificing accuracy for speed, and answering essay questions in as few words as possible. Any style, carried to an extreme, is likely to reduce a person's score. (In Chapter 8 we shall consider some more fundamental styles in intellectual work, and inferences about personality from style in drawing will be illustrated in Part III.)

Perhaps the most important maxim to ensure validity of content is this: *no irrelevant difficulty*. Reading is irrelevant to proficiency in engine repair (p. 414). Reading of long sentences is irrelevant to the task of a messenger, whereas reading everyday phrases is relevant.

Wherever a task can be simplified without making it a false example of the performance that is of interest, it should be simplified. Vision is not part of the construct of verbal ability, but elderly examinees have trouble reading the 9-point type that appears in many tests. Reprint the test in 14-point type, and their scores go up (Vanderplas & Vanderplas, 1981). Irrelevant easiness is also to be avoided. Particularly in multiple-

Table 5.8   CORRELATIONS OF TESTS SIMILAR
IN FORM OR IN CONTENT

Tests similar in form	
Verbal tests: mechanical vs. electrical	0.8
Pictorial tests: mechanical vs. electrical	0.85
Tests similar in content	
Mechanical: verbal vs. pictorial	0.7
Electrical: verbal vs. pictorial	0.75
Tests different in form and content	
Mechanical verbal vs. electrical pictorial	0.65
Electrical verbal vs. mechanical pictorial	0.6

Source: Conrad, 1944. All correlations are adjusted, to estimate the relations between perfectly reliable tests.

choice tests for domain-referenced interpretation, one wants to avoid clues that enable the test-wise student to detect the right answer.

33. *"Johnny gave 2 marbles to Tommy. If Johnny started with 7 marbles, how many does he have left?" That wording makes the task harder than "Johnny had 7 marbles and gave Tommy 2 of them. How many does Johnny have left?" Is the first word order a source of "irrelevant difficulty" in a test for third-grade arithmetic?*

34. *The Morse code consists of a short alphabet of characters. The receiver must respond to units made up of several characters in rapid succession; the most difficult part of the task may be to separate one letter from the next.*
    a. *Describe an appropriate test for a person learning to receive ordinary nonsecret communications in English.*
    b. *Describe an appropriate test for a person learning to receive encoded messages of the form GFVG JHBI YGTA FBSJ. . . .*

Statistical Properties of Items

Some test constructors try to make items harder by requiring fine discriminations or by offering alternatives that fool the test taker who does not read very closely. They believe that a good test "spreads out people." A content-valid test, however, need not discriminate among persons, and sometimes it should not. A test for applicant messengers ought rule out those who cannot read what messengers have to read, but above that level it is improper to give preference to superior readers.

The test constructor can learn something by correlating the score on

1. If $2x + 2x + 2x = 12$, then $2x - 1 =$

   (A) 2
   (B) 3
   (C) 4
   (D) 5
   (E) 6

2. If $\frac{1}{8}$ of a number is 3, what is $\frac{1}{3}$ of the number?

   (A) 24 (B) 8 (C) 3 (D) 1
   (E) It cannot be determined from the information given.

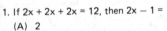

Note: Figure not drawn to scale.

3. In the figure above, if Q, R, and S are points on segment PT the distance from the midpoint of QS to the midpoint of PT is

   (A) 0 (B) 1 (C) 2 (D) 3 (E) 123

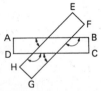

4. In the figure above, if ABCD and EFGH are rectangles, what is the sum of the measures of the marked angles?

   (A) 180°
   (B) 270°
   (C) 360°
   (D) 540°
   (E) It cannot be determined from the information given.

Figure 5.7. Four items from the Mathematics section of the SAT. (*Source*: These items appeared in Taking the SAT (1978) and are reproduced by permission of the Educational Testing Service.)

each item with the total test score. Thus, those who constructed Forms S and T of MCT tried 180 items (some new; some taken from older forms). These were given to high school juniors and seniors, and item scores were correlated with the total score. Only 136 items had correlations greater than 0.2, and the final forms were chosen from these items. Many of the items dropped had to do with electrical apparatus.

Another form of analysis is simple enough to be used routinely by teachers making up objective tests. Even if these items will not be banked for future use, the analysis can suggest how to prepare better items next time. Papers of students with high or low total scores are selected, and tallies are made of the groups' responses to each item. It is appropriate to contrast the highest and lowest quarters of the group, or, in a group of 60 to 100 examinees, the 25 cases at each end of the distribution. If the percentage correct is 70 in the high group and 50 in the low group, the item is consistent with the test as a whole. If the difference in percentages is small (or in the reverse direction), the item is called into question. Separate tallies for options keyed as wrong are also informative. A wrong option that is particularly attractive to high scorers should be reviewed.

Professional test developers elaborate this analysis into an "item characteristic curve" or "item response curve." We have already seen such curves at the end of Chapter 4. Here, a concrete example based on a simpler method will be suggestive. A number of SAT items are shown in Figure 5.7. The curves shown in Figure 5.8 were formed by dividing the group into fifths on the basis of total score, and counting correct responses in each subgroup. (Segment A had, on average, SAT-M scores 1.4 s.d. above the mean.) The slope of the line for Item 4 indicates that it is highly consistent with the total score; it measures what the test as a whole measures. Item 3 is not only extremely difficult but it is just as

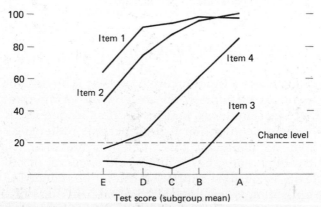

Figure 5.8. **Characteristic curves for the items in Figure 5.7.** (*Source*: Carroll, in Maslow et al., 1980, p. 38.)

hard for average test takers as for the lowest segment. Therefore, we say, it "fails to discriminate" over much of the range. Many test takers did not respond to Item 3, which explains why part of the curve fell below the chance level.

As Chapter 4 said, an item with poor statistics should not automatically be discarded. Statistical analysis spots questionable items. If a review finds a double negative, a too plausible false answer, or other source of trouble, the item should be rewritten, because the flaws tend to confuse able students and reduce validity. Danger arises when many items dealing with the same topic are discarded. That could *reduce* content validity by changing the way test content is distributed over the original domain. In fact, the screening of MCT items eliminated almost all the items related to electricity, thus narrowing the domain the test covers.

An achievement test usually samples mixed content. Dropping unusual items "purifies" the test, but the instrument then no longer represents the intended domain. A person might master the verbal portions of chemistry and still be badly confused about the quantitative parts of the course such as balancing equations. To drop the quantitative sections just because they correlate weakly with the total makes the test a poor sample of the content. On the other hand, if a question correlates poorly with the total because it requires knowledge of a certain chemical compound that few students have read about, the item is probably inappropriate.

35. *Evaluate Items 1 and 2 of Figure 5.7 on the basis of Figure 5.8.*

36. *A job candidate can be observed while directing a few workers in an assembly task. If the task and the standards for judging closely resemble those of the job, content validity could be claimed. It is argued, however, that content validation is insufficient because the persons hired will be trained, and poor performance at the time of application need not forecast poor performance after training. What do you think? (For a debate on the matter see Dreyer and Sackett, 1981, and Norton, 1981.)*

MORE ON CONSTRUCT VALIDATION

Construct validation is a fluid, creative process. The test constructor or any subsequent investigator works to develop an interpretation, persuade others of its soundness, and revise it as inadequacies are recognized. Self-criticism and criticism from persons preferring other interpretations play an important role. The interpretation has scientific aspects, but it often embodies policies and suggests practical actions. This complexity means that validation cannot be reduced to rules, and that no interpretation is the final word, established for all time (Cronbach, in Wainer & Braun, 1988; and in Linn, 1989b).

When the *Standards* were first developed in the 1950s, predictive and content validation were not hard to describe. But how should the validity of a test "of hostility" be defended? The scores might come from everyday observation, role playing, picture interpretation, or a questionnaire. No matter which, analysis of content would not guarantee that the test truly measured hostility. Someone might propose to count aggressive acts as a criterion of hostility. But clinicians believe that some persons are under stress just because they have strong hostile impulses that they dare not release in behavior. A count of aggressive actions would miss those cases. To get at covert hostility, highly indirect assessment may be needed.

The necessary validation process is like the one for scientific concepts and measures. A concept such as "mass" takes its meaning from scientific theory. The adequacy of a measure for mass is judged by whether the numbers it provides relate to other measurements as the theory says it should. When theory changes, a new measure may be needed; thus, Freud reoriented psychology when he produced evidence that absence of hostile behavior does not prove absence of hostile impulses.

An interpretation is to be supported by putting many pieces of evidence together. Positive results validate the measure and the construct simultaneously. Failure to confirm the claim leads to a search for a new measuring procedure *or* for a concept that fits the data better (Cronbach, in Thorndike, 1971; Cronbach & Meehl, 1955; Meehl & Golden, in Kendall & Butcher, 1982; Messick, in Linn, 1989a).

Creating a long-lived theory is an unreasonably lofty aspiration for present-day testers. Physical scientists needed centuries to shape concepts such as the atom and the force of gravity. The eternally patient refining process of pure science sets a standard that here-and-now studies of tests can only admire wistfully. Test interpreters employ a scientific logic but—like engineers and physicians—they have to do the best they can now with comparatively primitive theory.

One source of confusion about construct validation is the notion that the starting point has to be a "definition." How can psychologists claim to measure intelligence when they cannot define it? The eminent journalist Walter Lippmann (1923) made that critical comment when mental tests were first introduced, and it is echoed today. But the opposite question makes better sense. How can one reasonably define a construct until one has made many pertinent observations? Definitions evolve out of reflection on experience. Physical scientists were once content to think of "uranium" as a well-defined object of inquiry; discovering the difference between U-235 and U-238 rendered the old conception obsolete for some important purposes.

Many programs of research have refined the theoretical understanding of particular abilities and traits (Maslow et al., 1980; Sternberg, 1985)—and, of course, such research was going on long before the process was given the special name of construct validation.

Inquiries Contributing to Explanation

MCT Scores as an Example   Table 5.9 illustrates the variety of facts brought to bear in developing and supporting fairly simple explanations of a score. These notes (based on the MCT manuals) are illustrative but by no means complete; a thorough study of mechanical comprehension would consider other reports, including evidence from tests other than Bennett's. Much evidence about mechanical comprehension has accumulated, but almost no one has attempted to theorize about its nature and development. It remains a primitive construct that has been carried through only a "weak" program of research. (On weak programs, see pp. 183–184.)

What do we mean by "explaining" performance on MCT? Essentially, we mean being able to state what influences affect the score and what influences do not. To check whether MCT measures "mechanical intelligence," we would have to ask what is meant by that phrase. If we are told that mechanical intelligence is supposed to be an inborn ability to perform all tasks involving hardware, we can begin research. MCT correlates strongly with a pencil-and-paper test of reasoning with forms, but only weakly with dexterity tests. We are inclined, therefore, to interpret it as a measure of nonverbal problem solving rather than of manipulative skill.

Table 5.9   KINDS OF EVIDENCE OFFERED TO MCT INTERPRETERS

Procedure yielding evidence	Specimen evidence or suggested conclusion
Correlations with practical criteria	(See Table 5.3.)
Correlations with tests of other variables	MCT correlates 0.6 with a test of spatial reasoning and less than 0.4 with a test of dexterity in handling tools.
Demographic correlates	Scores of high school males exceed those of females on average, the difference increasing with grade level.
Content analysis	Most common content of items: hydraulics, structures, gears, pulleys.
Relationship to subjects' experience	Persons who have studied physics score, on average, modestly higher than others.
Experiment with varied testing conditions	Having taken MCT previously gives a subject little or no advantage on a new form.
Internal consistency	Correlations with the total score of items having electrical content are low.

Sources: Manual for the Bennett Mechanical Comprehension Test, 1969, and Manual supplement, 1980.

It is hard to believe that the ability MCT measures is inborn. MCT pictures mechanical devices that did not exist 200 years ago and that persons in a non-Western village have never seen. The test taker has to recognize common industrial devices to earn a good score, so MCT is probably not suitable for selecting factory trainees in a developing country. Even in the United States, not everyone has equal familiarity with the devices pictured. The finding that males tend to surpass females—coupled with our knowledge of traditional sex roles—leads us to suspect that experience is important. The comparatively small advantage associated with study of physics suggests that practical experience counts, not grasp of theory.

Investigators want to know how strong each influence is. I once suspected that much of the MCT score depended on knowledge of specific principles (e.g., gears, levers), each of which enters several items. But I found that a person good on gear problems (for example) was likely to succeed on other items. So my concept of subtypes of mechanical comprehension aptitude was unnecessary. On the other hand, the item analysis described earlier does imply that understanding of electrical processes is a distinct variable.

Before considering research procedures further, let me point a moral. We have just convinced ourselves that MCT does not measure the "mechanical intelligence" our informant offered as an interpretation. That person might say, "MCT is invalid"; we would be wiser to say, "The proposed interpretation is invalid, and we are not persuaded that your notion of 'mechanical intelligence' is a useful construct." Validity of test and validity of construct are inseparable. When a new test is considered for a well-accepted construct, the test is at risk more than the construct. Still, the evidence could compel revision of the construct. A particularly notable example is the abandonment of traditional ideas of "feeblemindedness."

A range of pertinent research techniques has been suggested by Table 5.9. Here is a somewhat fuller list—still not exhaustive. To add concreteness I shall suggest how each technique might be brought to bear on MCT.

- Inspecting items. Inspection alone rules out some explanations; thus, it is easily seen that ability in arithmetic is not a factor.
- Internal correlations (as in my study of items based on different mechanical principles).
- Stability of scores. Is mechanical comprehension a lasting, vocationally significant aptitude? Yes and no; the correlation between ninth- and twelfth-grade scores of boys is about 0.7. Ranks are far from fixed, so case histories of persons who change would be instructive.
- Administering the test to individuals who "think aloud." Perhaps some people succeed by a quick perception of answers that others reach by painstaking logic; if so, a good score means different

things in different persons. The character of errors would be noted. Errors that arise from impulsive response, for example, scarcely imply inability to comprehend machines.

- Varying test procedures experimentally. If it is suggested that having to interpret pictures creates irrelevant difficulty for some test takers, one could set up a "parallel" test in which the person sees the actual machines and responds to the same questions as in the pictorial form. If this change makes items less difficult for many people, doubt is cast on the printed test. Varying the test items, under laboratory controls, can lead to penetrating analysis of the roles played by perception, memory, visualization of motion, and other processes.
- Trying to improve scores. We might try to instruct low-scoring ninth-graders so that they will reason well about mechanical devices, even devices not covered in the instruction. If we succeed, that would have practical value and would suggest how mechanical comprehension develops.
- Correlation with practical criteria.
- Correlation with other tests. If MCT correlates highly with a general mental test, it need not be interpreted in terms of a specialized aptitude.
- Studies of group differences. For example, at what age does MCT performance tend to level off?

Convergence and Divergence of Indicators   To defend a proposition about what a test measures, one looks basically for two things. The first is *convergence* of indicators. To justify a trait label, one collects two or more kinds of data that are regarded as evidence of a person's standing on the variable. If these indicators agree, despite surface dissimilarity, the proposed theoretical interpretation is supported. The fact that Block Design correlates with a verbal reasoning test tends to support the view that both tests measure some general intellectual ability. This "multimethod" principle must be satisfied by any specific construct (Wimsatt, 1981).

Second, scores identified with supposedly distinct aptitudes or traits should not correlate too highly. A test said to measure "ability to reason with numbers" should not rank pupils as a test of sheer computation does, because the computation test cannot reasonably be interpreted as a reasoning test. The interpretation would also be challenged if the correlation with a test of verbal reasoning were very high; "with numbers" would be an inappropriate restriction on the interpretation. This principle of *divergence* of indicators keeps a science from becoming overloaded with many names for the same thing; divergence is sometimes referred to as "discriminant validity" (Campbell & Fiske, 1959). Correlation is not the whole story. Suppose that the students who are the best at writing French are also the best at speaking French. Despite the positive correlation, the tasks are not "the same variable." (This question is pursued further on pp. 493–497.)

I return to Embedded Figures (EFT; p. 16) for an example of research on convergence and divergence. Witkin employed several procedures intended to measure ability to free perception from the domination of a strong framework. Some of his tasks require attending to kinesthetic cues. For example, in Rod-and-Frame one is to turn a rod to the true vertical despite interference from visual cues provided by a tilted square frame. EFT has a moderate correlation (0.4) with Rod-and-Frame; this convergence implied to Witkin that both measured the same variable (which he called "field independence"). The variable correlated little with a conventional "intelligence test," Wechsler's vocabulary measure; that is, the two diverged. Later, EFT was checked against *nonverbal* reasoning tests such as Block Design, and the correlations were high. So Witkin accepted the fact that EFT measures the same adaptive ability that is usually regarded as a central aspect of intelligence. Apparently, only the tests of perception of the vertical measure something separate from the construct of intelligence. For a fuller summary of the hypothesis and evidence see the fourth (1984) edition of this book (pp. 264ff.).

Strong and Weak Construct Validation

"Almost any type of information about a test can make some contribution to an understanding of its construct validity." That statement from the manual of the fourth edition of the Stanford-Binet scale (Thorndike et al., 1986, p. 52) reflects what may be called a weak approach to construct validation.

A strong approach looks on construct validation as tough-minded testing of specific hypotheses:

> [T]heoretical concepts are defined conceptually or implicitly by their role in a network of nomological or statistical "laws." The meaning is partially given by the theoretical network, however tentative and as yet impoverished that network may be. Crudely put, you know what you mean by an entity to the extent that statements about it in the theoretical language are linked to statements in the observational language. These statements are about where it's found, what it does, what it's made of. Only a few of those properties are directly tied to observables [p. 136]. In [an early] theory sketch, based upon some experience and data, everything said is conjectural. We have tentative notions about some indicators of the construct with unknown validities [p. 144]. [When we check up empirically on predictions from the model] we are testing the crude theory sketch, we are tightening the network psychometrically, and we are validating the indicators. All of these are done simultaneously [p. 149]. [Extracted with elisions and some paraphrase from Meehl & Golden, in Kendall & Butcher, 1982.]

The Meehl-Golden statement calls for validation driven by theory; studies are favored that specifically challenge (hence offer the possibility of confirming!) the proposed interpretation.

The statement of Thorndike et al. refers to an essentially undirected and inductive process. On the "Dragnet" show, the good cop used to say, "Just give us the facts, ma'am." Indiscriminate interest in any and all facts makes for a weak program of construct validation—somewhat instructive, but not focused and not pointedly critical. Under the heading "construct validation," many manuals print loose compilations of miscellaneous information. Although the argument regarding the validity of MCT that I have just laid out has a decidedly omnidirectional character, it is not discreditable because the accumulated research *has* shaped a better understanding.

A strong program of construct validation tries to resolve crucial uncertainties. This research style has often been described as if the starting point is an elaborate theoretical interpretation. Few test interpretations, however, have been subject to the decades of persistent research that produce a network of formal theory. Strong challenges are equally appropriate for tentative interpretations.

The heart of the strategy is recognizing *plausible rival hypotheses*. That is, one tries to think of challenges to the interpretation that might be made by the advocate of another theory or of a competing test. The challenge usually takes the form of a counterinterpretation (as when I suggested that MCT was an inventory of scattered mechanical concepts rather than a measure of a unified mental ability). Having recognized an issue as important, the validator collects evidence that bears directly on it (as when I investigated whether items on comprehension of various machines converge). Not every rival hypothesis is checked out; there are too many of them. The focus at any time should be on those that make the best sense, in the light of prior experience, *and* that would have a strong effect on whether and how the test is used. Contradicting the original interpretation does not spell doom for the test or the construct; almost always, the theory can be revised or hedged so as to account for the new facts (Cronbach, in Linn, 1989b).

37. *Why would it be valuable to find out "what a test of pharmacy aptitude measures" if we already know that it predicts success in pharmacy school?*

38. *Kohs (1923, pp. 168ff.) wished to argue that his Block Design test measured "intelligence," defined as "ability to analyze and synthesize." He then offered the following types of evidence (plus others) for his claim. How does each of these bear on construct validity? (The Stanford-Binet test was at that time regarded as the best available measure of "intelligence" but was thought possibly to depend too heavily on verbal ability and school training.)*
   a. *Logical analysis of mental processes required by the items.*
   b. *Increase in average score with each year of age.*

c. *Correlations as follows:*

Binet score with age	*0.8*
Block Design score with age	*0.65*
Block Design score with Binet score	*0.8*

d. *Correlations:*

Binet score with teachers' estimates of intelligence	*0.45*
Block Design score with teachers' estimates of intelligence	*0.25*

e. *Correlations:*

Binet score with vocabulary	*0.9*
Block Design score with vocabulary	*0.8*

f. *Correlations between successive trials:*

On Binet	*0.91*
On Block Design	*0.84*

39. *For a test of computation given with a time limit, one significant aspect of interpretation is how "speeded" the test is. What would be learned from each of these studies?*
    a. *After the regular time expires, students continue work for 10 more minutes, using a different color of pencil. The changes in score are tabulated.*
    b. *Forms 1 and 2 are given with the regular time limit; double that time is allowed for Form 3. The investigator compares r_{13} with r_{12}.*
    c. *Having given Forms 1 and 3 described in b, the investigator waits for a measure C of success in bookkeeping and compares r_{3C} with r_{1C}.*

40. *The attempt to show that there is no irrelevant difficulty in a test amounts to a check on "rival hypotheses." Defend this statement.*

VALIDATION AS PERSUASIVE ARGUMENT

An interpretation or recommendation based on a test score requires a persuasive defense. Within an organization, one member may be persuaded that the test should be relied on. A second member, equally qualified but weighing up the risks and values differently, will prefer to rely on non-test information. The two have to argue it out. In validation, the bottom line is the collective judgment of a forum of critical users (Cronbach, in Wainer & Braun, 1988).

Employers defending tests whose validity is challenged in court often have to rely on indirect reasoning. Whenever their evidence departs from the ideal plan of a direct criterion-oriented or content-oriented study, interpretation brings in concepts and theoretical statements.

The Equal Employment Opportunity Commission has been reluctant to accept indirect reasoning, apparently regarding it as a verbal smokescreen (Gorham, in Maslow et al., 1980; Novick, in Wigdor & Garner, Vol. 2, 1982). Lawyers and psychologists are trying—with increasing success—to work out a style of indirect validation argument that courts find persuasive (Bersoff, in Glaser & Bond, 1981).

Many sentences are required to defend an inference from a score.

Some of these sentences are value judgments, some are appeals to common sense or prior evidence, and some are logical or legal premises. If the relevant audience finds the sentences plausible and the chain of argument coherent, it accepts the conclusion. A critic, replacing a sentence with a plausible alternative, can reach a contrary conclusion. When discussion is confined within the profession, it is fellow experts whom the interpreter must persuade. Other interpretations reach a public forum; the psychologist's view is adopted only if nonspecialists find her argument more reasonable than competing arguments.

Consider one of the simplest examples from early in the chapter. Students enter a law school, and their subsequent grades are cross-tabulated against test scores to form an experience table. When used for prediction, the experience table is reinterpreted as an expectancy table. Asked to defend the extension, you assert that nothing much in the situation is changing from year to year. Your argument becomes more impressive when you describe next year's applicant pool, faculty, and curriculum. The example hints at what it means to defend an interpretation by combining sentences.

With student motivation, grading standards, and instructional styles all changing, it would be foolish to assert that test-criterion relations never change (Rubin & Stroud, 1977). In law schools, as a matter of fact, the validity of undergraduate grades as a predictor declined by nearly 0.1 between the 1960s and the early 1970s (reported by Schrader, in Law School Admission Council, 1977, p. 530). In this same time span the validity of LSAT actually rose a bit. Distraction of undergraduates from study during the years of student protest is a possible explanation; grade inflation may also have affected the relation.

The person investigating a test would be wise to concentrate on counterhypotheses a critic could make plausible. The job of validation is partly to support an interpretation, and partly to detect anything wrong with it. A proposition deserves some degree of trust only after it has survived serious challenge. In the law school data, for example, it is important to check whether what has been true of applicants in general is true of the mature women who are being attracted to law schools in increasing numbers. A proposal to apply the test in a new site, before data are collected there, requires close comparison of the new situation with the one studied. Lacking that, only those who think all law schools are alike should believe the validity claim.

A validity coefficient supports an argument from only one corner (Figure 5.9). Other reports are needed, to answer challenges such as these:

- What justifies *this* criterion? What biases does it have?
- Does a steep regression imply that the ability measured is necessary for the course of study? Or could instructors adapt so as to make the course easier for the low scorers? (High predictive validity implies bad instruction, says the egalitarian critic.)

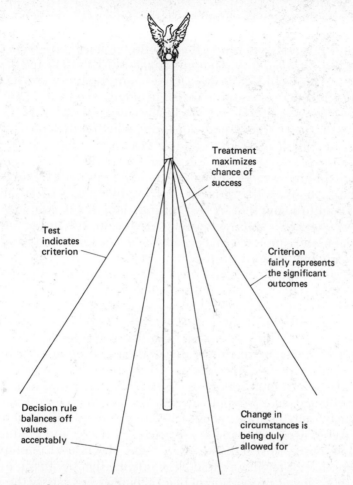

Figure 5.9. **Considerations supporting validity argument for selection program.**
(*Source*: This figure appeared in Cronbach, 1980, and is reproduced (as adapted)
by permission of Jossey-Bass, Inc.)

- Among the applicants who meet a reasonable standard, all of
  whom will probably be adequate students, what justifies creaming
  off the ones who scored highest?
- Present selection practices concentrate high scorers in prestige
  schools. In this mechanism better for the nation than one that
  would distribute qualified law students more evenly over schools?

The whole selection system is to be justified, not the test alone. Empirical propositions enter the defense of the criterion, of the instruction
or job requirements, and of the decision procedure, but values and prior
beliefs within the audience determine what is judged reasonable.

An argument focusing on test content is likewise subject to challenges. Proof that the test samples a stated domain properly is not a complete argument. The defense must be prepared to show that the domain is relevant. A good example is the scrutiny a court gave a test for fire fighters (*Vulcan Society* v. *Commissioners*, 6FEP 1045 [1973]). Many candidates who would otherwise have been eligible were blocked by the few arithmetic items in the test. The court asked how critical those items were to the fire fighter's work. Not very, was its answer. Certain physics items the court scorned, not caring whether they measured what the tester intended. The judge had this to say about the item pictured in Figure 5.10: "A high school physics student would know the correct answer is (C), but the wrong answer (A) might be more useful for a fireman on the job." About another item he said: [W]hile it may be of some value for a fireman to know that 'A ball rolling along level ground will slow down and come to a stop,' we cannot appreciate the importance of his knowing whether the force that accomplishes this is called velocity, momentum, friction, or equilibrium."

When the content of a test does pass scrutiny, the argument is far from finished. This is illustrated in Jaeger's review of tests as diploma requirements (in Linn, 1989a). As was said at page 172, courts have ruled that such a test abridges student rights if the school does not match the test to the curriculum; test content and instruction have been adjusted to meet that standard. The advocates of the requirement, however, had claimed that imposing standards would improve the economic chances of students by making them better qualified. According to Jaeger, evidence (collected on a competency test that did not control graduation) shows the employment rate at ages 20–25, and the earnings of those employed, to be nearly the same for average graduates and graduates who scored low on the test. On the other hand, the rate of unemployment among youths not having a diploma was twice that of others. Add, now, the fact that a lower proportion of blacks than whites satisfy the standard set by the test. It seems that requiring the test makes blacks less likely

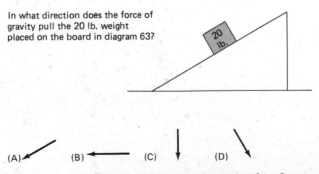

Figure 5.10. **Item from a test for fire fighters.** (*Source*: This figure appeared in Cronbach, 1980, and is reproduced (as adapted) by permission of Jossey-Bass, Inc.)

to graduate, and so *impairs* their economic future. Note, then, how a claim of validity made on content grounds is being challenged by an appeal to predictive evidence and to values beyond subject matter competence.

A test user's argument is specific to her own plans for interpretation. A test developer reasoning about validity, however, is expected to lay out evidence and argument that will help the entire profession make sense of scores from the test. Users will want to know about the processes required for successful test performance, about the relation of this score to traits that are better understood, about background factors associated with good and poor scores, and so on. Such information helps them to recognize what alternative interpretations of scores are plausible wherever they use the test. The test developer, not knowing the tester's particular subjects and local situation, cannot tell the tester what to think. The developer records experience with the test and brings out ideas the interpreter should consider. Also, she shows that certain interpretations that might come to mind should be rejected, in the light of that evidence.

This chapter has only introduced the types of reasoning that enter validation argument. The ideas will have to be extended through examples and explanations in many further chapters.

Chapter
6

How to Judge Tests: Reliability and Other Qualities

6A. The reliability coefficient and the standard error of measurement serve different purposes. Explain.

6B. How can a test interpreter use the information that the standard error of measurement is 4 raw-score points?

6C. Do all procedures that yield reliability coefficients for a test answer the same question?

6D. In what ways can the reliability of measurement be increased? Do these changes improve validity?

6E. A particular test is suggested to serve a certain purpose. The purpose will influence the evaluator's judgment regarding the test's administrative and statistical characteristics. Illustrate.

Abbreviations in this chapter: MCT for the Mechanical Comprehension Test (Bennett or Differential Aptitude Tests); SAT for the Scholastic Aptitude Test; s.e.m. for standard error of measurement.

ORIENTATION

This chapter first develops thoroughly the concept of reliability. The final section pulls together many considerations from this chapter and earlier ones.

The central concern of reliability studies is this: If people were tested twice, would the two score reports agree? How closely? In the section titled "errors of measurement," your major concern should be to understand five linked terms—*observed score, true score, error, standard error of measurement (s.e.m.),* and *reliability coefficient*. All the discussion down to page 214 revolves around them. In particular the s.e.m. will reappear often in later chapters. The subsection on generalizability illustrates how a measurement may contain errors of several kinds. An understanding of kinds of error is needed when we compare estimation procedures.

You need to associate the name of each procedure described in the second section with the question answered by the procedure. (That understanding will enable you to give meaning to a report on reliability found in a test manual or journal.) Note which procedures tend to give larger values and why. The formulas in the tables look forbidding, but they are easy to apply. With regard to Table 6.1, try to understand what features of a test or group of examinees make particular components larger or smaller. With regard to internal consistency, you need to know what questions such analyses can and cannot answer, and to see that differently named procedures usually reach the same conclusion. Note the warnings about when these coefficients overestimate and underestimate.

The section on interpreting findings makes many important points. Once you grasp fully the one main conclusion each subsection is developing, subordinate details will seem almost obvious. Pay attention to formula (7). Directly calculated validity coefficients can be misleading, and adjusting for measurement error usually provides a better answer to the validity question. Even if you never will make such a calculation, when you read reports on validity you should have this possible correction in mind.

The "further considerations" (p. 214) can make the difference between a successful testing program and an unsuccessful one, so they are important. But you will find the section easy to follow. Equally easy and still more important is the final section. In the checklist for reviewing a test, think through which entries should weigh most heavily in judging how satisfactory a particular test is likely to be.

ERRORS OF MEASUREMENT

In a 3-minute work sample, Mike types 162 words, or 54 words per minute; how well does this score represent Mike's skill? Suppose the teacher requires typing at 50 WPM before a student takes up shorthand.

Is Mike truly above this level? Mike scored 45 WPM last week. Does today's score of 54 show that he has changed his technique for the better? Or is the change a chance fluctuation?

There are many reasons for inconsistency from one measurement to another. Attention and effort change from moment to moment. Over longer periods, score changes come from physical growth, learning, or changes in health and personality. Using fresh questions for the second measurement introduces another type of variation. The person who finds the first set of questions easy may find some unfamiliar questions in the next set.

True-Score Theory

In test theory, the term *error* refers to unwanted variation. The tester would prefer to base conclusions on an ideal error-free score. Theoretically, testing could be continued until errors balance out, and one would have what is traditionally called the *true score*. Any particular testing produces an *observed score*. Because the behavior sample is limited, this observed score differs from the true score. The difference is, by definition, the error of measurement. Occasional lapses bring the observed score below the true score. An atypical success (luck? alertness? getting all the moves together?) can produce an observed score greater than the true level. (Technical statements in this chapter apply most exactly to raw scores of tests and items, and to standard scores. The same concepts apply to the other types of score introduced in Chapter 4, but the interpretations of the standard error and the reliability coefficient apply only loosely to, for example, percentiles.)

As a first example, suppose that students of physical education are being trained to time races with stopwatches. On one race, their times for the winner spread out: 23.7, 24.0, 24.2, . . ., 25.1, 25.2 seconds. Since they disagree, we say that variable error enters the measurements. The students probably vary in quickness of reaction, and they may not be attending to the same cues.

The mean of the times might be 24.7. This value approximates what true-score theory calls the "true" time of the winner.

The Standard Error   The set of measurements has a standard deviation (pp. 114–121). We call the standard deviation of a set of measures of the same event or object its *standard error of measurement* or s.e.m. The larger the s.e.m., the less accurate the measurement. The square of an s.e.m. is an *error variance*.

"Constant error" is ignored by those calculations. Suppose that a trustworthy electronic timer recorded the time for this trial as 24.0. On average, the trainees are wrong by 0.7 seconds. Constant error is usually left out of the s.e.m. because a constant error does not affect comparative standings.

Subtleties remain to be considered. We might want to track down kinds of error: starting the watch early or late, variation in reacting when the winner breasts the tape, and errors in reading the watch. Also, instead of being interested in this one race we might be interested in the runner's normal time for the distance. If that is the "true score" of interest, errors in timing are only part of the story. Whatever made the runner faster today than usual, or slower, is another source of unwanted variation. To answer subtler questions would require more elaborate data.

The s.e.m. tells how widely measures on the same person are likely to spread. It is customary to assume that errors have a normal distribution (p. 120). Then an error greater than 1 s.e.m. (considering both positive and negative errors) occurs one-third of the time. If the s.e.m. is 3.5 in a large set of measurements, two-thirds of the variable errors will fall between -3.5 and $+3.5$.

Robert Finchley scored 63 on a mechanical comprehension test (Figure 4.6, p. 122). Its s.e.m. is 3.5, so the odds are 2-to-1 that Robert's true score is in the interval 59.5–66.5. Those numbers were converted to percentiles to get the *confidence band*—88th to 98th percentile—which is shaded on Robert's profile. If Robert and his classmates are tested many times, with no practice effect or other change in ability, two-thirds of them will have average scores lying within the confidence bands formed in this way.

Norm-referenced testing is mostly concerned with comparing individuals. The accuracy of such comparisons is often described by a reliability coefficient. Reliability coefficients are valuable. But do not lose sight of the fact that the coefficient does not describe the accuracy of domain-referenced information or of comparisons of performance against a standard. The s.e.m. is far more relevant for those purposes, especially if any constant error is recognized alongside it.

The Reliability Coefficient   A variance is a squared standard deviation (p. 115). Because errors average zero when the constant error is ignored, the following formula holds. Variance of true scores plus variance of errors equals variance of observed scores. We may write that in another way:

True-score variance = Observed-score variance − Error variance

We obtain the variance of observed scores of a group of persons and subtract the error variance to estimate true-score variance. The reliability coefficient is a ratio:

$$r_{xx'} = \frac{\text{True-score variance}}{\text{Observed-score variance}}$$

The traditional symbol $r_{xx'}$ suggests the correlation of one measure X with a similar measure X'. Correlating scores from two forms of a test is one of several ways to estimate reliability.

The coefficient reaches 1.00 when the measurements contain no variable error. If there is as much error as true information in scores, the coefficient is 0.50. Thus (ignoring the decimal) $r_{xx'}$ directly answers the question "What percentage of the test-score variance is attributable to true differences rather than error?"

The coefficient and the s.e.m. have this relation:

$$\text{s.e.m.}^2 = \text{Observed-score variance} \times (1 - r_{xx'})$$

The s.e.m. is unlikely to change greatly from one group to another (unless the test is extremely easy or extremely hard for one group). But groups have different variances, so the reliability is likely to change with the group (see p. 206). That fact makes s.e.m. more fundamental than the coefficient.

1. *An employment interviewer asks, "How many jobs have you held since you left high school?" If we consider the response as an observed score, what is meant by "error of measurement" and "true score" in this case?*

2. *In speaking about hearing tests for children, a writer says: "Physical and psychological changes from day to day may make an average of half-tests at two sittings less valid than a complete test at one sitting. We find that we get worse results on cloudy days than on sunny days."*

   Can you defend the contrary statement that the combined scores from two sittings would be more valid than a complete test at one sitting?

3. *Why is the s.e.m. more relevant in domain-referenced interpretation than the reliability coefficient?*

4. *We could construct a confidence band that reaches out 2 s.e.m. on each side of an observed score. If we did this with Robert Finchley, we could make a firmer statement about his true scores; the odds change from 2 : 1 to about 20 : 1. What is the disadvantage of such high-confidence bands?*

5. *Figure 4.8 (p. 125) displayed scores of five children. In the group tested, the standard errors of the six subtest raw scores range from 1.1 to 1.6. The section raw scores have s.e.m. near 2.0 (about 0.5 point on the stanine scale). For the composite, s.e.m. is 3.4—again, about half a stanine unit. How should this information influence the teacher's decision about whether, in trying to develop these skills, her instructional emphasis for Emily and Kaveh should differ?*

6. *In former days SAT scores were reported to three digits: 772, 502,. . . . In recent years the reported score always has zero as the last digit, because admissions officers were taking too seriously the fact that Peter at 606 "had done better" than Paul at 604.*
   a. *Rounding to the nearest 10 points put Peter at 610 and Paul at 600. Whom did rounding help, on average?*
   b. *If 30 is the s.e.m. of SAT Total, what is to be said for or against rounding to the nearest 30 points?*
   c. *If Susan's score is 720, the s.e.m. implies a 2-to-1 chance that her true score is between 690 and 750. The comparable estimate for Daisy is 720–780. Should an admissions officer disregard the difference?*

7. *The Law School Admission Test is reported on a standard-score scale with*

a standard deviation of 8. On this scale, one unit is equal to about half the
s.e.m. Does choice of this scale avoid (or reduce) the problem of overinter-
pretation considered in question 6?

Generalizability Theory

The true-score theory just summarized is the basis for most reports on
error found in test manuals. Other procedures, more flexible and with a
different terminology, are prominent in research, particularly when everyday behavior is observed. Generalizability theory (Brennan, 1983;
Cronbach et al., 1972) distinguishes among sources of error. Resolving
error into components and finding out how large each component is tells
more about a measuring procedure than the traditional analysis does.

At 10:10 A.M. on May 5, Ms. Brown asked Mike to type a passage
from a news report on the United Nations; the paper was scored by Alice
Gates, Ms. Brown's student helper. No one was especially interested in
how well Mike could type at 10:10; a measure at any other hour of the
day would have been equally relevant. Nor did anyone wish to measure
him on this news report; any similarly difficult selection would serve.
Ms. Brown could accept a different tester and a different scorer. There
are at least five distinguishable influences on Mike's score: day, time
within the day, passage typed, tester, and scorer.

On some days Mike feels livelier. Some passages are easier for him
than others because he finds some words easier spell and some sentences easier to carry in mind. Probably tester and scorer effects are
small, but they should not be forgotten. Each of these variations in conditions is a *source of variance,* because if Mike were retested under a
new condition, his score would change.

The psychologist or educator setting out to measure a variable intends, almost always, to generalize to a relevant *domain* or *universe* of
observations. (The profession uses both terms.) Ms. Brown may require
ability to type at 50 WPM before a student takes up shorthand. For that
purpose, the average speed of *all* Mike's typing during May is of far more
interest than any one test. If it were possible to observe all typing, the
average of those scores would be the *universe score.*

The universe score is much like a true score. What is the difference?
True-score theory is worded as if error variance is all of a kind and as if a
person has one true score. Generalizability theory recognizes alternative
universes of generalization, hence many universe scores.

Only after the universe is defined can we say which sources of variance count as "error." If Ms. Brown intends to plot day-by-day records
to see which students have stabilized their skills, the universe for the
May 5 observation is limited to scores on that day. Mike has up days and
down days; that is a fact Ms. Brown wants the chart to represent, not
"error of observation." To decide whether Mike is proficient enough to

take up shorthand, Ms. Brown wants to know Mike's typical level. The relevant universe extends over several weeks. Today's "up"—a departure from the average over that universe—is now regarded as a source of error.

As a second example, consider ratings of preschool children on friendliness. An observer is to rate each child after observing him for 5 minutes in each of three situations: in the sandbox, on playground equipment, and at the juice break. The most evident sources of variation are these:

- Observer. Some raters are generous; some are not. Some are especially generous in rating cute redheads; some, in rating children belonging to racial minorities. An act that one observer considered to be "friendly" is counted as neutral by another.
- Situation. The three situations by no means exhaust the events of the preschool day. Some children would be less friendly in a competitive game.
- Occasion. Even in a defined situation such as the juice break, behavior varies from day to day as weather, companions and objects present, and the child's mood all change.

An investigator trying to assess effects of day care would want to generalize broadly—over observers, situations, and occasions

Generalizability analysis goes beyond classical reliability analysis by pointedly asking, "What does *this* analytic procedure count as error?" and "How much variation arises *from each source?*" Knowing which sources of variance are large contributes to construct interpretation. We find (let us say) that the extent to which a child engages in cooperative play depends on which companions are available. This finding denies that "cooperativeness" is a trait within the child's skin. We have to shift to a construct characterizing the children as pairs.

Generalizability studies help in designing measuring procedures. When we sample typing performance repeatedly, scores vary. Selections are not equally difficult, and the individual's efficiency fluctuates. One passage on one day is a tiny sample. To obtain a more accurate score, we might have the person type three passages on the same day. Or we might have each passage typed on a different day. Both observations are "three times as long" as the one-trial test, but they are not equally good bases for estimating the universe score over passages and days. The first plan samples passages three times; days, only once. Use of one passage on each of 3 days samples *each* source of error three times—a better basis for conclusions. Generalizability studies enable one to estimate how greatly scores are affected by each such change. (One application of this thinking appears on p. 608.)

8. *What sources might produce variation among scores when a person takes several similar block design tests?*

9. *A teacher's rapport with pupils is judged by asking pupils to respond to a number of questions, such as "Does your teacher give fair marks?" The most evident sources of variation are the questions (because other similar questions could be asked), the pupils, and the occasion. For what type of decision or investigation would one define the universe to include*
    a. *all possible pupils and questions, with observations limited to this particular semester?*
    b. *all similar questions, but only pupils in one class at this time?*

10. *Criteria as well as tests have error of measurement. What would be unwanted sources of variance—errors of observation—in first-year grade point averages at a particular college? (The answer depends on your concept of "true grade average.")*

ESTIMATION METHODS

Simple Correlational Studies

Physical scientists study error by comparing multiple independent measurements. Behavioral scientists use this method when they can, but retesting a person several times is not often practical. Moreover, a human characteristic tends to change over a series of trials. Fortunately, we can assess the magnitude of errors from just two comparable measurements on each of many persons.

One procedure applies equivalent ("parallel") forms of a test. Forms are *equivalent* if they have essentially similar content, structure, and statistical properties. Correlating equivalent forms estimates a reliability coefficient. Multiplying the coefficient by the observed-score variance estimates the true-score variance (as can be seen from the formula for $r_{xx'}$). Subtracting true-score variance from observed-score variance estimates the error variance. Taking its square root gives the s.e.m.

Two measurements per person can be collected in various ways, and each procedure answers a somewhat different question. I illustrate here with made-up (but realistic) numbers for ninth-graders taking the MCT. To simplify, assume that the observed variance is 116.6 in every set of scores. Here are three possible correlational studies:

1. Two forms given *on the same day*. Form S given in the morning correlates 0.92 with Form T given in the afternoon. The true-score variance is 0.92 × 116.6, or 107.3. When we subtract, the error variance is 9.3. Or, we might say, 8 per cent (= 100% − 92%) of observed variance is error variance; and 8 per cent of 116.6 is 9.3. Taking the square root, s.e.m. = 3.1.

2. Two forms given *4 weeks apart*. With 4 weeks separating the forms, the correlation drops to 0.89. Taking 11 per cent of 116.6 gives the error variance as approximately 13; s.e.m. = 3.6.

3. Two forms given *1 year apart*. Greater time lapse allows more

change in standings, and the correlation drops to 0.79. The error
variance and s.e.m. are approximately 25 and 5, respectively.

The three studies give reliability coefficients (and standard errors) with
different meanings. *To speak of "the" reliability of a test glosses over
fundamentals.* The first study tells about the consistency among measurements on the same day, a narrow universe. The second study samples
from a broader universe but one during which the students' development remains essentially constant. The third study moves to a question
not so much about accuracy as about student development: Will we
reach the same conclusions about students' mechanical aptitude if we
test in Grade 9 as we will if we wait a year?

Think through the following question. Which of the following
sources would Study 1 count as error variance? Study 2? Study 3?

a. Some testers give directions clearly and fully; some do not. The
tester in this school changes from one year to the next.
b. A student's alertness is affected by health and anxiety.
c. The test forms are not (let us suppose) equally difficult. Scores on
the second form tend to run 3 points higher for everyone.
d. One form (let us suppose) contains several items that require numerical reasoning; the other does not.

Influence *d* causes some persons to do better on one form than the
other. In Study 1, *d* adds to the s.e.m., but *a*, *b*, and *c* do not. The tester
is constant; health and mood ought not to change from morning to afternoon. Increasing everyone's score by 3 points does not affect the
correlation. . . . Among the sources listed, *b* and *d* enter the error variance for Study 2. . . . In Study 3, *a*, *b*, and *d* count in the error variance.
Differences in the students' development are a further large source of
inconsistency in Study 3.

In all the studies, the error variance includes moment-to-moment
fluctuation of efficiency and luck. An immediate repetition of, say, a tennis serve will not produce the identical result even though the performer
has not changed in any identifiable way. Another unsystematic influence
is borderline decisions of the scorer.

In general, the greater the time interval the lower the correlation. A
correlation of measures separated by a long interval reports the *stability*
of the characteristic in whatever environment the test takers experienced. To study short-term variation may seem trivial, but fine-grain
studies of behavior look at day-to-day change. (Recall Zuckerman's study
of state anxiety; p. 80.) Indeed, change from hour to hour is examined
in comparing drug effects or experimental variations in tasks. The less
stable the measure under any one condition is from hour to hour, the
more subjects the investigator must test to reach a firm conclusion.

The one-day study answers another important question: Do we have
a sufficient sample of items? If two forms on the same day disagree
badly, the test is inadequate.

If some aspect of the situation or measuring procedure changes from one observation to the next, its influence on the ranking of individuals is counted in the error variance. Some other aspect remains unchanged; its effect on the standing of individuals is not counted in the error estimate. This is a mistake, unless the universe definition calls for holding that aspect constant. Holding too much constant overestimates the coefficient, and underestimates the error of measurement. The reader of a study must ask the pointed question: Are there potentially important sources of error that this estimate of error ignores?

If scores are obtained by having two judges score every test paper, the agreement of the scores evaluates only one source of error: that coming from the judge. The coefficient tells how well we can generalize from one scoring to the score a universe of judges would assign to *that same performance*. It does not tell how well we have sampled the person's behavior; it tells how well we have sampled judgments.

Some key points of this section will be reviewed after procedures have been examined more fully. This book rarely gives formulas or notes on computation because that is the job of texts on statistics. Many formulas appear in this chapter, however, because texts on statistics usually say little about how to estimate measurement error.

11. *Interpret these facts about a test measuring "liberality" of political attitudes.*

Coefficient from two forms taken at same sitting	0.90
Coefficient from two forms, 1 year apart	0.60
Coefficient from test, and retest with same form, 1 year apart	0.65

12. *A tester presents questions such as "Do you make friends easily?" with the response alternatives* YES/NO/CANNOT SAY. *If there were two forms, correlational studies of types 1, 2, and 3 could be carried out. What would contribute to error variance in each study? (Is there any counterpart of "luck" in this kind of test?)*

13. *Some studies of error examine whether two procedures for sampling behavior agree (equivalence). Other studies examine whether behavior is consistent over time (stability). Considering observations of stammering, describe a study that would primarily bring out information on equivalence and another that would primarily check on stability.*

14. *The MCT examples discussed in this section compared scores on forms S and T. Thus alternate-forms coefficients were obtained, with various time lapses. Giving form S twice would have produced a "retest reliability." Would you expect it to be higher or lower than r_{ST} when the time lapse is 1 week? when the time lapse is 2 hours?*

Estimation from a Two-Way Score Table

Analysis based on generalizability theory can be quite elaborate; here I illustrate only some main ideas. Suppose that 25 persons have typed five passages, each passage on a different day (Table 6.1). From the table

Table 6.1   ANALYSIS FOR FIVE OBSERVATIONS OF TYPING SPEED

| Pupil (p) | Observed scores X_{pi} | | | | |
	A	B	C	D	E
Mike	54	57	51	50	51
Joe	52	55	56	53	52
Carlos	50	46	49	52	50
Bruce	52	51	52	43	54
Newt	53	53	43	47	50
. . . .					
. . . .					
. . . .					
Averages	52.2	53.0	51.4	51.2	51.7

Number of persons $N = 25$
Number of conditions $k = 5$

From analysis of variance:

MSp : Mean square for rows (persons)   = 50
MSi : Mean square for columns (conditions)   = 10
MSr : Mean square for residual   = 3

Estimated variance of person effects (universe scores):

$(MSp - MSr)/k = (50 - 3)/5 = 9.40$

> Component for persons

Estimated variance of condition effects:

$(MSi - MSr)/N = (10 - 3)/25 = 0.28$

> Component for conditions

Estimated residual variance:

MSr $= 3.00$

> Residual component

of scores informative "components of variance" are derived, leading to summary coefficients and standard errors. A standard computer package for analysis of variance turns out the mean squares in the table, and the formulas shown convert them to components of variance.

The investigator is interested in generalizing over many selections and over all occasions within a certain time span. The *component for persons*, 9.4, estimates the variance of universe scores, the scores that exhaustive measurement—many selections, many occasions—would produce.

The *component for conditions* tells how much the population average fluctuates from one selection and day to another. This component turned out to be small. This is usual. We find little variation in difficulty over same-level forms of a professionally developed ability test. Teacher-made tests on a body of content are likely to be less nearly equivalent; then the condition component can be large. Variation over conditions is often large in data from everyday life, as is illustrated by the nurses' state-anxiety scores (p. 80).

The *residual component* (ordinarily large) includes all manner of unsystematic effects: Several times in Selection E Joe encountered a word he found hard to spell; Newt, between Tests B and C, lost several days of practice on account of illness; Bruce slipped into typing *h-t-e* several times on Test D. The residual component assesses errors that affect individual differences when everyone is observed under any one uniform condition (here, the same selection on the same day). The variance component of 3 implies an s.e.m. of 1.7. This s.e.m. is relevant when individual differences on a particular testing are the main concern.

Error variance plus true-score variance gives observed-score variance: $3.0 + 9.4 = 12.4$.

The reliability coefficient is 9.4/12.4, or 0.76, according to the formula introduced earlier. It estimates the correlation to be expected if we choose two selection-and-day combinations, test everyone, and correlate the scores. The coefficient would be higher and the s.e.m. lower when the observed score being interpreted is the average of scores on two or more passages. The pertinent formulas will appear in the next sections.

Return to the question: Is Mike ready to take up shorthand? This decision depends on whether his universe score is above 50. Because the difficulty of the selection affects his observed score, the component for conditions adds into the error. The error variance for *this* use of a one-passage test is 0.28 plus 3.00; the corresponding s.e.m. is $\sqrt{3.28} = 1.8$. (The added component barely changed the s.e.m.) Mike's first score of 54 is more than 2 s.e.m. above 50. If the teacher has to base the decision on that one score, the conclusion must be that Mike's universe score qualifies him for shorthand.

Table 6.1 is, obviously, a two-way layout. Some data sets are more complex. With appropriate design and computation one can tease apart variances in children's social interaction, for example, associated with observers, days, situations, and playmates (Cronbach et al., 1972). If behavior varies from playmate to playmate, the investigator will plan in the future to collect data with several playmates (in turn) for each child. If, on the contrary, that component of variation is small, playmates can be regarded as interchangeable. The investigator will get an adequate reading by observing the child with any available playmate. For another example of such an investigation, see Figure 13.2 and the accompanying discussion (p. 502).

15. *Suppose that students type the same passage every day for 5 days. Would analysis of the table of those scores answer the same questions as the analysis of Table 6.1?*

16. *Suppose that, when samples from various sections of the newspaper are typed, scores show a large component for conditions. The tester might fix*

on one condition (such as the sports section) or combine conditions. For what purpose, if any, would you recommend each option?

17. *To investigate accuracy of scoring of a test administered individually, three observers watch the testing through a one-way window, keep independent records, and score. In this way, three scores are obtained on each of 20 children. What question is answered by each of the following?*
   a. *The variance component for persons.*
   b. *The variance component for observers.*
   c. *The residual component.*

Internal-Consistency Formulas

The usual observed score is a sum or average over items, trials, raters, or occasions or over a combination of these. The tester analyzing a composite can array the scores on the *parts*, and examine their consistency. Table 6.2 shows the form for a layout of item scores, adds two scores for half-tests, and reports several variances that we could calculate directly if all the scores were listed. The proportion passing P is the column mean for the data set, and Q is the remainder, $1 - P$.

Several convenient formulas produce what statisticians know as an intraclass correlation and testers know as an *alpha coefficient*. Using the Greek letter alpha (α), α_k symbolizes a reliability coefficient for an average or total of k observations. A reliability coefficient for average scores is the same as that for total scores, and it is essentially equivalent to the correlation between two such composites.

The s.e.m. for an average of several measurements of the same person is obtained by multiplying $1 - \alpha_k$ by the observed-score variance for the composite, then taking the square root. The s.e.m. for a total is k times as large.

Four internal-consistency formulas appear in the next three tables. Do not focus on the details; these are presented to help if you ever make the calculations. The important point is that, when used appropriately,

Table 6.2 DATA FOR ILLUSTRATIVE RELIABILITY ANALYSES

Item no.	1	2	3	4	5	6	7	8	Total	Odd	Even
				Item scores						Test scores	
Person 1	1	0	1	1	0	1	1	1	6	3	3
2	1	1	1	1	1	1	1	1	8	4	4
3	0	0	0	0	1	0	1	0	2	0	2
. . .									. . .	. . .	. . .
Proportion passing (P)	0.4	0.3	0.5	0.6	0.6	0.7	0.7	0.8			
(Q)	0.6	0.7	0.5	0.4	0.4	0.3	0.3	0.2			
Variance	0.24	0.21	0.25	0.24	0.24	0.21	0.21	0.16	9.60	2.45	2.67

Table 6.3   CALCULATING α FROM VARIANCE COMPONENTS

---

(1)
$$\alpha_k = \frac{k^2 s_p^2}{k^2 s_p^2 + k s_{res}^2}$$

1.1 Obtain mean squares by entering item scores into a computer program for analysis of variance. Estimate variance components s^2 as in Table 6.1. Suppose that these are the results:

Component for persons	= 0.14
Residual	= 0.08

1.2 For the numerator: Multiply the component for persons by k^2 to estimate true-score variance.[a]

$$0.14 \times 8^2 = 8.96$$

1.3 Multiply the residual component by k to estimate error variance.[a]

$$0.08 \times 8 = 0.64$$

1.4 For the denominator:

Add these two values to estimate observed-score variance:[a]   9.60

1.5 Divide true variance by observed variance.

$$8.96/9.60 = \mathbf{0.93}$$

---

[a]Variances are for total scores. Divide each variance by k^2 to get variances for average scores.

these four calculations produce essentially the same result. The many methods are really one.

Look first at Table 6.3, based on the method of Table 6.1. Entering the data of Table 6.2 and carrying out steps 1.1 to 1.5 with $k = 8$ gives α_8, the coefficient for a composite of eight observations. Setting k equal to 1 in formula (1) will estimate how well single observations agree. The formula can be used with any value of k.[1]

Table 6.4 presents two formulas. Formula (2) is the one test manuals and research reports usually refer to as "coefficient alpha." Formula (3)—"KR20"—is a specialized version of (2) that applies when every right answer counts one point and a wrong answer counts zero. Formulas (1), (2), and (3) give identical results.

Instead of working from item scores, we might split the test into two roughly equivalent parts. An "odd-even" split (items 1, 3, 5, . . . vs. 2, 4, 6, . . .) is usual, but a test can be halved in many other ways (e.g., 1, 4, 5, 8, . . . vs. 2, 3, 6, 7, . . .). Formula (4) is a version of the Spearman-Brown formula on page 208. (The half-test variances can be entered into formula (2) in place of item variances, and k is set at 2, to get almost

---

[1]A formula introduced by Cyril Hoyt reaches this result directly from the mean squares:

$$(MSp - MSr)/MSr$$

Hoyt's formula, however, applies only when k equals the number of parts entering the analysis.

Table 6.4   CALCULATING α FROM ITEM VARIANCES OR MEANS

Coefficient alpha

(2)
$$\alpha_k = \frac{k}{k-1}\left[1 - \frac{\text{Sum } s^2_{\text{items}}}{s^2_{\text{Total}}}\right]$$

2.1 For each column of item scores, calculate its variance (s^2_{item}). Add these k values.

$$0.24 + 0.21 + \ldots = 1.76$$

2.2 Calculate the variance for the Total column.   9.60

2.3 Substitute in formula (2).

$$(8/7)(1 - 1.76/9.60) = 1.14(1 - 0.183) = \textbf{0.93}$$

Kuder-Richardson formula KR20

(3)
$$\alpha_k = \frac{k}{k-1}\left[1 - \frac{\text{Sum } PQ}{s^2_{\text{Total}}}\right]$$

3.1 The column mean is P, the proportion of persons passing the item, and $Q = 1 - P$.

3.2 Multiply to form PQ, the variance for each item, and add.

$$\text{Sum } PQ = 0.24 + 0.21 + \ldots = 1.76$$

3.3 As above, s^2_{Total} $= 9.60$

3.4 Substitute in formula (3). As in 2.3,

$$(8/7)(1 - 1.76/9.60) = \textbf{0.93}$$

precisely the same result.) Because each split gives a somewhat different coefficient, the "split-half" method is usually less satisfactory than formulas (1)–(3). Still, split-half coefficients do approximate the result those formulas give—unless the test has sections with distinct content.

α_k underestimates the form-to-form correlation if a test has sections of distinct types. If a test is planned to include several areas of content or types of task, those "strata" ought to be recognized in the reliability analysis. The only formula in this section that can directly recognize strata is (4); we could distribute categories of content equally over half-tests. The other formulas can be modified to avoid an underestimate, however. (On "stratified alpha", see Cronbach, 1988, and Rajaratnam et al., 1965).

Reports most often speak of "internal consistency" when the analysis rests on parts of a test (half-tests or items). The method applies also

Table 6.5   CALCULATING A SPLIT-HALF COEFFICIENT

(4)
$$r_{xx'} = \frac{2r_{hh'}}{1 + r_{hh'}}$$

4.1 Calculate the correlation $r_{hh'}$ between half-test scores. Table 6.2 reports this as   0.876

4.2 Substitute in formula (4). $2(0.876)/(1 + 0.876) = \textbf{0.93}$

Table 6.6   WHAT "ERROR" MEANS UNDER SEVERAL PROCEDURES

	Sources of variation that increase the reported s.e.m. when the data come from			
	internal consistency	test forms given on same day	test forms given on different days	test and retest (same form, different days)
Momentary inattention, luck in guessing	x	x	x	x
Choosing a particular set of items to represent the universe	x	x	x	
Health, mood, or other temporary state of the test taker			x	x
Shift in motivation from occasion to occasion			x	x
Opportunities for learning that change pupil standings as time passes			x	x

to totals or averages of other kinds. With judgments made by k raters entered into the table, α_k reports on the expected consistency of one composite of k ratings with that from k other raters. Setting k = 1 assesses the typical consistency of single raters with each other. Observations on multiple occasions can also be analyzed in this way.

The method requires that the part scores be experimentally independent; that is, errors on one part must not be linked to errors on another. Independence is violated when a highly speeded test is scored in odd-even fashion, because the person who gets stuck on an odd-numbered item will not reach the end of the test and will thereby get a lower score on *both* the odd and even parts. There is a lack of independence also if success on one problem helps the test taker to solve the next.

Wherever such linkages are possible, it is advisable to divide the test into physically and logically separate parts to collect reliability data. The parts of a speed test would be given separately, each with its own prorated time limit. The part scores can enter any of the formulas in place of item scores. Anastasi and Drake (1954) gave half-tests with separate time limits in order to get a proper estimate for one set of speeded tests. They obtained coefficients as much as 0.15 below those calculated improperly from odd-even scoring of the intact test.

18. *Find the s.e.m. for the total score of the test in Table 6.3.*

19. *The scores on a test have a variance of 60. The two half-tests (odd and even) have variances of 20 and 22. Find the reliability and error variance of the total score.*

20. *For a 10-item test, the observed-score variance is 90. The respective items have variances 3, 1, 5, 2, 2, 4, 3, 3, 1, 4. Calculate the reliability coefficient, and say as much as you can about what it means.*

INTERPRETING FINDINGS

Some popular methods of analyzing error of measurement neglect sources of variance that should concern test interpreters. Table 6.6 compares three procedures, reviewing some of what has been said earlier on this topic. In general, of course, a procedure that takes into account more sources of error will yield a larger standard error and a smaller coefficient.

There is no objection to calculating an internal-consistency coefficient when a test is being used to measure a supposedly stable characteristic; if it turns out to be small, it raises serious questions. When the coefficient is large, the user must bear in mind that inconsistency over occasions is a source of error not yet investigated.

21. *A chemistry teacher gives a standardized test of knowledge of scientific facts. Several students make scores lower than she had expected.*
    a. *She asks, "Could it be that I gave a form of the test that included many questions these particular students happened not to know? Would their scores have changed much if they had been asked other questions of the same type?" What type of investigation answers this question?*
    b. *She asks, "Could the performance of these students be due to an 'off' day? Does a score on tests of this type vary much from day to day?" What type of investigation is most helpful in answering this question?*

22. *Add this row to Table 6.6: "Differences among scorers' conceptions of a good response." Add a column: "Scoring of the same test papers by two scorers." Check cells in this row and column to indicate what increases the s.e.m.*

Considering the Range of Scores

Recall that the reliability is the ratio of true to observed variance. The larger the true-score variance, the larger the coefficient. But this means that the reliability coefficient is higher in a wide-range group. (So is the validity coefficient; see p. 167.)

One MCT study gave the variances listed under "original sample" below. A class of more select students might have the variances listed at the right.

	Original sample	Select sample
Observed-score variance	116.6	82
Error variance	12	12
True-score variance	104.6	70
Coefficient	0.90	0.85

The change in coefficient can be far more dramatic when, for example, a test designed for representative children is administered in a remedial class.

23. *For a college-entrance test, the test manual reports a reliability coefficient of 0.95 for a college applicant population where the standard deviation is 20. What will the true-score, error, and observed variances and the coefficient be in a group of students actually admitted to a certain college if the standard deviation in that group is 10?*

24. *A reading test is to be used in Grades 4 through 6. The manual should report a coefficient calculated for each grade level separately. Why?*

Number of Observations: Effect on Accuracy

A long test is generally better than a short test because every question added improves the sample of performance. Likewise, six 15-minute observations of a child's social behavior provide a better sample of typical behavior than three.

When k uncorrelated errors are averaged, the variance of the average error drops to $1/k$ times the error variance of a single measure. The effect is illustrated in the second column of Table 6.7. As k increases, the coefficient approaches 1.0. The more observations we average, the more closely the result agrees with the true score. This kind of analysis can indicate how much accuracy is gained by going from two graders of an essay to three, for example, and how much is lost in going from a 40-item examination to a 30-item version. (It is assumed that a change in length does not change the nature of the test.)

The Spearman–Brown Formula   The Spearman-Brown formula embodies this reasoning. It changes a reliability coefficient for a k-part composite

Table 6.7   EFFECT ON ERROR OF MAKING ADDITIONAL OBSERVATIONS

Number of tests averaged[a] (k)	Variances			Coefficient	s.e.m.
	Error	True	Observed		
1	1.00	9.80	10.80	0.91	1.00
2	.50	9.80	10.30	0.95	.71
3	.33	9.80	10.13	0.97	.58
5	.20	9.80	10.00	0.98	.45
10	.10	9.80	9.90	0.99	.32
100	.01	9.80	9.81	0.999	.10

[a]If tests were summed, instead of averaged, the variances would be multiplied by k^2, and the s.e.m. would be multiplied by k.

to that for a composite of k' parts. It can convert α_1 to α_{10}, or α_{10} to α_1, or α_6 to α_4. Write n for the fraction k'/k. Then

$$\alpha_{k'} = \frac{n\alpha_k}{1 + (n-1)\alpha_k} \tag{5}$$

The formula also applies when the first coefficient is obtained by correlating two measures.

For the formula to apply exactly, the parts must be equivalent; but we get reasonable estimates so long as the parts are samples from the same universe. Likewise, if we are going from a long test to a short one (k greater than k'), the short one must be representative of the whole. We have here another instance of a practically useful theory resting on a troublesome assumption. In some domains it is not possible to prepare an indefinitely large number of items on the same subject matter, keeping the difficulty range constant.

Bandwidth versus Fidelity   Information from an employment interview can be reported simply as an interviewer's summary rating on suitability. Or the interviewer can rate the applicant on half-a-dozen qualities or mark a checklist of numerous specific characteristics. Similarly, a pupil's ability in arithmetic computation can be reported as a single score, or as a string of scores for subskills.

Tests that report multiple scores are hard to evaluate. The problem is partly technical and partly one of values. A certain time is available for testing. Should the tester go after a good measure of one dimension or make several less thorough measurements? It is hard to strike the right balance between the number of questions investigated and the precision of answers obtained.

This is the bandwidth-fidelity dilemma. We encounter it in debates about the proper number of aptitudes to take into account in guidance, about the wisdom of preparing a ten-subtest profile for a Wechsler scale, and about the usefulness of "diagnostic" tabulations of student errors in spelling. The argument is equally vigorous in the personality domain. Some investigators settle for a single "emotional adjustment" score; others prepare an elaborate descriptive profile.

The terms "bandwidth" and "fidelity" come from Shannon's information theory (Shannon & Weaver, 1949), developed for the study of communication systems. Home music systems have made "high fidelity" familiar to everyone. The complementary concept of bandwidth refers to the amount of information a message tries to communicate.[2] The

---

[2]As used here, "bandwidth" is associated with complexity and variability. A wideband assessment seeks information on many aspects or dimensions. Some writers on personality use the word as I do, but others give it the opposite meaning. Writers in the second group speak of a scoring system as "broadband" if it tries to sum up the person in a few broad dimensions such as "agreeableness."

fidelity of a tape recording depends upon tape speed. A slow recording has greater fidelity but less information per tape. With other things held constant, increasing the variety of information reduces fidelity.

When many decisions are to be made, each requiring a different sort of information, the best solution is to allow plenty of time for gathering information, giving the most time to the most important questions. When questions are of about equal importance, obtaining rough answers to most or all of them is more profitable than precisely answering just one or two (Cronbach & Gleser, 1965).

In trying to help an individual, one needs detailed information. Psychologists and educators try to identify the particular kinds of social situation or intellectual problem where the person's functioning rises above his usual level, and the ones where his performance lags. This kind of analysis pushes bandwidth upward. When the assessor makes numerous statements, each has to be based on limited information. Critics point to the risks inherent in interpreting unreliable differences among subscores. Practitioners mindful of these risks can make good use of subscores as *tentative* leads.

The classical psychometric ideal is the instrument with high fidelity and low bandwidth. The Law School Admission Test tries to answer just one question with great accuracy. It concentrates its content in a narrow range of verbal abilities. Because its parts are highly correlated, part scores are unenlightening. At the opposite extreme, an interview can have almost unlimited bandwidth. Questions can turn in any direction, different themes being pursued with each interviewee. The report can be individualized to such an extent that no two persons are described on the same variable. A technique used as a wideband method by some testers or organizations becomes a narrowband method for others. Even the interview can concentrate on a single variable.

Some purposes of testing demand greater accuracy than others. We do not want decisions to be appreciably influenced by temporary variations in performance or by the tester's choice of questions. An erroneous favorable decision—to terminate therapy, for example—may be irreversible and damaging. An erroneous unfavorable decision is unjust, disrupts the person's morale, and perhaps retards his development.

Reliabilities of the main scores in standard ability tests used for important decisions often are (and should be) 0.90 or higher. A lower reliability is entirely acceptable in many situations, however, as these examples show:

- Weekly quizzes—because no major decision rests on the single quiz, and errors of measurement tend to average out over several weeks.
- Tests used to assess classes or schools as a whole—because errors of measurement tend to average out over students, and the inaccurate score for the individual does not affect his fate.
- Outcome measures in statistical research on sizable samples—be-

cause erroneous scores do not harm the individuals, and group statistics can be adjusted for measurement error.
- Screening tests to identify members of a community who should be examined for a risky physical or psychological condition—because a reliable follow-up test will uncover the errors. (But unless there are proper safeguards, the inaccurate test can generate disturbing rumors and misunderstandings.)

25. *Illustrate how a screening test for persons at risk could generate rumors and misunderstandings, and suggest some safeguards. Would the safeguards be less necessary if the test s.e.m. is small?*

26. *The reliability coefficient for a single testing is 0.80. If two testings are combined, what will the coefficient be? (Use the Spearman-Brown formula.)*

27. *A 60-word spelling test has a reliability coefficient of 0.90. What reliability would be expected for a 20-word test?*

28. *In World Series baseball, some pinch hitters reach batting averages as high as 0.750, whereas the best regular players rarely exceed 0.400 for seven games. How can this be explained?*

29. *The KR20 formula is said to report on the homogeneity of the universe the items in a test represent. Why would α_1 be a better indicator of homogeneity?*

Accuracy for Particular Individuals

Accuracy as a Function of Score Level   A test is usually designed to fit a certain range of ability, and it will be most accurate in that target range. Persons for whom the test is very difficult are likely to have comparatively large errors of measurement because of guessing or variable response to stress.

The scores of recruits who took a pitch discrimination test twice are presented in Figure 6.1. If the test were accurate, the two scores for each person would be nearly the same, and all points would fall along the diagonal line. The test consists of 100 pairs of tones; in each pair, the person reports whether the second tone is higher or lower than the first. A score of 50 would be expected, on average, if all responses were guesses; 50 is the "chance score." According to the figure, high scores are fairly consistent. Recruits scoring 85 on the first test fell between 72 and 95 on retest. But those scoring near the chance level (e.g., 55) scattered widely on the retest (40 to 87). The broken line shows the average score on the second test corresponding to each score level of the first test.

The upcurve at the left indicates that many recruits with very low scores on the first test did well on the retest. Probably those having such low scores on the first test misunderstood directions and judged the first tone instead of the second. Following directions correctly on the retest would shift their scores from 70 items wrong to 70 items right.

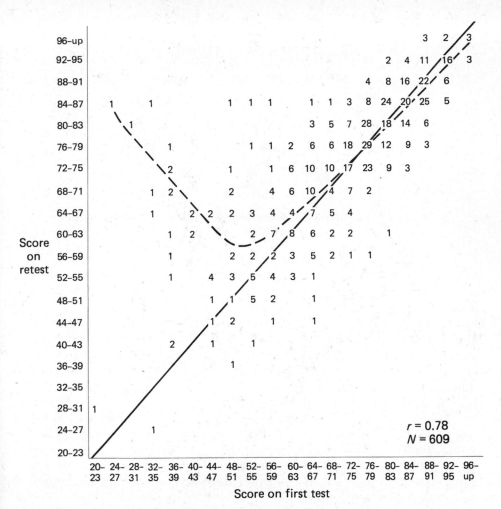

Figure 6.1. **Test and retest scores on pitch discrimination.** (*Source*: Ford et al., 1944.)

A test should be appropriate in difficulty for the decision to be made. Figure 6.2 shows distributions of scores on several tests given to the same group.

The very easy test A may be quite satisfactory for measuring at the lower end of the group. Test A is unsatisfactory for comparing abler persons because a change of only a few points causes a person to drop from the top of the group to the average. The test does not distinguish between the persons tying at 100, even though these people probably do not have the same ability. This failure to detect differences among (and shortcomings in) superior persons is a "ceiling effect."

A score distribution that tails off to the left is appropriate for a

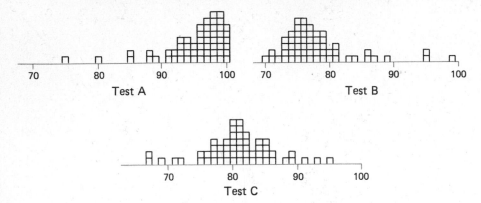

Figure 6.2. **Distributions for three tests given to the same group.**

screening test. A survey trying to identify persons who are at risk in some respect (or simply trying to obtain a count of them) ought to distinguish persons with low true scores from the general population, but there is no reason for a finely graded assessment of persons who are normal and above. Distribution A is also appropriate for "mastery tests" used in instruction and for tests used to certify competence. A checkoff test on congruent triangles identifies geometry students ready to move ahead to theorems on parallel lines. A test where nearly everyone "hits the ceiling" is suitable for this (and encouraging!).

Test B is difficult. The top scores spread out, but differences at the low end of the scale are too small to distinguish individuals dependably ("floor effect"). If we need only to distinguish the best members of an applicant group, Test B is efficient. Such a test could also be used to screen out able persons who will be exempted from certain training or considered for scholarships.

Test C spreads out cases at both ends of the scale. Tests yielding roughly normal distributions are preferred when it is necessary to distinguish all along the scale.

Individualized Standard Errors   The conventional procedure for obtaining confidence bands employs an s.e.m. that is a kind of average over a reference group. Estimates would be sounder if we could determine the individual's own s.e.m. An unusually large s.e.m. identifies a person the test did not fit properly (too hard? directions not understood?). The s.e.m. is greater (other things being equal) for a child who succeeds on some hard items but misses some easy ones.

The individualized s.e.m. (or the estimated band for the true score) can be derived in many ways (Feldt et al., 1985). Estimates of uncertainty for the individual are readily obtained when a test based on unidimensional scaling is administered by computer.[3] And, as was explained at p. 141, adaptive testing can continue measuring until sufficient accuracy is obtained. If a person is inconsistent, testing should continue—within the limits set by fatigue and boredom—until his scaled score has as small an s.e.m. as desired. The estimated s.e.m. refers to consistency across measurements on the same day, not to stability over time. It tells how adequate a sample of today's behavior was obtained.

Sometimes one wants precision to be the same for everyone. In screening or licensing, on the other hand, a short test may show some persons to be well qualified. Many items will be needed to be sufficiently sure about persons nearer the borderline. A large s.e.m. is acceptable for persons well above the borderline; it should be small for persons whose scores hover near the minimum qualifying level.

30. *Which distribution in Figure 6.2 would be most desirable in each of the following cases?*
    a. *A psychologist wishes to measure liberalness of attitudes, to study its relation to voting habits.*
    b. *A college wishes to pick out freshmen needing special training in reading.*
    c. *A test for college guidance measures interest in medicine.*
    d. *An employer wishes to select the best statistician from a group of applicants.*

31. *The Psychological Screening Inventory reports an Alienation score whose possible range is 0 to 22. A high score implies the advisability of an intensive psychological or psychiatric examination. Percentile ranks of males correspond to raw scores as follows:*

Score	0	2	4	6	8	10	12	14	16	18	20
Percentile rank	0	3	21	52	78	91	96	98	99	99+	99+

    a. *How would a person's percentile rank change if his score changed by 4 points?*
    b. *What is the shape of the raw-score distribution? What does this distribution imply regarding the usefulness of this test?*

Effect of Measurement Error on Correlations

Other things being equal, the more accurate a test, the stronger its correlation with other variables. Increasing the number of observations makes for higher validity.

Table 6.8 illustrates these important relationships, starting with a short test having a reliability coefficient of 0.40 and a validity coefficient

---

[3]Instead of determining the s.e.m., the usual calculation reports the likelihood that a person having true score 19 (or 20 or 21 and so on) would have passed and failed items just as this test taker did. This generates a kind of chart of true scores that are more or less plausible in the light of the performance. As testing continues, the likelihood curve becomes more sharply peaked at the test taker's probable scale position.

Table 6.8   EFFECT ON VALIDITY OF MAKING ADDITIONAL OBSERVATIONS

	Number of observations for predictor X				
	1	2	4	8	16
Reliability $r_{XX'}$	0.40	0.57	0.73	0.84	0.91
Squared validity r_{XY}^2	0.09	0.13	0.16	0.19	0.20
Validity coefficient r_{XY}	0.30	0.36	0.41	0.44	0.45

of 0.30. The validity coefficient creeps up slowly. The *square* of the validity remains proportional to the reliability; in every column the ratio is 0.225 (= 0.09/0.40). If we could extend the test to the point of perfect reliability, the squared validity would not exceed 0.225. The limit on validity is, therefore, the square root of 0.225 or 0.47. Estimating the correlation (or regression) coefficient for an ideally accurate measure is called *disattenuation* or *correction for attenuation*. For procedures, see Cronbach et al., (1972); Jöreskog and Sörbom (1979), and Lord and Novick (1968); see also pages 280 and 433. One basic formula takes this form:

$$r_{YX_{true}} = r_{YX}/\sqrt{r_{XX'}} \tag{6}$$

This estimates the validity coefficient for the true score of X against criterion Y. Because $r_{YX_{true}}$ cannot exceed 1.00, the correlation of the test with any criterion cannot exceed the square root of the reliability. This is a theoretical limit that we rarely come close to in actual data. Errors in the criterion keep the correlation from reaching the limit, and so do variables influencing the criterion that the test does not measure.

32. *What value would the validity coefficient in Table 6.8 approach as the reliability of X improves if the initial reliability was 0.6?*

33. *Two 30-item arithmetic tests for fourth-graders are studied by means of KR20. Test A has a coefficient of 0.70, and Test B has a coefficient of 0.85. Is it possible that Test A is more valid? Why?*

34. *Disattenuation formulas might be used in analyzing the relation of the adolescent's educational aspirations to attitudes expressed, say at age 8, by the person and his parents. Why do disattenuated correlations answer the scientist's question better than the coefficients directly calculated from scores?*

FURTHER CONSIDERATIONS IN CHOOSING TESTS

As stated in Chapter 5, the fundamental basis for choosing a test is validity. Can we interpret the test soundly? Does the information serve our purpose? Reliability is a supplementary consideration. Excellent reliability cannot compensate for unacceptable validity. If validity is acceptable, reliability information helps in interpreting scores, and it may suggest how to increase validity (by repeated measurement, for example).

Among the additional considerations entering into the selection of a measuring procedure are costs: monetary costs of materials and tester time; burdens borne by the test taker; and cost of scoring. Norms will be an asset in some testing programs as will the availability of comparable or equated forms. Two considerations require further discussion here. Appeal to nonspecialists—the clients, the persons who will use the report, the press and the public, and the courts—can make a world of difference in the success of a testing program. So can the assistance the publisher supplies the user.

Appeal to the Lay Person   The medicine a doctor prescribes loses much of its power when a patient loses faith in it. He may skip doses. In the end he may decide that doctors cannot help him and let treatment lapse altogether. For similar reasons, in selecting a test one must consider how worthwhile it will appear to the test taker and to others who will see the results.

If an applicant for a job is given an employment test that he considers unrelated to the job, he is likely to be resentful. This will make it difficult to obtain valid scores. If he is not hired, he may excuse his failure by criticizing the test; what he says to his friends damages public relations and makes it harder to obtain job applicants. Some satisfactory workers have had little schooling and are distrustful of tests that probe their weaknesses; catch questions and questions that seem childish are especially likely to arouse criticism.

If a test is interesting and "sensible," taking it is likely to be a pleasant experience. This not only tends to make the scores valid but also helps to establish good relations between the personnel worker and the candidate. An Italian bus company contracted with psychological laboratories in two cities to give tests to would-be drivers. After a few months, it was found that most of the applicants were traveling to Rome—going as much as 100 miles farther than necessary—because the Rome center had elaborate testing apparatus whereas the second center used simple equipment to measure the same aptitudes. The applicants thought the elaborate tests fairer and more dependable. British experience with selection boards in World War II is a second case in point. The selection board observed officer candidates during several days of field testing, apparatus tests, and discussions. Before this system was established, men from the ranks rarely applied for commissions. The tests previously used gave an advantage to applicants from upper-class homes and schools, they thought. Because the rank and file saw the selection board as a fairer system for recognizing talent, it became easier to recruit candidates for commissions.

A large audience passes judgment on a testing program. British officer selection had to satisfy a Labour cabinet insistent that poor youths have a fair chance to become officers, the parents of the candidates, and the old-line officers who trained the candidates accepted. A psychologist who installs a highly valid industrial selection program will find it in the ash can a year later unless she convinces management, the union, and government regulators that the test is fair. Recall the judge's scornful analysis of the test for fire fighters (p. 188). If a group of social workers is accustomed to reports from Test A, the psychologist may be unwise to rely on Test B. Even if Test B is more accurate than A, the social worker may disregard results from B because the test does not have her confidence. So important is user acceptability that the psychologist working with teachers, industrial staffs, or physicians must often use a test that would be her second or third choice on the basis of technical qualities. The increasingly widespread practice of bringing the individuals examined or their representatives into the decision making—as in working out an instructional plan for a child who has not prospered in school—also leads the tester to select tests whose relevance is easily perceived and that can be explained in lay language. Comparatively transparent techniques are also to be favored in research uses of tests, if the findings are likely to be debated outside the profession.

A test that *looks* relevant to the lay person is said to have "face validity." Adopting a test just because it appears reasonable is bad practice; many a "good-looking" test has had poor validity. Civil service examiners, for example, prepared two tests to measure ability in alphabetic filing. One gave five names per item—John Meeder, James Medway, Thomas Madow, Catherine Meagan, Eleanor Meehan—and asked which name would be *third* in alphabetical order. The other test required the subject to place a name in a series; for example:

Robert Carstens   A _____
                       Richard Carreton
                     B _____
                       Roland Casstar
                     C _____
                       Jack Corson
                     D _____
                       Edward Cranston

Though the makers were confident that the tests called on the same skill and though both tests had reliabilities above 0.8, they correlated zero (Mosier, 1947).

Such evidence as this (reinforced by the whole history of phrenology, graphology, and tests of witchcraft!) warns against adopting a test solely because it is plausible. Validity of interpretations should not be compromised for the sake of face validity. Consumers accept many esoteric technical procedures, for example, the things done behind laboratory doors to the blood drawn as part of a physical examination. Confidence in those procedures whose inner workings we know little about has been painstakingly established by physicians' communications, personal and published. Still, the psychologist who wishes to collect information that others will use, by procedures that seem mysterious to them, undertakes a more difficult task of explication than one who can find a method that has both technical validity and face validity.

Aids to the User   When test users are not test specialists, the developer is expected to provide suggestions regarding proper interpretation and warnings regarding likely misconceptions and incorrect applications. Responsibilities for test use devolve upon many who are not trained in testing: faculty members on a college admissions committee, parole boards, homeroom teachers pressed into service as counselors, ... The student himself belongs in the list insofar as he is using the scores for judgments of his own.

The test producer has many ways to make professional experience and wisdom available. These range from sentences in the manual, to booklets like *Taking the SAT*, to computer summaries and comments on local data that have been processed centrally, to whole training courses on a particular instrument. How large an effort is appropriate depends on the use to which the test is put and the subtleties (psychological, ethical, and practical) of the application.

35. *A clinical tester examines persons charged with or convicted of crimes, to provide data bearing on their ability to distinguish right from wrong. Some of the tests will provide reports for the guidance of a hospital psychiatrist. Others will be conducted at the request of lawyers on one side of a trial. What features or characteristics of a test would make it especially suitable for one of these uses and of no particular advantage for the other use?*

36. *A certain examination for French secondary school admission was deliberately made very difficult. A skewed distribution was wanted, as only a small number of places were to be filled. When the children told of the questions at home, parents organized protest meetings that ultimately brought the problem to the attention of the minister of education, who ordered a second test of those who had failed. Do you agree with this decision?*

37. *Why would it have been illogical to cover "face validity" in Chapter 5 on "validation"?*

EVALUATING A TEST

Nearly every concept used in judging the adequacy of tests has now been introduced. As later chapters apply these concepts, they will explain them more completely. A form useful in reviewing a test (Table 6.9) recapitulates those concepts. (Table 6.10, which applies the form to MCT, is briefer at several places than it would be if it were to be filed by itself. To avoid repetition, cross-references to comments in this book that the form would otherwise summarize have been inserted.)

Table 6.9   A FORM FOR EVALUATING TESTS

1. Title.
2. Author.
3. Publisher.
4. Forms; groups to which applicable.
5. Practical features.
6. General type.
7. Date of publication.
8. Cost: booklet, answer sheet, or diskette.
9. Scoring services available and cost.
10. Time required.
11. Purpose for which evaluated.
12. Description of test, items, scoring.
13. Nature of computerized interpretative reports.
14. Author's purpose and basis for selecting items.
15. Adequacy of directions; training required to administer.
16. Mental functions or traits represented in each score, whether relevant or sources of invalidity.
17. Comments regarding design of test.
18. Validation against criteria: number and type of cases, criterion measure, time interval, result.
19. Other empirical evidence indicating what the test measures.
20. Comments regarding fairness.
21. Comments regarding validity for particular purposes.
22. Generalizability (procedure, cases, result).
23. Long-term stability (procedure, time interval, cases, result).
24. Norms (type of scale, selection of sample).
25. Comments regarding adequacy of above for particular purpose.
26. Aids to the user.
27. Comments of reviewers.
28. General evaluation.
29. References.

Development of a testing program requires, first of all, a clear purpose. One searches for a test that fits the decision to be made, not just for "a good test of reading" or "a good personality test." For this reason, I suggest that any test manual be approached with a definite measurement problem in mind. The form in Table 6.9 carries a space (entry 11) for noting this purpose, which might be specific (selecting clerks who will be trained for computer data entry) or rather general (obtaining information to be filed for subsequent use in counseling high-school students as problems arise).

The top section of the form calls for simple descriptive facts (entries 1–10.) Date of publication (entry 7) is not highly significant. A new copyright date for test or manual may imply much revision, or next to none. Some older tests are excellent, and the interpreter benefits from the research that has accumulated. But some of the test items may be obsolete, and the manual is likely to be out of date. Regarding the date of norms, see entry 24.

The next step is to form an impression of the test by examining the items, the scoring principles, and the aims the author had in mind. Under entry 12 in the form, one can describe the items superficially and list the subtests separately scored. Attention should be given to the objectivity of scoring.

The author's stated intentions (entry 14) help in understanding the nature of the test. The manual will usually indicate whether the author was interested in selection, guidance, clinical use, or classroom evaluation and will often tell what aptitudes, traits, or categories of behavior she had in mind when preparing items. How items were selected is particularly important if the test is to be interpreted on the basis of its content.

Many test manuals report statistical studies used in selecting items. These reports are rarely significant to the test interpreter. The item selection procedure is best judged by its fruits, namely, the evidence on validity and generalizability. When content validity is of interest, statistics are less informative than an examination of the content.

Directions (entry 15) can be examined with regard to their clarity and the extent to which they standardize the test.

An armchair analysis of the test items (entry 16) suggests what abilities, experiences, work habits, or personality traits influence each subscore. The comment should list irrelevant variables thought likely to distort scores.

Empirical evidence of validity (entries 18 and 19) may be of various sorts. For some tests the volume of research is so great that it can only be summarized or sampled. Under heading 20 any study might be listed that helps establish what the score measures. Here particularly it is necessary to select the most significant information from that available.

"Fairness" applies more to procedures used to make judgments and to the judgments themselves than to the test in isolation. Some aspects of fairness fall naturally under other entries (as with the reference to "Western world" in entry 16); entry 20 provides a place for evidence or comments especially related to the purpose stated in entry 11.

The final evaluation of validity (entry 21) is the most important single entry. It is necessary to weigh positive and negative evidence, to decide which of several contradictory findings is most trustworthy, and to judge the body of evidence as a whole. It is important to note when evidence on an important aspect of validity is lacking. Attention should be paid to the adequacy of qualitative interpretations or decision rules if these are suggested in the manual or provided by scoring services.

Entries 22 and 23, on error of measurement, are usually summarized from the manual. Subscores as well as totals should be discussed. Norms (entry 24) are examined for relevance to the user's situation. If norms

Table 6.10 ILLUSTRATIVE SUMMARY EVALUATION

1. *Title.* Mechanical Comprehension Test (MCT).
2. *Author.* George K. Bennett and others.
3. *Publisher.* Psychological Corporation.
4. *Forms; groups to which applicable.* S, T. Primarily for job applicants and trainees. Can be used with students and experienced technicians. A version appearing in the DAT battery for students is of similar difficulty. Spanish versions available.
5. *Practical features.* Directions and items available on prerecorded tape make the test more suitable for applicants weak in verbal skills.
6. *General type.* Aptitude.
7. *Date of publication.* 1970. Earlier versions appeared from 1940 onward. Manual supplement, 1980.
8. *Cost: booklet,* $3.16; *answer sheet,* 78 cents (1989).
9. *Scoring services available and cost.* May be scored by hand or any automated system.
10. *Time required.* 30 minutes (plus directions).
11. *Purpose for which evaluated.* Vocational guidance of high school students.
12. *Description of test, items, scoring.* Pictures of simple apparatus. Has three-choice questions about what will happen to an object when force is applied, which of two structures is most stable, etc. Objective scoring (number right in recent forms). No part scores.
13. *Nature of computerized interpretative reports.* None.
14. *Author's purpose and basis for selecting items.* To measure an ability required in many jobs and training courses. Past experience affects scores, but the items require understanding rather than recall of isolated facts. Items were put through various stages of criticism and tryout; items retained were those discriminating persons scoring high on a pool of items from low scorers.
15. *Adequacy of directions; training required to administer.* Directions are unusually clear and simple. Classroom teacher or personnel clerk can handle.
16. *Mental functions or traits represented in each score.* General experience with machines common in Western world, understanding of simple principles of motion. Solutions can be intuitive or deductive. Unspeeded. No claim is made that the test measures an innate aptitude.
17. *Comments regarding design of test.* Highly efficient. As errors are not penalized, a person who marks every item has an advantage; directions mute on this point. Any test paper with several omissions should be flagged as questionable.
18. *Validation against criteria.* Manuals refer to numerous studies in which MCT was correlated with technical-training criteria. Coefficients mostly range from 0.3 to 0.6 (Table 5.3). Manual often unclear about time interval separating test and criterion. A separate compilation of studies by Ghiselli (1973) confirms these validities. Results against ratings of job proficiency are poorer.

   Evidently generally useful, though ordinarily MCT should be supplemented by a verbal measure. Information on usefulness of the test for prediction in high school courses, and on long-range predictions from high school testing, available for DAT version.
19. *Other empirical evidence indicating what the test measures.* Correlates about 0.5 with tests of general or verbal-numerical reasoning abilities. Correlations with spatial reasoning tests reach 0.6 and above. Some investigators question whether a distinct concept of "mechanical" reasoning is necessary.
20. *Fairness.* The tendency of females to score lower on MCT than males raises the question whether a given score has the same predictive significance for both sexes. Direct studies on that or on the comparable question about ethnic differences seem not to have been reported. PDRI study (p. 421) on another test found validity similar across ethnic groups.

21. *Comments regarding validity for particular purposes.* Test has predictive value for nonroutine machine operation. Overlaps general and spatial tests.

22. *Generalizability.* Standard error of measurement (across forms) is 3–4 points on the 68-point scale. Limited data on high school students suggest form-to-form correlations close to 0.9.

23. *Long-term stability.* Scores improve with mechanical training and experience. No stability correlations reported.

24. *Norms.* Manual and supplement (1980) give percentile distributions for several specific industrial samples. High school norms come from a single city, presumably in the 1970's.

25. *Comments regarding adequacy of above for particular purpose.* Though high school norms are much poorer than those for the DAT version, norms are not highly important. Counselor should develop within-sex norms for curricular groups within her own school.

    Accuracy of test is acceptable. But many a difference between MCT and other ability measures arises from error of measurement alone. Moreover, standing in mechanical comprehension changes during early years of high school.

26. *Aids to the user.* Like most older tests, MCT provides little information to assist users in deciding when and how to use the scores. This is not a drawback where the test is installed by a qualified personnel psychologist or guidance counselor.

27. *Comments of reviewers.* "Of limited value to educational counselors and to those setting up test batteries for *differential* prediction objectives. The test may well be most useful when used alone or when used with a few clerical aptitude and manual dexterity tests to predict current performance in a few relatively simple, mechanically oriented occupations" (H. P. Bechtoldt, in Buros, 1972, p. 1049: my italics).

    "The artwork . . . is shamefully old-fashioned. The artwork belongs in a 1940s test, not a test for the '80s. Also, the attempt by the publisher to create a 'balanced' racial mix of persons depicted by darkening a few faces is embarrassing." (Hambleton, in Mitchell, 1985, p. 504, speaking of the DAT version.)

28. *General evaluation.* The concreteness of the test makes it appealing. Being unlike tests commonly encountered in school, it dramatizes for the counselee the concept of special abilities.

    Forms S and T could be helpful in bringing the ninth-grader to examine his aptitudes, but the DAT battery, which includes a version of MCT, is preferable for this purpose; it gives comparable data on other abilities. The DAT battery is also useful later in high school, when more definite vocational and educational plans are being made. Even where a mechanical comprehension test is wanted by itself, the Bennett has no apparent advantage over the DAT version.

    MCT is a measure of understanding acquired through general exposure to tools and machines; it does not depend on training or specific technical experience. It is uncertain whether MCT information adds much of value if general and spatial abilities have been measured. MCT indicates whether the person has the concepts useful in profiting from training; it does not guarantee proficiency without training, and it has nothing to do with manual aspects of performance.

---

will be employed in interpretation, it is important to consider the adequacy of sampling and the date of the investigation. With rising educational standards, for example, adult norms rise, and old norms make a given performance look better than current norms would.

Entry 26 calls for an evaluation of the assistance given the user. This is especially important where tests will be used in planning instruction or clinical treatment and for score reports that inexperienced persons are likely to misuse.

Entry 27 provides for a summary of published reviews. Entry 28 is a final summary of the advantages and limitations of the test for the particular purpose, considering both technical and practical features. It is appropriate to compare the test with others having the same general function and to mention information to be considered along with the test.

A plan is more than a list of good tests. It should minimize wasteful overlap among procedures and should get each piece of information when it will be most helpful. Testing cannot be planned by itself. In industry or the armed forces, it must be dovetailed with recruiting, training, and assignment. In the clinic, testing is part of the whole therapeutic effort. Any plan should consider how the results will be used in assigning the person or in helping him to understand himself, or, in an evaluation, how the relevant public will be informed.

PART Two

TESTS OF ABILITY

Chapter
7

General Ability: Appraisal Methods

7A. Judging from the descriptions in this chapter, to what extent do scores on general mental tests reflect the examinee's educational experience and success?

7B. What are the principal differences between WISC and CogAT in what they measure and in the functions they best serve?

7C. Among the principal individual tests, what important differences are found in the ways subtests are organized into main scores?

7D. Are general ability, intelligence, mental development, and learning potential different names for the same concept, or are there important differences among the terms?

7E. Do the measuring procedures applied prior to age 3 measure the same psychological variables as tests for school ages?

Extremes of opinion about tests of mental ability and about the legitimacy of basing decisions on measured ability are found among psychologists and nonpsychologists alike (Brace and others, 1980; Houts, 1977; Jensen, 1980, Ch. 1). There is plenty of room for debate about "human nature" and about changes that might result if child rearing (for example) were altered. Conflicting concepts of merit fuel the argument. Intellectual excellence is valued, but critics stress the value in what the usual tests do not measure: warmth and social sensitivity or eccentric creativity or evenness of temperament or charisma, for example.

Part Two summarizes ideas about ability with which today's psychologists work and explains why certain other ideas have been discarded. It restates questions that, badly posed, have touched off unhelpful disputes. It describes lines of research and reasoning that begin to answer the scientific questions and that should influence educational and social policies. It describes traditional ways of using test data and emerging practices that may open greater opportunity to low-scoring individuals.

"General mental ability" (shortened here to "general ability") refers to all-round effectiveness in activities directed by thought. To speak of a person's "general health" is not to deny that many ailments are specific, but good health means more than absence of disease. Nor is a measure of health the average of scores for heart and joints and skin and so on. "Health" refers to the performance of a system, and so does "general ability." Some people perform better than others in solving problems, comprehending events and messages, and learning. This general ability is not fixed, even though performance rankings are fairly consistent from one year to the next. A vital question for psychologists is how growth in abilities comes about: why some individuals forge ahead of others and also why decline sets in—at different ages for different persons and tasks.

ORIENTATION

Chapter 7 is primarily introductory and descriptive. Neither the test descriptions nor the historical review that comes first requires the close attention that was needed in Chapters 4 to 6. The superquestions on page 225 are your best guide for studying the chapter, but I can add a few further hints about what to remember.

In the historical material, I point out the Binet definition of intelligence as especially important, because current thinking builds on that idea. Note too how schools of thought appeared; intellectual successors of Binet and Spearman are still at odds on some matters, after 80 years.

In the descriptive sections, no doubt the most important specifics are the names and meanings of major scores ("Performance IQ" in the Wechsler and "Simultaneous Processing" in KABC, for example). You need these names to follow reports on test findings. Fix in mind also the conclusions on prediction of college success, and think hard about Table 7.4.

THE EMERGENCE OF MENTAL TESTING

Measurement before Binet

Although a history of mental testing is in large part a history of Alfred Binet's scale and its descendants, psychological measurement began a century before Binet's work.

The first systematic experimentation on individual differences in behavior arose from the discovery that astronomers differ in reaction time. In 1796, an assistant named Kinnebrook at Greenwich Observatory was engaged in recording the instant when this or that star crossed the field of the telescope. When Kinnebrook consistently recorded times 0.8 seconds later than those his superior—the Astronomer Royal—recorded, Kinnebrook was fired for incompetence. Before long, however, it was established that competent observers respond at different speeds and that the variations are more or less normally distributed. Hence astronomers cannot consider one report strictly correct and all others wrong. Such differences gradually came to be recognized as significant facts about the processing of information.

Physiologists, biologists, and anthropologists were stimulated by the scientific climate of the nineteenth century to measure a great variety of human characteristics. Notable among these workers was Francis Galton, whose interest in individuality developed from the theory of his cousin Charles Darwin. Galton invented ways of measuring physical characteristics, keenness of the senses, and mental imagery. These methods, though not developed fully by Galton, served as models for later tests. In addition, Galton demonstrated that outstanding intellectual achievement occurred unusually often in certain families—the Bach clan, for example. Genius, evidently, was not an accident or a gift of capricious gods, but a lawful phenomenon to be investigated scientifically.

At this time, psychology was only beginning to emerge as a science. It was suggested that mental processes—or at least their products—could be observed under standard conditions. Scientific observations, supplementing or even replacing introspection and philosophical speculation, could describe exactly the relation between the mental and physical worlds.

This was the aim with which Wundt opened the pioneering psychological laboratory in Leipzig in 1879, and he and his colleagues did triumphantly establish quantitative psychological relationships. Believing that laboratory research should analyze behavior into its simplest elements, he measured very limited functions. Wundt, trying to identify general laws governing all minds, was not concerned with individual differences. His laboratory procedures, however, had a strong influence on early tests.

In the United States, as early as 1890, J. McKeen Cattell was using procedures from Wundt's and Galton's laboratories to measure sensory acuity, strength of grip, sensitivity to pain from pressure on the forehead, and memory for dictated consonants. Cattell came to the study of individual differences out of sheer curiosity, but he quickly became eager to use tests practically (Sokal, 1987, pp. 21–45). This early effort collapsed when the tests measuring elements of behavior proved to have no relation to practical affairs. The crucial study was Wissler's (1901) analysis on test scores of Columbia University students. He correlated their marks with many Cattell measures and found that marks correlated zero with reaction time, canceling a's rapidly on a printed page, and speed of naming colors. We now recognize that low correlations were certain to result no matter what mental functions were tested. Wissler's brief tests were inadequate samples of behavior; moreover, the students were so highly selected that differences among them were hard to detect.

Wundt tested narrow reactions that could be precisely defined, using stimuli that could be accurately controlled. The tests had validity in the same way that a chemist's measure of the freezing point of a substance has validity; the result describes a clearly defined characteristic and is readily interpreted at a superficial level, no matter how much remains to be learned about the underlying process. Tests of elementary reactions have an obvious content validity, and continued investigation in the laboratory spins a web of theory binding these measures to constructs. Their relevance outside the laboratory, however, has usually been negligible (except, for example, that in some task a defect in color vision or another sensory quality may be a handicap).

For practical prediction, tests constructed on quite another principle have been more successful. When a complex performance is to be predicted, performance on a task of similar complexity is often a good predictor. To minimize effects of specific training and to obtain a test of wide applicability, a psychologist measuring ability usually observes not the practical task directly but a performance calling on the same motor or intellectual processes as the criterion task does. The MCT is an example. Such a test serves as a "sign" (p. 52) of the quality of reasoning to be expected in encounters with new machines, not simply as a sample of information about common ones.

This kind of practical testing came into psychology from medicine. Clinicians dealing with mentally retarded and pathological cases needed diagnostic tests. Psychiatrists looked for tasks that would distinguish normal from abnormal subjects and distinguish among mental disorders. Kraepelin and other nineteenth-century psychiatrists observed reasoning, as well as steadiness of effort in continuous work. Their tasks had some resemblance to requirements of life outside the laboratory. Only a few tasks of this period survive in present-day diagnosis.

Binet Defines Intelligence

Binet knew that there must be something like intelligence because its everyday effects could be seen, but he could not describe precisely what he wished to measure. Binet was a research psychologist and not a practicing clinician, but he had spent several formative years with Charcot at a mental hospital in Paris. He studied differences among individuals, differences in the same person over the course of development, and changes within a patient from time to time. He was seeking to understand the functioning person rather than to isolate sensory processes and other "elements" (Wolf, 1973).

The French system had adopted the ideal of universal education in 1881, but by the turn of the century had made none of the systematic provisions for retarded children that other countries were adopting. Individuals and groups advocating more humane and suitable treatment of these children finally persuaded the government to appoint a study commission, with which Binet served.

Teachers' judgments about who should receive special education were not trusted. The concepts of the time were so vague that in one school a quarter of the children were called "abnormal," but not one child in the next school down the road was so identified. A teacher might so label the able child who was making no effort or the troublemaker he wished to be rid of. It was important to identify the dull from good families, whom teachers might hesitate to rate low, and the dull with pleasant personalities, whom teachers might favor. The commission said that a child thought possibly to be retarded should have a "medico-psychological examination," and Binet set to work on preparing a suitable procedure.

Having little preconception regarding the difference between brighter and duller children, he tried all sorts of measures: recall of digits, suggestibility, size of cranium, moral judgment, tactile discrimination, mental addition, graphology—even palmistry. He found most useful the tasks that required the child to make sense of objects, pictures, and stories. What such tasks (impure by Wundt's standards) measured was obscure, but scores corresponded to differences observed in everyday life.

Binet found quickly that children who were best in judgment tended also to be superior in attention, vocabulary, and so on. If various intellectual tasks usually rank people in the same order, it is convenient to think of a general mental ability; but that ability is not a single process. Like blood pressure, a test score is a surface indication of the way in which many parts of the organism are working together. Binet gradually identified the essential features of intelligent behavior as "the *tendency to take and maintain a definite direction;* the *capacity to make adaptations* for the purpose of attaining a desired end; and the *power of autocriticism*" (translation by Terman, 1916, p. 45; italics mine). Direction, flexibility, judgment—these *together* formed the arch. Nearly one hundred years of research leave this as the ruling conception: ability is a coordinated whole. A recent analysis of subordinate processes leads to a summary statement much like Binet's.

The basic skills . . . include

predicting the consequences of an action or event,

checking the results of one's own action (did it work?),

monitoring one's ongoing activity (how am I doing?),

reality testing (does this make sense?),

and a variety of other behaviors for *coordinating* and *controlling* deliberate attempts to learn and solve problems. (Brown & De Loache, 1978; see also p. 319.)

To say that one person is "more intelligent" than another can only mean that he or she uses information more efficiently to serve his or her purposes. The efficiency of a factory is not to be located in this or that part of the operation. Rather, the purchasing division, the mechanics, the operators, the inspectors, and the shippers do their tasks with few errors and little lost time. Efficiency is a summary statement of what they accomplish as a team. Knowledge, motivation, self-questioning, and so on team up to produce intelligent behavior.

When, as late as 1904, he was trying to separate knowledge, memory, and other faculties, Binet was pessimistic regarding the practical possibilities of testing. Binet's biographer Wolf (1973, p. 173) credits two practicing clinicians with shifting the attention of testers away from the parts and toward the whole. The right method, they said, was that of the clinic and not the dissecting table. Binet enthusiastically adopted their perspective and promptly assembled an assessment procedure.

The scale published in 1905 (by Binet, with Th. Simon) was a set of clinical procedures, with no summary score. Binet had tried and failed to locate differences in *kind* between normal and subnormal intellects. In the course of the work he realized that although both normals and subnormals can (for example) draw a shape after it has been displayed and withdrawn, the normals can handle shapes of a complexity subnormals can handle only when they are 2 years older. In other tasks also, normals have command of any particular level of difficulty at an earlier age. The Binet-Simon revisions of 1908 and 1911 provided a summary score, a "mental level." (Also, tasks were extended to assess the whole range of ability rather than to appraise low-end performance.)

Binet died in 1911 and the scale had negligible influence on educational practice in France. Binet's ideas were rapidly picked up in other countries, however.

Contrasting British Ideas

Throughout the latter part of the nineteenth century, ideas about social institutions were strongly influenced by the Darwinian conception that in an ecology the species best fitted for *that* ecology is most likely to thrive. Galton, Spencer, and others in England lost sight of the specificity of fitness, however. They saw education as preparation for responsibility and expected the fittest persons to go furthest in *any* situation. A sound system would be one in which the ablest persons were given greatest encouragement and greatest responsibility—helping "natural selection" along. In the United States, democracy had long cherished the ideal of an open system, as we saw in Jefferson's letter to Adams (p. 6). Hence U.S. social Darwinism was much interested in biological fitness *and* in improving opportunity (Hofstadter, 1944).

If some persons were naturally more "fit" intellectually than others and more likely to benefit from education, this seemed to imply that ability is unidimensional, that persons can be ranked. The influential British psychologist Charles Spearman spoke of a central general ability. Whereas Binet had been willing to consider personality and emotion as contributing to intellectual functioning, Spearman sought to isolate the purely intellectual element—that is, to observe "mind" at work.

Spearman's aim was to understand intellectual power apart from knowledge of content. The center of his concept of general ability was abstract reasoning—the ability to perceive and apply relationships. This he symbolized by g. (In most current writings psychologists give the term "general ability" a broad, rather loose meaning, closer to Binet's concept than to Spearman's. Even Spearman's symbol g is used for the mixture of processes common to whichever intellectual tests the investigator is analyzing. See, for example, papers in Gottfredson, 1986, and Horn's complaint about "mixture models" in Linn, 1989b.)

Analogy problems are a good match to Spearman's concept, requiring perception of relationships and their application. An analogy is a set of terms in which the same relation appears between terms A and B and terms C and D: "Father is to son as mother is to _____." Analogies can be made of words, symbols, pictures, or geometric forms. Spearman's followers invented the two-way figure-analogy or matrix task, illustrated in Figure 7.1. It is accepted as an excellent measure of general ability or (by some definitions) "intelligence." It is much less related to school lessons than the vocabulary and arithmetic tasks that Americans such as Terman and Thorndike emphasized in their early testing. Unlike Block Design (an equally excellent measure of general ability), matrix items

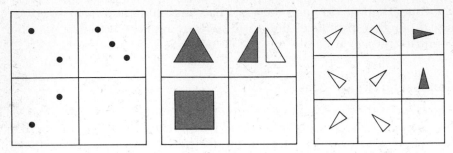

Figure 7.1. **Matrix items at three levels of difficulty.** Most matrix tests are in choice-response form. The response choices may be presented in a booklet or (in an individual test) as a set of tiles or adhesive squares. (*Source*: The item with nine cells is the stimulus part of a specimen item used to introduce adolescent examinees to the Matrices subtest of the Stanford-Binet, 4th ed. Copyright © 1986 by the Riverside Publishing Company and reproduced by permission.) (Somewhat reduced.)

can be used in group tests. Probably no single task is used more often in psychological reports on ability than the analogies task, usually in matrix form.

Spearman's successors have thought of intelligence as a "functional unity"—that is, as some one structure or process (probably physiologi- cal)—that explains most differences in efficiency. For more on this, see pages 301–302. The statement of Brown and De Loache quoted above is typical of the opposing view that ability is no more unitary than the current in a mountain stream. John Horn is one of those who use variants of the g concept in summarizing facts about individual differences; yet the following statement speaks for all but a handful of today's experts:

> Evidence from biology, from genetics, from sociology, from education, from anthropology, and from common sense, as well as from psychology, persis- tently suggests. . . . that what is called intelligence is a mixture of quite dif- ferent attributes having different genetic and environmental determinants, different courses of development over the life span, and different implica- tions for understanding human achievement, human failings, human creativ- ity, and human happiness (Horn, in Sternberg, 1986, p. 36).

1. *It has been suggested that almost everyone who reaches school age in West- ern culture has whatever knowledge the matrix test demands. What con- cepts or facts are useful in solving the problems of Figure 7.1? Is it conceiv- able that some of these concepts would be little known in a non-Western culture?*

Developments in the United States

At the start of the century, U.S. psychological research was dominated by introspection, anecdotes, and questionnaires, all of them as fallible as the person reporting. Educational and social research had been little more than the collection of opinions -and the recording of statistical trends, until E. L. Thorndike's group began to develop structured educational measures about 1905. American and British psychologists appreciated the value of studying how the child worked but placed far more emphasis on the score level than on the style of response. Thorndike defined intelligence as "the power of good responses ...," which pointed toward a numerical assessment of superiority or inferiority. Binet's clinical test, seemingly impartial and independent of preconceptions, fitted into this enthusiasm for "measurement" after he provided a summary score in 1908; Binet's method was welcomed as a research technique and especially as a means of examining below-average children. Terman's 1916 version prepared at Stanford University captured the spotlight. The acceptance of the Stanford-Binet was due to the care with which it had been prepared, its demand for complex responses, its identification of superiority as well as subnormality, and the seeming simplicity of the IQ concept, a step beyond Binet's "mental level." (The IQ proposal originated with a German psychologist, Wilhelm Stern.)

For decades, the Stanford-Binet was central to psychological research and practice. Indeed, from 1920 to 1940 the main function of the clinical psychologist was to "give Binets" in schools and other institutions. Periodically updated down to 1960, the SB remained popular with clinicians and school psychologists but was overshadowed by newer instruments. Terman and his chief collaborator Maud Merrill having died, the publisher commissioned a group headed by R. L. Thorndike (a son of E. L. Thorndike) to revise the instrument. A redesigned SB appeared in 1986.

Preliminary attempts at group testing had begun by the time the United States entered World War I, and leading psychologists proposed to screen men inducted into the army. Prospective misfits would be rejected, and the remainder sorted to receive training for high, low, or intermediate responsibilities. They quickly assembled Army Alpha, a measure of simple reasoning, following directions, arithmetic, and information. As is seen in Figure 7.2, soldiers rising to greater responsibility earned higher scores on Army Alpha. The psychologists considered this to be striking evidence of validity. (Historians now tell us, however, that the test was not highly regarded by the military and had little influence on the assignments given soldiers; Reed, in Sokal, 1987, pp. 84–85).

The psychologists of the time were proud of their contribution, and obtained considerable publicity for Army Alpha and the research findings about the distribution of groups of soldiers from different backgrounds. (In the process, they added the word "moron" to the popular vocabulary.) Figure 7.2 was widely reproduced, especially in textbooks for psychologists and teachers.

Public schools were eager to adopt the new technology (Chapman, 1988; D. Resnick, in Wigdor & Garner, 1982, vol. 2). American business had taken "scientific management" as a slogan, and school administra-

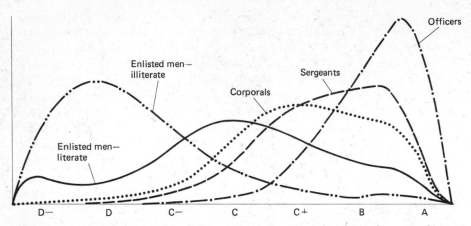

Figure 7.2. **Alpha scores of soldiers, by rank.** (*Source*: Data from Yoakum & Yerkes, 1920, p. 20.)

tors were endeavoring to put schools on a businesslike basis. Providing alternative curricula at several levels of difficulty was a response to the expectation—new in that day—that most adolescents would attend high school and to the new interest in fitting schooling to the learner's development. Tests were the obvious way to put each student "onto the right track." Mental tests for selecting employees were also widely accepted, but never on a scale comparable with the use of tests in schools and the military services (Hale, in Wigdor & Garner, 1982, vol. 2).

Army Alpha and most group tests that followed it did not exclude school-learned content. (Arithmetic subtests have been particularly common.) Nonetheless, these tests were generally regarded as measures of intellectual promise. A number of psychologists warned that the tests measure only the person's development to date and that inference about underlying capacity is hazardous. However, the general impression among test users during the 1920s and for some time thereafter was that the tests did indeed select those "fittest to survive" and most responsive to opportunity.

Figure 7.2 tends to support this view, but other data from the same source (Figure 7.3) suggest that the group tests of the period were reflecting past education rather than naked potential. Data classified in the manner of Figure 7.3 were much less widely reproduced than those of Figure 7.2. Psychologists making clinical interpretations, of course, tried to allow for any test taker's educational disadvantages, but only recently has the broader public become sensitive to the importance of experience in developing scholastic aptitude.

Criticism of tests has been vigorous from the earliest days. Back in 1867 Matthew Arnold (a notable poet, but also a school inspector) had complained that tests on what we now call "basics," mandated by a cen-

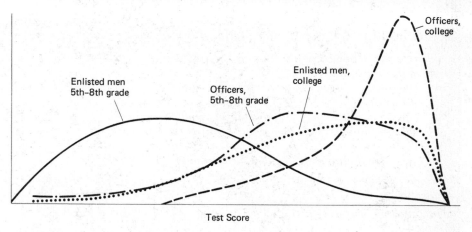

Figure 7.3. **Alpha scores of soldiers, by level of education.** The score scale does not correspond precisely to the "grade" scale of Figure 7.2. (*Source*: Data from Yerkes, 1921, pp. 766–767.)

tral authority, were reducing the quality of teaching. The enthusiasm of mental testers in the 1920s was opposed by such distinguished liberals as John Dewey and Walter Lippmann. Here is one of Lippmann's remarks (1923, p. 146):

> I hate the impudence of a claim that in fifty minutes you can judge and classify a human being's predestined fitness in life. I hate the pretentiousness of that claim. I hate the abuse of scientific method which it involves. I hate the sense of superiority which it creates, and the sense of inferiority which it imposes.

For a balanced and readable account of the pioneers of mental testing (and of the whole course of dispute regarding the importance of heredity), see Raymond Fancher's *The Intelligence Men* (1985).

It was a great mistake to adopt the words "intelligence" and "capacity" in test titles and in communications to the public. Binet knew full well that he was examining only present performance. Binet wrote eloquently of the hope of finding new methods of cultivation that would "produce a rich harvest" from children who seemed unpromising. For him, intelligence was no more and no less than a resource that had been developed.

In British and American discourse, "intelligence" seemed usually to refer to potentiality, as if the test score foretold what level the person would reach if given every educational advantage. The evidence is necessarily one-sided. Good ultimate performance proves capacity, but poor performance does not prove incapacity. The typical school-age test is best identified as a "test of general scholastic ability." It measures a set of abilities now developed and demonstrated (not a "potential"). It emphasizes abilities helpful in most schoolwork.

2. *What do the following definitions of "intelligence" include that Binet's definition does not, and vice versa?*
   a. *"The power of good responses from the point of view of truth or fact" (E. Thorndike).*
   b. *"The general tendency to consistently display effective responses to problems of an abstract or symbolic nature" (R. Thorndike).*
   c. *"The capacity of an individual to understand the world about him and his resourcefulness to cope with its challenges" (Wechsler).*

3. *Would the same sort of test items be called for by each of the definitions in question 2?*

4. *Is previous learning included in intelligence by these definitions? By Binet's?*

5. *Critics have suggested that mental tests have measured conformity to "middle-class" ideas and values. Would the qualities listed in the Binet definition be considered valuable in a community of poor agricultural workers? Would such a community value any qualities of thought or of coping behavior that do not appear in the definition?*

Appreciating the Diversity of Abilities

Tests of general ability are not interchangeable; each has its own emphases and its own blind spots. Some tests require command of school-taught tasks; in others the tasks are remote from schooling. This and the following chapters will stress both the variation and the consistency among tests of mental abilities.

Alongside tests intended to report general ability, measures of specialized abilities sprang up after World War I. Carl Seashore, for example, produced "Measures of Musical Talent," requiring discrimination of pitch, timbre, rhythm, and the like. Although these abilities are necessary to musical performance, the name of the test is unsatisfactory. It hints that these abilities are inborn and that a person who scores high could be made into a brilliant performer. Now we know that these discriminations are trainable, and that musicianship requires abilities subtler than those Seashore tested. Other special tests checked on perception of forms, dexterity, and ability to learn Morse code.

By the 1940s the variety of tests had convinced psychologists that ability has many dimensions, and L. L. Thurstone's influential research program identified seven abilities as "primary": verbal, reasoning, number, spatial, perceptual speed, memory, and word fluency. Applied psychologists came to believe that jobs require different aptitudes, and that guidance should match individuals and jobs. During World War II, the U.S. military relied on tests of specialized abilities to place recruits in assignments where they would perform well.

Complexity and diversity have been themes of recent cognitive psychology. Jean Piaget, following the French tradition of examining process rather than score level, traced how the child gains command of distinct concepts such as three-dimensional space, number, and probability. Each concept, mastered, permits the child to transform objects and symbols imaginatively. He or she can say, for example, how the layout of buildings on a table looks to someone seated on the opposite side. Piaget argued that these concepts do not merely "grow," nor are they handed down from elders. Rather, the child constructs them through explorations. Herbert Simon introduced in 1956 an analysis of problem solving that compares the mind to the computer. The two perform many of the same functions: storing information, restating it, identifying gaps, and incongruities, retrieving needed facts, and so on. Numerous codes and skills intermesh to produce the performance.

These lines of research do not discredit the concept of general ability as a *summary* description. But they—along with deeper understanding of genetics—indicate that there is no unitary endowment, strong in some persons and weak in others.

Alongside the theorists' discontent with the reduction of ability to a single dimension, a political opposition developed. To advocates for children in difficulty, the practice of classifying children according to level of intelligence ("educationally mentally retarded," for example) seemed simplistic and inhumane. Legislation and court decisions demanded individualized analysis and services. In many jurisdictions school psychologists were forbidden to use general-ability tests that yielded only a single summary score.

Wechsler's Scales for Clinical Appraisal   Wechsler's measures of general ability came to prominence largely because they highlight many facets of performance. In the 1930s David Wechsler, as a clinical psychologist at Bellevue Hospital operated by the city of New York, needed to test adult social derelicts. These people might be mentally subnormal, psychotic, adequately able but temporarily disturbed, or illiterate. Intellectual functioning was important to consider in decisions about disposition, and the psychological examiner was expected to appraise the disorder or handicap underlying any low score. The 1939 Wechsler-Bellevue scale was designed to serve in such clinical evaluation. Some Stanford-Binet tasks of that era seemed childish to adult subjects, and proper norms for adults were lacking. Furthermore, its predominantly verbal tasks elicited too limited a range of diagnostic clues for Wechsler's purpose.

To provide clinicians with tests of diverse functions, Wechsler reviewed tasks others had been using and selected a few for his subtests: block design, and holding digit strings in mind, for example. The Wechsler-Bellevue was long ago replaced by better-constructed and better-standardized forms, some of them geared to children. As with the Binet, there have been adaptations and translations throughout the world.

Wechsler's test became available at the moment when clinical psychology was emerging as a full-fledged profession. During World War II, military hospitals received great numbers of patients showing emotional disturbance or brain damage. Prompt diagnosis was wanted, and Wechsler hoped that his profile of subtest scores would help. Brain-injured patients, he postulated, would be especially low on certain subtests, schizophrenics on others. His test became the standard instrument in military clinical testing; and when clinical psychologists went to work after the war in veterans' hospitals, public mental hospitals, and guidance services they carried the test with them.

Wechsler emphasized that performance is a complex product of biological development and experience. Like Binet, he wished to consider the complete person and was unwilling to separate intellect from emotion. Emotion may heighten attention, persistence, and adaptability, or it may impair performance. Because anxiety, self-confidence, and desire to impress the tester are clearly learned reactions, Wechsler never saw his test as measuring potential independent of experience.

Ironies attend test development. Binet set out to identify subnormal children, yet the most famous piece of research with his scale was Terman's follow-up of superior children (p. 288). Wechsler designed his mental test for adults in the belief that adults and children differ in their interests and approach to work; yet today his technique is popular as a children's test. Wechsler's secondary hope in developing the test was that patterns of subtest scores would help to objectify clinical diagnosis of patients. Score profiles proved to have little diagnostic validity except when supplemented by a study of qualitative features of the responses (pp. 305–307). Moreover, psychologists and psychiatrists have come to realize that a diagnostic label is not sufficient to guide treatment (Kaufman, 1979, pp. 11–19).

The resemblance of today's most prominent ability tests to those of 1920 testifies to the pioneers' insight and ingenuity. Tests are like automobiles in this respect. The main working parts of today's machines were to be found in the cars of 1920—society is slow to supplant an invention that works. Kaufman (1979, p. 4), however, was right to say that mental testing failed to

> grow conceptually with the advent of important advances in psychology and neurology. . . . The impressive findings in the areas of cognitive development, learning theory, and neuropsychology during the past 25–50 years have not invaded the domain of the individual intelligence test. Stimulus materials have been improved and modernized; new test items and pictures have been constructed with keen awareness of the needs and feelings of both minority-group members and women; and advances in psychometric theory have been rigorously applied to various aspects of test construction,

norming, and validation. However, both the item content and the structure of the intelligence tests have remained basically unchanged.

Several tests of the 1980s have brought in new item types and new score structures, so a shift in content and interpretation has been picking up momentum. And the pioneers' intention to describe ability in a single number has given way to an attempt to characterize strengths, weaknesses, and needs.

Expertise   Whereas psychologists from Wundt to Wechsler and Kaufman have emphasized processes of perception and reasoning that apply to almost any content, much recent work examines the specialized comprehension an expert brings to particular subject matter.

Howard Gardner (1983) envisions "multiple intelligences," each embracing the concepts, facts, and procedures that facilitate response in some one domain. Linguistic, logical-mathematical, and spatial intelligences are at least partially represented in mental tests. Alongside them Gardner describes musical, bodily kinesthetic, and "personal" intelligences to illustrate kinds of expertise that are readily observed at work in the world but neglected in psychology. (The "personal" category includes insight into others and into one's own emotions.)

Interest in expertise of a still narrower sort was aroused by studies of chess players. The Dutch chessmaster-psychologist deGroot (1966) and Chase and Simon (1973) demonstrated that chess masters recognize common configurations of pieces at a glance and thus grasp complex layouts quickly and visualize changes in them. After a midgame chess layout has been exposed briefly, experts can place the pieces correctly on a board. Novices need a much longer exposure to take in the information. The masters are no better than novices at perceiving a layout of chessmen placed at random. The masters' advantage lies in their instant grasp of relationships significant for the game; almost literally, they see the chessboard through different eyes than do novices.

"Chess intelligence" is considerably narrower than Gardner's "spatial intelligence." Current studies of expertise are trying to explain supercompetence in even more limited domains—for example, high-speed mental multiplication (Staszewski, in Chi et al., 1988). This work, still in a formative stage, strongly suggests that with long-term practice on one intellectual task the expert builds an internal filing system. That system makes it easy to store and retrieve *bundles* of information like that he has been facing: chess layouts or numerical partial products. That is to say, specialized intelligence somehow relies on a specialized associative system. This conclusion suggests potential value in testing command of associations in particular fields. Strangely, this concept returns in a way to an early associationist psychology. E. L. Thorndike not only saw all learning as an associative process but said that higher intelligence amounted to having a greater store of associations. Most psychologists objected that Thorndike was equating degree of intelligence with extent of education. The new speculation about concentrated associational systems puts a different spin on Thorndike's idea.

The g Revival   From 1930 to 1980 there was a steady shift of interest from overall level of general ability to ability profiles; but in the 1980s a counterrevolution emerged. No one denies that abilities are patterned or that an individual's standing rises and falls as he goes from one task to another. The counterrevolutionaries are emphasizing that general ability contributes so much to performance—on almost any task requiring memory, judgment, comprehension, and reasoning—that it accounts for nearly all the predictive power of a narrower cognitive measure. (See a symposium presented to personnel psychologists; Gottfredson, 1986.)

Two questions will arise many times as we proceed: (1) Do present-day test batteries measure subordinate abilities well enough to offer useful predictive or diagnostic information, beyond that in the overall score? (2) With improved measurement *could* subordinate abilities produce appreciably better educational and vocational decisions?

6. *Comment on this statement by Lewis (1976, p. 8): "[S]ociopolitical influences . . . dictate our scientific requirements [our choice of tasks for measuring intellectual qualities]. . . . It may be that an authoritarian ideology requires tasks of rote memory, while an ideology of personal freedom requires tasks of creativity."*

7. *An agricultural experiment station tests varieties of corn. For hybrid G, specimens yield, on the average, 47 pounds per plant.*
   a. *Does it mean anything to say that hybrid G seeds have a "potential" of 47 pounds? What is required for the "potential" to be realized?*
   b. *Might seeds of hybrid F, measured at an average of 42 pounds, have a greater "potential"?*

SCORE SCALES OF MENTAL TESTS

This section reviews what was said in Chapter 4 about reporting of scores, and comments on some obsolete score scales.

After scoring almost any individual test of general ability, the tester can turn to a table translating the result to a 100 ± 15 standard score. Until recently this was called an "intelligence quotient" or "IQ"; current tests reduce misinterpretation with a label such as "Composite Standard Age Score." The numerical scale as well as the label is anachronistic. The only justification for the scale is like that given for measuring in pounds and feet instead of shifting to the metric system: The older generation is used to the old scheme.

The Obsolete Ratio IQ   When introduced, the IQ was truly a quotient. To understand how the quotient came into psychological tradition and why it faded from the scene, we go back to 1916. Binet had suggested describing each child in terms of the level reached on tasks of ascending difficulty. He might have attached labels such as "Level *d*" but instead he identified the levels with particular ages, and the description of present status came to be called the *mental age* (MA). To describe a child's *rate* of development, Terman divided the mental age by the chronological age. When the decimal was shifted, the ratio 1.25 became the IQ 125.

A 4-year-old with mental age 5, then, had a "ratio IQ" of 125. In a sense, he had developed 25 per cent faster than the average child. Interpreters presumed, in those days, that the child would continue to develop at this faster rate until adulthood. If this were true, the plot of his MAs in successive years would form an ascending straight line (but a wavering one, because of errors of measurement). A linear trend would have to break down in adulthood. The norm at age 40 is only a bit higher than the norm at 15; hence it makes no sense to speak of "mental age 40." It was for this reason that Wechsler, building a scale for adults, shifted to standard scores.

Standard Scores   "Deviation IQs" are nothing but standard scores. Ratio IQs on the original Stanford-Binet, for representative persons of any one age, had been more or less normally distributed, with a mean of 100 and an s.d. in the neighborhood of 15 (but varying from age to age). For deviation IQs, therefore, Wechsler chose a 100 ± 15 scale.

Almost all norm-referenced profiles for aptitude batteries use the 50 ± 10 standard-score scale, which does not echo the false "rate of development" theme. There is no point in continuing to report general ability on a unique scale, and there *is* a point in discarding the 100 ± 15 scale. I am in accord with Reschly's statement (in Glaser & Bond, 1981):

> The term IQ is bound to the myths that intelligence is unitary, fixed, and predetermined. As long as the term IQ is used, these myths will complicate efforts to communicate the meaning of test results and classification decisions. . . . The solution is to abandon the term IQ and replace it with a more accurate descriptor.

Outmoded regulations in some states define degrees of subnormality in terms of the IQ. Dropping the 100 ± 15 scale would discourage this practice.

To encourage modern thinking, I shall avoid the terms "intelligence," "IQ," and "mental age" whenever possible. I usually take the liberty of substituting 50 ± 10 standard scores (or percentiles) when summarizing data that were originally reported on the 100 ± 15 scale.

Mental Ages and Raw Scores   John's mental-age score purports to indicate the age at which the average child does as well as John has done. No matter how old John may be, he is assigned a mental age of 8 if he earns as many points as the average 8-year-old. The Wechsler and the

Stanford-Binet have both dropped the mental-age concept. (Tables that lead to something much like a mental age are still to be found, however, buried in the manuals for WISC-R and SB.)

It is wrong to think that children with the same MA (or the same raw score) have the same mental development. Among those reaching the same MA, the brighter children tend to go furthest on tasks that require analysis and judgment whereas the duller children earn much of their credit on tasks for which schooling or experience gives a marked advantage (e.g., information items). Children who are retarded but not brain-damaged can use the reasoning processes that normal children of the same MA have under control. They show this when the information-processing burden is reduced (Haywood et al., 1975; Weisz & Yeates, 1981). See also p. 319.

In research, tabulations are best made from raw scores. It is usually a mistake to calculate statistics from IQs or other age-normed scores because they summarize not ability but comparative ability. The following made-up numbers illustrate what happens when age is not uniform and a variable X is adjusted for age.

	Child A	Child B	Child C
Age	6	8	10
Raw score X	30	40	50
Standard score on X within age group[1]	58	50	42
Variable V	10	20	30

Variable V—whatever it is—increases with age. In this three-person sample, it correlates positively with X. Age differences are removed from X by the conversion to standard scores, and the correlation of V with the age-adjusted scores is negative.

8. *In the example just given, how do you think the V, X relation is likely to change if V is also expressed in standard scores?*

9. *Three children have the following scores on an ability test:*

	MA	Raw score	Standard score
Mack, age 7 yr, 6 mo	10	80	70
Ray, age 10	10	80	50
Ted, age 10	13	100	70

Which boys are most similar? Can one say that any two of them are truly alike in mental ability?

---

[1]One would reach these figures if the mean of X is 22, 40, and 58 at ages 6, 8, and 10, with s.d. 10 at each age.

ILLUSTRATIVE MENTAL TESTS

This chapter describes a few prominent tests. A close look at their content will provide a basis for recognizing what kinds of interpretation of mental tests are clearly warranted and what kinds are questionable (at least until supporting research is presented). These examples also provide a concrete underpinning for later examination of practices and research conclusions, inasmuch as several of the tests have been widely used in clinical case work and educational decision making or in studies of intellectual development.

Individual testing is fundamentally different from group testing. Group testing is impersonal and is usually intended to produce scores that will be interpreted by established rules. Individual testing is personal. The tester gets to know the examinee, interacts so as to encourage a good performance, observes how the person approaches tasks and responds to frustration, and usually prepares a personalized interpretation. The scores are given meaning by the examiner's careful observations of the style of performance (p. 306).

Until recently, group and individual tests differed substantially in content as well as in mode of presentation and interpretation. The dividing line is increasingly blurred. The most dramatic departure is in "dynamic assessment," where, instead of seeking the best performance the person can produce unaided, the intent is to give sufficient help to demonstrate his full ability to learn (p. 87). Dynamic procedures often use test tasks originally designed for group administration; and the coaching process may be conducted either one-on-one or in a small group.

The first description here is of the Wechsler, which has long been the dominant individual test. It now has a group test cousin, the Multidimensional Aptitude Battery, proposed as a cost-effective alternative. I also discuss Mercer's variations on the Wechsler, which recast interpretations according to the child's social background. The second subsection takes up the recently introduced Kaufman battery. The third subsection describes a representative group test, the Cognitive Abilities Test (CogAT). The recent revision of the Stanford-Binet also enters that subsection. Although some tasks introduced by Binet and Terman survive in modified form in the new Stanford-Binet, it is equally a descendant of CogAT. Thus we see an individual test, the Wechsler, providing the model for a group test and tasks from a group test, CogAT, being grafted onto the pioneer individual test of Binet.

Later sections of the chapter move on to tests for admission to advanced education and tests for early ages.

The Wechsler and Its Cousins

The current tests of the Wechsler system are WPPSI-R for ages 3–7, WISC-R (6–16), and WAIS-R (16–74). WPPSI-R is a 1989 revision. Modification and restandardization will produce a test tentatively titled WISC III to replace WISC-R in the early 1990s. Important sources on the Wechsler are books by Kaufman (1979), Matarazzo (1972), and Sattler (1988), chapters in Wolman (1985), and reviews of WISC-R and WAIS-R in the *MMY* (Mitchell, 1985). The descriptions here will rely on facts about WPPSI and WISC-R because their successors were not available when this book went to press.

The three instruments have the same pattern, with five or six subtests producing a Verbal score (hereafter denoted V) and another set generating a Performance (P) score. These combine into a Full Scale score. The subtests are similar but not identical across age levels (Table 7.1). The table follows tradition in listing "alternate" subtests; for example, Digit Span is available if one of the "regular" verbal tests is somehow spoiled during administration. Digit Span and Mazes probably should be included in any WISC-R administration because of the light they can shed on mental processes.

The Wechsler is given by a trained examiner and requires about 1 hour. Verbal and Performance subtests usually are alternated. The examiner is directed to start with the easiest items or—as with Block De-

Table 7.1   SUBTESTS OF THE WECHSLER SCALES FOR VARIOUS AGES

Young children (WPPSI-R)	Children of school age (WISC-R)	Age 16 and up (WAIS-R)
VERBAL		
Information	Information	Information
Comprehension	Comprehension	Comprehension
Arithmetic	Arithmetic	Arithmetic
Similarities	Similarities	Similarities
Vocabulary	Vocabulary	Vocabulary
(Sentences)	(Digit Span)	Digit Span
PERFORMANCE		
Block Design	Block Design	Block Design
Picture Completion	Picture Completion	Picture Completion
	Picture Arrangement	Picture Arrangement
Object Assembly	Object Assembly	Object Assembly
(Animal Pegs)	Coding	Digit Symbol
Mazes	(Mazes)	
Geometric Design		

NOTES: Parentheses indicate tests often treated as alternates or supplements. Tests appearing in the same row are psychologically similar even when they differ in content and title.

sign—to start with intermediate items expected to be easy enough for the present examinee. The examiner shifts to the next subtest when the person has clearly gone as far as he can. The stopping rule ordinarily takes such a form as "Stop after two consecutive failures," but the examiner must make rather sensitive judgments.

Some practitioners, wishing to shorten the testing time, propose to substitute three or four subtests for the whole scale. It is reasonable to use a short form to confirm that a person is not notably below the norm for his age, but no composite score should be reported. A report from an abbreviated version is not comparable to a true Wechsler examination. The same statement, of course, can be made with regard to any test.

Chapter 4 pointed out that test norms go out of date. The Wechsler scales and nearly all other major ability tests are renormed periodically, with or without revision. It is important, when an instrument has been renormed, that any score report indicate what norms have been used. That practice aids in making comparisons across research reports or across the cumulative record of an individual.

Verbal and Performance Sections Table 7.2 exhibits items similar to the verbal tasks in Wechsler scales. For many items there are follow-up questions to elicit a fuller answer if the first one is inadequate. The items shown here represent a medium level of difficulty; they do not reflect the range of actual questions for the same scale.

Among the performance subtests, we have already examined Block Design (p. 57); Figure 7.4 introduces some others. These tests are varied, because Wechsler saw intellectual functioning as a mixture of diverse processes. Block Design, for example, requires analysis of a complex whole, breaking a pattern into elements. Object Assembly gives the parts and requires the person to discover how they go together to make an object. Picture Completion requires inspection of a whole to identify the essential missing part. In Picture Arrangement, cartoon panels that tell a story are laid out in incorrect sequence. To arrange them, the test taker must identify a complex whole from disorganized parts and also reason correctly about the time sequence of events.

Digit Symbol and Coding require the person to put the proper symbol in each place, doing as much as he can in a short time. The code remains in front of him as he works. My illustration of Digit Symbol shows only five symbols; the actual test uses nine. Animal House requires the young child to hold a code in mind as he matches colored houses with the animals that "live" in them.

Performance tasks are especially helpful in studying persons whose behavior or emotional responses are unstable, mentally retarded individuals, adults with limited education, children suspected of inefficiency in learning, persons with poor hearing, and those whose command of the tester's language is limited. Such tasks make minimal

Table 7.2   WECHSLER VERBAL TASKS AT THREE LEVELS

Information
How many wings does a bird have?
Who was Thomas Jefferson?
Who was Huckleberry Finn?

Comprehension
Why should we wear shoes when we go outside?
Why is it important to use zip codes when you mail letters?
Why do married people who want a divorce have to go to court?

Similarities
Puppies grow up to be dogs, and kittens grow up to be _____.
In what way are corn and macaroni alike? How are they the same?
In what way are a book and a movie alike?

Vocabulary
What is a hammer?
What do we mean by 'protect'?
What does 'formulate' mean?

Arithmetic
The examiner places 10 blocks in front of the child, then says:
    Give me all of the blocks except three. Leave three of the blocks here.
Dick had 13 pieces of candy and gave away 8. How many did he have left?
How many hours will it take to drive 240 miles at the rate of 30 miles an hour?

Sentences
I'm going to say something and I want you to say it after me just the way I say it:
    Karen has two dogs and a new blue wagon.

Digit Span
I'm going to say some numbers. Listen carefully, and when I am through say them right after
    me.
    3-6-1-7-5-8.
Now I'm going to say some more numbers, but this time when I stop, I want you to say
    them backwards.
    1-9-3-2-7.

NOTE: The three rows represent, respectively, the difficulty found in WPPSI-R, WISC-R, and WAIS-R. Digit Span items in WISC-R and WAIS-R are similar. I thank Alan Kaufman for supplying these items.

demands on verbal facility, permit significant observations of the process of performance, and appeal to examinees who resist schoollike tasks.

Nearly all current mental tests provide subscores representing bundles of abilities. The subvariables may have different predictive and clinical implications if measured well; but distinguishing them is not worthwhile unless the score difference is reliable. At the start of Chapter 8 we shall look at the reliability of differences within a profile. Here, it is sufficient to note that the Verbal/Performance difference is reasonably

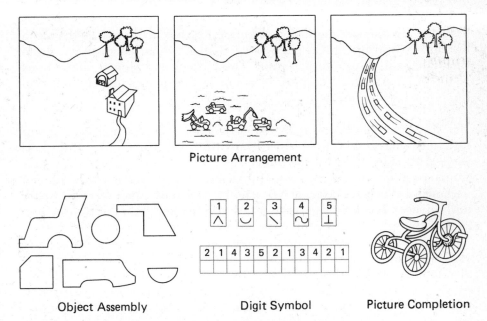

Figure 7.4. **Wechsler performance tasks.** The items illustrate the general form of the subtests. Color is being added to the pictorial subtests in WISC-III.

well measured, and that differences across subtests generally are not. Inconsistency between Verbal and Performance standings was once considered a sign of abnormality. But many persons whose behavior is normal show sizable V/P differences. It is better to think of the two kinds of test as surveys of overlapping domains of ability, as tests that examine "the same thing" by different methods. (See pp. 280, 294.)

Variation across subtests or sections of the test is sometimes highly suggestive. Here, in simplified form, is an example recounted by Matarazzo and Herman (in Wolman, 1985); for details see Matarazzo (1972, pp. 414–417).

A 21-year-old woman was referred to the medical psychology consultants by the chief of neurosurgery with a request for any leads that might help him decide between a differential diagnosis of brain tumor (of a type clinically difficult to verify) and one of catatonic schizophrenia. Each condition, he felt, was compatible with her history and with clinical findings. The psychologist's Wechsler findings included a Verbal IQ of 98 and Performance IQ of 70. Based only on clinical experience, the clinician could say that such a 28-point VIQ-PIQ difference in a high school graduate of average ability had never been observed even in the most disabling forms of acute schizophrenia or other major psychiatric disorders. However, such a discrepancy was not infrequent in patients with traumatic or other head injuries. Surgery found a large tumor in the patient's right hemisphere and removed it. Reexamination three months later produced a Verbal IQ of 104 and a Performance IQ of 104.

Clinical judgments do not rest on scores alone. Wechsler examiners tend to view the test more as a setting for observing behavior than as a measuring instrument. On page 306 I shall draw on Matarazzo again to illustrate qualitative interpretation. The Jackson and Mercer adaptations of the Wechsler that I take up here are in the quantitative rather than the clinical tradition.

The Multidimensional Aptitude Battery   Douglas Jackson devised a group test somewhat similar to WAIS-R. His Multidimensional Aptitude Battery (MAB; ages 16 and up) produces ten subtest scores, Verbal and Performance IQs, and a Full Scale IQ. Nine subtests are multiple-choice variants of Wechsler tasks. MAB contains no counterpart of Digit Span, and replaces Block Design with a task requiring rotation of figures in a plane. (See p. 382 for a similar task.)

The Verbal score is a good match to Wechsler's V, at least for responsive test takers. In a modest sample who took MAB in small groups and also took WAIS-R individually, the two scores correlated 0.94. P scores of MAB and WAIS-R correlated 0.79, so Jackson's Performance simulation is less successful. Picture Arrangement and Picture Completion were ingeniously converted to multiple-choice form. The rotation task, however, does not require as much reasoning as Block Design.

MAB was constructed well and all scores have good reliability, but much research will be needed to flesh out its interpretation. Until such research is in hand, it would be a mistake to carry over Wechsler profile interpretations. There is no way to judge, for example, whether the features that make WAIS Comprehension meaningfully different from other V tasks are captured in the MAB format. Also, whether administered by live tester or computer, MAB does not serve for as wide a range of clinical cases as the individual Wechsler. Jackson advises against using it with the retarded and with psychotics. In many run-of-clinical-practice cases, an MAB profile that is inconsistent with other facts will simply signal the need for an individual test.

Mercer's Multicultural System   In the 1970s, Jane Mercer, a sociologist concerned with the opportunities offered to children of minority background, introduced a System of Multicultural Pluralistic Assessment (SOMPA) for ages 5 to 11, in which WISC-R data are central. SOMPA tries to systematize a practice that has always been recommended—of interpreting a test score in the light of other information.

Dissatisfaction with past services to the handicapped has stimulated careful planning for children who have, or are expected to have, difficulty with the usual school program. Traditional practice was to shunt the handicapped child to a special class or institution for those having that kind of disability. Federal law now requires that schoolchildren lead lives "as little restricted as possible." Schools try to keep the child in a classroom that enrolls a full cross section of the local child population of his age, if he can be served there. (See pp. 350–352.)

Classes "for the retarded" have been under particular criticism because, in many localities, disproportionate numbers of children from Hispanic and black families were placed in them (Heller et al., 1982). In many schools, unstimulating offerings were serving these children badly.

Some states adopted a rule forbidding special placement unless the mental test score fell below a certain level. But in some school systems this seemed to produce automatic assignment to special education when the test score was low, without regard to the suitability of the test for that child. To make this less likely, Mercer's SOMPA collects information on the child's background and brings norms for children of similar background into the interpretation.

From the child's parent, SOMPA collects a health history, information indicative of the child's maturity and adjustment, and information on educational, economic, and cultural characteristics of the family. The interview generates numerical indicators of family size, family structure, socioeconomic status, and urban acculturation (use of English in the home, parents' sense of efficacy, community participation, etc.).

In addition, the Adaptive Behavior Inventory for Children (ABIC) covers such questions as[2]

> How many of the children and families living around the neighborhood (ranch or farm) does _____ know by name?
>
> 1 SOME OF THEM   2 MOST OF THEM   0 NONE OF THEM
>
> When _____ cannot have what he/she wants immediately, how often does he/she get angry and fuss about it?
>
> 0 MOST OF THE TIME   1 SOMETIMES   2 ALMOST NEVER

The response choices (but not the numbers) are read to the parent. The responses yield six scores: Family, Community, Peer Relations, Nonacademic School Roles, Earner/Consumer, and Self-Maintenance.

The child takes six tests of motor coordination, one of vision, and one of hearing. The Bender Gestalt test, in which the child copies lines of various shapes, is given as a crude check on perceptual maturity and neurological functioning (see p. 624).

Alongside the scores so far mentioned, Wechsler standard scores are considered. Significantly, they are plotted under "School Functioning Level (SFL)." Mercer's next step is to construct an "Estimated Learning

---

[2]Selections from the System of Multicultural Pluralistic Assessment Parent Interview Manual reproduced by permission. Copyright © 1977 by The Psychological Corporation. All rights reserved.

Potential (ELP)"—the label implicitly claims that statistics can disclose unobserved talent. Her statistical procedure (described on p. 133) does no more than compare the child with others of somewhat similar family background. Mercer's adjustment lowers the standard score if the child's family is small, intact, and integrated with mainstream culture and raises it (perhaps by quite a lot) where the opposite is true.

Bernice, a black 9-year-old, had a Wechsler IQ of 68, with V and P also at that level. Bernice scored average or above on the ABIC scales, apparently being unusually able to care for herself. But her school record was very poor, and, as Mercer says, that fact plus the WISC-R scores would have led many schools to consider placing Bernice in a class for the retarded. From the ELP↔(Figure 7.5) and background information, Mercer and Lewis (1977, p. 88) concluded that

> the average WISC-R Full Scale IQ earned by children having Bernice's configuration of scores on the Sociocultural Scales is 77. Her WISC-R Full Scale IQ of 68, therefore, is only 9 points below the mean for her normative group. This is not an important variation from the mean, and her Estimated Learning Potential, expressed as an ELP Full Scale score of 89, argues against placing Bernice in a class for the mentally retarded.
>
> In Bernice's case, there is much to build on. She does not have a history of serious health problems, her sensory-motor abilities do not appear to be impaired, and her vision and hearing are good. As evidenced by her scores on the ABIC, Bernice exhibits a degree of personal independence and social

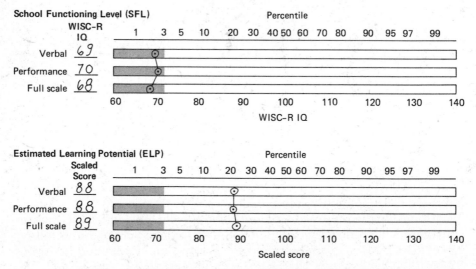

Figure 7.5. **Profiles based on general and differentiated norms.** A score in the shaded region at the left would conventionally be considered a markedly weak performance. (*Source*: Profile form and description of Bernice reproduced by permission from the System of Multicultural Assessment Parent Interview Manual (pp. 87–88). Copyright © 1977 by The Psychological Corporation. All rights reserved.)

responsibility greater than one ordinarily finds among children her age. Although her *WISC-R* IQs are low, her ELP scores are within the normal range. When all of these factors are considered, it seems likely that Bernice can benefit from a program of educational instruction that takes differences between her background and the culture of the school into account.

This benign interpretation does seem to be more appropriate than a prediction of school failure. The paragraph glosses over the difficulties of inventing an educational program suited to Bernice, but a test manual lacks room to develop such a theme.

Psychologists know that performance at the 2d percentile does not have the usual implications when a child demonstrates adequate functioning in home and community, so they advise considering the child's adaptation to his or her own subculture. But the ELP conversion is flawed. Mercer's Hispanic data were obtained by testing in English; testing should be in Spanish when the child has better command of that language. Mercer's samples were small and not geographically representative. At best, the formulas that fit one community would not be best for a distant community (Reschly, in Reynolds & Gutkin, 1982). Nor would a true national sample give a formula appropriate to a local clientele. Moreover, better statistical methods (Darlington, 1978) would have changed the adjustment formulas.

Mercer's techniques boost black scores by about 11 IQ points on average and those of Hispanics by 7. Scores of a few white children are adjusted upward by similar amounts, but small downward adjustments are made for most white children. Mercer implies that children with the same ELP are equally ready to learn, and hints that proper education would bring them the same final attainment. That goes too far. The words *potential* and *capacity* again cause trouble. Mercer offered no evidence for the optimistic prediction that children like Bernice will, with appropriate nurturance, achieve as much in school as a child for whom both SFL and ELP stand at 89. (See Sattler, 1981, pp. 280–282.)

Mercer compares three models of score interpretation: "medical," "social system," and "pluralistic." Table 7.3 introduces ideas from several of her chapters. In medical diagnosis, testers locate defects (in hearing, for example). All but four of Mercer's variables, she says, seek out defects. WISC-R IQs (= SFL) and ABIC, she says, address questions posed by the "social system" model. ELP and the sociocultural scales embody a "pluralistic" conception.

Adaptive Behavior Whatever the problems in Mercer's overall scheme, the Adaptive Behavior Inventory (p. 249) has value. It is one of several well-regarded instruments of the type. In addition to Mercer's, I draw attention to the Vineland Adaptive Behavior Scales pioneered in the 1920s and recently revised, and the AAMD Adaptive Behavior Scale.

Those planning for persons with substandard intellectual development generally agree to restrict use of the labels "retarded" and "mildly

Table 7.3 MERCER'S THREE ASSESSMENT MODELS

Elements of models	Medical model	Social system model	Pluralistic model
Other names for models	Pathological model, Disease model, Deficit model.	Social deviance model, Social adaptivity model, Social-ecological model.	General intelligence model.
Purposes	To screen for biological anomalies.	To identify behavioral deviance.	To estimate learning potential.
Definition of normal/abnormal	Normal = absence of pathological signs. Abnormal = presence of pathological signs.	Normal = behavior that meets social norms. Abnormal = behavior that violates social norms; social deviance.	Normal = scoring average for own group. Abnormal = scoring high or low on test of learning compared to own sociocultural group; a normative classification.
Assumptions of the models	1. Symptoms are caused by biological pathology. 2. Sociocultural factors are not relevant to diagnosis or treatment; human organisms are similar across cultures.	1. Multiple definitions of "normal" behavior are role- and system-specific. 2. Behavioral norms are politically, not biologically, determined; values of the dominant group are enforced.	1. All tests measure learning and are culture-specific. 2. Inferences regarding "intelligence" are based on comparisons among children who have had similar sociocultural experiences.
Ethical code governing interpretation	It is a more serious error in assessment to overlook a pathology that is present than to falsely suspect a pathology that is not present, since untreated pathology may lead to more serious pathology.	It is a more serious error in assessing behavior to falsely label behavior as deviant than to falsely label behavior as normal, since negative labeling may result in the placement of a child on a disabling trajectory.	It is a more serious error to underestimate than to overestimate learning potential, since underestimates may result in the placement of a child on a disabling trajectory. Overestimates may enhance educational options.

retarded." Such a label is acceptable only if the person is far below the norm in tested general ability *and* in a measure of so-called adaptive behavior: clothing and feeding oneself, staying with a chore, and the like (Coulter & Morrow, 1978). In this usage, "adaptive behavior" is a palatable label for adequacy in coping with *recurrent* everyday situations. As can be seen from Mercer's questions, the emphasis is on typical behavior and not on maximum performance. Many persons, though classed as retarded in childhood by the usual mental tests, have succeeded as adults in jobs and family living. It follows that intellectual ability, narrowly defined, is not a sufficient basis for judging the seriousness of suspected retardation.

Nihara (in Coulter & Morrow, 1978) finds that most questions in such scales fall into three categories: personal self-sufficiency, personal-social responsibility, and community self-sufficiency. The first category has to do with elementary functioning (walking, dressing oneself, hearing, . . .). The second is more motivational and social (consideration for others, work habits, care of personal property). "Community self-sufficiency" includes concepts of time and number, basic literacy, and such skills as using public transportation and handling work assignments of some complexity.

The communication aspect of adaptive behavior overlaps considerably with an individual mental test, but the sections on social and living skills do not (Keith et al., 1987, p. 37).

10. *Consider Mercer's models as described in Table 7.3.*
    a. *If a person drinks alcohol frequently and in large amounts, how would that behavior be described in Mercer's language? Which of the three value judgments (at the bottom of the columns) seem(s) appropriate for such a case?*
    b. *Recent immigrants from countries where English is not spoken have difficulties in the school and community. Describe them in terms of Mercer's second and third models.*

11. *What do you understand "learning potential" to mean? Would Mercer's concept be adequately validated by a check on how well ELPs recorded 3 years ago, when children entered school, correlate with scores on a current achievement test?*

The Kaufman Batteries

The Kaufman Assessment Battery for Children takes a fresh approach (KABC; Alan and Nadeen Kaufman; ages $2\frac{1}{2}$ to 12). A volume interpreting research on the test (Kamphaus & Reynolds, 1987) and a symposium review in the *Journal of Special Education* (Miller, 1984) are important sources of information.

There are 16 subtests, some suited to young children and some to older ones. The tasks are generally attractive to children and easy to administer. Figure 7.6 lists the subtests and the scores they enter. Items call for nonverbal or very brief answers, so the clinician has little opportunity to evaluate verbal production. Therefore the Kaufmans recom-

MENTAL PROCESSING

Sequential Processing (Memory)

Hand movements. Examiner gestures; then child is to make same movement.

Number recall. Like Digit Span.

Work order. Examiner reads off names of pictures or color spots; child is then to touch them in the same order.

Simultaneous Processing (Fluid ability)

Face recognition.[a] Child studies photo of a face, then page is turned to a group picture where he is to pick out the same person.

Magic window.[a] Child to name a picture turned past a slit (Fig. 7.7).

Gestalt closure. Child is to integrate drawing (Fig. 7.7).

Triangles. Like Block Design.

Matrix analogies. Task resembling Figure 7.1.

Spatial memory. After child studies a layout of objects (Figure 7.7), page is turned. On the grid, child is to point out where objects were located.

Photo series. Like Picture Arrangement. (Example: Eight colored photos of a cake being iced, to be placed in time order.

ACHIEVEMENT (Verbal and quantitative)

Expressive vocabulary.[a] Pictured objects to be named.

Faces and places. Child is to name famous persons and buildings in photographs.

Arithmetic. Questions calling for basic concepts from "more" to "three-fourths"; computational items are few and simple.

Riddles. Example: "What is shaped like a tube, is used by plumbers, and carries water?"

Reading/Decoding. Single words and letters to be read.

Reading/Understanding. Child is to act out printed command. ("Form a circular shape, using your thumb and the finger that is adjacent to it.")

---

[a]Used only for ages below 5.   *Counted in Nonverbal Score.

mend giving Wechsler's Comprehension subtest alongside KABC in most cases.

The manual emphasizes that KABC measures current functioning and not innate abilities. The two main scores are labeled Mental Processing and Achievement; the Kaufmans purposely identified "intelligence" with the former. On page 2 of the manual they say that KABC

> is predicated on the distinction between problem solving and knowledge of facts. The former set of skills is interpreted as intelligence; the latter is defined as achievement. This definition represents a break from other intelligence tests, where a person's acquired factual information and applied skills frequently influence greatly the obtained IQ.

Within Mental Processing are subscores for Sequential Processing (SEQ) and Simultaneous Processing (SIM), the division being based on recent ideas from neuropsychology and cognitive psychology. SEQ tasks call primarily on short-term memory. The SIM section looks mostly at pattern detection and nonverbal reasoning. Figure 7.7 illustrates three SIM tasks. Two short-term memory tests are included in SIM; the Kaufmans cite evidence that these require more organizing and verbal encoding than the SEQ tasks. The Nonverbal score (see footnote to Figure 7.6) is most pertinent for children with language handicaps, being based on those processing tests that can be administered in pantomime and responded to by pointing or moving pieces. I shall take up the Achievement section a bit later.

A review of KABC by Das (in Miller, 1984) is instructive, because Das was a principal developer of the concepts of simultaneous and sequential processing. Das prefers not to think of these as "abilities"; rather they are processes, both of which can help in almost any intellectual task. Two children who do well on one of the tasks may apply SIM and SEQ processes to it in different proportions. Das would prefer to have tests identify a child's actual approach. Also, he suggests giving greater attention to planning and decision making than KABC does.

Interpretation at the subtest level can be illustrated by a condensed account of one case (KABC interpretative manual, 1983, pp. 219–220; I put scores on a 50 ± 10 scale). Gary had all his main scores in the 54–61 range, with no important variation. Most subtest scores were in the neighborhood of 57, but there was a remarkable difference between 70 on Hand Movements and 40 on Word Order—both part of SEQ. The Kaufmans have found that Hand Movements is about equally likely to call upon simultaneous and sequential processing. When a child describes the tester's gestures to himself in words in order to hold them in mind, the theory calls this processing simultaneous. If Gary took this

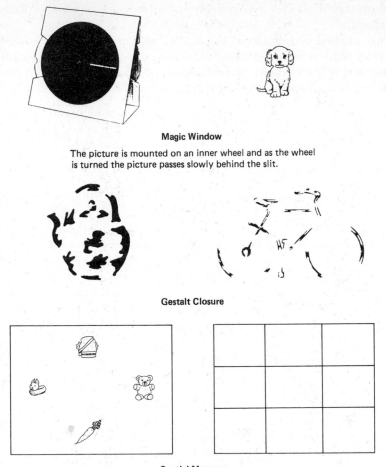

Magic Window

The picture is mounted on an inner wheel and as the wheel
is turned the picture passes slowly behind the slit.

Gestalt Closure

Spatial Memory

The figure at left is exposed for study. After it is
removed, the grid is presented for the child's response.

Figure 7.7. **Item types used in three Simultaneous Processing subtests.** Pictures
are much reduced here. The dog occupies about half the width of the slit.
(*Source*: Kaufman Assessment Battery for Children by Alan S. Kaufman and Na-
deen L. Kaufman. Copyright © 1983, 1988 by American Guidance Service, Circle
Pines, MN 55014. Items reproduced with the permission of American Guidance
Service, Inc.)

approach, it would be best to evaluate his memory only from Word Order
and Number Recall. Judging from them, Gary is a bit below the norm in
memory. His record is superior otherwise.

The Achievement section of KABC is not an achievement test in the
usual sense, as can be seen from the content listed in Figure 7.6. KABC
Achievement correlates above 0.85 with the Verbal score of SB4. Also,
the Achievement score is saturated with whatever central element is

shared by WISC-R and KABC—more so than the Mental Processing score (Naglieri & Jensen, 1987). The "Achievement" label for this score has drawn severe criticism (see Anastasi, 1988, p. 269; Page, in Mitchell, 1985, p. 775; and Sternberg, in Miller, 1984). Test users may fail to appreciate that the Achievement score is a significant indicator of aptitude. The plans for a forthcoming adolescent-adult battery call for attaching the label "Adaptive Intelligence" to this kind of score.

This Kaufman Adolescent and Adult Intelligence Test (KAIT), for ages 11 and up, retains many features of KABC. More of the Mental Processing tasks will be verbal, but a separate score based on the less verbal tasks will also be reported. The Kaufmans expect to add a Planning section (as Das recommended).

The emphasis on memory and the small emphasis on verbal conceptualization in KABC is partly a consequence of deliberately seeking tasks on which blacks and whites have similar means. Whereas most other tests report a black/white difference of 15 IQ points, the difference is near 2 points on SEQ, 6 on SIM, and 8 on Achievement, for ages below 8. At higher ages, the differences are 7, 12, and 12.[3] In addition to the usual type of national norms, scores can be converted to percentiles relative to a socioeconomic group—for example, black (or white) children with at least one parent who went beyond high school. Consider a 10-year-old whose national percentile on Sequential Processing is 75 and whose most-educated parent finished high school. The "sociocultural percentile" is 90 if the child is black; 75 if he is white.

12. *Just after the passage quoted from p. 33 of the manual, the Kaufmans criticize Binet's Dissected Sentences item (used in the 1960 SB) for the weight it gives to "reading comprehension." The item has this form:*

    hose   out   with   fires   can   their   put   firemen

    To what extent is the criticism reasonable? Does the Kaufmans' distinction between problem solving and knowledge of facts apply to this task?

13. *Does the character of the Spatial Memory subtest justify including it in SEQ rather than SIM?*

14. *Gestalt Closure has appreciably lower correlations than the other KABC subtests have with WISC-R subtests (Kaufman & McLean, 1987). What does this suggest regarding the contribution of this subtest?*

15. *What could be learned from the KABC Achievement section when a pupil is referred for testing because of poor academic progress in Grade 2, after an average record in Grade 1?*

16. *The black/white difference in SIM standard scores increases between early childhood and middle childhood. What explanations can you suggest?*

---

[3]These figures combine medians for socioeconomic groups (scoring manual, pp. 207–231), using group sizes from the U.S. census (KABC interpretative manual, p. 69).

The Cognitive Abilities Test and the Stanford-Binet

Here we shall look at a representative modern group test, CogAT, and the current Stanford-Binet, an individual test that resembles CogAT in many ways. Mental tests prior to the 1937 version of the Wechsler rarely offered more than a single score, usually an IQ. A few tests such as Raven's famous Progressive Matrices employed a single type of item. There were also single-task vocabulary tests; each item might present a word pair (e.g., *frugal-lavish*) and ask whether the meanings are the same or opposite. In contrast, modern instruments have diverse parts and report a composite score for each family of subtests. (Sometimes, attention is paid also to the separate subtest scores.)

The early group tests were highly speeded. In contrast, current practice favors "power tests," with items of one kind presented in sequence from easy to hard. Time limits are sufficiently generous that nearly everyone finishes all the items on which he is likely to succeed.

CogAT   The three sections of the Cognitive Abilities Test (Robert L. Thorndike and Elizabeth Hagen) yield Verbal, Quantitative, and Non-verbal scores. (On this patterning, see pp. 375–377.) No overall score is provided. The authors hoped to focus teachers' attention on patterns of ability and to discourage simple bright/dull classifications. A version of this test appeared in 1954 and it took essentially its present form in 1971: it is periodically revised and renormed.

Each part contains three subtests; two from each part are illustrated in Figure 7.8. The three tasks not shown are verbal analogies, number series, and paper folding ("Figure Analysis").

A single booklet serves Grades 3 through 12. (There is a separate test for the primary grades.) Thanks to an adaptive procedure that allows testing with only part of each subtest, the examinee is given few items that he is likely to find very hard or very easy. This saves time, and reduces frustration and boredom.

Within a subtest, items are arranged according to difficulty. All the specimens in Figure 7.8 are from Level C, where a typical fifth-grade class would start work. For every starting level, there is a corresponding stopping point. A class might start Number Series at Level C with the item having an "add 5" rule in Figure 7.8. That class would stop just short of Level H, whose items have rules like this: "Add 2, subtract 3, add 4, subtract 5, . . ."—e.g., 10 12 9 13 8 . . . . Whereas most fifth-graders stop short of level H, typical twelfth-graders start there.

CogAT allows "out of level" testing. Very able fifth-graders score high on a test planned for the usual fifth grade; harder items would better test their limits. And a comparatively easy test is advisable for the least able members of a class. Starting levels can be fitted to pupils individually if the exceptional ones are identified in advance, perhaps by their achievement. A pupil *in any grade* whose grade-equivalent score

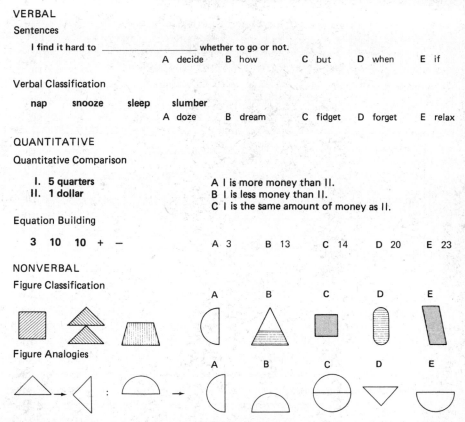

VERBAL

Sentences

I find it hard to _____ whether to go or not.

    A decide   B how   C but   D when   E if

Verbal Classification

    nap   snooze   sleep   slumber

    A doze   B dream   C fidget   D forget   E relax

QUANTITATIVE

Quantitative Comparison

    I. 5 quarters   A I is more money than II.
    II. 1 dollar   B I is less money than II.
                    C I is the same amount of money as II.

Equation Building

    3 10 10 + −   A 3   B 13   C 14   D 20   E 23

NONVERBAL

Figure Classification

    A   B   C   D   E

Figure Analogies

    A   B   C   D   E

Figure 7.8. **Selected tasks from CogAT.** (*Source*: Some of these items are copyright © 1971 or 1978 by the Riverside Publishing Company and are reproduced by permission.)

is 12.0 would start with Level H. An adept tester can start pupils on different levels; the time allowance is the same regardless of the starting point. The several levels are mapped onto a common score scale by the Rasch method (p. 139).

Items progress so steeply in difficulty that few scores are affected by the time limit (see p. 303). On tryouts, children given extra time did not improve their scores appreciably. The total working time is 90 minutes plus time for giving out materials and presenting directions. Spacing the sections over 2 or 3 days is advised.

Computer scoring uses norms to generate several kinds of report, as is seen in Figure 7.9. The computer will also calculate percentiles and stanines (see p. 117) relative to class, school, or community groups. When raw scores are obtained by hand, percentile and standard-score equivalents are read from tables. Because comparisons across variables

PROFILE NARRATIVE REPORT
Cognitive Abilities Test
Published by THE RIVERSIDE PUBLISHING COMPANY

Abilities	GRADE SCORES National		National Percentile Rank						
	Stanine	Percentile Rank	Low 1	10	25	Average 50	75	90	High 99
VERBAL	5	56	/////////////////////						
QUANTITATIVE	7	86	/////////////////////////////						
NONVERBAL	8	94	/////////////////////////////////						

Score Detail	RAW SCORE		AGE RELATED SCORES		
	Number Attempted	Number Correct	Standard Age Score	National Stanine	National Percentile Rank
VERBAL	75	51	99	5	48
QUANTITATIVE	60	49	115	7	83
NONVERBAL	65	57	126	8	95

Predicted Achievement	
VOCABULARY	ABOUT AVERAGE
READING	ABOUT AVERAGE
LANGUAGE TOTAL	SOMEWHAT ABOVE AVERAGE
WORK-STUDY TOTAL	SOMEWHAT ABOVE AVERAGE
MATHEMATICS TOTAL	ABOVE AVERAGE

Figure 7.9. **CogAT score report for Patrick Blanch.** (*Source*: This is the left portion of the printout intended for parents. The form is slightly simplified here, some detail being removed. Patrick was tested in Grade 6 (Spring), at age 12-9. I thank the Riverside Publishing Company for this example. The original form is copyright © 1986 by The Riverside Publishing Company and is adapted by permission. The right portion of the form (p. 261) describes Patrick's performance in words.)

can be more secure when all are normed together, CogAT and two achievement batteries were normed on the same samples.

Testing companies vie in preparing ingenious computerized reports. There are adhesive labels for the pupil's file record and score lists for the teacher. A one-page report for the pupil can serve (along with other information) as a basis for a conference with the parents, and is intended for them to take home.

Figure 7.9 shows the left half of one such report. The right half appears below, with boldface type used for the words inserted to describe Patrick. (These words do not stand out in the actual report.)

Your **son, Patrick,** was given the Cognitive Abilities Test (Form **4,** Level **D,** in **March 1986. Patrick** is in the **sixth** grade at **Lincoln Spec Educ Cedar Rapids Communi.** The test results are shown on the left. Scores under the section headed "Abilities" are reported and then graphed on the profile. This narrative will help explain the test results.

Different students bring different patterns and levels of abilities to learning tasks. To help find out about **Patrick's** abilities, **he** has been given the Cognitive Abilities Test. The test covers three different kinds of abilities: verbal, quantitative, and nonverbal. Most school work has to do with one or more of them.

Patrick was tested in all three areas: verbal, quantitative, and nonverbal abilities. **Patrick's** national percentile rank on verbal ability is **56.** This means that compared with other **sixth** grade students nationally, **Patrick** did better than **56** percent. **Patrick,** therefore, appears to be **about average** in verbal ability. **Patrick's** national percentile rank is **86** in quantitative ability and **94** in nonverbal ability. Patrick seems to be **above average** in quantitative ability and **well above average** in nonverbal ability.

To a certain degree, abilities can be used to predict success in school subjects. How well **Patrick** might do in different school subjects can be predicted using **his** scores on the Cognitive Abilities Test. A subject that may be a relative strength for **Patrick** is **mathematics,** and his achievement score will likely be **above average.** Subjects where **Patrick** may be relatively weak are **vocabulary and reading. Patrick's** achievement here may be **about average.** Some students' achievement is higher than that predicted from ability scores and some lower. Much depends on the study environment, student effort, and motivation for learning.

If you would like more information about **Patrick's** performance in school please contact **his** school.

The Stanford-Binet   The present-day descendant of Binet's pioneer scale retains some items Binet devised and others that Terman introduced; but its structure is entirely new (R. L. Thorndike, Elizabeth Hagen, & Jerome Sattler). This is a fourth (1986) edition, the earlier dates being 1916, 1937, and 1960. Sattler's 1988 book is a valuable supplementary source.

The new test (here coded SB4) is efficiently designed for measuring overall ability at ages from 2 to 23. (SB4 can be given to older persons, but norms for older persons are lacking.) The main score (on a 100 ± 16 scale) is labeled CSAS—Composite Standard Age Score. Four sections contribute to CSAS, and for each of these an SAS is reported on a 100 ± 8 scale. (The compressed scale is chosen to play down small differences in these comparatively unreliable scores.)

An examinee takes subtests, and items within subtests, appropriate to his age and ability. The Vocabulary subtest is presented first, increasingly difficult items being given until the person fails three out of four items. The level reached on Vocabulary indicates which subtests are too easy or too difficult to be given to this person, and also indicates which difficulty level to start with in each remaining subtest.

An 8-year-old of average ability would usually be given the following subtests (subtests from the several sections being presented in mixed order):

Verbal section: Vocabulary, Comprehension, Absurdities

Quantitative section: Quantitative, Number Series

Abstract/Visual section: Pattern Analysis, Copying, Matrices

Memory section: Bead Memory, Memory for Digits, Memory for Objects

Three subtests match Wechsler tasks; moreover, Quantitative and Pattern Analysis resemble Wechsler Arithmetic and Block Design.

A few of the subtests have no easy items and drop out entirely for most children under 7. Some others, for which difficult items were hard to create, are replaced around age 13 with distinctly different, harder tasks. Most SB items for early ages employ pictures and objects. Items within a subtest are likely to change in character as difficulty increases; Figure 7.10 illustrates changes within the Copying subtest.

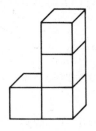

Level B. Block tower to
be imitated

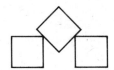

Level D. Flat block layout
to be imitated

Level H. Simple pattern to be
copied with pencil

Level M. Complex design
to be copied

Figure 7.10. **Easy and hard items for a Copying subtest.**

At school ages, the CSAS score is a well-balanced combination of memory tasks with three types of reasoning. For preschoolers, however, there are few Quantitative and Memory subtests. Section scores are strongly influenced by general ability (p. 281). Although not enough is known about its reliability and correlations with other measures, the CSAS score apparently will serve the same purposes as the Wechsler Full Scale IQ or the SB IQ of earlier years. Special functions and special limitations of the new SB will become clearer as experience and research accumulate.

Earlier editions of SB employed only a few items of any one type. All the types were thought to reflect general mental ability from various angles, and a single score was reported. Small clusters of items having similar difficulty were assigned to an age level. Level VIII (suited for 8-year-olds), for example, included the following tasks: vocabulary, memory for stories, verbal absurdities, similarities, comprehension, and naming the days of the week. Harder tasks (mostly of other kinds) appeared at Level IX and above. A 10-year-old might be started at Level VIII, and then moved forward until, perhaps at Level XIII, he failed consistently. There, testing would stop. An important defect was the predominantly verbal nature of tasks for later childhood and adolescence. In contrast, several tasks in SB4 employ abstract drawings at higher ages and allow nonverbal response.

17. CogAT scores "can help students and parents to understand the students' strengths and weaknesses. . . . [which] can then be matched with the cognitive demands made . . . by careers," says the manual. Assuming that the differences interpreted are reliable and stable, what vocational implications—if any—would the following profile patterns suggest? (At what age would such an interpretation be sensible?)
    a. Verbal and Quantitative in normal range; Nonverbal superior.
    b. Quantitative and Nonverbal in normal range; Verbal superior.

18. In question 17, what evidence about CogAT would need to be supplied to justify use of the profile in thinking about career plans?

19. The three sections of CogAT are influenced substantially by a common or "general" factor (p. 375). Yet CogAT provides no overall score, and the manual recommends against forming composites for purposes of case interpretation. What risk would there be in bringing to a case conference the three part scores plus an overall score?

20. Patrick's parents may be confused by having several sets of scores for him (Figure 7.9). Which of the sets should the teacher emphasize in talking to them?

21. The report for parents could be framed in terms of local rather than national norms. What is to be said for and against this choice?

22. What does the descriptive report add to the parents' understanding, beyond what is evident in Figure 7.9?

23. SB4 is advertised as the only test measuring the same variables on a continuous scale in the age span from 2 to 23. For what purposes could this feature be important?

24. *The Absurdities subtest of SB4 shows drawings such as a group of birds in flight, with one bird flying upside down (not an actual item.) The examinee is to say what is "wrong" or "silly." This is counted in the Verbal section, not the Abstract/Visual section. What evidence or reasoning could justify that decision?*

TESTS FOR ADMISSION TO ADVANCED EDUCATION

The two prominent tests for college admissions are the Scholastic Aptitude Test (SAT) and the American College Testing Program (ACT). Both measure the high school senior's intellectual readiness for college work.

These tests loom larger in the minds of students anxious about admissions than in the minds of admissions officers and faculties. Most colleges have flexible admission rules, not a minimum score for admission; and most accept a very high proportion of their applicants (Manning & Jackson, in Reynolds & Brown, 1984). Although a school with a surplus of applicants will scrutinize closely an applicant with poor test scores, admissions committees look beyond ability, seeking a good mix of applicant interests and backgrounds. Two national committees have recommended against selection by formula, that is, against automatically accepting those above a certain predicted grade average and rejecting those below it (Carnegie Council, 1977; Wigdor & Garner, 1982, vol. 1, pp. 199, 202). Such a practice turns away applicants with adequate academic promise who are outstanding along other lines. A questionnaire on musical, scientific, literary, and leadership activities (e.g., Have you ever won an award in a science fair?) identifies promising cases. The self-report can, of course, be checked. Records of such accomplishments correlate negligibly with grade record or with test scores (Wallach, in Messick, 1976), but they do correlate with subsequent accomplishment in the same fields.

Features of SAT   SAT is required by most of the colleges where admission is competitive and by many that accept nearly all applicants. Copies of questions from past examinations and booklets that advise on test taking are available to the prospective test taker. High schools can also purchase filmstrips plus audiotapes for orienting those who will take the test, and diskettes that provide exercises in test taking. A Preliminary Scholastic Aptitude Test is offered to high school juniors. It provides practice, helps in decisions about which colleges to apply to, and certifies eligibility for certain scholarships.

SAT-M measures mathematical thinking up to a high level—as is necessary, for instance, in awarding scholarships. SAT-M ingeniously avoids giving an advantage to students who have taken many math courses. Items such as those in Figure 5.7 (p. 176) call for algebraic and geometric reasoning. The student with insight has a great advantage.

(Note that the thinking student can solve the difficult Item 3 in Figure 5.7 with very little calculation.) The test taker need not remember formulas and theorems. Those pertinent to the items are printed as part of the test and also in the orientation booklet sent out in advance. SAT-M asks not "How much math do you *know*?" but "What can you *do* with math that everyone has studied?"

SAT-V is not so successful at the upper end as SAT-M. Superior college applicants have such highly developed verbal skills that the best scarcely differ from the next best. Wisely, the developers avoid rare words and avoid comprehension tasks that depend on knowledge of ideas from, say, economics. Analogies are made difficult by requiring subtle analysis of relationships of rather common words—an appropriate technique.

The game of trying to fool all but the ablest applicants carries item writers onto thin ice. A strong argument can sometimes be made for what the writers considered second-best and did not credit. David Owen (1985) entertainingly proves this in Chapter 3 of *None of the Above*, an informative but less-than-fair assault on the Educational Testing Service.

The items have been criticized also for too often drawing concepts from the lives of the socially privileged. Weiss (1987) complains about an analogy item: "*Runner* is to *marathon* as . . ." This is to be completed by choosing "*oarsman* is to *regatta*." (The analogy is not close but is probably the best of the choices offered.) The item measures reasoning *if* the respondent knows the meaning of "regatta." The example might be dismissed as an isolated misjudgment by the item writers if Weiss did not also point to items in which "bridle," "polo," "tympanist," and "heirloom" figure.

Features of ACT   The ACT assessment was changed substantially in 1989, and the remodeled instrument was not available when this book went to press. From the statement of plans, it appears that the new test is much like the old in overall character, and that the predictive validity will not change notably.

ACT has been and will be more nearly a test of achievement than the SAT. It seeks to measure *general* educational development rather than content likely to be covered in one student's curriculum and not another's. The emphasis is on intellectual skills rather than knowledge from particular lessons. As in SAT, all items are in multiple-choice form. The new version has four parts:

- *English.* One subscore reports on "usage": punctuation, agreement of verb with noun, ordering of phrases within a sentence, and the like. The second subscore, Rhetorical Skills, has to do with economy and clarity in writing, order of development of ideas, and matching style to audience and purpose.

- *Reading.* Includes literal comprehension and recognition of implications.
- *Mathematics.* Includes skills such as solving equations and also (to measure understanding) analysis of novel problems. Three subscores refer to course levels, one being Intermediate Algebra and Coordinate Geometry.
- *Science Reasoning.* The examinee is to interpret research summaries and tables, and to analyze conflicting hypotheses.

The most novel section is the last one, intended to assess a competence toward which scientific courses aim without favoring students who have studied any one field of science.

The test of 1988 and earlier had two reading sections, covering social-science and natural-science content. Reading ability is a suitable predictor, but reporting these separate subscores was not helpful to colleges in selection and guidance. The developers hope that the new profile will provide a suitable basis for placing college entrants in appropriate courses or course levels.

Many nonselective colleges, including statewide public systems, have required or recommended that applicants take ACT. The program provides extensive statistical services; with that help, a college can build up its own experience table to identify, for example, how the several scores relate to later success in its engineering department.

Predictive Power Findings on validity of predictions from admissions tests appear in Figure 7.11. Grades from high school alone had predictive coefficients of 0.5 on the average. Prediction improved dramatically when the score from a standard test was combined with the high school record, presumably because the test is not subject to the vagaries of local grading practices. The coefficients for ACT considered alone had much the same range as those for the school grades alone. Prediction tends to be better for women than for men (Sawyer & Maxey, 1982). An elaborate study of SAT data compared validities across types of colleges (Ramist, in Donlon, 1984). Most differences between types were small.

Table 7.4 summarizes typical experience in another way; these numbers are worked out on the assumption of a normal distribution. It is assumed, for purposes of the mathematical demonstration, that the college fills the available places by selecting from the top of the predictor distribution, and that all those admitted to the college enroll there.

Persons who acknowledge that SAT measures academic abilities sometimes challenge its practical worth. Crouse, among others, questions whether the college needs the information, which is obtained at some cost to applicants (Crouse & Trusheim, 1988). I can indicate his line of thought with going into detail as he does. Look at the last two rows in Table 7.4 (he would say). In the 0.5 column, taking SAT into account raises the hit rate from 76 to 78 per cent. Is that benefit sufficient to warrant imposing the test on applicants?

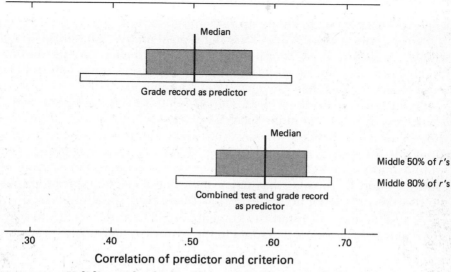

Figure 7.11. **Validity with which college marks are predicted.** Distribution of correlations in 312 colleges relating freshman grade average to high-school grade average and to a predictor that combined grades with ACT scores. (*Source*: Data from Linn, in Wigdor & Garner, 1982, vol. 2, p. 348.)

Misuse of Group Averages   In addition to their use in decisions by and about individuals, SAT and ACT results are brought into debates on policy. The arguments are often unsound. When the chief school officer of a state brags that his regime has been effective because the average SAT score of the state's test takers has been rising, his inference is unjustified for two reasons.

Although schools can improve reasoning ability as well as more "basic" skills, out-of-class life has a large effect. The student's hobbies, and

Table 7.4   PRACTICAL CONSEQUENCES OF SELECTIVE ADMISSIONS

Basis for prediction	Typical validity coefficient	Percentage of admits who reach 40th percentile in college GPA		
		SR = 0.2	SR = 0.5	SR = 0.8
Chance	0	60	60	60
SAT-V *or* SAT-M	0.37	79	72	65
SAT-V *and* SAT-M	0.41	79	73	66
High school grade average	0.49	86	76	67
SAT-V, SAT-M, and high school grades	0.56	88	78	68

Source: Adapted from Kaplan, 1982, p. 21.

NOTE: SR (selection ratio) is the proportion of applicants admitted.

conversations with friends and family, can be more influential than whatever teachers do to shape up reasoning.

Second, those who take SAT are not representative. Students choose whether to take SAT, ACT, or neither, according to what is requested by the colleges they are considering. Change in the average may reflect those choices rather than any change in competence.

In the early 1980s the federal Department of Education produced a dramatic wall chart that ranked states by average SAT scores; at the top were midwestern states, with New York and California far down the list. Alongside the scores, data on school expenditures were displayed. The Administration, lobbying to hold down appropriations for education, used the chart to "prove" that states spending more on education (per pupil) were producing no better results than states spending less.

Self-selection corrupted the comparison. Where the state's university requires ACT scores (common in the Midwest), most college-bound

State mean on SAT V + M	Mean percentile rank-in-class of SAT test takers in the state				
	70–74	75–79	80–84	85–89	90–91
1100					
1080					IA SD
1060					ND
1040				KS MT NE	
1020			MN WI	UT WY	
1000			NM TN	AR ID OK	
980		IL	AZ CO LA MI MO WA	KY MS	
960			AL OH	WV	
940					
920	NH		AK	NV	
900	CT DE NY	CA OR VT			
880	MA MD PA RI VA	FL ME			
860	HI IN NJ	TX			
840					
820	DC GA	NC			
800					
780	SC				

Figure 7.12. **Rank order of SAT means of states, with an indicator of self-selection by test takers.** States in italics are those where college-bound seniors are more likely to take ACT than SAT. A high mean rank-in-class indicates that the SAT group was a highly select fraction of a state's seniors. (*Source*: Data from Wainer, 1986.)

students take ACT. The fraction who take SAT are mostly applying to out-of-state, prestige schools. In a state where the dominant colleges ask applicants to submit SAT scores, however, the SAT population is a broad cross section of the college-bound. Figure 7.12 shows that higher SAT means come from the states where the SAT population is self-selected from the top of the graduating classes.

Although the wall chart's abuse of test data has now faded into history, I have given space to it because many policy studies of group means on tests fail to adjust for selection into the groups. It is possible to make reasonable (but imperfect) allowance for selective factors (Bryk & Raudenbush, 1986; Wainer, 1986).

25. *One of the committees referred to earlier concluded that probable accomplishment should not be overemphasized in college admissions. "When there are many applicants capable of succeeding admissions decisions should be based on social and educational values broader than . . . grade averages." Attention is drawn to "diversity" in the student body as a value, and minority representation is on the committee's mind. What other values or what other kinds of diversity should an admissions committee care about?*

26. *Admissions tests have been designed to predict grades, and applicants with the highest predicted grade averages have been preferred over others. A study commission has advanced a "value-added" concept as an alternative. It advises an institution to seek those applicants whose later value to society will be most enhanced by participating in the institution's program (Higher Education Research Institute, 1982). Whom would this policy favor? What do you think of the proposal?*

27. *The assumptions underlying the calculations in Table 7.4 are somewhat unrealistic. In what ways? Would you expect the consequences to change if the assumptions were closer to reality?*

28. *On page 85 we saw that SAT-M scores are easier to improve than SAT-V. Suggest possible explanations.*

29. *The College Board recommends that employers not request SAT scores of college graduates applying for positions. What are the arguments for the policy? (The candidate can obtain an official copy of his scores for forwarding; the firm cannot request the report directly.)*

TESTING IN THE EARLY YEARS

Testing young children is difficult. It is hard to hold their attention on a task. They have not yet learned to follow instructions as they do after a year or two in school. And their limited verbal comprehension complicates interpretation of essentially nonverbal tasks. The individual tests described earlier in this chapter, by simplifying tasks, reach down to age $2\frac{1}{2}$ or 3. "Floor effects" limit the evaluation of the youngest and least able children. On SB4, a score of zero on a subtest is not uncommon; the child did not understand the directions or was unable to cope with the easiest items. Attentiveness and cooperation vary from day to day at age

3—another source of inaccuracy. Instability is an even greater problem at very early ages. The long history of infant testing and interpretations of the research are fully treated in books edited by Lewis (1983) and Osofsky (1979).

Assessment is important in planning early education, especially of children whose development is slow or uneven, and there are a number of special tests for this purpose. Typically these appraise specific aspects of development such as auditory memory, right-left orientation, and motor coordination, as well as the broader verbal and reasoning domains. How such measures fit into educational planning will be discussed in Chapter 9.

Testing in the early *months* is becoming increasingly feasible. Intellectual developments begin long before the grasp of language makes conventional testing possible, so early performance is receiving much research attention. Pediatricians trying to assist infants who seem likely not to progress at a normal rate need tests for screening and diagnosis. (Sometimes tests show reassuring normality where a pediatrician had suspected abnormality; Honzik, in Lewis, 1983.) Psychologists are testing out programs of stimulation, in home or care center, intended to foster perceptual and cognitive development. Analysis of an infant's development can perhaps guide the choice of activities or evaluate their effects (Seibert, in Uzgiris & Hunt, 1987). Kahn (in Uzgiris & Hunt, 1987) suggests similar use of the infant scales with the seriously retarded at ages beyond infancy.

One cannot set a task for the infant. To study the first year of life is to study spontaneous behavior or conditioned reactions and habits. In the second year, limited tasks can be set. We may regard the child's reaching for a ring as purposive, but we credit him with visual-motor coordination rather than abstract analysis. He is perceptive when he imitates the examiner and places one block atop another, but this is not the kind of problem solving we test at age 4 and above. Critics make remarks such as this: "When the psychologist assesses ability by asking whether the infant follows a ball visually or uses a spoon in eating or seeks a lost toy, she looks at behavior that neither the lay person nor the psychologist would regard as integral aspects of intelligence at a later age."

The age at which a response emerges may be as much a reflection of special stimulation or lack of stimulation as of the child's ability to develop the response. Twins, for instance, are slower to speak, very likely because their attention is going into nonverbal interaction when other children are practicing sounds to themselves. Mental development has many facets, and progress in sensorimotor imitation may proceed on a different schedule from that of verbal development. Indeed, enthusiastic exercise of one skill may delay emergence of another. Even when developments A and B are logically linked and achieving A is a necessary preliminary to B, the date at which the infant succeeds on B does not come a predictable number of weeks after the achievement of A.

B is a new performance whose date of consolidation depends on many variables in the child's experience.

The greatest cumulation of findings on abilities prior to age 2 comes from the Bayley scales. Bayley had been a student of Terman and she extended the Binet tradition. Two emerging procedures look at the infant in new ways. One, derived from Piaget, tries to observe progress toward several kinds of competence. The second takes the child's attentiveness as an indicator of what is in his mind. This method has not yet been standardized or widely disseminated, but it seems likely to become practically important.

Bayley's Scales   The Bayley Scales of Infant Development are standardized. Samples were tested at 14 levels: 2, 3, 4, 5, 6, 8, 10, . . ., 24, 27, and 30 months. Smoothing the developmental trends produced norms for intermediate ages such as $4\frac{1}{2}$, 9, and 28 months. To test 1400 infants individually on controlled dates was a large and indeed unparalleled undertaking. Bayley's two scores, Mental and Psychomotor, intercorrelate near 0.6 at 2–6 months and near 0.3 after 18 months.

The following observations represent the "mental" content at 6 months (each item being accompanied here by Bayley's suggestion as to the function measured):

Sustained inspection of ring (alertness of an exploratory type).

Turn to observe moving spoon (goal-directed attention).

Vocalizes displeasure (extrovertive responses, not goal-centered).

Smiles at image in mirror (social response).

At 12 months, the emphasis is on communication and concepts, including imitation and obedience to simple commands, though a substantial number of the items require controlled movement. Imitation, of course, is both evidence of learning and a means of further learning.

The Uzgiris-Hunt Scales   In the Infant Psychological Development Scales (I. C. Uzgiris & J. McV. Hunt) each scale is an "ordinal" representation of one aspect of development. Items are strongly ordered; an infant who cannot perform one task is unlikely to pass consistently an item higher in the scale. The following paraphrase of items from the 11 stages in the scale for Construction of object relations in space illustrates the ordered character of the scales (but does not give an adequate impression of the testing procedure). Each item is identified here by the age at which the majority of infants "passed" the test.

2 months   Confronted with two objects, infant alternates glances between them.

3 months   In that same situation, infant alternates glances rapidly.

4–5 months   Presented with a graspable object, infant reaches and grasps.

7 months   Tester displays an object and allows it to fall; infant directs his eyes toward its probable location on the trials when it falls out of view.

9 months   Seated before an empty container and several beads or blocks, infant places objects in container and turns it over to dump them out.

The seven scales include Visual pursuit and permanence of objects, Vocal imitation, and Development of operational causality. Among normal children of the same age the scales are not strongly correlated; correlations are higher for retarded children (Curcio and Houlihan, in Uzgiris & Hunt, 1987). Uzgiris-Hunt scores correlate appreciably with the Bayley mental score in the second year of life (Sexton and Uzgiris, in Uzgiris & Hunt, 1987).

An important aim of the plural scales is to get away from the notion that early development is growth in a unitary "mental ability." Considered separately, the several scales can trace how lines of development relate to specific elements in the infant's environment and activity. It remains useful to think of the overall level of development (as in a finding that progress across the board is inhibited by life in a bleak orphanage nursery).

Inferences from Attention   The acquisition of words, and thus of categories and abstractions, might seem to mark the beginning of truly intellectual processes. The investigators making inferences from visual responses believe that the infant's information processing is similar to and a forerunner of ability to perform analytic tasks at later ages. (See p. 284.)

These methods have evolved from the pioneer work of Robert Fantz in the 1950s (see Fagan, 1985). A baby lying on his back can be tested, but I shall speak of one on his mother's lap. A frame is mounted a foot or so in front of the child, and a light beside it reflects off the eye surface. The tester, watching through a peephole, can easily recognize when the baby's gaze shifts.

One testing routine makes use of the satiation phenomenon. One or two "targets" are dropped into slots in the frame. If one target is novel and the other one is familiar, a person tends to look at the novel one. So, to begin, target A (perhaps a straight-up square) is exposed. After a 2-minute "study" period the target is removed. Perhaps 30 seconds later target A is shown at the left and target B—perhaps an identical square set at an angle—appears at the right. The child "passes" if his gaze settles down on B, the novel target. With other targets, right-to-left counterbalance, and changes in the delay interval, one gets a sensitive indicator of delayed recognition memory. If the degree of similarity between A and B is varied, one can infer when shapes are discriminated, or colors.

The testing session has to be brief, so an accurate measure can be obtained only by testing on several days. Ordinarily, when mother and child have to be brought to the apparatus or vice versa, a single session of no more than five items is the source of data. This is suitable for studies that accumulate many cases to investigate a hypothesis; however, with day-to-day correlations near 0.4, one session is an insufficient basis for evaluating individuals.

The technique extends to the measurement of ability to think "abstractly." Fagan familiarizes the baby with a red diamond, then after a brief delay exposes red and green squares side by side. Older infants look mostly at the green square; they are taking into account the general property, color. This performance has a strong resemblance to the ability required in the Figure Classification task of CogAT (p. 259).

30. *The Figure Classification example requires recognition of the difference between cross-ruled and plain figures. Could an infant's ability to make this distinction be tested by Fagan's procedure? What is required in the Figure Classification test that is not required in the infant test?*

31. *McCall et al. (1972) see infant tests as analogous in function to birth weights. The birth weight of a child does not predict childhood weight (even after adjustment for premature birth), yet for the pediatrician that measure is a significant signal of developmental status. How can one validate infant tests if they do not predict?*

32. *On the Bayley scale, retests after 1 week showed high consistency for most items including Lifts cup by handle, Looks for fallen spoon, and Imitates words. Low consistency was found for such items as Holds cup to drink from (in response to examiner's example), Cooperates with examiner in games, and Vocalizes displeasure. How do the two sets of items appear to differ? Can you explain the variability of the second set?*

Chapter
8

The Meanings of
General Ability

8A. What are the advantages of the overlapping longitudinal design for studying changes in ability over time?

8B. Why is the reliability of the difference between two tests usually lower than their separate reliabilities?

8C. What advantages do psychological tests have over grade averages for predicting educational success?

8D. In examining a new psychological test and statistical reports on it, how could you decide whether it measures general ability and, if so, where it belongs on the *Gf-Gc* spectrum?

8E. What constructs help to explain individual differences in rate of learning?

Abbreviations in this chapter: ABIC for Adaptive Behavior Inventory for Children (Mercer); ACT for American College Testing Program; CogAT for Cognitive Abilities Test; EFT for Embedded Figures Test; *Gc* and *Gf* for crystallized and fluid ability; KABC for Kaufman Assessment Battery for Children; SAT for the Scholastic Aptitude Test; SB for the Stanford-Binet, with SB4 for the fourth edition; WAIS-R and WISC-R for the revised Wechsler scales for adults and children, with V and P for Verbal and Performance IQs; WPPSI for the Wechsler preschool scale.

Our understanding of "general mental ability"—that is, of whatever lies behind thoughtful, adaptive performance—evolves steadily. Binet invested 15 years in research before arriving at his characterization of mental ability (p. 230). His ideas are still being refined and extended.

I said earlier that "ability" is like "efficiency"; such terms refer to multiple coordinated processes. It is appropriate to assess general ability "as a whole" and also to identify processes within good or poor performance. Maturing consists of more or less simultaneous small advances along a broad front, accompanied by gains in an "executive" or "managerial" skill that ties together these resources. This statement, and indeed almost all the facts and conclusions presented in this chapter, apply with equal force to achievement tests.

This process interpretation and its implications are the central topic of Chapter 8. I seek to place main issues in a broad context and to clarify them, not to report all that research has learned. Chapter 9 will look at the role of education and culture in fostering ability, and at some uses of tests in education. Chapter 10 explains how the ability domain can be subdivided, and considers the role of aptitude profiles in counseling.

ORIENTATION

The first section of this chapter reports on the reliability of mental tests. Conclusions, including those listed on page 277, are much more important than the tabled data used as illustrations. Figure 8.1 and the accompanying text deserve emphasis; many mistakes in test interpretation result from insufficient awareness of the errors in differences and gains. Formulas are given for reference, but your goal should be understanding *why* most differences are comparatively unreliable. I spell out in some detail the application of this logic to three tests from Chapter 7. The test-specific conclusions are of some importance, but mostly I am demonstrating the importance of asking this type of question about *any* test's subscores.

With respect to effects of age, understand why longitudinal studies cast doubt on old beliefs about the decline in ability during adulthood. The conclusions from Figure 8.2 are to be noted, along with Horn's dissent. The quotation from him is your first introduction to the "process" interpretations to be developed later. Capture the viewpoint; don't memorize the list. Figures 8.3 and 8.4 present the modern answer to the timeworn question "Is the IQ constant?" You cannot remember all the facts, but you should come to recognize what predictions are possible and what cautions are necessary. The facts connecting test scores to later accomplishment are basic to discussions of policy. Even though the text is simple, each paragraph carries its own important message.

A bridge section explains briefly how correlational, clinical, and analytic investigations differ. To the question of whether general ability is unitary, correlational studies provide a delicate answer: "Yes and no." The fluid-crystallized spectrum takes a first step toward sorting out subtypes of mental ability, and the subsequent note on achievement tests looks at practical implications. A number of conclusions are then offered on mental speed and on ability to learn.

Clinical thinking is pointed less toward general conclusions than toward understanding cases individually. Instead of concentrating on scores, the clinician looks at the character of a performance, as my brief account illustrates.

The analytic approaches sketched in the last main section are making possible precise measurement of some elements within problem solving. A recurrent theme is control processes: planning a line of attack, coding information for easy storage and modification, segmenting a task, and checking possible answers against powerful concepts or standards of a good response.

RELIABILITY OF SCORES AND SCORE DIFFERENCES

Test and Subtest Scores

Interpretation of correlations across ages or across abilities must allow for errors of measurement: errors in the total score, in part scores, in subtest scores, and in the differences between these.

For illustrative purposes, I review findings on WISC-R. The reliability studies in its manual come from split-half scoring of a single testing or from a test and retest about a month apart. Except for the details, what will be said about the Wechsler holds for other full-length tests.

Table 8.1 offers a simple, inexact summary of findings. (In some samples, the standard errors fell outside the range stated in the table.) The

Table 8.1   MEASUREMENT ERROR OF WISC-R

Score	s.d.	Standard error of measurement	Reliability coefficient (within age group)
Full Scale IQ	15	3–4	0.95
Verbal IQ	15	3–5	0.94
Performance IQ	15	4–5	0.90
V/P difference	11	6	0.76
Verbal subtests	3	1–1.5	0.81
Performance subtests	3	1.5–2	0.73

NOTE: Estimates are based on two testings about a month apart (WISC-R manual, 1974, pp. 32–33). A calculation on page 281 defines reliability of scales differently, in terms of consistency of standings across subtests.

following conclusions are derived from the summary table and other data.

- Scores on retests average higher than scores on initial tests: about 0.2 s.d. higher for Verbal, 0.6 s.d. for Performance, and 0.5 s.d. for the Full Scale.
- Full Scale and Verbal scores are more reliable than the Performance score.
- The Verbal subtests are somewhat more reliable than the Performance subtests, and more highly correlated with each other. Within each set some subtests are more accurate than others.
- Reliability prior to age 8 is somewhat lower than at later ages.

An observed score locates the person only approximately. A standard error of 5 points implies that the observed IQ may be as much as 15 points from the person's universe score. Most errors will be 5 points or less, and for practical purposes the tester probably should report an IQ scored as 90 by saying, "The IQ is estimated to fall in the range from 85 to 95." Or, with a 50 ± 10 scale, "in the range from 40 to 46." The universe score falls outside those limits for about a third of those tested (as was explained on p. 193).

Because performance is unstable when behavior patterns are being acquired, we would expect a pencil-and-paper test score to be unstable in the earliest school years. For one first-grade test the correlation between two forms given at about the same time was 0.9—but the retest correlation over a 4-month interval was only 0.75. Once children are accustomed to school and have stabilized their work habits, group tests for successive ages give fairly stable rankings.

I point out the potential importance of the "practice effect" seen in the gains on retests. Research into the value of an operation intended to increase blood supply to the brain found that WAIS scores rose in many of those who had the operation. Skeptics complained of having inadequate information on the likely test-retest change among *unoperated* persons of similar age and presurgery deficit. Pursuing this question, Matarazzo and Herman (1984) found that gains of normal adults on retest after 2–7 weeks average 3 IQ points on V, 8 on P, and 6 on the full scale. To be judged favorably, the operation should beat this record, but apparently it does not (Parker et al., 1987). Matarazzo and Herman make another important point: An individual's change in score should be regarded as "real" only if it is confirmed by other tests or by observations of improved functioning.

1. *The manual for Progressive Matrices summarizes reliabilities for Chinese, Malay, and Indian children in Singapore (from a thesis by Khatana). Use principles from Chapter 6 to explain the remarkable variation among the coefficients.*

Test-retest, 1-year interval, ages 7–11, 100 cases   0.71

Test-retest, 1-year interval, age 7, 20 cases   0.41

Test-retest, 1-year interval, age 9, 20 cases   0.44

Split-half, ages 7–8, 79 cases   0.88

Split-half, ages 8–12, 71 cases   0.99

Differences and Gains

When two tests correlate highly, it is rarely profitable to compare a person's standings on them; differences are mostly attributable to measurement error. Even when the observed correlation is far from perfect, the correlation might be quite high if the variables could be measured accurately. In mental testing it is important to recognize when two scores are truly giving distinct information and when they are reporting the same variable under two names; and also when a difference between similar measurements on two occasions implies a real change.

Standard Error   The first question is how the accuracy of a difference relates to that of the original scores. The random errors of measurement in both scores enter the error of the difference. *The error variance of a difference equals the sum of the error variances of the two variables.* Hence, typically, the standard error of the difference is about 1.4 ($= \sqrt{2}$) times the s.e.m. of either component. For two Verbal subtests of WISC-R, the s.e.m. of the difference is near 2 points, compared with 1.5 or less of the single subtest.

     To show how true and error variances enter the difference, Figure 8.1 decomposes the score variances of two tests and their difference. We make these assumptions:

Both initial scores have the same s.d.

$r_{AB} = 0.5$ and $r_{CD} = 0.25$.

Each test has reliability 0.75.

The first assumption implies that the test intercorrelation tells how much variance the tests have in common. Here 50 per cent of the A variance is due to whatever is common to A and B. From the reliability, we know that 25 per cent of the A variance is due to error. This leaves 25 per cent of the A variance for whatever A measures and B does not. Similar statements apply to B.

     An important warning follows from this reasoning. When a school gives a standardized reading test each year, it is natural to interpret the change in a pupil's standing as telling that he learned faster or slower than others. Successive levels of a standard achievement test are usually placed on a single continuous scale to help the teacher look at such gains. The differences are likely to be highly unreliable, however, because the common variance is large. After Grade 2, the year-to-year correlation of achievement scores is usually above 0.80. The situation is no

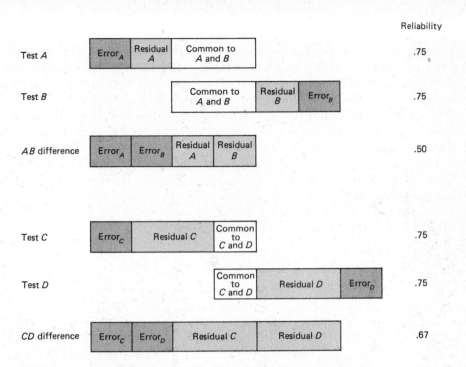

Figure 8.1. **How overlap of tests reduces the reliability of their difference.** In each bar, the variance of a score is divided into independent segments.

better when an inaccurate measure is used (as is often the case in assessing progress in therapy). Any interpreter of gains, then, must be mindful of the s.e.m. of difference scores.

Reliability   Taking the difference between two standard scores cancels out the common part. The A and B residuals and the two errors make up the variance of the differences. Because error is a large fraction of the difference, the reliability of the A/B difference is 0.50 (compared with 0.75 for the original scores). Overlap being less for C and D, that difference has reliability 0.67. You can experiment with other combinations of numbers.

Figure 8.1 represents this formula:

$$r_{A_{\text{true}} - B_{\text{true}}} = \frac{r_{AA'} + r_{BB'} - 2r_{AB}}{2 - 2r_{AB}}$$

If the tests have unequal s.d.'s the formula takes this form:

$$r_{A_{\text{true}} - B_{\text{true}}} = \frac{V_A r_{AA'} + V_B r_{BB'} - 2C_{AB}}{V_A + V_B - 2C_{AB}}$$

Here, V is the variance (s.d. squared) and C is the covariance (product of the two s.d. values and r).

Divergence of Constructs

We move now from the scores to a question about underlying constructs. How distinct would the two variables be if they were measured with great accuracy? That is, how much of the *true* variance comes from the independent residual? In A, the overlap with B (stated as a decimal) is 0.50 and the true (nonerror) variance is 0.75; so also in B. Thus the overlap accounts for 0.67 of each true-score variance, and the correlation of the A and B true scores is 0.67. The independent residual in A or B accounts for only one-third of the true variance. The variables converge far more than they diverge. The corresponding values for the C,D pair are 0.33 and 0.67, so these measures represent distinct constructs.

If the reliabilities of A and B had been unequal, the following formula for the true-score correlation would apply:

$$r_{A_{\text{true}}B_{\text{true}}} = \frac{r_{AB}}{\sqrt{r_{AA'}}\,\sqrt{r_{BB'}}}$$

This is a correction for attenuation equivalent to applying the formula from p. 214 twice, once with each reliability.

Eysenck (in P.A. Vernon, 1987, p. 56) comments on the importance of making this correction when a variable is not highly reliable: "Such corrections, of course, are not very relevant from a practical point of view, but from a theoretical point of view they are all-important." That is because the theorist is interested in the variable the measurement is sampling—not in the fallible score. Relations among latent variables are now evaluated in many research reports on ability and personality. For a long time correction for attenuation was in somewhat bad repute, because sampling errors sometimes produced an unbelievable "corrected" coefficient greater than 1.00. That result indicates a need for better data, but it is also a clear signal that the two latent variables diverge little if at all.

When reliabilities are reported alongside a correlation we can usually judge overlap adequately without calculation. If the two reliabilities are appreciably greater than the intercorrelation, the scores reflect two distinct kinds of individual difference.

Findings on Part Scores of Mental Tests

Because case interpreters and theorists tend to take unreliable differences too seriously, this is a vital kind of reasoning. Therefore, I offer findings from three major individual tests.

Wechsler V and P   Let us begin with Wechsler's V/P contrast. Think of the subtests that enter the Verbal scale as a sample from the domain of possible verbal tasks; likewise for Performance. The appropriate reliability coefficient is of the kind Tryon (1957) called "domain validity," an α coefficient derived from subtest intercorrelations.[1] The computation (using data for $9\frac{1}{2}$-year-olds from the WISC-R manual) gives coefficients of 0.89 and 0.78 for V and P respectively. The variance of each score is 225 in Wechsler's system.

Reasoning as in Figure 8.1 we reach this partitioning:

	V	P
V, P common (r = 0.72; 72% of 225 =)	162	162
Error (1 − 0.89 = .11; × 225 =)	25	
(1 − 0.78 = .22; × 225 =)		50
Independent part of V (remainder)	38	
Independent part of P (remainder)		13
Variance of difference	126 (s.d. = 11.2)	
Error variance of difference	75 (s.e.m. = 8.7)	
Reliability (domain validity) of difference	0.41 = (1 − 75/126)	

The correlation of the V and P constructs if the domains were to be exhaustively measured is estimated as 0.86 ($= 0.72/\sqrt{0.89}\sqrt{0.78}$), confirming that mental ability is not entirely unitary.

Still, modest observed V/P differences are untrustworthy. (Compare the s.d. and s.e.m.) The tester can reasonably try to explain any V/P difference that exceeds 12–15 points (Kaufman, 1979; Matarazzo & Herman, 1984). The examinee's observed style of response (p. 306) may suggest an explanation, and score differences across subtests may also.

KABC   Here are correlations of the main KABC scores:

	SIM	SEQ	Achievement
SIM		0.47	0.60
SEQ			0.62

The respective retest reliabilities are 0.82, 0.88, and 0.95. The domain validities are 0.74, 0.75, and 0.87. The intercorrelations are enough below the domain validities to imply that the three measures are reporting somewhat distinct variables.

SB4   For SB4, I put the question in another form, examining differences of the form Verbal-minus-Composite (CSAS). From age 8 to 14, the domain validity coefficient for this contrast for Verbal is in the neighborhood of 0.45. The same is to be said about Memory. The corresponding figure is about 0.25 for Quantitative and Abstract. Each section is con-

---

[1] The average intercorrelation is entered in the Spearman-Brown formula along with the number of subtests. I did not use the reliabilities from Table 8.1, which came from a split-half analysis within subtests. Using them would treat subtests as fixed rather than as representatives of a domain.

ceptually somewhat distinct from the composite or general ability, but the distinctions are not well measured.

To see the practical significance, suppose that Ms. Green wishes to identify children with a difference of 0.5 s.d. (or more) between true scores on Verbal and Composite. To hold down misinterpretations, she considers the standard error and flags only cases with somewhat large observed differences, whose true scores are unlikely to be equal. Out of 100 cases, Ms. Green flags 15 children; just 5 of these children have true differences of the size she *wishes* to identify. Five children having so large a true difference would be missed. So Ms. Green must accept 15 errors to get 5 correct reports. Ten false flags are mixed indistinguishably with 5 valid ones; and there are 5 misses. (These are long-run figures. The numbers would not be the same in every sample of 100.)

2. *Form a diagram like Figure 8.1 for KABC Sequential Processing and Simultaneous Processing at age 7, taking error percentages from the domain validities. Calculate the reliability of the difference.*

3. *KABC combines Sequential Processing and Simultaneous Processing into a Mental Processing Composite. In view of the intercorrelation, what can be said for and against this decision?*

4. *Three WISC-R subtest differences have the following reliabilities at age 9: Block Design-minus-Object Assembly, 0.4; Vocabulary-minus-Information, 0.5; Vocabulary-minus-Digit Span; 0.75. Suggest why the Vocabulary/Digit Span contrast is so much more reliable than the other two.*

CHANGES WITH AGE

A *longitudinal* study is the direct way to trace growth and decline in ability (Baltes & Nesselroade, 1979). The same persons are tested repeatedly. Few investigators can wait a generation for data to ripen, however. The most common alternative is a *cross-sectional* design: samples at several ages are tested in the same year. A cross-sectional study gives means and standard deviations for each age but not age-to-age correlations. A compromise—the *overlapping longitudinal* (or "cross-sequential") design—uses several samples, following each of them for a few years. For example, one might test 4-, 7-, and 10-year-olds and retest annually for at least 3 years.

The longitudinal design follows a fixed group of subjects. The several samples of a cross-sectional study may not be fully comparable. A sample of 4-year-olds obtained from preschools may not be as representative as a sample of 7-year-olds from the elementary schools of the same community. The overlapping design guards against this. Comparing the original 6-year-old distribution with that for original-3-year-olds-turned-6 warns the investigator when the groups are not comparable.

Even if the groups are sampled from the same population, the cross-sectional comparison is ambiguous. If, in 1990, 20-year-old females do better on a math test than 30-year-old females, is aging a cause of decline? Perhaps the decline comes from failure to use the skills once schooling ends. Or the "decline" could mean that in the late 1980s more females studied math before age 20 than in the 1970s.

Change in Level of Performance

The age trends depicted in Figure 8.2 come from measures of word knowledge and symbolic reasoning. Schaie has collected similar data on several other abilities. Other data sets also have led to widespread acceptance of the following main points:

- Persons born earlier and later (different "cohorts") differ notably. Because they have had more education, later-born cohorts do better than earlier generations.
- The cross-sectional trend gives a false impression of rapid decline with age.
- Individual decline is slight on average, at least to age 60 or thereabouts. (A study of the Wechsler found no average decrement down to age 75; Botwinick & Siegler, 1980.)

Although Schaie's results have been widely accepted, one expert argues that nonverbal reasoning declines steadily from about age 20. For the basic research report see Horn et al. (1981). Horn has studied many subordinate processes that contribute to general ability, and concludes (in

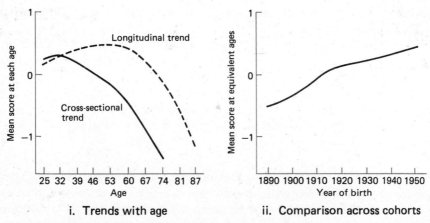

Figure 8.2. **Trends over time in general ability.** All curves have been smoothed. Each unit on the vertical scale represents 1 s.d.; the zero point is arbitrary. In panel i the two curves have been arbitrarily matched at age 32. (*Source*: Based on Schaie, 1983, pp. 89, 93, 100.)

Sternberg, 1986, p. 56) that decline is particularly associated with reduced efficiency in the following processes:

Concentration: Maintaining close attention, as in very slow behavior.

Encoding organization: Classifying incoming information in ways that facilitate subsequent recall.

Incidental memory: Remembering small things—i.e., things that would seem to be insignificant.

Eschewing irrelevancies: Not attending to what has proved to be irrelevant.

Dividing attention: Attending to other things while remembering a given thing.

Working memory: Holding several distinct ideas in mind at once.

Hypothesizing: Forming ideas about what is likely.

Inspection speediness: Speed in "finding" and "comparing."

Many of these variables seem to reflect attitude toward the tasks presented by the psychologist rather than maximum performance. It is conceivable that Schaie elicited an especially responsive attitude during his long association with his subjects, and so got something more like a maximum performance than would be obtained in ordinary testing.

Consistency of Individual Differences

Figure 8.3 summarizes typical retest correlations. Stability of scores is much greater after age 8 than before. Score at age 8 is predicted with $r = 0.6$ from a test at age 3, and less well from infant tests. Prediction from early tests is somewhat better for girls than for boys (Honzik, in Lewis, 1983; McCall, in Osofsky, 1979). (Age-to-age correlations are comparatively easy to interpret. Some analyses of retest studies have correlated standing at age 8, say, with gain over the next several years. These analyses are misleading; see p. 303.)

The increase in stability of these scores with age fits facts about development. By age 4, language functions are well established in most children. Some are exhibiting superiority that will last, and some are showing vocabulary and comprehension poor enough to be a serious handicap. Still, standings will change. An old mental test is not to be relied on for a critical decision. At any age, a few rankings change considerably in 3 years.

Children Who Change Radically Although the characteristics associated with rapid growth differ with age and sex, one arrives at a strong impression that gains are larger among those who vigorously and independently engage in exploring their world. Gainers are described as comparatively aggressive, nonconforming, willing to work for a reward, and, of course, as having intellectual interests. The warmth and authority pattern of the home contribute complexly to development.

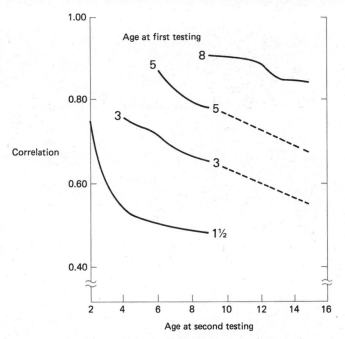

Figure 8.3. **Prediction of mental-test standings from earlier tests.** (*Source*: Scores at ages $1\frac{1}{2}$ to $2\frac{1}{2}$ came from the Bayley scales, at 3 to $3\frac{1}{2}$ from the SB with 1972 norms, at 4 to 6 from WPPSI, and at 7 to 9 and at 15 from WISC-R. Each correlation is based on 300 or more children (Wilson, 1983). The line marked 8 comes from retests of approximately 80 children with the 1960 Stanford-Binet (data from McCall, reported in Jensen, 1980, p. 279). All curves are smoothed.)

Simple hypotheses about causes of change are likely to be false, as the individual cases in Figure 8.4 illustrate.

- Case 946 was far below the norm during the school years, yet she had performed well in early childhood. She came from an unhappy home; her parents divorced when she was 7, and she appeared insecure after her mother remarried a year or so later.
- The standing of 783 is nearly constant, slightly above the group mean. Yet he had a history of poor health, an insecure and impoverished home background, poor grades, and symptoms such as stammering and enuresis. "There never was a time in his history when he was not confronted with extreme frustrations."
- Case 567 shows consistent improvement. During this girl's early years there were grave illnesses in the family, and she was sickly and shy. After age 10, her social life expanded, and she became interested in music and sports. This blossoming is paralleled in the test scores.

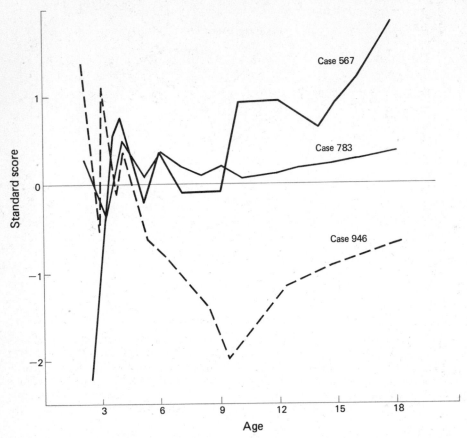

Figure 8.4. **Test standings of three children from age 2 to 18.** (*Source*: Honzik et al., 1948.)

In general, large changes in intellectual standing seem to be associated with radical changes in the child's opportunity for learning or his emotional readiness to profit from them. These factors work together, as is illustrated by the case of Danny.

Danny was tested when he adapted poorly to kindergarten. Danny's low score supported a decision to keep him out of school for the year. Lowell (1941) reports a record covering the next several years. On a 50 ± 10 scale, he had these Stanford-Binet scores:

Age	5–0	6–4	8–5	11–11
Standing	39	49	57	70

Because Danny scored at the norm after his sixth birthday, he was placed in the first grade in spite of poor social adjustment. The teachers complained that Danny seemed to live in a world of his own, was poor in motor coordination, and had a worried look on his face most of the time. The mother was called in, and only then was light thrown on his peculiarities.

The mother explained that while Danny was still a baby his father had developed encephalitis. In order for the mother to work, they lived in the grandparents' home, where Danny could be cared for. Danny's high-strung, nervous old grandfather was much annoyed by the child's noise and at times expostulated so violently that Danny became petrified with fear. The grandfather's chief aim was to keep things quiet and peaceful at any cost. When Danny was excluded from kindergarten, the mother took him from the grandparents' home.

The next few years were a period of educational and emotional growth. Danny amazed teachers with his achievement. He became an inveterate reader and could solve arithmetic problems far beyond his grade level. He was under a doctor's care much of the time and was also treated by a psychiatrist because of his marked fears. He made friends with boys in spite of physical inferiority.

I add one further upbeat story (from Cantoni's follow-up study, 1954; see p. 288).

Though a group mental test in Grade 9 placed Alex at about the 30th percentile, Alex eventually became a lawyer. (The test score was confirmed on a retest a few months later.) Alex had lived in a boarding home during his early school years following the death of his mother and suffered from a sense of inadequacy that led him into aggressive, offensive behavior. A counselor felt that Alex had ability even though his tests and grades were poor. An *individual* mental test placed Alex at the 75th percentile. Under the counselor's encouragement, Alex improved his marks to the B level and transferred to a college-preparatory curriculum. His personal adjustment also improved. After war service, Alex entered college and completed his law course successfully.

Stability in the Early Years   From the lowest line in Figure 8.3 we see that infant tests such as the Bayley are highly unstable. This does not tell the whole story about prediction from infancy. Longitudinal reports following up on babies' attention to the familiar and the novel (p. 272) are just beginning. The present limited data suggest that such measures in the first 6 months of life correlate 0.4 to 0.6 with mental tests at 6 years (Bornstein & Sigman, 1986; Fagan, 1985). This finding is especially impressive because the infant tests are so unreliable. The reports suggest that accurate infant measurements could predict school-age ability as well as accurate measurements at age 3 would.

Not all the fluctuation in early childhood that is illustrated at the left side of Figure 8.4 comes from errors of measurement or haphazard changes in health and interests. A longitudinal study of one-egg twins (identical heredity) shows remarkable within-pair similarity in the patterning of change in Bayley and WPPSI scores (Wilson, 1983). For one pair we have these norm-referenced scores (on a 50 ± 10 scale):

Age in months	3	6	12	18	24	36	48	60	72
First born	50	43	47	62	44	59	56	52	52
Second born	50	45	39	63	44	56	56	59	61

These scores appear to provide evidence that heredity influences the timing of lags and spurts in mental development, although the strength of the influence is debated (McCall, in Osofsky, 1979, p. 720).

5. *Differences between older and younger samples in a cross-sectional study may arise from social changes. What changes other than in length of schooling might cause the test scores of 50-year-olds to average higher (or lower) in 2000 than those of similar 50-year-olds in 1980?*

6. *Danny improved markedly during the 15 months between his first and second tests, at a time when he was not yet in school. What explanations can you suggest?*

7. *Because of the way tests are normed, persons who decline in ability standings must be about as numerous as those whose standings rise. What might account for declines between age 5 and 12?*

Ability and Later Accomplishment

Test scores are collected because (with some margin of error) they indicate what can be expected in the practical world. The original SB and Wechsler were accepted as relevant to decisions largely on the basis of unsystematic evidence. They were supported by the consistency between test scores and clinical impressions of observers working, for example, with retarded children. With the passage of time, case histories of children who had been tested piled up.

Terman and his successors (see Oden, 1968; R. Sears, 1977) followed up some children in the top 1 per cent of their age group. Ninety per cent entered college and 70 per cent graduated. By the age of 40 or so, the 800 men had published 67 books, more than 1400 scientific and professional articles, and more than 200 short stories and plays. They had more than 150 patents to their credit. Some of Terman's bright boys— not very many—failed in college or served a prison term or had unhappy marriages and careers. As Terman's last report said (1954): "Nearly all the statistics [on achievements] of this group are from 10 to 30 times as large as would be expected for 800 men representative of the general population." The better-than-average academic, professional, marital, and financial success and adult mental health are impressive (even after allowing for the advantages their parents provided many of Terman's high-scoring children). The key to adult achievement seems to have been amount of education; variation in completion of college and in advanced training was strongly predicted by the early test scores. Among equally educated adults in the sample, the early test scores had no relation to the level of career achievement. For a report specifically about the women, see P. Sears and Barbee, 1977.

A Terman associate estimated from recorded biographical facts how some historical personages would have scored if tested in early life. "Voltaire wrote verses from his cradle; Coleridge at 3 could read a chapter from the Bible; Mozart composed a minuet at 5; Goethe, at 8, produced literary work of adult superiority" (Cox, 1926, p. 217). The IQs presumably required to account for the recorded facts: Voltaire, 180; Coleridge, 175; Mozart, 160; Goethe, 190.

Other investigators followed low-scoring children. In one study information was compiled at age 50, and some of the adults were retested. Table 8.2 compares three groups: "very low" (more than 2 s.d. below average in early years, educated in classes for the retarded); "low"; and "average" (not more than 1 s.d. below average). Many childhood retardates performed in the normal range as adults. Low scorers supported themselves in semiskilled labor and low-level supervision. (The education of the low group probably was not as stimulating as the education that would be recommended today.)

Outside school, a performance test sometimes predicts better than a verbal test. Among children classified as "borderline defective," the ones who as adults succeeded in holding down jobs outside an institution were those with Wechsler P greater than V. This observation is supported by the correlation of nearly 0.8 between a childhood maze test and a rating of adjustment to the community in adulthood (Appell et al., 1962; see also Cooper et al., 1967).

Long-term forecasts are not very accurate. A person in the middle range of ability may do well in school and college and enter a profession or may drop out of school and remain in an unskilled job.

Figure 8.5 reports on students who graduated from high school in Flint, Michigan, in 1943. Ten years later the investigator obtained information about the subsequent careers of 97 boys. The boys are divided

Table 8.2   INDEPENDENCE IN ADULTHOOD OF PERSONS WHO SCORED LOW ON MENTAL TESTS IN CHILDHOOD

	Very low	Low	Near average
Institutionalized or totally dependent	11%	3%	0%
Entirely self-supporting	65%	93%	96%
Mean or median, childhood standard score	25	40	55
Mean, adult standard score	40	45	55

Source: Adapted from Baller et al., 1967.

Superior on mental test (30 cases)

High-school grade average:	Below 1.5 xxx		1.5-2.4 xxxxx xxxxx xxxxx xx			2.5+ xxxxx xxxxx			Total 30		
	No college xxx	Entered college	No college xxxx xxxx	Entered college xxxxx xxxx		No college xxxx	Entered college xxxx xx		No college	College, no degree	Degree
				No degree xxxx	Degree xxxxx		No degree x	Degree xxxxx			
Occupational status:											
Business, professional	0		2	2	5	2	1	5	4	3	10
Skilled	0		6	1	0	2	0	4	0	1	0
Unskilled or semi-skilled	3		0	1	0	0	0	0	3	1	0
									15	5	10

Average (49 cases)

High-school grade average:	Below 1.5 xxxxxxxx		1.5-2.4 xxxxxxxxxx xxxxxxxxxx xxxxxxxx			2.5+ xxxx			Total 49		
	No college xxxxxx xx	Entered college	No college xxxxxxxxxx xxxxxxxxxx x	Entered college xxxxxxxxxx xxxxxx		No college x	Entered college xxx		No college	College, no degree	Degree
				No degree xxxx xxxx	Degree xxxx xxxx		No degree x	Degree xx			
Occupational status:											
Business, professional	1		3	5	8			2	4	5	10
Skilled	6		9	2	0			0	15	2	0
Unskilled or semi-skilled	1		9	1	0	1	1	0	11	2	0
									30	9	10

Below average (18 cases)

High-school grade average:	Below 1.5 xxxxx		1.5-2.4 xxxxxxxxxx			2.5+ xx			Total 18		
	No college xxxxx	Entered college	No college xxxxxxxxxx	Entered college x		No college	Entered college xx		No college	College, no degree	Degree
				No degree	Degree x		No degree x	Degree x			
Occupational status:											
Business, professional	1		2		1		0	1	3	0	2
Skilled	2		4		0		1	0	6	1	0
Unskilled or semi-skilled	2		4		0		0	0	6	0	0
									15	1	2

Figure 8.5. Educational and occupational histories of 97 boys. (*Source*: Data supplied by L. J. Cantoni; see Cantoni, 1955.)

according to a group-test IQ in Grade 9. High-school marks, college history, and occupation 10 years after graduation are tabulated.

Grades do correspond to test scores; practically no one in the lowest tier earned superior marks. Boys in the lowest group were more likely than others to go into unskilled jobs. A very few, with good grades, entered college. About one-third of the average-ability group entered college, and half of them graduated.

In the two upper tiers, the occupational status of persons *who went to college* averaged out the same. Regardless of test score or high school average, every student who finished college was in an upper-level occupation 10 years after high school. Among those who did not go to college, occupational level corresponded somewhat to test score. From a report by Eckland (1980) it seems that the story remains much as Cantoni (1955) told it, except that more students are entering college.

Secondary schools and colleges with diversified programs try to route students into courses they are ready to handle, which makes good sense. Too often there are rigid barriers—between the academic track and the commercial track in a high school, for example. A student sorted into a less demanding program has difficulty in meeting requirements for admission to a regular college program when, midway through high school, he and his teachers realize that he is capable of the heavier load. They are many "late bloomers" who seem to get the knack of academic work and develop strong motivation only belatedly. It is essential that plans for sorting students keep access open for those initially regarded as poor candidates for a tough program (Wigdor & Garner, 1982, vol. 1, p. 175).

Obviously, tests are used comparatively in admissions. Aptitude and achievement tests correlate highly. Therefore, it makes little difference which is used in comparing students who have taken the same courses. The general-ability test is more suitable for comparing the developmental level of persons coming from *different* educational backgrounds because it has little to do with lesson content. Correlations of predictors with grade averages were reported on page 267.

Every comparison shows higher mental-test averages in more prestigeful, more demanding occupations. For example, World War II soldiers who had been lawyers in civil life had a median on the General Classification Test of 62 (on a scale where the population median was 53); the median for general clerks was 58, and that for plumbers was 51. The lowest medians (around 45) were for farm workers, miners, and laborers. The overlap of groups is equally noteworthy. The plumbers (disregarding the extreme 10 per cent at each end of the distribution) ranged from 36 to 61. Some were far below the median for laborers, and some did as well on the test as the average lawyer.

Amount of schooling explains most of these differences. Children of the well-to-do have a good chance to stay in school and also to get a good position; that contributes to the correlation. The person who does badly on mental tests—particularly on verbal tests—is likely to do badly in school. One can scarcely say that poor ability causes poor learning or that poor learning causes poor ability. There is a spiral relationship. The person who gets off to a poor start fails to learn and then is ill prepared for the next demand. Those with poor school records tend to leave school earlier. Completing college gives a license to enter the path toward executive-professional work regardless of whether the college course increased competence for it. The dropout who learns on a job can perform in some occupations just as well as the person who survived additional years of schooling.

A unique follow-up study traced workers in the home office of an insurance company. Nearly 700 workers hired between 1937 and 1949 were tested on a short general mental test at the time of hiring. New workers entered in the lower job categories and presumably were promoted on the basis of performance. The correlation between responsibility held in 1954 and score at time of hiring was 0.6. Fifty-four per cent of those in "decision-making jobs" had had scores of 120 and over; only 5 per cent with scores 0–99, and 19 per cent in the 100–119 range held these high-ranking jobs (Knauft, 1955). The insurance company found a high correlation because the level-of-responsibility criterion spanned many jobs. Within one job (e.g., office manager), the correlation of the test with a later merit rating would surely be lower.

Predictive validities for any job title range from substantial to negligible, depending upon the range of ability in the group tested and the demands of the specific job—and, of course, statistical sampling error. Ghiselli (1973) averaged validities for group tests of general ability against measures of job proficiency and also against training criteria. Prediction of training outcomes is easier, but less important. Ghiselli's results for job proficiency fell in the following ranges:

Definitely below 0.25	Packers and wrappers, sales clerks, vehicle operators
Near 0.25	Service occupations, trade and mechanical work, some clerical work
Definitely above 0.25	Managerial, sales, and some clerical positions

Superiority in technical occupations is also associated with superior general ability. Hunter and Hunter (1984) concluded that the importance of general ability is closely related to job complexity.

Comparative studies indicate that in most situations aptitude predicts more accurately than educational level, interviewer judgment, and reports from previous employers. Biodata (p. 511), work samples of job tasks, and peer evaluations (p. 601) do compare well with tests (Hunter & Hunter, 1984; Reilly & Chao, 1982).

8. *In view of what is known about the stability and forecasting power of data on ability (including school records), at what age should superior children or youths be encouraged to aim toward a profession or other demanding occupation?*

9. *Entry jobs are often used to identify persons who can be promoted to higher levels of responsibility. A person who scores low on a general ability test may be fully qualified for the entry job and yet be unlikely to qualify for promotion. Is it fair for the company to give preference to high-scoring persons in filling vacancies in the entry job?*

10. *Why are training criteria easier to predict from tests than on-the-job criteria? Consider police officers as an example.*

THREE LINES OF INQUIRY

Case reports and statistics in preceding pages have already begun to develop explanations for performance on general-ability tests. The remainder of the chapter draws on three kinds of studies to build up a theoretical understanding: analytic, correlational, and clinical.

- The analyst dissects performance. The research is, in a broad sense, experimental; it contrasts scores across specially arranged, systematically varied conditions. It asks how varying wording or timing or other stimulus conditions modifies scores, and then tries to explain.
- A correlational study asks how strongly *other* individual differences (in personal background, in tested characteristics, or in performance at a later date) are associated with rankings on the measure under study. The reports on school and work records in the preceding section illustrate correlational research (but with a practical, rather than theoretical, focus).
- The clinical investigator is concerned primarily with understanding each individual in turn. The data she collects and the themes of her interpretation are likely to change from case to case.

The analytic investigator typically concentrates on one task at a time, to understand precisely what plans of attack, transformations of information, and attention to feedback produce good performance. Piaget thus did several studies with Binet's bead-chain task—not because the task is especially important, but because it is easy to modify and responses are easy to observe. Processes detected in one kind of performance are likely to be significant for many other tasks.

The statistically minded think in terms of individual differences. They concentrate on a few main streams of ability and not on all the tributaries. Various kinds of intellectual performance are strongly correlated (when each one is reliably measured). Therefore, statistical investigators ask how general ability, or some broad segment such as spatial ability, is related to heredity, educational history, emotional stability, and to comparatively simple variables such as reaction time. Little more would be learned by considering specific abilities such as bead-chain performance, one after the other.

For the clinician, a profile of even a dozen scores provides merely a starting point. The meaning of the scores depends on the person's background, reaction to the testing situation, and style of work. Composites such as Wechsler's Verbal and Performance scores are, as it were, the first strokes on a paper where an elaborate portrait will be developed. The first lines may be erased from view as the final portrait takes on its individual character.

HOW UNITARY IS GENERAL ABILITY?

Consistency Across Tasks

An ambivalence runs through all interpretations of mental-test correlations. The correlation between two ability measures implies both a similarity and a difference, and both have to be attended to. It is encouraging to find correlations in the neighborhood of 0.8 between the Wechsler and SB, for they claim to perform similar functions. But the correlation would have to be higher to convince us that the Wechsler and SB are reporting on exactly the same variable (save for random errors of measurement). We are seeing plenty of evidence—for example, in the analysis of SB part scores a few pages back—that some common or general ability has a pervasive influence. Yet each such study shows also that ability is not indivisible.

Wechsler Subtests as an Example   Table 8.3 summarizes intercorrelations for Wechsler subtests. The tests have been grouped to bring out some important variations. The first two rows relate the V and P totals to the subtests, within age groups. The verbal subtests in Set 1 correlate a bit more with the Verbal total than with the Performance total; that is true also of Arithmetic. At these ages, the correlation between the Verbal and Performance totals is close to 0.7.

Block Design, a performance test, correlates substantially with the Verbal score; on the basis of such results, Block Design is regarded as a particularly good measure of *general* ability. The tests in Set 2 correlate about as high with verbal subtests as they do with each other, but that anomaly is accounted for by their lower reliabilities. Allowing for that, we conclude that these tests do have something special in common with each other (and with Block Design). That common element is weak.

Arithmetic, Digit Span, and Coding seem to link up; it is said that they are influenced by distractibility (Kaufman, 1979; Kroonenberg & ten Berge, 1987). "Distractibility" appears to be an alternative name for

Table 8.3   CORRELATIONS AMONG WISC-R SUBSCORES

	Set 1 subtests	Set 2 subtests	Block Design	Arith- metic	Digit Span	Coding
Verbal Scale	0.70–0.80[a]	0.40–0.55	0.55–0.60	0.60–0.65[a]	0.35–0.45[a]	0.35–0.40
Performance Scale	0.55–0.65	0.50–0.65[b]	0.65–0.75[b]	0.50–0.55	0.30–0.35	0.25–0.35[b]
Subtests singly[c]						
Set 1. Information, Similarities, Vocabulary, Comprehension	0.60–0.75	0.30–0.55	0.50–0.55	0.45–0.60	0.30–0.40	0.25–0.30
Set 2. Picture Completion, Picture Arrangement, Object Assembly		0.30–0.50	0.45–0.60	0.25–0.40	0.10–0.25	0.15–0.30
Block Design				←	0.30–0.50	→
Arithmetic, Digit Span, Coding				←	0.30–0.40	→

[a]This is based on the correlation of each subtest with the Verbal total, excluding the subtest in question and Digit Span.

[b]This is based on the correlation of each subtest with the Performance total, excluding the subtest in question and Mazes.

[c]The lower part of the table summarizes correlations each of which relates one subtest to another subtest.

NOTES: Estimates are based on tables in the WISC-R manual. The range shown includes at least 60 per cent of the pertinent correlations for the six ages from 9 to 14, and often includes 90 per cent. Comparatively large correlations are shown in boldface.

failing to "maintain a mental set" (Binet). Coding and Digit Span are so simple that mobilization of attention is a main ingredient in efficiency. Slippage of attention is also bound to reduce the score in Arithmetic, although that subtest demands knowledge and analysis as well. Weakness in this cluster is fairly common among children who have special difficulty in learning to read (Bannatyne, 1974; Rourke, in Filskov & Boll, 1982). On the whole, the distractibility interpretation seems too simple; no one process accounts for the links between these three tests (Stewart & Moely, 1983). Kaufman warns against overemphasis on "distractibility"; in particular, he would let the nature of the child's errors guide interpretation.

Verbal subtests measure a verbal ability in addition to general ability. The concept of a "performance ability" is poorly supported. Each Performance subtest is strongly influenced by specific components its fellow subtests do not require. Figure 10.2 will offer further insight into this diversity.

11. *In a general mental test, why is a high correlation among subtests not wholly desirable?*

12. *Comment on this statement: "A person's true level of mental ability is shown by whichever IQ, verbal or performance, is higher."*

13. *One of the subtests of an "intelligence test" developed abroad requires the test taker to cross slanting lines, making X's as rapidly as he can, thus:*

    XXXXX//////

    Such a subtest is rarely used in American tests measuring general ability. On what basis could the inclusion of such a test be criticized? What argument or evidence would justify including this subtest in a general mental test?

14. *Terman and Wechsler both discarded tasks that showed a consistent difference between males and females. A fair measurement could not be made, they said, if items were better suited to one sex than to the other. Did the elimination of such items make the scale more valid or less valid*
    a. *as a predictor?*
    b. *as a measure of the intended construct?*

The Fluid-Crystallized Spectrum

A continuum from fluid abilities *(Gf)* to crystallized abilities *(Gc)* (Figure 8.6) provides a preliminary sorting scheme. Tests at the same level in Figure 8.6 tend to be more highly intercorrelated than tests that are distant from each other (Cattell, 1971; Horn & Cattell, 1966; Vernon, 1979; see also p. 381).

The tests at the lower end of the spectrum require information and practiced skills; a brilliant but uninformed person could not do well. When a task corresponds closely to past lessons, response can be nearly mechanical. We can call such an ability "crystallized" or "automatized." Some skills are practiced so thoroughly that the person can act with almost no reflection. The test items call up practiced responses that are "in stock, nearly ready for delivery."

Knowledge and specific skills are no more than a starting point in a task at the upper end of the spectrum (Figures 1.2, 3.2, and 7.5). The person has to extract or construct an answer. Even with choice-response, the answer cannot be reached by recall.

"Fluid" ability is a short label for the adaptive process of apprehending an unfamiliar configuration and rearranging it to satisfy some requirement (or extending it). In Block Design the person must direct his attention, break up the given pattern into small squares, select and rotate blocks to match those elements, and assemble the whole, with a minimum of wasted time. One who works by trial and error will score low; one who plans ahead will be fast and accurate (see p. 308). The terms "direction", "judgment", and "self-criticism" from Binet apply here. It

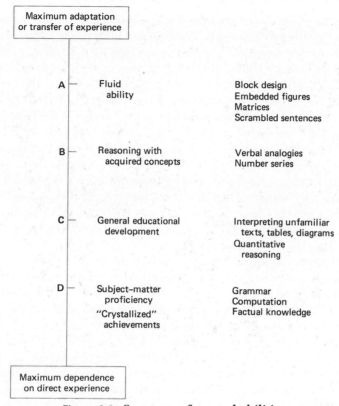

Figure 8.6. **Spectrum of general abilities.**

is convenient to speak of fluid ability in the singular, even though it is a composite. Many processes must function at once to produce good performance.

The *Gf/Gc* distinction is not a nonverbal/verbal contrast. Some verbal tasks require considerable adaptation; recall the Dissected Sentences example (in question 12 on p. 257). Recognizing commonplace figures such as squares is a crystallized *nonverbal* ability.

Ackerman (1987) distinguishes consistent from inconsistent tasks. In a *consistent* task such as counting, the same stimulus-response or pattern-response associations are appropriate in one problem after another. Counting can be automatized to the point of being performed without deliberate attention. Driving a car also reaches the point of making little demand on attention even though the stimuli are always changing. In contrast, in highly inconsistent tasks one must contend with novelty, and only a small part of the response can be automatized. A series of jigsaw puzzles is an example.

Crystallized abilities are demonstrated in speed of computation, recognition of word meaning, and other consistent, familiar tasks. Intercorrelation among those performances derives from the shared educational experience to which most persons are exposed. When first encountered, any task is problematic, so any crystallized ability develops out of *Gf*. When persons with equal *Gf* differ in *Gc*, the explanation presumably lies in the extent of their schooling or the effort they have put into schoolwork (Undheim, 1981).

Some discussions seem to suggest that fluid ability is contentless, and that crystallized abilities are elementary and not very intellectual. But fluid ability uses knowledge in formulating and checking hypotheses. An architect designing a building, even at his or her most creative, is relying at every moment on a bank of knowledge. At the crystallized end, basic language and number skills are important. But much specialized knowledge (within celestial navigation, say, or the law on contracts) can be crystallized. The expert is at home with the material in his field and his initial analysis relies on "consistent" elements no matter how novel the question to be resolved.

How much adaptation a task requires depends on the culture and the individual's history. In principle enough practice could be given to make Block Design performance a crystallized skill. Conversely, if children practiced no number skill beyond counting, making change efficiently would remain a demonstration of fluid ability.

The tasks at Level D in Figure 8.6 ask for familiar reactions to familiar content. Level C, increasing the demand for adaptation, requires application of practiced skills to new content. In paragraph reading, each stimulus is new to the reader, but there is little demand for ingenuity.

Level B demands reorganization of knowledge. A difficult verbal test at Level C or Level D introduces uncommon words or ideas; the advantage goes to the person who is well informed. At the B level, the problem is constructed of words all examinees should know well; difficulty is introduced by making relations more complex.

Whereas some mental tests concentrate on Level A—or on A and B together—many are like the Wechsler, covering much of the spectrum. Many an aptitude test for adolescents and adults is predominantly verbal, making demands on both reading and vocabulary. A poor reader's score is sure to be limited no matter how well he thinks. Conversely, a nonverbal or performance task demands ability to think with verbal concepts. In EFT, for example, search obviously goes faster if the person can hold in mind a good verbal description of the target figure. The test is nonverbal in the limited sense that one does not take in words from tester or test booklet and does not give back the answer in words.

Are Aptitude and Achievement Distinguishable? Many educators call a pupil an "underachiever" when his normed achievement score is lower than his normed general ability. A pupil who reads better than most others with the same general ability is labeled an "overachiever." It is true that a large discrepancy suggests atypical development of abilities. But it would make equally good sense to reverse the formula. The first pupil is "superadaptive"; he solves problems better than others who have equal command of the school subjects. The second one, by the same logic, is "underadaptive." Comparison of one test with another runs afoul of technical and logical difficulties. (I take up some of these in Chapters 4 and 9; see also Thorndike, 1963.)

The terminology of "over- and underachievement" should be abandoned. Teachers should do what they can to identify specific weaknesses that can be overcome, whether these lie at the Gc end of the spectrum or the Gf end. The student who ranks at the same level on both types of test also is likely to have some weaknesses!

Let us look in more detail at the overlap of individual standings. Scores on a test like CogAT correlate strongly with an achievement battery given at about the same time. For a national sample, typical within-grade correlations (Grades 5 to 8) with the composite score on the Iowa Tests of Basic Skills are CogAT Verbal, 0.85; Quantitative (Q), 0.8; Nonverbal (NV), 0.7. The lower correlation of nonverbal (Level A) tasks is a usual finding.

Taking reliability into account, in an analysis like that made earlier for Wechsler V and P, I estimate that 15 to 20 per cent of the variance in the Verbal or Quantitative score arises from some reliable characteristic the achievement test does not measure. For Nonverbal, however, the percentage is at least 35. When we compare children of equal achievement, most of their differences in fluid ability are due not to measurement error but to a real difference in problem solving.

In the early days of mental testing it was thought that innate abilities were being directly assessed. Failure to understand that *both* fluid and crystallized abilities are nurtured by experience and instruction has led to a peculiar asymmetry in interpretation. This is seen in the elaborate scoring scheme for the Iowa Test of Basic Skills (ITBS). When CogAT and ITBS are given at about the same time, a "predicted" score in Mathematics, for example, is calculated. This is essentially the national average of pupils in this grade who matched this pupil's CogAT performance. The actual Mathematics score and the "predicted" score are printed on the report to the teacher, and special attention is drawn to the difference if it is considered too large to be explained by measurement error.

There has been endless argument about the overlap among ability tests. Some have complained that whoever applies the label "aptitude" to one set of tests and the label "achievement" to another is a victim of the "jangle fallacy," of the illusion that things having different names must be distinct. Today few measurement specialists would say that no fluid/crystallized distinction is to be made. I limit myself to a few comments.

First, the fact that variables are highly correlated does not mean that they are indistinguishable. In samples of natural water, the amount of heavy water has a correlation with the number of molecules of ordinary water that considerably exceeds 0.999. Even so, it is scientifically and technologically important to distinguish the variables.

Second, most children have plentiful opportunity to develop the abilities that enter the usual achievement battery and to develop the ones aptitude tests call for. Turn to content that some persons have experienced and others have not, and the variables are less correlated. Thus high school seniors differ in their command of theory of music: reading of musical notation, naming the notes in this or that scale, working out elementary harmony. This achievement would correlate highly with general intellectual development *if* every senior had been exposed to the same amount of instruction in music theory.

Third, although tests of modest length are poor at assessing an aptitude/achievement difference for an individual, averages of groups are measured accurately. Differences across tests can be important in the study of developmental trends and in evaluation. Baughman and Dahlstrom (1968), for example, found that boys and girls in a certain community had about equal averages on the Stanford-Binet at each age from 7 to 14. On the Stanford Achievement Test, the sexes again tied—up to age 12. At ages 13 and 14, the boys' average lagged noticeably behind that of the girls. This trend almost certainly reflects an adolescent reaction to the schooling offered.

Fourth, although the *Gf/Gc* distinction is useful it is a mistake to align it with the terms *aptitude* and *achievement*. These refer to ways of using scores, rather than to different kinds of variables (Anastasi, in Plake, 1984).

15. *To what extent is each of these tasks consistent?*
    a. *The same 250-piece jigsaw puzzle is assembled once a day for two weeks.*
    b. *Playing tennis.*
    c. *Playing bridge.*

16. *Would it be possible for schooling to vary so that fourth-graders in one community advance in tests at both ends of the spectrum whereas in another community gains are great in crystallized abilities and small in tasks at Levels A and B?*

17. *Insofar as you can, locate the Wechsler subtests on the spectrum.*

18. *What sort of directions and associations would have to be stored in order to enable a computer to solve problems of each of the following types? How does this relate to the classification of items on the continuum? (Assume that the computer can "read" words and drawings, call on a memory, and "hear" commands.)*
    a. *Backward recall of digit strings*
    b. *Retrieving synonyms from memory*
    c. *Verbal analogies*
    d. *Mazes*
    e. *Naming pictures of shop tools*

19. *A spectrum like Figure 8.6 might apply to a comparatively narrow field in which a person develops expertise. Suggest problems or tasks within the*

domain of preparing meals that would probably fall at Levels D, C, B, and A for
a. *a person who regularly prepares family meals.*
b. *a person whose specialty is gourmet cooking.*

20. *Norms for class averages are available, and it is possible to compare the achievement average of a particular class with the average over classes that match their level on a general-ability test. What would be a reasonable conclusion or line of further questioning if, at the start of seventh grade when children come from several feeder elementary schools, class averages tell the following stories:*
    a. *Class A is at the 50th percentile of seventh-grade classes nationally in general ability and at the 25th percentile on achievement in computation and use of references.*
    b. *Class B averages at the 50th percentile in general ability and at the 75th percentile on most achievement measures, including reading and mathematics.*
    c. *Class C averages quite high in verbal ability and only average in fluid ability.*

How Central Is Speed?

Hans Eysenck, a leading British scholar, sees today's theorists as following either a Binet tradition or a Galton-Spearman tradition (Eysenck, in P. A. Vernon, 1987). One school of thought stresses the complex, multifaceted character of general ability, and stresses purpose and process. That view will be developed in the sections that follow this one.

The second school sees general ability as having inner unity that probably can best be explained by physiology (after more has been discovered). Some of the attempts to link brain physiology to ability will be taken up in Chapter 9. Here I examine whether neural speed is at the core of intellectual efficiency.

Early in the century, some workers explained fluid ability as a product of speedy neural transmission. Speed of response was distinguished from the "altitude" of ability, the highest level of task the person can cope with. A contemporary version is the statement that speed, persistence, and error-checking are "major, independent aspects of the IQ, with speed the most fundamental" (Eysenck, 1979, p. 188; see chapters by Furneaux and White in Eysenck, 1973).

In principle, speed and power of intellectual activity might correlate positively, negatively, or not at all, depending on conditions. A test taker can work faster at the risk of a higher error rate, or vice versa. It is not easy to measure speed and altitude separately, because experimental subjects do not fully comply with directions to work with maximum care and persistence, or to sacrifice accuracy for speed (Lohman, in Kanfer et al., 1989).

A two-part measuring procedure does give independent measures of speed and altitude. For example, two similar shapes, or the same shape rotated into two positions, can be exposed briefly. After the exposure ends, the subject is to say whether the figures were the same. Keeping figure complexities constant and varying the exposure, we find out how long an exposure the person needs to reach 90-per-cent success (at the chosen complexity level). We can also present shapes at various levels of difficulty, with no time pressure. An adaptive procedure will find out what complexity the person can handle with 90-per-cent success.

Intellectual efficiency arises not from sheer speed but from sensitive encoding and memory search (Cooper & Regan, in Sternberg, 1982; Lohman, in Sternberg, 1988). Ackerman (1987) varied conditions in reaction time experiments over a range from consistent (weak demands on information processing) to inconsistent (strong demands); see page 297. When the information burden was heavy, individual differences in reaction time were large, and strongly predicted by ability tests. On consistent tasks, however, reaction times following practice were rather uniform and differences were not predicted well.

Many current studies (discussed in P. A. Vernon, 1987) examine correlates of choice reaction time. Typically some number of lights and push buttons (eight, perhaps) are arranged in a semicircle around a home button. All the person has to do is move his arm quickly from the home position, to push the button beneath the light that comes on. Vernon (1983, p. 69) makes the telling point that this requires no knowledge, no problem solving, no rearrangement of information. Yet a thorough measure of choice reaction time will correlate 0.5 with Gf and Gc. (Higher correlations are sometimes reported, but there are technical reasons to discount many of them.) This evidence persuades Vernon, Eysenck, and Arthur Jensen that Spearman's g arises from basic physiological differences among individuals; knowledge and problem solving are associated with this base just because physiological efficiency prepares the ground for mental development. (They also say that heredity accounts for much of the variation.)

Controversy is heightened when it is suggested that speed is more important than other facets of performance, that it is not just a correlate but "the essence of intelligence." Biological variation in neural conductivity may be important; however, in problem solving, *what* one does is more important than how fast response is. Reactions that were published alongside a paper by Jensen (1985) raise this and other issues; see also Widaman & Carlson, 1989). Rabbitt (1987) challenges the procedures used to measure reaction time; he does not consider Jensen's score a clean measure of processing speed. His questions apply to some studies from other investigators also.

In practical testing, most current group tests have a time limit that allows at least three-fourths of the target population to reach the end of the test. Scores then reflect altitude and inconsistency more than speed; but differences in speed have some effect. A substantial study of CogAT correlated its scores with equally reliable computer-administered measures of quickness in making easy judgments (Levine et al., 1987). The correlation of speed scores with CogAT had a range of 0.1–0.4. The strongest correlation was for speed of same/opposite judgments on pairs of familiar words. Sections of CogAT correlated 0.6–0.7 with each other in this sample, and there were strong correlations among the speed tests. This is strong evidence that the two sets of measures diverge. Although speed of processing had a very weak connection with what CogAT measures, some experimental speed tasks have correlated with verbal test scores (Snow & Lohman, in Linn, 1989a, esp. p. 277). It is an open question whether speed in simple judgments is worth measuring as a separate aspect of ability.

21. *To what extent is the choice reaction time measure consistent with Binet's definition of intelligence?*

22. *Perhaps fast choice reaction reflects intensity of concentration more than physiological efficiency. Could evidence on this hypothesis be obtained?*

23. *In which of these tasks does it seem that speed and altitude can be assessed separately, using the computer timing described in the text:*
    a. *arithmetic word problems?*
    b. *analogies?*
    c. *Gestalt closure?*

Ability to Learn

From the beginning, the foremost aim of aptitude testing has been to estimate ability to learn—either in school or on the job. Psychologists accepted and promoted the tests without truly direct validation; rather, they originally settled for indirect evidence such as agreement with teachers' reports and with rank attained in the army. When, in time, mental test scores were correlated with direct measures of learning or progress over time, the results did not show the obvious correspondence that would be expected if general ability *is* ability to learn.

One type of study from 40 years back was badly misinterpreted, sometimes by eminent psychologists. Schoolchildren were tested twice on the same scale, with a time interval of perhaps 2 years. In such a study the change $(Y - X)$ between testings correlates negatively with the first score (X). The investigators wrongly inferred that the first score, reflecting development to that date, could say nothing about probable future learning.

In truth, the negative correlations of the $Y - X$ gain with the baseline X came from measurement error. Properly analyzed, the data indicated a modest *positive* correlation of about 0.4 between the *true* score (on the test scale) at first testing and the true change. By stretching the measurement scale in various ways, however, we could change that correlation upward or downward; so the finding is meaningless (Cronbach & Snow, 1977, pp. 149–150; Thorndike, 1963).

A number of studies of cognitive laboratory tasks of an "inconsistent" character—concept attainment, for example—show that general ability predicts performance early and late in practice (Cronbach & Snow, 1977, Ch. 5). Ability to learn from practice alone is not the same as ability to learn from instruction, and different instructional content or methods may call upon different aptitudes (Carroll, 1980). If we measure successful learning by performance *on the task practiced,* making no demand for further analysis or adaptation, general ability will have much less to do with ranking on the posttest than it does when the posttest requires comprehension and analysis. (Ferrara et al., 1986).

The cumulated research has supported the original hopes for mental tests. Persons who are intellectually efficient ordinarily learn more than others on tasks that require comprehension (Jensen, 1981, p. 31). Also, their learning is more flexible, more transferable (Campione et al., in Sternberg, 1985). This finding cannot be reduced to a single summary correlation between test score and "ability to learn" because of the variety of learning situations and the range of learning outcomes we could measure.

In contrast to learning with understanding, a limited kind of learning is measured in the short-term-memory subtests that appear in the major individual tests of general ability. Scores such as Digit Span have weak correlations with Gf and Gc.

It is not surprising that memory for digit strings, resistant to meaningful interpretation, has little relation to general ability. Memory tasks, however, can easily become meaningful (p. 37). A resourceful learner remembers a word pair by building a sentence around the words. Laboratory learning of unfamiliar principles correlates consistently with general mental tests, and so does programmed instruction, where lessons try to supply complete and easily grasped information.

Memory scores have comparatively little relation to home background; the children of the poor perform in the normal range. Some educators recommend giving plentiful drill to children who are near average in memory and subaverage in reasoning. A closely related line of thought is seen in Benjamin Bloom's recommendations on mastery learning (1976). He suggests that any person can learn anything, given sufficient time and excellent instruction. Foreign languages may be difficult for American adolescents, but infants learn those languages easily when they grow up with them. Measures of Gf or Gc forecast how lengthy an instructional immersion the student will require to reach satisfactory competence, not whether he can reach that level. This argument asks teachers to be patient and diligent, not giving up on slow learners. And, because time for instruction is limited, the argument encourages schools to concentrate the school day of the slower learner on a few "basic" competences, to pile up the extra time-on-task he needs. Drill methods do indeed succeed in teaching consistent skills—but not comprehension and problem solving. For a discussion of the latter, see pages 343–345.

PERFORMANCE THROUGH THE CLINICIAN'S EYES

Nearly all the evidence on the nature of general ability in the first part of this chapter has come from correlational analysis of group statistics. Clinicians, observing test takers one at a time, notice things that do not show up in statistics and therefore are able to explain a different aspect of ability.

A tester picks up information over and above the count of successes. One person approaches a task slowly and methodically. Others adopt tentative trial responses or display brash confidence. These are differences in style. Style can be seen as a temporary coping strategem, a reaction to this testing situation; or it can be seen as a sample of *typical* response to intellectual challenges. An inference about style generates suggestions for the teacher, case worker, or other professionals. Also, feedback sometimes can be given the examinee to help him see how a style is reducing his efficiency. Clinical testers use stylistic clues in evaluating pathology (pp. 623–630).

Looking at style is profitable even in assessing basic skills (Glaser, in Glaser & Bond, 1981). Very poor performance in arithmetic or writing does not usually imply total incompetence. The person's attack on alternative versions of the same task will show knowledge of many elements and command of many processes. Crucial gaps in technique or specific misconceptions are the likely sources of frequent errors.

One striking example is the written composition of a college student (from Bartholomeo, 1980), which begins:

> This assignment call on chosing one of my incident making a last draft out of it. I found this very differcult because I like tham all but you said I had to pick one so the Second incident was decide.

At first glance, this student seems hopelessly ignorant of the rules of sentence structure. When the student was asked to read his paper aloud, he produced sentences with good structure though not without error. He inserted word endings and even added words that the structure required (e.g., "was decided on"). What this student most needed was the proofreader's skill of seeing precisely what *is* on the page rather than what he intended to put there. Once such a fault is identified, targeted reteaching can often produce rapid improvement.

For decades, specialists in the teaching of arithmetic, reading, speech, and writing have used informal clinical methods to pinpoint difficulties as a first step in remediation. Glaser holds out the hope that today's frontier efforts to analyze problem solving will be extended into comparatively formal assessment of microprocesses within the pupil's tool skills. One such microassessment is described on page 404.

The main aim in clinical assessment of ability should be to understand where the person is efficient and informed, and where and why he lapses (Moriarty, 1966). This is illustrated in an examiner's notes on an 8-year-old (Biber et al., 1952). Mark scored not far above average on the largely verbal Stanford-Binet of that era. He rose to the 80th percentile or better on some performance tests.

> The most striking feature of Mark's examination was his extreme lack of confidence and his desire to do what was expected of him. This was manifested by his constant reference to the examiner. . . . to see whether the expression on the examiner's face indicated approval.
>
> In the Healy Completion [fitting small blocks into square holes to complete a picture] the examiner noticed that once when she gave him a friendly smile he was content to leave an inferior solution, as if he were guided much more by his wish to please than by his own good intelligence. Although she busied herself with papers and tried to pay as little attention as is compatible with a test situation, it was impossible to prevent this. The directions in the Healy Completion to look the work over carefully and see if there are any changes to make seemed to imply criticism to Mark, and he removed a block which was correctly placed and substituted a blank. His first responses were all good. In this test, he placed the first three accurately; then, apparently, he began feeling anxious or uncertain, and the last three he placed were blanks. It seemed that he was using the blanks as a way of avoiding committing himself to a mistake, and that he felt that he would rather do nothing than to get the wrong result. This test was the most plainly motivated by his desire for approval, although there were indications of it throughout the other tests as well. . . .
>
> Probably no test results on Mark are completely accurate because other factors besides ability are so definitely involved in his behavior. Difficulty . . . simply discouraged him and left him tense and uneasy. He was responsive to praise, but always with a questioning expression, as if he were trying to ferret out what one really thought of him.

Wechsler examiners learn much about the person. Earlier (p. 73) I described the testing of an executive who was masking acute depression. On the surface—good grade record, good military record, positive report on business and family affairs—the man was a fine prospect for a responsible post. At his educational level, the standard scores of 57 Verbal and 55 Performance (only a little above average) signaled that something was wrong. The jagged profile—Comprehension and Arithmetic near 70; Digit Span, Picture Arrangement, and Digit Symbol near 40—hinted at pathology. One warning sign was the many "Don't know" responses on Information. This traveled and educated man could not identify *Genesis* or *yeast* and said that the capital of Italy is Florence. Other overcautious responses and passivity were noted.

The older research literature was filled with proposals to categorize clinical patients by adding and subtracting Wechsler subtest scores. In today's diagnosis, the Wechsler is a means of observation and not a source of scores to be treated by formula (Filskov & Leli, in Filskov & Boll, 1982; Wood, 1979). The computational approach failed because diagnostic categories are crude, and background and qualitative features of test performance were left out of account. What Matarazzo said in 1972 (p. 432) remains true:

> [N]o . . . Wechsler subtest pattern or . . . index has been reported which reliably differentiates "schizophrenic" patients from . . . normal individuals. . . . Using information from the Wechsler Scales, in *isolation*, to date has failed to separate patients diagnosed schizophrenics . . . from patients diagnosed neurotic, or sociopathic, or . . . brain diseased.

24. *What description of the patient's thought processes is suggested by each of these responses to "Why should we keep away from bad company?" (Schafer, 1948). (The response in a was given by an adult of average ability; the other two patients were well above average.)*
    a. *Your friends will talk about you; if we want to live in a good environment, we must choose good company.*
    b. *I don't know if that necessarily holds true. To prevent picking up their bad habits, I guess.*
    c. *It's a trend toward living the same kind of a life, get bad yourself.*
25. *Match the responses in the preceding question to these answers to "Why do we have laws?" given by the same three patients.*
    a. *Govern the behavior of people. [E asks for elaboration.] There has to be some maintenance of order by which government policies are carried out as well as personal behavior of individuals.*
    b. *To have a law-abiding group of people; otherwise they would corrupt the city.*
    c. *To make good citizens out of us; to keep the unruly under control.*

INFORMATION PROCESSING: THE VIEW FROM THE LABORATORY

Analytic techniques for studying abilities have been contributing more and more understanding, and may soon lead to new assessment methods (Snow & Lohman, in Linn, 1989a). Today's "cognitive psychology" is trying to understand how minds interpret the world and regulate responses; the study of individual differences is only a part of the activity. The central concept is that humans "process" information: recording, comparing, compressing, reconstructing a whole from recollected parts. The central technique is that of the laboratory: systematic variation of a well-standardized task, to see how responses change.

The techniques used to explain why some people are good at general problem solving are also applied to narrower abilities, but this book cannot pursue that research. Among the many subdomains of aptitude, spatial, verbal, and reasoning abilities have been most thoroughly examined. I draw attention to several introductory chapters on verbal abilities (with syntactic, semantic, and perceptual aspects) and reasoning (with inductive, deductive, and other branches) by writers in Sternberg (1985), and to a chapter on verbal processes by E. B. Hunt (in Vernon, 1987).

Reviews on spatial performance are provided by Cooper & Regan (in Sternberg, 1982) and Lohman (in Sternberg, 1988).

Analytic research programs often extend over several years and frame conclusions in terms of models of mental activity, in the form of computer programs or mathematical equations. I shall next present two comparatively simple pieces of analytic research to illustrate the general nature of the studies. Then I turn to some process-centered explanations of ability.

Two Illustrative Studies

Evidence from Task Variation   The person who decomposes a block design and builds his replica one block at a time is likely to do better than the person who tries to grasp the global pattern and assemble it by trial and error. Some kinds of brain damage seem to prevent patients from decomposing the pattern.

Experimenters have varied block designs to find out why some are harder than others of the same size (Royer & Weitzel, 1977; Schorr et al., 1982; for clinical studies, see Diller & Gordon, in Filskov & Boll, 1982). E. B. Hunt (1974) has done similar research on matrix items.

Schorr et al. asked college students to construct four- and nine-block patterns (easy for them). Figure 8.7 illustrates the basic approach. The student was to pick the block that belongs where the asterisk appears. After a "ready" signal, the display was presented and the person pressed a button to indicate his choice. Because errors were rare, the response times were the main data. Subjects were not scored on the test or questioned about their style. The experimenter investigates mental processes by comparing stimulus conditions rather than persons.

Responses tended to be rapid when the pattern contained more single-color squares, was more symmetric, and—especially important—had few "interior-edge cues." A checkerboard pattern, with four interior cues, is easy. An illustration will clarify this key notion. In the pictured pattern, the lower-right block has four edges: the obvious outside edges

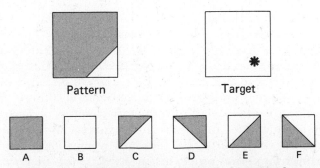

Figure 8.7. **Choice format for block design task.**

and two interior ones that can only be imagined. The pattern has no interior cues. If the starred block were turned to point the white triangle toward the center, the interior edges would be obvious; two cues.

When there are few interior cues and many solid squares, the global approach works as well as the analytic approach. The test developer can choose patterns that a global approach can handle fairly well or can choose patterns that demand decomposition.

Strategies Inferred from Eye Movements.   Confronting a multiple-choice item, a person may move "forward." He thinks about the stimuli that pose the problem (the "stem"), works out an answer for himself, and then looks for that answer among the choices offered. Another person works "backward." After glancing at the stem, this person focuses on the answers, eliminating the ones that seem not to fit and choosing among the reminder. These "strategies" are detected in various ways, including photographs of eye movements.

Adolescents worked on Paper Folding items including the one at the top of Figure 8.8 (Snow, in Snow et al., 1980, vol. 1). The instructions

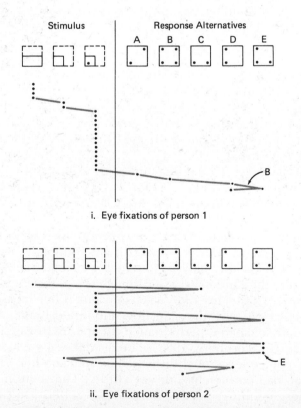

Figure 8.8. **Two styles of response to a paper-folding item.** (*Source*: Based on Snow in Snow et al., 1980, pp. 46, 48.)

went like this. "A square paper is folded twice to produce the third shape in the row, then a hole is punched through all layers. Now, how will the sheet look when unfolded?" This task is a good measure of Gf; spatial reasoning also counts. (A similar test appears at upper levels of SB4.) Person 1 moved forward. He invested 7 seconds in thinking about the folded paper, presumably imagining the unfolding. Then he marched briskly across the response options. As soon as he had glanced at the last one, he made his choice (correct). Snow calls this "constructive matching." Person 2 seemed intent on comparing response C to the folded pattern (but it is possible that, looking toward C, he was taking in its neighbors also). Next, it seems, he jumped impulsively to E, convinced himself that it could match the folded paper, and gave a wrong answer. Eliminating mismatches is not the best line of attack, though some persons apply it more systematically than did Person 2.

A line of attack is often referred to as a strategy rather than a style. The word "style" connotes typical behavior. Rather often, a person uses constructive matching on some problems and then changes to eliminating mismatches. Line of attack is not necessarily habitual.

Line of attack to some extent determines what a task measures. Some tasks can be approached by reasoning with verbal symbols *or* by forming a mental picture. That is true of this logical problem:

Town A is north of B, and C is south of B; what can you say about A and C?

Timing of elements in problem solving can identify which strategy the person adopted (Bethell-Fox et al., 1984). It turns out that excellence of performance correlates substantially with tested verbal ability for those students who are thinking verbally—and with spatial ability for those using visual imagery (Cooper & Regan, in Sternberg, 1982; Sternberg, in Reynolds & Willson, 1985).

Not everyone chooses the mode of analysis best suited to his or her aptitudes; there is much to be said for making students conscious of alternative strategies for problem solving. Choice of strategy can then become deliberate.

The tradition in psychometrics has been to ask "what ability" a test measures, or, perhaps, what *fixed* mixture of abilities it measures. That is the thrust of the factor analyses to which we come in Chapter 10, and of (for example) the Kaufmans' identifying certain tests with Simultaneous Processing. Clinicians like Wechsler and Biber have long held a quite different view, and they are now supported by laboratory analysis—particularly of spatial performance (Cooper & Regan, in Sternberg, 1982; Lohman, in Sternberg, 1988). The test taker, by choosing a "strategy," draws upon one set of abilities rather than another. (Thus, he may place a great load on memory, or very little.) The score measures how well the chosen abilities served the test taker. Because examinees are calling upon different competences, scores do not compare them on the *same* ability—in any psychological sense (Snow & Lohman, in Linn,

1989a, p. 283). We cannot even determine what ability of Person P is being measured by Paper Folding during this session. The person shifts strategy within the test and even while working on a particular item. To speak of "an ability," then, is to use a loose summary term, not to refer to a single attribute. We can think of "visualization," for example, only as efficiency in coping with a certain category of tasks. It is, like a pitcher's won/lost record, a product of countless causes. The "high spatial" performer has extra powers not in the repertoire of a "low spatial" performer. But it will be surprising if that difference is ever identified with a few particular processes.

26. *For a general mental test such as Wechsler's, is the influence of style of approach on a Block Design score a source of validity or invalidity? To get the best measure of Gf, should the Wechsler subtest use patterns suited to one of the styles, or should the effect be balanced out?*

27. *Suppose that the timed-choice procedure for Block Design is standardized for administration by microcomputer. If cost and convenience are disregarded, would that procedure or Wechsler's constructed-response procedure best serve the purposes for which Wechsler's test is now given?*

Piaget's Account of Intellectual Development

Jean Piaget's studies of children employed what he called a "méthode clinique," and his success did depend heavily on the observer's insights. His work nonetheless fits in this section; it *was* laboratory research. Small aspects of tasks were altered in order to trace and explain the effects on difficulty. I shall describe Piaget's method and some main interpretations, and then restate some findings in terms of the modern computer analog.

Piaget believed that mental "structures" are the tools of judgment and reasoning. Structures of a sort are present from an early age. As the child progresses, crude and indefinite concepts are supplanted by exact and powerful ones.

One kind of structure consists of conservation principles. The child comes to know, for example, that true shape does not change when something is viewed from a new angle, or volume when some liquid is poured into a new container. Children have to acquire these principles. The aim in Piagetian testing is to inventory what intellectual structures the child has on tap.

The concept of order is one of these acquired structures. "Order" is at first limited to the concrete world; thus, the young child can compare bead chains laid side by side. He can compare a straight chain with one twisted into a figure eight only much later, when able to put the order into words. When the concept is sufficiently developed, he can quickly encode the Town A/B/C problem (p. 310) as one of logical ordering.

Piagetians modify tasks of a particular kind subtly, to learn which complications the child takes in stride. The remarks the child makes as he works (and in justifying answers) are more important than the count of successes. The statement that the child is following such-and-such chain of reasoning is a complex inference about events inside the child's head.

The person who imposes on events a mature conceptual structure detects misperceptions and so reduces overt error. Do Piagetian tasks measure the general ability that conventional tests measure? Yes, but—. Piagetian tasks are of two types. Logic-based questions correlate strongly with general-ability tests. Superior command of conservation principles is somewhat distinct from both *Gf* and *Gc* (Carroll, Kohlberg, & DeVries, 1984).

It is certainly possible to teach conservation principles, by methods suited to the child's development (Siegler & Richards, in Sternberg, 1982). Berland (1982) has reported on his experiences with Pakistani children who had been trained from infancy to perform in a nomadic band of entertainers, adept in sleight of hand and acrobatics. These children not only performed excellently on Piagetian tasks but would make up their own conservation tests and instruct Berland in them. They were particularly fond of pinching off a tiny bit of mud from one of the objects to fool him, and prove that he did not know how to pay close attention!

Correct responses to a conservation test could be drilled in, and, in principle, could form a crystallized ability. But surface "mastery" may not be true command of a concept, as Smedslund (1961) demonstrated. He asked 5-year-olds and 8-year-olds to judge the comparative weight of two lumps of clay, originally identical, after one had been flattened. The 5-year-olds said that the two were unequal. Then Smedslund "trained" the children, using a balance so they could check their own judgments on trial after trial. After training, these children did indeed call the round lump and the flattened lump equal. But Smedslund tested the limits with "extinction" (contradiction) trials. He secretly pinched off some of the clay or added an extra bit, so that the judgment of "equal" was contradicted by the balance. The young children accepted their errors with a sort of "you can't win 'em all" reaction; they had not truly been forming a mental representation of constancy of weight. Eight-year-olds, though, responded as the concept of weight dictated: "Something is wrong with the scales" or "Some got lost"—and scrambled down from their chairs to look on the floor for the missing clay. The training, then, served not to erase the superiority of the older children but to expose it more clearly. The older children had "expert knowledge" about conservation of volume, which shaped their perceptions.

Modeling Bead-Chain Performance

I now use the bead-chain task—a measure of command of ordering that Piaget borrowed from Binet—to illustrate how mature and immature external responses can be explained as a "program" of simple steps within the mind. The task sequence in Figure 8.9 derives from Piaget and In-a.

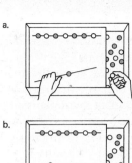

Child adds one bead at a time, putting copy alongside model to check, regulating by touch or short eye movements.

b.

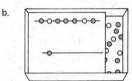

Rod is fixed by tester in offset position. Child adds one bead at a time, regulating by back-and-forth eye movements.

c.

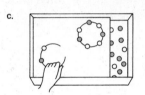

Child breaks circle into parts. Tends to lose his place and reverse direction. Has no concept of "between."

d.

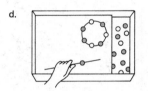

Response is mediated by image of the circle "opened out," transforming the task to one resembling that in *b*.

Operational Thought (about ages 6–7)

Child is told to make a chain with the order reversed. He must extract the order, neglecting appearance. The performance is regulated by verbal mediators such as "next to" and "between."

e.

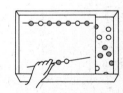

f.

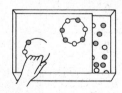

Child is told to make a chain with the order reversed from a given starting point.

g.

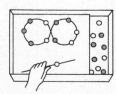

Starting point is given. Child mediates response by naming colors in order while working on each section.

Figure 8.9. **Successive stages in command of bead-chain tasks.** Problems are arranged here in the order in which the child masters them, according to Piaget and Inhelder (1956). The child is to construct, on the rod he holds, a chain exactly like the model. Shadings indicate three colors of beads. (*Source*: Educational Psychology, 3d ed., by Lee J. Cronbach. Copyright © 1977 by Harcourt Brace Jovanovich, Inc.; reprinted by permission of the publisher.)

helder (1956). My restatement of their explanation (Figures 8.10 and 8.11) leads to the schema a programmer could use to generate childlike responses, stopping short of a program ready to run.

How would a computer generate the same intellectual response to a problem that a human gives? Asking what the computer would need by way of storage facilities, codes, and orders for rearranging symbols leads to an imaginative construction of steps in information processing. The research is not like ordinary computer programming, which directs the computer efficiently to the right answer. The program efficient for a computer is likely not to be efficient for a human test taker. The psychologist observes a person at work on a certain intellectual task, infers his thought processes, and then spells out that inference in the form of a program. Her model is judged satisfactory if the computer, directed by

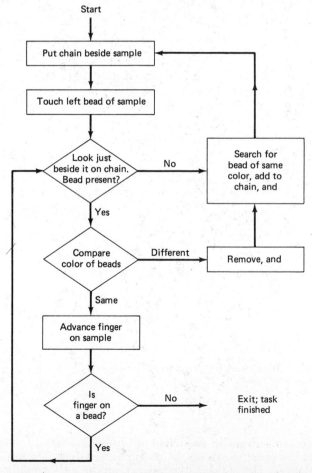

Figure 8.10. Actions making up bead-chain performance at the preoperational level.

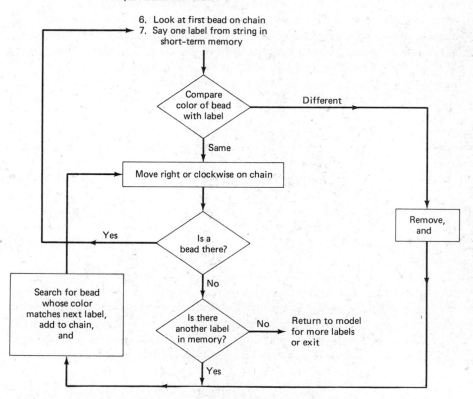

Impose frame of reference

1. Choose a starting point on sample
2. Label it
3. Store label in long-term memory

Fix order of beads in mind

4. Name colors of beads on sample, from
   starting bead right or clockwise
5. Put names in short-term memory

Compare beads with order

6. Look at first bead on chain
7. Say one label from string in
   short-term memory

Compare color of bead with label

Different

Same

Move right or clockwise on chain

Remove, and

Yes

Is a bead there?

No

Search for bead whose color matches next label, add to chain, and

Is there another label in memory?

No

Return to model for more labels or exit

Yes

Figure 8.11. Actions making up bead-chain performance at the operational level.

her program, reacts to the problems as the human did, making similar errors and pausing at the same places in the sequence.

Assume that the child and the computer understand the directions: they are to string beads into a chain that matches a sample. Assume also that the computer can represent the bin of loose beads in its memory, "move" a bead from bin to end of chain, and display the chain on the screen after each move. The psychologist varies the sample chains. She increases the load on the system, perhaps by adding beads or colors to the sample, or by twisting the sample chain. The test taker must bring additional control processes to bear as bead-chain tasks increase in difficulty. Which complications cause failure at earlier and later ages, and what does that suggest?

Young children proceed impressionistically and make frequent errors. It is not easy to simulate a haphazard process, so I move on to about age 5, when thought is "preoperational." The child is not yet able to regulate performance adequately with abstract concepts of order and color names; instead, he picks a bead, mounts it on his chain, and then moves his chain closer to the sample to check the correspondence of colors. He does not use a verbal recoding such as "red-blue-blue." Direct sensorimotor comparison enables him to reproduce a long chain under condition *a* of Figure 8.9 (though he may eventually lose his place). When the wire on which he is to mount beads is anchored, he cannot make a direct comparison; then he is very likely to lose his place and make errors. He tries to get sensorimotor control by pointing with his finger; but this control breaks down when sample and chain are kept separated.

Figure 8.10 sketches a process that might account for the successes and failures at this stage. It is a series of steps, all of one form: try, check, and correct if necessary.

Figure 8.11 simulates (incompletely) the behavior of an older child using "operational thought." Actions are regulated by labels carried in mind, sensorimotor feedback playing little part. The simulation is a bit indefinite; we would have to learn how long a string of labels he carries in mind, how he chooses a starting point, and so on, before the program is a true simulation.

Simulations suggest types of individual differences that might be worth recognizing. A dozen skills or habits appear in Figures 8.10 and 8.11; it should be possible to develop a measure for each one. Knowing exactly where a child is weak, one could teach techniques such as the use of a fixed starting point. Some of the abilities and habits in these programs are fairly general—for example, the older person's tendency to say to himself what he needs next.

28. *Solution of advanced bead-chain problems partly reflects typical behavior. Illustrate.*

29. *Sketch a model for block design performance similar to that for the bead-chain task. Do the same processes enter?*

Sternberg's Componential Analysis

Robert Sternberg's work is representative of modern attempts to measure elements of information processing by altering test tasks in the laboratory. His "componential analysis" was first developed by modifying simple analogies (Sternberg, 1977). One item can be presented in three ways:

RED : BLOOD :: WHITE :   A. COLOR
                                 B. SNOW

RED : BLOOD ::   A. WHITE : SNOW
                                 B. BROWN : COLOR

RED :   A. BLOOD :: WHITE : SNOW
                                 B. BRICK :: BROWN : COLOR

In one of his procedures (for others see Sternberg, in Reynolds & Willson, 1985), Sternberg exposes the left portion of an item for study. Timing of response begins when the right portion is flashed on the screen. Each person receives some items in each form. After responses to items of all three types have been clocked, subtraction of one working time from another indicates how much time each extra step requires. Sternberg's is one among many analytic approaches. (For an introduction to a wide array of experimental studies that tease out the structure of abilities, see papers by Earl Hunt, Campione et al., Kosslyn, Pellegrino, and others in Sternberg, 1985.)

Sternberg identifies six "performance components": encoding, inference, mapping, application, justification, and response. Speaking of the preceding analogy, he would say (Sternberg & Gardner, in Eysenck, 1982, p. 238; paraphrased and abbreviated):

> According to the theory, a subject [seeing the analogy all at once]
>
> *encodes* each term of the analogy, retrieving from semantic memory and placing in working memory attributes that are potentially relevant for analogy solution;
>
> next, the subject *infers* the relation between RED and BLOOD;
>
> then, the subject *maps* the higher-order relation between the first and second halves of the analogy, here recognizing that the first half deals with the color of blood and the second half deals with the whiteness of some substance;
>
> next, the subject *applies* the relation to the third term, WHITE, to form . . . an image of the ideal solution;
>
> then the subject compares answer options, seeking the ideal among the options presented and, if none of the options fits exactly, he *justifies* one option as being closest to the ideal;
>
> finally, the subject *responds* with his answer.

Sternberg has applied this scheme not only to analogies but to syllogisms, series completion, and classification, and has applied it to both verbal and figural items.

The experimenter assessing information processing typically lays out a diagram (somewhat more detailed than Figure 8.11) intended to describe steps a person might perform in sequence. Then, having timed each process, she determines whether the time required by all the separate processes matches the person's overall working time on a problem of specified complexity. Alternative models of the same task are needed to account for responses of different persons. See Sternberg and Rifkin (1979) for a succinct illustration of the techniques. Their paper also illustrates conclusions reached by these methods. For example, "second-graders appear to have used . . . [incomplete] encoding, inference, and application, and either have omitted mapping or perform it at a constant rate, regardless of [item complexity]." Fourth-graders use a mapping step that does vary with item complexity, and fully take stimulus features into working memory.

Proficiency in problem solving is not accounted for very fully by timing Sternberg's six components. Sternberg attributes the large remainder to the efficiency of "executive functions" by which elementary processes are organized and monitored.

30. *Sternberg lists six processes in the analogy performance. Which of the processes can also be found in bead-chain performance?*

31. *Could each of the following tasks be analyzed in terms of components like Sternberg's?*
    a. *Mechanical comprehension items that present gear chains; the question is: In which direction does the final axle rotate?*
    b. *Wechsler Object Assembly.*
    c. *Pitch discrimination.*
    d. *Finding the shortest route from A to B on a map.*

MARKS OF EXCELLENCE

It is time to sum up. The current understanding of "the meanings of general ability," the outcome of the decades of research sampled in this chapter, is neatly encapsulated in four propositions describing how abilities develop (Sternberg & Powell, 1983, pp. 400ff.). During development, problem solving changes in the following significant directions:

the available information is taken into account more completely;

rules are applied more sensitively, with a better fit to any change in conditions;

increasingly complex relationships, including relations among relations, are comprehended and used; and

executive or control strategies become more complex and more goal conscious.

Glaser & Bassok (1989), summarizing how experts attack problems, make essentially the same statements. They add that the expert in a domain commands several kinds of domain-specific competence. An expert encounters certain subjects or malfunctions or puzzles over and over.

Many elements in such a situation have become so familiar that the response is automatized, and hence the expert becomes free to concentrate attention on whatever is novel. Moreover, the expert brings a readily accessed, intelligently structured store of knowledge. In that store, particular facts are subordinated to general principles. This structure enables a "top-down" control process, in which figuring out the nature of the problem precedes interpretation of elements.

Such insights into content structures are too recent to have affected tests. Most psychologists concerned with aptitude have tried to present tasks that depend little on specific experience. Mechanical comprehension is an exception, because it does call on expertise. Tests of this character are likely to receive more attention in the years to come.

This summary, which equates intelligence with excellence in processing novel material, would seem familiar to Binet. Ann Brown, as discussant in a conference where Sternberg, Glaser, and other leaders presented two dozen papers on "thinking and learning skills" (Chipman et al., 1985), presented an "interview" (pp. 319–337) in which she asked for Binet's opinion on the themes of the conference. She answered each question by quoting a pertinent passage from *Les idées modernes sur l'enfant* (Binet, 1909). The match of Binet's ideas to the current ones is so great that Brown had to add a section to prove that theory has made *some* progress since 1909!

32. *The traditional Similarities item asks, for example, "In what way are an orange and a banana alike?" The child has to supply a general concept, fruit. Mentally retarded children do poorly on such items. Haywood and his associates (see Haywood et al., 1975) found that, on "enriched" items, the retarded children, if not brain-damaged, do about as well as younger (normal) children of the same mental age. Enriched items took this form:*

   In what way are an orange, a banana, a peach, a plum, and a pear alike?

   What does this finding indicate about the strengths and limitations of the retarded child?

33. *Some "domain-specific competences" of an expert are found at intermediate levels of development. Can you illustrate with reference to a person who has been engaged in some partly intellectual activity for 3 years (playing sandlot baseball, perhaps, or baking cookies)?*

34. *Is there any similarity between Piaget's conception of operational thought and the Glaser-Bassok description of expertise?*

Chapter
9

Influences on Intellectual Development

9A. The heritability coefficient for ability T is twice that for ability U. Suppose that is the finding in several investigations on American samples. What does the statement mean?

9B. Many features of conventional mental tests have been criticized as likely to underrate the average mental ability of non-Western or lower-class populations. In the light of accumulated evidence, which criticisms should be taken most seriously?

9C. Are there sound reasons to believe that giving appropriate experience to children can raise general ability?

9D. What policies for giving and interpreting individual mental tests are most likely to contribute to better instruction in the early years of school?

9E. In an Advanced Placement course the teacher is expected, by the students and by the College Board, to "teach for the test." What features of the Advanced Placement system make this educationally sound?

Abbreviations in this chapter: CogAT for Cognitive Abilities Test; ETS for Educational Testing Service; *Gf* for general-fluid ability; KABC for Kaufman Assessment Battery for Children; MCT for Mechanical Comprehension Test; SAT for Scholastic Aptitude Test; WPPSI, WISC-R, and WAIS-R for the preschool, child, and adult Wechsler scales.

ORIENTATION

This chapter is concerned almost entirely with the two-way traffic linking mental development to experience. Early in the chapter, after assessing the roles of heredity and environment, I tuck in some recent explorations of the physiological base for ability. I shall go more deeply into the part culture plays in developing abilities and in shaping test performance. This brings us to questions about the meaning of test scores for persons of differing cultural background and about the improvement of assessments and the improvement of abilities themselves. Much of the chapter, then, bears on such important topics as race differences and compensatory education. As the chapter proceeds, attention shifts to educational policies and educational uses of tests: pupil classification, planning of instruction, evaluation of student progress, and program evaluation. Tests serve in the management of national, state, and local school systems, as well as in planning within the schoolroom; the chapter considers both aspects of education.

I cannot offer advice on which parts merit closer study than others because each topic will be of special concern to some readers. There are seven sections, all dealing with recurrent controversies; indeed, sometimes one section reviews three or more controversies. Regarding each subsection, I suggest that you ask: Is there controversy about this topic? If so, just what is the question in dispute? Is there now a "best answer"? If not, why is the answer uncertain? You will have to judge for yourself, even when I have stated my own conclusion. Almost every controversy in this chapter is still alive, and both sides have vocal supporters.

HOW NATURE AND NURTURE COMBINE

The hereditary aspect of mental development has little relevance to educational practice and social policy, but misunderstandings about heredity distract attention from matters of greater practical importance. So it is important to get the main ideas straight.

The Continuity of Development

Today's organism grows out of yesterday's. Yesterday's health, alertness, food intake, and experiences influence today's actions which, in turn, produce tomorrow's organism. Mental processes, being carried out by physiological mechanisms, are subject to biological laws. Chemical messages lodged in the genes regulate metabolism and growth and point the way for development. Not even early effects are predetermined, however. Characteristics at birth are influenced by prenatal physical conditions and possibly by stimuli received in the womb.

Superior development cannot be attributed simply to the combination of "good" heredity with "good" environment. Environments cannot be scaled from rich to poor, good to bad. Environments differ in myriad ways. Potentially important are the presence of certain substances in the diet, the ability level of the young child's companions, the extent to which the culture stresses individual excellence, the extent to which parents press the child to take independent responsibility, the use of two languages in the child's home, and so on. Conditions considered advantageous to development by some psychologists are seen by others as impediments.

Darwin's message was that a successful species fits a particular ecological niche. Genes that suit a species to one environment make it unsuited to another; thus, plant species require specific soils and climates. The genes an organism received at conception leave a wide range of developmental possibilities open (Davis & Flaherty, 1976; Dobzhansky, 1973). Heredity could not possibly fix the level of ability the individual will attain. If—inconceivably—a set environment were imposed on everyone, some gene pattern would be especially suited to *that* environment. There is no reason to think that the same gene pattern is best for intellectual growth in all human environments. Nor is there any reason to think that one environment makes the most of every set of genes.

Controlled experiment is needed to trace the joint action of heredities and environments, but in studies of humans only gross controls are possible. Let us pause, then, for two illuminating studies of animals.

The demonstration long ago by Berkeley psychologists that rats can be bred for "maze brightness" was impressive. Generation 1 ran a maze repeatedly, and rats who had the best error records were interbred. Rats with poor records were likewise interbred. In generation 2, the two sets of offspring differed little. The same procedure—test, select, interbreed—was repeated. By generation 7, the ablest rats in the "dull strain" barely equaled the least able in the maze-bright line (Tryon, 1940). The difference reflected heredity, but it did not simply mean: "Rat intelligence is hereditary."

The meaning of the effect became clearer when the range of tests was widened (Searle, 1949). The "dull" rats outperformed the other strain when an underwater path was to be learned. Searle found the "bright" strain responsive to food as incentive, not especially eager to escape from water, and not much inclined toward exploratory wandering. The "dull" rats had the opposite motivational pattern. A further study with a conventional maze showed that dull-strain rats were dull when trials came in quick succession, but equaled "bright" rats when practice trials were 5 minutes or more apart (McGauch et al., 1962). Breeding had selected, then, on attributes advantageous in one particular learning situation.

Freedman (1958) arrived at a similar conclusion when he contrasted indulgent and disciplined rearing of puppies. In a matched pair from a given breed, one pup was encouraged by the handler in whatever activ-

ity the pup initiated, including aggressive games. The pairmate was formally trained to sit, stay, and come on command. The test at age 8 weeks
was this:

> Each time a pup ate meat from a bowl placed in the center of a [test] room,
> he was punished by a swat on the rump and a shout of "No." After 3 minutes
> the experimenter left the room and, observing through a one-way glass, re-
> corded the time that elapsed before the pup again ate.

A dog that did not eat within 10 minutes was removed from the test
room.

In Figure 9.1 each data point averages the scores of four pups with
the same breed and training. Breeds differed conspicuously, sheepdogs
learning quickly and basenjis refusing to learn. Indulgent rearing pro-

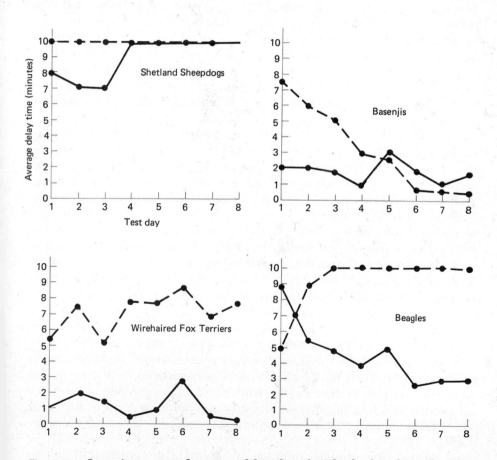

Figure 9.1. **Learning curves for pups of four breeds.** The broken line identifies
pups who previously had been indulged, and the solid line identifies pups who
had been subjected to discipline. (*Source:* Adapted from Freedman, 1958. Copyright © 1958 by The American Association for the Advancement of Science and
reproduced by permission.)

duced superior obedience in terriers and beagles—the breeds that, during the training, showed greatest interest in contact with the human trainer. The result is an effect of heredity *under particular conditions*—a heredity-treatment interaction.

What Kinship Correlations Do Not Mean

No scientist thinks that rank in ability is fixed at conception. Jensen (1973, p. 164), a foremost hereditarian, acknowledges that among children with the *same* genes intellectual performance at school ages spreads over about a 28-point range of IQs (2 s.d.). But tracing the sources of variation has proved difficult.

Studies on human heredity look at similarities among close and distant kin and at the development of children reared apart from their natural parents (adopted, or in orphanages). Much is learned from the "natural experiment" that twins offer. Identical twins develop from identical genes: the test scores of twins raised in the same home correlate at the same high level as two testings of the same person. Fraternal twins, like brothers and sisters, share half their genes (more or less). Scores of these twins correlate only a bit higher than do scores of brothers or sisters born separately.

A few studies located identical twins who had been separated at an early age and reared apart; despite the separate upbringing, the correlation of the twins' test scores in adulthood was high. There are reasons for discounting this as evidence of hereditary influence (P. E. Vernon, 1979). The environments of the identicals reared together must have been similar. When families were split up, the children usually moved to relatives who represented a similar culture and presumably gave the twins similar advantages. Among twins reared apart, those whose adoptive environments differed most tended to differ most in adult ability. Technical disputes about statistical procedures in research on heredity do not justify disagreement regarding the conclusions in general.

Where relevant environmental variables have a wide range, inheritance will be responsible for the lion's share of the differences in performance *only* if inherited advantage is the gateway to environmental advantage. Upgrading of deficient environments would make outcomes less related to family background than they have been. A finding in line with this remark is that black children of underprivileged mothers, adopted into white families at an early age, later perform at the same level as the natural children of the adopting middle-class parents (Scarr, 1981).

Correlational studies produce a "heritability coefficient." This would be 1.0 for a quality wholly determined by heredity—for eye color, the coefficient exceeds 0.95. It would be zero for a trait unrelated to heredity. Heritability of weight (clearly subject to environmental influence!) has been calculated at about 0.8. For ability, most estimates made a generation ago were near 0.8. Values calculated from recent data range from 0.3 to 0.8; the inconsistencies have not been adequately explained (Loehlin et al., 1988; Vandenberg & Vogler, in Wolman, 1985, p. 34). Even the highest of the values implies that rank in mental ability in our culture is far from predetermined by heredity. Scarr (in Linn, 1989b), after reviewing the statistical comparisons, argues that when persons of similar heredity turn out differently the cause is each individual's personal experience and the use made of experience, not "being in a good (or bad) home."

Research on the genetic background for abilities will in time trace *how* genes affect microanatomy and internal chemistry and *how* these, in turn, affect specific responses. (For a review, see Scarr and Carter-Saltzman, in Sternberg, 1982.) The most famous success along this line is the tracing of a particular mental defect to a failure of enzymes in the liver to break down molecules of phenylalanine (which are part of a normal diet). Subsequently, investigators devised a chemical test to detect the disorder in newborn infants, and devised a maintenance diet that enables children with the faulty gene to develop at nearly the normal rate (Willerman, 1978, pp. 216–298).

1. *Scarr (in Linn, 1989b) suggests that—except perhaps for the severely disadvantaged—the important "environmental differences" are those between children within a family, not differences across families. What events within a family seem likely to affect differently the development of siblings of the same sex?*

2. *The Supreme Court ruled against the parents of Amy Rowley, who asked the school to provide an assistant who would relay to Amy in sign language what was said in class* (Board of Education v. Rowley, 50 L.W. 4925 [1982]). *Amy's hearing was impaired, but she had a satisfactory school record. When Congress voted that handicapped children were to receive a "free appropriate public education," it did not intend, said the court, to require schools to give every handicapped child "an opportunity to achieve his full potential." If Congress is asked now to require that schools strive toward "full potential," what arguments pro and con should it bear in mind?*

3. *An athletic coach pays no attention to a player's ancestry; he does whatever is possible with the player's muscles and skills as of the present date. Ability in sport is affected by heredity, and there is no dispute about this—even though excelling in sports brings great rewards. Why does the role of inheritance in performance with words and symbols generate much more controversy than its role in performance with muscles?*

PHYSIOLOGICAL BASES FOR INTELLECTUAL DIFFERENCES

Mental processes are carried out in the brain, so individual differences in performance must somehow correspond to differences in physiological events. Eysenck and his adherents (see p. 301) see superior performance as resting primarily on physiological differences, and they hypothesize that heredity strongly influences the physiology. The related evidence deserves a brief review.

In principle, information about activity in the nervous system could provide a better indication of what the brain can do than can be inferred from behavior itself. Some form of this attractive hypothesis arises in each generation (Berger, in Eysenck, 1982). Modern electrophysiology offers increasingly sophisticated ways to measure physiological bases of mental activity.

Hemispheric Specialization

Modern studies assign responsibility for logical processes primarily to the left brain, whereas the right brain seems to handle most recognition and transformation of patterns. There is speculation that left-brain processes produce well-defined, exact responses whereas right-brain processes are more continuous, their correctness being a matter of degree. The distinction is similar to that between digital and analog computers. The left brain, it is suggested, works with abstracted elements; the right brain, with general impressions or gestalts. Loose-coupled, intuitive machinery is needed in generating fresh ideas; possibly the right brain is best at that function. A recent suggestion, not yet much investigated, is that sequential and simultaneous processing (p. 255) are associated respectively with the left and right hemispheres (Dean, 1984).

This set of hypotheses sums up notions from a research frontier, notions that can easily be overstated (Berent, in Filskov & Boll, 1982; Bradshaw & Nettleton, 1981; Federico, in Snow & Farr, 1987). The suggestion that the left brain processes verbal material and the right brain visual material is only weakly true. One cannot identify a task as the job of one hemisphere rather than the other because most tasks can be handled in both the symbolic and holistic modes. Moreover, in some persons the left brain seems to have taken over so-called right-brain functions, and vice versa.

Some test interpreters suspect that fluid processes depend on the right hemisphere whereas crystallized performances can rely on the left hemisphere (Reitan, 1985). Adults and children with damaged left hemispheres usually earn better standard scores on performance tasks like Wechsler's than on the verbal tasks. The opposite is found when the damage is on the right side. Some samples fail to confirm this conclusion (small samples? difficulties of locating lesions? the confounding effect of other variables?).

Study of hemisphere differences is of great scientific interest. Interpreting an individual's performances in terms of brain laterality, however, adds nothing to the interpretation in terms of process, except when more direct indications of organic pathology appear. It has been suggested that the Wechsler V/P difference is a sign of hemispheric imbalance, but the observed difference no more than hints at a possible physiological cause (Farr et al., 1986; Kaufman, 1979, pp. 6–7, 27–29; Matarazzo & Matarazzo, in McReynolds & Chelune, 1984, pp. 92–94). Numerous specialized tests are used in neurological diagnosis, but such clinical work is still much more art than science.

Evidence from PET Scans and Electric Potentials

Reports on findings from positron emission tomography (PET) are just beginning to appear. The technique, using radioisotopes, records blood flow or glucose metabolism in each part of the brain (which reflects activity) and generates pictures that highlight the regions active at any instant. In preliminary results on a tiny sample (Haier et al., 1988), brain activity (during the test) of persons having superior matrix scores differed markedly from that of less able persons.

One of the fascinating features—which will in time add a physiological facet to the experimental analyses Chapter 8 introduced—is that images recorded from two performances can be subtracted (electronically) from each other. Then one can see how small changes in task requirements shift the work assignments of parts of the brain (Petersen et al., 1988).

Study of the electroencephalogram has a longer history than the PET scan, marked both by enthusiastic claims and by failures to replicate. The history, the currently active theories, and the conflicting findings are reviewed by Eysenck (with Barrett, in Reynolds & Willson, 1985, and more briefly in Sternberg, 1986). There probably is significant information in tracings, made from electrodes on the scalp, of "evoked potential" (electrical response to controlled stimuli). The one conclusion solidly established at this point is that findings are much affected by small differences in technique (the placement of electrodes, the conversion of the complex wave form to a numerical index, the intensity of the stimulus, and so on).

Studies done in Eysenck's laboratory by A. E. and D. E. Hendrickson (in Eysenck, 1982) reported correlations with WAIS-R IQ of 0.7 for certain measures derived from the tracings. Eysenck properly emphasizes the need for true, independent replications. He finds some studies by other investigators consistent with the Hendricksons', and discounts contradictory findings as resulting from changed techniques. The Hendrickson correlations are probably too high to hold up, but correlations of 0.3 to 0.5 would pose important questions for theorists.

Callaway (1975) believes that the electroencephalogram can someday identify persons at risk for schizophrenia, and it already serves in studying brain lesions and tumors. As an objective measure of the fine structure of attention, the brain recordings should play a role in laboratory research on information processing (Donchin & Isreal, in Snow et al., 1980).

4. *It is possible that several years of complex experience would modify physiological reactions of the brain?*

CULTURAL INFLUENCES

How Culture Channels Motivation

When facing an ability test, children from some cultures and subcultures may be less inclined to do their best than typical Western students are. Holding oneself in is a defense many people use in alien situations. I speak of a cultural phenomenon, not shyness or withdrawal in single cases; children in an alienated group define for each other a barrier that separates them from the institution. The school and all that goes with it is alien for some children, as was suggested by Labov's anecdote regarding verbal performance (p. 75).

The failure of school observations to disclose these children's abilities is not specific to "testing." The verbal inhibitions Labov reported would impair the child's dealings with the teacher and classmates and so reduce the amount learned in school. The classroom observations of speech were a relevant indication of probable difficulty in school, but invalid as a measure of linguistic *skill*.

Motivations taken for granted in typical Western examinees run counter to the tradition of some cultural groups. Goodnow (in Resnick, 1976) notes that a culture may not value working out complete answers or formulating general principles or doing problems in one's head. The tester's formal question may then seem irrelevant, even absurd. The classic example is the experience of Glick in Liberia (cited in Triandis & Berry, 1980, p. 283). Adult Kpelle farmers were asked to group objects that "belong together." Theory says that intellectually mature sorters use "logical" categories: articles of clothing, containers, tools, and so on. The farmers formed "immature" functional groupings: rice with cooking pan with stirring spoon. The farmers insisted that this grouping made sense. Finally, Glick asked one of them to group the objects as a *stupid* Kpelle would. The response was a perfect logical sorting—"mature" according to Western, Piagetian theory. Berland's report from Pakistan (p. 65) is similar in its implications.

Time is not of the essence in many traditions. Wober (1972) found that advanced students in Uganda had accepted the Western idea: Quickness is a sign of intelligence. Villagers, however, typically identified intelligence with "slowness" (reflection? inhibition of impulse?).

The Zuñi teach cooperation rather than competition. Zuñi children have races. But a child who wins several races is scolded for having made others lose face. He is taught to win some races to show he is capable and then to hold back and let others win. White teachers sent Zuñi children to the blackboard for arithmetic drills, with instructions to do a problem and turn their backs to the board when finished. Instead, the pupils faced the board until the slowest had finished; then all turned. This was to them simple courtesy; in their eyes, the teacher had asked them to show off. Obviously, a group speed test gives misleading results among the Zuñi. An individual test fares no better. The first child tested may fail some items deliberately, because he fears that the next child will be unable to answer.

Adapting Testing to the Culture

Psychologists studying mental development in Third World cultures started with the idea of standardization. They learned the hard way that one should *not* keep the test operations the same in every setting (Irvine & Carroll, in Triandis & Berry, 1980). Content and procedure usually should be modified.

Consider block design tests as an example. Ord (1971, pp. 21–22) found the traditional tests useless in New Guinea.

> [M]any subjects, particularly in the Highlands, did not seem to appreciate how two-dimensional designs could be represented by three-dimensional material. They tried to use the tops and sides of blocks concurrently to make a design. There was also some manipulative difficulty. . . .

Excessive dependence on the tester was a further source of trouble; Ord's adults responded much as Mark did (p. 306). Ord went on to revise the test. He replaced the blocks with flat tiles. He compensated for lack of dexterity by making the tiles large and by providing a tray whose sloping sides kept the tiles in place. And he had the tester construct the first patterns, so that the examinee, by imitating, could get off to a running start.

Experience with groups round the world has led to suggestions for obtaining more valid information on abilities in preliterate societies (Brislin et al., 1974; Ord, 1971; Schwartz & Krug, 1972; Irvine & Carroll and other chapters in Triandis & Berry, 1980; P. E. Vernon, 1969). Not all the following suggestions can be adopted at once, and their usefulness varies with the population.

Base test content on words, stories, and objects familiar in the culture.

When a function such as memory or visual perception is of interest, go beyond imported tests. Observe members of the community performing the function in their usual activities. Arrange standard tasks that bring controlled variation into these activities.

Use objects rather than pictures. Pictures or diagrams can create an irrelevant "reading" difficulty.

Do not set time limits or allow bonuses for fast work unless your intent is to measure speed.

Reduce variation in style. For example, pace any timed test, so that persons who would otherwise work too hastily or too methodically do not suffer.

To the extent possible, make the test a game—convivial, dramatic, cheerful.

Depend as little as possible on verbal directions, even in the native language. Use visual demonstration.

Present instructions by film or videotape (to standardize).

Adapt all language and simplify all requirements to the point where a native can grasp the task and act as tester.

Do not intermix item types. Present each type as a subtest with its own introduction.

Teach every technique the examinee is expected to use (e.g., placing and turning blocks).

Teach the standards for judging a response good or bad.

Unless respondents fully command the rules of the game, their scores cannot be interpreted. In the West Indies, Uganda, and occasionally in England, children tested by Vernon were satisfied with designs they had made even though the responses had only a vague resemblance to the prescribed pattern (Figure 9.2).

Traditionally, testers introduced novelty or surprise, so as to observe adaptation rather than a practiced, specific competence. Opinion is now

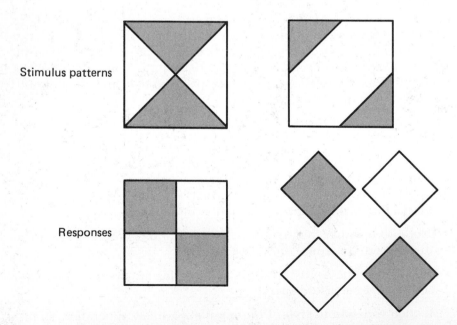

Stimulus patterns

Responses

Figure 9.2. **Block Design responses accepted by non-Western subjects.** Adapted from P. E. Vernon, 1969, p. 102.

moving in the opposite direction. Cross-cultural testers in particular recommend leading the person into the task by easy stages that amount to
instruction, so that the test proper will contain no surprise beyond the
particular stimuli of each item (Biesheuvel, in Cronbach & Drenth,
1972). Such testing still requires adaptive response insofar as each item
requires analysis, retrieval of knowledge, or organization of responses.
But the score no longer depends on quickness in adapting *to the test
situation*. Conventional procedure tends to give a considerable advantage to persons who have previously faced testlike tasks or lessons.

Logically, the level a person reaches when thoroughly prepared for
the test task should validly predict success in schooling or job training
because weeks or months of instruction allow time for coming to understand what is wanted. In a few scattered studies, scores obtained after
familiarization have shown superior predictive validity (Dague, in Cronbach & Drenth, 1972; Ombredane et al., 1956).

A warning must be voiced. After extended practice, standings on
consistent tasks reflect sheer speed of response or the efficiency of whatever routine the person has developed for this specific task. Thus, Digit
Symbol, on early trials, depends to some extent on Gf; on later trials,
differences are due to motor speed.

5. *In what ways, if any, might cultural experience affect performance on each
   of the following tests?*
   a. *Formboards (fitting blocks into variously shaped holes).*
   b. *Wechsler Picture Arrangement.*
   c. *Porteus mazes.*

6. *One could modify the Picture Arrangement test to fit other cultures by re-
   drawing the pictures to represent scenes in each type of community. Would
   such adapted tests provide a suitable basis for cross-cultural comparisons.*

7. *Assume that Picture Arrangement is adapted as described in the preceding
   question. Then would Picture Arrangement or Block Design be more nearly
   "culture fair"?*

8. *Irvine (cited in Triandis & Berry, 1980, p. 222) found that coaching on matrix tasks raised the correlation of such a test with concurrent school examinations and with a test of numerical ability among eighth-graders in Masho-
   naland. If admission to secondary school is selective, and tests are used to
   compare children from different villages, does this evidence support coaching prior to testing?*

9. *Which of the suggestions for testing in Africa would be likely to improve
   the validity of tests in the United States for job applicants who have attended school irregularly?*

Cultural Shaping of Profiles

By making particular activities important, providing opportunity to engage in them, and providing appropriate vocabulary and other intellectual tools, a culture promotes certain kinds of intellectual development.

Children in more industrialized communities tend to be superior on many kinds of test. However, groups widely separated on one set of tests are close together on others. Children of the isolated Shilluk, living on the edge of the desert in Egypt, fell far below European norms—except on a test rather like Ord's version of Block Design. On that test, the Shilluk performed above the European norm. Fahmy (1954) attributed this finding to the large role played by color in ceremonies and games with which the children were familiar.

Further evidence that cultural differences cannot be summed up simply comes from a longitudinal comparison of children in Austin, Texas, and in Mexico City (Holtzman et al., 1975). The samples were essentially equal at the start of school on several Wechsler subtests, but the Texans steadily pulled ahead as years passed. Here are means on Block Design:

Approximate age	Texas	Mexico
7	7.7	8.0
10	22.2	14.9
13	35.9	29.6

The averages in Arithmetic stayed close together over the years, however, and on a measure of rote associative learning the Mexican average was definitely higher.

A particularly understandable example of cultural shaping of an ability is the report that Samoans are outstanding at judging whether monotone rhythmical patterns are the same or different (J. B. Ford, 1957). This result almost surely is explained by the importance to Samoans of music that consists largely of rhythmic beating on tins, logs, or bundles of reeds. The U.S. Navy found Samoans exceptionally competent at sending and receiving radio code. Indeed, before tape recording was available, it was necessary to transport Samoans to Hawaii to act as receivers; no one else could keep up with the fast transmissions from Pago Pago.

The educated sector in most nations is accustomed to looking at systems of symbols: balance sheets, blueprints, legal syllogisms, maps,. . . . A principal feature of cultural advances—many of them non-Western—has been abstract schemes like the calendar, which capture essential relations and detach them from the ever-changing context. In many cultures, children and adults who cope well with village life do badly on tests that ask for analysis independent of context or for reasoning about imaginary cases. This is especially true of persons with little formal schooling (Scribner & Cole, 1973; Sharp et al., 1979).

Kpelle farmers in Liberia would not produce logic on demand (Cole et al., 1968, 1971). Witness the following interchange between tester and respondent (Cole et al., 1971, pp. 187–188):

EXPERIMENTER: Flumo and Yakpalo always drink cane juice [rum] together. Flumo is drinking cane juice. Is Yakpalo drinking cane juice?

> SUBJECT: Flumo and Yakpalo drink cane juice together, but the time Flumo was drinking the first one Yakpalo was not there on that day.
>
> EXPERIMENTER: But I told you that Flumo and Yakpalo always drink cane juice together. One day Flumo was drinking cane juice. Was Yakpalo drinking cane juice that day?
>
> SUBJECT: The day Flumo was drinking the cane juice Yakpalo was not there on that day.
>
> EXPERIMENTER: What is the reason?
>
> SUBJECT: The reason is that Yakpalo went to his farm on that day and Flumo remained in town on that day.

This apparent lack of disciplined thought is offset by other findings. Kpelle children who had had more schooling scored higher. (Some villages provided more opportunity for schooling than others, so this is not a simple effect of selection.) Also, children and adults were relatively successful when, instead of having to *construct* responses about Yakpalo and his friends, they were to judge the suitability of responses the tester suggested. Finally, Cole et al. (1971) point to instances of "what if . . . .?" thinking in everyday Kpelle activities. The conclusion is not that the Kpelle are incapable of logic but that they find it relevant only in particular activities or settings. Note the resemblance to Labov's argument.

A natural question is whether, across the wide range of the world's cultures, abilities can be found that Westerners have not developed strongly and that Western tests neglect. One can have great respect for the Samoans' superior ability to discriminate rhythm and for the ability of Bushmen to detect in their desert environment the minimal cues that make survival possible (Reuning, in Cronbach & Drenth, 1972), without regarding those abilities as resources on which alternative civilizations could be built.

Some commentators speak of the lower scores of minority groups in Western countries and of tribal groups elsewhere as signs of "difference, not deficit." They imply that, although members of these groups are not prepared to use the commonplace tools of symbolic thought, they probably are proficient in some other important kinds of thinking. Since evidence of these alternative abilities has not been presented, little can be said here. An example can be suggested, however, to keep the idea open.

It is reported that some cultures stress mutually supportive social relationships. P. E. Vernon (1969) quotes Jomo Kenyatta: "To the Europeans, individuality is the ideal of life, to the Africans, the ideal is right relations with, and behavior to, other people." Recall also the behavior of the Zuñi. A group-oriented culture must develop techniques that lead to reasoned decisions; otherwise, it could not thrive in a problem-laden world. Perhaps some non-Western cultures are superior to Western cultures in developing the kinds of interpersonal sensitivity that make groups effective.

10. *In which of these features of modern life is "decontextualized" reasoning especially valuable?*

    Political participation   Do-it-yourself home repairs
    Investment   Child rearing   Architectural design
    Computer programming   Medical practice

11. *The Russell Sage Social Relations Test (Damrin, 1959) is a block design test in group form. The teacher remains on the sidelines as the tester distributes about 20 blocks of several colors among the pupils, displays a comparatively large pattern that can use so many pieces, and tells the children that they are to construct it as rapidly as possible. "Before you begin, you can take as much time as you need to talk about it and to figure out a way in which the class can do it. I will not begin timing until you tell me that you are all ready to start."*

    a. *Can Binet's definition of intelligence (p. 230) apply to a group? Rephrase it if necessary. Does the Russell Sage test measure group intelligence in Binet's sense? If not, what?*

    b. *If several classes are ranked according to the average scores of their members on WISC-R Block Design, would you expect the classes to rank similarly on Damrin's test?*

    c. *For what purposes, if any, could this test provide more relevant information than the CogAT Non-Verbal section administered in the usual way?*

CULTURAL LOADING OF ABILITY TESTS

Comparisons of U.S. Ethnic Groups

Score differences between culturally different groups cannot be attributed to heredity. Reasoning about "group heredity" breaks down because indefensible assumptions about environments are smuggled in. If girls have a gene that helps in mechanical reasoning—one that boys lack—yet the culture gives boys experience with machines and gives girls little or none, most boys will outscore most girls on MCT. Males will develop scores toward the high end of whatever range their heredity permits. Females will develop scores toward the low end of their possible range. If two groups, from conception, had indistinguishable biological and social environments, we could draw a conclusion from observed differences; otherwise, not.

Innumerable surveys have reported average test scores for U.S. ethnic samples. The findings, essentially consistent, require careful interpretation. Blacks average about 1 s.d. below the white population on general mental tests. Both groups spread over the range of test scores; at school ages about a sixth of blacks exceed the average of the white population. Every kind of test within the *Gf-Gc* spectrum shows about the same difference (Loehlin et al., 1975, pp. 177–188; Reynolds et al., 1987). Eysenck (in Reynolds & Brown, 1984) reviews studies on "racial" differences from many parts of the world. One consistent finding (in the

United States as well as in Asia) is that persons of Chinese and Japanese stock average higher than the population as a whole. Jensen (1985) finds some indication that tests calling for more complex information processing show larger race differences. (A critical discussion by many experts is published with Jensen's paper.)

The difference in averages of racial groups is greatly reduced when samples are matched on parent education, occupation, or income. The difference between blacks and whites at the same socioeconomic level is about half the difference prior to matching. Even more important, when the analyst equates families on child-rearing styles (including intellectual stimulation), the average IQ difference between black and white children drops to about 0.2 s.d. For a review of this research on home processes, see Elliott (1987, pp. 46ff.). The fact remains that poor black children average lower than children from impoverished white families.

Social scientists do not agree about the likely explanation.[1] Some would say that the test scores systematically underrate the true present ability of poor black and Hispanic children. Others would say that cultural traditions in some sections of the community leave their children, on average, ill prepared to meet demands of the school—less prepared than is the case in other economically pinched households, in any ethnic group, where the child's intellectual growth is nurtured. Some say that a history of prejudice and discrimination impairs development of young members of a group in subtle ways. And, finally, some believe that a fraction of the observed difference in means is an outcropping of differences between the gene pools of the subpopulations.

All explanations but the last relate the performance difference to factors in the culture; and those factors change. The average score for blacks on achievement in reading and arithmetic is steadily overtaking that of whites, according to national surveys (Appleby, Langer, & Mullis, 1989; Jones, 1984). The mean difference in mathematics for 9-year-olds tested in 1986 was about 2/3 of the difference found 13 years earlier, in a survey of 9-year-olds born in 1964.

One WISC-R item asks a child what he or she should do if a smaller child starts a fight with him or her. The city streets do not value avoiding aggression as the middle class does, and "Shove him (or her) in the face" is not an unreasonable answer. Wechsler himself said that a Harlem child deserves credit for responding "Fight back" but he did not modify the scoring key, which credits "Walk away" or the like. A slightly differ-

---

[1] A National Commission on Testing and Public Policy, funded by the Ford Foundation, is studying tests and test use with particular attention to differences across ethnic groups. An early product will be a multivolume series of papers by psychologists and nonpsychologists, many of them updating or extending views of authors cited in Part II of this book. Two volumes of conference papers (Gifford, 1989a, b) have been completed; subsequent volumes will contain fully developed position statements.

ent criticism is made of Wechsler's Information subtest. "Who wrote *Paradise Lost?*" asks for a fact that not every American adult has encountered. Using such evidence to draw conclusions about "intelligence" has deservedly been satirized. Alternative tests have been devised on which only a person who knows the argot of the black ghetto (alternatively, of the barrio) could succeed. These tests make white college graduates look "unintelligent."

Criticisms of cultural loading are sometimes too hasty. The black/white difference is *not* especially large on many items that critics call unfair. One target has been a Stanford-Binet item, used until 1985, that asks the child to pick the prettier of two faces; one has regular features and is well groomed, whereas the other is puffy, slack-jawed, and untidy. Critics complain that the judgment "is loaded with white middle-class values." In fact, black children find this the easiest of all the items placed at the same level. (It is third easiest for whites; Jensen, 1980, p. 5.) Likewise, the Wechsler "fight" item turns out not to be especially hard for blacks.

Another overstated criticism has a statistical slant. Minority performance suffers, it is said, because most of the data used in selecting items come from whites. If so, choosing items on the basis of data from blacks would reduce or reverse the group difference. Hickman and Reynolds (1986) reprocessed KABC subtests, selecting items for a B form on the basis of black data and items for a W form using white data. In a fresh sample the B and W Sequential scores gave essentially identical reports on the (small) black/white differences. The B Simultaneous test reported a mean race difference about 40 percent smaller than the W Simultaneous test. (Whites significantly outperform blacks on both Simultaneous scales.) The criticism, then, has some validity but does not explain away the group differences.

Should Cultural Experience Count?

Although some culture-loaded items are indefensible, others have a legitimate function if interpreted correctly. The test on ghetto slang is a valid (though partial) test of familiarity with ghetto culture. The test taker who possesses this resource is better able to adapt in that culture than a person who does not. Moreover, the test taker gives evidence of having learned successfully in it. Such a test might reasonably play a part in the clinical examination of a black teenager. Wechsler deliberately opted for an information subtest, believing that a person who reasons at a normal level will be handicapped in the community without a normal store of information. A similar justification lies behind Wechsler Comprehension items; a person unacquainted with the social norms of a culture is going to encounter difficulties. A fraction of the Wechsler total score, then, comes from acquaintance with the predominant culture. Testers are dead wrong if they assign the same meaning to all IQs of 70 regardless of the examinees' backgrounds.

Much of the same issue arises in achievement testing. On a test that one must pass to receive a high school diploma, is filling out a bank check a proper task? Plaintiffs in *Debra P.* (p. 172) pointed out that comparatively few blacks have checking accounts and, therefore, the item is hard for black students. The question is one of relevance. If education is to prepare students to enter the general community, it must acquaint them with the skills of that world, especially if they are unlikely to acquire them in and around their homes.

Some tests do give excessive weight to culture-specific elements. As was noted in connection with the SAT (p. 265), when verbal analogies items are intended to measure reasoning, using uncommon words is a mistake, a source of irrelevant difficulty. In a pioneering analysis of cultural loading, W. Allison Davis (1951) contrasted the following items (among others):

A symphony is to a composer as a book is to what?
                paper   sculptor   author   musician   man
A baker goes with bread, like a carpenter goes with what?
            a saw   a home   a spoon   a nail   a man

On the first item, 81 per cent of children from well-to-do homes passed, compared with 51 per cent of those from poorer homes; on the second item, both percentages stood at 50. The first item seems to require mostly familiarity with the word *author;* the second requires sharp discrimination of relationships, but only the commonest of knowledge.

Davis and colleagues (Eells et al., 1951) contrasted items strongly associated with social background with items weakly related to background. The former set included more verbal items than pictorial items. Many of the errors suggest failure to hold multiple facts in mind or to process facts carefully, as is illustrated in Table 9.1. Only a few items—such as the "author" item above—seemed to impose a specific content handicap. Davis and Eells produced their own test, making every effort to use words and pictures familiar in poor homes and neighborhoods. Their test, however, correlated with the social level of the home just as conventional tests of general ability did (Charters, 1963).

To sum up: The fact that an item is difficult for or strange to a cultural group or that the group averages below the American national norms is not proof of invalidity. But many test items have, for no good reason, included content with which well-to-do children are more familiar. Recent tests have been improved in this respect. Recall especially the reduced black/white differences in the mental processing sections of KABC (p. 257).

Detecting Questionable Items

Eliminating irrelevant difficulties is always an aim in test construction. Test makers now strive particularly to weed out items that present special difficulty for minority examinees (Berk, 1982). There are basi-

Table 9.1   RESPONSES OF PUPILS CLASSIFIED BY HOME BACKGROUND

Item stem, age, and status group of students	Percentage of status group giving each response					
If I have a large box with 3 small boxes in it and 3 very small boxes in each small box, how many boxes are there in all?	6	7	3	12	13[a]	Omit
13- and 14-year-olds						
High status	2	29[b]	1	13	51	1
Low status	13[c]	37	3	18	23	1
If the letters e l i c a d e t were arranged properly, they would spell	elucidate	dedicate	elegance	elevate	delicate[a]	Omit
9- and 10-year-olds						
High status	21	8	3	4	61	4
Low status	28	10	11[c]	9	35	7

[a] Correct answer.

[b] Wrong response significantly more attractive in high-status group (as percentage of their errors).

[c] Wrong response significantly more attractive in low-status group.

Source: Eells et al., 1951, pp. 269, 276.

cally two approaches to the screening of items: judgmental and correlational.

Especially in the preparation of examinations for admission to professional school, for a public job, or for a high school diploma, it is common to enlist a review committee from pertinent sectors of the community. These informants are invited to challenge items that might be poorly understood by test takers from the subcommunity they know best. The acceptability of the test is heightened by the removal of items perceived as unfair (even if some of them are valid) and by the participation of community representatives in making the test.

The correlational approach is, essentially, a check on the order of item difficulties. Is the difficulty ranking of the items the same in each demographic group? Groups might be defined by age, sex, education, and ethnicity—alone or in combination. Before taking this up, we must look at a simpler alternative that is dubious.

Advocates for minority interests have recently pressed for laws mandating a "Golden Rule" procedure in constructing tests for certification or school graduation. The name comes from the Golden Rule Insurance Company in Illinois, which brought suit against a state examination on which black applicants for licenses to sell insurance tended to do badly.

In a 1984 settlement, the maker of the test (ETS) agreed to changes that would increase the pass rate for blacks.[2]

The ETS official who negotiated the agreement has now called it "an error of judgment"; for extended pro and con discussion see Haney and Reidy (1987). The American Psychological Association has condemned attempts to mandate wide use of the procedure, in part because of its weakness and in part because every profession objects to laws that regulate details of its work (Committee on Psychological Tests and Assessments, 1988).

In many circumstances, the Golden Rule tends to discard the strongest items, the ones most related to the central dimension of the test. Also, the statistical filter might remove certain difficult topics when, to protect the public, a test for licensure ought to cover them.

Professional analysis uses sophisticated methods (see Angoff and Ironson, in Berk, 1982; Cole & Moss, in Linn, 1989a, pp. 208–212; Wainer, in Wainer & Braun, 1988). The basic notion (p. 141) is to select black and white subgroups matched on the ability the test is to measure, and flag items where these matched groups differ. If a test is intended to measure quantitative reasoning, for example, rather than command of particular mathematical techniques, one would want the rank order of items to be the same for males and females. The finding that on most items males outscore females would be credible if in the relevant population males have studied math for more years. But if items that touch on surveying are *especially* difficult for females, the difficulty is probably irrelevant and should be removed.

Items have to be judged one by one. The test maker might discard an item or revise it. Sometimes she can defend an item whose ranking is "out of place" in one group on the grounds that it measures highly relevant content. And sometimes she can keep the test in balance by offsetting items that favor group A with other items that favor group B.

No method of item selection yields "culture-free" tests. In former times that term was applied to tests that do not on the surface demand language or school learning. Nowadays it is agreed that no behavioral evidence is "culture free." Where modifications described in this chapter have been made, tests are "culture reduced." The stronger term "culture fair" makes a dubious claim. Judgment on the claim has to look beyond the test technique and toward the questions: "Fair when used

---

[2]The Golden Rule principle is to favor items that are comparatively easy *and* show a comparatively small or no difference between majority and minority test takers. More specifically, "Type I items" are to be favored. Items would fall in this category if, in a tryout, at least 40 per cent of each group gets the item right, and the difference is 15 per cent or less. Thus the black and white percentages correct might be 40 and 50 (or 60 and 74, or 91 and 99). In choosing items for the final test, those with the smallest differences are to be chosen first. All items are to be of Type I so long as this produces enough items for each content category in the test blueprint.

in what manner? And for what purpose?" An example of reasoning about fairness is useful here; I shall have more to say in Chapter 11.

In the early 1970s, officials in Washington, D. C., set out to recruit additional black police. They screened applicants on vocabulary and reading comprehension, and many failed, especially among blacks. A court was asked to stop the testing, but in the end the Supreme Court accepted it (*Washington* v. *Davis*, 96 S. Ct. 2040 [1976]; see Lerner, 1977). Vigorous recruiting had brought many poorly prepared applicants into the pool, and that was partly responsible for the high failure rate. There was no willful or irrelevant discrimination.

12. *One set of guidelines (Educational Testing Service, 1980) illustrates "offensive" items that reviewers should reject. What might be objections to the following item? Could it be repaired? (Assume that the test is intended for social workers. The response options, not listed, are irrelevant to the criticisms of the stem.)*

    A Puerto Rican welfare mother with ten children needs help in paying her winter utility bills. Which agency would be the most likely to provide assistance?

13. *When an Unusual Uses test asks the child from an impoverished home to suggest uses for a newspaper, he tends to get a high score because he thinks of things like soaking up spilled grease or putting on the floor when you take a bath. Is Unusual Uses biased in favor of the poor child? Or is the higher score valid?*

14. *Shepard (in Berk, 1982) constructs several instances that might, if actually observed, lead to a charge of bias. Here is one of them:*

    On a math computation test, the largest difference between blacks and whites is on the word problem subtest. When items are presented orally, the differential difficulty disappears.

    Give an example of use or interpretation for which the printed test is informative and unbiased and then an example where the charge of bias is justified.

15. *In describing the Golden Rule I included the phrase "enough items for each content category in the test blueprint." In some statements of the Rule that phrase is omitted. Why is it important?*

16. *Valencia (personal communication) finds that Hispanic children in California do less well on KABC Arithmetic items referring (for example) to fractions than Anglo children who match them on the rest of KABC. He suggests that the Hispanic children may have received less instruction on fractions than Anglos of the same age, because of class time diverted to teaching English. Does this argue that the Arithmetic score is biased?*

INTERVENTION TO MODIFY ABILITIES

Using codes, distributing attention, making logical comparisons—these skills develop out of experience. Whether deliberate educational efforts can accelerate the development has been disputed since modern testing began. At one extreme (reviewed in Spitz, 1986) are enthusiasts prepared to claim near miracles for some training program, yet lacking trustworthy evidence of the effects. At the other extreme are those who see general ability as a by-product of miscellaneous experience, its rate of accretion being strongly influenced by heredity and exceedingly difficult to change.

Evaluation Results for Compensatory Education   The result shown in Figure 9.3 is fairly typical of experimental evaluations of American compensatory education where training was carefully planned and supervised by a knowledgeable person. Two years of prekindergarten instruction were given to children from poor families. This study, like many others set up around 1970, focused on whether the preschool experience raised Stanford-Binet scores. (The scores were adjusted according to age norms before plotting; hence year-to-year change attributable to normal development is removed from the picture.)

The experimental group was measurably superior at the end of the treatment. However, the control group "caught up" during the ensuing year. The many further years of follow-up added greatly to the value of the investigation.

The evidence in Figure 9.3 does not prove the intervention worthless. These test results strongly suggest that there was no lasting change in general ability; but that represents only one of many possible benefits (Travers & Light, 1982). Even the temporary elevation of scores the figure shows greatly reduced the chance of a child's being permanently classed by the schools as retarded, because most such assignments are made during the first years of schooling.

Theory from Vygotsky   Increased understanding of processes underlying efficient performance has generated a new hopefulness (Borkowski & Cavanaugh, 1979; Campione et al., in Sternberg, 1982; Lidz, 1987). In particular, professionals dealing with children who seem to be at risk

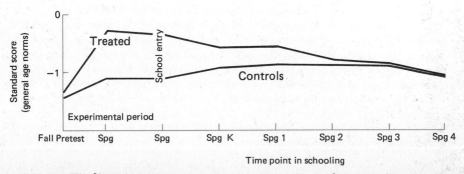

Figure 9.3. **Findings in an experiment on compensatory education.** (*Source*: Data from Weikart et al., 1978.)

for educational failure are exploring dynamic assessment as a training method, sometimes working on a large practical scale. Inspiration for the efforts have come from many sources. To mention only a few:

It is known that some children who can function well intellectually freeze up when formally tested.

Intellectual resources among schoolchildren who show the same low standing on conventional mental tests vary considerably, and school psychologists are charged with recognizing and providing for these differences.

There is a belief, supported by fragmentary evidence, that slow-developing children can be moved ahead much faster by tutoring in skills of problem solving (enhanced by the motivation that success brings).

Recent theories about mental development suggest giving greater attention to processes in a formative stage than to processes that are well established (or those seemingly absent).

Among those theories, Vygotsky's has been particularly influential. There is an affinity between Piaget and Vygotsky, inasmuch as both see a higher performance as growing out of simpler ones, and both see progress as the piecemeal acquisition of insights and structures. Unlike Piaget, Vygotsky focused on what could be done to promote those changes.

A person's powers are incomplete. At any point in development one can plot an elaborate profile of the concepts and skills available to him. The next concept acquired does not grow out of nothing. Rather, the person's experience today stimulates roots lying beneath the surface of behavior, which prepare him to grasp this or that next idea tomorrow. There is, then, what Vygotsky called a "zone of proximal development," a range of tasks that at the moment the person is ready to learn.

Minick (in Lidz, 1987) gives an extended account of this thought, starting with a translation from Vygotsky (1934/1986, pp. 203–204).

Assume that we have determined the mental age of two children to be eight years. However, we do not stop with this. Rather, we attempt to determine how each of these children will solve tasks that were meant for older children. We assist each child through demonstration, through leading questions, and by introducing the initial elements of the task's solution. With this help . . . one of these children solves problems characteristic of a twelve year old while the other solves problems only at a level typical of a nine year old. This difference between . . . actual level of development and the level of performance that he achieves in collaboration with the adult, defines the zone of proximal development.

A wide zone implies that the child can profit greatly from instructional help now. A narrow zone promises much less response to instructional help at this time. Vygotsky sees no need to forecast whether that child's zone will widen in time. The emphasis is on present readiness.

Chapter 8 cited evidence that a "static" conventional test indicates something about ability to learn. The thesis of dynamic assessors is that the level of performance attained *with* prompting tells a great deal more about responsiveness to instruction. And, whereas Vygotsky summarized the zone as a number, most dynamic assessors are attentive to what kinds of shortcomings the child quickly corrects and what kinds persist despite the tutor's efforts.

Training in Information Processing   Among efforts to base instruction on such assessments, the greatest amount of experience has been accumulated by Reuven Feuerstein and his followers in many countries. Feuerstein, an Israeli psychologist, has worked for decades with adolescents from a disadvantaged background. Jews whose families come from North Africa and the Middle East tend to score low on tests, and to fare much less well in school and jobs than those of European background. Feuerstein's teachers work with apparently retarded adolescents from such families over periods as long as 2 years.

The Israeli instructional program extends over hundreds of hours and has two aspects. General Enrichment (GE) is the instruction ordinarily given to these youths; it concentrates on arithmetic, Hebrew, history, and so on, plus field trips. For Feuerstein's trainees Instrumental Enrichment (IE) replaces 300 hours of the GE program. IE seeks to develop self-regulation—an understanding of the nature and criteria for intellectual effort plus a consciousness of, and willingness to correct, one's own procedures.

The Learning Potential Assessment Device (LPAD) is both a test and a vehicle for training (Feuerstein, 1979; Feuerstein et al., 1982). The materials have been used in the United States and Canada for some time, and more formal publication of LPAD is planned. LPAD includes a matrix test, number series, verbal analogies, and several other measures of *Gf*. The assessment technique adopts many of the suggestions for testing in non-Western cultures. The items of each type ascend from easy to difficult. The respondent is encouraged to concentrate and analyze, is given hints when he loses sight of the goal, and, if necessary, is guided through to the solution. Less credit is assigned when success comes only after much help has been given. The examinee who profits from help on one item, making a more independent attack on the next, is judged likely to be responsive to instruction. The dynamic version of, for example, the matrix task can be administered to groups of students. In the group version, the teaching is more standardized than in the individual version. In the individual version the examiner is on the lookout for styles that make the person inefficient, and responds accordingly. There is little difference between dynamic "assessment" and the instructional procedure, save that the instruction is extended over a long period. Feuerstein and his collaborators say this about the aim of assessment (in Lidz, 1987, p. 46):

> Interpretation focuses on the peaks in the functioning, . . . which may . . . [stand out in] splendid isolation from otherwise low functioning. Rather than discarding these incidents as random or chance, or, at best, as . . . over-learned behavior . . ., peaks in performance are to be considered as indications of the capacity of the individual. The responsibility for explaining their appearance, or rather, their lack of pervasive presence falls upon the evaluator. . . . [T]he peak performance is [to be studied] by inducing its recurrence, and by producing insight into the conditions of its appearance. . . .

This is accompanied, of course, by an attempt to understand deficiencies. Different exercises tell different stories, generating a nonnumerical "profile of modifiability."

Traditionally, measurement of ability or a fuller case workup was part of initiating instruction or other treatment. Assessment and remediation both go on at once in a program like Feuerstein's, assessment continuing as long as the child is in the program. The instructor, even in the midst of tutoring or conducting a group session, is making observations that update the profile of modifiability.

Dialogue is the heart of the Instructional Enrichment procedure—supporting, challenging, leading, recapitulating. Table 9.2 illustrates this concept with extracts from an 18-step interaction of tutor and beginning trainee. The first nine steps led a young person who had no conception of the task to a solution. When the right answer ("Four") was given, the tester did not stop. She led the youth to explain why one of the options was incorrect and then to pick the very worst response and give two reasons for rejecting it. Leading the student to be articulate about reasons is considered highly important.

Six goals guide the teacher's effort (Feuerstein, 1980, pp. 115–144):

Strengthening any process identified as weak or faulty—for example, planning, use of time.

Developing vocabulary to describe concepts and relationships. (The student is pressed to describe all manipulations in words.)

Teaching habits of attack that apply to problems generally. ("Find out what is needed!")

Promoting interest in intellectual challenges.

Producing self-observation, reflection, and inhibition of impulsive action.

Bringing the performer to realize that he should actively generate information, not passively receive it.

Three Canadian case reports on young adults (Barr & Samuels, 1988) illustrate the variety of conclusions that can emerge from LPAD and the conversations that flow naturally in the interaction.

Table 9.2   DIALOGUE TO ORIENT A LAGGARD YOUTH TO AN EASY MATRIX ITEM

Instructor's question	Rationale	Response
1. "Look at this page. What must be done here?"	Request for definition of a problem.	"I don't know" (or incorrect or irrelevant response).
2. "Look at this rectangle. What do you see in it? Look at the bottom, and you will see 6 pieces."	Produce in the child a state of disequilibrium.	
3. "This square is gray. Is it all gray?"	Produce explicit analytic perception of a whole and a missing part.	"No. There is a white part. Some gray is missing."
4. "Yes. You are right. There is a missing part. What must you do about it?"	Orient the child toward the need to solve the problem.	"I have to color it gray."

[Steps 5 and 6 lead the subject to connect the six options to the task and say, "I can take one of these and put it here."]

7. "Yes. Right you are. Now could you show me the one that you could put in there to make it look like nothing is missing?"	Induce the child to compare on relevant dimensions (e.g., an irrelevant dimension in this task is the shape).	"Number two."
8. "It's almost good; it is the right color. But there is a better one."	Minimize the child's failure. Point to the need for a more appropriate answer.	
9. "If you want to find it, look at all the possible choices at the bottom of the page, from 1 to 6. Look at each one to see which one of them is the right one." The examiner "models" systematic looking for the best answer among the various alternatives by pointing to each in order from 1 to 6.	First attempt to produce systematic exploration, accompanied by gestural modeling.	"Four."

Source: Adapted from Feuerstein, 1979, pp. 353–355.

NOTE: The item presents a square with an overall polka-dot pattern of light gray circles. A blank area appears in the square, and six patterns that fit the area are offered. The five incorrect choices differ greatly from the main pattern.

- Beth was withdrawn and noncommunicative. When she worked on her own, she was erratic and inattentive. With encouragement and gentle pressure to focus, Beth did engage the task fully now and then; one-word responses gave way to full, appropriate sentences. The examiner concluded that Beth's emotional problems were more significant than any weaknesses on the cognitive side, and recommended counseling.
- Bill had come through schooling for the retarded, and as an adult had had low-level jobs. He wanted to train for something better. Initially his LPAD responses were slow and vague. A combination of positive feedback with pressure for precise labeling and orderly analysis quickly elicited better results. Again, it turned out that emotional factors mattered more than intellectual ones. Bill was ambitious and resented having been treated as incompetent all his life. Counseling improved his self-image, and at last report he was succeeding in a math course.
- Pat, a 37-year-old secretary, also had a bad school history, not even having mastered the alphabet until Grade 3. Her LPAD displayed impulsiveness and failure of organization. Pat believed that normal people react quickly and that if she worked systematically through information before responding, it would be evidence of inferiority. She was brought to understand that her style was self-defeating, and gained enough confidence to enroll in a computer course. Further counseling to raise self-esteem was recommended.

Evidence on Effects Feuerstein's evidence on effects of IE was culled from files built up under field conditions. Impressive case studies of change in retarded, disturbed adolescents are offered. Those who had been school failures prior to the intervention became adult successes as manager, skilled printer, executive secretary, and so on (Feuerstein, 1979).

A formal comparison of matched cases shows IE trainees ahead of GE-only trainees on several tests not used in the training. The difference on achievement tests was tiny; still, the IE trainees held their own in areas where GE trainees had many more hours of instruction. On vocabulary and verbal reasoning, IE outdid GE by very little. On EFT and spatial tests, the IE group was ahead by nearly 1 s.d. A similarly favorable result appeared on tests given during army induction, 2 years after the end of the training (Feuerstein, 1980).

A large number of other studies in Colombia, Canada, and several U.S. communities are reviewed by Savell et al. (1986). The findings are mixed and hard to interpret. Programs varied in duration and other features—and where outcomes seem to have been positive, the reports often fail to indicate whether the change was large or small. Savell et al. are impressed by the score increases produced on nonverbal ability measures (with tasks not covered in the training), but they question whether these increases represent fundamental change or only greater test-wiseness. We lack well-controlled studies on whether IE activities increase educability.

17. *Which elements of Feuerstein's program, if any, could reasonably be made a part of the elementary school curriculum for average pupils in the United States, to be checked out along with what are ordinarily called "basics"?*

18. *When effects of "Sesame Street" were studied, it appeared that all children benefited, but that students from average homes benefited more than disadvantaged, slow developing children. Arguing that "Sesame Street" widened the gap, Cook et al. (1975) questioned whether making the program freely available was in the best interest of society. What do you think?*

19. *Staats and Burns (1981) trained preschool children to trace and then copy letters of the alphabet (6 hours of training). Account for each of the following results in terms of change in processes.*
    a. *The children became efficient; it took them only a few trials to learn letters introduced late in the training.*
    b. *On a WPPSI subtest where geometric shapes are to be copied, the scale score mean of controls changed from 10.7 to 11.2 from pretest to posttest; the experimentals changed from 10.6 to 13.0. (A similar gain on all subtests would raise the IQ 14 points.)*
    c. *On WPPSI mazes, the control means were 11.2 and 10.9 (a small decline). The experimental means were 10.7 and 12.7.*

20. *Do you think Staats and Burns were improving the child's "intelligence"?*

21. *The three Canadian cases are similar to Matarazzo's case of the executive whose emotions were a source of intellectual malfunction. What advantages does LPAD have over the Wechsler as an aid in understanding such cases?*

TESTING AND EDUCATIONAL DIFFERENTIATION

In a society where roles are differentiated, education is also differentiated. Sometimes the program is uniform for all students up to the age where weaker (or less wealthy) students drop out. Sometimes the program is branched long before the school-leaving age; thus, it has been common to route one fraction of adolescents into a high-level academic program and the remainder into a general or vocational track. Further differentiation occurs after high school as students sort themselves into more and less demanding postsecondary institutions and major fields. Especially in English and math, colleges and secondary schools sort students into advanced, regular, and remedial sections. In elementary schools the rates at which students are pushed along in the basic subjects depends on their performance.

Tests of general or scholastic aptitude can be used to sort entering pupils into fast and slow tracks and to identify some as handicapped. They can define eligibility for options open to "gifted" pupils, and they can count heavily in the choice among curricular options in high school.

They play an obvious role in admission to college and to postgraduate training. The same decisions, of course, could be based entirely on achievement tests or on teachers' impressions. Although critics have complained about mental tests, most of the issues—and most of the arguments in favor of systematic testing—would be the same if decisions were based on achievement tests. (Whatever test is used, information of other kinds, including teachers' impressions, should be taken into account.)

No one seems to think that the schools should hold all students to the same pace or teach them exactly the same courses. "Tracking" or "streaming" refers especially to setting up "fast," "regular," and "slow" classrooms in each grade. Efforts to group students by readiness levels are condemned for their inflexibility and for the damage that can result from labeling a person as "slow." (But children in a full-range classroom are well aware that this or that classmate is "slow.")

Routing certain learners into a slow track guarantees that, after months or years have passed, the regular students will have learned far more than the "slow" group, simply because their lessons covered more ground. The slow pace of instruction offered—in all kindness—puts the student farther behind his agemates with each passing month and makes a transfer into an average class less and less practicable. The case of Alex (p. 287) and other such evidence indicates that students who at one age are not ready for brisk instruction may be fully capable at a later date.

Any sorting plan that does not provide for frequent shifts of classification, on the basis of updated judgments, should be challenged. Plans that place students in slow or fast levels for the whole school day are especially hard to reverse.

Decisions about Learners with Intellectual Handicaps

The greatest sin in the treatment of the child who shows poor intellectual development is the common assumption that he is doomed forever to be substandard. This concern more than any other has produced support for "mainstreaming," for keeping the slow-learning or otherwise handicapped child with his agemates in most school activities (Heller et al., 1982; Hobbs, 1975). Federal legislation (the Rehabilitation Act of 1973 and the 1974 law on handicapped children generally referred to as P.L. 94–142) has tried to increase the opportunities of persons with handicaps. The law, as Shepard says (in Linn, 1989a, p. 545), "took poorly formed, consensual definitions of vaguely understood concepts and made them the basis for entitlements. Scientific understanding of the disorders has not progressed much since then."

The legislation supported mainstreaming. Schools are expected to provide an "appropriate" education. This calls for a case review using a wide range of information (often including an elaborate test battery but by no means limited to tests). Once the handicapped pupil's needs are identified, an individual plan (IEP) is developed in cooperation with the parents and any professional advisers they bring in (Kennedy & McDaniels, in Travers & Light, 1982). Any diagnosis or plan is to be updated from time to time. I shall briefly discuss policies related to "learning disabilities" and "retardation." For recommendations on analysis of learners with physical, emotional, or cognitive handicaps, see the handbooks of Filskov and Boll (1982) and Reynolds and Gutkin (1982). For research on tests of physically handicapped or learning-disabled college applicants, see Willingham et al. (1988).

Learning Disability   The "disability" category is essentially a residual; it makes a place for those whose uneven intellectual development is not understood, and for whom Congress has wanted to provide "categorical" funds. A national committee had this to say (Sherman & Robinson, 1982, p. 13):

> "Learning disabilities" is a very heterogeneous and ill-defined category that covers a wide range of difficulties in speaking, understanding speech, reading, and writing. The National Advisory Committee on Handicapped Children developed the following definition, which is used in the Education for All Handicapped Children Act (P.L. 94–142; Wepman et al. 1976:301–302):
>
> *Children with special learning disabilities exhibit a disorder in one or more of the basic psychological processes involved in understanding or using spoken or written languages. These may be manifested in disorders of listening, thinking, talking, reading, writing, spelling, or arithmetic. They include conditions which have been referred to as perceptual handicaps, brain injury, minimal brain dysfunction, dyslexia, developmental aphasia, etc. They do not include learning problems which are due primarily to visual, hearing, or motor handicaps, to mental retardation, emotional disturbance, or to environmental disadvantages.*
>
> There seems to be little consensus among physicians or educators about how to identify and classify learning-disabled children. The most commonly accepted indicator is a marked discrepancy between general learning ability, or "intelligence," as measured by standardized tests, and educational achievement, as measured by tests or grades.

A typical rule resurrects the misguided concept of "underachievement" (p. 298), flagging the child of average mental ability who is about "two grades behind" on an achievement test. A study group recommends more subtle assessment, with attention to the difference between the child's standard score in achievement and the average achievement score of children with a general-ability score equal to the child's. This is estimated by a simple regression equation. Additional calculations are made before the discrepancy is considered large enough to justify the "learning-disabled" classification (Reynolds, 1984; see also criticism of the commonplace rules by Lopez & Yoshida, 1987).

The achievement lag could result from poor motivation, emotional disturbance, or inadequate instruction rather than any neurological handicap. The confusing "learning-disabled" designation is bound to persist, if only because parents are pleased with the list of explanations for their child's lack of achievement ruled out by the Committee's definition. Children with weakness in a single subject may be classified as having a "*specific* learning disability." Using, instead, a dignified label such as "dyslexia" removes none of the mystery (White & Miller, 1983). The confusing and poorly justified labels sometimes have to be applied simply because certain government funds can be used only for pupils who "have a diagnosis."

Learning disability remains a political-bureaucratic concept having no scientific meaning. Those unhappy with the definition in the federal law offer alternatives, and each proposal is rejected by one or another agency or advocacy group. As Shepard says, policy cannot make sense until the heterogeneous category is subdivided along scientific lines. *That would mean identifying groups suited for particular treatments.*

The most significant recent definition is this:

> Learning disabilities is a generic term that refers to a heterogeneous group of disorders manifested by significant difficulties in the acquisition and use of listening, speaking, reading, writing, reasoning, or mathematical abilities. These disorders are intrinsic to the individual and presumed to be due to central nervous dysfunction. Even though a learning disability may occur concomitantly with other handicapping conditions (e.g., sensory impairment, mental retardation, social and emotional disturbance) or environmental influences (e.g., cultural differences, insufficient or inappropriate instruction, psychogenic factors), it is not the direct result of those conditions or influences.

This definition has been endorsed by a committee of federal officials asked by Congress to make recommendations (*Learning disabilities,* 1987).

22. *In what ways does the definition from the federal committee differ from the one in P.L. 94–142?*

Retardation   There was a time when children whose mental test performance fell below a level chosen by school officials were automatically placed in "special education." During a childhood stay in the United States, Jan Masaryk—later eminent as a Czech statesman—was classified that way. (A competent tester would have recognized his language problem and made a more detailed study.) We have come a long way from those practices, but no one is content with present practice.

Special classes have been called into question repeatedly, as in the case of *Larry P.* (495 F. Supp. 926 [1979]); also C-71-2270 RFP, Order modifying judgment, Sept. 25, 1986). Mental testing was the surface issue. Advocates for black children, including organizations of black psychologists, protested the use of mental testing that routed children into classes for the "educationally mentally retarded (EMR)." The proportion of black children so classified was shockingly high. The heart of the matter was that the classification seemed to be doing harm, not good. California policy directed teachers to assume that it was "impossible" for EMR children to learn the content of regular lessons. Teachers were to develop in them the minimal skills for low-level employment and survival in the community. Almost no EMR pupil ever returned to the regular classroom; understandably, the judge's decision said over and over that these were "dead-end" classes and that a child's rights were violated if his EMR placement was invalid. The state's overemphatic directive made its practices hard to defend. How could one cope with "the validation burden of showing that it is impossible for those who score low to profit from the regular classes even with remedial instruction" (words from the court opinion, rearranged)? Jane Mercer, as a witness, called the regulations an instance of the conception that retarded persons suffer from an incurable disease or disorder.

The judge ruled that California could not continue to use the Wechsler and similar tests in deciding which black children were to go into EMR classes. (He did not question their use with whites.) Skills of retarded children do not grow faster in special classes than in regular classes, according to comparisons across school systems with differing policies. Therefore, testing specialists called in by the state could not convince the judge that the classification was valid.

The court's reasoning in *Larry P.* and the arguments put forth by psychologists for each side have been forcefully criticized, particularly in the light of a diametrically opposed Chicago decision (*PASE* v. *Hannon*, 506 F. Supp. 831 [1980]). The reader interested in the interplay of science, politics, and law will be amused and dismayed by the story told in *Litigating Intelligence* (Elliott, 1987). This book should be read alongside an equally critical but quite different evaluation by Bersoff (in Plake, 1984).

The criticism of the ruling most pertinent here is that reducing the amount of information available about a child makes for less adequate judgments.

Banning tests does not, in itself, benefit black children. For several years while *Larry P.* was in the courts, California schools were enjoined from mental testing of blacks. The number of black children classified as EMR did not decline in most school districts. (The percentage of blacks among those given the EMR label, in years with and without mental testing, were 51 and 50 in Los Angeles, 85 and 84 in Oakland, 79 and 43 in San Francisco, 21 and 34 in San Diego.)

Mainstreaming is not advocated for the tiny fraction of children who, intellectually, are markedly below nearly all of the school population. Figure 9.4 is representative of current thinking about those children whose limitations do not keep them out of school altogether. As you can see, the recommended plan puts a heavy burden of proof on whoever recommends special-class placement.

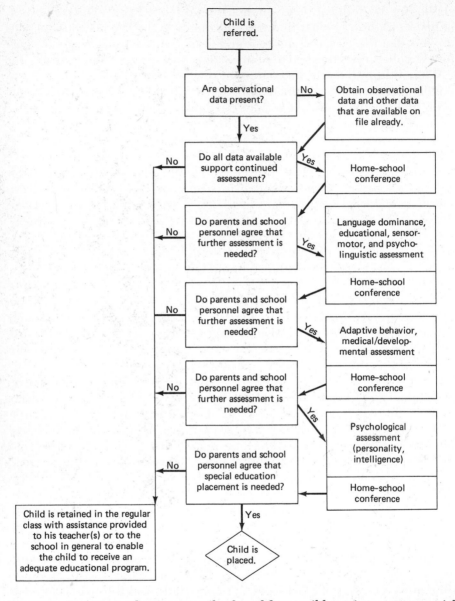

Figure 9.4. Steps in evaluating a pupil referred for possible assignment to special education. (*Source*: Tucker, 1977, p. 96.)

Fitting Instruction to the Child

Many school systems give a standardized test of general ability or general achievement early in the school year. One purpose is to advise teachers so that they will demand neither too much nor too little of their pupils. It is on the basis of such expectations that a teacher paces the instruction (standing ready to give special assistance to the slow and to challenge the able). Expectations are formed by cumulative experience in daily activities and by records on teacher-made tests, as well as by standard tests of achievement and ability. (See also p. 88.) There are two particular hazards in the process: teachers may have biases (for example, expecting intellectual inadequacy from unruly boys), and the expectations may not be updated as new evidence comes in.

Teacher Expectations   Standard tests given at the start of the year—and especially "intelligence" tests—have been much criticized. It is alleged that once his score labels a child as bright or dull, the teacher pitches lessons to that level even when daily performance contradicts the expectation.

As a part of the attacks on mental testing in the 1960s and 1970s, many investigators set up experiments to demonstrate a "Pygmalion effect." Supposedly, reporting a test score (valid or invalid) to a teacher biases the teaching process. In an attempt to demonstrate the effect, teachers were given false high scores for some children; the claim was that teachers would help these flagged children more than the control children, so that they would outdo their classmates. In fact (considering all the investigations together), if the teacher had known the child for as little as 2 weeks, no effect appeared. A report supplied during the teacher's first week with the child did have an effect—indexed by an average gain of about 5 IQ points (and presumably some extra subject matter achievement) at the end of the term (Raudenbush, 1984).

Observations by Rist (1970) show how teacher expectations lead to miseducation. An important part of his tale is that in these classes impartial tests were ignored. Testing could not prevent improper teaching, but it could have corrected some of the teachers' false impressions. Rist observed a group of black children, taught by successive black teachers, from school entry to the end of second grade. The kindergarten teacher assigned children to three tables after the first week of school; the great majority of children were kept with these same trackmates during all three years. Rist believed that the initial grouping was influenced by the mother's report on home background and by the child's dialect, appearance, and body odor. The children the teacher saw as superior were given every opportunity. The third-place table was neglected; for example, when writing on the blackboard, the teacher typically wrote on a panel these children could not see. The first-grade teacher taught reading directly to those who had been favored in kindergarten—so their readiness had developed—and started the others at a slower rate. Sometimes a Table B child made rapid progress. That child was not allowed to shift to Table A until he had read all the books on the list for Table B. And so on. The children in the lowest group were not socially accepted and showed emotional disturbance.

The sorting expressed a teacher's social-class bias. Ability tests were actually given at the end of kindergarten, but filed and ignored. On the tests, several children in the lower two groups had come within the range of the top group—even after a year of adverse treatment.

Teachers today seem not to give much thought to the reports on general-ability tests and achievement tests that reach them from a central office. Teachers say they are most likely to pay attention when a mental test reports a better score for a pupil than they anticipated from his classwork; that alerts the teacher to the possibility that better classroom performance could be elicited. When the test score is lower than a teacher had anticipated, on the other hand, the teacher does not lower her estimate of what the child can do (Salmon-Cox, 1981; Yeh, 1978).

Current Practices and Recommendations   Schools and teachers vary greatly in their policies regarding differentiation of instruction and regarding testing (Anderson, in Wigdor & Garner, 1982, vol. 2). It is no longer common to assign able and less able children to different elementary classrooms. Rather, differentiation takes place within the classroom and by "pull-out" arrangements to give advanced experiences or remedial help during part of the school day. The tests that influence groupings are almost always achievement tests—except when adolescents are being advised whether to take college preparatory courses.

Instructional grouping within a classroom is common. There will be groups in reading or arithmetic or groups working on science projects of varying complexity. Such grouping allows extra time for a pupil who needs a slow pace, as well as special assistance in one school subject, or allows a pupil to advance rapidly in some subjects. Moreover, frequent regrouping is possible. Such arrangements are not easy for teachers to manage; they are facilitated by team teaching, by use of more advanced students as tutors, and by availability of both simplified and advanced teaching materials. Standardized tests contribute little to this kind of instructional planning. When grouping is flexible, test scores collected in September become almost irrelevant to the decisions of November; by that time the teacher has detailed information from the pupil's handling of daily assignments.

Testing for microlevel decisions is increasing. Some parts of the school curriculum can be reduced to small elements, for example, recognizing where to use a semicolon. A checkoff test can demonstrate that a student has "mastered" that skill (though mastery comes in many degrees). And tests of this sort can be developed in numerous forms: the learner can test himself and judge his own adequacy. Published tests administered once or twice a year can report scores on subsets of items; the scores for individuals are unreliable, but the teacher who finds 40 per cent of the class at a low level on punctuation and only 20 per cent at a low level on capitalization will take that into account in daily instruction.

General mental tests have identified many children who possessed

exceptional general ability but whose school records were barely satisfactory. Many such pupils are not challenged and do not realize that they
can achieve more. Nonroutine assignments often stimulate such
children.

Also, there may be a significant message in the standing of the class
as a whole on a test of general ability. When last year's teacher set too
easy a pace, the group will probably have a lower standing in the conventional subjects than in the abilities that develop more spontaneously.
The message to step up the pace comes through clearly.

But teachers ought also to try to promote fluid reasoning, not accept
its level as a given. Underdeveloped skills of information processing
should concern teachers just as much as underdeveloped skill in computation. No one cares about tasks such as block design, matrices, embedded figures, or scrambled sentences; they are not "subject matter"
worth teaching. But skills of analysis, systematic search, self-checking,
and so on, are valuable. Tests of fluid ability would remind teachers of
that part of their responsibility—if we had not fallen into the habit of
regarding standings on such tests as indivisible composites, somehow
fixed in advance. Obviously, we want teachers to think about specific tasks and processes, not about the remote construct of "factor
score Gf."

M-MAC, A Computerized Planning System   School psychologists are now
offered a microcomputer program for case interpretation. The McDermott Multidimensional Assessment of Children (M-MAC; P. A. McDermott and M. W. Watkins) has two modes: classification and program design. Although applicable from age 2 to 18, M-MAC is most fully
developed for primary-level children who seem to have educational
handicaps.

The system is interactive. The user is prompted to type in information on the child's background; she has opportunities to choose among
options or to override. For example, at one point the user either bypasses
the mental-test option or indicates the test for which scores will be provided. (In this category the system is prepared to analyze scores from
four instruments, including Wechsler and Stanford-Binet.) Having chosen WISC-R, the user can ask that primary interpretation be based not
on Full Scale scores (as is usual) but on the Verbal or Performance score.
Adaptive behavior, basic achievement, and problem behavior scores or
judgments can be taken into account.

In classification mode, M-MAC invokes norms and reliability information to identify significant patterns. For some purposes cutting scores
are applied. If suitable standardization data are available the program
will calculate "expected achievement." (The user has the opportunity to
replace the built-in M-MAC rule with local norms or an experience table.) Among more than 30 intellectual labels are these, one or more of
which may be applied:

Severe educational retardation (as distinct from mental retardation)

Specific learning disability in arithmetic

Developmental arithmetic disorder

With regard to maladjustment, severity is judged. Then the profile is compared with profiles of various types and one label is picked (e.g., "Conduct disorder undersocialized aggressive"). Sixteen labels are available, the sixteenth being "Good adjustment." The classification report does not suggest what action to take. A final page summarizes facts and inferences that seem most likely to influence decisions.

The program design mode processes information related to abilities and learning skills, then lists perhaps a dozen objectives for this pupil's near-term instruction (e.g., "can suggest synonym for unfamiliar word presented in context—upper Grade 3 level"). The list derives from a fine-grain achievement test, and the user has the option of overriding the machine's choice of objectives before the list is printed. The program design mode is conservative in aim and method, and has been favorably reviewed from the standpoint of special education (Glutting, 1986).

How good is M-MAC? It is a first try, sure to evolve and sure to attract competitors. A good many faulty details (Bracken, 1986) will no doubt be corrected; here we should be evaluating not the details but the style of test use. Computer interpretations are hard to validate (pp. 579–581), and the argument for M-MAC classification probably has to be that it generally leads to conclusions a sophisticated psychologist would also reach. No systematic evidence has been offered on that point. The developer obviously paid close attention to relevant research literature and applied generally sound technique. (For example, M-MAC refuses to interpret score differences that lie within the likely span of measurement error.) To an able school psychologist M-MAC is a reminder of factors to consider, a handy source of technical information, a time-saving processor, and a fine source of hypotheses to push against.

There is considerable risk that inadequately trained users will fail to recognize pitfalls buried in this kind of system. The system is much too limited to be taken as the final authority. M-MAC is rooted in an obsolescent "labeling" approach. It has no way to use the tester's personal observations. Most disturbing, it classifies emotional disorders, hard to do even with much better data than the schools usually possess. M-MAC does print out cautionary messages about this—but the warnings should be five times stronger.

Problems in Evaluating Assignment Schemes

Educators and policymakers would like hard evidence on the effectiveness of alternative plans for differentiation. Many comparative studies have attempted to assess whether students make greater progress with or without tracking.

Such studies are nearly uninterpretable because of a dilemma in measurement (Leinhardt & Seewald, 1981). What accomplishments are to be assessed? Some evaluators reason that the only fair basis for comparison is an achievement test confined to the lessons covered by all the sections, fast and slow. Others favor a test over the full reach of lessons covered by *any* of the groups. Testing on what everyone studies gives fast sections no credit for the breadth of their learning. Fast students in a fast section probably spend less time polishing elementary skills than equally fast students in a wide-range class. The first testing plan, therefore, is likely to conclude that ability grouping is bad for abler students and beneficial for weak students. The second suggestion, a wide-range test, tends to show that even weak students in a wide-range class have learned more than their ability-grouped counterparts because the wide-range class exposed them to more of the test content.

One solution is to build the test on the second plan but to make an analytic comparison. When students at a particular ability level are compared across treatments, some competences will have developed fastest under one condition and some under the other. These crisscrossing indicators show effects much more truthfully than any summary statistic. The summary statistic hides within it a value judgment as how heavily each outcome should count. The first test plan accepts the concealed value judgment that only the most elementary lessons should count; a total score on the second kind of test values supplementary topics as much as basics. If the full profile of contrasts were laid out, citizens would argue about the weightings, as they should. "Which is the better educational plan?" calls as much for judgment as for science.

A test that has predictive validity may be useless for classification. To justify teaching individuals in different ways, an aptitude-treatment interaction has to be demonstrated (or, at least, presumed). Educational psychologists conduct experiments following the plan suggested in Chapter 5 (p. 169). Such experiments are more a source of insight than a source of rules for teaching.

Consider the distinction between verbal (V) and spatial (S) abilities. One hypothesis is that "high V" students will learn more from verbal presentations and "high S" students will profit from visual presentations. The findings are mixed: some studies show that trend, and some show just the opposite. Diagrams in text materials may place a load on spatial abilities, but if the diagrams are easily grasped, they lighten the burden of visualizing and spatial reasoning (Cronbach & Snow, 1977; Gustafsson, 1976). The same is true of words. Given a lucid verbal explanation, persons with low verbal ability can recall it; a complex explanation communicates only to high-V students, but it may leave them with a deeper understanding than they would get from a simpler explanation.

Formally sorting students into groups for instruction would make sense if we could assess aptitude or learning styles and then teach the same school subject in ways that fit different students' patterns. Research findings on aptitude-treatment interaction do not justify that kind of direct application of mental-test scores (Corno & Snow, 1986; Cronbach & Snow, 1977). The evidence does suggest that teaching step-by-step, patiently and with regular feedback, is advantageous for less able students. Such teaching, however, sometimes causes superior students to achieve *less* than they would from instruction that presents a greater demand for analysis. The greatest successes in adapting instruction come through individualized shaping of lessons on the basis of qualitative diagnosis of assets and weaknesses (pp. 344, 404–405).

This is the direction also in which instruction by computer is moving (Snow & Lohman, in Linn, 1989a). An "intelligent tutor" takes information from the student's responses and moves into new ground, or backtracks, according to the progress shown. The rules that choose the computer's challenges and prompts amount to predictions of the student's next responses. Unlike a year-long assignment, an erroneous short-term prediction is quickly corrected.

23. *In what way can a teacher make use of the conclusion that having to organize subject matter for themselves benefits some students and handicaps others?*

24. *If a test were used formally to divide students between instructional methods A and B, would Test 1 or 2 work better? The following facts are available for equivalent groups assigned to each treatment:*

The mean of outcome Y is the same in A and B; the s.d. of Y is the same in A and B;

r_{Y1} is 0.4 in A and 0.0 in B;

r_{Y2} is 0.3 in A and -0.3 in B.

ACHIEVEMENT TESTS IN EDUCATIONAL MANAGEMENT

Much is said nowadays about "accountability"—of the schools to the public, of individual teachers to their superiors, and of school officials to the central governments that supply funds. When someone in authority decides that a test shall be given, one principal reason is to press persons at lower levels to strive harder to develop whatever competence the test measures. This statement is true of Regents' examinations imposed on high school seniors in New York State, of test reports that districts receiving federal funds must send to Washington, and of any teacher's quizzes and examinations.

Topics in endless array compete for time in the classroom. There are pressures to cover new subject matter (the Third World, effects of drugs) along with pressures to concentrate on so-called "basics." Authority over curriculum is divided. The United States has traditions of local control of education and of respect for the teacher's judgment, but state and federal legislators desire to set priorities. Tests are one way to influence what will receive emphasis.

For a teacher, tests are an integral part of instruction. Telling a class "what will be on the test" causes them to spend their time on those topics. Marking standards tell what level of performance is respectable, and comments on papers point out the features that make a performance excellent or inadequate. Students take in these cues. Indeed, they go to great lengths to foresee how they will be evaluated so that they will not "waste time" on what is not to be tested. When a higher authority imposes a test on the class, the teacher plays the same defensive game. It is common to set aside the usual curriculum during the weeks preceding the Regents' exam, to force-feed students with whatever appears in the test outline. The student who seems likely to fail a "minimum competency examination" is given a concentrated dosage of the skills that test covers. In each of these instances, "teaching for the test" (and studying for it) is precisely what was wanted by whoever imposed the examination.

Concentrating student and teacher effort on what will be tested is good insofar as the test content is worth the effort. Sometimes the influence of tests distorts the curriculum. The chemistry teacher may say that a main purpose of the course is to teach "scientific method," but if the examination questions are limited to technical terms, facts, and such skills as balancing equations, the students will not study reading materials on the processes of science. The teacher of literature may aim to help students develop their own tastes and standards of criticism—but she will discourage that development if tests give credit for parroting *her* opinions about works of literature. An anecdote from a large evaluation of competing instructional packages in primary arithmetic provides a further example. The test on addition included not only sets of numbers lined up vertically but also tasks in horizontal form:

$$3 + 2 + 3 = ?$$

When, in the first year of the study, children found such items difficult, one of the competing teams rewrote its lessons to provide practice on the horizontal format. The team had originally considered horizontal addition unimportant, so the test-driven change of emphasis may have been educationally unwise.

The Role of Objectives

Educators choosing tests do pay attention to content in the narrow sense of the word. They would be critical of a chemistry test that contains many items on the rare-earth elements when the instruction barely touches on them. They would be critical of a history test that emphasizes the Reconstruction period and neglects the modern civil rights movement. And so on. But much that the student is intended to learn cannot be identified with particular chapters of a text or particular segments of the course of study. Understanding the nature of science or of literature or of historical change—themes such as these cut across all the topics of a course, yet may not appear at all in a "content" outline.

For this reason, educational testers amplify the notion of content validity by asking how well the test tasks cover the "objectives" of instruction. Many of the most important educational objectives—intended outcomes—are generalized concepts, attitudes, and skills. Students who acquire the ability and habit of identifying the bias of a writer can apply that learning to almost anything they read, and it can be acquired as a by-product of instruction with almost any reading materials. Likewise in science or history, general concepts may be acquired by the class that studies *its* local geology, or *its* community history. The evaluation of student progress ought to be concerned more with main ideas than with specific lesson content.

Ralph Tyler (1950; Smith & Tyler, 1942) was particularly responsible for introducing the idea of "behavioral objectives." The function of education is to change behavior, not merely to equip the person with answers to a limited number of fixed questions. If educators and citizens say what they wish graduates to be able (and motivated) to do, mapping what graduates can (and do) accomplish identifies where the educational program has succeeded. Not all the evidence can or should come from tests. What students read after they leave the course, what arguments they advance in a conversation about political matters, and how faithfully they discharge responsibilities—those kinds of evidence may contribute as much to an assessment as evidence from set questions. But here let us concentrate on knowledge and skill, which lend themselves to conventional testing.

The adjective *behavioral* forces informants to describe objectives concretely. "I want graduates to understand scientific method" is an ambiguous reply. The inquiry should be pushed further: "What might a person do or say that would indicate satisfactory understanding?" The informant might say any of the following things:

- Students will express confidence in statements about the planets that are attributed to an astronomer and express doubt about statements attributed to an astrologer.
- Students, when trying to measure the solubility of a chemical in water, follow accurately the directions in the laboratory manual.
- When a student is asked to comment on the report of an investigation, he notes and mentions how the investigator's wishes or preconceptions may have influenced the report or mentions precautions taken against such bias.

Each suggestion implies a different kind of test. Educators would disagree as to which gives relevant evidence on command of scientific method. Reducing the discussion to behavioral terms was valuable just because it permits pointed disagreement about the appropriate test. No one could have disagreed about the lofty original objective.

Behavioral objectives can be subdivided finely, and then the desired responses can be directly taught. This is easiest to do for factual knowledge and tangible skills. Skill in map reading, for example, can be subdivided into specifics such as this one: "The students, given a map in Mercator projection, with marks that indicate longitude at 10-degree intervals, can estimate the longitude of a point on the map within one degree." For those aspects of learning to which it applies, listing detailed objectives can guarantee good correspondence between the description of what is to be taught and the test items.

Objectives having to do with subtler interpretation or with creative problem solving cannot be so specified. One test outline, for example, includes statements such as this among objectives for which items are to be written (and subscores reported): "The student will analyze the feelings, traits, or motives of characters in a passage." This is a useful reminder that reading comprehension goes beyond facts and events, but it does not "specify" themes, levels of difficulty, or standards for judging a response. It is therefore impossible to say whether a set of items represents the objective adequately. Nor is it sensible to say that anyone reaches "mastery" of such an open-ended task. Behavioral objectives, then, help to bring the process to test planning down to earth, but they are no cure-all.

In a debate about educational evidence, a professional may ask whether a test that obviously covers basic skills in mathematics has *curricular* validity. (See also p. 172.) The questioner may be asking whether the balance of content and difficulty in the test is a match to what the teacher(s) actually worked on. Or the question may be whether it matches what planners in the school system said their mathematics instruction should teach. The planners may have good reasons to emphasize some topics more than schools elsewhere do—and some topics less. A test used to determine whether the plans are working out ought to have curricular validity in the second sense. Sometimes the lessons do not cover all that was planned because the plans were too ambitious or suitable teaching materials were not found. Both teachers and pupils are disturbed when the test includes what the lessons neglected. Reducing the test to what the lessons covered adequately is fair for some purposes, but it can hide the fact that instruction fell short of the plans.

Item banks are beginning to provide professionally developed items that fit the local curriculum. The publisher lists the skills and topics for which items have been banked, and a committee of teachers or school officials decides how many items to use from each category. Although such a custom-made test cannot have norms in the usual sense, the publisher has tried the component items on more or less representative samples of students. The record of difficulty from this tryout provides some basis for interpreting results in the local district.

25. *An English teacher takes up metaphors with an eighth-grade class. What might be some reasonable behavioral objectives for that instruction? Which could be investigated with choice-response questions?*

26. *In the area of consumer economics, illustrate instructional objectives concerned with maximum performance and objectives concerned with typical behavior.*

27. *Where an evaluator is to report on the performance of a group of students (not on students individually), are printed questions adequate to assess the kinds of behavior listed in response to question 26?*

28. *"After reading a scene from* Merchant of Venice, *the student will be able to suggest two alternative answers to the question, 'How did Shylock feel during this scene?'" From the viewpoint of a test developer, how does this statement differ from the objective ". . . will analyze feelings of characters"? How could the objective be stated so that it does not press the teacher to spend time on* Merchant of Venice?

Standard Tests

Traditionally, standard achievement tests have represented the common-denominator content of curricula across the country. The test authors examine courses of study for (say) Grades 4 to 6 and identify subskills or topics that are nearly universal. Test development has generally been successful for tool skills, including language usage, spelling, reading, vocabulary, arithmetic and general mathematics, and map-reading and library skills. Although the tests cannot include all the subskills that some teachers and parents consider important, what is included is a part of almost every school's curriculum. The tests meet the needs of administrators trying to keep track of the system as a whole, of the problems of schools within a district, and of curricular areas where the district may need to make a special push.

The reports sent to each pupil's home and the reports on the district as a whole perform an important public relations function. All such reports, however, are open to misinterpretation (pp. 126, 298). Moreover, the schools have responsibilities and aims that reach far beyond the basic skills, and one risk in standardized testing is that teachers will focus on the tool skills to the point of neglecting the remainder of the pupil's development. Tests covering the rest of the curriculum would provide a desirable balance of pressures.

The National Assessment of Educational Progress has attempted to provide a balanced picture of the full range of the schools' collective accomplishment. To do this, it has tested in all the following areas: reading and literature, writing, math, science, citizenship and social studies, music, art, and career planning and development of vocational skills. Questions have reached beyond facts, skills, and problem solving to questions about experiences and actions. Thus a high school senior may be asked if he has ever written a letter on any policy to an official or a newspaper and also asked whether he has visited an art museum in the past year. The assessment produces several test booklets, draws a sample of schools and a sample of students at ages 9, 13, and 17 within the schools, and has each student respond to one booklet. Instead of reporting on single students or schools, the report covers geographic regions or types of community or types of students. The public is told what level students reached on various subskills, and how today's 9-year-olds compare with those of 2 years back. (Several reports are distributed each year—e.g., Appleby et al., 1989.) Unfortunately, policymakers and the public have been far more interested in the three or four basic skills than in the remainder of the assessment. Collecting balanced information, then, is beside the point if the public is not sensitive to the full range of school responsibilities.

Standard tests in high school subjects such as U.S. government are available, and some teachers use them as a cross-check on their own more informal assessments. Tests of "general educational development" in particular fields have succeeded at the high school level. These tests—in social studies, literature, science, and other areas—present passages test takers are unlikely to have seen previously and ask them to make inferences, criticize arguments, and otherwise exercise the intellectual skills *any* course of study in that field should develop. Much the same strategy is seen in Advanced Placement testing, to which the next section will turn.

Some achievement tests for elementary grades and high school attempt rather unsuccessfully to survey achievement in broad fields. Understanding of the social world is surely important, for example, and is included in curricula everywhere. The curricula are not at all standard, and, therefore, a standard test fits no local curriculum. The publishers string together items on topics that appear frequently in courses of study. One of the prominent tests for the middle grades contains 60 social-studies items (multiple-choice) whose heterogeneity is illustrated by these paraphrases:

On which continent is Spanish the language of many countries?

A law Congress has passed can be overturned by what group?

Which [among silhouettes of four skylines] shows a dead volcano?

[A chart of average incomes for 1950 through 1985 is shown.] If the trend continues, what level will income probably reach in 2000?

Which of these men won a Nobel Prize for peace? [Names of four black men follow.]

Obviously, such a test lacks unity and represents no construct.

Many recent standard tests of tool skills shred a complex skill into narrow subskills and offer "criterion-referenced" or "mastery" scores for each of these. Such a label usually implies that the scoring service will flag any subskill on which the student's percentage-correct score falls below some specified level. Figure 9.5 displays items from two sub-subtests of Reading Yardsticks, which is one of several current instruments of this character. In all, 40 scores are reported for sub-subtests; testing time is about 5 minutes per objective, on average. The items are intended to be fairly easy for most students in the grade tested; the main purpose is to signal gaps that should be repaired. Prior to the scoring, the

---

Syllabication: Identify the number of syllables in a word of 1–6 syllables. **Choose the answer that tells how many syllables are in the given word.**

1. spirit   (A) 1   (B) 2   (C) 3   (D) 4
3. route   (A) 1   (B) 2   (C) 3   (D) 4
6. especially   (A) 3   (B) 4   (C) 5   (D) 6
8. imaginary   (A) 3   (B) 4   (C) 5   (D) 6

Possessives: Choose the correct translation of a possessive phrase, discriminating the object owned from the owner of the object, a singular possessive from a single plural, or singular possessive from a plural possessive.

11. The kitten's muddy paws made everyone laugh.
    What was muddy?
    (A) the paws of the kitten   (C) the kitten
    (B) the paws of the kittens   (D) the kittens

13. The trains' whistles kept Pat awake all night.
    What kept Pat awake?
    (A) the whistles of the trains   (B) the whistle of the train
    (C) the whistles of the train   (D) the whistle of the trains

15. The _____ flames flickered and died in the wind.
    Which form of the word <u>candle</u> is correct in this sentence?
    (A) candle's   (B) candles   (C) candle   (D) candles'

18. The first pitch bounced off the _____ glove.
    Which form of the word <u>catcher</u> is correct in this sentence?
    (A) catchers'   (B) catchers   (C) catcher's   (D) catcher

---

Figure 9.5. **Items matched to specific objectives of language instruction.** The typography has been altered in several respects from the original source; most important, in the actual test more white space separates items, and the phrases in items such as 11 and 13 are arranged vertically for easier comparison. (*Source*: These items are taken from two 8-item sections of Level 13 of Reading Yardsticks, Form 1. Copyright © 1981 by The Riverside Publishing Company and reproduced by permission.)

school district specifies the level below which scores are to be flagged. It might pick 40 per cent for all subtests, or a figure as high as 70 per cent. The level of this test intended for Grade 7 has four main sections; the objectives in Figure 9.5 fall within the "Structural Analysis" section. For the sections, both raw scores and percentiles are reported.

Identifying the number of syllables in a word probably is a unified ability; a pupil who has learned to listen for syllables should report the right number for almost any word he can read and pronounce. The interpretation of possessives, on the other hand, is divisible—as the statement of the objective indicates. Some sub-subscores refer to broad domains, for example, ability to "interpret information given in a table." The score comes from just three questions referring to a single table. When the test has flagged a pupil as weak in an area, a large task of diagnosis remains for the teacher. And the signal system is crude; a good many pupils who get 2 items out of 3 correct are no better than those who miss 2 out of 3.

29. *If, at the end of the year, a fourth-grade class does poorly on the social studies test described (compared to its standing on achievement in tool skills), should that information influence how the teacher covers social studies next year? If so, how?*

30. *Achievement batteries may be given either in early fall or late spring and have norms for both dates. What purposes can be served by fall testing? Spring testing? (Assume that students move to a new teacher at the end of the spring term.)*

31. *With two 8-item subtests, the standard error of measurement of the difference in percentage-correct scores is approximately 25 percentage points. Why should a teacher be mindful of this fact?*

32. *A teacher (or even a committee of students) could easily make up dozens of tests of either objective in Figure 9.5. What advantages or disadvantages does the standardized test for these objectives have?*

An Advanced Placement Test

Constructive use of testing in educational management is particularly well illustrated by the advanced placement program of the College Board. A student works with a teacher's help, possibly in a small group, to study some field not regularly taught by the high school. At the end of the year he takes a test set by the board. If he succeeds, the college he attends will probably exempt him from the equivalent college course and allow him to enroll in a more advanced course.

For each course, the board distributes a prospectus to interested schools. I shall use the European History description for 1989 as example. Three pages describe and outline the range of topics; major events and trends from 1450 to 1970 will be covered, with cultural, social, and political history equally weighted. The remaining 25 pages consist of test questions, with brief information on how the test is graded. The student is told that passing 60 per cent of the multiple-choice items is normally considered acceptable. The items listed are illustrative; other items will of course make up the official test. Figure 9.6 illustrates that many factual questions press for comprehension of trends and concepts, not sheer recall of names and dates. Other items ask for interpretation of a map coded to show population change in France and interpretation of a political cartoon. The effect of these exhibits is to encourage wide reading plus an attempt to integrate. They do not identify topics for cramming.

The greatest beneficiary in the Thirty Years' War (1618–1648) was
  A. France
  B. Spain
  C. Russia
  D. Sweden
  E. the Holy Roman Empire

All of the following are associated with the commercial revolution in early modern Europe EXCEPT:
  A. An increase in the number of entrepreneurial capitalists
  B. The appearance of state-run trading companies
  C. A large influx of precious metals into Europe
  D. An expansion of the guild system
  E. A "golden age" for the Netherlands

The economist John Maynard Keynes did which of the following?
  A. He urged governments to increase mass purchasing power in times of deflation.
  B. He defended the principles of the Versailles Treaty.
  C. He helped to establish the British Labor party.
  D. He prophesied the inevitable economic decline of capitalism.
  E. He originated the concept of marginal utility to replace the labor theory of value.

All of the following statements about the Renaissance are true EXCEPT:
  A. The preeminence of medieval Scholasticism was challenged.
  B. The papacy became increasingly ascetic, promoting mystical contact with God.
  C. People looked increasingly back to the classical period for ideas and models.
  D. Wealthy merchant princes patronized the arts.
  E. There was interest in broadening the range of education.

Figure 9.6. **Multiple-choice questions on European history.** (*Source*: From Advanced Placement Course Description, History. College Entrance Examination Board, 1989. Reprinted by permission of Educational Testing Service, the copyright owner.)

Essay questions are included because many college instructors are skeptical of choice-response tests and because such questions point the student's preparation in desired directions. A conventional essay test asks the student to write on one of six broad topics, for example, the reflection of (or departure from) enlightenment ideals in the first years of the French Revolution. The student is to bring specific examples to bear—another encouragement to wide reading. The other essay is to respond to a "document-based question"—on witchcraft, in one recent booklet. The documents begin with the testimony of a midwife about an alleged confession of one Walpurga Hausmannin, progress through a quotation from Luther (". . . witches are the Devil's whores who steal milk, . . . and force people into love and immorality. . . ."), ending with a table of demographic statistics on suspected witches—over 2000 words in all. The examinee is to identify three major reasons for the persecution of individuals as witches and use the sources to justify the answer. (This is a practice test; witches will not be the topic in the actual test.) This is a prime example of testing a generalized ability, one that students must prepare for by engaging in historical interpretation and not by digesting history others have written.

Beyond the brochure, a teacher can obtain further document-based questions from past years and a report from the previous year's examination. The report shows the rating scale used to define the several levels of adequacy of answers, and reprints a student response that received a high mark and another that was rated inadequate. The fact that a committee of high school and college teachers developed the overall plan and standards makes it likely that the plan, announcement, student-teacher collaboration, examination, grading, and report will converge to serve the intended purposes. The external examination transforms the high school teacher, in the student's eyes, from a taskmaster and standard setter to a collaborator whose only responsibility is to help the student do well. The elaborate procedure is made necessary by the fact that colleges have agreed to use the test for an important decision about a student with whom they have no personal experience.

33. *What would be gained or lost if students and teachers were supplied a file of questions three times as long as the actual test and promised that all test questions will be taken from that file?*

34. *What features of the advanced placement plan would be appropriate when*
    a. *a state imposes an examination that all students must pass to receive a high school diploma?*
    b. *a national board in a medical specialty requires practitioners to demonstrate up-to-date knowledge before their certification is renewed?*

35. *What is to be said for and against setting up an "external examiner" for all the principal first-year courses in a college? (Some colleges have done this by establishing an examiner's office that prepares tests much as the College Board examiners do.)*

Constructed-Response vs. Choice-Response Tests

In the discussion of advanced placement we returned to a topic introduced in Chapter 2, the adequacy of choice-response tests. Critics of standardized achievement tests frequently complain about the predominance of choice-response items.

There are two issues. One has to do with the role of the test in directing teaching and learning; the other, with the statistical correlates of scores. Warning students that they will be expected to organize facts to support an argument seems very likely to lead them to practice that while studying history. Probably no defender of choice-response tests believes that all educational activity should consist of convergent thinking. Solving a problem requires a sharp-eyed comparison of alternatives, but *generating* alternatives is a distinct art, learned through another kind of practice.

The statistical question is whether persons who are identified as superior by a multiple-choice test are also the ones picked as superior by a constructed-response test. Basically, the answer is yes. The correlation of essay test with multiple-choice test is usually about as high as the test reliabilities permit.

A particularly striking result comes from an objective test of skills used in writing (the student being asked to select clear expressions as well as grammatically correct ones). The choice-response test correlates well with a careful summary of the quality of a college student's writing during a course. Indeed, because it is reliable, the choice-response test correlates higher with the summary than does the mark assigned to a composition the student produces as a writing specimen (Breland, 1979a). Hogan and Mishler (1980) find similar evidence on writing in Grades 3 and 8. Also relevant is an unpublished College Board report on an Advanced Placement test in calculus: Free-response and choice-response sections correlate 0.85; that is as high as the correlation between two tests of either kind.

The methods are not indistinguishable. Two small experiments are suggestive. In one, the respondent saw the stem of a choice-response item, constructed a response, and only then was shown alternative answers and asked to pick the best. It appears that each version is more valid for some students (Pellegrino et al., in Embretson, 1985). The second study found that choice response is better at bringing out the ability of students who have high test anxiety, especially if the problems are difficult. Constructing a response usually requires more information processing than comparing alternatives; this seems to overload anxious examinees intellectually and emotionally (study by Schmitt and Crocker, summarized in Embretson, 1985).

Constructed responses ought to be a part of instructional evaluation. That is obviously true of handwriting; of artistic, musical, and literary composition; and of the ability to speak French. It is probably true of the planning of experiments, the translation of French, and the criticism of works of art. (See pp. 387–389 on divergent thinking.) In selective admissions on the basis of general academic abilities, however, a multiple-choice test that deals with generalized intellectual skills appears to be entirely adequate.

Chapter
10

Multiple Abilities
and Their Role
in Counseling

10A. What does it mean to say that a test with 8 or 9 scored parts "measures only four factors"? How should this knowledge influence the test interpreter?

10B. How do measures of spatial visualization differ from measures of general fluid ability?

10C. How are the concepts of "divergent thinking" and "creativity" alike? How are they different?

10D. For purposes of adolescents' self-understanding, as it relates to career planning, which ability or abilities is it most valuable to measure?

10E. When used with high school juniors, what purposes does DAT try to serve beyond those of CogAT? Why is it difficult for the 8-score battery to accomplish more?

Abbreviations in this chapter: CogAT for Cognitive Abilities Test, with Verbal (V), Nonverbal (NV), and Quantitative (Q) sections; DAT for Differential Abilities Tests; EFT for Embedded Figures Test; ETS for Educational Testing Service; GATB for General Aptitude Test Battery of the United States Employment Service (USES) with G, V, N, and S (general, verbal, number, and spatial) scores, among others; Gf and Gc for general fluid and crystallized factors, respectively, with g for Spearman's general factor; KABC for Kaufman Assessment Battery for Children; MCT for Mechanical Comprehension Test; SB4 for the Stanford-Binet, fourth edition.

ORIENTATION

How is the domain of abilities organized? Tests differ in content. Tests with similar content may have large or small correlations. (Recall the alphabetizing tasks on p. 216.) Tests dissimilar on the surface may rank pupils similarly (for example, Block Design and EFT). It should be possible to group tests into families whose members tell consistent stories.

Among three main parts of this chapter, the first explains the technical methods that have been used to group tests. Factor analysis (a form of correlational research) has played a large role in organizing ability and personality variables. A summary on page 377 lists main ideas of the section. The text and diagrams up to that point are all illustrative, giving background for understanding this meaty summary. Next, confirmatory analysis is covered briefly, primarily for the benefit of readers who will be encountering the method in research reports. Zoom in on the "multilevel" findings at the end of the section; they are today's preferred summary of two generations of research on how to classify abilities.

In this chapter we make a transition from general abilities to the multiple abilities considered in counseling and personnel selection. Practice and theory continue to use the materials and ideas described in the middle section of the chapter, which emerged mainly from 1930 to 1970. Read to get the "flavor" of the primary abilities, the ETS kit, and the Guilford structure. (A course instructor may want you to fix specifics of these schemes in mind.) Testing divergent thinking stands today as a bright idea that somehow has had little practical payoff—so far at least. The story is short and simple.

The last long section is important for all practical testers. Although the content centers on career counseling, it bears directly on personnel selection and on interpreting profiles from educational and clinical tests. What is said about each test battery is less important than the general picture. The results in Tables 10.7 and 10.8, for example, are typical of aptitude batteries; these results say a lot about how useful tests of this kind are. On page 397 we enter rougher terrain. GATB is in the midst of radical change. Many of the changes are controversial, and the ultimate evaluation of the proposals will affect all practical use of ability tests. The central issue is whether multiple abilities deserve much consideration in vocational psychology. Reread this material to make sure you understand why there is disagreement. You can delay reaching a conclusion because Chapter 11 will pick up the topic. The "limitations" on profile interpretation, which follow, are vital knowledge for any reader who will be interpreting profiles; each subsection has its own message.

"Short and simple" again applies to the final pages on microanalysis, one of the directions in which testing is moving.

SORTING TESTS BY FACTOR ANALYSIS

Factor analysis lives in two worlds. It and its close relatives are indispensable in reducing statistical data. A field study in social or behavioral science may measure hundreds of variables. Forming clusters or composites makes the data compact enough to think about, and smooths out fluctuations. Second, factor analysis is an explanatory technique; this is the concern here.

In a sense, scores having high correlations "measure the same thing." Factoring a large set of tests indicates how many distinguishable kinds of individual differences enter the set of scores and how strong the influence of each such dimension is. Beyond that, factoring sorts tasks into sets, each supposed to measure one ability or complex of abilities. Similar analyses have been made of interests, attitudes, and personality.

The first factor analyst was Spearman. He assembled tests that correlated with each other, hypothesized a "general" factor (a process required in all the tests), and calculated which tests best represented it. He assumed that a test combines a demand for general ability with its own specific demands; one could speak of Block Design as measuring the general factor plus a "Block Design specific" ability.

Before long, "group" factors, present in several tests but not all, were recognized. Block Design and EFT and Figure Analogies all intercorrelate, but the higher correlation between the first two suggests the influence in them of a shared spatial or figural ability. Thurstone, who did the most to extend and popularize factor analysis, assumed at first that general ability was best interpreted as a bundle of group factors. He tried to develop tests of verbal ability that make little demand on reasoning and tests of reasoning that make little demand on word knowledge, number knowledge, or figural perception. In the end, he concluded that most group factors do interrelate; intellectual efficiency, then, extends over tasks of many kinds. But Thurstone showed that group factors can be measured reliably and advised attending to them in guidance and personnel selection.

Factor analysis is not so dominant in research as it was from 1930 to 1970; additional styles of inquiry have ripened. Today there is discontent with the assumption that tests fall into "kinds." When some persons approach a test with style A and others with style B or when a test is closely related to the experience of some persons and not others, the test is "measuring different things" in these groups. Still, testers should know how to interpret the reports that come out of factor analysis and the explanatory concepts it has produced.

How Factor Analysis Is Carried Out

A factor analysis starts with correlations among tests. The resulting description of any one test depends on the companion tests, the group of persons, and the technique of analysis. Despite this, accumulated research has produced consistent interpretations.

How to group abilities is rather like the question, "How many kinds of animals are in the zoo?" One might consider mammals as a "kind"— or carnivores or hyenas or the species *Crocuta*. Some analysts ("splitters") favor small categories and some ("lumpers") favor large ones; moreover, alternative category systems cut across each other. The choice derives from the purpose of a test user or theorist. From one point of view, a child's ability to tell right from left is a trivial factor within the spatial domain; from another point of view, it is a major developmental achievement.

Table 10.1 displays correlations among four tests given to job applicants. In this simple case, inspection can anticipate the findings.

Is there a general factor? No more than a trace; all the correlations are positive, but four are near zero. Therefore, no common element such as ability to understand directions plays a large role in all four tests. The absence of a general factor may seem strange because all tests have directions that must be understood. When directions are well suited to the group, however, ability to understand them will not affect score *differences*—and correlations reflect only differences among persons. These correlations come from a particular population, most of whom graduated from U.S. high schools. Apply the tests to an applicant pool that includes a large number of newcomers from Central America or Hong Kong, and understanding of directions would account for differences. A moderately strong general factor would appear because that source of difficulty would affect all tests.

It is important to distinguish "*a* general factor" from "*the* general ability" of Spearman. A general factor is common across a set of measures; a set of bodily measurements shares a general factor ("body size"). "General factor" changes its meaning with each new set of variables. In contrast, Spearman's g is conceived of as independent of particular variables, as a process or set of processes thought to pervade intellectual performances.

The largest correlation in Table 10.1 implies that Vocabulary and

Table 10.1   INTERCORRELATIONS OF FOUR MEASURES
FOR ADULT WORKERS

	Arithmetic reasoning	Turn	Assemble
Vocabulary	0.65	0.05	0.15
Arithmetic Reasoning		0.05	0.15
Turn			0.40
Assemble			

Source: GATB manual, 1970, III, p. 29. (Rounded.)

Table 10.2   FACTOR LOADINGS OF FOUR TESTS

	I	II	h^2
Vocabulary	0.85	0.05	0.72
Arithmetic Reasoning	0.80	0.00	0.64
Turn	0.05	0.70	0.49
Assemble	0.15	0.50	0.27
Variance	1.39[a]	0.74[a]	2.13

[a] Sum of squares.

Arithmetic Reasoning share a group factor, the crystallized ability Gc discussed in Chapter 8. The Turn test (placing pegs in holes) shares a second group factor with Assemble (putting rivets and washers together rapidly). (A serious study uses many more tests. With more tests, more than two factors would probably be reported.)

I use this example to demonstrate the main features of a factor analytic report. Table 10.2 and the equations that follow are based on uncorrelated factors. The equations change when the analyst employs correlated factors.

A factor is a hypothetical or "latent" variable; every person is assumed to have a true score on that variable (his "factor score"), and each loading describes the correlation of test score with factor score. Vocabulary correlates 0.85 with factor I, Turning correlates 0.70 with factor II, and so on. As with other correlations, there are sampling errors in factor loadings. Because loadings will change from one sample to another, we need not take seriously the fact that (for example) Assemble loads higher than Turning on factor I.

The *communality* h^2 tells what proportion of the test variance is accounted for by common factors. The equation for the communality of Test i is

$$h_i^2 = r_{iI}^2 + r_{iII}^2 + \cdots$$

(The dots indicate that common factors beyond I and II might contribute to Test i.) For Turning, the two-factor communality is

$$h^2 = (0.05)^2 + (0.70)^2 = 0.00 + 0.49 = 0.49$$

Suppose now that the reliability of Turning is known to be 0.70; then 30 per cent of the variance is error variance. This carries us one step further. The variance divides into three parts:

49 per cent due to the two common factors

30 per cent due to error of measurement

21 per cent remaining, owing to the specific factor or to common factors not yet extracted

In sum, 100 per cent.

Table 10.2 describes the first two tests as measures of *I* and not *II*; if it were not for their specific content, they would be pure measures of *I*. When several such measures are combined, the specific factors tend to balance out, and hence the composite score is indeed "saturated with" the factor.

1. *Confidence may be manifested in a variety of situations: making a speech to a club, taking one's car apart to repair it, piloting a jet plane, or going to a movie instead of cramming for a test. Give three alternative explanations of the nature of confidence: one in which it is considered as a general factor, one in which it is divided into group factors, and one in which it is considered as a number of highly specific factors. Which theory do you think is most adequate?*

2. *R. Gardner (1960), factoring abilities involved in using a second language in French-English Montreal, found that abilities taught in school grouped together and that abilities used outside school in interacting with speakers of the second language formed a separate factor. Explain.*

Pictures of the Makeup of CogAT

The nine subtests of the Cognitive Abilities Test (p. 258) are designed to measure three correlated group factors. To provide a simple initial example, I have factored intercorrelations among only six subtests, retaining just two uncorrelated factors. (All data are for Level E, suited to Grade 7.)

Bringing Out a General Factor The computer prints out loadings for many factors, possibly as many as there are tests. The analyst decides how

Table 10.3 FACTOR ANALYSIS OF SIX CogAT SUBTESTS

Test	Loading on factor I	II	h^2	Squared loading on specific factor	Error
1. Verbal Classification	0.80	−0.27	0.71	10	19
2. Sentence Completion	0.80	−0.30	0.73	11	16
3. Verbal Analogies	0.82	−0.28	0.75	3	22
7. Figure Classification	0.70	0.24	0.55	21	24
8. Figure Analogies	0.76	0.38	0.72	16	12
9. Figure Analysis	0.60	0.38	0.51	26	23
Sum of squares	3.38	0.58			

NOTE: The figures given for specific factors and error are percentages. Removing the decimal in the h^2 column would convert those numbers also to percentages, so that the last columns add to 100.

many to keep, discarding those she attributes to sampling error or considers unimportant for some other reason. With six subtests, the third and later factors were extremely small.

The first interpretation examines "unrotated" factors, whose loadings appear in Table 10.3. Factor I is strong, and, because all loadings are appreciable, it is "general." The second factor can be labeled "Verbal-minus-Nonverbal." (Logically, it is akin to the Wechsler V/P contrast. The direction of subtraction is arbitrary.) The first factor is far more powerful than the second; the strength of factors is indicated in the sums of squared loadings, at the foot of columns in this table.

Rotation   For interpretation, an analyst almost always "rotates," substituting new reference axes (factors) for those the computer first generated. This is much like reorienting a map on the page. In geographic maps, up-down means North-South. But some road maps of the San Francisco peninsula bring the NW-to-SE line around to vertical position, to match the way the land lies and the traffic flows. Deciding how to rotate calls for judgment. Computer programs place axes according to rules; the investigator ought to judge whether its result is sensible, not accept it trustingly.

The dots in the left panel of Figure 10.1 plot the loadings from Table 10.3. Panel ii displays the rotated result. The figural tests have substantial loadings on whatever the verbal tests have in common. The new factors I' and II' obviously can be labeled Verbal and Nonverbal; the general factor was absorbed into them.

Correlated factors make better theoretical sense, and one obtains them by placing reference axes at an angle. In panel ii of Figure 10.1 we could place axis II' through the 7–8–9 cluster. Then large loadings on II' would account for those tests, and their loadings on I' would become

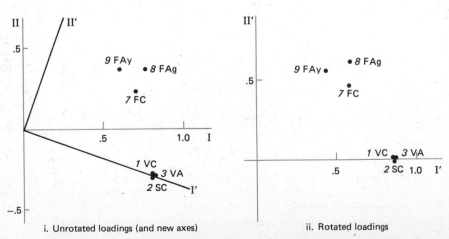

i. Unrotated loadings (and new axes)   ii. Rotated loadings

Figure 10.1. **Two plots of CogAT factor loadings.**

negligible—a "cleaner" picture. (In the multilevel analyses discussed on p. 382, all factors below the top level are defined by this kind of rotation.)

Options with All Nine Tests We need not examine in detail the analysis with nine subtests; the following paragraphs serve chiefly to illustrate that there is no one "right" factorial picture. With nine subtests the sums of squares for the first four unrotated factors are 5.3, 0.9, 0.6, and 0.5. Because the last two sums are well below 1.00, an analyst unaware of the developer's theory would ignore them. The Quantitative tests load heavily on factor *I* (general) and they could be added into Figure 10.1 roughly midway between the other two clusters. (The positions of the original six points move very little when all subtests are considered.)

Because the theory envisions a third factor, an analyst might rotate the first three factors. With the axes at right angles, the large loadings on factor *I* are for Verbal subtests, on *II* for Nonverbal, and on *III* for Quantitative. But several subtests load on all three factors. Again, the picture is cleaner with axes placed at an angle. Then there is one strong loading for each subtest. That picture is like a cluster of arrows, with V and *NV* 50° apart and *Q* between them, offset from the plane by 20°.

The test developers decided to extract *four* factors, forcing the general factor and three uncorrelated group factors to appear. This echoes their conception of the test as a measure of general ability (symbolized G because no effort was made to match Spearman's g) plus three narrower abilities. The third and fourth factors turned out so small that the conception was poorly supported (Technical manual, p. 45). The quantitative subtests loaded mainly on the general factor. Their loadings on a *Q* factor were trivial, the largest being 0.18. Since *Q* failed to separate out, this test does not measure a distinct quantitative ability. Interestingly, that matches a finding about SB4, which the same developers produced (p. 281). But, whereas the Composite/Abstract distinction did not work in SB4, the General/Nonverbal distinction does hold up in CogAT. Probably the overall SB4 is closer to the *Gf* end of the spectrum (p. 287), and CogAT closer to the *Gc* end.

Summary These principles have been illustrated:

- How many factors are reported depends on the tests that enter the analysis, and on the analyst's preference.
- The analyst places axes to fit her preferred interpretation.
- In a set of ability tests the first unrotated factor typically accounts for a great deal of variance. Specific factors can carry more weight in a test than the second and later factors.
- The "general" factor does not necessarily have the same meaning from one ability battery to another.
- The developers may intend a test to measure more factors than it actually distinguishes.

- With correlated factors, just one of them can often "explain" a test; but with uncorrelated factors a test's loadings are likely to spread over two or three of them.

For all its mathematical formality, factor analysis is partly artistic. A photographer brings out particular features of a cathedral by placing the camera at a chosen spot. The features are real, but the photographer can control their prominence. That is what the factor analyst does with a set of scores.

3. *The numbers in each row of Table 10.3 decompose the subtest variance. In the first row, 71 + 10 + 19 = 100 per cent; and 0.71 is the sum of squares of 0.80 and −0.27. Prepare a bar diagram to show the percentage breakdown of Figure Classification.*

Confirmatory Analysis

In *exploratory* factoring, the investigator twists and turns the factors until satisfied with the pattern. Panel ii of Figure 10.1 was obtained that way. *Confirmatory* factor analysis, an alternative procedure, is much used nowadays in test development and is being reported in test manuals. To use the technique (Jöreskog & Sörbom, 1979), the test author writes down the factor loadings that represent her hypotheses in constructing the test, and asks whether the test intercorrelations are reasonably in line with them. More precisely: If the set of hypotheses is true in the population, is it believable that sampling error accounts for all departures of the data from the pattern? A positive answer does not prove that the author's structure is best; it says only that the data do not contradict her idea. (In the case of CogAT, the data did contradict the four-factor hypothesis.)

The contrast shown in Table 10.4, between the two kinds of analysis for KABC, is typical of studies on all tests. In the right-hand part, the authors are claiming that the missing loadings can be regarded as zeros. The confirmatory result looks neater and *seems* to provide stronger support for the test structure. That is because confirmatory analysis forces the data to tell as favorable a story as possible. Note, however, that on the left (exploratory) side, Hand Movements loaded equally on both factors. The ambiguity of this score was psychologically significant in the case of Gary (p. 255). The confirmatory analysis hides this ambiguity because it was not part of the authors' presuppositions.

4. *Factorial decomposition implies that intelligence has verbal, spatial, and other elements. So it is "not unitary." Many writers therefore say something like this: "Intelligence cannot meaningfully be subsumed under a single construct or assessed in terms of a single index." Would it be sensible to make similar statements about the following variables with compound origins:*
   a. *Household income (economics)?*
   b. *Protein intake (nutrition)?*
   c. *Brightness of white light (photosynthesis)?*

Table 10.4 EXPLORATORY AND CONFIRMATORY FACTOR LOADINGS COMPARED

Subtest	Exploratory analysis Age 10		Confirmatory analysis Age 9	
	Sequential	Simultaneous	Sequential	Simultaneous
Hand Movements	0.37	0.43	0.41	
Number Recall	0.92	0.13	0.96	
Word Order	0.69	0.24	0.70	
Gestalt Closure	0.04	0.52		0.53
Triangles	0.18	0.69		0.72
Matrix Analogies	0.23	0.62		0.64
Spatial Memory	0.27	0.54		0.57
Photo Series	0.22	0.75		0.78

Source: KABC Interpretive Manual, 1983, pp. 105, 108.

NOTE: Loadings for the empty cells in the confirmatory analysis were not reported in the manual because the hypothesis that in the population they equal zero was not disproved. The sample values, however, may have been as large as 0.20. (Each analysis is based on 200 cases.)

5. One student says, "It seems to me the factor analysts are like astronomers trying to discover planets. The astronomer finds a new planet by detecting the pull it exerts on already known bodies. Then he makes more careful studies to check his conclusion and locate the planet exactly. The factor analyst locates one test against already established abilities." How satisfactory is this comparison?

Multilevel Structures

The tests of Binet, Spearman, Terman, and their contemporaries emphasized a single score. This gave way to scores at three levels in the Wechsler scales and SB4 (subtest, section, and overall summary).

Not even three levels provide a full account of task similarities. Items within a subtest such as Vocabulary can be factored, and they fall into clusters. Words from science and art define subabilities (Coffman, 1966), and Marshalek (1981) distinguished subfactors for abstract words and concrete words. Knowledge shreds out finely; a person can rank high in science vocabulary and still know few technical terms from brain physiology or oceanography. Even verbal ability regarded as a process (rather than a vocabulary store) has subprocesses: decoding in reading, using cues from syntax, "making sense" by supplying context from experience, and others (Hunt, in Sternberg, 1985). These processes work together and they are likely to be intercorrelated; but they are distinguishable achievements.

The distinction between group and specific factors is not fundamental. The psychologist who becomes interested in an ability specific to one test can probably invent additional tasks that measure it. Then it becomes a "group" factor. The dictionary of factors can expand forever.

Group factors are not distinct and unified kinds of competence but locations within an essentially continuous ability space. A geographical space can be described in terms of large chunks (continents), smaller units (watersheds, perhaps), and so on down to particular hillsides; so with the map of abilities. The number of distinguishable levels is endless. Interpreters of tests go up and down the hierarchy just as medical specialists shift from gross anatomy to X-ray picture to microscope and back.

Test interpreters live with a paradox. Wide-reaching abilities develop as assemblies of bit-by-bit achievements such as possessing the concept "clockwise." But it is the broad abilities that dominate measurements. In any collection of diverse items measuring knowledge or reasoning, the first factor (before rotation) accounts for a large proportion of the variance, and each successive factor accounts for less. Any one subordinate factor carries little weight in a higher-level score.

Figure 10.2 maps out many relations among tests and test clusters. For emphasis I have drawn in arbitrary constellations. Tests that call for much the same concepts and processes become near neighbors; tests that *look* dissimilar may fall close together if the abilities they call for develop in tandem. (This map was developed by a scaling technique rather than by factoring, but that matters little.)

At the center of the picture are tests heavily loaded on g. These tests require comparatively complex processing, whereas tests toward the edge (weakly loaded on g) are simple in their demands. Note for example that Digits Backward is closer to the center than Digits Forward. Figural tests fall toward the right; verbal tests, toward the lower left; and tests that present meaningless symbols appear in the upper left. Other samples and other test sets confirm the broad picture but fill in details differently (Snow et al., 1984).

Multiple levels can be displayed in a "hierarchical" system. The structure in Figure 10.3 is based on a suggestion from P. E. Vernon (1965) and on a formal multilevel analysis by Gustafsson (in Sternberg, 1988). No one hierarchical picture has been established as fully adequate, and no flat picture could do justice to all the interrelations. My picture omits many branches and many twigs are left unlabeled; that avoids any hint of a finished structure.

Finding fluid ability *(Gf)* indistinguishable from the general factor g, Gustafsson places it at the apex. The best measures of it are abstract reasoning tasks including matrices, series, and induction (e.g. CogAT Figure Classification). Although these tasks have "content", individual differences are mostly differences in process. To understand that sentence, consider these series problems:

4 5 5 6 6 6 — —

△ △ ☐ ☐   — —

March May July September ———— ————

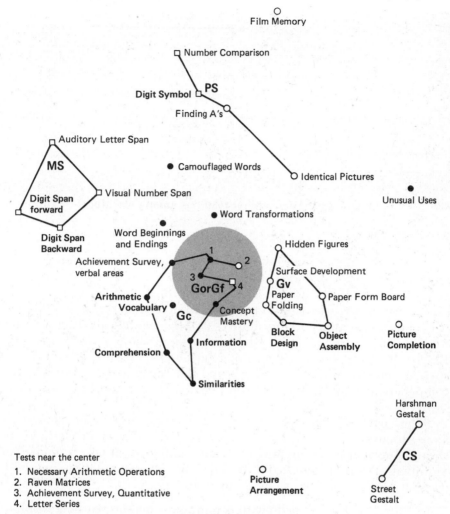

Figure 10.2. **A two-dimensional mapping of diverse tests.** Open circles denote figural or pictorial tests, closed circles denote verbal tests, and squares denote tests using meaningless symbols. Names in boldface identify Wechsler subtests; nearly all other tests are from the ETS Kit (p. 384). The shaded area includes tests where half the variance is attributed to the first (general) factor. PS = perceptual speed; MS = memory span; CS = closure speed. (*Source:* Adapted from Marshalek et al., 1983.)

On the surface, these are numerical, figural, and verbal. But for mature subjects in the normal range, all the items measure *Gf* because such persons have excellent command of the relevant knowledge. Crystallized abilities are multiple, and fall at lower levels of the scheme.

There is a danger of misreading Figure 10.3; *Gf* is *not* a combination of *Gv* and *Gc*. Rather, it is what *Gv* and *Gc* have in common. The habits and skills described in the latter part of Chapter 8, which make up *Gf*,

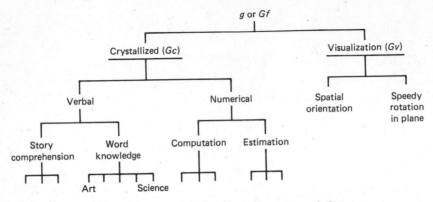

Figure 10.3. **Hierarchy of relations among abilities.**

contribute—along with narrower kinds of competence—to performance on verbal, numerical, and spatial tasks.

Broad stimulus categories appear at the third and fourth level. The spatial complex has to do with transformation of shapes. There probably is a companion "fluid auditory ability" (taking in and evaluating auditory signals), and this may have educational significance (Horn, in Linn, 1989b). It would be possible to add further factors at the same level, such as perceptual speed, memory, and fluency. These, however, have comparatively low *Gf* loadings and perhaps do not belong in this hierarchy.

The spatial domain at the right of the figure deserves somewhat more discussion. It is not easily subdivided, as intercorrelations are strong. But people do not rank the same on all spatial taks (Lohman, in Sternberg, 1988; McGee, 1979). Four factors deserve mention, but there was not enough space to show them all in Figure 10.3.

- *Visualization* has to do with comprehension and rearrangement of relatively complex forms. This cluster recognizes the strong convergence among the spatial test of DAT, EFT, Block Design, and Paper Folding (see, respectively, Figures 10.5, 1.3, 3.2, and 8.8), and other tests requiring processing of visual information. This is the "spatial" factor most often reported, because tests in the other subcategories are not entered into many analyses. Whether the following factors are subdivisions dependent on this factor is unclear.
- *Spatial Orientation* is the ability to say how a scene will look when viewed from another position. One test shows two views of the shore as seen from the cockpit of a boat, and asks what turn the boat made in the interim.
- *Speed of Rotation* is measured by timing simple judgments. (For example, could ⌐ be rotated into ⌐ without turning the block over?)

- There is a "dynamic" factor (perhaps more than one) in making judgments about figures that change or move (Hunt et al., 1988; Snow et al., 1985). Correlations among these tests—presented on film or on a computer screen—tend to be higher than their correlations with static tests (whether pencil-and-paper or computer-administered).

6. *Suggest subcategories that might be useful in a detailed analysis of*
   a. *Computation.*
   b. *Visualizing in three-dimensions.*

7. *Defend the following statement: At every level of the hierarchy there is a cell in which the Embedded Figures Test fits. Can this be said of every verbal or figural task?*

8. *Which K ABC subtests have near counterparts in Figure 10.2? How does the K ABC structure differ from this figure?*

VARIABLES AND TESTS IN THE THURSTONE TRADITION

Let us drop back now to the older research programs of Thurstone and his disciples, which reported all factors at one level. That work left a large residue of research findings, and dozens of tests.

The seven factors that came to the fore in Thurstone's early explorations he called "primary": Verbal, Reasoning, Number, Spatial (speed of rotation in a plane), Perceptual Speed, Memory, and Word Fluency. Word Fluency first directed attention to "divergent" thinking (p. 387). Choosing the best synonym for "reconcile" measures the Verbal factor; one Fluency test calls for supplying three synonyms for an easy word, such as "house," under time pressure.

In echoing the phrase "primary colors," Thurstone deliberately suggested that the group factors combine in various proportions to produce any complex intellectual process, just as green, red, and blue spotlights can be mingled to produce any other hue or white. Thurstone's primaries have been compared also to the chemist's list of elements, but that is not a sound comparison. There is only one answer to the question: What elements make up table salt? In factor analysis there are many answers, sound but not equally appealing.

The PMA Tests   Among the batteries Thurstone organized to measure his "primary mental abilities" (PMA), two are in current use. His wife Thelma Gwinn Thurstone, a school psychologist, coauthored the tests now known as PMA Readiness Level (Grades K-1). Verbal, numerical, perceptual, and spatial abilities are separately scored.

Schaie, having accumulated much information about performance of adults (p. 283), has produced the Schaie-Thurstone Adult Mental Abilities Test. Form A, made up of tests originally published by Thurstone, has one test for each of these factors: verbal, number, spatial, reasoning, fluency. Form OA is specially designed for older adults. The test taker marks a large-print booklet instead of using a separate answer sheet. Because older persons respond more positively to meaningful materials, two tests have been added: one in which drawings of recognizable objects are rotated, and one in which names of months form series to be completed.

The ETS Kit A factor does not become important just because several measures are invented. A list of "chief" factors has to grow out of a consensus that certain abilities deserve attention in psychological research or practical decisions. Some years back, J. W. French, a follower of Thurstone, asked colleagues to judge which factors were important for research and which tasks best measured them. The consensus provided the design for the so-called ETS Kit, to which improved tests were later added. Although the Kit is incomplete, not covering measures or concepts from recent cognitive psychology, the variables it does include are still actively investigated.

The present Kit of Factor-Referenced Cognitive Tests (Ekstrom et al., 1976, 1979) provides 72 measures—at least 3 for each of 21 factors and 2 tests for 2 more factors. The 23 factors are named to suggest a best interpretation. The rubrics in Table 10.5 (Reasoning, etc.) serve to make reading easier. Not all of these groupings correspond to correlations. The multidimensional scheme of the Kit recognizes more constellations than the flat chart of Figure 10.2, and fewer than will shortly be encountered in Guilford's system.

An investigator wanting to measure a factor would apply at least two Kit tests for it, to reduce the influence of specifics. The tests are kept short so that many factors can be included in the same investigation. The manual warns against use of the tests for purposes other than research.

In most Kit tests the items present one pervasive type of difficulty and only one. Necessary Arithmetic Operations is an example of such a purified test.

> A store marked down the price of a TV set from $200 to $175. What was the per cent reduction? To solve this one would
> A. multiply and divide
> B. subtract and divide
> C. divide and add

Nearly all American adolescents should be able to read this and should possess the concepts of pricing, percentage, division, and so on. The item makes no numerical demand. So differences among most subjects come from "reasoning pure and simple" (in the context of arithmetic). It should be noted that Necessary Arithmetic Operations (an indicator, say Ekstrom et al., of General Reasoning) is in the center of the map in Figure 10.2.

9. *Insofar as you can judge from the information presented, which Kit factors represent fluid ability and which represent crystallized abilities?*

Table 10.5   NOTES ON THE KIT OF FACTOR-REFERENCED COGNITIVE TESTS

Factor name	Presumed Guilford category	Tests matched to the factor and page where a similar test is described
Reasoning, General	CMS	Necessary Arithmetic Operations (p.384)
Induction	CSC CSS CFC	Figure Classification (p.259); Letter Sets
Reasoning, Logical[a]	EMR EMI	Nonsense Syllogisms
Verbal Comprehension	CMU	Vocabulary
Number Facility	MSI	Addition; Division
Spatial Orientation	CFS	Card Rotations (p.382)
Visualization	CFT	Paper Folding (p.309); Surface Development (p.391)
Spatial Scanning	CFI	Maze Tracing Speed (p.39)
Perceptual Speed	ESU EFU	Number Comparison (p.390); Identical Figures
Closure, Flexibility of[a]	NFT[b]	Hidden Figures (p.18)
Closure, Speed of[a]	CFU	Gestalt Completion (p.256)
Memory Span	MSU	Number Span (p.246); Letter Span
Memory, Associative	MSI	Picture-Number
Memory, Visual	MFU MFU MFR	Map Reading
Fluency, Figural	DFU DFI	Ornamentation
Fluency, Expressional	DMS	Arranging Words
Fluency, Word[a]	DSU	Word Beginnings and Endings (p.383)
Flexibility of Use[a]	DFT NFT	Different Uses (p.388)

[a]The Kit includes one additional reasoning factor, one additional closure factor, and two additional fluency-flexibility factors.

[b]This column is taken from Ekstrom et al. (1979). This one entry I have added from Guilford's research.

10. *WISC-R places little emphasis on the Associative Memory, Visual Memory, and Closure Speed factors. Would the test be improved by inserting subtests involving these factors in place of some present ones?*

11. *What has happened to the traditional distinction between verbal and nonverbal tests in the listing of Table 10.5?*

12. *"Necessary Arithmetic Operations, instead of measuring 'reasoning pure and simple,' measures the extent to which a young person has accepted the conventions, values, and styles of thought of the dominant middle-class culture." What justification can you offer for that comment?*

Guilford's "Structure of Intellect"

From 1950 to about 1975, the most extensive research on individual differences was that of J. P. Guilford. Following Thurstone's lead, Guilford assumed that talent takes many forms (Guilford, in Wolman, 1985; and references cited therein).

The scheme displayed in Figure 10.4 guided Guilford's efforts to investigate a much wider array of aptitudes than others had tested. The structure envisions 120 abilities; Guilford hoped to produce two or three pure measures for each cell, and to explain traditional tests as composites of the 120 factors. Each cell definition is intended to suggest a combination of task characteristics that can be built into tests; Guilford ultimately "filled in" 100 of the 120 cells. At the end of his work Guilford (1988) made two modifications. He divided Memory into Memory Recording and Memory Retention. He relabeled "Figural" content "Visual," and he placed an "Auditory" rubric beside it. (I retain the symbol "F" in what follows, as I use "V" elsewhere for "Verbal").

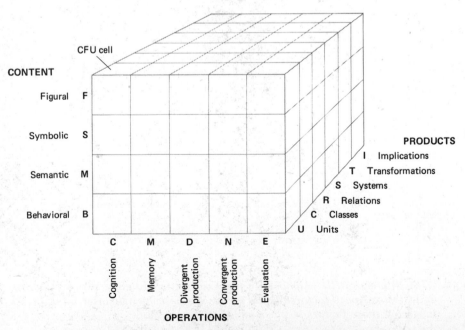

Figure 10.4. **Guilford's categories for test tasks.**

The first cell (CFU = Cognition of Figural Units) refers to tests that call for

C: recognition or simple interpretation of

F: diagrams or pictures, where

U: response is to well-defined elements.

The ETS Kit identifies CFU with speed of closure (see Figure 7.7). "Semantic" tasks deal with word meanings and with verbal or quantitative relations (hence, with aspects of Gc). "Symbolic" tasks use letters, numbers, and other symbols without regard to meanings; Digit Span, Digit Symbol, and Letter Series are examples. The "Behavioral" category presents social scenes and communications—pictures of people, or recorded dialogue, for example.

Among operations, Guilford's Divergent rubric matches Thurstone's Fluency; it will be the topic of the next subsection. Evaluative tasks require close comparison of alternatives. For example, an Evaluative-Symbolic-Relations task presents the pair GRAND–RAN and asks which of the following pairs has most nearly the same relation:

    COUNTRY–COT
    RESPITE–SIT
    LOVING–LOG

The second is considered correct because the letter rearrangement is most nearly like that in GRAND–RAN.

Factors at the cell level account for little variance. Whereas, for me, Matrices, EFT, and Number Series all measure Gf, Guilford identifies Matrices with CFR, Embedded Figures with NFT, and Number Series with CSS. It is impractical to measure many of the Guilford factors on any one group. It would take 4 hours of testing to distinguish convergent symbolic classification NSC reliably from divergent symbolic classification DSC.

At the "slice" level, Guilford's conceptual separation of operations and content will have to be taken seriously as theory evolves. (See Jäger, 1982, 1984.)

Divergent Thinking

Among the Thurstone primaries and the Guilford operations, the "divergent" or "fluency" factor merits separate discussion because it is not a component of the conventional mental tests described in Chapter 7, on which most research has focused. It has been suggested that fluency of ideas plays a significant role in creativity, because testimony from artists and other creators often speaks of the need for fresh combinations of observations and ideas.

A contrast is made between "convergent" and "divergent" questions; a convergent question has one best answer, whereas there are many good answers to a divergent question. Only constructed responses give clear evidence on divergent thinking. Psychology students, for example, have been asked to offer hypotheses to explain research results. The students who produce responses judged superior are also superior when they rate hypotheses that the tester supplied. The free-response form, however, displays the fluency with which students form hypotheses; that divergent ability differs among students who are equally good at the convergent judging task (Frederiksen, 1986; Ward et al., 1980).

Much research has accumulated around the Torrance Tests of Creative Thinking (E. P. Torrance), which can be applied from kindergarten to adulthood. The verbal section contains subtests such as these:

Product Improvement. A picture of a stuffed animal toy is shown. The test taker is to suggest changes, each of which would make the toy more fun to play with. ·

Unusual Uses. This test, which originated with Guilford, asks for many possible uses for a kind of commonplace object such as empty tin cans. (Space is provided for 50 answers!)

Torrance's figural tasks ask for drawings that tell a story or depict an object, given initial starting points. One test, for example, consists of a page of circles. The directions tell the child to make as many different pictures as possible with the circle a key part of each picture. Responses can be scored for one or more of these qualities: fluency (total acceptable responses), flexibility (i.e., variety of content), originality, and elaboration. Scores on these qualities correlate highly, so perhaps the distinctions are pointless.

Torrance's data suggest that divergent figural performance does not improve during the school years and that divergent verbal performance improves little after Grade 6. Scores on convergent tests hold up until age 50 or later. Word fluency, however, drops off steadily after about age 30 (Schaie, 1983).

Is divergent thinking distinct from convergent thinking? Table 10.6, based on a follow-up of 1000 Swedish youngsters, provides support for the distinction. There were several tests of each type for age 13 and for ages 15–16. The convergent and divergent totals correlated about 0.25. The types of scores from convergent tests are kept separate in my summary; thus the top line in the table is a median for verbal-with-verbal, logical-with-logical, and spatial-with-spatial scores. It can be seen that divergent tests predict other divergent tests—not well, but better than convergent tests do.

The evidence suggests that the advantage of the person with well-developed knowledge and intellectual skill can be neutralized by some inhibitory process. (Greater conventionality? Sterner censorship of flawed responses?) Children with high scores in divergent thinking tend to be expansive and spontaneous in their everyday activities; children

Table 10.6   STABILITY AND CONSISTENCY FOR CONVERGENT
AND DIVERGENT ABILITIES

Test type, age 13	Test type, age 15–16	Correlation[a]
Convergent	Same convergent ability	0.65
Convergent	Another convergent ability	0.5
Convergent	Divergent	0.2
Divergent	Convergent	0.2
Divergent	Divergent	0.4

[a]Approximate median, over sexes and over test pairs.

Source: Magnusson & Backteman, 1978.

who do well on conventional tests and badly on divergent tests seem to be cautious and insecure (Getzels & Jackson, 1962; Wallach & Kogan, 1965).

Some popular writings leave the mistaken impression that fluidity of association *is* creativity. Fluency, however, ought to be integrated with the purposiveness and critical thinking that Binet emphasized. Novel ideas are of little value if not accompanied by intellectual control. Pouring out unrealistic, ill-considered ideas is not meritorious.

Creativity is specific; composers of music are not architects. Knowledge and conceptual systems are as useful in original thinking as in other thinking—see Guilford's particularly good statements (1965) on this point. The creative producer, then, has ability in Binet's sense plus rich experience in a field plus something extra. Perhaps, say some writers, the creative person will not be found in the highest ranges of academic success: dutiful learning of school lessons may not be congenial to or conducive to a free-ranging intellect. To put the suggestion differently, rank in convergent tests corresponds to rank in creativity up to the high-average level; in the highest range, however, there seems to be a lack of correspondence between convergent tests and rank in creativity (Barron & Harrington, 1981).

Partly because criteria of creative performance are hard to come by, the predictive value of divergent tests remains in doubt. A sympathetic review (Barron & Harrington, 1981) could not go beyond this carefully hedged conclusion:

> On the basis of those few studies [that compare predictions from divergent and conventional tests] one can say that some divergent thinking tests, administered to some samples, under some conditions and scored according to some criteria, measure facets relevant to creativity criteria beyond those measured by indices of general intelligence.

Inasmuch as divergent tests are hard to score and standings are unstable, perhaps their main function is to dramatize for teachers that convergent abilities are not the whole of intellectual development.

MULTISCORE APTITUDE BATTERIES

Instruments providing profiles to guide career exploration grew largely out of practical experience with prediction of vocational and educational criteria. Neither factor analysis nor theory of processes greatly influenced their design, although Thurstone's writings on group factors stimulated interest in multiscore measurement.

The Differential Aptitude Tests

The profile of Robert Finchley (p. 122) came from the widely used Differential Aptitude Tests (DAT). That battery is intended primarily for high school counseling. The tests measure complex abilities that have a fairly direct relation to job, families, and curricula. Spelling and Usage sections are included because of their relevance to clerical and other occupations. The Verbal and Number scores are averaged to produce a further point in the profile.

All sections are illustrated in Figures 3.2 or 10.5, except for Spelling (Sp) and Clerical Speed and Accuracy (CSA). Here are examples of those remaining sections.

Is the word spelled correctly?
    cautious   ajustment

Mark the choice at the right that matches the underlined group at the left.
    XY Xy XX <u>YX</u> Yy   Xy Yy YX XX XY
    6g <u>6G</u> G6 Gg g6   g6 Gg 6g G6 6G

The publication in 1947 of DAT, the first integrated battery, is a landmark in testing history. Previously, the counselor had to assemble her own collection of tests, which would have been normed and validated on different samples. Percentile conversions for all DAT scores were calculated on the same samples to give profile shapes as much meaning as possible. The 1986 version for administration and reporting by microcomputer (see pp. 61 and 141) is another "first" in testing for the purpose of counseling.

In the printed version, the battery requires nearly 4 hours. The computerized DAT Adaptive is usually completed in less than 2 hours, with no loss in accuracy.

Many intercorrelations (Table 10.7) are sizable. Comparatively few students will have differences large enough to consider seriously when an intercorrelation of two scores is 0.7 or larger (nearly equal to the self-correlations in the diagonal).

The computer format for CSA items departs considerably from the one shown above, and scores from the two versions correlate only about 0.3. The older CSA is understood as a measure of perceptual speed. A fresh program of validation will be required to understand the new ver-

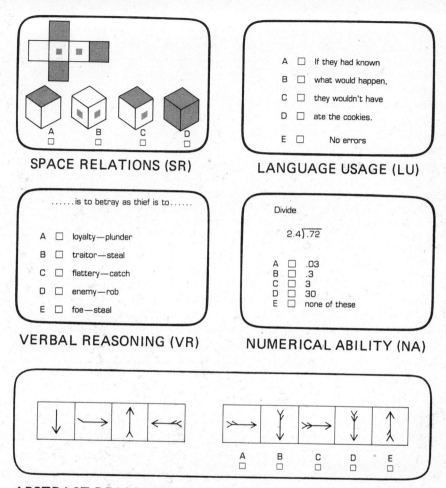

SPACE RELATIONS (SR)

LANGUAGE USAGE (LU)

VERBAL REASONING (VR)

NUMERICAL ABILITY (NA)

ABSTRACT REASONING (AR)   Which figure is next in the series?

Figure 10.5. Items representing DAT subtests. (*Source:* These items, and the Spelling and Clerical items listed in the text, are practice items from the orientation booklet of the DAT. They are reproduced by permission. Copyright 1972, 1973, 1975, 1980, 1982 by The Psychological Corporation. All rights reserved.)

sion. (Correlations between the two versions of the other sections are close to the reliabilities in Table 10.7; McBride et al., 1987.)

Table 10.8 goes on to report correlations of scores with marks. The large sampling errors must be kept in mind. The first entry, for one of the larger samples, implies a population correlation in the 0.4–0.6 range, not a precise 0.5. General ability predicts grades rather well in all the courses except shop; the crystallized Verbal and Numerical scores predict a bit better than the fluid AR. The manual's fuller tabulation for English marks in many schools shows VR, LU, and NA to be equally

Table 10.7 CORRELATIONS WITHIN THE DAT

	MR	SR	AR	NA	VR	LU	Sp	CSA
Mechanical (MR)	0.77							
Spatial (SR)	0.6	0.77						
Abstract (AR)	0.6	0.7	0.78					
Numerical (NA)	0.5	0.6	0.7	0.82				
Verbal (VR)	0.6	0.6	0.7	0.7	0.88			
Language Usage (LU)	0.6	0.5	0.6	0.7	0.8	0.81		
Spelling (Sp)	0.3	0.4	0.5	0.6	0.6	0.7	0.88	
Clerical (CSA)	0.2	0.2	0.2	0.2	0.2	0.2	0.2	0.74

Source: DAT technical supplement, 1984, pp. 3, 7. All values were calculated within grade and sex, and a midrange value was selected for this summary. Intercorrelations are based on a total of about 5000 cases who took the booklet version. Reliability coefficients in diagonal cells come from the ninth grades of a single school district; two forms were given, 2 weeks apart.

good predictors, with Sp only slightly behind. The surprising success of NA indicates that the prediction rests on a *Gc* factor, not on verbal ability as such. Spatial scores have no special relation to marks in geometry; indeed, in the Arlington sample SR predicted English marks as well as it did geometry marks. The one clear success in course-specific grade prediction is that NA is a better predictor of math grades than the other subtests are.

13. *Linn (in Buros, 1978, p. 659) says this:*

Possibly the most serious nagging doubt regarding the DAT comes from the lack of empirical evidence regarding the degree of the *differential* validity

Table 10.8 DAT CORRELATIONS WITH COURSE MARKS ABOUT 6 MONTHS LATER

Course	Grade	Location	Number of cases	Correlation of marks with				
				VR[a]	NA[a]	AR[a]	SR[a]	VR + NA
Geometry	10	Arlington, TX	315	0.5	0.6	0.4	0.35	0.6
	10	Columbus, MS	58	0.25	0.6	0.4	0.3	0.4
Shop[b]	9	Lodi, CA[c]	114	0.2	0.4	0.25	0.3	0.35
	10	Baltimore Co., MD	44	0.35	0.45	0.5	0.3	0.4
Accounting[b]	11	Baltimore Co., MD	76	0.45	0.5	0.4	0.3	0.5
English	10	Baltimore Co., MD	208	0.55	0.5	0.4	0.35	0.55
	10	So. Pasadena, CA	332	0.45	0.5	0.4	0.2	0.5

[a]Abbreviations are explained in Table 10.7.

[b]Shop correlations are for males only. Accounting correlations are for females only.

[c]The Lodi grades were given about 12 months after the DAT.

Source: DAT technical supplement, 1984, pp. 14–31.

of the subtests in predicting various criteria. Such evidence will not be forth-coming without the development of adequate differential criterion measures.

In this context, "differential validity" is present when each criterion is pre-dicted by a different test or combination of tests. What academic or job criteria might bring out such validity for specialized abilities?

14. *DAT-Abstract can be thought of as a measure of g that is affected little by reading, vocabulary, and knowledge of arithmetic. Why is VR + NA consistently a better predictor of grades? Is the finding that a student has AR higher than VR and NA of no importance?*

15. *How might the substantial correlation of VR with accounting grades be explained?*

16. *If an adolescent being counseled has been tested with the Wechsler, which of the Differential Aptitude Tests would add the most useful supplementary information?*

The Armed Services Vocational Aptitude Battery

Very large numbers of young people take the Armed Services Vocational Aptitude Battery (ASVAB) each year. Military recruiters arrange to give it without charge in cooperating high schools, and all students in certain grades whose parents sign a consent form are tested. A score report is returned to the student, and a copy goes to the counselor's file. The recruiter uses the scores to identify capable young persons whose enlistment she encourages, to offset the tendency of the armed services to attract students with poor academic records.

ASVAB subtests cover abilities somewhat like those in DAT; however, there is no spatial subtest, and mechanical comprehension is supplanted by subtests on knowledge—about machinery (particularly cars and trucks) and electricity. Score patterns have changed repeatedly in the past; the score combinations now reported for guidance do not resemble the combinations used in selection and classification by the several armed services.

I cannot speak neutrally about ASVAB, inasmuch as I have had occasion to condemn some of its features and to criticize some of the validation research (Cronbach, 1977b, 1979; in Wainer & Braun, 1988). The faults derived in part from interservice rivalries, in part from excessive recruiter zeal, and in part from misjudgments by psychologists engaged with the activity. A chief complaint in recent years has been that score differences within the profile reported for counseling of students have little or no reliability. I am not alone in my criticism; another textbook says this (Murphy & Davidshofer, 1988, p. 208):

ASVAB . . . fails the acid test of a multiple aptitude battery. The ASVAB does not provide the information about multiple abilities needed for successful job placement. For most of its major goals, the military would do just as well with a short test of general intelligence.

A change is in the making. The Army is in the midst of a mammoth 9-year research program known as Project A (Campbell, 1986), and has engaged many top-flight specialists in personnel psychology and psychometrics as contractors or consultants. The main concern is (in the spirit of Figure 1.5) with classification into specialties rather than merely screening overall quality of recruits. Findings from an initial trial of many newly designed tests along with ASVAB became available in 1986. The battery was revised and a new study was launched; about 50,000 soldiers in 21 military specialties were tested, and their performance in training and on the job is being appraised (with greater accuracy than in previous army research). Results are emerging slowly; some of those now available are examined on pages 398 and 556.

The General Aptitude Test Battery

The General Aptitude Test Battery (GATB) was developed by the United States Employment Service (USES) and is administered by state employment services to persons seeking work. Versions of GATB are in use in many foreign countries. Schools can arrange with the local employment office to use the test in counseling.

When an employer asks the employment service for referrals, he wants applicants likely to succeed. The applicant to the employment service wants referral not to the first opening he qualifies for but to an opening where his best talents will be used and rewarded. The test developers study psychological characteristics of jobs and accumulate information on the meaning of test scores. The variety of occupations studied is endless: accountant, aircraft mechanic, appliance cord assembler, artificial breeding technician, asparagus sorter,. . . .

Several of the tests are descended from research of the 1920s that produced a famous "Minnesota" series of vocational aptitude tests. A separate aptitude test for each job title is impracticable. USES once started to build a test for each type of job. But when the number of tests passed 100, it became clear that such a collection could not be used for guidance or placement—that is, for finding a job opening suited to each individual. Such service requires a limited number of diversified tests that can be given to everyone and that can be combined to predict for all the firms served. A thorough review of GATB by a national committee, covering innovations recently proposed and studies not in the test manual, is to be found in Hartigan and Wigdor (1989).

Test Features   GATB, as currently used in high schools, reports nine scores:

> G—General (a composite of Vocabulary, Three-Dimensional Space, and Arithmetic Reasoning)
>
> V—Verbal (Vocabulary)

N—Numerical (Computation, Arithmetic Reasoning)

S—Spatial (Three Dimensional Space)

P—Form Perception (Tool Matching, Form Matching)

Q—Clerical Perception (Name Comparison)

K—Motor Coordination (Mark Making)

F—Finger Dexterity (Assemble, Disassemble)

M—Manual Dexterity (Place, Turn)

Tests in sections V, N, S, and Q resemble those of DAT. Tool Matching calls for rapid comparison of pictures of tools, alike save for differences in black-and-white markings. Picturing of tools is intended to increase the appeal of the test. In Form Matching, several dozen size-and-shape combinations, each one lettered, are scattered within a rectangle. The same patterns appear—numbered, rearranged and rotated—in an adjacent panel, and the test taker matches numbers to letters, as many as possible within the time allowed.

The coordination tests are designed brilliantly to serve a program that tests a million persons each year. In Mark Making, the respondent is asked only to fill squares with a simple pattern of tally marks, as many as he can make in 60 seconds. For the manual dexterity tests, 48 pegs are mounted in a board, and there is a second board with holes. In the Place test the person transfers pegs from one board to the other as fast as possible, working with both hands. In the Turn test (single-handed), he inverts each peg while transferring it. Assemble and Disassemble call for finer coordination. A board contains 50 holes. Using both hands, the person fits a rivet and washer to each hole. In Disassemble, he replaces the rivets in their bin and puts each washer onto a rod.

GATB is efficiently designed. The working times for pencil-and-paper tests are close to 6 minutes each. The psychomotor tests require even less working time, but several minutes are used for demonstration and practice. The entire battery can be given in about $2\frac{1}{2}$ hours. The simple procedures allow trustworthy administration by relatively untrained testers, to persons who have limited education or poor command of English. In the psychomotor tests each test taker leaves all the materials as he found them, ready for the next examinee. A price is paid for this efficiency. The marked speeding of nearly all GATB subtests may reduce their validity. And several scores lack the precision attained in DAT by means of longer sections or adaptive design.

USES is now changing the way scores are used in hiring. It proposes to discard a practice that reviewers have long condemned (see Keesling, in Mitchell, 1985). To be recommended as an egg candler (for example) under the old system, the job seeker had to reach 80 on P, 85 on K, and 100 on M. (The score scale is 120 ± 20; the other six scores did not enter the rule for egg candlers.) This multiple-cutoff rule relied on unreliable single scores. Merging scores into composites is sensible, but the new plan may go too far. (See p. 453 for another innovation proposed for use of GATB in selection.)

Three Scores? or Nine? For making decisions about persons seeking employment, USES now recommends combining the 12 tests into 3 scores. Three factors capture much of the score information. The psychomotor M, F, and K overlap negligibly with the intellectual measures. A general factor runs through the other six scores, but cognitive and perceptual factors *VN* and *PQ* can be separated. (As elsewhere in this chapter, italics refer to factors.) The *VN* and *PQ* true scores (not the measures) correlate 0.88, and the *PQ* component is almost perfectly estimated by a combination of *VN* and *MFK*. S can be described as *VN* plus *PQ* plus a strong specific factor (USES, 1983a; report written by J. E. Hunter). If Hunter had factored tests rather than composite scores like P, and had not chosen a "confirmatory" approach (p. 378) that specified absence of an S factor, he very likely would have found a clear Spatial factor (see Hammond, 1984). The three scores now recommended for use are a GVN composite, an SPQ composite, and an MFK composite. The net effect of the three-score plan is to ignore V/N, S/Q, and many other score contrasts. (As S enters the G score, it is part of two composites. This oddity obscures the interpretation of Hunter's statistical reports.)

Hunter (see USES, 1983c) pulled validity reports on some 500 jobs from GATB files and summarized them. Small samples and rough-and-ready criteria made the data far from ideal, and Hunter had to adjust coefficients quite a bit. To examine the usefulness of, for example, the V/N distinction, he paired their adjusted validity coefficients on any job, then correlated across jobs. Wherever V is a strong predictor, N also tends to predict (*r* of validities is about 0.7). In contrast, the value for V and S is 0.3; that for V and F is 0.0.

Aided by job analyses, Hunter formed five categories of jobs; jobs within a group have rather similar aptitude requirements (Table 10.9). Any job opening is closer to one of those families than the others, and the formula for that family—a weighted average of one, two, or three of the composites—is taken as a predictor. As can be seen, GVN is the determining factor for about 80 per cent of the job referrals. Although USES analyzes jobs in terms of their emphasis on people as well as data and things (see p. 465), Hunter found no correlational evidence that people-centered jobs differ in aptitude requirements from other jobs assigned to the same row of Table 10.9.

For counseling applications, USES still reports nine scores, and retaining most of these scores seems wise. The V/N distinction is clearly significant, whether in suggesting jobs to avoid or in suggesting which of the two competences needs to be built up if a young person is to make good in a preferred career. V and N have meaningfully different relations

Table 10.9   JOB FAMILIES AND THEIR APTITUDE REQUIREMENTS

Family	Percentage of U.S. workforce	Name	Code and complexity	Validity			Prediction weights		
				GVN	SPQ	KFM	GVN	SPQ	KFM
T1	2.5	Setting up	Things, high	.17	.15	.08	.40	.19	.07
T2	2.4	Feeding, Offbearing	Things, low	.21	.18	.24	.07	.00	.46
D1	14.7	Synthesizing, Coordination	Data, high	.28	.24	.19	.58	.00	.00
D2	62.7	Analyzing, Compiling, Computing	Data, middle	.23	.18	.13	.45	.00	.16
D3	17.7	Copying, Comparing	Data, low	.20	.20	.18	.28	.00	.33

NOTE: The weights are for z-scores and indicate relative emphasis. Weights for the SPQ composite were set low because it is redundant with the other composites. The validities (which are corrected for criterion reliability) are based on more recent studies than were used in choosing weights.

Source: United States Employment Service, 1983c, p. 39, and Hartigan and Wigdor, 1989, p. 168.

to jobs. We can see this if we start down the alphabet of the GATB manual and note that the validity of N is higher than that of V in these jobs: accountant, audit clerk, bookkeeping-machine operator, cabinetmaker,. . . .

The three-score system embodies controversial theses that will be discussed further on page 43 in connection with the topic of validity generalization. Hunter leaves the impression (e.g., in Gottfredson, 1986) that general ability is the only cognitive aptitude worth taking seriously—that is debatable. When USES commissioned a review of the scheme, the panel said this (Hartigan & Wigdor, 1989, p. 143):

> The case for rejecting specific aptitudes is weak. Not enough is known about predicting job performance to conclude quickly that two composites alone are sufficient, however convenient it is to work with only two variables [as in most rows of Table 10.9] in classifying jobs and constructing regression equations.

Why the Relevance of Group Factors Is Underestimated   Hunter and USES lost sight of the fact that employment services perform a *classifying* function. The contrasts among V, N, and S, and perhaps other subscores are the most promising basis for classification whenever one is working *within* a high level of g (college graduates), or a low level (no college), or an intermediate one.

Hunter's conclusions about the irrelevance of factors beyond the first ignore the selection processes that tend (for example) to keep low-spatial persons out of spatial careers. Selection by institutions and self-selection have steered the person over many years toward lines of work he or she handles relatively well. In a sense, a test can only predict failure. Architects prove during their training that they can handle spatial work; if not, they drop out. The survivors have adequate spatial ability, and the differences that remain are not the basis of stardom or failure.

One of many studies to document this selective effect is the longitudinal Project TALENT (Flanagan et al., 1973). High school sophomores took a test similar to DAT Space Relations. Five years later a follow-up sorted the youths according to the jobs they were in or were preparing for. The *majority* of those within certain job categories came from the top quarter of the national distribution on the spatial test. Among males, high spatial ability greatly increased the probability of gravitating into a career as architect, engineer, or physicist and, among females, of gravitating into high school mathematics teaching, physical therapy, or the visual arts. (There were not enough cases to provide clear evidence on both sexes in every occupation.)

Another point: Spatial reasoning is only one aspect of the work even of an architect or a geometry student. Global criteria, affected by all the aspects, tend to lose sight of any specialized competence (see p. 416).

Some data from Project A bear on this question. Criteria were available in nine military specialties; there were 500–700 soldiers per group. One criterion, an evaluation on "General soldiering," was global. It was predicted about equally well (0.5–0.6, after correction for range restriction) by verbal, quantitative, technical-knowledge, and spatial scores (Campbell, 1986, p. 170; McHenry et al., 1987; Wise et al, 1987). The patterning of correlations was similar in all specialties, so the result looks very much like successful prediction on the basis of general ability.

"Core technical proficiency" was evaluated within each specialty, and the relevance of predictors changed with the specialty (Campbell, 1986, pp. 169 and 171). Strangely, the spatial score made an appreciable contribution to prediction in every specialty (except radio operator); probably this occurred because many spatial tests were tried, producing a score of exceptional reliability. For vehicle mechanics and operators, the technical-knowledge part of ASVAB was the most relevant predictor; the verbal part was most relevant for medical specialists; and the quantitative part for administrative specialists. For radio operators, verbal and quantitative carried the predictive weight. The data could be recast in Hunter's manner to show relevance everywhere of the general factor, with lower-level factors raising each particular validity coefficient only a little. But for purposes of classification and career planning, the important thing to predict is the *difference* in probable outcome in Job Family A and Families B, C,. . . . That, the general factor by definition cannot predict.

17. *GATB-S correlated substantially with success of cabinetmakers, but the corresponding correlation for carpenters was low. Can you explain?*

18. *For what types of guidance does the content of GATB seem more useful than that of DAT? For what types is it less useful?*

Limitations on Interpretation of Profiles

To choose among educational and vocational options, the individual needs a sense of his strengths and weaknesses. Profiles are intended to bring differences among abilities to the surface, yet over and over we have seen that differences across scales are difficult to pin down and make sense of. The reader should keep in mind the cautions voiced earlier, alongside those this section develops.

Specificity of Norms   Rarely, a profile based on raw or percentage scores is interpretable. Some sense could be made of percentage comparisons in a diagnostic readiness test (Figure 4.8). Examples where such contrasts are even more suitable appear on pages 364 and 475. But aptitude profiles are charted against norms.

Insofar as a vocational plan is based on norm reference—that is, on a concept of a competitive world—it is important to compare the person with the group he will compete against, not with "people in general." Changing the reference group changes the story.

The GATB profile is ordinarily plotted against norms for adult workers. The profile of a student engineer plotted in the usual manner (Figure 10.6, upper profile) implies outstanding G, V, and S abilities, with several other scores above average. The lower profile, based on norms for engineering students, is strikingly different. This student is strong

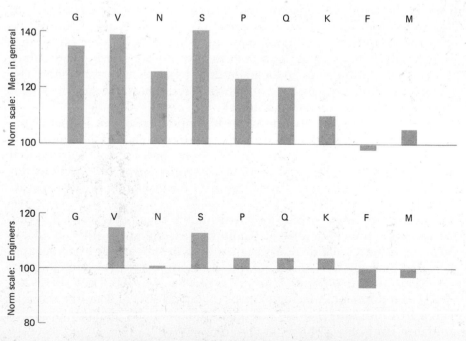

Figure 10.6. **Two GATB profiles for a student engineer.**

on V and S. He is only average in G and N. The obvious next step is to check his academic history in mathematics, and perhaps test further in that area.

Uncertainty in Prediction   Eric, with a standard score of 60 on some test, is considering a certain occupation. The counselor knows that 30 people out of 100 having Eric's score fail in that work. Even so, the counselor cannot give a firm prediction. Perhaps Eric would do better if tested again. Perhaps qualities unknown to us put Eric among the 30 per cent who will fail rather than the 70 per cent who succeed.

The counselor who is conscious of unreliability takes precautions. She starts by reporting scores as approximate rather than exact, perhaps by the "confidence band" technique illustrated in Robert Finchley's profile (p. 122). She looks to the case history to confirm the impressions the profile gives. If in doubt about a critical finding, she checks it with a second test or other sources of information. She looks for factors such as language handicaps or unusual training that might make the usual meaning of the score inapplicable.

Clients and professional workers may trust test data too much. Even when the tester's report is carefully hedged, the person receiving the report is likely to remember only portions of it. A parent, learning that his child stands at the 25th percentile in fluid ability, may forget the tester's cautions about what the test does not measure, the possibility of growth or decline in ability, and the approximate nature of predictions from it. The number may stick vividly in mind and be used as a basis for significant decisions for years to come. (Worse, the basic logic may escape the layperson. A congressman and successful lawyer once complained mildly to me about how tests he took decades earlier at Stanford showed his "aptitude" to be for an outdoor job such as forest ranger. The test was an *interest* measure, and surely the counselor said loud and clear that it hadn't measured ability.)

A rule of thumb for working with confidence bands is that if the bands do not overlap the difference is worth drawing to the client's attention. If you look back at Robert Finchley's profile, you will see that none of the differences among his high scores meets this standard for interpretability—nor does any of the differences among his low scores.

Redundancy of Scores   Multiscore instruments have been accused of picturing mountains that are really mole hills. General abilities obviously do account for a great deal of variance both in school and in an occupation, and perhaps DAT and GATB profiles are excessively detailed.

I have already reported Hunter's criticism of GATB. DAT scores are similarly redundant. A factor analysis (Nanda, 1967) of data like those in Table 10.7 indicates that the information dependable enough for use in guidance could be captured in just four scores:

A verbal composite emphasizing Verbal Reasoning, Spelling, and Language Usage

A composite emphasizing Abstract, Spatial, and Mechanical

A numerical factor[1]

A clerical factor

Weak specific factors that appeared in several tests are not measured accurately. As was seen earlier (p. 279), when two tests correlate substantially, only a modest fraction of the differences in observed scores imply a meaningful difference in true scores. Among typical students, about 20 per cent have clearly nonchance differences between DAT Verbal Reasoning and Language Usage. Still, the fact that (for example) DAT Verbal, Spelling, and Language Usage overlap does not make reporting all three scores inappropriate. Sampling three aspects of verbal abilities broadens the composite, and it reminds the counselee that verbal development has many aspects. For the 20 per cent with a reliable Verbal/Language difference, it says more.

Humphreys (1981), reflecting on the efforts of the armed services to sort enlisted personnel for specialized training, concluded that nearly all the valid information is carried by three types of score: general-scholastic, mechanical knowledge or reasoning, and speed in arithmetic and clerical tasks. The first indicates the probability of succeeding in comparatively difficult courses and assignments involving words and ideas. The second predicts quickness in learning "dirty hands" jobs. And the third predicts for routine clerical tasks. Once these three variables have been assigned weights to match a training program, Humphreys says that scoring other aptitudes is pointless. (Humphreys sees a larger role for specialized tests within an academically superior group, either at the college level or in advanced military specialties. The enlisted population has generally come from a nonacademic high school track emphasizing shop *or* clerical subjects.)

The critics rightly place the burden of proof in guidance and employee classification on whoever proposes a job-specific interpretation of specialized factors. The old Complex Coordination test (p. 40) provides an example that cuts both ways. The designers thought they were getting at a psychomotor aptitude required by pilots, one not tapped by other tests. The test proved to be one of the best single predictors of success in pilot training (p. 439). Four-fifths of its validity, however,

---

[1]A recent analysis employing both the computer and booklet versions also reports four factors; but Numerical is associated with the first two factors and the third factor is identified with Mechanical (McBride et al., 1987). Separation of Mechanical as the third factor is probably a consequence of mixing the sexes in McBride's analysis.

came from general and spatial abilities tapped by pencil-and-paper tests. That result does not prove that the psychomotor test was a bad idea; the fraction of the validity that did come from the coordination component was economically significant in reducing the failure rate. (For detailed evidence, see Cronbach, 1970, p. 390.)

How Early Do Profiles Stabilize?   The student is continually revising his self-concept as he goes through school, forming an impression of the fields in which he is specially strong and weak. In judging where talents lie, the present profile can be taken too seriously. Patterns become increasingly stable, but they are reversible even in adulthood.

Illuminating evidence on general academic abilities comes from a longitudinal study in 17 communities where "aptitude" and "achievement" batteries were given in Grades 5, 7, 9, and 11. Table 10.10 covers a small fraction of the information, on males only. Patterning is weak; most r's within the same column are of similar size. Competence in mathematics in Grade 11 is predicted nearly as well by verbal abilities in Grade 5 as by fifth-grade mathematics. The person whose Grade-5 reasoning is superior to his achievement score in the same area tends to show a similar fluid/crystallized difference in Grade 11, but the main message of the table is the stability of all-round academic-intellectual performance.

A rolling readjustment is going on in every area. Some students are rising in rank while others are dropping back. In reading, for example, the retests correlate 0.78–0.80 over a 2-year span, 0.77–0.78 over 4 years, and 0.73 over 6 years. A profile in Grade 3 will report reliable within-profile differences for many children, but even without directed reme-

Table 10.10.   GRADE-11 SCORES PREDICTED FROM GRADE-5 TESTS

| Grade 5 | Grade 11 | | | | | |
	V^a	Reading	Social studies	Q^a	Math	Science
Verbal tests						
V^a	**0.79**	0.69	0.70	0.58	0.58	0.62
Reading	0.76	**0.73**	0.70	0.61	0.62	0.65
Social studies	0.74	0.69	**0.70**	0.59	0.59	0.60
Quantitative tests						
Q^a	0.63	0.63	0.59	**0.70**	0.64	0.56
Mathematics	0.70	0.67	0.64	0.69	**0.66**	0.61
Science	0.73	0.68	0.67	0.61	0.61	**0.67**

[a]These two scores emphasize general intellectual development and reasoning more than the other scores do.

Source: Data supplied by T. L. Hilton. For the design of the study, see Hilton et al., 1971; see also Hilton, 1980.

dial efforts a large fraction of those differences will be weak or even reversed a year later. Table 10.11 is based on retests of thousands of students initially tested in Grade 9. The readjustment of ranks, and of profile shapes, is drastic for the perceptual and motor tests. Courses of study affect profile shape in high school. There is less change after adolescence. In a 3-year retest of adults around age 30, all the correlations between corresponding test and retest were 0.75 or higher (GATB manual, p. 269).

The adolescent correlations are high enough to warrant interpreting differences within a Grade-9 profile. Advice in the early years of high school, however, should center on helping students fill in weak spots significant for their employability and personal interests. It is one thing to say, "You will be severely handicapped in these career lines that interest you if you do not strengthen your math (or spatial reasoning, or motor coordination)"; it is quite another to say, "Don't consider those careers; let us find one that matches your profile." Emphasizing developmental experience is especially important if the student has had little exposure and encouragement in an area where his score is low—mechanical reasoning, for example. Standing is least likely to change in an area where the student has already had plentiful learning opportunities.

In the early days of testing, it was hoped that a test profile would permit a definite, final choice of vocation at the time the tests were given. If this were the case, the counselor and client together could reach a decision, the client relying on the counselor's interpretation of the tests. Today it is recognized that vocational choice is not a single throw of the dice; rather, it is a long-term process of development. Even after leaving school, a person has many occasions to narrow his or her field of concentration or to transfer to a new one. The engineer in a tech-

Table 10.11.   STABILITY OF GATB SCORES

	Measures having coefficients in each range, when Grade-12 scores are compared with scores earned	
	3 years earlier	1 year earlier
0.08–0.85		G, V, N
0.70–0.79	G, V, N, S, K	S, Q, K, M
0.60–0.69	P, Q, M	P, F
0.50–0.59	F	

Source: GATB manual, 1970, p. 327.

nical firm, for example, may become a manager, a salesperson, a creative designer, or an expert on specifications. Wise choice requires self-understanding; no prescription filled out by a tenth-grade or freshman-year counselor could properly anticipate later choices. On this, Chapter 12 will have more to say.

POSSIBILITIES IN MICROANALYSIS

For conventional applications of tests in selection, career planning, and the like, a broad-stroke picture of the individual is sufficient. But fine detail has its uses.

The practical promise of microanalysis lies in clinical work that can use precise measurements of the *present state* of the individual. Research on psychoactive drugs, for example, can take advantage of fine-grain data; if some processes are slowed and others are not, that sheds light on the physiological effect of the drug and on its clinical suitability. Moreover, microanalytic psychological measurement can help in the day-to-day management of medication for the individual patient, especially when the testing can be computerized. Most of these developments are far in the future.

One present-day example of practical, efficient microanalysis is the Porch Index of Communicative Ability (PICA). This instrument for the study of aphasia and similar disorders grew out of an elaborate conceptualization that the concentrated effort of neuroanatomists and clinical practitioners had built up.

In many ways, the design of PICA departs from the tradition of psychological testing, having more in common with physical and physiological assays. The speech clinician sometimes is asked for a one-time diagnosis, but she often monitors patient progress—either to guide case management or to evaluate a kind of treatment. PICA is, therefore, designed to be used repeatedly; it has no element of novelty.

A particular commonplace object—a key, for example—is the basis for 18 items: "Point to the key." "Write the name of this [tester points to key]." "Say what I say: *key*," and so on. Ten objects (or their names), used 18 times, produce 18 subtest scores. Using the same object or concept in several ways facilitates comparison of functions. A 16-point scoring scheme is applied to every response. A response that is "intelligible but incorrect" is rated 6; 11 signifies "accurate but delayed and incomplete." The scheme draws attention to degrees of failure and to the nature of a fault. It is sensitive to improvements from session to session.

Certain profile shapes suggest the presence of specific kinds of brain dysfunction and their severity, others are suggestive of nonphysical disorders, and still others are characteristic of malingerers (who may be making a case for compensation). Decades of clinical experience have indicated the likely rate of recovery from each type of disorder and the suitability of alternative treatments at each stage of recovery. (Beside the point from the standpoint of measurement but of interest nonetheless: the tasks have been automated for computer delivery. The patient can practice on a prescribed task; he is sufficiently aware of the speed and adequacy of his response that he benefits from the trials. This not only extends treatment far beyond what the therapist's time permits, but offers help to patients in remote areas who can visit a therapist only infrequently.)

Sternberg (in Glaser & Bond, 1981) has suggested that the payoff for testing from the current research on processes is likely to be a microanalytic battery adapted from laboratory measures of elements within perception, memory, and so on. If that were to come to pass, it would be belated vindication for the Wundtian approach. I do not regard such a development as likely (nor does Carroll, 1980). Tasks low in a hierarchy cover narrow domains but—even in a Porch subtest—numerous processes affect any one task. Tests of elementary processes have a role to play—in audiometry, for example, and in neurological workups. But as I see it, Porch's microanalysis pays off just because it is based on long study of the field of application. I note also that the Schorr study of Block Design (p. 308) grew out of an established clinical use of the test. Microanalytic tests that contribute to the teaching (for example) of mathematical reasoning will not, I think be borrowings from the psychological laboratory. They will be invented by someone who has studied the errors learners make and has devised instructional techniques to help them.

Glaser (1977, Chap. 5) presents several examples of primary-school teaching procedures in which lessons on microskills are linked to tests of highly specific processes. A test on a certain element may be given every week (or oftener) until the child demonstrates proficiency and is routed to a nex mix of lessons. The tasks include aspects of fluid ability (figural analysis, for example) as well as conventional skills such as letter naming. On educational microanalysis, see also page 364.

Even more detailed in their adaptive processes are some computer programs now being developed that act as tutors (Glaser & Bassok, 1989). In teaching students to prove geometric theorems, for example, the tutor keeps track of which rules, checks, and search principles a student has command of and chooses a next problem that pushes him to add just one new subskill to that repertoire. An account of other recent successes, and a projection of possibilities, is given by Bunderson et al., in Linn, 1989a.

19. *According to a retest study (over an interval of a week or so), s.e.m. for a PICA subtest score is about 0.8. [The subtest score is the average of the item scores, hence is on a 1-to-16 scale.] How adequate is this degree of accuracy, for the intended uses of PICA?*

Chapter
11

Personnel Selection

11A. What should an investigator take into account in choosing a criterion for an employment test?

11B. If a firm plans to carry out a full tryout before adopting a selection plan, what can job analysis contribute?

11C. An investigator who tries out ten predictors on present employees might retain all those that correlate with the criterion, form the weighted sum that gives the best prediction, and thereafter hire the persons who score highest on that composite. What are the limitations of this approach?

11D. Explain why a low selection ratio enables a test of modest validity to pick far more good workers than bad.

11E. If applicants belonging to one race score higher on an employment test than members of another, why do psychologists not take this as proof of bias? What could be evidence of unfair discrimination in hiring?

Abbreviations in this chapter: ACT for American College Testing Program; EEOC for Equal Employment Opportunity Commission; ETS for Educational Testing Service; GATB for the General Aptitude Test Battery, including scores V for Verbal and N for Number; MCT for Mechanical Comprehension Test; PDRI for Personnel Decisions Research Institute; UFG for Uniform Federal Guidelines.

ORIENTATION

On the surface, this chapter is about selection of employees, and it does cover such decisions as thoroughly as one chapter can. But readers not interested in business management will find much of the chapter useful. Selection in education and the military adopts similar logic and faces similar challenges. Likewise, the screening activities of mental health professionals resemble selection, and such topics as the combining of test scores apply directly to clinical tests. The final topic, equity in selection, merits close study by anyone concerned with social issues.

Your personal aims will determine how much you want to take away from the first two sections, on planning for selection. All readers will, I hope, come to appreciate the difference between thorough professional work and a superficial procedure. Readers who expect to engage in selection ought to become aware of sensible ways to carry out each of the steps. I flag for attention Figure 11.1, one of the most illuminating pieces of research in this book. The section on two examples is a concrete extension of the first section. The PDRI work demonstrates how the many steps dovetail. Believing that multiple aptitudes are needed by programmers, the developers of CPAB applied traditional techniques for assembling the best indicators into a composite score. Think especially about why certain tests were discarded; they were not bad tests of their kinds.

In what follows, the short subsection headed "What level of validity ...?" deserves close attention. The ideas help in deciding when selection testing is appropriate. The subsection on adjustments reviews and reinforces messages from Chapters 5 and 6.

Validity generalization (introduced in Chapter 10) is of more concern to industrial psychologists than to other test users. Most readers can concentrate on the points of agreement listed on page 436 and the few paragraphs that follow.

The section on multiple predictors presents three key ideas: weighted composites, "pattern" interpretation, and cross-validation. You should understand the intent of each approach. The short section on classification decisions bears on assigning pupils, vocational choices, and clinical diagnosis, as well as military classification. Digest it.

As a minimum, the section on fairness will teach you how complicated the question is and what subtopics ought to be considered in setting policy. You will probably have to reread this, and perhaps refer to earlier parts of the book, before everything in the summary table is clear in your mind. The seriousness of the topic warrants the effort. (If I had made the topic seem simple I would have been misleading you.)

DEVELOPING A SELECTION PROCEDURE

Establishing a sound selection program is not easy. When a firm wants to fill Job X, it would be convenient if the boss could look in a test catalog, find a test labeled "Test of Aptitude for Job X," and begin choosing among applicants on the basis of the test scores. But tests with similar names measure different things, and sometimes the test intended to predict Job X predicts less well than a test made for another purpose. A job demands many abilities, so more than one test may be needed. And, on the other hand, it is pointless to test what all applicants can do or can learn quickly on the job.

The ideal system matches person and job, personnel workers say. This process calls for more than sorting; changes in the person and in the job may be necessary. Sound management integrates selection with recruitment of applicants, design of jobs, training, organization of teams, performance appraisal, staff development, promotion and transfer, and so on. Having plenty of applicants increases the contribution selection can make. Improving training or reducing turnover reduces the importance of selection. Another "system" aspect is the extent to which misuses of predictive information undercut validity. On this and other realities of selection practice, see Thayer's (1977) history of what is now called the Career Profile (p. 510).

Note that whereas the term "selection" suggests an accept/reject decision *by the institution*, the applicant also makes judgments about his suitability and probable satisfaction with the job. Processes of recruitment, selection, and assignment, therefore, can profitably contain a large element of guidance ("job previews").

The *Principles for the Validation and Use of Personnel Selection Procedures* (see p. 148) advise psychologists to devote considerable initial thought to the characteristics of the job and the criteria so as to decide what kinds of tests are promising (Society, 1987). Although less-reflective work can produce an acceptable, defensible selection plan, balanced analysis reduces cost and generates greater understanding. This chapter gives much space to criterion-oriented methods, just because there is an elaborate lore to communicate. A user of selection procedures who will not carry out follow-up studies should nonetheless know the logic of validation. Understanding how to determine the suitability of a selection plan helps her judge how much to trust a procedure and helps her defend her practices.

Data gathering typically starts after a number of tests have been chosen for tryout. The study finds out how well each of them predicts success. Traditional selection research can be outlined in eight steps:

1. Analyzing the job to form hypotheses about characteristics making for success or failure.
2. Determining that a study will produce adequately persuasive evidence at an acceptable cost.
3. Choosing (or devising) tests expected to measure some or all of the listed characteristics.
4. Administering the tests to workers already on the job or to new applicants.

5. Collecting reports on the adequacy of these workers.
6. Analyzing how test scores and information on the worker's background relate to success on the job.
7. Devising an operational selection plan.
8. Compiling later data, regularly or periodically, to check on the continuing soundness of the plan.

Step 2 is important, but it can be disposed of in a few words. Sometimes there are so few vacancies that it would take years to compile stable statistics; sometimes no way is found to collect trustworthy criterion data (e.g., because employees are scattered); and so on. A selection procedure then has to be defended by a wholly indirect argument.

Job Analysis

Analysis of a job seeks to identify personal qualities that contribute to or limit success. The search is for KSAOs, the trade jargon says, referring to knowledge, skills, abilities, and "other characteristics" (including attitudes and habits). Job analysis can be systematic but not machinelike. The analyst brings psychological theory and her own insight to bear in developing a theory of the job. Several styles of job analysis have been developed (Dunnette, 1976; McCormick, 1979); they vary in cost and in the degree of expertise required of the analyst. Experimental comparisons do not show one technique to be consistently superior.

A first step is preliminary identification of a job category. "Salesperson," for example, is too broad; it is better to look at "representative of a drug firm who calls on physicians." Research engineers may differ from development engineers, word processors from clerk typists. When jobs prove to be similar, the ultimate selection plan may apply to a broad category such as "general clerical tasks" (see Pearlman, 1980).

The job analyst's report should be specific. She should not state that successful workers have "mechanical ability"; she should specify to the level of "knowledge of and ability to apply principles of gears," or "speed in routine two-handed manipulation, not involving much finger dexterity or adaptation." Such definitions guide the search for a directly pertinent test.

Fleishman and his associates have developed a list of 52 abilities that fit into task descriptions and have also developed rating scales to record how much demand a task makes for each of these. The task being analyzed is assigned a number between 1 and 7; reference points give meaning to the scale numbers for both raters and recipients of the information. The Arm-Hand Steadiness scale, for example, has these anchor points (Fleishman & Quaintance, 1984, p. 469):

Cut facets in diamonds 6.3
Thread a needle 4.1
Light a cigarette 1.7

Observing workers' motions and analyzing the cues and signals to which the worker responds suggest relevant perceptual or motor abilities. The analyst asks just what superior workers do differently and what difficulties newly hired workers have in learning the job. Reports from other firms help.

Direct observation is necessarily limited in scope, and analysts therefore rely on informants. But supervisors' remarks about what is important are usually vague and incomplete. Instead of asking about broad traits, job analysts ask about acts.

Analysts often employ a version of the "critical incident" technique (Fivars, 1980; Flanagan, 1954). An informant familiar with the job is asked to think of an individual who has done excellently on the job and then to recall one particular incident that showed this person's superiority. The informant then recalls a poor performer, perhaps one who had to be discharged, and the incident that led to the final verdict of unsuitability. The incidents are only one stage removed from field observation, as can be seen in these examples of good and poor performance from one of the earliest reports (Preston, 1948):

> This officer was instructed to land his P-80 on runway 15. He pedaled on the right runway but lined up to land on runway 9. He was told to go around and line up and land on runway 15 again. This time he overshot and had to go around. He was getting dangerously low on fuel so I personally talked him around the pattern, putting him on his down-wind leg, and instructed him when to turn on base. I asked him if he had runway 15 spotted and he said "Roger." After acknowledging, he flew right by runway 15 and almost "spun-in" trying to turn in on runway 9. Being low on fuel, I told him to go ahead and land. He came in hot and ran off the end of the runway.

> In meeting and acting as a pilot for general officers this lieutenant has brought favorable comment upon himself through the accomplishment of the mission. One specific case, when, through no fault of his own, an aircraft was allowed to depart without a retired Major General on board. Immediately upon being confronted by the general—a rather crusty old bird—he, without calling on me or any other superior, arranged for his departure to the original destination in time to overtake his original aircraft.

In one version (Dunnette, 1976, p. 490), the informants are brought together in a workshop where remarks of one participant can trigger the memory of another, and ultimately hundreds of incidents pile up. The incidents are then sorted. In summarizing incidents on performance of naval officers, 13 categories were used, including training of units and individuals, handling stressful situations, and fairness with subordinates. The incidents gave concreteness to such qualities as "fairness to subordinates."

Although recalled incidents provide richly suggestive data, the method is not truly objective. If the folklore of the business says that truck drivers must have stamina but need not be very bright, the informant is likely to bring to mind incidents where stamina counted and to forget the drivers who made themselves valuable by recognizing mix-ups in delivery orders.

1. *List aptitudes that might enter into one of the following: making pie dough; learning to use a word processor; driving a taxi.*
2. *If someone should try to define the psychological requirements for success in college faculty positions, can all such positions be analyzed together? If not, what would be an appropriately narrow category?*
3. *What practical conditions would a department store chain consider in deciding whether a published test for salespersons in general is more suitable than a separate test for salespersons in a given department?*
4. *Skeptics have suggested that a qualified psychologist, looking into the job briefly, may do as well in devising test batteries and criteria as can be done after an expensive formal analysis (Levine et al., 1980). What are the costs of accepting this as a policy?*

Choice of Tests for Tryout

The investigator next seeks ways to appraise relevant characteristics. Perhaps the abilities the job seems to demand are measured in published tests. Not every test with a relevant name will be suitable; for example, the difficulty of the test may not fit the usual educational level of applicants. If the job calls for an ability that no test on the shelf matches, it may be better to construct a new test than to obtain a pale image of the ability from an indirect measure. When time and cost permit the development of a work sample covering important job elements, validity typically is better than that of off-the-shelf tests (Asher & Sciarrino, 1974).

Information need not come from tests. Grade records are considered in academic predictions, and work history in decisions about employment. Tests play a particularly prominent role in selection for entry level jobs just because past activities are not directly relevant. Work history is usually appraised informally through an interview, but it can be reduced to scorable variables. Thus Hough (1984) describes an adaptation of the critical-incident approach. Candidates for advanced responsibilities (from outside the organization or inside) are asked to describe incidents in their own work histories that illustrate their highest level of performance to date on certain dimensions. Attorneys, for example, are asked to describe incidents of "planning and organizing" and "oral communications and assertive advocacy." Asking for names of associates who can confirm each such account discourages distortion. Systematic scoring of the incidents permits validating the relevance of the dimensions just as test scores are validated.

Some studies try collections of heterogeneous items, most commonly biographical ("biodata"; Owens, in Dunnette, 1976; see also p. 439). Questions touch on work and educational experience, hobbies, athletic background, social activities, and home conditions. A "merit key" counts up the answers associated with success in a certain kind of job. For example, a firm may find that its satisfactory office managers typically had 1 to 2 years of education beyond high school—not more. Then an office manager key would assign one point to that educational level and zero to any other. In former times, weights were often based purely on statistical associations. Today not many psychologists would favor counting "played in a football league" in favor of an applicant for a police job even if (among males) that does correlate with on-the-job ratings; logical as well as empirical justification is wanted (Pace & Schoenfeldt, 1977; Wernimont & Campbell, 1968). Some life history questions are not proper bases for selection because they introduce bias. Experiences most familiar to persons who grew up in a well-to-do family probably should not be counted even if they correlate with a criterion.

5. *If keys were to be built for the following roles, in which would it be proper to count foreign travel experience as a positive sign? (Assume that the item correlates moderately with each criterion.)*
   a. *TV newscaster*
   b. *Computer programmer*
   c. *Life insurance salesperson*

6. *The direct cost of clerical turnover in a bank can be more than 1000 dollars per instance. Application blank information was scored by counting items on which long-tenure and short-tenure (female) employees differed. Applicants were assigned lower scores when they had these characteristics: between ages 20 and 25; mother worked; no family responsibilities; attended college; record of frequent job change (Robinson, 1972). Is it fair to eliminate otherwise qualified employees on these grounds?*

Experimental Trial

Unfortunately, in many instances tests that psychologists considered relevant have proved to be of no value in selection (Parry, 1968). A tryout of proposed procedures and rules *before the plan is made operational* is the best way to arrive at a superior plan and assess its effectiveness. Ideally, one tests typical *applicants*, hires them without considering their scores, and observes the correspondence of test scores to success. When the job analyst suggests that Test X will eliminate weaker prospects, the boss would prefer to install the test and benefit from it at once, not to withhold judgment during weeks or even years of investigation. A common compromise is to eliminate applicants who are poor prospects and then to determine predictor-criterion relations within the group of high scorers who are hired.

During World War II, U.S. Army Air Corps psychologists thought it so important to demonstrate the greater level of validity in an unselected group that they chose 1300 eligible recruits at random and sent them through training. They made this investment to pin down evidence on validity, although they knew that a large fraction would fail (DuBois, 1947; see also p. 432). Test scores were sealed up until the experiment was complete so that they could not influence trainers and raters. The trainees' success matched the predictions well enough to convince the generals to take test scores seriously in the future. Evidence of the same kind can be obtained less expensively by hiring just a few of those who satisfy most requirements but who score below the recommended cutoff on the tests. Again, no one is to be told the test scores. Later criterion data will make evident whether the scores give a useful early warning.

Experimental trial has practical limits. Neither the employer nor the public wants unscreened workers in responsible positions. The employer tied by seniority rules will properly refuse to hire low scorers that the firm cannot get rid of. Fortunately, within a group that has been subjected to some screening, sufficient differences remain to indicate whether scores relate to job performance, so one can try the instruments on present employees instead of applicants.

Comparing current rankings of employees with scores on a test they take now is a concurrent validation. Under some circumstances concurrent correlations agree with what a predictive design would report (Barrett et al., 1981; Schmitt et al., 1984). Such agreement is to be expected when all of the following are true:

1. One sample is not more restricted than the other.
2. The abilities under test matured prior to the testing.
3. In the predictive study either the time between testing and criterion measurement was rather short *or* little was done to improve job proficiency in the predictive sample.

A concurrent correlation can falsely make validity look bad. Workers are lost as time passes, and they tend to be the ones who cannot handle the job. A study carried out on survivors does not credit the test for its ability to identify likely dropouts. Also, higher ratings go mostly to workers with seniority. Workers out of school for a long time tend to score poorly on a written test, which pulls test scores out of line with the ratings. The validity of the test might be fine for current applicants of uniform age. Interpreting concurrent evidence, then, embraces assumptions that should be examined closely. Doing without a predictive trial on a full-range sample is easiest to justify when a test is supported by tryouts elsewhere.

7. *Suppose that an employer sets a cutting score on a test and puts the rule into use without tryout. What harm can result from this, assuming that the test has some degree of validity?*

8. *Could a concurrent study report good validity when a predictive study would find little validity?*

The Criterion

After collecting predictor data, the experimenter waits for evidence on job performance to ripen. In due time, data on success are obtained. Ideally, the criterion (or set of criteria) would cover all aspects of the job in which there are economically or socially important differences in work-ers' contributions. Partial criteria are acceptable, but imbalance is not; history speaks badly of generals who win all their battles yet lose cam-paigns by reluctance to stand and fight.

A bad criterion may make inappropriate tests look good. Tests that predict training criteria differ from those that best predict job perfor-mance, the former putting more stress on verbal and reasoning abilities. The fault probably lies in the typically verbal nature of both training and posttest for even essentially nonverbal jobs. Norman Frederiksen (1981) calls this "the *real* test bias" because the overly verbal training criterion is a barrier for less educated applicants who could do the job itself.

Frederiksen refers to U.S. Navy experience such as Figure 11.1 re-counts. When grades on ship's engine operation were based on instruc-tors' judgments, predictor tests did not correlate well with them. When grades were based on highly valid achievement tests, the classification tests were satisfactory predictors. The subjective judgments were most strongly related to academic and intellectual abilities. The valid crite-rion of job knowledge and skill was predicted best by mechanical knowl-edge and aptitude. The valid achievement tests asked the sailors to do

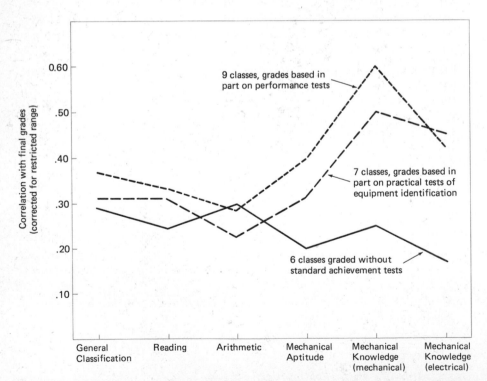

Figure 11.1. **Predictive validity with three sets of criteria.** (*Source*: Stuit, 1947, p. 307.)

what they would have to do on shipboard, handling objects and not words (see also Table 5.8). When the new criterion was made the official standard, the training itself changed. The instructors stopped lecturing on theory and set the trainees to practicing the shipboard tasks.

The criterion was at fault when tests given to journeyman electricians correlated zero with supervisor ratings. After the supervisors were trained by means of videotapes to observe accurately and to communicate what they observed, the test validities jumped to around 0.5 (Pursell et al., 1980). In general, supervisor ratings agree poorly with "results-oriented" criteria; Heneman (1986) places the typical correlation at 0.27.

Ratings are much used because they are cheap to collect. Performance measures are likely to be more meaningful. The U.S. Army has installed about 900 mastery tests of occupational specialties. These "hands-on" performance tests were introduced, in the spirit of Frederiksen's observation, in order to "drive" training. The data are useful also in setting cut scores for assignments and in evaluation of training (Vineberg & Joyner, in Landy et al.,1983).

In some firms, the excellence of employees can be judged by the rate at which they are promoted or given greater responsibility. In one such follow-up, 2 years after assessment, the progress criterion correlated 0.4 with the predictor whereas supervisor's rating correlated negligibly (Meyer, 1987).

Judgmental criteria become contaminated if the judge knows the predictor data. A supervisor may rate a worker higher than performance warrants because the supervisor knows the worker has had considerable experience. A therapist may be quicker to note signs of progress in the patient whose intake record included a favorable test report. Such influences spuriously raise the validity coefficient and sometimes cause an irrelevant measure to appear valid. The only way to prevent contamination is to keep predictor data secret until criterion scores have been collected.

Time Considerations   There is always the possibility that good short-term predictors have limited long-run validity, or vice versa. Correlations change in puzzling ways as the time between test and criterion measurement increases. Admission tests correlate with first-year college grades. They correlate much less with grade average in the junior and senior years, partly because students spread out into courses that vary in difficulty and in grading standards (Humphreys & Taber, 1973). In some studies relating college success to career success, correlations have increased with time. Employees entering with good school histories did no better in the first 10 years than those with middling records; subsequently, those who had done well in college pulled ahead (Roe, 1963). It seems likely that the later, fuller record is the better criterion.

Helmreich et al. (1986) report limited evidence of a "honeymoon effect." A job performance criterion for travel agents collected in the 3 months following training showed a small s.d. and negligible correlation with motivational variables; criterion data collected later had a larger s.d. and the correlations rose to 0.3. The suggested interpretation: People are willing to play a role that is not natural for them when new on the job; then they relapse.

Sackett et al. (1988) make a related point. Many criteria assess maximum performance, but productivity depends on typical performance. Typical speed of supermarket checkout clerks was assessed, without their knowledge, by analyzing records from the cash register. Maximum speed was assessed by presenting a number of loaded carts to be rung up; the clerk knew this was a test. Both scores were reliable, but they correlated only 0.14. It is a good bet that motivational predictors are more relevant to typical performance than to a maximum-performance criterion.

Hypothetically, there is an "ultimate criterion" that fully represents the outcome the selector desires. The medical school would, if it could, judge the success of its graduates by their lifetime contribution to the health of the communities where they practice. This contribution probably depends more on personality than on intellectual level; it certainly is not closely related to grades in biochemistry. For practical reasons, however, medical school grades are likely to be the criterion in evaluating selection plans of medical schools.

One effort to get a near-ultimate criterion was made during the Korean War. Observers and interviewers went to the theater of combat to obtain information on performance; these data were supplemented by ratings from field commanders. A test battery developed to predict performance in training and in maneuvers correlated 0.27 with these peacetime criteria, but only 0.17 with the combat criterion. A battery designed to fit the combat criterion correlated 0.36 with both training and combat criteria. The important difference was that the combat-valid battery included a personality questionnaire (Willemin et al., 1958).

Multiple Criteria In place of the single "ultimate criterion," it is more realistic and more illuminating to think of criteria of different kinds, becoming observable at different times (P. C. Smith, in Dunnette, 1976). The more criteria the test is compared against, the more light is shed on selection policy.

There can be many patterns of success in a position. Consider teachers, for example. One develops into a friend and counselor for youth; one stimulates independent thinking in the few brightest students; one overcomes the blockings that cause failure among weak students. To try to score these performances on a single scale is pointless; both information *and* predictability are lost. With diverse and dependable criteria, it is appropriate to find out what predicts each one.

Psychological Interpretation When criterion data become available, the time arrives for a serious effort to understand why newly hired employees succeed or fail. Far too often validation research is treated purely as a formal statistical check on a fixed hypothesis. The psychologist ought to be trying to understand the processes that generated the data, by every available means. When a worker is rated far below (or above) what was predicted, it may make sense to interview him and his supervisor or even to observe him at work. Likewise when predictions are confirmed, an effort at explanation may still improve the characterization of the job. Sometimes a variable that proved to be important was weakly measured; if so, the set of tests can be revised. A way of altering the training to overcome a weakness may emerge—or a plan for reducing the emphasis supervisors place on qualities irrelevant to production. (Similar comments apply to clinical, correctional, and educational predictions and also to evaluations of treatments in those fields.)

9. *In each of the following situations, trace how contamination might occur, and suggest an improved procedure to avoid it.*
    a. *Tests for selecting salespersons are being tried experimentally. Because they are thought to be valid, the results are given to the sales manager for guidance in assigning territories to the salespersons in the experimental group. After a year of trial, each salesperson is judged by the amount of sales in relation to the normal amount for the assigned territory.*
    b. *Flight instructors' ratings are used as a basis for promotion from primary to advanced training. It is desired to check the validity of these ratings as predictors of success in advanced training. Advanced training is taken at the same field with a different instructor, whose judgment supplies the criterion.*

10. *In industry, does one wish to predict an employee's maximum performance (proficiency) or typical behavior? Criteria of both types are in use; illustrate that fact.*

11. *List several criteria that might be appropriate for judging branch managers of an equipment firm. Branches are responsible for both sales and service.*

12. *PACE is a general-verbal ability measure formerly used as an entrance examination for the professional civil service. (Because minority applicants tended to fare badly on the test, it was forced out of use.) One validity study correlated PACE with three criteria for customs inspectors; the coefficients were 0.6, 0.6, and 0.0 (Trattner, 1979). The first two criteria were a job information test and a work sample where the person judged what to do in situations presented by videotape. Both of these were designed in the light of a job analysis. The third criterion was a supervisor's rating. (Levin, 1989, evaluates the criteria in this study.)*
        Account for the discrepant validities
    a. *on the assumption that PACE is valid for job performance.*
    b. *on the assumption that PACE has little validity for the job.*

Translating Predictions into Decisions

Predictor scores have to be translated into decisions according to some plan. The plan describes how scores are to be combined across tests or subtests, how tests are to be combined with nontest information, and what decision will be made for any given combination of facts. For the moment, we consider decisions based on a single test score.

When the number of vacancies to be filled is fixed, the obvious strategy is to rank applicants and fill vacancies from the top of the list. If there is no limit on the number to be selected, one could, in principle, set a "cut score" and reject all persons below it. For nonroutine jobs it is more usual to examine files individually rather than to let the decision rest entirely on the scores. I can best explain the logic of decisions, however, by speaking as if only the scores are considered and assuming that a select-from-the-top rule will be applied in a strictly impersonal manner. (Also, I take as an example a data set that is too small for making policy).

The cutting score is determined from the scatter diagram or experience table relating scores to a criterion. Considering what fraction of persons at each score level are expected to perform adequately, the interpreter sets an acceptable level of risk and fixes the critical score accordingly. Figure 11.2 shows how engineering marks at the University of Idaho in a certain year corresponded to aptitude scores. A grade average below 2.0 was regarded as unsatisfactory. The probabilities plotted in Figure 11.3 led the investigator to set the critical score at 85. This sug-

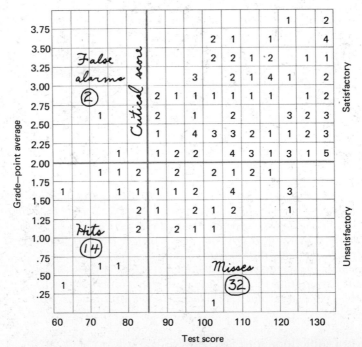

Figure 11.2. **Engineering grades tabulated against a predictor.** (*Source*: Sessions, 1955.)

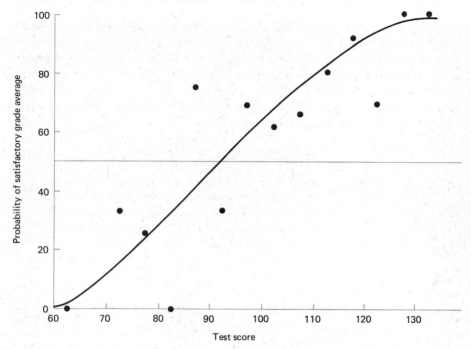

Figure 11.3. **Success in engineering as a function of test score.** Dots show what proportion of students in each column of Figure 11.2 had grade averages of 2.00 or better.

gested that in subsequent classes, applicants scoring below 85 should be discouraged.[1]

One method of evaluating such a selection rule divides the predicted failures into "hits" (actual failures) and "false alarms." Among those accepted by the cut score, the ones who turn out unsatisfactory are "misses." Finally, there are those who succeed as predicted, ordinarily much the largest fraction of the sample. (We could call them "hits" also; but there is a tradition of counting the persons flagged as problems. In medical research, "true positives" for syphilis have that disease and "false positives" were wrongly given that label by the diagnostic test.)

Among the 147 engineering students, 16 failures were predicted by a cut at 85. Two predictions were false alarms. Among the 131 persons above that cut, 32 did poorly in school (misses).

Setting a cut score requires a value judgment. A cut at 85 flags applicants who have fewer than 38 chances in 100 of doing adequate work. If

---

[1]The trend line in Figure 11.3 is curved. That is logically necessary, with an upper limit of 100 per cent and a lower limit of zero. But you can see that a straight line could fit most of the points.

the policy is to challenge those whose chances are below 70 per cent, the cut score goes up to 105. Another policy might leave the choice to the student unless the probability of failure is very high. Then a cut score of 75 might be set to rule out those who have only one chance in five of surviving. The administrator who lowers the cut score gets fewer false alarms and more misses.

Some of the arguments that push the cut score downward (accepting more students who will fail) are these:

- A "failure" is not a total loss. The student will gain much from a year of college, even if he then drops out. If admitted, he will become worth more to society because of whatever he learns.
- An applicant refused admission may be a total loss to higher education. If he is enrolled, further investigation can perhaps identify deficiencies to be removed or can help him work out a plan in which he has a greater chance of success.
- When the country needs engineers badly, it is important to process even low-grade ore to get a few extra graduates.
- Tests are fallible. A decision to admit is really a decision to continue testing by considering class performance. There is no way to continue testing one who is rejected. Erroneous decisions to reject cannot be corrected.

The arguments for a high critical score include these:

- Accepting someone who is unlikely to succeed wastes educational resources. He overloads the staff, and takes time that might better be spent on more promising students. His presence in the group lowers the level of discussion and thus robs the better students.
- The person who is going to fail is better off facing the fact at once rather than after a year. He can use the year to get started in a less demanding institution or in a job.

In industry, a particularly desirable approach is to screen at two or three stages rather than to promise a permanent job at the time of first hiring. Eliminating a fraction of those initially selected, after further information comes in from training sessions or work as probationer, greatly reduces the cost of initial misjudgments.

13. *In Figures 11.2 and 11.3, what cut score would identify students with one chance in three of failing?*

14. *The following is taken from a letter to* The New York Times:
    "I submit that 'slaughter on the highway' will continue until state licensing authorities recognize some simple facts: To drive a car on today's highways demands a rather complex set of sensori-motor skills. These skills are 'normally' distributed; i.e., some folks have them, some do not. Instruments are available to measure these skills. Authorities have responsibility to see that such instruments are used before licensing."

a. *What degree of validity should be required before tests are used as proposed?*

b. *If scores are normally distributed, how should the cutoff score be fixed?*

15. *A screening test is applied to schoolchildren to identify those in poor mental health so that they can be given intensive study by the school psychologist. What factors argue for a high cut score? What factors argue for a low cut score?*

16. *Which is to be preferred, false alarms or misses, in each of these situations?*

   a. *A company puts newly hired control room operators for a nuclear power plant through an expensive training program; success cannot be observed until the end of the course.*

   b. *Candidates for admission to teacher training are screened for competence in arithmetic and use of language.*

   c. *It is important to hire skilled sheet metal workers to fill vacancies during a time of tight labor supply. Workers cannot be trained on the job.*

   d. *In inducting soldiers, a test is used to determine which recruits are too dull to be useful to the service.*

TWO EXAMPLES

Selecting Power Plant Operators

Much selection research consists of small and partial studies, but research in a large organization or an industry-wide project can be thorough and substantial. I describe here a study representative of excellent contemporary personnel research (which is not to say that identical tactics would be followed by other experts). In a "cooperative study," the electric utility industry asked the Personnel Decisions Research Institute to develop a selection system for operators at various levels in electric power plants (hydro, fossil, and nuclear). For convenience I label it the PDRI study. Data were obtained from more than 70 firms and thousands of individuals. Even this 3-year study with good support compromised, first, by limiting the study to persons already employed. The summary volume (Dunnette *et al.*, 1982) describes four phases of work.

Identifying Job Requirements   The following steps were taken to identify variables:

- Literature review, covering "human factors" research on all process control jobs, and studies conducted specifically in power plants (often drawn from within-company memoranda). A schematic outline identified broad functions such as "vigilance," and KSAOs were listed beneath these ("auditory acuity," "compulsivity," etc.).
- The PDRI staff read job descriptions, then visited plants and talked with operators. Lists of tasks so identified went into a form

on which supervisors indicated requirements of particular jobs. Supervisors also filled out McCormick's Position Analysis Questionnaire. The importance of functions and KSAOs in each job was rated.

- A procedure akin to factor analysis grouped occupations with similar requirements and separated those that differed (e.g., turbine operators were separated from boiler operators). Two dozen abilities and personal characteristics emerged as seemingly important in some or all categories.
- Because emotional stability seemed important, workshops were held to define the concept by critical-incident techniques. Experts were asked to suggest screening methods for use in hiring and in periodic checkups.
- Judgments as to the dollar value of good performance. The difference in payoff between a 15th percentile worker and a 50th percentile worker is great in some jobs, modest in some others. (Quality in one role in a nuclear plant was judged to be 5.6 times as important as quality in the same job in a fossil plant.)

Developing Predictor and Criterion Measures   The second phase began with a search for measuring procedures.

- A literature search was made with the aid of *Mental Measurements Yearbooks* and other sources. Fifteen diverse tests considered adequately reliable and relevant were chosen, some from a commercially distributed set of aptitude tests, and some from the ETS kit.
- Where it was desired to match more exactly the content of power plant jobs, PDRI developed new instruments, e.g., for numerical ability and for mechanical comprehension.
- Biographical items and self-descriptive statements describing personal characteristics were borrowed from older instruments or written afresh. This became an Opinion and Attitude Questionnaire (OAQ) of more than 500 items, split between two packages.
- Criteria were derived from supervisors' statements. Statements relevant to emotional stability ("willingly admits own mistakes") were assembled into a rating form that could be scored for six aspects of personality. A more elaborate rating form (Figure 15.2) dissected job performance.

Field Trial   Consideration of available materials and time reduced the collection to 17 ability tests, OAQ, and supplementary forms. A plan for choosing cases was drawn up, with careful attention to random sampling of nonminority males and oversampling of minorities and females to obtain more stable data on these subgroups. Workshops were held to train test administrators and raters. For each person tested, ratings were filled out by two or three supervisors, working independently.

Statistical analyses examined the reliability of scores and ratings, the overlap among tests, and the range of workers' abilities within job categories. Factor analysis reduced the ratings to a few composites, and validity coefficients were determined within jobs. Scoring scales for the OAQ were developed. Elaborate studies were made to determine which jobs differed sufficiently from the others to justify distinct selection batteries. A check was made to ensure that test criterion relations found in workers from the mainstream held up in minority samples. And ratings were checked for possible race bias, particularly by considering workers who had one white rater and one minority rater. (Some bias was found.)

Constructing and Evaluating the Final Plan   The staff devised several possible packages of tests and used the statistics to evaluate how each such package would perform, considering not only its screening effectiveness but its cost and the stability of relationships across jobs.

PDRI recommended three cognitive batteries as worthy alternatives; they differ in length and makeup but have similar (and satisfactory) validities. Also, there is a score from biodata and one from self-reports on emotional stability.

To demonstrate the overall effectiveness of the battery, a possible decision rule was translated into an estimate of the financial return to the industry if it were to adopt the selection procedure. Expectancy charts were produced for various kinds of plants and jobs. Recommendations were made regarding practical use of the several scores in various circumstances a company might face.

17. *In what ways might the relevance of the PDRI study to future operations have benefited or suffered from the following features of the design?*
   a. *Multiple ratings on each case were collected.*
   b. *Test administrators were given a common training.*
   c. *Comparatively few poor employees were found within the group of subjects. (Many of these had survived on the job for decades.)*
   d. *The OAQ form carried the statement that replies would be held in confidence and used for research only.*
18. *Match the eight steps listed at the start of the chapter with the four phases of the PDRI outline. Do the lists overlap completely?*

An Aptitude Test for Programmers

The PDRI report said comparatively little about the content and relative usefulness of its tests. For a fuller example of test development, I turn to the Computer Programmer Aptitude Battery (J. M. Palormo; CPAB). This work, carried out on a comparatively small scale with samples of convenience, is much less systematic than the PDRI study.

Learning to write computer programs is hard for some people, and thus it is important to select good prospects for training. The original impetus for CPAB came from the desire of certain firms making computers to help their customers; an inept programmer can make the best system look bad.

The first step was a job analysis that relied in part on earlier research on programmers. This analysis led to a fairly long list of possibly relevant abilities. Because it was not practical to try out all of them, the list was reduced to seven kinds of task. For each task, a large set of trial items was prepared.

The tests investigated were:

- Verbal Meaning. Words were taken from documents advanced programmers have to read, in fields such as business management and systems engineering. Although the programmer's own job is not primarily verbal, the programmer *does* have to communicate with specialists in these related fields.

  This find-the-synonym item illustrates the lowest level of difficulty in the test:[2]

  RECIPIENT   donor   owner   performer   receiver   borrower

- Letter Series, with items as difficult at this:

  s c a g s c d j ___   g   s   c   e   p

- Number Series. Another reasoning task.
- Number Ability (computational tasks). The test taker is often to select a closest approximation—and, to encourage estimating, the test is speeded. A typical item has this character:

  .882% of 576 (approximate):   5   50   70   700

- Reasoning (formulating and interpreting quantitative relationships). Items are generally harder than this specimen:[3]

An office manager ordered a conference table which cost S dollars, a dozen chairs which cost P dollars each, and three bookshelves which cost Y dollars apiece. The total cost of the order in dollars is	$S + P + Y$ $SP + 3Y$ $S + 12P + 3Y$ $S + \dfrac{(P + Y)}{4}$ $S + P + 3Y$

- Ingenuity. A problem is stated, usually referring to an object or machine. The examinee generates a solution; if he hits on the

---

[2]From the *Computer Programmer Aptitude Battery*. Copyright © 1964, 1986, Science Research Associates, Inc. Reprinted by permission.
[3]From the *Computer Programmer Aptitude Battery*. Copyright © 1964, 1986, Science Research Associates, Inc. Reprinted by permission.

keyed answer he can recognize the best response choice, as in this illustrative item:[4]

As part of a manufacturing process, the inside lip of a deep, cup-shaped casting is machine-threaded. The company found that metal chips produced by the threading operation were difficult to remove from the bottom of the casting without scratching the sides. A design engineer was able to solve his problem by having the operation performed

i ___ ___ ___ ___ p	h ___ ___ h
m ___ ___ ___ ___ n	c ___ ___ e
f ___ ___ ___ ___ r	w ___ ___ l
i ___ ___ ___ ___ d	b ___ ___ k
u ___ ___ ___ ___ e	d ___ ___ n

- Diagramming. To test the ability to think systematically about sequences of operation, the items employ flow diagrams similar to Figure 11.4. (Test items are more complex than this warm-up item.) The person is taught the code (e.g., Y implies a "yes" answer). He chooses an entry for each numbered cell. Cell 1, for example, is to be matched with choice C: "Is it the range 3.5 to 4.4 ounces?"

The tryout was conducted with employed programmers, and with supervisor ratings as criteria. The validations were concurrent, as there was no opportunity to test unselected persons entering training. It was exceedingly difficult to obtain a sufficient number of programmers in comparable assignments. A single office or laboratory is likely to employ only a few programmers, and no supervisor knows many of them. Therefore, several small studies were made.

In the best of the initial studies, the seven subtests were given to 186 programmers working at installations within the same corporation. This provided fine data for studying test intercorrelations. A solid criterion (ratings from four or more supervisors, averaged) was available for only 46 cases.

Two decisions were based on these early data. The Ingenuity subtest did not correlate with the criterion. When this was confirmed in other samples, the subtest was dropped. In retrospect, Ingenuity presents problems more concrete than those facing the programmer. Number Series showed some validity, but it was dropped because it correlated strongly with other tests and so added little information. Four of the remaining tests looked promising by both standards: validity and nonduplication. Verbal Meaning did not correlate with the criterion in

---

[4]From the *Flanagan Aptitude Classification Test*, Ingenuity, Form A. Copyright © 1957 by John C. Flanagan. Reprinted by permission of the publisher, Science Research Associates, Inc., Chicago, IL.

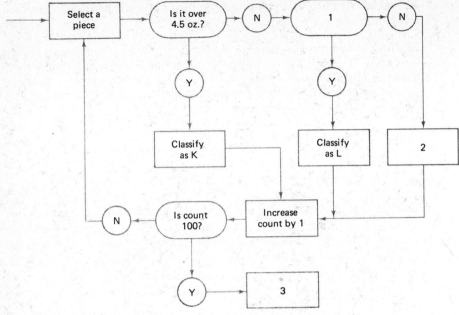

Problem and conditions

A. A company inspects and classifies its products in lots of 100.

B. It is necessary to classify the individual pieces within each lot of 100 into three classes by weight:

Class K— 4.5 oz. or over
Class L— 3.5 to 4.4 oz.
Class M— less than 3.5 oz.

Cell 1. A. Is it less than 3.5 oz.?
         B. Select a piece.
         C. Is it 3.5 to 4.4 oz.?
         D. Classify as M.
         E. Classify as L.

Cell 2. A. Classify as K.
         B. Classification of lot complete.
         C. Select a piece.
         D. Classify as M.
         E. Classify as L.

Cell 3. A. Select a piece.
         B. Classification of lot complete.
         C. Classify lot as K.
         D. Classify lot as L.
         E. Classify lot as M.

Figure 11.4. Diagramming task for prospective programmers. (*Source*: From the Computer Programmer Aptitude Battery. Copyright © 1984, 1986, Science Research Associates, Inc. Reprinted by permission.) (Proportions and typography altered.)

the 46-case sample, but this result was thought to reflect the use of a highly select, well-educated group. These five subtests, then, went into the further trials and eventually into the operational test.

All subtests share a common factor of which Reasoning is the best measure, but Diagramming seems to require a specialized ability, in addition. Because Diagramming appears to be valid, one might wish to use more problems of this type in a future edition of the test.

The first two editions of the test manual urged prospective users to validate the test in their own situations. Such local validation can be illustrated by a study carried out by Perry (cited in the CPAB manual, 1985, p. 6). 114 trainees who had passed the screening procedures already in use took a test battery essentially like CPAB. (Two substitutions of similar subtests were made.) The criterion came from marks in a programming course. Correlations were adjusted statistically (p. 432) to estimate validities in a full-range applicant group. In this sample, education had essentially no predictive value. Diagramming, and two reasoning tests, had validity 0.6–0.7; and a best-weighted composite had validity 0.75. When weights are based on a sample, the coefficient calculated from that sample is inflated (p. 444). Therefore, a second coefficient was obtained from a fresh sample. This best estimate of validity is 0.66.

Verbal and Number scores did not help to predict. Very likely the reason is that almost all the applicants to this firm had completed college. In this instance, retaining all five subtests did no harm, but sometimes a subtest that does not work in a firm's applicant pool will dilute predictive accuracy.

Studies compiled in the third edition of the manual (8 with training criteria and 14 with job ratings) produced the uncorrected correlations summarized in Table 11.1.

Some of the criteria were seriously faulty. In one group of slightly over 40 workers, the test did not correlate with supervisor's rating, but correlated 0.46 with grades assigned during an advanced training course. The rating criterion is suspect because older workers received much higher ratings but had lower test scores. The older workers were highly experienced and were taking more responsibility; this did not mean that they were superior programmers.

The newest CPAB manual (1985) does not recommend local validation, arguing that local samples are usually small and the coefficients poorly determined. Using procedures from Schmidt and Hunter (see p. 434), the publisher's staff estimated the validity for selection situations "in general." The calculation increased each coefficient by compensating for range restriction, criterion unreliability, and test unreliability. Correcting for measuring error in the test forecasts the predictive power of a test that has zero error of measurement—a test that will never be available to decision makers. Therefore, I reduced the developers' estimate to the values in the last column of Table 11.1.

Table 11.1   VALIDITY COEFFICIENTS FOR THE CPAB

Score	Internal consistency reliability	Median correlation with other subtests	Median of actual validities Training	Job	Estimate of generalized validity[a]
Verbal Meaning	.86	.5	.3	.25	.25
Letter Series	.67	.5	.2	.25	.3
Number Ability	.85	.5	.25	.25	.35
Reasoning	.88	.6	.45	.4	.6
Diagramming[b]	[a]	.4	.35	.3	.6
Total			.45	.4	.55

[a]I have lowered values given in the manual; see text. This estimate mixes information from training and job criteria.

[b]A proper estimate for Diagramming is not available. It would have been desirable to compute an alpha coefficient with scores for diagrams as parts, but the developers calculated from responses within diagrams which are not independent. The developers split the speeded tests, administering two separately timed parts; so coefficients for them are not overestimated.

Source: CPAB manual.

19. *According to limited data, nonwhites average lower on CPAB than whites, and criterion scores of blacks at a given score level are not superior to those of whites at the same level. The manual suggests that a firm committed to opportunity for minorities should set a cutting score on the basis of ethnic-group norms. Thus, if whites scoring above 95 are hired (70th percentile of white norms), blacks scoring above 72 (70th percentile of nonwhite norms) would be hired.*
    a. *What do you think? (I discuss such proposals on page 453.)*
    b. *Less educated persons tend to score lower on CPAB. Would you favor a similar use of percentiles for each educational level?*
20. *In 2 of the 22 studies summarized in the CPAB manual, the validity coefficient for Verbal was close to −0.1. How can these negative coefficients be explained?*

INTERPRETING PREDICTIVE VALIDITIES

What Level of Validity Is Acceptable?

As validity coefficients have been presented you have probably been classifying them as "good" or "poor." Many predictors do not seem very satisfactory at first glance. But the fundamental question is, Does the predictor information permit a better judgment than could be made without it—sufficiently better to justify its cost?

Coefficients as low as 0.3 usually imply definite practical value (see

Table 11.3), and measures with even lower validities may improve decisions. One psychologist commented that the test critic who is contemptuous of low positive correlations is quite willing to accept information of no greater dependability when he plays golf or employs a physician. The correlation of golf scores between the first and second 18 holes in championship play is about 0.3, he said, and correlations between two physicians' initial diagnoses are near 0.4.

The personnel psychologist can evaluate a selection device by comparing high- and low-scoring applicants with respect to number of failures in training, average length of training required, rate of turnover, average production, and so on. Such analyses show that tests with validities in the range from 0.3 to 0.5 make a considerable contribution to the efficiency of the institution even though they forecast wrongly for many individuals. (If you go back to Figure 5.3 you can count up the number of high and low criterion scores, with various cut scores and various values of r.)

The significance level of the validity coefficient does *not* tell how useful the test is. Significance levels (e.g., $P < 0.05$) have to do not with worth but with certainty. A good-sized correlation that is not "significant" nonetheless argues for accumulating further experience with the test.

In evaluating a selection test, one should ask the following questions. Each question is so worded that an answer of "no" encourages consideration of tests having relatively low validity.

Are individual differences in job performance or other outcomes fairly small?

Is the number of vacancies so large that a large fraction of the applicants have to be accepted?

Does this test measure an ability that is fairly well covered in information already taken into account in screening?

Is the reliability of the test high? (If not, lengthening the test should raise validity.)

Is the test costly to administer?

Is it feasible to discharge or transfer to other duties workers who turn out to be unsuccessful? That is, can the firm adapt when a favorable prediction "misses"?

The best single rule of thumb for interpreting validity coefficients in selection is Brogden's (1949). Making certain reasonable assumptions, he showed that the benefit from a selection program increases *in proportion to the validity coefficient*. Suppose 40 applicants out of 100 are hired. Take as a baseline the average production of randomly selected workers. An ideal test would pick the 40 applicants who later earn the highest criterion scores; the average production of these workers is the maximum that any selection plan could have pulled from this pool.

A test with validity 0.5 will select workers whose average production is halfway between the base level and the ideal. To be concrete, suppose that the average, randomly selected worker assembles 400 gadgets per day, and the perfectly selected group of workers turns out 600, on the average. Then a test with validity 0.5 will choose a group whose average production is 500 gadgets, and a test of validity 0.2 will select workers with an average production of 440 gadgets. The assumptions underlying Brogden's rule are these:

The job to be performed remains the same, whether workers of high or low ability are selected.

Production (or other measure of benefit) has a linear relation to test score.

Tests of low validity have considerable value when a great surplus of applicants can be recruited, when individual differences in job performance are large, and when small increases in production have a large dollar value.

The benefit from selection depends on the selection ratio, as well as on validity. The *selection ratio* is the proportion of persons tested who are accepted. If there is a large labor supply, the selection ratio can be very low, but when applicants are scarce, the selection ratio is forced up toward 1.00. Even an ideal test does not raise the quality of workers when every applicant must be hired. If the employer can pick and choose, average output can be much improved. Figure 11.5 shows the

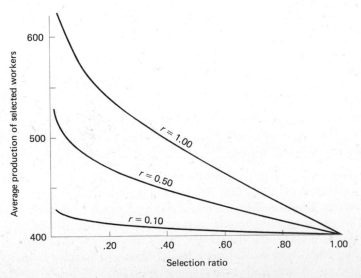

Figure 11.5. **Benefit from selection.**

relation of production to selection ratio for the gadget assemblers. It is assumed that among unselected workers the average production is 400 gadgets, and the standard deviation is 100.

Utility analysis, a method of appraising the economic benefits from selection, is reviewed by Hunter and Schmidt (1981) and by Cascio (1987). Where a worker's contribution can be expressed in dollars, careful accounting might, theoretically, determine the benefit from the selection rule. This, however, proves not to be straightforward because accounting practices embody many judgments (Green & Cascio, 1987).

Current applications follow Hunter and Schmidt in relying on estimates made by managers, as in the PDRI study. The last paragraph of the PDRI report reads as follows (Dunnette et al., 1982, p. 263):

> In effect, it does not seem to be too great a stretch of the imagination to expect a potential annual gain in the neighborhood of $800,000,000 when these selection procedures are adopted by the companies participating in this research project.

Bolder projections have been made. Schmidt et al. (1979) figured that if the selection ratio were 0.2 and the validity of a programmer aptitude test appreciably higher than the validity of the selection procedure previously in use, the test would produce a benefit to the employer of $64,725 per programmer hired. Multiplying this by the number hired, they calculated that if the test had been used to select all the programmers in the American economy, the productivity gain would reach nearly $11 billion.

This projection is a fairy tale. The economy utilizes most of the persons who are trained as programmers, and only the most prestigious firm can reject 80 per cent of those who apply. If 90 per cent of the programmers are hired somewhere, the tests merely give a competitive advantage to those firms that test (when some other firms do not test). A much subtler analysis would be needed to assess the benefit to the whole economy. Essentially, that benefit would come from routing each person in the labor market into the career where he or she could make the greatest contribution, not from creaming off the best workers and discarding the others (Hartigan & Wigdor, 1989).

21. *In one study, the predictive validity of pencil-and-paper tests for selecting persons to be trained as military pilots was 0.64 against an elimination-graduation criterion. The coefficient rose to 0.69 when apparatus tests were added. Is such a small increase worthwhile?*

22. *State employment offices use tests to guide workers into appropriate positions. A very low selection ratio may be used because a particular unemployed worker may be directed into any one of hundreds of job families. In a particular insurance agency, on the other hand, it is necessary to employ about 60 per cent of those who apply for clerical jobs. Are the same tests equally suitable in both situations?*

23. *In which of these situations is there likely to be a fixed number of vacancies, and in which can the decision makers set the critical score as high or low as they judge appropriate?*

  a. *A parole board decides which prisoners may be released.*
  b. *An engineering school admits well-qualified applicants.*
  c. *A school psychologist identifies mentally handicapped children to be placed under a special teacher.*
  d. *A college counseling bureau identifies clients likely to profit from psychotherapy.*

Adjusting Validity Coefficients

In most personnel research, the validity coefficients directly calculated can mislead. Adjustment methods can offset various defects, but they rest on assumptions. Therefore they are dependable in some circumstances and shaky in others. Only an expert can judge, in each particular application, how near an adjusted value is to the true value of the quantity it estimates. Ordinarily, both the original coefficient and the one obtained by formula should be reported. Even though questionable, the adjustments have the important function of warning against face-value interpretations of unadjusted coefficients. Here I take up corrections for restricted range and for error in the criterion. "Shrinkage" corrections fall within a later section on cross-validation.

I have noted repeatedly that a correlation coefficient obtained on a previously screened group will underrate the power of the test for sorting applicants. In the U.S. Army Air Corps, the correlation with the criterion of one test composite for trainees selected by those tests was 0.37. In the completely unscreened sample sent into training for experimental purposes, the coefficient rose to 0.66. A second irrelevant cause of a low validity coefficient is an unreliable criterion (p. 607). Unreliability is to be expected when criteria must be collected inexpensively, under field conditions, with few controls.

Adjustment formulas transform an observed correlation or regression coefficient into an estimate of what would have been found if the study had been made with one or more of these ideal features:

Representative applicants.

A fully reliable criterion.

A fully reliable test.

The formulas most commonly used date back to the turn of the century. One, introduced by Karl Pearson, allows for "restriction of range" (i.e., for preselection). The Pearson formula assumes that one knows how persons who provided complete data differ from the applicant pool (or other population of interest). Recent technical work, by adding assumptions, makes correction possible even when unspecified judgments and self-selection caused some loss of cases (Gross & Fleischman, 1983; Olson & Becker, 1983). Violation of assumptions is a problem with both old and new formulas (Brown et al., 1988). The formulas probably adjust in the right direction, but they can overshoot or undershoot.

Spearman introduced the correction for unreliability that appears on pages 214 and 284. For additional formulas see Jöreskog and Sörbom (1979) and Lord and Novick (1968). This approach, you will recall, recognizes that errors of measurement hold down validity coefficients. The formulas allow us to estimate three correlations:

1. Predictor with true score on criterion
2. True score on predictor with actual criterion
3. True score on predictor with true score on criterion

The second and third can be important sources of insight. Sometimes a second-best predictor is more relevant to the criterion than a measure with a greater validity coefficient; differences in the reliabilities are responsible for the reversal of validities. Because one never has a true predictor score with which to make personnel decisions, corrections 2 and 3 address a hypothetical question. On the other hand, when we want to know how well a predictor works, we do not want errors in the criterion (rater inconsistency, for instance) to lead to an inappropriately discouraging conclusion. So correction 1 is pertinent in evaluating a practical selection plan.

24. *Consider the probable success in industrial jobs of graduates from an engineering school. What characteristics have a restricted range (compared to the entire population of the same age) owing to preselection? What characteristics relevant to the job probably have not been restricted?*

25. *The Flanagan Industrial Tests were validated by collecting test scores and on-the-job criteria. In the analysis for at least one job, the sample was divided into fourths on the criterion, and the two middle groups were discarded. The correlation was calculated from the remaining cases. Why does this procedure give a falsely large coefficient?*

VALIDITY GENERALIZATION

Whoever applies a selection rule is generalizing from the original validity study or studies. As Chapter 5 pointed out, a decision to select this year's law students on the basis of last year's experience requires assumptions about the stability of the local situation.

In a stable environment it does appear safe to generalize from data analyzed in one year to applicants of future years. A follow-up study in many colleges found that a regression equation developed in one year had the same validity over at least the next 4 years (Sawyer & Maxey, 1979). A predictor of law school grades has similar validities in different schools and years (after allowing for statistical fluctuations). Even so, coefficients are appreciably higher in some schools (and years) than in others (Linn et al., 1981).

A far bolder extrapolation is a new user's claim that a test is valid for her on the basis of positive evidence collected elsewhere. Employers would like to rely on the validation research others have reported, because it takes time and money to study their own workers in each new site. When the number of workers in a job category is small, firm-by-firm validation is impracticable.

An increasingly common resolution is for a consortium of firms to apply the same test or tests to their applicants, collect similar criterion data, and interpret all the data together. This procedure—seen in the PDRI study—enlarges the sample and produces comparable data across several firms. Whoever analyzes the data does have a responsibility to check out whether the requirements for satisfactory performance appear to be similar from firm to firm.

"Validity generalization" refers to the working hypothesis that a selection rule found valid in one setting will be valid in the next. A firm that installs a test on the basis of experience reported in other places and makes no follow-up of its own is trusting the generalized power of the test to predict for all jobs with the same title. But no hypothesis is to be trusted blindly.

Cautious professional opinion urged for decades that any selection plan be validated afresh in each setting. In 1977 Frank Schmidt and J. E. ("Jack") Hunter staked out an opposing position favoring validity generalization. With rare exceptions, they asserted, a test whose validity is established on a large sample in one setting will be valid for all jobs in the same broad category and in all firms. (They say that the validity will be positive, not that the test will work equally well in all situations.) To them, local validation seems useless. It adds nothing if it matches the average finding of many studies in other places; and, if it disagrees, it is unpersuasive, because it comes from a small sample.

A second thesis of Schmidt and Hunter is that all ability tests are (more or less) equally valid, hence choosing different test combinations for different jobs is pointless. On most jobs, success is forecast by general ability. (Their eye is on Gc more than Gf.) A psychomotor factor predicts in some jobs, but they consider it the only other important predictive measure. Observed correlations of verbal, spatial, and numerical tests with a given criterion usually differ. Schmidt and Hunter attribute this to sampling fluctuations rather than to differences in relevance.

The new plan for using GATB in hiring (discussed on p. 396) reflects these theses. Not more than three abilities enter prediction for any job family. A formula will select candidates suited to any particular job on which no criterion validation had been carried out. A job analysis assigns the new job to one of five families (Table 10.9), and the formula for that family is adopted.

I argued in Chapter 10 that the numerical component (for example) is greater in some jobs than others within the same family, so ignoring lesser factors seems to oversimplify. In actual correlations, however, the sampling error swamps out nearly all the true variation from job to job. Only a huge study could identify statistically the jobs where numerical ability is especially relevant.

The case for generalizing over jobs has been made mostly by compiling studies from old files, with the aid of elaborate statistical reasoning. Technical criticisms of the analytic methods have not overturned the main conclusions, but it does seem that conclusions are often worded more strongly than the data warrant (Linn, in Berk, 1986).

In one compilation, clerical jobs were sorted into what are ordinarily regarded as distinct families; here, I confine attention to two categories: stenographers, typists, file clerks; and bookkeepers, accounting machine operators, tellers. Table 11.2 shows average validity coefficients for several kinds of tests. These averages must be highly accurate because the number of coefficients is large. Although the categories seem to describe distinct kinds of work, the average coefficients are almost the same— with one exception. The reasoning tests had greater validity in one job category than the other.

If the argument that evidence of validity for one job justifies using a test for jobs with *other* titles is accepted, employers will be relieved of much of the burden of validation (Goldstein & Patterson, in Gottfredson & Sharf, 1988).

E. J. McCormick and his associates, taking a more conservative position than Schmidt's group, defend the use of a test battery without tryout when a *local* job analysis identifies relevant dimensions *and* tests have been validated elsewhere as measures of those dimensions. McCormick speaks of "job component" validity; others have spoken of this type of informal judgment as having "synthetic validity" (McCormick et al., 1979; Mecham, 1985; Mecham et al., 1983). Mossholder and Arvey (1984), reviewing the research on this approach, see it as promising but undeveloped. It is, of course, the *favored* approach to building a tryout battery that will have a local criterion validation.

The Schmidt-Hunter position runs counter to the long-standing American interest in the diversity of aptitudes and to the undeniable fact that jobs within a category—even jobs with the same name—differ in the talents they demand. Therefore it is hotly disputed, as is best illustrated by a 100-page discussion (Schmidt et al., 1985). Schmidt and three coauthors try to dispose of 40 challenges, and Sackett and three coauthors reply.

Table 11.2   MEAN VALIDITY COEFFICIENTS IN TWO CATEGORIES OF CLERICAL JOB

| Job family | Relation of proficiency criterion to test | | | | |
	Perceptual	Quantitative	Verbal	Reasoning	Memory
Stenographic	0.22	0.23	0.19	0.18	0.18
Accounting	0.24	0.25	0.20	0.32	0.20

Source: Pearlman et al., 1980, p. 382.

The strenuous "debate" style tends to obscure the basic agreement on these important matters:

- Personnel researchers have been overinterpreting correlations based on small or unrepresentative samples, or weak criteria.
- Single studies reporting that Test A is more relevant for situation X than for Y, or that in situation X Test A predicted better than Test B, would have had little credibility if the statistical uncertainty of each correlation were displayed prominently.
- Statistical integration of results from weak studies is an interim attempt to "make do." Better studies, particularly studies with better criteria, are much needed.
- Characteristics of jobs or work settings do alter aptitude requirements. The only well-documented, powerful result, however, is the connection between general ability and job complexity.

A particularly well-balanced statement on these points is found in the *Principles for the Validation and Use of Personnel Selection Procedures* (Society, 1987, pp. 26–28). The *Testing standards* accept validity generalization when proper local validation is not available, and add: "The integrity of the inference depends on the degree of similarity between the local situation and the prior set of situations."[5] Schmidt and his colleagues do not truly believe that the world of jobs and aptitudes is flat and featureless. But it must be agreed that no one knows how many continents there are or where the tectonic plates begin and end.

It is important to return to a point made in connection with GATB (p. 397). The validity-generalization literature has paid *no* attention to the use of tests in classification. A general-ability score may have validity 0.4 for selecting trainees to be either word processors or programmers. Using a verbal score to pick word processors and a mathematical-reasoning score to pick programmers would probably raise the within-job validity by 0.05 or less. More important, using distinct tests for the two jobs locates a greater number of satisfactory workers in the labor pool. (Recall Figure 1.5.)

Future personnel research will surely reinstate appreciation of multiple aptitudes (Prediger, 1989). A main source for Schmidt et al. (1981) was the U.S. Army data of Helme et al. (1957). The Schmidt group concluded that the profiles of validity coefficients for the markedly diverse military jobs differed no more than would profiles calculated on random samples of soldiers all in the same job. That might be true of the old data, as Helme et al. used catch-as-catch-can data with criteria of uncertain value. Reports from the current Project A (p. 398) change the picture.

---

[5]From the *Standards for Educational and Psychological Testing*, p. 16. Copyright © 1985 by the American Psychological Association. Reprinted by permission.

Another hint about future lines of advance is found in a study applying Schmidt-Hunter methods to biodata (p. 411). Brown (1981), compiling data from 12,000 salespersons hired by a dozen insurance firms, showed that validities varied across companies far more than sampling error could explain. The higher validities appeared in better-managed companies. When Brown sorted the companies on objective evidence, the validity was about 0.3 in superior firms, compared with 0.2 in the others.

26. *Tenopyr and Oeltjen (1982) suggest that, when a supervisor's rating is the criterion, validity coefficients are more likely to be similar from one job to another than when a direct measure of job performance is the criterion. Why might this be true? (Figure 11.1 may help with your answer.)*

27. *In what ways is better management of a firm or subdivision likely to increase the validity of a relevant predictor?*

USING MULTIPLE PREDICTORS

Linear Composites

Two or more scores can be combined in a weighted sum. The weighting that gives the highest correlation with the criterion is defined by a multiple-regression equation; the corresponding validity coefficient is the multiple correlation R.

As a first example, let us consider prediction of college marks again. Figure 7.11 (page 267) reported that combining a predictor test with high-school marks yields a multiple correlation of college grade average that is about 0.10 higher (on average) than the simple r for marks alone. Here are the r's for one year's class in one college (from the ACT Technical Manual, 1988):

	High-school GPA	College GPA
1. Aptitude score	0.53	0.51
2. High-school GPA		0.58

If we simply add the two z scores, predictive validity rises to 0.623. The formula that predicts best in this sample is

$$0.28z_1 + 0.43z_2$$

The corresponding multiple correlation is 0.626. The best weights, then, did not work appreciably better than equal z-score weights, and even that advantage would probably fade when we try to predict for next year's applicants. (See p. 444 on cross-validation.) With general-ability and educational measures as predictors, uniform weights are advisable—usually but not always (Dawes, 1979). Two side comments: In this sample, using both predictors gained less than Figure 7.11 led us to expect, but of course there are also samples of college data where gains are larger than 0.10. Second, "uniform weights" means equal z-score weights. The corresponding weights for raw scores will usually be unequal because each of those weights equals the corresponding z-score weight divided by the s.d. of the predictor. For an example, return to the SOMPA formula on page 133.

When several predictors carry information of much the same kind, combining a few of them improves reliability and therefore validity (p. 214). But adding more of the same to a reliable predictor is unprofitable, as is seen in the following correlations of predictors with elimination from flight training (DuBois, 1947, p. 194):

Pilot stanine (i.e., composite score on selection battery)	0.653
Stanine plus Qualifying examination	0.655
Stanine plus Qualifying plus General Classification Test	0.655

Adding information about a component of the job not already covered by tests in the set raises the multiple correlation. Table 7.4 displayed this increase in validity for predicting college grades: from an r of 0.37 with one test score to 0.41 with two scores to 0.56 when high-school marks were added in. A multiple correlation quickly reaches a ceiling; combining more than three or four variables rarely is valuable.

In the PDRI study their mechanical comprehension test had the best validity of any measure (0.33 against rated problem-solving ability, all cases pooled) and the validities of batteries that added in five or six more scores reached only 0.34. The reason for recommending a battery rather than the MCT alone was to obtain stable validity in various subsets of plants, jobs, and so on.

Elaborate formulas can be worthwhile when each added test measures a new factor, combining weights are based on more than 250 cases,[6] and conditions of work are unlikely to change. Although only a few tests will enter any one prediction formula, it may be desirable to try out many more tests, especially when one wants to predict each person's success in a variety of jobs (as in guidance or military classification).

Table 11.3 shows how tests were weighted to predict graduation from pilot, bombardier, and navigator training during World War II. In the selection of bombardiers, Discrimination Reaction Time and Finger Dexterity counted heavily, whereas Reading and Arithmetic deserved very little weight. The navigator composite, on the other hand, de-

---

[6]This figure comes from a little-known report by Campbell (1974). For samples of 150–250 (and for larger samples if R is below 0.5), he recommends making z-score weights proportional to the simple test-criterion r's. He finds that with fewer than 150 cases it is better to base weights on judgment than on statistics.

Table 11.3   VALIDITY DATA AND COMBINING WEIGHTS IN AIRCREW CLASSIFICATION

Test	Correlation with criterion			Relative weight		
	Bomb.	Nav.	Pilot	Bomb.	Nav.	Pilot
Printed tests:						
Reading Comprehension	0.1	0.3	0.2	8	2	—
Spatial Orientation II	0.1	0.35	0.25	—	10	5
Spatial Orientation I	0.1	0.4	0.2	—	9	6
Dial and Table Reading	0.2	0.55	0.2	14	18	4
Biographical Data—pilot	—	—	0.3	—	—	15
Biographical Data—navigator	—	0.25	−0.05	—	9	—
Mechanical Principles	0.1	0.15	0.3	—		8
Technical Vocabulary—pilot	0.05	0.1	0.3	—	—	13
Technical Vocabulary—nav.	0.05	0.2	0.1	—	—	—
Mathematics	0.1	0.5	0.1	—	18	—
Arithmetic Reasoning	0.1	0.45	0.1	8	12	—
Instrument Comprehension I	—	—	0.15	—	—	9
Instrument Comprehension II	—	—	0.35			
Numerical Operations, front	0.15	0.25	0.0	—	—	—
Numerical Operations, back	0.1	0.3	0.0	—	—	—
Speed of Identification	0.1	0.2	0.2	—	—	—
Apparatus tests:						
Rotary Pursuit	0.15	0.1	0.2	12	—	4
Complex Coordination	0.2	0.25	0.4	12	—	17
Finger Dexterity	0.15	0.2	0.1	19	6	—
Discrimination Reaction Time	0.2	0.35	0.2	27	6	4
Two-Hand Coordination	0.1	0.25	0.3	—	11	4
Rudder Control	—	—	0.4	—	—	12

Source: DuBois, 1947, pp. 99, 101.

NOTE: The criterion for the various validity coefficients is graduation or nongraduation from training.

pended primarily on intellectual abilities. The jobs have been redefined as new equipment and tactics altered crew duties; weights have changed accordingly.

Essentially the same logic is being used nowadays to combine tests for optimum allocation. The army data in Figure 14.7 were combined in this manner, and Bartram (1987) is using this kind of procedure to combine scores from the computerized tests illustrated on page 50. In British training for naval aircraft duty, it is desired to rule out probable failures, and then to identify whether a recruit will do better as a pilot or as an observer. Intellectual (especially mathematical) tests apparently are most relevant to the observer role. There are preliminary indications, requiring accumulation of more cases and cross-validation, that the computerized coordination test is especially relevant to advanced pilot training (and more relevant than the old electromechanical tests such as that on p. 38).

28. *A predictor for success in accounting could use the simple GVN composite of GATB or could apply regression weights to G, V, and N. Why would the validity coefficient not increase greatly? (Think of the weighting formula as GVN plus some amount of N.)*

29. *What is the apparent psychological meaning of each of the following regression equations? They combine standard scores on the Armed Services aptitude battery to predict grades in a training course:*
    a. *Drafting grade predicted by Clerical Speed + 2 Spatial + 0.5 Arithmetic Reasoning.*
    b. *Machine Shop grade predicted by Arithmetic Reasoning + 1.5 Tool Knowledge + 1.5 Automotive Information + .01 (all other tests).*

30. *Consider the weights in Table 11.3.*
    a. *Why, in the navigator composite, are different weights assigned to the first two tests when their validity coefficients are similar?*
    b. *Consider the tasks making up each job. Which weights are open to suspicion as possible statistical flukes that would not cross-validate?*

Patterns and Configurations

The basic methods of combining predictors assume that a linear trend relates outcome to any test score. Many less simple relationships are recognized in theory and sometimes in practice.

First let us reconsider the regression of outcome onto a single test. Brogden's rule assumed that each increase in test scores implies a corresponding increase in payoff. But it would be a remarkable coincidence if the regression of utility on score were linear. Suppose, for example, that the number of gadgets produced per day *is* linearly related to Test X. The worker who produces 400 gadgets is worth more than twice as much to the firm as the worker who produces 200 because the latter's cost of equipment and overhead is much higher (per gadget produced) than that of the first worker. If the production criterion were mapped onto a utility scale, the curve would resemble panel i of Figure 11.6. This comparatively flat trend at the left would also be seen where the failure rate during training is high for low scorers; the cost of failures being more or less uniform, utility is much the same across the high-risk region.

Panel ii describes the opposite case: utility increases with score up to a certain level, and then the rise tapers off. This occurs, for example, when a particularly fast worker on an assembly line cannot produce more because he must wait for others to supply parts. Among workers who can keep up with the standard pace with little spoilage, there is not much difference in utility.

This casts a sidelight on validity generalization. No doubt typing skill has general relevance over many jobs and firms, but the utility very

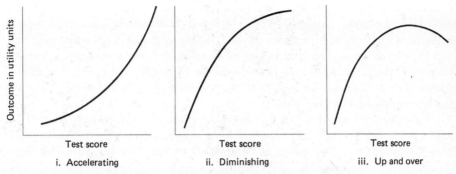

Figure 11.6. **Possible nonlinear relations of outcome to test score.**

likely tapers off as in panel ii. The cut score that eliminates inadequate workers probably varies, however; only in straight "production typing" would better-than-average speed be a worker's most important asset.

Panel iii represents the possibility that workers who are "overqualified" are poor investments. This kind of regression is most likely when turnover is weighted into the criterion; better qualified workers leave for more rewarding jobs, and the employer benefits less from the investment in training them.

If panel iii describes the situation, the employer could logically prefer to hire persons in midrange. Where panel ii describes the facts, the employer may set a cut score at a moderate level to rule out high-risk applicants and hire at random—or on the basis of non-test characteristics—within the group who survive the cut. Where panel i tells the story, it is desirable to push the cut score as high as possible. Intensifying the effort to recruit excellent applicants would be logical.

Considering two variables (or more), various nonlinear trends are possible. One is illustrated in Figure 11.7, where outcome goes up as test scores W and X increase. The composite $W + X$ is the predictor suggested by conventional regression methods; it would define a cutoff line slanting from upper left to lower right. But persons along that line are not equally promising. The curved contour line identifies equally promising cases; for every score combination along that line, the expected outcome is 12.5. The best workers are those for whom W and X are in balance.

The term "configural prediction" refers to forecasting from a pattern of scores, not a simple weighted sum. Another common term is "moderator variable"; the slope of regression onto X depends on the level of W, so W "moderates" the Y-on-X regression. (And X moderates that of Y on W.) Not only may one ability influence the predictive power of a second ability, but personality variables, sex and race, and life history variables may act as moderators.

Statistics can generate an equation for a curved line that identifies equally promising workers. A simpler approximation is to use two cut-offs. Hiring everyone whose X and W scores both reach 3 or better would include nearly all the persons above the curved line in the figure.

It should be added that multiple cutoff rules are sometimes used in place of linear composites—not because they are more valid, but because they are easier for clerks to apply. An example is the old scheme for interpreting GATB (p. 395).

Configural formulas are not easy to justify. The nonlinearity in Figure 11.7 is not trivial; the regression of outcome on X is three times as steep when W = 6 as when W = 2. Yet very nearly the same persons would be hired under the W + X rule as under a double-cutoff or curvilinear rule that accepts the same number of applicants. In cross-validation, nonlinear rules usually turn out not to predict better than linear equations (Dunnette & Borman, 1979).

The personnel worker should nonetheless keep the possibility in mind. If strength in W compensates for weakness in X, and vice versa, a simple combination of W and X is probably a suitable predictor. If compensation is not a plausible hypothesis, linear combination may be a bad idea.

During World War II the U.S. Navy asked psychologists to select recruits suitable for training as sonar operators. All sailors whose general-ability scores qualified them for specialized training were screened. The selectors looked at a weighted sum of MCT and several tonal discrimination tests. Many of the men above the cut score were sent to sonar training. If they failed there, it was standard practice to reassign them to general sea duty. It was a serious matter when a sailor with good

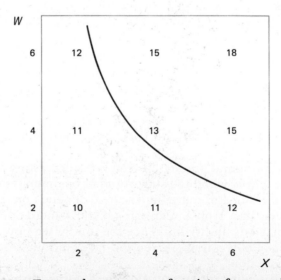

Figure 11.7. **Expected outcome as a function of two predictors.**

general ability was sent to a school for which he lacked special abilities because his general ability would not then be fully used. Many of those who failed in sonar school did so because of poor tonal judgment. They had been selected because their high mechanical comprehension raised the composite score, offsetting their weakness. Such men were doomed in sonar training, whereas they could have been excellent in, say, radar maintenance. (After a time, the composite was replaced by a multiple cutoff.)

31. *If it is unfair to reject an applicant because his ability scores are very high, what legitimate use can be made of the finding that an ability predicts length of stay on a job as shown in panel iii of Figure 11.6?*

32. *In a situation described by panel ii of Figure 11.6, what does a firm sacrifice if it sets a very high cut score?*

33. *Considering the following responsibilities, would you expect a deficit in either of the named abilities to be compensated for by superiority in the other ability?*
    a. Baseball player: hitting, fielding.
    b. Opera singer: vocal range, ability to memorize roles in many languages.
    c. Newspaper reporter: writing skill, ability to win confidence of strangers.

34. *I have said that much of this chapter is relevant to clinical classification, although most examples have come from personnel selection. Which sections apply to such clinical decisions as screening and diagnosis?*

35. *Figure 14.7 (p. 557) shows that, in the military, job competence can be well predicted and responsible conduct can be predicted (less well but usefully) by other predictors.*
    a. Prepare a diagram like Figure 11.7 to represent the relation of the value, in time of war, of mechanics repairing armored vehicles to these two aspects of performance.
    b. For screening recruits, would a linear predictor have advantages over a two-way cutoff (or a nonlinear predictor that approximates such a double cut)?

Cross-Validation

It is usually unsafe to accept a combining rule on the basis of a satisfactory coefficient in a first sample. The particular critical score or the combining formula that gives the very best result is certain not to be best in a second sample. The investigator should be particularly skeptical of weights that make little psychological sense because they are likely to have come from sampling errors.

Although regression weights give the best prediction for the sample, the weighting best in the population (hence best for future samples) would be somewhat different. Therefore, the validity coefficient for a statistically derived formula shrinks in an independent sample. Shrinkage is relatively small when the predictors are chosen initially on the basis of substantial past experience and theory and relatively large in a "shotgun" study where miscellaneous predictors are tried with no particular rationale.

"Robust" procedures that hold shrinkage to a minimum are widely accepted (Darlington, 1978; Dunnette & Borman, 1979; Wainer, 1978); see also page 438.

Cutting scores, combining weights, and multiple correlations derived from modest samples ought to be confirmed. This is to be said also of the "criterion keys" applied to many measures of interests and personality. A rule or formula is cross-validated by trying it on a sample not used in selecting the elements (tests or items) and establishing weights. Conceptually, cross-validation requires two full-size validation studies, and the cost becomes discouraging. Some investigators, trying to avoid this cost, turn to "shrinkage" formulas. Under some circumstances, however, the formulas give misinformation even about the relationships they were developed to estimate (Marshall & Klimoski, 1986).

Fortunately, internal-consistency methods such as those for studying reliability can be applied. A traditional shortcut has been to split the original sample at random. Weights are determined using data from half the sample, and the population validity coefficient for the resulting predictor is estimated from the other half. Keys based on half-samples, however, are ordinarily less valid than the full-sample key one intends to use.

Some new "resampling methods" permit split-sample cross-validation with negligible downward bias. The methods apply only when the rule is based strictly on the data; they cannot be used when judgment shaped the rule after the data were examined. Some statistical work in psychology has made use of these so-called jackknife and bootstrap techniques, but no application to scoring keys or psychological prediction rules has yet appeared in print. (A reference to begin with is Efron & Diaconis, 1983; for further information, see Cooil et al., 1987, Efron, 1983, and Mosteller & Tukey, 1977, pp. 36ff., 148ff.)

One procedure is close to the old half-split idea. First, we divide the sample randomly into 10 nearly equal blocks. Holding out Block 1, we form a predictor composite that fits the remaining data, and then predict criterion scores of Block-1 cases with that formula. Next we create a formula using all cases save Block 2, and use it to predict for Block-2 members. We repeat to give each block its turn. Then, having predictions for all cases, we correlate them with criterion scores to estimate the population validity for a formula based on these variables. The coefficient is not inflated because no case played a part in shaping the prediction rule applied to it. A key based on 90 per cent of the cases will have nearly as much validity as a key based on all cases. (The estimate can be improved by carrying out the entire operation many times, with new random divisions of the cases. These repetitive techniques were expensive in the past, but personal computers can run them for next-to-nothing in their spare time.)

CLASSIFICATION DECISIONS

A test that predicts success on *many* jobs is likely to have little value for classifying applicants. The general test does not tell which job the person can do best. From a formal standpoint, classification attempts to predict a difference between two criteria. A composite predictor can be found for each of the criteria. A value comparison is required: How good a navigator must one be to be as useful as an average pilot? Once the scales are matched up, the predictions indicate which route is most promising for a person.

The ideal classification test has a positive correlation with performance in one job and a zero or negative correlation with performance in other jobs. For a simple example, I assume that the criterion standard deviations for pilots and navigators are about equal—that is, that the difference in value to the air force between an ace pilot and a borderline pilot is equal to that between an outstanding and a mediocre navigator. According to Table 11.3, Two-Hand Coordination has a validity close to 0.3 for *both* navigator and pilot. Therefore, it is useless for classification. Numerical Operations has a validity near 0.3 for navigator and zero for pilot. It is, therefore, a good classification test. The Mathematics test, with validities 0.5 and 0.1, is even better.

Under Brogden's assumptions (p. 430), the value of a test used to assign persons to one of two treatments is proportional not to validity but to the difference between its two validities or, more exactly, to the difference in slope between the two criterion-on-test regressions (Brogden, 1951). Figures 1.5 and 5.5 extended this reasoning.

It should be possible for employers to capitalize on differential abilities by, for example, designing two forms of training for a production task. One could be heavily verbal, and the other might rely more on concrete and visual experience. The verbal training probably would be quicker and cheaper, but the second approach could make good use of applicants who are less educated or less familiar with English. Another obvious type of differentiation is to give training in specific skills (dial reading, say, or use of calipers) to each person who appears capable of learning the job but would fail if these specific deficiencies were not repaired.

In clinical diagnosis there is no fixed number of places to fill. Every person assessed can be called "normal," or everyone can be called "schizophrenic" if such uniform classification appears correct. When the clinician is trying to identify a rare condition, classifying everyone as not having that condition is often the best strategy—even when some test has appreciable validity.

Meehl and Rosen (1955) took prediction of suicide as an example. If a test identifies a person as having a high probability of suicide, the clinician will probably recommend giving him closer attention and more intensive treatment than a probable nonsuicide. Suppose that 5 per cent of those tested in a certain clinic later attempt suicide ("base rate" probability = 0.05). A person with a low test score (on a hypothetical test) has probability 0.001 of a suicide attempt, and one can confidently place him in the nonsuicide category. With higher test scores, probability of suicide increases, so the test is somewhat valid. The highest score in the clinic sample, however, may indicate only probability 0.2 of a suicide attempt. The high-scoring person is not a "probable suicide." In labeling such persons suicide risks, we raise four false alarms for every correct decision. To put a special watch on the high scorer drains the clinic's resources. Very likely it cannot invest this effort in four false alarms in order to forestall one suicide. On the other hand, one person saved may be seen as outweighing the cost of guarding all five.

The use of information in classification is basically similar to that underlying the setting of cut scores in selection (p. 420). The cost of each kind of error is to be considered. Misclassifications are easily tolerated when further work with the person will disclose the error and the temporary misclassification does not significantly damage the person's interests.

36. *What tests had greatest validity for distinguishing pilots from bombardiers, according to Table 11.3?*

37. *A 20-point test for parole prediction gives these expectancies for violating parole: for a score of 20, 40 per cent; score 10, 20 per cent; score 0, 5 per cent. Can this test be used practically by a parole board, or should all prisoners be classified as likely to obey probation rules?*

38. *Could two treatments have equal means and equal test-outcome correlations, but very different outcome standard deviations? If so, which treatment (assignment) is advisable for a person with a high test score?*

FAIRNESS IN SELECTION

Poor, less educated persons tend to score lower on ability tests than those with advantaged backgrounds, and women average lower than men on tests where mechanical experience helps. Sometimes these unwelcome differences reflect real differences in qualifications. Which tests and test uses discriminate unfairly has had to be argued out in the courts.

Some History and Law

Title VII of the Civil Rights Act of 1964 prohibited disparate treatment of workers and job applicants from different sex, racial or ethnic, or religious groups. The Senate inserted an amendment pointedly stating that the act did not prohibit selection on the basis of "professionally developed tests," where there was no intent to discriminate. Administrative guidelines were issued and revised, charges were brought from time to time against private and public employers, and cases were settled administratively or in court. A second body of law and policy has evolved with regard to educational selection.

Although much has been settled, doctrine is still evolving. A small fraction of challenges reach the courts; very few reach the higher courts. Some employers promptly abandon or amend a plan that is challenged; sometimes the enforcement agency decides that a plan is defensible and drops the challenge. Courts take divergent positions about the cases that reach them. In one region the appeals court lays down precedents that are tough on employers; in another region the appeals court hears employers sympathetically. The Supreme Court resolves contradictions, but it tries to progress slowly, and keeps its rulings narrow (Hartigan & Wigdor, 1989, Ch. 2).

Sources on the history and legal theory include Gorham (in Maslow et al., 1980), Lerner (1979), papers by Hollander and Wigdor (in Wigdor & Garner, 1982, vol. 2), and Part I of Wigdor and Hartigan (1988). Handbooks on employment law (Larson & Larson, 1987; Schlei & Grossman, 1983) are revised frequently, and recent rulings can be traced in the periodical *Fair Employment Practices Cases* (FEP). For a summary by psychologists see Nathan and Cascio (in Berk, 1986).

Federal Guidelines   The Equal Employment Opportunity Commission was set up as advocate for groups that might be discriminated against. Several other federal agencies with missions of other kinds take conflicting positions. Their *Uniform Federal Guidelines (UFG;* EEOC et al., 1978, 1979) are a compromise, open to divergent interpretations.

The EEOC has pressed toward a "representative work force." Ideally, its officials have said, all groups in the community would be represented in a job category in proportion to their availability. Other agencies place greater stress on merit hiring, opposing both deliberate discrimination and quotas. Even the Office of Personnel Management— formerly the "Civil Service Commission," whose name was almost synonymous with merit hiring—yielded to pressure and agreed that the percentage of blacks and Hispanics accepted into administrative and professional lines of the federal service is to match the percentage of applicants from those groups. The court-approved plan discarded a test that seemingly predicted success but on which the average minority applicant (less educated?) fell below the overall average.

In explaining the issues, I shall refer to blacks (or to "plaintiffs" as advocates for blacks) and to whites (or to employers as "defendants"). This permits brevity and recognizes that treatment of blacks has been at issue in most cases. But the rules protect any race, sex, or ethnic group; white males can be plaintiffs under them. Moreover, selection based on evidence other than tests must meet these standards also, say the *UFG*.

An employment case turns on three successive questions:

1. Is there adverse impact? The plaintiff must show that the rejection rate of (otherwise eligible) blacks is greater than that of whites. Rule of thumb: A selection practice is challenged when the rate of black hiring is less than four-fifths the rate for whites.
2. Is the selection rule valid? If the procedure fails standard 1, the defendant has to show that the basis for selection is related to the job.
3. Can an alternative selection procedure be found that has less adverse impact? If Test X is valid but has adverse impact, the *UFG* urge the employer to seek a procedure that has validity but not adverse impact.

According to the *UFG*, criterion, content, and construct validation are equally legitimate. Courts are impressed by criterion validation. Courts have been equally receptive to content validation if no irrelevant difficulty in the test is detected (see p. 188).

On construct validation, the *UFG* and the court decisions are conflicting, confusing, and not a good reflection of the relevant psychological literature (Maslow et al., 1980). Construct-related arguments in employment cases face a fundamental difficulty. The match of test to construct can be firmly established only when the construct is rooted in a well-ripened, well-substantiated theory. But theory, hence the support for this kind of validity argument, ripens slowly (Cronbach, in Wainer & Braun, 1987, and in Linn, 1989b).

Court Rulings   In five key Supreme Court decisions the chief points were these:

- *Griggs* (401 U.S. 424 [1971]). A pencil-and-paper test given to would-be coal handlers was struck down. Employers must show "business necessity" for selection, and employment tests that have adverse impact must be relevant. (The law does not require validity otherwise!)
- *Albemarle Paper Co.* v. *Moody* (422 U.S. 405 [1975]). A selection rule with adverse impact was struck down because the firm's hastily assembled validation did not meet professional standards.
- *Washington* v. *Davis*[7] (426 U.S. 229 [1976]; see p. 340). A majority of the court accepted a selection rule that had adverse impact, noting that the test predicted final marks in police training and measured a logically relevant variable at a reasonable level. Two dis-

---

[7]*Washington* v. *Davis* was not judged under the Civil Rights Act, and the legal rationale differed from that of the other cases. The same was true of *Bakke*.

senters objected that the job relevance of the training criterion had not been established.

- *Bakke* (98 S. Ct. 2733 [1978]). A system that reserved a number of law school places (a "quota") for minority applicants was struck down. But selection need not ignore race, the court said; diversity in a student body has recognized educational value.
- *Weber* (99 S. Ct. 2721 [1979]). Reserving places for blacks as trainees for supervisory positions was accepted as a remedy when a firm confessed to past discrimination.

Appellate courts are suggesting further principles (Cascio et al., 1988). One line of thought is to make a random (hence color-blind) choice at the last stage of selection, after the pool has been reduced to persons who are adequately qualified. In *Guardians* (23 FEP 909 [1980]), a rather unsatisfactory test was upheld as of some relevance to police work. Because the measurement error was substantial, said the court, the test should be used only to eliminate definitely unqualified applicants. Above that cutoff, random selection should be considered as less discriminatory than hiring from the top. Another plan added 250 points to the score of every black applicant for police sergeant prior to ranking the eligibility list. (The score difference between means of white and black applicants was near 250.) The court in *Kirkland* (23 FEP 121 [1980]) accepted the plan, saying that the bonus was not a quota in disguise (!). For a similar opinion, see *Navaho Refining* (19 FEP 184 [1979]).

The psychological community has viewed this history with mixed feelings (Glaser & Bond, 1981; Wigdor & Garner, 1982). Psychologists surely supported the civil rights principles of 1964 and the demand for valid selection methods. They agree that selection rules have at times set unreasonably high and irrelevant standards that blocked the path of competent but less-educated applicants. Many psychologists are strongly committed to the merit principle, hence to "color-blind" hiring, and are opposed to quotas and special preferences. Many are distressed that employers have abandoned testing to avoid complaints and the costs of defense, when interviews should be at least as suspect as tests (Arvey, 1979). It is hard to believe that all the unvalidated selection methods used by employers who do not test are fair to the applicants rejected. The Supreme Court indeed has ruled (*Watson* v. *Ft. Worth Bank & Trust*, 108 S. Ct. 2777 [1988]) that subjective bases for judgment that have adverse impact are open to attack if not validated (Bersoff, 1988).

39. *High school students who score high on the Preliminary Scholastic Aptitude Test are eligible for National Merit scholarships. The cut score is set separately for each state so as to make the number of awards proportional to their high school populations. Which national interests are served by this policy? What national interests suffer?*

Psychometric Issues

Do regressions in subpopulations differ? When a test is valid for white
male applicants, is it likely to have predictive validity for other subpopulations? Yes indeed. A formula for predicting an educational or employment criterion, worked out on a typical applicant pool, holds up for black
applicants considered separately. A formula worked out for men usually
holds up for women.

Bad reasoning confused past discussions; this paragraph is intended
to clear away that underbrush. (I draw especially on critiques by Hunter
et al., 1979, and Linn, 1978.) The standard research design is to collect
data in the same setting, on whites and blacks who have been accepted.
Some studies reported that certain validity coefficients for blacks were
"not statistically significant," implying that the tests in question were
invalid for blacks. Other studies reported coefficients for blacks that
were positive, but lower than those for whites. The small samples and
the comparatively narrow range of scores for the blacks accepted could
easily have generated such findings, even where population validity coefficients would be the same for unselected black applicants and unselected white applicants. Comparisons of correlation coefficients across
population subgroups are beside the point, however.

The real issue is *differential prediction:* Are the Y-on-X regression
lines the same for blacks and whites (or other contrasted groups)?

Suppose that whites who score 75 on predictor X average +1 on
criterion Y. Then if blacks who score 75 on X average +2 on Y, a formula
based mostly on white employees would seriously underrate these black
applicants (*UFG*, Sec. 1607.14 A.(6)(a)). (Similar inquiries about test
items considered singly were discussed earlier; see pp. 141 and 339.
Item analyses—usually made during test development—relate the item
score to what the test as a whole measures, because no criterion is
available.)

Differential prediction does occur at times, as Figure 11.8 shows.

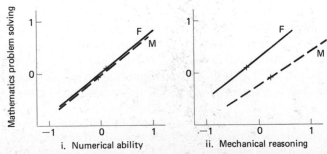

Figure 11.8. Prediction within sexes from two aptitude measures. Each score is
expressed relative to the mean and s.d. of the sample (sexes combined). (*Source:*
Calculated from data in the DAT manual, 1974, p. 139.)

Using a numerical predictor, the regressions for males and females are the same. With mechanical reasoning as predictor, the two regressions differ. Females are underpredicted. That is, they do better on the criterion than is forecast by an equation calculated from males or from males and females together. This dramatic contrast occurs because the mechanical test measures something, irrelevant to the problem-solving criterion, on which males are superior. The irrelevance makes the predictor biased. (In this study, DAT was given at the start of the school year, and proficiency in arithmetic problem solving was measured in the spring. Mechanical reasoning correlated about 0.6 with the criterion in each sex group.)

In such a study of blacks and whites, the picture comes out much like panel i of Figure 11.8, though the lines are rarely so neatly parallel. Sometimes there is a modest separation, smaller than that shown in panel ii. Where separation is found, the white regression line is higher. See summaries by Breland (1979b) of college data, and by Jensen (1980) and Linn (in Wigdor & Garner, 1982, vol. 2, pp. 374–384). I know of *no* study of appreciable size where the regression describing criterion performance of black workers (or students) lies above the white regression lines. Expectancy tables based on data from whites do not underrate black applicants. (For a similar conclusion on Hispanics, see Schmidt et al., 1980.)

Sweeping generalizations are not warranted and indeed are not logically defensible. The disparity between regressions would change if the test were lengthened or shortened (other things being equal). Moreover, if regressions calculated on selected workers coincide, regressions in applicant populations probably would not (Cronbach & Schaeffer, 1981; Linn, 1983). Validators should be conscious of these complications, but it would be absurd to propose that they calculate regressions separately for old, educated, native speakers of English, ... or young, educated, native speakers of Spanish, ... and so on ad infinitum. Such fragments of data are too small for serious statistical analysis. The properly curious, properly cautious investigator will form an overall regression equation and then examine the roster of persons for whom the formula overpredicts and those for whom the formula underpredicts. Insofar as either list seems to be unrepresentative of the pool, pointed questions can then be asked. The finding may have nothing to do with test bias; it may turn out that criterion ratings from a particular supervisor led to many instances of underprediction. A common finding is that white and black supervisors tend to rate members of their own race above other workers (Kraiger & Ford, 1985).

Setting Cut Scores   If regressions indicate validity within each group, how should cut scores be set? Clearly, it is sensible to prefer applicants who rank appreciably above others from the same demographic group. Any desire to take group membership into account can be satisfied by setting group-specific cut scores. I shall consider the propriety of treating groups differently after reviewing some theory.

In both panels of Figure 11.9, use of the test greatly reduces the number of unsatisfactory workers, compared to what would occur with chance selection. Hiring the best 20 per cent of blacks and the best 20 per cent of the whites would produce only 7 per cent failures in panel i, compared with a peak value of 4 per cent if race is ignored. In panel ii the numbers are 32 and 31. The figure is based on specific assumptions, but much the same results would be found in most real situations (Cronbach & Schaeffer, 1981; Hunter et al., 1977; Wigdor & Hartigan, 1988). Black applicants are assumed here to be less qualified, on average, than whites.

Various policies for setting cut scores have been recommended. Rather than give extensive references, I draw attention to Petersen and Novick (1976) and the comments published with it.

1. *Group-blind hiring.* Traditional practice is to look at scores without regard to group membership. The same cut score is applied to both groups. Then if blacks score lower on average, a smaller proportion of blacks are hired.

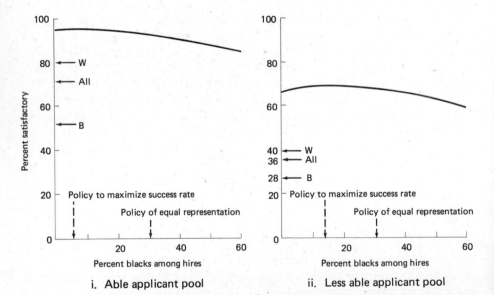

i. Able applicant pool   ii. Less able applicant pool

Figure 11.9. **Change in adequacy of work force with increase in minority hiring.** In both panels it is assumed that 30 per cent of the applicants are black, that the selection test has validity 0.55, and that only 20 per cent of applicants will be hired. Cut scores will be set to choose the highest scorers within each group, but the percentage taken from each group (bottom scale) is allowed to shift over a wide range. The horizontal arrows indicate the assumed proportion of white (W), black (B), and all workers who would be satisfactory if selection were at random.

2. *Quota hiring.* The most direct way to get a representative work force is to hire the same fraction from each group of applicants, guaranteeing zero "adverse impact."
3. *Quotas based on group merit.* One has a sense of injustice when persons who would be satisfactory are less likely to be hired if they come from a minority group. When we know what fraction of each group would be satisfactory if hired, we can adjust cut scores to equalize the chance that satisfactory applicants are hired regardless of group membership.
4. *Equal marginal risk.* We could set a cut score in each group so that the last persons hired—the lowest-scoring applicants among those hired from each group—have equal probability of success. This is"merit hiring" in the most literal sense, and it is the policy that produces the greatest number of successful workers.

As Figure 11.9 indicates, in the typical employment situation, one can move a long distance from policy 4 toward policies 2 and 3 with little loss in productivity. How policy 1 affects productivity depends on the group means, but it is bound to give worse results than policy 4—unless the regressions coincide.

Job proficiency is not the only economic consideration. An employer could regard having a racially mixed staff as valuable in itself for winning community or customer acceptance. Also, as Dunnette (1974) has pointed out, all members of the community share the dollar costs of social disorganization that follow when some group finds itself unable to get ahead economically.

Race-conscious plans have received much encouragement. The *UFG* (Sec. 14B, para. 8d) appear to advise equal-marginal-risk cutoffs, and many less direct plans for increasing minority participation are in effect. Law schools and selective undergraduate colleges admit many blacks whose test scores matched those of white applicants who were rejected (Linn, 1982; Willingham & Breland, 1982). This is in keeping with *Bakke.* In employment also, appellate courts have accepted disparate cut scores for racial groups, and the Supreme Court (*Johnson* v. *Transportation Agency*, 107 S. Ct. 1442 [1987]) endorsed employers' voluntary plans for giving preference to workers from underrepresented groups.

In the 1980s USES proposed a "race-conscious" plan for nationwide use. GATB (p. 394) is used in state employment offices to refer workers to employers trying to fill jobs of all kinds. To increase minority hiring, USES planned to convert scores to percentiles based on the local applicant pool, building *separate* conversion tables for Hispanics, blacks, and "others." The persons with the highest own-group percentiles would be referred to the employer. How this would work is illustrated in Table 11.4, with made-up numbers. The employer has five vacancies to fill. Under a traditional meritocratic plan, workers A, B, C, D, and E would be judged most promising and sent forward. Under the USES proposal, person J has a higher within-group percentile than D, so J would be sent

Table 11.4   TWO STRATEGIES FOR REFERRING EMPLOYMENT SERVICE APPLICANTS
TO AN EMPLOYER

			Percentile rank in		Referred, if policy is	
Applicant	Group	Raw score	Total pool	Own group	Race-blind	Race-conscious
A	X	70	95	99	X	X
B	O	70	95	96	O	O
C	O	66	92	92	O	O
D	O	65	92	92	O	
E	Y	64	91	96	Y	Y
F	O	62	89	88		
G	O	60	87	86		
H	O	60	87	86		
I	O	58	85	84		
J	X	57	83	93		X

forward along with A, B, C, and E. (The employer would not be told the scores of applicants.)

After the Department of Justice challenged the plan as unfair to the D's who would have been referred under the meritocratic policy, a non-government panel was asked to review the issue. The reports recognized legal, political, economic, and psychometric concerns and stated this broad principle (Wigdor & Hartigan, 1988, p. 51):

> If the will of society is to pursue both high levels of productivity and a ra-cially balanced workforce and if a valid test that produces an adverse impact is used in the referral process, then a race-conscious referral policy is neces-sary.

The group suggested that USES follow *both* plans up to the point of sending A, B, C, D, E, *and* J to the employer. This plan, in the spirit of Figure 11.9, leaves the policy decision to the employer. The firm, not the government agency, determines the desired balance between max-imizing production and minority representation.

A lawyer speaking for the Department of Justice argued that the re-porting of race-conscious scores is unconstitutional (Delahunty, 1988), but failed to persuade the review group. The language of recent deci-sions suggests that the present Court is shifting the burden of proof away from the employer. Instead of having to prove "business necessity", the firm may win the case if it only states a "legitimate employment goal" for the selection practice (*Wards Cove Packing*, handed down June 5, 1989).

An important feature of the recommendation (Hartigan & Wigdor, 1989) is that for each person referred two scores should be sent to the employer. One is the within-group percentile, which encourages hiring of minorities. The second is an estimate of the probability that the applicant will be above-average in job performance. Comparison on this basis enables the employer to recognize how much or how little risk attends the hiring of a candidate such as J. In the absence of a directly relevant, large-sample experience table, the committee proposes to fall back on an estimated validity coefficient and an assumed normal distribution (Fig. 5.3).

Main Points Reviewed

"Test bias" has received more attention from the press and from general works on testing than any other aspect of psychology. The reason for not giving it a *separate* chapter in this book should now be clear. Every aspect of testing might lead to a charge of unfair or unwise practice, and that accusation might or might not be well grounded. Some debates are about facts, some about social policy and the law. Some are essentially about the logic of validation, as a biased interpretation lacks validity.

Table 11.5 reviews several main points. A symposium on techniques of evaluating single items (Berk, 1982), a chapter by Reynolds concerned chiefly with school psychology (in Reynolds & Gutkin, 1982), a symposium on minimum competency tests (Madaus, 1983), Jensen's (1980) massive analysis of relevant facts, and papers in the Glaser-Bond (1981) symposium, plus chapters by Jaeger, and Cole and Moss, in Linn, 1989a, extend the discussion. Table 11.5 emphasizes themes that have concerned blacks and Hispanics; it would require far more space to review the concerns of women, Jews, Asiatic immigrants, the physically handicapped, and so on.

The succinct comments in the third column are intended only to remind the reader of better developed statements made on the pages referred to. Do not fix attention on these sentences out of context; they are no more than headlines to cover complex stories. If these statements were put to a vote among the dozens of psychologists who have written on bias, surely nearly every statement would be endorsed by a strong majority. Universal support for a statement, however, would be a sign that it is vague. On this topic, everything is controversial (Gottfredson & Sharf, 1988).

One further comment did not fit into the table. Whenever the suitability of using ability tests as a basis for a decision is under discussion, the debate should not focus on testing alone. As a minimum, these questions should be added:

Is this a decision that should be made (no matter on what basis)?

If yes, what will be the basis for the decision if testing is not used?

And how would such questions as those in Table 11.5 be answered with regard to that alternative kind of information?

Table 11.5   TEST BIAS AGAINST MINORITIES: SOME QUESTIONS AND ANSWERS

Central concern	Question	Comment	Relevant pages
Score distribution	Does one group score lower than another on average?	A common finding. Implies bias only where there is solid evidence that the groups do not differ on what the test is said to measure.	132f. 251 332 334f.
Test administration	Are scores lowered when the test taker belongs to a minority group and examiner does not belong to that group?	Probably true for some test takers. Evidently not a major source of observed group differences in the United States. Scores should routinely be flagged when the tester sees the examinee's effort as weak.	74f. 306 330
	Are scores lowered when the person is not tested in his own language?	Yes, in general. But "testing in own language" is an incomplete solution.	75 330
	Do standard conditions bring out the best in minority test takers?	Performance may be improved when conditions are altered. If conditions are modified, renorming and revalidation would be needed to support many interpretations.	49 75f. 87–89 328–331
Test content	Does the test contain irrelevant content that holds down minority scores?	A major difficulty in cross-cultural research. Not a major source of differences between groups in the United States. Review of items by minority members a potential safeguard.	265 329–333 412 448
	Does the selection of items favor majority subjects?	Statistical analysis can locate items that present special difficulty for minority persons (and vice versa). Whether that difficulty is irrelevant and biasing depends on the proposed interpretation.	141f. 171–173 335–340

Table 11.5   Continued

Central concern	Question	Comment	Relevant pages
Predictive validity	Do minority members tend to do better on the job or in school than majority members with the same test score?	"Differential prediction" is investigated by a follow-up study in each group. Discrepancies are typically small and work to the advantage of minorities.	450f.
	Does the test predict because the institution (or its criterion) in itself handicaps minority participants?	A lively possibility. Test validators should be alert to irrelevant difficulty in a treatment or bias in a criterion.	8f. 351 414–445 417–451
Selection rule	Does the rule accept a smaller fraction of minority applicants than of other applicants?	"Adverse impact" is a preliminary consideration; it may occur when the selection rule is valid.	340 447f.
	Does the rule accept persons from one group who are below the cutoff applied to another group?	Justification can be offered for preferential hiring of this kind.	449 452–455
	Does the rule neglect some valued quality on which the minority group shows to advantage?	A meaningful challenge once such a quality is pointed out and a measure of it suggested. Both law and the selector's self-interest require attention to a plausible suggestion of this kind.	251 253 264 333

40. *Assume, in each of these cases, that the test is reasonably valid and that the courts would accept any policy between equal marginal risk and zero adverse impact. What policy would you favor?*
  a. *A test is used to select persons for training as operators of cranes used in construction. Trainees who seem not to catch the knack or are careless are discharged before they operate the machine by themselves. Most discharges occur within the first 2 weeks. The discharge rate serves as the criterion for the test.*
  b. *A public health official is expected to exercise considerable judgment and to be alert to detect unsanitary conditions and other hazards. Many*

persons who seem to grasp the regulations and skills used in entry level jobs do not demonstrate the desired qualities when promoted to independent responsibility. A test is, therefore, used to screen those applying to enter the service.

41. *Using within-group norms in USES referral is an "affirmative action" plan. Why is the proposal more defensible than Dr. Good's use (p. 132) of within-group norms in prescribing treatment for an individual?*

42. *To fill two places, an employer receives four referrals from the employment service, with scores on the most relevant aptitude composite as follows:*

	Group	Within-group percentile	Expectancy of above-average job performance
Allen	Minority 1	88	54
Bell	Minority 2	86	58
Cole	Nonminority	88	65
Doe	Nonminority	76	59

What reasoning could lead the employer to hire Cole and Doe? Bell and Cole? Allen and Bell?

PART Three

MEASURES OF TYPICAL RESPONSE

Chapter
12

Interest Inventories

12A. "How many dimensions are needed to describe interests?" That question has no definite answer. Why not?

12B. Why is a norm-referenced profile likely to differ from a profile of percentages of LIKE responses?

12C. Why, as a basis for promoting self-understanding, are homogeneous interest scales more satisfactory than scales keyed against occupational membership?

12D. A student says that he is interested in Occupation X, but scores in midrange on the criterion-keyed scale for Occupation X. His score on several other keys is higher. How should a counselor trying to give advice evaluate this apparent contradiction?

12E. In what major ways does today's Strong blank differ from Strong's original blank? (Consider the test form and score report and also the validity argument.)

Abbreviations in this chapter: ACT for American College Testing; DAT for Differential Aptitude Tests; JVIS for Jackson Vocational Interest Survey; KOIS for Kuder Occupational Interest Survey; MIG, WIG for men in general, women in general; MMPI for Minnesota Multiphasic Personality Inventory; RIASEC for the Holland system in Figure 12.1; SDS for Self-Directed Search (Holland).

ORIENTATION

After the solidly packed Chapter 11, this chapter offers a breather. This one tells you what interest inventories are like and takes you behind the scenes to look at judgments that go into making up a questionnaire and designing a score report.

The introduction includes ideas worth remembering, but I suggest that you read it once lightly and then review the material after you complete the chapter, in order to spot what is most significant. In the section on "dimensionalizing," you should grasp fully the RIASEC system of Figure 12.1. The "hierarchical" conception of abilities, sketched in Chapter 10, has its counterpart in this section. The details are unimportant; concentrate on the larger idea that no one solution is complete.

In the section on choices, pick out the several matters on which the experts disagree, and try to see both sides of each argument. Pay particular attention to Table 12.1 and the accompanying text. Criterion keying is widely used and is probably new to you. Be sure that you get the point of Figure 12.3; that kind of dilemma arises with many measures of typical behavior.

Reflect on Figures 12.4 and 12.5, not so that you can reproduce the content but so that you will appreciate the complex thinking behind one of the prime examples of testing technology. Scores from the Strong inventory are a recurrent topic throughout the chapter.

The research findings that begin on page 476 are to be remembered in terms of the broad conclusions and the kinds of evidence used, not the numbers from this or that study.

The section on counseling draws attention to what a score report means to the person receiving it. It extends the discussion of testing as an interactive process to which much of Chapter 3 was devoted. The ideas are straightforward, but practitioners sometimes overlook them.

Read quickly about the three "technical issues" and then decide which ones you want to think about. They are specific to interest testing, and the book will not return to them.

FUNCTIONS OF INTEREST MEASUREMENT

Interest inventories are important in their own right; 3 million young people take them each year. Beyond that, because interest inventories and personality questionnaires are based on the same range of techniques, much that is said in this chapter is broadly applicable.

The inventory is a way to help a person confront what he already knows about himself, for who else can say what his interests are? The inventory is more convenient than an interview and presents more questions, perhaps indirect ones. The standardized questions are objectively scored, and norms can be provided.

Most questions ask about degree of liking for commonplace activities with which respondents have had personal experience. Inventories also ask for responses to occupational titles or abstract descriptions of work; these may or may not have much concrete meaning. One wonders whether adolescents have a clear image of what it means to "be a juvenile delinquency expert" or to "go on expeditions to fight diseases among natives."

Unlike nearly all other psychological measurements, interest inventories are intended primarily to inform the respondent, not to provide information enabling someone else—teacher, policymaker, or clinician—to make wiser judgments. Occasionally someone proposes to use inventory scores in institutional decisions—in medical school selection, for example. Whether or not this improves prediction, the practice is questionable. To favor applicants whose interest pattern matches the one most common among today's successful students or alumni makes the profession more uniform in membership and more static. Also, asking applicants to testify about themselves could reward dishonesty. The interest inventory is best left as an aid to self-examination.

The variety of scoring scales and interpretative materials draws the respondent's attention to many vocations he or she might not have considered. The inventory thus becomes an instructional device, leading to exploration of career options. Although interest inventories are most used in high school and college, they are increasingly being applied to counsel adults in midlife and those thinking about prospective retirement activities.

The appropriate outcome of a counseling episode or a study of careers is greater self-knowledge, not a career choice. It takes many years to settle into a career; successive decisions are made along the path. The adolescent should be encouraged in wide-ranging exploration that identifies promising alternatives. Concentration comes gradually, first as choice of a broad area, then of a vocational line, and ultimately of a specialty or a personalized role.

Innocuous as interest measurement seems, it has recently been controversial (Zytowski & Borgen, 1983). Inventories can perpetuate cultural stereotypes—for instance, about occupations suitable for one sex or the other. Though agreeing that each individual should shape his or her own fate as fully as possible, measurement specialists disagree sharply about the best way to recognize that occupations do not appeal equally to women and men. Whereas domain-referenced interpretation is highly regarded in much testing of abilities, some critics condemn domain-referenced interpretation of interest scores as sexist. They contend that only interpretations based on norms for *like-sex* respondents are suitable for guidance. (A dozen years ago, whether to prepare separate inventories for males and females was also an issue. No investigator has defended sex-specific forms since separate pink and blue blanks came under attack as sexist.)

1. A firm finds substantial turnover among its salespersons. The interest pattern of those who quit differs from the pattern of those who stay (validity coefficient 0.4). Which (if any) of these uses of the information seems appropriate?
   a. Use the interest pattern as an "aptitude" measure, and reject applicants for whom short tenure is predicted.
   b. Give the inventory after hiring, and notify the sales manager that short tenure is predicted for applicants A and B but not for C.
   c. Show the applicant his interest scores and the distributions for salespersons who stay and for those who quit before the applicant commits himself to the job.

DIMENSIONALIZING INTERESTS

An occupational choice assumes a fit between personal style and work. A person's specific interests cannot be matched one by one to a catalog of occupational duties. Categories or dimensions are needed.

Six dimensions (R-I-A-S-E-C in Figure 12.1) that John Holland distilled from accumulated research now enter into most interpretations.

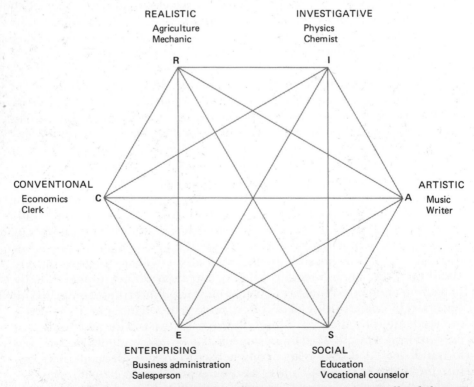

Figure 12.1. **Themes in the RIASEC system.** At each vertex is a Holland theme, a related college major, and a related occupation.

The themes are considered singly or in pairs or triples. As artistic motivation (for example) is easily combined with scientific investigation, these are adjacent in Holland's diagram. Few occupational duties encourage both artistic self-expression and conformity to conventions, so these dimensions are opposite in the diagram. The six interest scores have low intercorrelations; at the highest, a pair of neighbors such as R and I correlates about 0.3.

After all dimensions are scored, interpretation typically centers on a summary code: AEI (for example) when the person's highest scores, in order, are Artistic, Enterprising, and Investigative. A similarly coded list of occupations opens a way to interpretation. The list for AE suggests such possibilities as advertising manager, public relations, fashion model, and lawyer.

Holland's inventories have no indirect or disguised questions, and he brings no norms into the interpretation. These, then, are face-valid, domain-referenced procedures. Although Holland has produced instruments that stand by themselves, his Self-Directed Search (SDS) is today the most prominent of his offerings, and it is a multifaceted self-examination, not just an interest inventory. The person lists occupations he has been vaguely considering, checks off activities he would like (for example, "work on a scientific project"), checks off competences ("can use a microscope"), and rates occupations as attractive or unattractive. Each page is scored on RIASEC scales, and these scores are totaled across sections. If in several sections positive responses pile up on Investigative items, that gives a strong indication of the respondent's self-concept. Having self-reports on ability as well as interests mixed into the final summary score on which interpretation is based makes SDS unlike any other current instrument. (Counselors are encouraged to look at the section scores separately, to note discordant information. The materials for self-interpretation, however, rely entirely on the coded summary score.)

The ACT inventory, widely used in high school guidance, also derives from Holland's work, but it is norm-referenced.

The dimensional scheme of ACT (Figure 12.2) comes from the old notion that most occupations emphasize ideas *or* things *or* people. This structure was compressed to two main dimensions by factor analysis (Prediger, 1976, 1981a). A score near the top of the report form—high on "data" as contrasted with "ideas"—indicates preference for definite, tangible work materials. Scores plotted at the left indicate preference for dealing with people rather than things. Turn the Holland hexagon of Figure 12.1 to bring Realistic to the 3 o'clock position, and you see that the two diagrams place occupations similarly. The pie-shaped regions of the report form probably do a disservice by breaking up the continuous space. A student ought to give attention to all occupational types near his position, not focus on one piece of the pie (Latona et al., 1987).

In organizing the Jackson Vocational Interest Survey (JVIS; D. N. Jackson), the author, working from his own factor analysis, made such

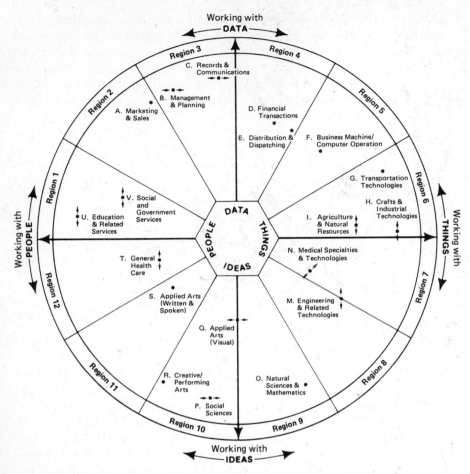

Figure 12.2. **A map of the world of work.** This diagram is part of an interpretative report supplied for career planning programs of the American College Testing Program (ACT). An arrow indicates that jobs within an occupational field range widely in the direction shown. (*Source*: From the ACT Assessment Program Technical Manual. Copyright © 1989 and used by permission of ACT.)

distinctions as Expressive/Communicative and Logical/Inquiring, so he has ten scales in place of Holland's six. An unusual feature is a cross-cutting arrangement of the items to describe preference for jobs demanding Stamina or Planfulness or Accountability. Obviously, this complex profile is best suited to mature respondents; Holland's simple one is geared to early career exploration.

2. *What occupations seem likely to suit interests with Holland code AIS? In view of the limited reliability of differences between scores, would your answer have been the same if the pattern had been SIA (S highest instead of A)? Would an SIA person like SA occupations?*

3. *Locate professional occupations and others requiring a college education in Figure 12.2. What does this suggest about the interpretation of Prediger's factors?*

CHOICES IN CONSTRUCTING INVENTORIES

Interest inventories are constructed in a variety of patterns. Vocational interest measurement began with simple occupational checklists, but E. K. Strong's 1928 Vocational Interest Blank asked also about recreations, persons admired, and other preferences indirectly related to occupations. For this he devised a scoring system that reported how closely the respondent's interests resembled those of, for example, bankers; I shall explain this "occupational" keying later in this section. As reshaped over the years by Strong and his successors,[1] this inventory has commanded great respect and has had wide use. In 1939 G. F. Kuder produced an instrument quite different from Strong's using factor analysis to group items with similar content ("homogeneous" keys). Easy to use and interpret, the Kuder Preference Record became highly popular. As late as the 1970s the story of interest measurement could be told almost entirely in terms of Strong/Kuder contrasts.

Today, the picture is scrambled. Computers made it possible to build ever-more-elaborate score reports. The Strong persisted with its original technique but added scales to measure dimensions in the traditions of Kuder and Holland. Kuder, meanwhile, shifted to occupational keying and heterogeneous scales, but gave the system a twist of his own. His Kuder Occupational Interest Survey (KOIS) has evolved so that it too reports occupational scores and homogeneous scales of the two kinds. Where once there was conflict between the advocates of the two approaches, the view today is that each type of profile enriches the interpretation of the other type.

This chapter will end with a close look at some construction techniques; here, I consider broad issues significant for personality inventories as well. They are easier to grasp in the interest context, because theories of personality structure are controversial, whereas theories about interests stick close to common sense.

Techniques matter. Possibly it is true that the different kinds of instrument are equally valid, on average, but scales constructed on different principles are bound to disagree. This point deserves several examples:

---

[1]The original Blank was revised and extended by David Campbell, and the 1974 revision was called the Strong-Campbell Interest Inventory. Jo-Ida Hansen (1978, 1988) has been the principal developer in the 1980s. The 1985 manual, signed by Hansen and Campbell, refers to the instrument as "SVIB-SCII." I shall speak of "the Strong" without attending to these nuances.

- At the extreme, two scales describing interest in a career as printer were found to correlate *minus* 0.7 (Zytowski, 1968).
- Even two scores from the same answer sheet can be discordant. Thus, a correlation of only 0.6 is reported for the Artistic and Artist scales of the Strong. The items in the Artistic scale refer to liking for artistic activities. The Artist scale examines whether the person's preferences among miscellaneous activities (algebra, tennis, selling, etc.) correspond to the preferences of the majority of artists.
- Holland interest scores correlate only 0.35–0.6 with corresponding scales of the ACT inventory.
- In one study, the "basic interest" scales of the Strong were scored along with the JVIS. The most nearly corresponding scales did not correlate above 0.5, and sometimes r dropped to 0.3 (for example, Office Work with Office Practices).

Discrepancies of this magnitude imply that any instrument is just a partial indicator, which inevitably limits validity. This is a persuasive reason for looking on an inventory as a stimulus to conversation rather than as a definitive "measurement."

Simplicity vs. Complexity

Developers have to decide how many items to include and how simple to make the scoring. Short-and-simple implies lower cost but less thorough measurement. A form that test takers can score for themselves appeals to purchasers who want quick, inexpensive returns. At the opposite extreme, a client may be happy to pay for, and perhaps wait some days for, a computer printout that offers dozens of scores and several pages of "personalized" interpretation. The more elaborate the profile, the more necessary computer scoring becomes.

Computers can be brought more directly into the act. They not only can present the scores but can conduct a question-and-answer session simulating a conversation with a counselor about the report. The computer program is especially adept at bringing in information on occupations. Many clients counseled by computer come away better satisfied than similar clients who have met with a human counselor. (This difference, however, may have been created by the human counselor's pressing clients to consider inconsistencies in their vocational thinking.)

There is an increasing emphasis on self-scoring and self-interpretation, and for many inventories one can obtain a booklet that leads the person through a limited interpretation. Some descriptive interpretations printed out by computer aim to give the respondent all the understanding the inventory can provide.

Despite the painstaking work behind the complex Strong and KOIS, many specialists in guidance have come to prefer simplicity to high technology. If an interest profile is generated primarily to stimulate the client to study careers and himself over an extended period, the information can be much less precise than what a one-time effort to "choose a career" would need. A short, simple, self-scoring instrument may engage the young person more fully than a mysterious and remote technical procedure and may carry more the flavor of self-examination than of assessment by an authority. Holland argues that simple instruments are generally as effective as technically refined instruments in advancing career development (Holland, in Plake & Witt, 1986; see also Zytowski & Borgen, 1983).

Bypassing the services of a counselor becomes a realistic necessity when counselors are few; but the risk of misinterpretation goes up. The Self-Directed Search is not fully successful in providing for self-interpretation. College students go astray when digesting the materials without a counselor's help (Dolliver & Hansen, 1977), and high-school students make a good many errors even at the relatively simple self-scoring stage (Holland, 1985, p. 9).

An ever-present hazard in test interpretation is oversimplification. Older practices such as routinely calling persons with IQs under 70 "feebleminded" and categorizing everyone with a certain personality score as "paranoid" are now in disrepute. Interest scores sometimes stereotype occupations; to say "You are like a biologist" suggests incorrectly that biologists are all alike psychologically. I shall later illustrate how the full profile can help the counselee understand the diversity within an occupation and take that into account in his planning. Self-interpretation cannot be so sensitive.

Holland's SDS introduces additional risks by inviting those receiving reports to consider personality descriptions associated with RIASEC categories. One can scarcely quarrel with attaching to the Investigative category the adjectives "curious," intellectual," and "precise." No one who has known many scientists, though, would be ready to generalize that persons in investigative careers are "cautious," "modest," and "reserved." The trait-career associations may have been "statistically significant" in studies Holland reviewed; but in self-interpreting materials there is no way to convey how weak such associations are.

Item Form

Regarding format, there are three major decisions. The first has to do with the kind of item: Endorsement? or comparison? The second has to do with organizing items into a scale: Homogeneous? or criterion-keyed? The third has to do with the basis for plotting profiles: Raw response counts (or raw percentages)? or norm-referenced conversions? I shall argue that the advantage lies with homogeneous keying and with interpretation of a raw-score profile. Both item forms have a place. With directly interpretable homogeneous keys, endorsement items probably serve best. Choice items probably serve best where indirect criterion keys are applied.

An endorsement item presents a single stimulus ("Repairing a bicycle"). The person is to check what he likes or to respond LIKE/INDIFFERENT/DISLIKE (L/I/D) or to rate on a 5-point scale (LIKE VERY MUCH, etc). A comparison or forced-choice item presents two to four stimuli and asks the person to choose the most liked and perhaps the least liked, as in

Make a speech to raise funds for a cause   M L
Write letters to raise funds for a cause   M L
Persuade friends to volunteer as fund raisers   M L

Another forced-choice form is represented by

I have more admiration for someone who
  A   Knows a lot about astronomy
  B   Can pick profitable investments

Respondents can answer endorsement items faster than choice items and they find endorsing more comfortable than making hard choices. Forcing choices rules out the influence of yea-saying and nay-saying styles. With the endorsement format, one person will blandly endorse nearly everything, while another may reject all but the few occupations he already has centered on. A person who usually responds LIKE or YES or AGREE is said to be "acquiescent." With endorsement items that person's profile bumps the ceiling, and differences across scales become unreliable. Persons with many INDIFFERENT responses to endorsement items likewise generate uninformative profiles.

Organizing Items into Scales

Holland's interest scales—Investigative, for example—are homogeneous; items counted within a scale refer to similar activities and correlate positively with each other. The alternative technique, criterion keying, counts up responses that correlate with a criterion (usually membership/nonmembership in an occupation).

To arrive at a homogeneous set of items, the developer uses logic and correlations. Suppose that the developer's original hunch is that some work is predominantly "verbal." A checklist of verbal activities could be presented:

Writing a poem
Persuading passersby to donate to a charity
Translating for speakers at the UN
Reporting a soccer match for a newspaper

The psychological demands of these activities differ; persons who like one might dislike others. When the interitem correlations are not consistently positive, it may be possible to salvage the original category by dropping a few activities whose correlations run low. The original category could be split if, for example, "persuasive" uses of words hang together. Other coherent categories might be "self-expressive writing" and "word processing."

Criterion keying, like the regression weighting described in Chapter 11, is strictly data-based. Ideally, the prediction-minded psychologist developing a scale would allow a long lead time. She would first try likely items on many young persons, later finding out which ones became airplane pilots (say) and enjoyed the life. Those in today's generation who respond as these aviators did would be judged most likely to pursue and enjoy an aviation career.

Long-term follow-up is a slow way to develop a scale, and an enormous initial sample would be needed to finish with a suitable number of satisfied persons in each occupation. The shortcut is to collect responses of adults who have been in an occupation for some time and who appear to be successful and satisfied. The developer locates a few hundred professional fliers and collects inventory responses from them. Whatever responses most of them share are counted as symptomatic of "aviator interests."

Criterion keys are not confined to vocational interests, as items can be keyed against any external criterion. The Strong inventory offers an Academic Comfort scale, based on interests expressed by college students who have good grade records. In principle, a scale assessing accident-proneness of customers could be constructed for an insurance company (Kunce & Reeder, 1974).

The Strong's occupational keys are formed by comparing responses of men satisfied in an occupation with responses representative of all men—"men in general" or MIG; similarly for women (WIG). Table 12.1 illustrates the method. The difference in L percentages is large for "Manufacturer," so the person who marks that item L adds one point to the Engineer(m) score. The key for Engineer(f) has nearly the same pattern. In that key, however, liking to be manager of a child-care center is counted -1, because 41 per cent of WIG and only 14 per cent of female engineers gave that response. The difference among males was too small to justify counting the item in Engineer(m).

The keys cover diverse occupations: Accountant, Beautician, Chef, Dental assistant, . . ., YMCA (or YWCA) director. The Strong now has male and female keys for 101 occupations. Prior to 1985 the vast majority of keys were for occupations into which college graduates go. An important recent addition is a set of keys for jobs that require few academic credentials: bus driver, for example.

The developers considered it necessary to prepare an entirely fresh set of keys for the current revision to recognize generational change. Weights for items were therefore determined anew, from contemporary samples. The effort required is suggested by the statement that responses of nearly 50,000 persons were used in building the various keys. (Actually, 140,000 persons filled out the blank. But the number of cases per occupation was often too small to support building of a key.)

Table 12.1   HOW ENGINEER(m) SCORING WEIGHTS WERE ESTABLISHED

| Item | Response distribution (%) | | | | | | | | | Scoring weight assigned | | |
| | Engineers | | | MIG | | | Difference | | | | | |
	L	I	D	L	I	D	L	I	D	L	I	D
Life insurance agent	2	16	82	8	23	69	− 6	− 7	13	0	0	0
Machine shop supervisor	30	47	23	20	37	43	10	10	− 20	1	1	−1
Machinist	38	43	19	22	35	43	16	8	− 24	1	0	−1
Manager, Chamber of Commerce	14	43	43	27	40	33	− 13	3	10	0	0	0
Manager, child-care center	4	25	71	15	31	54	− 11	− 6	17	0	0	0
Manager, women's style shop	2	11	87	5	20	75	− 3	− 9	12	0	0	0
Manufacturer	58	38	4	39	39	22	19	− 1	− 18	1	0	−1
Mechanical engineer	71	27	2	42	34	24	29	− 7	− 22	1	0	−1
Military officer	27	32	41	27	25	48	0	7	− 7	0	0	0
Minister, priest, rabbi	12	29	59	16	30	54	− 4	− 1	5	0	0	0
Musician	46	29	25	46	29	25	0	0	0	0	0	0
Newspaper reporter	20	42	38	38	38	24	− 18	4	14	−1	0	1

Source: Data supplied by Jo-Ida C. Hansen.

Homogeneous scales are transparent. The respondent is well aware of the interests his response expresses. Criterion-keyed scales are opaque. Therefore, the respondent can only partially guess the meanings a criterion key will attach to a response. The key evaluates the item by its correlates rather than its content. The woman saying "I would dislike managing a child-care center" is adding a point to her Engineer score, even though the topic is remote from technical work.

A criterion-keyed scale may be something of a hodgepodge. According to Campbell (in Zytowski, 1973, pp. 38, 40; edited):

> The only way to score high on the [homogeneous] Military Activities scale is to respond LIKE to "be an army officer," "drill a company of soldiers," and similar items. In contrast, the [criterion-keyed] Army Officer occupational scale . . . [includes] clusters of items; one concerns engineering and construction activities; another deals with legal power . . .; a third has items of a general managerial nature; yet another contains straight math items. Finally, a small cluster of items deals with military activities.

On the Military Activities scale, the respondent knows what responses indicate liking for an officer's job; hence the score is open to faking. On the indirect criterion-keyed scale it is much harder to obtain the score one would prefer by deliberate distortion in responding. (Campbell was speaking of a key that has now been replaced, but the basic point remains true.)

4. *Under what circumstances would anyone wish to paint a false picture of himself on an inventory?*

Score Reporting

Interpretation of interests has traditionally emphasized comparison across the person's scores: what does he or she like *most?* The number of positive responses depends on the number of items in a category, the attractiveness of the activities chosen to represent it, and, with forced-choice, the way pairs or triads are assembled. There are several ways to make scores somewhat comparable across categories.

- Raw percentages: positive responses in a category as a percentage of the maximum possible. A scale for a Likes-minus-Dislikes formula can run from -100 to $+100$.
- Percentiles or standard scores based on a general reference group. An interest inventory can offer norms within sex and grade or for a broader group.
- Percentiles or standard scores based on an occupational reference group. A high school senior can be told how his interest scores compare with those of college engineering students or those of adult engineers. A manual might report the range of engineers' scores on every scale or just on the Engineer scale.

Interest norms are commonly tabulated within sexes but, as with the DAT (p. 131), a profile may be presented with both same sex and opposite-sex percentiles.

In my opinion, general norms should play little part in interpreting interests; if a person likes the work, it makes no difference whether 50 per cent or 90 per cent of other persons would also like it. The emphasis on norms reflects the prominence of competition in U.S. thought, which presumes that you have a competitive advantage when you like your work better than others would—even if you hate it! On the other hand, raw scores depend on the list of items. Positive responses can be increased by adding popular activities to the scale, and dropping unpopular activities can conceal important aversions. If raw scores will be reported, a thoughtful policy for choosing items is required.

Norms for persons in an occupation can play a useful role, not because a high comparative standing is good in itself but because the norms tell what the occupational world is accustomed to. If a person's interest in Realistic activities falls at an extreme of the distribution for engineers—beyond the 15th or 85th percentile, perhaps—the person is unlike most engineers. Such a signal is thought-provoking. But it is not the final word, inasmuch as outliers may fill special niches.

Terwilliger (1960) contrasted profiles based on counts with profiles based on norms. He sampled job titles in four fields from a census list, then edited brief definitions, to form a domain-referenced instrument.

He defined response categories more carefully than is usual, as degrees of liking. I report on responses to the question, "Assuming that you had suitable training, would you think quite seriously about an offer of this job and *probably accept* it?" High school boys endorsed 17 per cent of occupations in the "artistic" field and 48 per cent of "mechanical" occupations. Mechanical and persuasive activities were popular; clerical and artistic work, unpopular. Figure 12.3 describes Jim and Nick in two ways. The left panel shows that Jim is mild in his endorsement of all four fields. Because most boys reject two of the fields, the percentiles at the right give the mistaken impression that Jim is attracted to artistic work and clerical work. Nick's norm-referenced profile suggests that he lacks any particular interest. In fact, his response to mechanical jobs was positive, but being positive about machines is not exceptional.

Data such as these lead me to emphasize raw scores. Among producers of inventories, however, only Holland agrees with me. His reasoning is laid out in the SDS manual.

Prediger (1981b) directly challenges Holland, urging counselors to interpret norm-referenced profiles. Prediger's evidence is summarized in Table 12.2. Women who had taken SDS were asked 1 to 3 years later what occupation they were planning to enter. Among the four women now headed for R occupations (presumably as a consequence of both counseling and satisfaction with college courses), three had originally given more positive responses to I items than to R or any other category. One had her highest raw score in S. When percentiles were plotted instead of raw scores, three of these women had peaks in R and one in I. For this small subgroup, then, the normed profile was more indicative. But the normed profile tended to be off-target with respect to popular fields (as in Figure 12.3). So, overall, it located fewer persons correctly.

Figures 12.4 and 12.5 illustrate how the report for the Strong, with its enormous number of facts, is organized. The halves of the profile

Table 12.2   RAW SCORES AND NORMED SCORES OF COLLEGE WOMEN AS PREDICTORS OF OCCUPATIONAL CHOICE

Holland code of occupation	Number of women choosing occupation	Number having that code highest when profile is		Per cent correctly predicted from	
		raw	normed	raw	normed
R	4	0	3	0	75
C	24	7	13	29	54
E	48	2	10	4	21
A	117	57	54	49	46
I	139	63	72	45	52
S	657	481	155	73	24

Source: Data from Prediger (1981b). I have italicized the better percentage in each row.

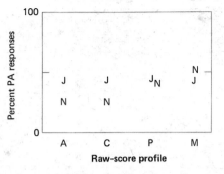
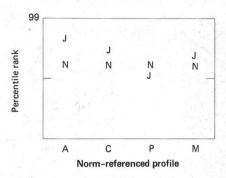

Figure 12.3. **Direct and norm-referenced profiles.**

have been put on two pages here for ease of reading. I display sections for only two of the six RIASEC categories. The scores charted are averages for female office managers, but an individual's report would look much the same.

I mentioned earlier that the Strong now augments occupational scales with homogeneous scales. Figure 12.4 represents these. In the Conventional section the office managers are high, which fits Holland's concept. Social interests are not high, even though office managers deal with people; their average is close to the population mean. In the schematic distributions of Figure 12.4 the thin line stretches from the 10th to the 90th percentile; the thick bar stretches from the 25th to the 75th.

Whereas basic scales are normed against MIG and WIG, occupational scores (Figure 12.5) are expressed relative to persons in the occupation. The highest average score among these office managers is Secretary, at 49—almost exactly at the average of female secretaries. The wide "Midrange" column identifies a near average degree of interest, which is of course below the mean of the criterion group. Women in general average 32 on the Secretary scale, a value falling in that column.

5. *If the raw-score profiles J and N of Figure 12.3 were for Jane and Nelly, would you expect the norm-referenced profiles to differ from those pictured? Should that alter the interpretation?*

6. *Most scoring services resolve the problem posed by Prediger's data by printing both raw scores and norm-referenced scores on the report form (but diagramming only one profile).*
   a. *Is there any argument against presenting both diagrams (somewhat as Figure 12.3 does)?*
   b. *If you were being counseled and were given both sets of numerical scores but only one graphic profile, would you prefer a picture of the raw or the norm-referenced profile?*

7. *When an inventory has norms, it is possible to display two profiles, in terms of own-sex and opposite-sex percentiles. What can be said for and against this practice?*

8. *A college woman has S highest in her raw-score profile and E highest in her normed profile. What does Table 12.3 imply about the field where she will be satisfied?*

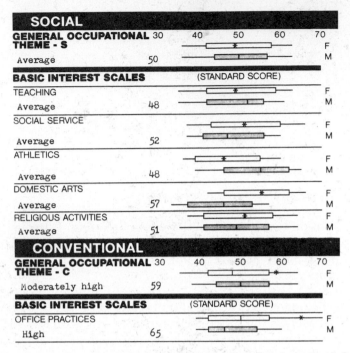

Figure 12.4. **Part of the basic Strong profile.** Two sections from the left side of a Strong score report, with data describing the average response of a group of female office managers. A score of 50 matches the average of "persons-in-general." These scores are charted against own-sex norms, with the opposite-sex norms alongside. The label at the left is based on own-sex norms; the "high" Office Practices score would be labeled "very high" if earned by a male. (*Source*: Reproduced by special permission of Consulting Psychologists Press, Inc., Palo Alto, CA 94306, agent for the publisher, Stanford University Press. Reprinted from the Manual for the Strong-Campbell Interest Inventory, Form T-325 of the Strong Vocational Interest Blank, 4th ed., by David P. Campbell and Jo-Ida C. Hansen. Copyright 1974, 1977, 1981, 1984, 1985 by the Board of Trustees of the Leland Stanford Junior University. Further reproduction is prohibited without the agent's consent.)

9. *Because school budgets are strained, little counselor time is available for most students; hence school policies capitalize on counselors' scarce expertise. What policies would you suggest regarding which kind of inventory to use, who should be encouraged to take it and when, and what interpretative support to provide?*

PREDICTIVE SIGNIFICANCE

Stability

Interest inventories seek to predict satisfaction over years to come, but interests develop. The ordering of broad areas sometimes changes, and preferences within an area come into focus.

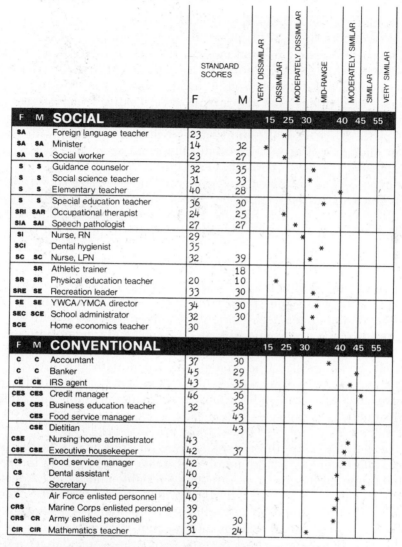

F	M	SOCIAL	Standard Scores F	Standard Scores M	Chart position (15 25 30 — 40 45 55)
SA		Foreign language teacher	23		* Moderately dissimilar (30)
SA	SA	Minister	14	32	* Very dissimilar (~15)
SA	SA	Social worker	23	27	* Dissimilar (25)
S	S	Guidance counselor	32	35	* Moderately similar (40)
S	S	Social science teacher	31	33	* Moderately similar (40)
S	S	Elementary teacher	40	28	* Mid-range
S	S	Special education teacher	36	30	* Moderately similar (40)
SRI	SAR	Occupational therapist	24	25	* Dissimilar (25)
SIA	SAI	Speech pathologist	27	27	* Moderately dissimilar (30)
SI		Nurse, RN	29		* Mid-range
SCI		Dental hygienist	35		* Moderately similar
SC	SC	Nurse, LPN	32	39	* Mid-range
	SR	Athletic trainer		18	
SR	SR	Physical education teacher	20	10	* Very dissimilar
SRE	SE	Recreation leader	33	30	* Mid-range
SE	SE	YWCA/YMCA director	34	30	* Moderately similar
SEC	SCE	School administrator	32	30	* Mid-range
SCE		Home economics teacher	30		* Mid-range

F	M	CONVENTIONAL	Standard Scores F	Standard Scores M	Chart position (15 25 30 — 40 45 55)
C	C	Accountant	37	30	* Mid-range
C	C	Banker	45	29	* Similar (45)
CE	CE	IRS agent	43	35	* Moderately similar (40)
CES	CES	Credit manager	46	36	* Similar (45)
CES	CES	Business education teacher	32	38	* Moderately similar (40)
	CES	Food service manager		43	
	CSE	Dietitian		43	
CSE		Nursing home administrator	43		* Similar (45)
CSE	CSE	Executive housekeeper	42	37	* Similar (45)
CS		Food service manager	42		* Similar
CS		Dental assistant	40		* Similar
C		Secretary	49		* Very similar
C		Air Force enlisted personnel	40		* Moderately similar
CRS		Marine Corps enlisted personnel	39		* Moderately similar
CRS	CR	Army enlisted personnel	39	30	* Moderately similar
CIR	CIR	Mathematics teacher	31	24	* Mid-range

Figure 12.5. **Part of the Strong occupational profile.** This figure shows two sections from the right side of the score report, with average data for female office managers. The first two columns indicate RIASEC codes for the occupations. The numbers are scores on the male and female keys for the occupation; a score of 50 equals the average of the within-sex occupational group used in keying. A blank in the column of numerical scores indicates that there is no occupational key for that sex. Asterisks chart scores from own-sex keys. A few details of the layout are changed here for ease of reading. (*Source*: See Figure 12.4.)

Broad tendencies—at the people/data/ideas/things level—are firm enough by the midteens to be a basis for preliminary discussion of the self-concept as it relates to occupations. Among adolescents not bound for college, interests appear to stabilize comparatively early. But teenagers, comparatively inexperienced, respond INDIFFERENT to more items than adults do; they have not yet developed some of their interests. (Schletzer, 1963, 1966). For the college-bound in particular, discussion of careers should stress options to be kept open.

The current Strong manual reports stability correlations of 0.85–0.9 over 3 years for most occupational scales. These recent figures (based on small samples) are strangely higher than the values from Strong's earlier studies, which the manual also summarizes. Taking 19- to 21-year-olds as example, correlations in the older studies were about 0.75 over 2–5 years. After 18 years, half—only half—of Strong's retest profiles were similar enough to suggest essentially the same occupational advice as the originals. Just 6 per cent of "very similar" reports changed to midrange; just 3 per cent of midrange reports to "very similar." In a few cases, however, a profile peak became a valley in the interval or vice versa (Strong, 1955, p. 64; see also Darley & Hagenah, 1955, p. 43).

Agreement of Inventories with Claimed Interests

Inventories often tell a story different from the response to "What job would you like?" In one study, students were asked to estimate their standings on the dimensions scored for an inventory they had taken. The average correlation between estimated interest and inventoried interest was 0.5 (Crosby & Winsor, 1941). In another investigation (Darley & Hagenah, 1955, p. 67), the inventory agreed with the estimates of roughly two-thirds of those who claimed interest in business detail, business contact, or a technical field, but agreed with only one-third of those who claimed dominant scientific, social service, and verbal-linguistic interests. (See also Super & Crites, 1962, pp. 437–441.)

There are at least three explanations for such apparent disagreements. The inventory's large number of items, many of them indirectly related to the job in question, provides a reliable and penetrating sampling. Second, "strong" interest on a normed scale refers not to degree of interest but to comparative standing. It is not logically comparable to the self-estimated of strength of interest, but statistical studies report that kind of comparison. Third, the low—sometimes scandalously low— correlations between scales bearing near-identical titles in different inventories imply that the client could not hope to predict his inventory score without knowing the peculiarities of the inventory in question.

When disagreement arises, the profile probably is saying something important, but the counselor would be unwise to dismiss the self-estimate as "wrong." Her task is to help the counselee to an emotionally acceptable reconciliation of claimed and measured interests.

Relations with Criteria

Occupational Choice and Satisfaction   Prediction of career choice is most accurate when claimed interests and inventoried interests point in the same direction (Holland, in Plake & Witt, 1986, p. 252; see also the references listed there). When the two disagree, according to two substantial studies (Bartling & Hood, 1981; Borgen & Seling, 1978), the actual job is far more likely to match the expressed interest than the inventory peak; but evidence in the opposite direction is reported by Crowley (1983). More intensive study of cases of disagreement, looking at job satisfaction as well as occupational title, is needed. One other point is worth noting: Many adolescents have only vaguely defined interests, and the inventory is especially pertinent for them (Hough, 1986, p. 149).

About half the middle-aged men in an occupation had scored, in college, near or above the average on the Strong key of the relevant occupational group. The available figures for women run lower, particularly because many of the workers were not in long-term careers.

Interest scores discriminate persons who will like a job from those who will not. A guidance service tested high school seniors and adults and a year later asked what work they were doing and how they liked it (Lipsett & Wilson, 1954). The investigators then judged whether the person's measured interests were "suitable" for the job. Interests predicted satisfaction reasonably well; interests and ability taken together gave an excellent forecast.

Further evidence is found in studies of men who changed fields after leaving school. Strong (1943, pp. 114ff.) and Zytowski (1974, 1976) found this:

> Those who remained in an occupation for 10 years or more averaged higher scores for that occupation than for any other.

> Those continuing in an occupation had higher scores in that interest than those who tried the occupation and changed.

> Those who changed from one occupation to another changed to one in which their interest scores were about as high as for the first choice.

Success   Few studies compare interest scores with excellence on the job. Strong's investigations of insurance agents (1943, pp. 486–500) are still notable. The value of new policies written by men with high scores in sales interest was three times the value of sales by those with low scores. A few men in midrange reached the minimum level required to support themselves by commissions; none got much above it. The correlation is only 0.4, no doubt because most men with midrange interest had dropped out of the sample during their first unproductive years. Once again we see the practical significance of a score whose correlation with a criterion is moderate. Reviewing all the available literature, Hough (1986, p. 167) puts the typical correlation of interest with proficiency in a field at 0.2–0.3.

E. L. Kelly and D. W. Fiske (1951; see also Kelly & Goldberg, 1959) tested students entering training for clinical psychology. Four years later they collected grades, scores on performance tests, and ratings by training supervisors. Particular interest attaches to the ratings on overall clinical competence and research competence. Among the many scores, only verbal reasoning predicted better than the Strong. Clinical ratings correlated 0.3 with Strong's Author and Lawyer keys. Ratings on research competence correlated around 0.3 with scientific interests and with lack of business or office work interests. (These results might not hold up in further samples; chance plays a large part when—with many scales and criteria—hundreds of correlations are run.)

Interests predict (usually at a modest level) who stays in training and who drops out. In training for dentistry, among students whose inventory responses were like those of dentists 92 per cent graduated from dentistry training, compared with 25 per cent of those at midrange and below (Strong, 1943, p. 524). The median correlation in published studies is 0.3 between course completion and the relevant inventory score. Correlations with grades or instructor's ratings are at about the same level (Hough, 1986, p. 168).

It adds up to this: Interest cannot offset a lack of ability, and lack of interest does not spoil the chances of those with high aptitude. But a person is most likely to put his full abilities into a job when the work and work conditions appeal to his needs (Dawis & Lofquist, 1984; Lofquist & Dawis, 1969).

10. *Follow-up studies on vocational choice and satisfaction almost always use persons who initially were told the implications of their score profiles. Discuss this as an example of "contamination" (p. 415).*

11. *It is possible to form occupational keys for subcategories within an occupation. What would appear to be reasonable subcategories for psychologists?*

12. *Barnette (1951) examined whether men who planned to enter engineering continued in such training. A score on mechanical interests had no relation to continuance; it was high for those who dropped out as well as for those who continued. A score on computational interests had a marked relation to continuance. Explain.*

13. *Several investigations have reported the following configural pattern: when students are classified as compulsive or noncompulsive, interest in science predicts grades in engineering for the noncompulsive group only. (See Frederiksen et al., 1972, p. 5.)*
    a. *Make a chart somewhat like Figure 11.9 to illustrate this finding.*
    b. *Suggest an explanation.*
    c. *Could the finding be of use in counseling or selection?*

INTEREST MEASURES IN COUNSELING

As I said earlier, counselors aim to promote self-understanding. The individual is to make choices as new facts become available, as he matures, or as his social circumstances and opportunities change. The student in high school may set down a definite plan to study certain subjects, to enroll in a certain college curriculum, to complete training in a certain professional school, and to seek a certain type of practice. This plan is unlikely to be carried out. Somewhere along the line instructors will open new vistas or arouse new interests. Somewhere along the line concrete experience will show that he does not enjoy some aspect of the work, or talent in another direction will surface. Counseling should generate plans with many branches. The significant goal in counseling is to equip the student to make later decisions. The aim should be to give the student a more sophisticated view of the world of work, of the choices open to him, and of his range of potentialities for achievement and satisfaction. Those counseled do not always welcome this missionary enterprise. Students come to an interest inventory seeking "reassurance" that their present plans are suitable; desire to extend their list of options is not a prominent motive (Holland, in Plake & Witt, 1986, p. 254).

The interest inventory can be given to entire classes, and interpretation of profiles can be carried out in group discussions. Leading each student to list career possibilities suggested by the inventory is an excellent preliminary to group study of careers or to individual counseling.

It is unwise to concentrate the interpretation on a few occupations. This gives the student far too narrow a description of himself. It is essential that the student go beneath occupational stereotypes, that he understand the diversity of roles within an occupation, that he understand the differences between demands of the training program and demands of the occupation.

Nowadays homogeneous scales are thought to be a better starting place for counseling than criterion-keyed occupational scales. A high score in verbal interests, for example, leads to follow-up questions to clarify whether the interest is in reading, writing, or speaking and whether the interest is in face-to-face communication or in writing in a quiet room. The discussion will come round to vocations. The examples brought forward should be consistent not only with the scores but with the counselee's claimed interests, probable ultimate level of education, and abilities. A string of scores based on homogeneous scales invites the student to think of himself as an individual rather than to concentrate on an occupational label.

In college Mary Thomas filled out a Kuder inventory with homogeneous scales. She was above the 90th percentile on Computational and Clerical scales, and below the 20th on Persuasive, Scientific, and Social Service interests. Her major at the time was child development. Her grades were mediocre, and her work with children was not especially successful. When questioned regarding her choice of major, she explained that she had set her heart on work in an orphanage. This desire arose in childhood when she read a book about a woman who helped orphan children—a "wonderful" lifework. Her low Persuasive and Social Service scores suggest a somewhat withdrawn personality, and the high Computational and Clerical scores suggest a liking for conventional, uncreative activities. When questioned about office work, Mary enthusiastically described her previous summer's work as a file clerk; her duties apparently consisted solely of alphabetizing folders; yet she had "just loved it." Moreover, she had done well in office skills courses. Evidently both ability and interest fell in an area she had not considered as a vocational goal.

To tell Mary, "You don't really want to work in child development; you want to be a secretary," would precipitate emotional conflict. No one can abandon a long-standing self-concept easily. An authority who bluntly contradicts firm beliefs invites rejection. In Mary's case, it might be best to inquire as to the reasons for her choice of child development, to ask her to envision the activities she may be engaged in 10 years hence, and to compare them with the activities rated high in the interest blank. The fact that the inventory contains only her own ratings brings her to face self-contradictions. The counselor is no longer the "authority"—she is merely holding the mirror. The counselor can go further, pointing out that agencies serving children need devoted clerical staffs. Such work is in line with Mary's ideals *and* her interests.

Interest scores should be considered as a set. Taken together, they support a portrait. Criterion scales were designed to be used one at a time, to predict for single occupations; but they can be interpreted as a set if one brings insight to bear. To be "like the average engineer" means little. In fact, whereas research engineers scored high on the SVIB Engineer scale, production engineers and sales engineers (engaged with people) tended to score fairly low (Dunnette, 1957). Occupations are not homogeneous. Persons in the same occupation use it to satisfy distinctly different personal bents.

I offer myself as example. Early in my career I filled out the Strong, and Campbell has rescored the blank with modern scales. College Professor and Psychologist (my ostensible career lines) were among the highest scores assigned my responses given at age 32; so were Lawyer, Journalist, Mathematician, and Political Scientist. Homogeneous keys applied to the same answer sheet tell a similar story. At the top are Public Speaking and Teaching, followed by Writing, Law/Politics, and Mathematics. Science was exactly average. Either *set* of scores taken together matches my career. I probably am more at home on a platform and have gotten more into public-policy discussions than most psychologists of my generation. I have written a lot. I have analyzed data and developed mathematical theory for such analysis. I did no laboratory research and no clinical work after age 30. So the Strong gave a valid picture, not of my "similarity to psychologists" but of a role I could enjoy within that variegated profession.

The current *Users Guide* for the Strong encourages the interpretation of scores all together, as a story about a life-style. This goes far beyond the concept that the counselee should pick "an occupation" for which his score is high.

14. *"The reason for using an interest inventory in counseling is not to rank a number of people but to rank a multitude of occupations for one person. . . .*

[T]he variation that is relevant to the individual is one that exists within the person" (Kuder, 1977, p. 9). *What type of score best serves this purpose? Could some other purpose be stated for interest inventories?*

15. *The scoring keys for earlier editions of Strong inventories were available to the profession, but current ones are not. Scoring must be done by computer today, and firms buy a license to provide that service. The publisher makes keys available only to licensees. What consequences would the policy have with regard to*
    a. *ability of psychologists to interpret the profile?*
    b. *quality of scoring and computerized interpretations?*
    c. *availability of funds to support continuing research?*

TECHNICAL ISSUES

Two Types of Criterion Key

Criterion keying has been popular because it does not require validated theory. The counselor can make predictions without any claim that she "understands" the interests of (say) male bankers. No matter what makes for happiness in a male banker's life, the client can be advised that he (or she!) is attuned to that life if the marks on the answer sheet resemble the responses common among male bankers. Many psychologists who distrust human judgment (pp. 569–573) favor criterion keying for interest and personality inventories.

The criterion-keying principles of Strong and Kuder differ. As Table 12.1 illustrated, the Strong tallies responses where the occupational group differs from the same-sex reference group—a discriminant key. In contrast, KOIS counts responses given frequently by members of the occupational group; I call this a commonality key.

It would overcomplicate this discussion to describe fully the KOIS technique. Instead, I describe a procedure that will make Kuder's main principle apparent. Consider the items in Table 12.1, and suppose that Sherlock Jones responded L to the first four items, I to the next four, and D to the last. Then on Strong's Engineer(m) key he picked up 2 points on the first four items and 1 point on the last item, for a raw score of +3 on this bit of the scale. To get a score more like that of KOIS, look only at the responses of the engineers in Table 12.1, and add up the percentages of engineers agreeing with Sherlock: 2 per cent on the first item, 30 per cent on the second, . . ., 38 per cent on the last. The average is 29 per cent; to bring norms into the picture, divide by the maximum possible. 82 + 47 + . . . gives an average of 57 per cent, and Jones's ratio (29/57) is close to 0.5. Note that the response L on the first item did not affect Jones's discriminant score but pulled down the commonality score.

A KOIS engineer score tells how closely the person's interests resemble those of the typical engineer of like sex. The profile highlights occupational groups the person *most* resembles. A high score on a Strong occupational key indicates that the person's interests depart markedly from those of average persons *in the direction* of the typical engineer. Two persons who depart equally from the modal response of engineers score alike on KOIS, but the Strong score is lower for the one whose interests are more commonplace.

Some detail will clarify this. Assume that on a certain dimension engineers have stronger interest than the average person of like sex. Figure 12.6 denotes this by putting E to the right of PIG (persons in general). On the discriminant key (broken line), interests definitely to the right of PIG are scored as "like engineers." The greater the distance from PIG, the higher the score. The solid line behaves like Kuder's score; persons *nearest* E are scored as most "like engineers." On the commonality key the top score goes to persons at Level 2. Persons at Level 1 are scored high on the discriminant key and rather low on the commonality key. If one wants a high score to represent "interests similar to engineers," commonality keying is logically superior. Because persons of radically different types earn *low* scores on such a key, it has little psychological unity.

16. *On a certain item, female engineers divide their responses evenly (33/33/33). The L/I/D distribution of WIG is 60/30/10. How would this item affect engineer scores calculated in the Strong manner? a score of the KOIS type?*

17. *Discuss the scoring of responses at Level 3 of Figure 12.6.*

18. *Suppose that physicists' interests locate their average to the right of E in Figure 12.6. How would discriminant keys and commonality keys for P describe Person 2?*

19. *What interpretation can be given to a low score on a homogeneous Investigative key? On a commonality key for Chemist? A discriminant key for Chemist?*

Changes from Decade to Decade

Over time, items change in popularity; the correlation between items changes; and the interests typical of men or women in an occupation

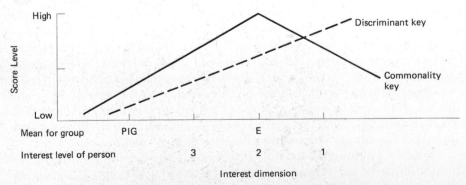

Figure 12.6. **Comparison of two criterion-keying techniques.**

may change. This may make it necessary to reconstruct the scales. Items found homogeneous in one generation seem likely to cohere in the next; a "realistic" item is unlikely to shift to "enterprising" or "social." Criterion keys probably are more vulnerable.

Occupations change in some of their fundamentals—recent years have seen the advent of television journalism, poverty law, and the electronic office. This could make an occupation attractive to some who formerly disliked it and vice versa. Radical changes in interests of an occupational group from one generation to the next are rare (Campbell, 1971; J.-I. C. Hansen, in Goldstein & Hersen, 1984, p. 172; Hansen, 1988). Still, there is evolution.

Campbell compared ministers questioned in 1927, for example, with the ministers serving in the same churches in 1965. The average scores on six of the keys were:

	Minister	Social worker	Lawyer	Rehabilitation counselor	Psychiatrist	Chemist
1927	48	40	36	36	32	17
1965	46	48	36	42	37	13

Along with a marked consistency, there was clearly a drift toward interest in personal service. (Each s.d. among ministers is near 10.)

Campbell (1965) reported the interest profiles of certain prominent psychologists. Among 10 who were presidents of the American Psychological Association around 1930, just one reached a score of 52 on the 1965 Psychologist key; among the presidents for the period 1955–1965, only one scored below 52. So, sooner or later, criterion keys have to be overhauled from the ground up.

Erasing Sex Differences

Everyone agrees that Strong's original inventory for women had unfortunate social effects. Drawing the young woman's attention to occupations many women entered (librarian, psychologist, buyer, nurse) tended to narrow the options she considered. That fault has been overcome in today's instruments.

The contemporary issue is whether interest inventories should be blind to sex or should make specific allowance for sex in selecting items, constructing keys, and interpreting profiles (Tittle & Zytowski, 1978). No doubt about it, responses of females collectively differ from those of males. One reasonable answer is blind to sex: a man and a woman who express the same likes and dislikes should be encouraged to consider the same list of occupations.

A second reasonable answer brings sex differences into the interpretation. It argues for sex-specific criterion keys and, if norms are used, for sex-specific occupational norms. Female physicians (for example) have tended to manage different kinds of practice and responsibility than male physicians. A criterion-keyed instrument can reasonably report whether the counselee's interests match the interests of physicians of *like* sex, as the Strong now does. This position is conservative; within many a profession, the two sexes are coming to have more nearly the same range of responsibilities. Men differ from women in the same occupation much as MIG differ from WIG. When persons are scored on the same-sex key and the opposite-sex key for the same occupation, the correlation is usually in the range 0.75–0.9.

Some persons who accept the second answer go further, objecting to inventories that allow sex differences. In particular, the protest is against homogeneous scales on which the sexes differ (Diamond, 1975). There is more than a hint in these statements that in an ideal society women would collectively have the same interests as men—which goes beyond the ideal of open opportunity and positive encouragement to be oneself.

To produce a seeming equality, some authors search for items that males and females like equally or items balanced so that male and female scale means are close together. One instrument developer discarded items that were more popular with one sex than the other, but had to stop short. *After* discarding the items with the largest sex differences, the proportion of L responses to the remaining Humanitarian items was 33 for males, 60 for females. To erase the difference, the developers would have had to abandon the attempt to measure that interest. Or perhaps they could have reasoned as another developer did. She tried this item:

> If you were to become a teacher, which would you rather teach, history or chemistry?

The second alternative was to be counted in a Science key and the first in a Culture (verbal-humanistic) key. Females chose the science option infrequently, so it was changed from "chemistry" to "biology." This did not eliminate the sex differential; it reversed it. Now men chose the science option less than women. The developer reasoned that this was all to the good as the change tends to attract females to a traditionally male career. In my opinion, such selection of items falsifies the report of interests by refusing to mention whatever part of the vocational domain is unappealing to females.

20. *In what ways is the proposal to construct scales on which both sexes have the same score distribution similar to (or different from) a proposal*
    a. *to use within-sex norms to interpret a RIASEC profile?*
    b. *to partial social background out of mental-test scores (p. 133)?*
    c. *to set hiring quotas to ensure proportionate representation in a firm (p. 453)?*

21. *Would it be sensible to develop two criterion keys for a field such as health services, one using a college-educated criterion group (and reference group) and one using less educated respondents?*

Chapter
13

General Problems in Studying Personality

13A. Any two sources of information about an individual's personality have somewhat different stories to tell. Illustrate. Is this an indication of invalidity?

13B. What assumptions are made when reports from informants (for example, persons in the same student residence) are taken as describing the ratee's typical behavior?

13C. If observers have paid attention to the actions of Person A and Person B and rate the two similarly on aggressiveness, can we expect A and B to behave similarly if exposed to the same provocation?

13D. What advantages and disadvantages (compared with other systems) does the Big Five list of traits have as the basis for describing individuals?

13E. What techniques of investigating personality are likely to invade privacy? Under what circumstances is it legitimate to employ them?

Abbreviations in this chapter: MMPI for Minnesota Multiphasic Personality Inventory; RIA-SEC for the Holland code for occupations.

ORIENTATION

This chapter provides a framework for examining inventories and observations of many types. An initial section indicates the variety of purposes such devices serve. Give close attention to the last paragraphs, on "impact."

The overview of data sources distinguishes types of observations and offers preliminary information on the advantages of each approach. The subsection on convergence and divergence develops further an aspect of construct validation. Learn to read reports like Table 13.1 and to draw conclusions about validity from them.

The subdivisions under "Conceptualizations" sketch perspectives on personality: interactional, trait, clinical-dynamic, and criterion-oriented (actuarial). You should see how these types of thinking differ but should also recognize that they can be used in combination. Most paragraphs in this section have "topic sentences" (for example, on p. 499, "We need to bound the class of situations"). You should grasp these general ideas well enough to explain them or give your own examples. Table 13.2 merits special attention because its "Big Five" dimensions appear often in score systems and research findings. With regard to the two "sign" approaches (pp. 508–512), concentrate on the question of trustworthiness. The information on stability is really a supplement to the section on conceptualizing, but I separate it because it is not an "alternative" approach.

Coming to self-reports, I emphasize threats to validity. Disregard of these simple points has often generated incorrect interpretations. Once the problems are called to your attention, you can probably recall examples from your experience as test taker. Toward the end of the section, note some nonobvious research findings about subtle scales and about correction keys.

The section on ethics is intended to build sensitivity regarding the transaction between personality tester and client (or other test taker). The aim is to help you recognize practices that may be upsetting or inappropriate, and to suggest some constructive tactics.

THE RANGE OF INQUIRIES

Interests, motives, beliefs and attitudes (including views of the self and others), habits of action (punctuality, for example), sources of emotional distress, and so on all fall under the heading of personality. "Typical response" includes both actions, which are observable, and feelings and motives, which can only be inferred from words and actions.

There are many reasons for appraising typical response. Businesses assess the functioning of their staffs and size up candidates for new responsibility. Service agencies seek to help individuals, and communities assess their needs and prospects. Evaluators are asked to appraise responses to stress, to medication, and to psychotherapy.

Some clinical psychologists dealing with an individual proceed directly to work on improving his life situation and actions. Others seek to understand "the personality" and, where appropriate, to change it. Some clinicians and institutions make case workups a regular preliminary to recommendations for treatment, then retest to assess progress and to redirect treatment. Periodic rereading of test reports can help the therapist maintain perspective on the patient. In decisions about a patient's release from the hospital, the person's recovery must be appraised. When the staff sees two patients as functioning equally well, a psychological workup may show that one has returned to emotional balance whereas the other is maintaining his demeanor only by a great effort at self-control (Schafer, 1978).

Aims, variables, and targets of inquiry have a wide range, as the following incomplete list illustrates. The list is deliberately presented in haphazard order, and the code letters are explained at the end.

1. What habits and attitudes of individual members are causing discord in this family? (S,P,L)
2. Children growing up in certain cultures or subcultures are strongly motivated to achieve; how does this come about? (S,M)
3. What relation is there between the duration of breast-feeding and the child's later personality? (S,P,M)
4. Is this prisoner's plea of "diminished responsibility" valid? (P,L)
5. Under what circumstances do citizens have a sense of political efficacy, a sense that they are capable of influencing government actions? (S,M)
6. What are the effects of electroshock? And for which emotionally disturbed persons, if any, should it be used? (S,P)
7. This individual, who is in continuing psychotherapy, is today expressing exceptional depression and speaks of suicide; is the risk so great that temporary hospitalization would be wise? (P,L)
8. Is it true that in many cases scientific or artistic genius is an outlet for hostile feelings built up during the early years? (S)
9. Is this counselee now keeping to a more regular schedule of work than before? (P)
10. Does method X of teaching science reduce the extent to which students accept without question the pronouncements of "authorities"? (S,M)
11. Which work crews are effective and why? (S,M)
12. How can our medical school select students who as doctors will be more concerned with community welfare than with personal gain or a scientific career? (S,M)

The letter code is as follows:

S   A type of information likely to interest scientists (not limited to psychologists)

P   Information of a kind practitioners use in helping individuals or making recommendations about them

L   An inquiry that could be relevant to legal proceedings

M   Information that would be important to managers of institutions or to makers of broad policy

But perhaps every question could (with slight rephrasing) qualify for every one of the codes. Some questions refer to overt acts, and others to inner feelings. Either a behaviorist or a psychoanalyst could rephrase almost every question so that it would come within her sphere of interest.

An inquiry may have an effect—good or bad—on the respondent, the person under study, or the institution where data were collected. Every effort should be made to reduce impact, unless the investigator is engaged as a change agent. To recognize possible impact, questions such as the following are to be raised when the inquiry is planned.

Will the individual report, or the general research conclusion, be communicated to the individual assessed?

If so, will he comprehend the report? Will it threaten him?

Is the assessment likely to be used by some person in authority to influence the fate of the individual?

If so, what kind of information is this recipient qualified to use?

Exquisite judgment is needed in deciding what findings to transmit to whom. Suppose that we could pick adolescents "at risk" for suicide attempts (say, those for whom the chance is as high as 1 in 50). We certainly would not warn these youngsters directly, as we would warn a person at risk from diabetes. Would we alert their parents and schoolteachers to the risk? Only in rare circumstances, surely. Perhaps, however, we could encourage them to protect these youngsters from stress without saying anything about suicide. Or we might propose such a general policy as trying to help *all* adolescents to make friendships. As you see, it is easier to think of significant questions about personalities than to decide what to do with the information.

1. *Which of the inquiries listed in this section could enter into program evaluations?*

ALTERNATIVES TO SELF-REPORT

I turn now to an overview of procedures that approach the person from the outside. A later section of this chapter will focus on self-report.

The most direct way to investigate behavior is to observe. To study interests, one could observe how the person spends free time. To appraise generosity, one could observe responses to charitable appeals, dealings with subordinates, and tipping.

Observations on many occasions can show what response is typical in a specific situation or class of situations. If we repeatedly see a new acquaintance engaged in quarrels, we size him up as irritable. Perhaps, however, a current worry has agitated him, and what we observed is a temporary deviation. Ups and downs—"states"—are of interest in their own right.

An investigative procedure that affects behavior is said to be "reactive" or "obtrusive" (Webb et al., 1981). A police car on the freeway raises drivers' performance above their habitual level. Presence of the observer may cause the person to try harder even when no penalty or benefit is in prospect. When typical behavior is of interest, it is almost never appropriate to let an observer's presence affect what the person does—unless, of course, the observer is regularly part of the situation.

In a *performance test* the measurer sets up an evocative stimulus. Standardizing the stimulus permits direct comparisons across persons and times. A summary report of everyday leadership may reflect differences in opportunity to lead rather than differences in readiness. Opportunity is essentially uniform when, in a performance test, each person being assessed directs a group that has been assigned a standard task. The standardized leadership task does not observe "typical behavior." It samples response to a very special situation—namely, a leadership opportunity set up by a tester whose good opinion will have certain consequences.

Some performance tests simulate a social situation and ask the person to respond as he normally would—a kind of self-report! Thus, to assess assertiveness, McReynolds et al. (1976) used the following script in an "improvisation" technique:

> *Tester says:* "You took an expensive suede coat to the cleaners. When you pick it up, you notice some spots on the back that weren't there when you brought the coat in."
>
> *Actor of same sex as test taker reads:* "Does it look okay?"
>
> *Subject reads from script:* "No, there are two white spots here on the back."
>
> "Oh, yes. Those look like bleach spots. I'm afraid we can't do anything about those."
>
> "But they weren't here when I brought the coat in."
>
> "Well, it certainly couldn't have happened here. . . . There's nothing I can do about it now."

At this point the script ends. Test taker and actor are to continue the dialogue, the actor having been told in general terms how to keep the conversation going. (For more on such techniques, see J. R. Hall, and McReynolds & DeVoge, both in McReynolds, 1977).

The same script can be used to assess *ability* to play an assertive part, by directing the examinee to respond assertively. Following a trial under "typical performance" directions with a trial under these "maximum performance" directions can help in planning an attempt at behavior modification (Nietzel & Bernstein, 1976, p. 500):

> Clients who display appropriate assertion only under high-demand could then be assigned to treatment oriented toward removal of inhibitory factors. . . . Those whose assertion remains inadequate under both demand conditions could be exposed to skill-building experiences.

Projective techniques are far more indirect. An ambiguous stimulus is presented, and the test taker is asked what he sees in it or what he thinks will happen next. For example, the tester displays a picture of people at work in a hospital operating room; thoughts and feelings attributed to characters in the pictures disclose the respondent's attitudes about work roles or about surgery.

Instead of using the person assessed as the source of data, the psychologist often turns to a third party. She may solicit *reports from informants:* from "peers" (acquaintances of the subject or co-workers at the same level) or from persons with a special opportunity to form impressions.[1] Supervisors supply information about workers, mothers about children, nurses about patients, patients about ward attendants.

Reports from others shed light on corners of the person's life where the professional observer may never go, cover past behavior no longer observable, and take into account incidents that could not be observed directly. Self-reports have these qualities, also, but there are bound to be discrepancies between a person's report on a significant event and the report of an outside observer.

A report is one individual's perception, as filtered as is any perception of a fluctuating, ambiguous stimulus. When pupils describe the practices of their teacher, the reports add up to a picture of the classroom "climate." Although adult observers may not see events as the children do, the reports of pupils are significant information about the psychology of their classroom.

The process of reporting on a rating scale or checklist is complex (Cooper, 1981). Errors can enter at every stage. Not everything in the original stream of behavior is noted, and what is noted is interpreted (e.g., as aggressive). So the memory trace departs from the facts at the outset. And memory is faulty. In making the report the informant enters into a social transaction with the investigator she reports to, and her mo-

---

[1]In this and subsequent chapters, female pronouns are used for raters and informants as well as for testers and investigators.

tives in that exchange modify the response. Moreover, informants may give somewhat different meanings to the variable names they are asked to rate or to the response scale—a communications problem.

Ratings are sometimes excellent sources of data. A striking example is a study where ratings of "ascendance" (dominance) by nursery school teachers correlated 0.8 with a score derived from objectively recorded observations on the playground (Jack, 1934).

The Q sort for eliciting reports from informants deserves mention at this point because of its special value in validation research. Statements such as the following are printed on cards:

Is fastidious

Enjoys sensuous experiences (including touch, taste, smell, and physical contact)

Extrapunitive, tends to transfer or project blame

An informant (who may be a layperson or a trained assessor) is directed to sort the cards into perhaps nine piles. (The same cards can be used for self-report.) At one end go the few statements judged particularly characteristic of the ratee; at the other end go those that are emphatically untrue of him. The middle pile catches "Don't know," "Does not apply," and half-and-half responses. The statements typically cover many aspects of style and emotional response. Indeed, the procedure is not worth the trouble if statements mostly measure a good/bad factor. (For more detail, see pp. 576, 593.)

Should Methods Agree?

Clinicians are committed to "methodological pluralism" and research on personality also should be (Craik, 1986). Within a multiscore instrument, a score gains a great deal of meaning from other scores (and also from supplementary information about the person). When claimed interests disagree with inventoried interests, it is wiser to take both facts seriously than to call one source invalid. If, in evaluating an attempt to reduce a pupil's hyperactivity, classroom observers report a decrease in restless behavior but the teacher's ratings do not change, the contradiction is instructive. The intervention evidently addressed one part of the problem and not the other.

"Convergence" of two indicators of a construct (p. 182) supports the validity of both indicators. If two scores truly measure the same construct, without impurities, they give the same answer in any comparison of persons or treatment groups (to the extent reliabilities permit).

Important though it is to investigate convergence, excellent convergence is not to be expected. Correlations between measures of a trait obtained by two methods are usually modest. Scored self-descriptions on an inventory were correlated with scored descriptions from several close acquaintances (averaged) on the same items. The correlations ranged from 0.3 to 0.6. These self-other correlations are about as high as can be obtained, the authors said (McCrae & Costa, 1987), because the data are of superior quality.

Broad characteristics such as adaptiveness and morale should appear under many circumstances, and various methods should be able to provide evidence on them. Each method, however, views the person from its own angle and filters the information in a particular way. Any two sources of information have, to some extent, different stories to tell.

Evidence that two methods of evaluating the same trait concur is, of course, welcome when it comes. For example, a role-playing test of assertiveness was checked against a sample of everyday response. Some time after the role-playing, an experimenter posing as a salesperson telephoned each subject and tried to "hard sell" magazine subscriptions. The assertiveness of the subjects' responses correlated nearly 0.8 with the score from the laboratory simulation (McFall & Marston, 1970).

When convergence is found in one range of data, that does not prove universal convergence. Someone with a new theory, introducing a new twist, may demonstrate inconsistency among supposedly similar measures. Thus Feather (1961) showed that persistence is strongly dependent on the *perceived* difficulty of a problem. Increasing task difficulty increases persistence of some persons and decreases that of others.

The call for convergence suggests that when two methods disagree, one or the other is defective. Something *is* wrong if speedometers in automobiles typically register lower speeds than does the radar apparatus in a patrol car. In the personality domain, however, what is an error for one purpose may be a significant fact for another purpose. Raters disagree because they have sampled different aspects of the person's behavior and because they feel differently about him. The interpreter can consider each rating as a report on that particular social relationship or—treating the reports as samples from a domain of informants—can average several of them. Likewise, when a self-description departs from the person's actual behavior, the discrepancy is a fact. To expect the two kinds of data to be in complete agreement would be psychologically naive.

McClelland (in Rabin, 1981, p. 93) goes so far as to say, "Campbell and Fiske . . . were wrong in arguing that theory requires . . . consistencies across methods of measurement." Yet Campbell and Fiske were not wrong, I would say, in urging investigators to find out which variables show consistency across methods and which do not.

Lack of convergence most often implies a need to develop subtly shaded interpretations for each procedure. The two ways of enacting a script to appraise assertiveness (pp. 491–492) illustrate constructive use of methods that do not converge.

MTMM Analyses Table 13.1 illustrates the Campbell-Fiske multitrait-multimethod design (MTMM; p. 182) for checking on convergence and divergence. Note these features of the study:

Table 13.1   CORRELATIONS OF RATINGS IN A MULTITRAIT-
MULTIMETHOD STUDY

		Participation rated in		Cooperation rated in	
		Cottage	School	Cottage	School
Participation rated in	Cottage	0.7	*0.4*	**0.0**	−0.1
	School		0.5	0.1	**0.0**
Cooperation rated in	Cottage			0.7	*0.5*
	School				0.5

Source: Koretzky et al., 1978.

Note: Disturbed and delinquent adolescents in a residential institution were rated by counselors in their small living groups and by teachers. Reliabilities in the diagonal report agreement among raters in the same situation, corrected by the Spearman-Brown formula. The two variables are more completely described as interest and participation vs. apathy and withdrawal, and cooperation and compliance vs. hostility and defiance.

- Two traits were assessed—"Participation" and "Cooperation." Whether these are distinguishable is a first issue. (A study can of course include more than two traits, or more than two methods, but it is advisable to examine each pair in turn.)
- Two methods were applied. Here the "measuring instruments" were informants who had seen the adolescent subjects in distinct settings. Situational differences, and differences in what the professionals in different roles consider, are possible sources of "method" effects.
- Observer agreement within methods and traits, a type of reliability, was evaluated.

Reliability coefficients are a baseline against which to interpret cross-correlations (Widaman, 1985). Here, the reliabilities (diagonal cells of the table) tell us that raters in the same situation did not agree excellently. The consistency of either characteristic across situations—reported by the numbers in italics—was remarkably high in view of the variation among observers. Note also the zeros in boldface (correlations across traits, within methods). These tell us that the traits were distinct in the minds of the raters, that they "diverged."

A correlation table cannot reveal complex convergences such as the one illustrated in Figure 13.1. Four sources of data are represented: self-report, report of peers, report of teacher, and a sample of performance (expansiveness vs. constriction in drawing). No two methods are strongly correlated, but the *pattern* of peer report and drawing, for example, is associated with the teacher's impression and also with the image the child offers in self-report.

Because multimethod validation cannot be exhaustive, two precautions are desirable, especially in research. First, testers and those who

Peer report:

Not chosen

Popular

Self-report:

admits im-
perfections

Teacher says:

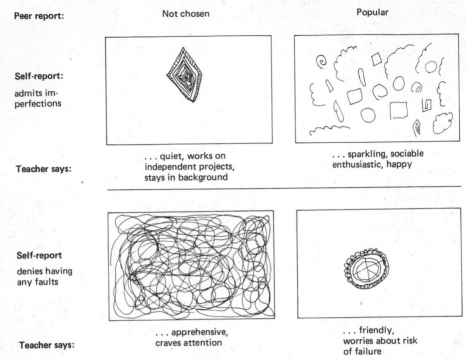

. . . quiet, works on
independent projects,
stays in background

. . . sparkling, sociable
enthusiastic, happy

Self-report

denies having
any faults

Teacher says:

. . . apprehensive,
craves attention

. . . friendly,
worries about risk
of failure

Figure 13.1. **Data reflecting four personality types found in first-grade girls.** (*Source*: Wallach et al., 1962, pp. 15–17. Copyright 1962 by the American Psychological Association. Adapted by permission of the publisher and author.)

read their reports should keep in mind the method that generated the score. Second, it is advisable to measure a variable by at least two procedures. Persistence in rolling a tiny ball through a tiltable maze may or may not go with persistence on a crossword puzzle. In research on factors affecting "persistence," the investigator ought to use two or more such techniques (possibly using each with a different random subgroup of subjects). If her experimental intervention has a similar effect on each measure, she can interpret with some confidence.

2. *How well can the four procedures—observation in representative situations, report from others, self-report, and performance tests—satisfy the following requirements? Rank the procedures from best to poorest in each respect.*

   a. *The data reflect differences in personality rather than differences in environment and opportunity.*

   b. *The data reflect the individual's behavior, undistorted by the perceptions of those who provide data.*

   c. *The data provide a summary or estimate of the individual's behavior during all moments of his current life.*

   d. *The results are the same regardless of whether the individual wishes the assessor to reach a highly favorable conclusion.*

3. *Zest and Vigor of aging persons might be measured by self-report (S) and reports of observers (O). A multitrait-multimethod study produces the following correlations:*

	ZS	VS	ZO	VO
ZS		0.6	**0.1**	0.5
VS			0.1	**0.6**
ZO				0.3

   a. *Do the trait scores show consistency across methods (convergence)?*
   b. *Do the persons rank differently on Z and V (divergence)?*
   c. *Internal-consistency coefficients are 0.7 for ZS and VS. Correlations between observers are 0.7 for ZO and VO. Taking all the correlations into account, how many of the reports would be worth collecting in subsequent research? (If fewer than four, which?)*

4. *In Table 13.1, the correlation of 0.4 for <u>Participation</u>, across methods, is less than the theoretical maximum of $\sqrt{0.7 \times 0.5}$ (about 0.6). What does this tell us about the children, or about the observers?*

CONCEPTUALIZATIONS OF INDIVIDUALITY

How observations and reports are interpreted depends on the user's purpose and her confidence in a personality theory (or her distrust in theories). This section amplifies and restates points made in Chapter 2 in describing styles of test use. A few lines about schools of thought will tie in what follows with Chapters 2 and 12.

- Behaviorists are the least "theory minded" of interpreters. Evidence is taken at face value. For them, behavior is behavior; a label such as "depression" merely obscures the user's view of procedures that defined the scope of the information. They prefer to define a narrow category of situations and count responses of a specified kind.
- The actuarial or sign approach is statistical and, again, not at all theoretical. Responses are reduced to numbers and—when the method is applied in its pure form—the conclusions are generated by a formula or a set of rules a computer can apply. Again, evidence is taken at face value. Actuaries see being "like army officers" in that career as forecasting satisfaction regardless of the content of the items that entered the key.
- The "trait" approach emphasizes somewhat abstract descriptive dimensions. The approach is illustrated by the homogeneous keys of interest inventories, where items were grouped in broad categories and responses summarized in a numerical profile. As we shall see, theories of personality have generated many trait systems. A personality theory often sets up a trait system, but the system may be created by factor analysis and then, perhaps, theory begins to

accumulate around it. The RIASEC system is developing in that second way.

A trait may be conceived simply as a statistical summary of a response tendency, but interpreters tend to think of a unified force within the person. A score may be a count of "responsible" acts; but saying "Fumiko is responsible" hints at a self-discipline Fumiko is expected to bring to new tasks.

- The phenomenalist approach is concerned with what events mean to the person more than with "facts." It can be argued that social interactions and emotional crises are shaped less by objective reality than by the individual's perception of events, of himself or herself, and of others.

  Though preferring direct observation, a behaviorist might ask a mother, "Does your child hang up his clothes without being prompted?" So might a phenomenologist. But whereas the behaviorist would focus on the evidence as describing the child, the phenomenologist would speak of the mother's *image* of the child.

- Psychoanalytic or "dynamic" interpretations explain behavior in terms of motives. This is again a "sign" approach because the interpreter looks for the "significance" of an action, rather than taking it at face value. The meaning emerges from theory rather than from statistical tables.

Examples scattered through the remainder of the book will demonstrate these styles.

I shall speak mostly about trait approaches because they have been most prominent in practical testing and theoretically oriented research. Much that I say about trait measures carries over to other styles of data collection and interpretation.

It is unfortunate that a book like this, and the research literature on validation, generally has to focus on one instrument at a time and to take up singly the scales within an instrument. It is hard to compile systematic data on combinations of scores, or on combinations of scores with life history. If we tried to study three scores or background variables, and coded each by High/Medium/Low levels, that would define 27 cells. The number of cases available for most cells becomes too small for convincing conclusions. The practical tester has to draw on her theoretical understanding, however patchy that may be, to develop a coherent story out of a combination of facts where interpretations have never been validated *as a combination.*

5. *When a highly reliable composite report from acquaintances was correlated with self-report, Woodruffe (1984) found much closer agreement of an extroversion score with the rating on "reserved/outgoing" than of neuroticism score with "relaxed/tense" (r's 0.7 vs. 0.4). For more information on these trait names, see p. 505. Why might greater convergence for the first pair of variables be expected?*

Traits as Response Tendencies in Situations

Behaviorists have stressed that a person's response depends on the immediate situation encountered on each particular occasion, which is true. Even so, there is plentiful evidence of consistency and stability, which I shall discuss later. As a preliminary example I cite Olweus (1979). He inquired repeatedly about the aggressiveness of a number of boys; each rater saw the boy under somewhat different conditions, and his life situation changed in some respects. Nonetheless, "true scores" an aggressiveness (see p. 192) correlated 0.75 over a 1-year interval and 0.6 over 10 years.

Defining a Variable   "Aggressiveness" is an abstraction, an interpretation and synthesis of several kinds of action. To obtain data that are comparable over persons and over time it is necessary to identify the acts or internal reactions that are relevant to the trait, to communicate that definition clearly to observers or informants, and, if direct observations are to be made, to observe on a sufficient number and variety of occasions. Even a response category that appears to be specific and objective can be defined in several ways.

Let us consider typical legibility of handwriting (TLH) as an example. It is reasonable to suppose that TLH changes; therefore, a definition requires a time frame. Suppose we restrict ourselves to the upcoming calendar month; whether TLH is the same from month to month and year to year (in a particular population) is left open to investigation. Suppose for the sake of the example that we invade privacy and collect, without the person's knowledge, a photocopy of everything he writes during the month. Once we assess the legibility of those specimens, the median figure represents TLH. Even so, there are decisions to make.

- What is an episode of handwriting? A page? A document? (The latter counts the briefest memo and the draft of a whole essay as equals.) Let us agree to weight time slices equally, ignoring those during which the person does no writing. Perhaps, then, we settle on one score per hour. (We may sample hours instead of evaluating all a person writes.)
- How define legibility? If we collect ratings, we must choose raters. Perhaps those familiar with the person's writing read it easily but then TLH becomes a property of writer and reader jointly, not of writer alone. So let us agree to select some judges who read the papers from everyone, legibility being scored as positive for a document they can read aloud at 100 words per minute with no more than one misreading per 100 words. The readers now are standard instruments and we have an operational definition of legibility.

Finally, we need to bound the class of situations from which handwriting specimens will be taken. Suppose that Curt scores 70 (percentage of writings counted as legible) during December, but brings a new typewriter to campus after the holiday break. What he used to write for the eyes of others with careful penmanship he now types. His TLH score may well drop to 30 if his January writing consists of notes taken in class, memoranda at the telephone, and other hasty jottings. Perhaps his score on jottings alone would have been 30 in December. The change in the TLH average is real, yet we can scarcely say that there was a change in Curt. When we compare two persons or two groups on TLH, we can easily draw a wrong conclusion if we did not collect data in similar situations.

Cultural norms define roles and shape styles of acting and feeling. Psychologists who study personality traits concentrate on stable differences among persons within a culture. Anthropologists, however, are most impressed by the similarities among members of a culture. Each culture encourages its members in certain responses (or, rather, defines a style proper among those in a particular status—e.g., among males prior to puberty). The same objective behavior means something different for persons in different cultures, in different statuses within the culture, and in different momentary roles.

Typical behavior cannot be defined independent of the person's life space. Our measure of TLH was based on a representative sample of Curt's life. In today's jargon, Curt's ecology changed when he acquired a typewriter. The measurer who wants to come closer to what is "in the person" will have to hold situations constant in some manner. He narrows the variable to the response typically made when a situation in the chosen range occurs (or is arranged experimentally).

The TLH measure can be improved if we divide the life space along suitable lines. An obvious first split is between messages written for the person's own use and messages for others; it should not be difficult to sort Curt's writings and obtain two scores. Many other lines of division suggest themselves: note taking (externally paced), academic papers turned in for a grade, drafts prepared for a typist, and so forth. Likewise, it is possible to subdivide the domain of stress situations or leadership opportunities.

Consistency Across Situations   Ordinarily, the psychologist assessing typical behavior wants a homogeneous category, one where persons who respond positively to one situation within the category are likely to respond positively to others. Then the category describes a response tendency that appears in many settings. Correlations of scores based on behavioral observations in supposedly similar situations are characteristically low; most investigators have to settle for values of 0.3 and lower. Some persons are consistent across the category. But a person's response will vary when the situations have different meanings for him (Bem & Allen, 1974).

Cross-situation correlations are like correlations of single items in ability tests, which also run about 0.2–0.3. When many situations (or samples on many days) are combined in a single score, two such composites can have a high correlation (Epstein, 1979).

Consider this question: How closely do actions match stated attitudes? Persons who claim religious beliefs differ very little from others on any single behavioral criterion such as saying grace before meals. But a composite score covering 70 acts—saying grace, donating money to a religious organization, being a conscientious objector to war, and so on—correlates 0.6–0.7 with stated attitude toward religion (Fishbein & Azjen, 1974). It makes sense, then, to speak of "a tendency toward religious actions" even though the attitude score (or a composite behavioral score) is a poor predictor of any one type of action.

A narrow variable can be appraised with fewer observations than a broad one, but broad variables are more satisfactory both for characterizing individuals and for generating theory. Narrow variables are most useful in monitoring the progress of behavior modification or other treatment that focuses on particular undesirable responses in specific settings. Even there, they have limitations. Because of situational influences, it is hard to reason from results in the experimental or intervention setting to the same variable in daily life (Strohsahl & Linehan, in Ciminero et al., 1986).

Instead of enlarging the sample of behavior to improve data, Buss and Craik (1984) propose to intensify it. They start with acts that might reasonably be called (say) extrovert, and ask laypersons how well each act fits that construct. A "prototypical" extrovert item is one that hits the community's image of extroversion on dead center—for example, "At a party I talk with nearly everyone." Self-reported extroverts, when observed, exhibit considerably more of the prototypical acts than others do. But on extrovert acts that are nonprototypical (that is, diluted with other factors), they depart little from the average. Mischel and Peake (1982) find that people rated high on a trait by peers show the prototypical acts consistently, but are not consistent on less prototypical acts.

Person-Situation Interaction   In the 1970s there was hot debate about the comparative "importance" of person, situation, and person-by-situation interaction in determining responses. The debate faded away as it came to be recognized that no general answer can be given. When a 1983 symposium brought together leading representatives of the several camps, the prevailing opinion was captured in Bem's remark, "There's nobody here but us interactionists" (West, 1983, p. 572).

Situation and person have understandable joint effects, as a high school study shows. Students were asked the same questions in English, math, biology, and government classes. One of the questions was, "Do you speak out in class?" Figure 13.2 reports just a fraction of the information obtained after a statistical analysis like that of Table 6.2.

- One of the questions was, "Do you speak out in class?" The average participation was nearly the same in every class. (Someone has

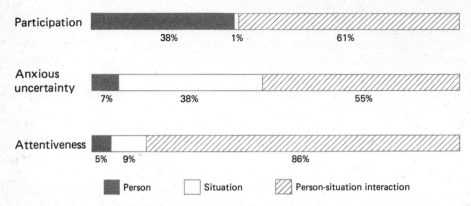

Figure 13.2. **Sources of variation in student behavior.** Sampling errors and errors of measurement were eliminated before adjusting totals to 100 per cent. (*Source*: Based on an analysis by Trickett and Moos, 1970.)

to answer the teacher's questions!) The large component for persons says that some students spoke up more than others. The sizable interaction indicates that few pupils were equally responsive across all classes.

• On anxiety, no "person" factor appeared; that is, few pupils expressed anxiety (or the opposite) all across their classes. Some classes elicited more anxiety than others. The interaction indicates that *who* was anxious changed from class to class.

• On attentiveness, the interaction is overwhelmingly larger than the other components. The attentiveness of the pupil depended on the class. Average attentiveness was about the same in all classes.

A strong interaction makes it advisable to report scores in narrower categories (e.g., anxiety in connection with mathematical tasks).

When the same response scale fits many situations and many occasions, something akin to the content-referenced analysis of abilities becomes possible. One can map ups and downs of anxiety (or some other state) and link them to conditions. In this vein, O'Leary and Wilson (1975, p. 18) wrote that behavioral assessment should "identify the environmental and self-imposed variables which are *currently* maintaining an individual's maladaptive thoughts, feelings, and behaviors."

Situationist criticisms warn against expecting people to behave consistently in accord with a "type" label pinned on by an assessor. Mischel (1977) makes the point that socially effective persons are *not* consistent. The person who changes from passive to aggressive or from affiliative to task-centered is discriminating one situation from another. If a person does so on the basis of role demands and considers his or her goals and resources, this fluctuation is far more adaptive than an unchanging style. In children, consistency with respect to aggression or withdrawal is a reflection of inability to meet the demands of situations; the same children are inconsistent when observed in several less demanding situations (Mischel, 1984).

A behavioral repertoire is both established and developing. After we have observed Sam, the best prediction is that Sam's style in the future will resemble his recent style—*and* that he will change. To say that Sam's present personality has deep roots still allows for change in his internal system of meanings, his external coping practices, and the balance of physiological forces. As with abilities, specific aspects are easier to change than broad patterns of adaptation. It is easier to decondition fear of snakes than to modify "fearfulness," easier to teach self-scheduling than to overcome "impulsiveness." On the other hand, communications to counselees, employers, and other lay persons usually must use broad language.

6. *Define the range, in time and situations, of the behavior one should study to answer these questions:*
   a. *How well does this supervisor handle grievances?*
   b. *Does study of philosophy make one more rational in his adult life?*
   c. *Does viewing a film on nutrition improve housewives' practices in menu planning?*
   d. *How anxious is this patient at this point in therapy?*
7. *Criticize the trait "responsibility" from the situational standpoint. Suggest a type of inventory that might satisfy the criticism to some extent.*
8. *A person may be "stubborn" in some situations and not in others. Both actions may be typical of him. Illustrate, and suggest a rational explanation for his consistency.*

Systems of Traits

Regarding ability, some psychologists think that one general factor tells nearly the whole story, yet a kit of tests offers to measure two dozen factors. In the interest domain, the general factor—tendency to like many activities—is unexciting; the domain is described by two-dimensional and six-dimensional schemes and by profiles with two dozen scores. We have already seen that personality dimensions can be finely subdivided by categorizing situations—but how many dimensions would permit a reasonably complete description? Again, some psychologists find a few dimensions adequate; others measure a dozen or more to pick up nuances (Wiggins, 1973).

Figure 13.3 starts us off with a map derived from factor analysis. There is a good/bad (evaluative, social desirability) factor and an active/passive factor. Persons judged "sociable" are typically judged active and good. Adding weakness/strength as the front-to-back dimension generates a spherical representation. The location of "sociable" on the rim implies that sociability is not associated on average with strength or weakness; it lies on an equator midway between the strong and weak poles. "Deferential" combines weakness and goodness. (In any such

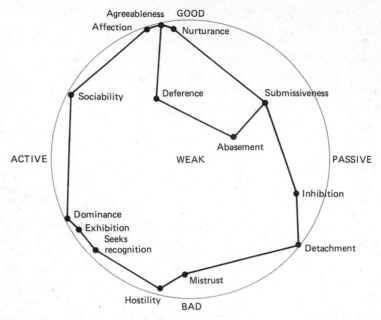

Figure 13.3. **An interpersonal circle.** The configuration was derived from ratings of acquaintances. The "front-to-back" dimension of the spherical plot represents a weak-to-strong factor; all traits in this set fell on the weak side. (*Source*: Data from Lorr & McNair, 1965.)

framework, rotation is possible. Figure 13.3 could be turned 45° to make warm/cold and dominant/submissive the axes instead of goodness and activity.)

Wiggins (in Kendall & Butcher, 1982; see also Kiesler, 1983) compares many circular and spherical schemes for summarizing parent-child and therapist-patient relationships as well as individual characteristics. To a remarkable degree, systems having different purposes have arrived at the same primary dimensions.

Correlations among traits reflect our language, a conceptual structure that has evolved for sizing up others. Ratings of strangers, based on negligible amounts of information, show the same factors as ratings of longtime acquaintances. Some theorists (Shweder & d'Andrade, 1979) contend that the dimensions are linguistic conventions and do not reflect facts about behavior. I prefer the view (Block et al., 1979) that words are associated because they correspond to associations in behavior. "Kind" and "gentle" do not refer to identical behavior, but many an act has both characteristics. Moreover, a person generally tries to be consistent with a verbally framed self-concept ("I criticize gently"); self-labeling *produces* some generality in behavior. A further point: What traits are found together will change across cultures, an obvious example being components of "masculinity."

The dimensional system is enriched by moving to the five factors summarized in Table 13.2. This prominent "Big Five" system provides a framework for rating scales and for some recent inventories, although versions coming from different investigators differ in their details. Every factor has a "good" pole; the good/bad dimension of Figure 13.3 has become a higher-order factor. As in Figure 13.3, it is possible to find adjectives that describe mixtures of the dimensions.

The first four dimensions are easily understood. The fifth needs to be distinguished from ability. It refers to a life-style of variety seeking, curiosity, and cultural interests (or the opposite). It correlates modestly with divergent thinking and academic ability (McCrae, 1987).

Despite the agreement among correlational studies, present terminology is chaotic; indeed, Goldberg refers to the synthesis as an attempt to "decode Babel." The emotional-stability factor appears in the literature under such aliases as anxiety, neuroticism, emotionality, lack of ego resiliency, and lack of confidence. Complicating matters further, authors use the *same* word differently. "Introversion" represents for one author a brooding neurotic; for another, anyone who would rather be a clerk than a carnival barker. "Surgency" ranges from spontaneous social responsiveness, in one theory, to inconsiderate and overbearing behavior in another.

As matters stand, the only sensible way to discuss data is to speak of "the Atkinson TAT *n* Achievement score," "the Spence-Helmreich

Table 13.2   THE "BIG FIVE" PERSONALITY DIMENSIONS

Factor, with alternative labels	Relevant polar adjectives
I. Extroversion,[a] Surgency	bold/timid sociable/retiring
II. Agreeableness, Affiliation, Compliance, Nurturance	warm/cold soft-hearted/ruthless
III. Conscientiousness, Responsibility, Will	organized/disorganized
IV. Emotional stability, Negative affect, Neuroticism	relaxed/tense unemotional/emotional
V. Culture, Openness to experience, Intellect	intelligent/unintelligent original/conventional

Source: Digman & Inouye, 1986; McCrae & Costa, 1987; Peabody & Goldberg, in press. A "sociability" component is sometimes separated out of I and II.

[a]Both "extroversion" and "extraversion" are used as titles for scores; the former is more common in instruments developed in the United States.

Mastery score," "the CPI Achievement-through-Independence score," and so on according to the measure used. McClelland (in Rabin, 1981) sees this incoherence as a reflection of reality rather than as a failure of psychologists to settle on a standard language. Specifically, he says, the motive expressed in fantasy (TAT), the valuation the person puts on hard work (a conscious ideal or value), and the effort he typically puts into work (typical behavior) are distinct. The three need not be equally strong in the person.

The dimensions most prominent in the literature do not capture all that can reasonably concern psychologists (Waller & Ben-Porath, 1987). Indeed, Peabody and Goldberg point out that the language with which lay persons talk about personality has evolved through everyday communications that inevitably simplify. The dimensions in Table 13.2 capture the differences people are most likely to talk about. Thirty-five "needs" (Abasement, Achievement, Affiliation, Autonomy, . . .) were required to capture the nuances teased out by an intensive study of normal adults that looked more at motives behind behavior than at actions per se (Murray et al., 1938).

The other complex system in most active use is that of R. B. Cattell. Having applied factor analysis to self-reports, ratings, and performance tests, he arrived at the following list of pervasive dimensions:

Warm	Impulsive	Suspicious	Radical
Intelligent	Conforming	Imaginative	Self-sufficient
Emotionally stable	Bold	Shrewd	Self-disciplined
Dominant	Sensitive	Insecure	Tense

These factor names tell Cattell's story too simply. What I list simply as "warm" is for him "Source trait A," which he unpacks as in Table 13.3.

9. *Becker and Krug (1964) extracted five factors from reports on children: Calm (vs. emotional-rebellious), Submissive, Sociable, Loving (vs. distrusting), and Cooperative. What information carried in the five dimensions is not carried in the good-strong-active dimensions?*

10. *Name two adjectives that would fall in the bad-strong-active sector. Do the two have distinct meanings? Could a person exhibit one of the traits and not the other?*

11. *How do the dimensions of Table 13.2 relate to Figure 13.3?*

12. *On a certain inventory each scale has a possible score range from zero to 30. A person who scores 15 points on Irritability falls at the 80th percentile; a person who scores 15 points on Punctuality falls at the 15th percentile. Suppose that Jeff earns 15 points on each scale; is it correct to say that he is more irritable than punctual? Can any meaning be given to score-to-score differences in a personality profile?*

Clinical Inferences

Clinicians are limited in their remedial efforts if they know only the person's level of adjustment and the problems he acknowledges. Under-

Table 13.3 DESCRIPTION OF A CATTELL FACTOR

Sizothymia (Reserved, Detached, Critical, Aloof, Stiff)		Affectothymia (Warmhearted, Participating, Easygoing)
Critical	vs.	Good Natured, Easygoing
Stands by His Own Ideas	vs.	Ready to Cooperate, Likes to Participate
Cool, Aloof	vs.	Attentive to People
Precise, Objective	vs.	Softhearted, Casual
Distrustful, Skeptical	vs.	Trustful
Rigid	vs.	Adaptable, Careless, "Goes Along"
Cold	vs.	Warmhearted
Prone to Sulk	vs.	Laughs Readily

Source: Cattell et al., 1970, p. 80. Adapted from the Handbook for the 16 PF. Copyright © 1970 by IPAT, Inc. Reproduced by permission.

standing the sources of behavior can point out advisable situational changes or goals for retraining. Deeper analysis is expressed in terms of inner characteristics that generate interpretations, emotional reactions, and coping behavior.

Phenomenologists try to comprehend the person's self-image and his image of other persons in his life and to learn what meanings he puts on situations central to his life. The response depends on how the situation is perceived. See pages 565–568 for examples of such analyses.

Hypotheses about Motives Dynamic interpreters try to understand needs or motives. Psychoanalytic interpreters, in particular, expect to uncover motives of which the person is unaware. Such an interpreter assumes that acts represent an organized system of motives; she tries to construct a coherent story to resolve the contradictions and inconsistencies in behavior. She is more likely than others to turn to the person's life history for a causal explanation.

Remarks by a university counselor provide an example. Many students with distressing academic records who come for help are found to have good aptitude. Barbara Kirk (1952) characterizes many of these cases. (Her account is drastically condensed here.)

The explanation and the excuses [given] for the academic deficiency are unrealistic, superficial, and largely implausible. The counselee demonstrates no real recognition or admission of the reasons for this deficiency, but, on the other hand, he evidences no surprise at the results of the tests. He may be surprised that he was not tense or bothered on tests administered to him during counseling because he frequently has been tense or bothered during academic examinations.

[A particularly frequent MMPI pattern] is "psychoneurosis with compulsive and depressive features." Such [persons] tend to be pervasively resistant on an unconscious level to any externally imposed task. Since childhood, however, they have concealed such resistances from themselves and

others by a façade of hard-workingness, meticulousness, and earnest dutiful-
ness. In the unstructured environment of a university, the loss of the continued external pushing of teachers and parents permits the overthrow of the
process of grudging achievement, and the resistances then manifest themselves in nonperformance.

The academic failure probably has meaning in terms of unconscious
satisfaction of the hostility usually directed towards some member of the
family who demands success, while the excellent scores on tests taken in a
counseling situation may be interpreted also as hostile gestures. Because no
importance is attached to these tests, the counselee is free to do with them
as he wishes. It is a declaration, perhaps, of the lack of significance of his
academic failure.

The chief limitation of the dynamic approach is the immaturity of
personality theories. Interpretation depends on two inference systems—
one that runs from observations to latent explanatory characteristics and
one that leads from that description to predictions or recommendations
(p. 643). For many reasons, improvement of either type of theory is slow
(Meehl, 1978, 1979).

Clinical Signs Any description that does not stick close to the kind of
behavior observed is a "sign" interpretation. Many performance tests
are given sign interpretations. The hypotheses are based on experience,
but they are not backed by "actuarial tables" as Strong keys are. The

(a)
Lack of
self-confidence

(b)
Strong
will power

graphologist tells us, for example, that in these two specimens the low
bar on the *t* at left shows lack of self-confidence whereas the high *t* bar
in the second specimen shows strong will power. Crumbaugh (1980),
after laying out the system of signs, says that it is the graphologist's integrative portrait that can be validated and not the statements based on single signs. (See also Crumbaugh & Stockholm, 1977.) That is true, because any one sign occurs infrequently. Yet a system can be no sounder
than the signs and interpretations it relies on.

For Rorschach interpreters, *m* responses (inanimate movement; e.g.,
water flowing, fireworks) to the blots are a sign of a state of stress, probably a transient sense of helplessness (Exner, 1986, pp. 317f., 334). The
support for this kind of interpretation comes from a program of construct
validation. Thus Exner compiles studies showing a rise in *m* responses
in conjunction with impending surgery or a parachute jump. This kind
of validation often stops with evidence that a relationship is present.

Then two questions about inanimate movement remain unanswered: Among those who give (say) four or more *m* responses, what fraction are currently under stress? And what leads to *m* responses in persons not under stress?

Despite scattered positive findings such as the one just cited, graphology, the Rorschach, and similar sign interpretetations have a poor track record. On graphology, see Goldberg (1986); on the Rorschach, see R. A. Peterson (in Buros, 1978).

One argument for criterion keying of personality measures is the inadequacy of psychologists' theories. They hold some incorrect ideas about even the long-familiar category of psychoneurosis. At least, when Gough (1954) asked professional clinicians and advanced trainees to mark an inventory as neurotics would, the clinicians' responses were significantly out of line with what most neurotics said. Too often, for example, Gough's clinicians expected complaints about being misunderstood and about health.

Figure 13.4 details another example of misjudgment. In patient management it is important to assess the risk of assaultive behavior, whether in the institution or after discharge. To pose a definite question, Werner et al. (1983) asked psychologists and psychiatrists to judge which patients would probably commit a violent or assaultive act within 7 days of admission, basing the judgment on 19 characteristics evaluated by the

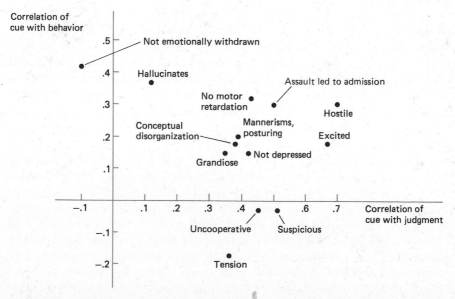

Figure 13.4. Relation of patient characteristics to assaultive behavior: Clinicians' estimates and actual validity. Six cues with correlations less than 0.3 are not displayed. (*Source*: Werner et al., 1983.)

intake interviewer. Many of these characteristics were relevant; combining them in a regression equation did indicate likelihood of actual assault in the next 7 days with validity 0.8. (This correlation would have dropped quite a bit on cross-validation.) The composite judgment of 30 clinicians correlated only 0.2 with the actual behavior of the 40 patients. (Psychologists and psychiatrists reached highly similar composite judgments.) The figure shows that the judges placed great weight on disturbed social relationships and ignored several cues that were valid indicators of risk of assault, at least with this sample and criterion.

13. *"In all clinical assessment procedures the validity is primarily in the clinician rather than in the technique" (Crumbaugh, 1980, p. 927).*
   a. *If this is true, how should an institution desiring to use assessments arrange to get dependable ones?*
   b. *How can the soundness of Crumbaugh's statement be investigated?*

Interpreting without Theory: Criterion Keying

The sign approach treats a test response as behavior that may have interesting correlates. Clinical signs are based on past experience and impressions, but they generally lack formal support. "Actuarial" interpretation, on the other hand, is based on careful records of associations between items or scores and other information. Criterion keying of items was illustrated in some interest inventories discussed in Chapter 12, and some formal systems of interpretation by computer will be illustrated at the end of Chapter 14.

The logical justification for making a criterion key is the intent to predict a particular criterion in a particular population. It should be possible to make keys that distinguish, at better than a chance level, moderate drinkers from alcoholics and applicants for legal training who will make extended use of it from those who will leave the profession at an early age. Such a key capitalizes on the fact that a group that has one distinctive psychological quality differs from the population on other qualities. Even small differences permit moderately accurate sorting when enough differences are counted up.

The actuarial method is illustrated at its best in the Career Profile (formerly called the Aptitude Index Battery; Brown, 1981; Thayer, 1977). As the failure rate of beginners who try to sell life insurance is high, a central agency supported by the industry has developed a screening device. Some 300 items are administered to each candidate and scored at national headquarters with a key that is secret; the score is returned to the local manager who, aided by experience tables, hires or rejects the candidate. Thousands of persons fill out the form each year, and an excellent bank of data for revising the instrument builds up. The validity coefficient, with amount of insurance sold as criterion, is about 0.2. (Restriction of range is partly responsible.) Because failures are costly, accepting only applicants above a certain cutoff increases profit by $10,000 per year for each agent hired. The score seems to be far better at predicting failure than at predicting success. Few of those with low scores succeed. Among those who score in the top 10 per cent, about half have poor sales records.

The items have to do mostly with personal history, so the Career Profile is sometimes spoken of as a "weighted application blank" or as "biodata." Tabulations of past data show how (within an age-sex bracket) insurance sales vary with, for example, the number of children a salesperson has. Questions on personality were part of the instrument at the beginning, but—although valid when a test form was constructed—they lost their validity within a few years, presumably because of social change. Today's Career Profile touches on "typical behavior" only by asking about such activities as participation in sports.

Criterion keying has most often proceeded in the fashion of the Strong blank (Table 12.1), weights being assigned to items that two keying groups (e.g., engineers and nonengineers) respond to differently. Item weights derived on the basis of a given criterion do not work out better (in a fresh sample) than a regression composite that assigns weights to "testlets," homogeneous *sets* of items (Burisch, 1978; Goldberg, 1972; Jackson, 1975).

A second approach holds down redundancy. The Career Profile selected items in a manner much like Strong's, but then reduced the weight given to items having comparatively large intercorrelations. This method, making the scale less homogeneous, reduces the influence of any one content theme. This strategy is logical for criterion keying, but it can be recommended only when the contrasted groups have a thousand cases or so, because of sampling error in the numerous intercorrelations. A "tree" methodology that has been useful in medical contexts Breiman et al., 1984) probably could be used successfully with psychological testlets.

A case can be made for a third strategy. Having located criterion-related items, the developer discards those *least* correlated with the set as a whole. This practice produces a shorter, more homogeneous, more interpretable scale, perhaps with no loss in validity. (Recall the Buss-Craik finding on prototypicality; p. 501.) Paunonen and Jackson (1985) shortened a scale of achievement motivation, and found that validity dropped very little—from 0.62 (16 items) to 0.58 (5 items selected as central). This finding is not a contradiction of the Spearman-Brown rule; that applies only to random shortening.

Large and relevant keying samples and a valid criterion are crucial. When the key is based on an inadequate sample, chance plays too large a part in determining scoring weights. Note the importance of cross-validation or a statistical substitute (p. 443). As for the criterion, it will not do to have a predictor of delinquency that counts responses common to *all* lower-class boys just because lower-class boys make up most of the keying sample of delinquents (and not the nondelinquent sample).

An actuarial key, relying on indirect information, has moderate validity at best. Unlike the insurance company, the diagnostician rarely intends to predict the original criterion. The actuarial key that best predicts aggression of patients in the 7 days after admission (even if developed on a properly large sample) may not be valid for longer-range prediction or for short-range prediction in another institution. It is far removed from a more significant problem, the prediction of assaultive behavior subsequent to release. For personality measurement, criterion keying of items may be at a dead end (Burisch, in Angleitner & Wiggins, 1986).

14. *The Adjustment scale of an inventory to be described on p. 597 asks parents to check items describing their child as a part of his evaluation. The original actuarial keying was done on suitable samples of boys aged 6 to 12. The authors say that the scale may be used with boys aged 3–5 and 13–16, and with girls. How could this extension be justified? (Consider defenses based on new evidence that might be collected, and defenses based on theory that may be available.)*

STABILITY OF PERSONALITY

During adulthood, broad personality characteristics are about as stable as abilities. Correlations are near 0.8 for 6-year retests on Neuroticism, Extraversion, and Openness (Costa & McCrae, 1988). A small study with 6-month retests gave only slightly higher correlations, implying that there is little change in true scores over a 6-year interval. Correcting for short-term fluctuations in responding would raise the 6-year correlations well above 0.9. Considering evidence from other studies spanning up to 30 years, McCrae and Costa (1984, p. 61) draw a forceful conclusion: Styles of social, emotional, and intellectual response are resistant to change:

> Many individuals will have undergone radical changes in their life structure. They may have married, divorced, remarried. They have probably moved their residence several times. Job changes, layoffs, promotions, and retirement are all likely to have occurred for many people. Close friends and confidants will have died or moved away or become alienated. Children will have been born, grown up, married, begun a family of their own. The individual will have aged biologically, with changes in appearance, health, vigor, memory, and sensory abilities. Internationally, wars, depressions, and social movements will have come and gone. Most subjects will have read dozens of books, seen hundreds of movies, watched thousands of hours of television. *And yet, most people will not have changed appreciably in any of the personality dispositions measured by these tests.*

This evidence does not deny that change in life circumstances can change one's prevailing mood or that a permanent change in role alters external behavior. Nor is the stability during maturity matched by stability in youth. A long-term study that began with field observations and careful clinical assessment of normal adolescents found both consistency and change (Block, 1981; Bronson, 1966; Macfarlane et al., 1954; Block, in Magnusson & Endler, 1977). Reassessed at age 40, some gave impressions highly consistent with those recorded in their early teens, but others "were nearly unrecognizable" from the earlier descriptions. Assessors' perceptions of 40-year-old adults correlated 0.4 with similar ratings made during junior high school on the following traits (among others): high aspiration level, values intellectual matters, self-defeating, and "pushes limits to see what he can get away with." The changes in males were far greater than those in females. For a more recent study of females see Helson & Moane, 1987.

Some life courses change dramatically. McClelland (1979; in Rabin, 1981) describes the academic psychologist who turned to mysticism and transformed himself into Ram Dass. For all the change, says McClelland, in many ways "the same person" shows through the new identity.

15. *What events might produce a marked increase in level of aspiration between ages 13 and 32? A marked decrease?*

16. *It is a reasonable bet that those whose level of aspiration was low at 13 and high at 43 had profiles at age 13 different from those who remained low. What traits might be precursors of adult striving?*

17. *Normal males' rankings on most personality traits at age 17 correlated 0.0 to 0.3 with rankings on the same traits at about age 35. For females the correlations ran from 0.3 to 0.6. What might explain the sex difference? (The data came from judgments of trained observers and interviewers, the early data having been collected in the 1930s; Haan, 1981.)*

SELF-DESCRIPTION: REPORT OF TYPICAL BEHAVIOR?

The self-report is a "published" self-concept—a deliberate self-presentation—not a factual description. Historians, examining the diary of a public figure, refuse to assume that all statements made therein are true reports of beliefs and feelings. Unless it is clear that the document was intended never to reach the eyes of others, the safest assumption is that it represents an image the person wished to write into history. The assessor can regard questionnaire responses as a statement of the reputation the test taker would like to have or of how he requests others to regard him at this time.

This edited information may be of considerable value, especially because what is not said can be indicative. A person who presents too perfect an image may be expressing fear of losing respect. Unless the immediate situation offers a special inducement for halo-waving, the report of so perfect a self hints at a similar facade in other social relations. As a facade of control and freedom from impulse is a brittle one, maintained at considerable emotional cost, the facade itself has significance. Heaton and Pendleton (1981) point out that some persons with neurological damage or other deficits seriously overestimate or underestimate their capabilities. This is important to know: the overestimators may take on responsibilities they cannot handle and be laggard in seeking help.

Candid reporting can be hoped for when the tester is helping the test taker to solve his own problems. Also in research, the investigator can hope for an honest effort to introspect; subjects want to explain themselves. But even then it is natural to give responses that will be judged favorably insofar as respondents can guess the investigator's standards for judgment. Full candor is unlikely if certain responses will gain reward or support for the examinee's desires. Promise or threat is implicit in institutional uses of tests.

18. *Industrial workers filled out identical health questionnaires under two conditions. One questionnaire was turned in to the company medical department as a preliminary to a medical examination designed to improve the worker's health. The other questionnaire was mailed directly to a research team at a university. The workers listed far more symptoms on the research questionnaire than on the other despite the fact that an honest report to the company physician might bring them medical help and the research questionnaire would not. Account for the discrepancy.*

19. *Distinguish in each of these cases whether the investigator is assuming that self-reports are truthful:*
    a. *The clinical symptoms of condition X are determined by observation. A list of symptoms (swollen feet, rash, etc.) is prepared. This list is used to determine how frequent condition X is in several localities. Each informant is asked to check whatever symptoms he has.*
    b. *A psychologist administers to a group of applicants a checklist in which each marks the adjectives that describe him. The success of these workers is observed, and a record is made of the characteristics checked by the successful applicants but not by the others. This checklist is then given to further applicants, and those who check the same characteristics as the previously successful workers are given preference in hiring.*

20. *A questionnaire is filled out by all parents belonging to a study group as a means of identifying problems to be taken up in group discussion. Mr. Smith checks many problems having to do with developing the child's honesty, respect for the property of others, and care for his own property. The school counselor knows, however, that his son has been in difficulty several times because of fighting on the playground, window breaking, and other aggressive offenses that have been called to Mr. Smith's attention. Can the counselor draw any useful conclusion from Mr. Smith's self-report?*

21. *An attitude questionnaire is given to first-line supervisors as part of a study that might lead to reorganizing the shop or to retraining the supervisors. It presents problems that might arise on the job and asks what action the respondent would take if he were supervisor. Scores are based on response patterns (e.g., "takes quick action," "seeks facts," "emphasizes morale," "emphasizes cost cutting"). What use can be made of the responses in view of the obvious temptation to give a desirable picture?*

Limitations of Inventory Responses

Interpretations Made by the Respondent Even when the respondent wants to cooperate, not all questionnaire responses are adequate communications. A first difficulty is that questions cannot be fully specified. "Do you make friends easily?" seems straightforward. But it is hard to say just what behavior the question refers to and what is meant by "easily." The respondent is unable to count up positive and negative instances in his past. He will recall some people who became warm friends quickly and other acquaintances who remained distant for months. A try for literal interpretation bogs down. What does "friend" mean—intimate companionship? pleasant interaction without emotional involvement? or something in between? The respondent does not ask such fussy questions; most of his answers come from an inarticulate self-concept. If the person regards himself as the type who makes friends easily—hang niceties of definition!—he marks YES. Another equally popular respondent applying a different standard marks NO.

Questionnaires ask about the hypothetical "typical" situation, not about specific ones. "Do you seek suggestions from others?" is a fairly clear question, but most people would have to answer, "Sometimes, not always." This might be further qualified: "I do on difficult problems"; "I do if someone is around whose ideas are especially good"; "Not if I'm supposed to make the decision myself." These qualifications would have to be stated if the respondent tried seriously to report typical behavior. Since he cannot average his memories to determine what percentage of the time he has sought suggestions, the question will be answered offhand (perhaps biased by a sense of what answer the test interpreter will consider a good one).

Response terms require interpretation. Terwilliger (1960) asked high school boys about their job interests in two ways. He asked one sample, "Would you probably accept . . . ?" (p. 473) and asked another, "Would you make a great effort to seek out . . . ?" work of each kind. On average, the "probably accept" endorsement rate was close to 27 per cent for both clerical and artistic activities, but the number of "seek out" endorsements for artistic items doubled that for clerical items (17 per cent vs. 9 per cent). The person who defines LIKE stringently rather than broadly will thereby alter the shape of his profile. Other response terms used in inventories: YES, AGREE, OFTEN, and so on are similarly equivocal.

An instrument for assessing the quality of students' college experiences used items of this form:

How often have you had serious discussions with students having different values?
NEVER   OCCASIONALLY   OFTEN   VERY OFTEN

As a crosscheck, C. R. Pace and J. Friedlander (1981) asked a sample to fill out this survey and, on a later page, to say how many times they had engaged in each activity during the year. Students who had marked NEVER nearly always responded "Zero" on the second version. Meanings for OFTEN ranged widely. On the item above, OFTEN translated into

Weekly or more often	41 per cent
Once or twice a month	33 per cent
Less than once a month	26 per cent

Moreover, students in selective liberal arts colleges tended to equate OFTEN with a high frequency. Obviously, that systematic difference in response definition confounds an evaluative survey.

Chapters 12–14 are chiefly concerned with lengthy inventories. Considering the time and effort required, such a "test" may be less suitable than a few short scales or one-item self-ratings (Burisch, in Angleitner & Wiggins, 1986). The inventory does allow more precise comparisons between persons and brings norms to bear; neither of these may be of first importance in, for example, opening up counseling. Extensive research on published inventories provides a helpful background for interpretation, but of course single questions could be standardized and made the focus of research. This has been common in sociological surveys of, for example, morale of population groups. Although I concentrate on psychological data, psychologists have much to learn from the efforts of opinion pollers to identify unwanted influences on the responses they collect (Bradburn et al., 1979).

Response Sets   A set to say TRUE when in doubt is a nuisance when knowledge is tested with true-false items: the acquiescent respondent earns undeserved points if the test presents more true statements than false. Bias toward saying LIKE, YES, and OFTEN—or INDIFFERENT—is a nuisance in personality measurement. Similar persons reach different interest scores if they locate differently the boundary between LIKE and INDIFFERENT. An instrument developer who sees ambiguity of directions as the source of response biases will try to reduce that influence, as Terwilliger did.

To some degree, however, response sets express significant personal styles. The person who is submissive and conformist at heart may tend to say YES more often. Some of those who evade questions with CANNOT SAY also are wishy-washy in daily life. Indeed, a criterion-based key gains some of its validity by capitalizing on behavioral differences between yea-sayers and nay-sayers. On the Strong inventory, ministers mark L rather often; physicists do not. Yea-saying raises the scores on all the general and basic-interest scales and probably introduces invalid information. But yea-saying may loom large in the life role of a minister, so it could be a valid element in the Minister key. On questions about morale, the maladjusted mark D more often than A—even where AGREE implies positive morale on just half the items (Rundquist, 1966). Hence disagreeing is a diagnostic indicator of sorts. How much validity is enhanced or diluted by response tendencies varies with the set of items.

Faking   A structured question dealing with emotional health, responsibility, or interpersonal relations typically has one answer option that the culture considers good, and the majority of respondents are likely to pick that "socially desirable" option. The person who consistently gives desirable responses may be admirable. It is also possible that he has been less than frank or that he is deceiving himself.

A respondent may "fake bad." Draftees have been known to report impressive arrays of emotional symptoms, hoping for discharge. In an ordinary clinical questionnaire, exaggerating symptoms may be a gambit to enlist sympathy and attention. An unsuccessful student may prefer to have the counselor believe that his troubles are caused by an emotional disturbance rather than to be thought of as stupid or lazy.

The "hello-goodbye" effect complicates evaluation of psychotherapy. The entering client tells a sad story. His symptoms are at such a peak that they have brought him to treatment, and full display of them bids the clinician to take his problem seriously. Just the opposite is often noted at discharge: the self-description glows, and some of the change may have come from self-deception. It would be ungrateful to dwell on symptoms the therapy did not relieve, so the exiting client gives himself and his therapist the benefit of borderline decisions. True improvement is not easily distinguished from change in test-taking attitude.

To learn how susceptible a questionnaire is to faking, one can ask some persons to fill it out honestly and ask others to give a false picture—a socially desirable report, a socially undesirable one, or one that fits a particular role. Wesman (1952) gave a personality inventory with the instructions: "I want you to pretend that you are applying for the position of salesman in a large industrial organization. You have been unemployed for some time, have a family to support, and want very much to land this position. You are being given this test by the employment manager. Please mark the answers you would give." The next week, the same inventory was filled out "as if you were applying for the position of librarian in a small town." The instrument carried a bland title, so students could only guess what variables would be scored. Self-confidence scores on the two occasions differed spectacularly, as Figure 13.5 illustrates. The applicant can beat the test, and, not surprisingly, faked scores lack predictive validity (Dunnette et al., 1962).

Faking good on a test has an everyday counterpart which social psychologists study as "self-presentation" or "impression management." One manual promoting an inventory for selection of salespersons and security personnel argues that faking is a source of validity rather than invalidity. Ability to convince others that one is outgoing, responsible,

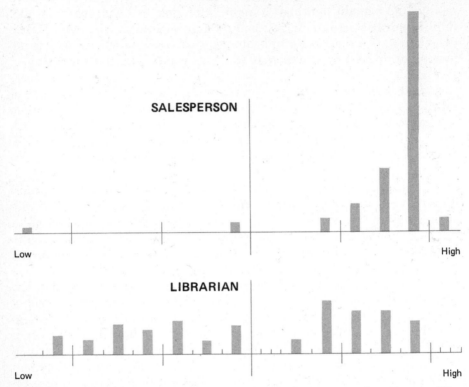

Figure 13.5. "Self-confidence" scores of students playing two roles. (*Source*: Wesman, 1952.)

or whatever a particular job requires contributes to success on the job and, it is said, the inventory that allows (invites?) faking samples this ability. Paulhus (in Angleitner & Wiggins, 1986) regards impression management as an enemy to validity of inventory responses but considers *self*-deceptive bias meaningful. The person who represses thoughts about minor faults and failures describes himself more favorably than events warrant; but this tendency seems to contribute to adjustment. Having "too positive" a self-concept is not faking. (But see p. 514.)

22. *Educational research tries to trace how teaching practices affect student gains. Hook and Rosenshine (1979) checked studies in which teachers had reported their own practices or styles and in which observers had recorded classroom practices. The two sources of information rarely agreed. There were a few negative(!) correlations, for example, between teachers' statements as to whether instruction was individualized and observers' records on the point. What explanations can you offer for the discrepancies?*

23. *Evaluate the argument that successful faking on an inventory is likely to be associated with effective response to the wishes of an employer.*

Coping with Biases and Distortions

Openness   The simplest way to get interpretable results is to make the purpose of the questioning and the questions themselves completely transparent. This is the usual approach in opinion polling and in the surveys conducted to evaluate human services. Candor is encouraged by the fact that respondents are anonymous and no judgment will be passed on them.

A transparent inventory where the respondent can see what he is disclosing suits the inquirer who views the questionnaire as a straight-forward communication. She would like the client to record what he would be willing to say face-to-face. She expects to start counseling or therapy by conversing on matters the client is ready to talk about, not secrets and self-delusions. "Behavioral" assessors in particular rely on openness. When a student is being helped to systematize his study habits, particular acts or patterns of behavior (for example, deliberate course-by-course allocation of each day's study time) are specified as targets for improvement. The student is asked to keep a daily record of these actions; this not only informs him and the counselor of his progress but strengthens his motivation. Of course, the student could untruthfully report actions close to the ideal; but that would not contribute to the improvement *he* is seeking.

Transparent inquiry assumes that the person's own purposes are being served by it and that he has the maturity, insight, and motivation to comply. It is easier to report on acts than on feelings. One cannot expect full disclosure on all topics or to all questioners (Chelune, in McReynolds, 1977). The person who does not feel strongly affiliated with the counselor or other inquirer cannot be expected to be open about matters tinged with shame or guilt.

Gibbons (in West, 1983) suggests that the frankness of self-report, even in guilt-laden matters, is greater under "self-focus" conditions. One device for inducing this mental set is to have the person fill out the inventory while seated before a mirror. Self-reports given "in front of oneself" correlate more with observed behavior than reports collected with no mirror.

Concealing the Purpose of an Inquiry   Naturally, the inquirer prefers not to threaten the respondent. For this reason, the usual self-report blank carries an unrevealing title. Ordinarily, the person is told the reason for making the inquiry, but not what scores will be recorded or what interpretations they will permit.

Sometimes the investigator states a plausible but false purpose for the questions. The F scale of Adorno et al. (1950) was devised to study the motives underlying a world view or personal style called "authoritarian"; the inventory, however, called only for opinions about public affairs and people in general. The interpreter focused on indications that the respondent looked down on the weak and powerless and was unduly trusting of established authority. Another investigator asks children to check titles of books they have read, seemingly to learn about reading interests. Fictitious titles sprinkled into the list make this a test of character; the child who checks many of them is suspected of exaggerating to make a good impression.

In a mixed inventory, the purpose of some single items is hard for respondents to recognize. An item that appears irrelevant to the decision being made is said to be "subtle." Criterion keying of interests counts any answers that engineers tend to give. In that context, "Do you like ice hockey?" is a subtle item; the respondent cannot foresee how it will count, if at all, in the Engineer score. Subtle items are difficult to fake. Indeed, on MMPI subtle items, persons asked to "fake bad" give fewer responses keyed as abnormal than do persons "faking good" (Burkhart et al., 1978)!

Although advocates of criterion keying expected subtle items to produce greater validity than transparent ones, research has torpedoed those hopes (Gynther & Burkhart, 1983; Hough, 1986, p. 13). Graham (1987, p. 159) in his authoritative text on MMPI, concludes from the research that "most of the subtle items would not have remained in the clinical scales if Hathaway and McKinley [the originators] had cross-validated the scales at the item level." Even with strict criterion keying, if the sample is large most of the items that pick up weight have an obvious relevance to the variable scored. (This is evident in the Strong inventory; see Table 12.1.)

Verification and Correction Keys Almost all modern inventories employ one or more supplementary keys to identify test takers who respond in an unusual manner. The Strong counts up the following control scores:

Total responses—If this falls far short of the possible number, scores are dubious; the person omitted many items or did not blacken spaces properly.

Infrequent responses—A person who gives many rare responses may have lost his place on the answer sheet. He may have responded in an arbitrary manner because he resented the test. Or he may be truly idiosyncratic in his interests.

Counts of L, I, *and* D *responses*—A count far from the norm warns against direct application of the usual interpretative rules.

Nearly all the inventories to be discussed in Chapter 14 provide such verification scores. Some also provide a count of socially desirable responses; a high count suggests the possibility that the person is "faking good" or lacks insight into himself. In a personality inventory, a count of implausible claims to saintliness ("I never avoid people I'd prefer not to talk to") is sometimes called a "lie scale." This label seems a bit harsh; the respondent may have tried to describe his general style and ignored the exaggeration in the inventory's "never" and "always."

The primary use of control scores is to flag profiles that should not be taken at face value. Correlations of peer ratings with self-reports on neuroticism and extroversion were considerably lower for respondents flagged by a lie scale than for persons not flagged (Borkenau & Amelang, 1985).

In theory, formal corrections can adjust for unusual response sets. Even the best researched procedure of this type, the "K correction" of the MMPI, is about as likely to reduce the quality of the information as to improve it (Meehl, in Butcher, 1972; see also Borkenau & Amelang, 1985, and McCrae & Costa, 1983). This was a bright idea that didn't work; the K correction is nonetheless used routinely nowadays in MMPI scoring (Graham, 1987, p. 25). Once test users take a wrong course, there is no going back to the choice point. (Recall the history of the mental age, and the IQ scale.)

Sometimes a control score can be interpreted directly. Thus, the Strong manual suggests that many persons with a high L count are enthusiastic or unfocused (or both). And persons who give many socially desirable responses are seen in performance tests as comparatively conventional and persuasible (Crowne & Marlowe, 1964).

Forced Choice   Casting items in choice format keeps most response sets from operating. Thus, in an interest inventory, the choice format requires everyone to express the same number of "likes." In a questionnaire on motives or reactions to stress, "faking good" is difficult when the choices within an item are equally "desirable." It is not difficult, however, for the person to portray himself as "like a librarian."

The "Have you stopped beating your wife?" character of forced choice arouses legitimate objection. Imagine yourself deciding what to say when someone with power over a job or parole asks which of this pair describes you better:

> I feel like blaming others when things go wrong for me; or,
> I feel I am inferior in most respects.

24. *Biases and distortions similar to those in self-report occur in third-party reports from an employer or parent. Which devices mentioned in this section seem likely to work well in collecting third-party reports on descriptive scales?*

25. *Rather commonly, a clinician's written interpretation of a questionnaire begins with "This is a valid profile." The basis for the statement is that none of the verification scores was unusual. Why is this phrase questionable as a communication to someone who is not a testing expert?*

ETHICAL ISSUES

Practical personality measurement has flourished in two contexts—one institutional, the other individual. Valid information about personality would presumably be of great value to employers, college admissions officers, and others who carry out institutional policies. Institutional appraisal tries to determine the truth about the individual, whether he wants that truth known or not. In noninstitutional appraisal, measures are applied solely for the benefit of the person tested. Here also the measurer believes that learning the truth will be valuable, but she does not feel free to violate the person's wishes. The client who comes wanting the psychologist's assistance may be quite unprepared to pay the price of unveiling his soul.

Any test invades privacy when test takers do not wish to reveal themselves. The personality inventory is more often regarded as invasive than the ability test. Everyone has two personalities: a social role and a "true self." If, for example, aggression and open expression of emotion are discouraged by the culture, there is certain to be some discrepancy between inner feeling and outward expression. Some techniques probe into feelings and attitudes people normally conceal. Indeed, virtually all measures of personality seek information that in normal social intercourse is regarded as private. The respondent is willing to admit the inquirer into these private areas only if he sees the relevance of the questions to *his* goals. A psychologist is not "invading privacy" when she is freely admitted and has a genuine need for the information.

Psychologists were shocked during the 1960s to find themselves accused of wholesale violations of human dignity (Amrine, 1965). Congressional investigators and editorial writers pilloried the psychological tester alongside the industrial spies who had been planting microphones in cocktail olives. At one point the Senate voted that "no [guidance] program shall provide for the conduct of any test . . . to elicit information dealing with the personality, environment, home life, parental or family relationships, economic status, or sociological and psychological problems of the pupil tested." Attacks came from those antagonistic to social services and also from advocates for civil liberties. Pressure from critics has at times forced reputable investigators to destroy research questionnaires that had not been tabulated.

The central question is whether it is objectionable to assess personality directly when the data *are* interpreted as well as possible. But first let us dispose of contentions that are *not* central.

- "Psychologists have made indefensible claims regarding the validity of their tests." True, and important; but most test developers and users are reasonably conservative in their claims today. Many violations come from inadequately trained testers. Some come from nonprofessionals—anyone with a printer can prepare a questionnaire and use it to find you a soul mate.

- "The interpretations have low validity." In many applications this statement is true, but from an ethical standpoint valid appraisal could be more objectionable. A test with nearly perfect validity for forecasting treason, embezzlement, or sexual offenses would be unthinkably dangerous—a clear invitation to cast out someone who has committed no objectionable act.

- "Inventories award high scores to conformers." This is an attack on the values of decision makers in schools and business, a proper enough matter for debate. Inventories, however, are an expression of the values, not a cause. An employer who wants yes-men will get them, with or without the inventory. Personality inventories find it no harder to identify the independent-minded than to pick conformers. Admittedly, some interpreters have been too quick to define the healthy personality as one free from emotional conflict. Conflict is a price one pays for independence.

- "Situational tests that put temptation before the person constitute improper entrapment." In some tests a child is given an opportunity to steal, not knowing—before or after—that he has been observed. Should the psychologist risk creating even transient guilt? (Kelman, 1967; Klass, 1978). This is a serious criticism, but it applies to only a few procedures.

Now to the central issues, the first of which is dignity.

Respecting the Dignity of Those Tested

Has an employer the right to question an applicant about matters not directly related to the work? Yes, if workers' private lives affect their usefulness as employees. It is not good for the bank when its teller is seen regularly at the racetrack (but is that *private* behavior?). At least one court (see Dahlstrom, 1980) upheld psychological evaluation of would-be fire fighters (with the self-report MMPI) because their being likely to withstand stress is so much in the public interest.

Has a teacher a right to ask children about their emotions, friendships, and home life? As with any of its testing, the school's justification must be that the information will lead to better educational services. The public has repeatedly urged schools to develop character and promote mental health—and instruction should be guided by facts about the learners. On the opposite side is the argument that no one should be asked to testify against himself. Moreover, parents' privacy is invaded when the child is asked, "Do your parents quarrel frequently?"

Observations and performance tests invite criticism on ethical grounds chiefly when the person is unaware of the observations or believes that he is revealing less than he is. Where techniques require cooperation, no major issue arises when the inquirer requests responses, explains how they will be used, and leaves the person genuinely free not to respond. Teachers and employers have sufficient power that the person may anticipate unwelcome consequences if he does not respond; hence the consent is sometimes given under compulsion. Imposing questions is difficult to justify, and the information obtained is suspect. No investigator will be allowed to impose questions for long unless she can convince the educated public (including advocates for the helpless) that the questioning serves the public interest and violates no recognized right of the individual. In general, an employer inquiring into attitudes and typical behavior had better be able to demonstrate that every question has genuine relevance to ability to perform the job in question. A school board can reasonably approve an attempt to identify maladjusted individuals when there is a responsible program for helping them, and it can approve an unsigned inventory as part of program evaluation. It ought to be outraged by an assessment intended to detect troublemakers in advance.

The inventory developer can remove a good many objections simply by discarding items objectionable to her public. Employees in a manufacturing firm were asked to check items about which they would "feel personally offended" if asked to respond (Winkler & Mathews, 1967). In a typical questionnaire, the usual person objected to no more than 1 per cent of the items. Moreover, objections are reduced when the respondent understands that interpretation is based on consistent responses running through many items and that the psychologist does not draw conclusions from single responses (Fink & Butcher, 1972). The person then feels more comfortable with questions where no response choice fits him exactly. To be sure, encouraging respondents to omit items they object to makes the procedure less standard and scores become harder to interpret.

26. *In the decision regarding fire fighters, the judge gave favorable consideration to the fact that the employer saw only the psychological report, not the scores or the responses to items. Why did the judge regard this as important?*

How Permissible Is Deception?

The second issue is the acceptability of disguise. The psychologist should ordinarily introduce procedures with as frank an account as the situation allows. The typical person seeking therapeutic help can readily understand the aim of diagnosis and that transparent diagnostic questions would invite him to choose his own diagnosis. It is harder to give a frank account of a test that observes style of work (e.g., impulsiveness); the person, knowing what is sought, will try to display that style. An investigator privileged to interview a genius about his childhood would ruin the inquiry—a difficult one at best—by explaining in advance her hypothesis about disguised hostility. Except with cooperative volunteers, legitimate uses of disguised procedures are extremely few.

Rules cannot define when disguise is justifiable. Universities require committee approval of plans for research on human subjects. Similar judgment by independent colleagues is advisable in clinics, prisons, advertising agencies—wherever typical behavior is investigated by standardized methods. But much is left to the judgment of the individual psychologist or counselor, especially when the data are collected by loosely structured methods such as interviews.

To keep matters open and above board in testing persons entering therapy, the psychologist can begin in this manner: "It should help to solve your problem if I collect a good deal of information. Some of these inventories use straightforward questions whose purpose you will readily understand. Other procedures dig more deeply into the personality. Sometimes they bring to light emotional conflicts that the person is not even conscious of. Few of us admit the whole truth about our feelings and ideas, even to ourselves. I think I can help you better with the aid of these tests." The client who is not ready to trust the psychologist may refuse to take disguised tests. If this is the case, the information probably could not be used constructively.

Persons who have taken a personality inventory naturally ask what the interpreter found out. Reporting from face-valid, transparent instruments will probably be safe, particularly if the report is content-referenced rather than norm-referenced. It seems safe enough to say, for example, "On the items inquiring about dominance and submission, about three-fourths of responses pointed in the dominant direction." The respondent must have known what he was saying, so the summary is that and nothing more. In contrast, even in a therapeutic setting one would hesitate to say that the inventory responses hint at disguised hostility. An important part of clinical skill is recognizing which interpretations will be beneficial at a given time, and which harmful. Baumrind (1978) uses the phrase "inflicted insight" in warning psychologists against carrying candor too far.

Limits on Scientific Inquiry

A third issue is freedom of research. It is important to understand why persons break under stress. Citizenship education is bound to remain impotent unless effects of various approaches on behavior are verified. Social scientists, having a high sense of social purpose, are puzzled by the public objections to some of their probings. Knowing that their intentions are pure and that the anonymity of respondents will be safeguarded, they are inclined to stress their right to inquire. If their probings threaten to expose weak spots in the society, they go further, insisting on their *duty* to inquire.

This is as it should be. On the other hand, the scientist must accept some restraints, if only to keep her study from being shot down in mid-flight. Patiently explaining the study to respondents and to other segments of the community is one of the costs of doing business as an investigator.

Psychologists and educators must be particularly mindful that their records are not proof against subpoena. "Good data" for a study of adolescent rebellion might be used against the respondent in a later trial for some alleged offense as an adult. Anonymity and simple coding of records is not a full safeguard. Identity can be detected by matching facts from the coded questionnaire with other facts that are openly recorded. There are enough anecdotes of malign detective work of this kind from the precomputer days of Nazi Germany to justify sober thought about the risks inherent in data banks.

Among many devices for protecting respondents (Boruch & Cecil, 1979), the virtue of random bundling should be noted. If data from individuals are coded and the records are sorted strictly at random into sets of uniform size (perhaps sets of five), average data for each bundle can be calculated (for example, average age, proportion female, proportion endorsing each item). Only these averages go into the research file; they can answer any statistical question as well as the individual data could but they cannot be used against any individual.

27. *Can there be ethical objections to requiring newly employed engineers to fill out a questionnaire on their attitudes and style of behavior, to aid the personnel manager in deciding whether to assign them to sales, research, or other responsibilities?*

28. *Discuss the following advice from an older textbook. Is it acceptable today? "Whether serving an institution or serving an individual client, the tester should not use indirect and misleading techniques unless the respondent clearly understands that anything he says may be used against him. To be sure, an employer may regard his refusal to submit to tests as grounds for denying him employment, but this is ethically preferable to obtaining deceitfully information he does not wish to give."*

29. *Investigators sometimes asks the respondent to mark a list of statements to indicate the responses the majority of people would give; that is, they present a task of social insight rather than of self-description. The responses he attributes to persons in general may correlate with independent evidence on the respondent's behavior better than his self-description does (Goldberg & Rorer, 1966). Suppose that this indirect and disguised technique is valid. For what purposes would you consider it a proper way to measure beliefs, fears, and so forth?*

30. *To find out if questionnaires "would have utility for screening and selection decisions," an investigator gave anxiety and ego-strength questionnaires to Peace Corps volunteers during training. Correlations with criteria of performance in Nigeria were higher than correlations of the criteria with ratings by the training faculty (Mischel, 1965). He had told respondents that the questionnaires were being given for research use only and would play no part in Peace Corps decisions; he adhered to this promise. Would the*

evidence warrant giving tests to future trainees without the promise of privacy?

31. *A firm needed to make a prompt promotion to a position in senior management. It pressed the psychologist on its staff to assess the several eligible persons as rapidly as possible and recommend a choice. The psychologist argued that she needed time to investigate the job requirements. Told bluntly that no delay could be allowed, she administered the California Psychological Inventory and used the scores as the sole basis for the recommendation (Eyde & Quaintance, 1988). What ethical questions do you see? What might the psychologist better have done? (Assume that CPI is as adequate in this situation as any questionnaire.)*

Chapter
14

Personality Measurement through Self-Report

14A. Are the inventories that best promote self-understanding in adolescents and adults likely also to provide the most useful information for counselors and personnel psychologists?

14B. What features of MMPI, as originally developed, have been questioned? Why has it remained popular for so long?

14C. In considering use of a test for screening, how should the local base rate, the hit rate, and the false positive rate be taken into account?

14D. In an elaborate (Level III) characterization of a person by computerized interpretation rules, to what extent are the topics or dimensions tailored to the individual and the problem that led to his being assessed?

14E. What are appropriate ways to validate a narrative description of a person based on self-report? What are the limitations of each approach?

Galton devised the questionnaire technique in the 1880s as a standard procedure for studying mental imagery. G. Stanley Hall extended the method a bit later, using retrospective information from large samples of adults to delineate normal trends in adolescent development. (For techniques reaching back to Pythagoras and beyond, see McReynolds, 1975; for the history in the present century, see Goldberg, in McReynolds, 1971.)

The first personality inventory primarily concerned with appraising the individual was the Woodworth Personal Data Sheet. At the beginning of World War I, the U.S. Army wanted to detect soldiers likely to break down in combat, but psychiatric interviews were not practicable when recruits were processed by the thousands. Woodworth listed some of the symptoms psychiatrists touched upon in screening interviews— "Do you daydream frequently?" "Do you wet your bed?"—and turned the list into a scored instrument. Men reporting many symptoms were singled out for further examination. The score detected numerous maladjusted soldiers quickly and cheaply, despite the insensitivity of mass processing.

As decades passed, instrument developers reworded Woodworth's items and shifted the content according to particular personal or institutional interests. Items chosen for simple measures of adjustment reappeared in multiscore inventories, sorted into such rubrics as sociability and emotional stability. The single score is a kind of synopsis, a first glance. Self-report procedures differ in many ways. Some are designed to help nonclinicians recognize emotionally troubled persons in groups they deal with, and offer little or no analysis of the cases identified. Others, used by clinicians, are designed to describe pathology. Still others are primarily an attempt to tell what a person in the normal range is like, perhaps as an aid to self-understanding or perhaps for the guidance of a teacher or employer.

ORIENTATION

The tests described in this chapter are representative of widely used types. The MMPI is so prominent that you ought to fix in mind both the descriptive facts about it and the main evaluative comments. The other instruments serve to illustrate principles presented in Chapter 13 and introduce further ideas that apply to many instruments. Thus on page 531 you will find a paragraph that starts "Personality measures are hard to validate. . . ." Because that thesis is not limited to the test just described, the paragraph calls for attention. The same is to be said of Figures 14.1 and 14.2 in that subsection. I suggest that in each descriptive section you locate such general points and study them more than the particulars of the test.

Following the descriptions are two sections on validity: first clinical, then nonclinical. Together they address these questions: How can we judge how well an inventory serves a purpose? For what purposes do inventories perform satisfactorily?

An insert follows on "structural" approaches that have little in common with methods described previously. These approaches never "caught on," but I hope that you will see promise in this way of thinking about personality.

The conclusions of research on human decision making surprise and distress most people, including many psychological practitioners. In some ways that is a "bigger" topic than computer interpretation, which follows, but other psychology courses take it up. The computer gets more space in this textbook because one of today's largest concerns in the testing field is whether the risks in automated interpretation undercut the benefits. Here, treat the examples as background; concentrate on problems of overinterpretation and misuse and on possible safeguards.

SPECIMEN INSTRUMENTS

Evaluative Scales

We begin with comparatively simple evaluative scales whose main function is to draw attention to individuals who are at risk for emotional or behavioral problems.

Various purposes are served by evaluative self-reports. Periodic surveys of morale in a community or organization alert policymakers and managers to problem areas. Self-reports can provide criteria for assessing housing arrangements for the elderly or the tone of a desegregated school. Self-reports can indicate the severity of difficulties in incoming patients and later can assess improvement. Some inventories follow Woodworth's lead, screening incoming waves of recruits or students or prisoners. In research on motivation, group process, and the like, simple inventories identify "similar" persons; this makes it possible (for instance) to check whether anxious and nonanxious persons respond differently to a certain teaching style. Measures in this broad category thus serve as social indicators, as evaluative criteria, as signs of individual stress, as measures of individual improvement, and as indicators for explanatory variables.

Questions in evaluative instruments vary somewhat, but almost all of them come down to "How well are you doing (or feeling)?" Broad topics can be subdivided; there are test-anxiety scales, for example, and scales for anxiety in social situations or in situations of physical threat.

A Self-Esteem Scale   Educators are urged to take responsibility for the mental health of students, both because stresses imposed by the school can be a significant source of unhappiness and because many children and adolescents who are at risk will not be helped unless the school recognizes their need. Use of inventories in schools was particularly stimulated by research that found schoolteachers equating quietness and dutiful behavior with good adjustment, reserving the term "maladjustment" for disruptive behavior. Some of the withdrawn children are more likely to break down than the rowdy ones.

The Piers-Harris Children's Self-Concept Scale (PH; E. V. Piers [and, earlier, D. B. Harris]; *WPS;* ages 8–18) began as a single-score instrument and changed to a profile report. The questions are concerned with a child's judgments of and feelings about his behavior, rather than with behavior as such. The instrument is in no way disguised; respondents see this title: "The Way I Feel about Myself." The 80 YES/NO items[1] are of this character:

> I do many bad things. (−)
> I am obedient at home.
> People pick on me. (−)
> I am an important member of my class.
> I am dumb about most things. (−)

In this listing, a minus (−) sign indicates that saying NO adds to the self-esteem score. Answers in the traditional booklet can be hand-scored, or mailed in for a computerized report, or keyed by an adult into the local microcomputer for scoring. The instrument can also be administered and scored by microcomputer.

The repeat reliability of the overall score is in the neighborhood of 0.75, over an interval of 4 months or so. Internal-consistency coefficients are near 0.90, so the instrument is obtaining a good measure of the message the child wants to send today. It is not surprising to see shifts over 4 months, whether the shift is in attitude during response or in feelings about oneself.

Self-esteem inventories are not consistent with each other. Among 93 cross-correlations between self-esteem inventories, only 7 exceeded 0.7, and the average was 0.4; values for the PH fit this picture. Self-esteem has several aspects including academic confidence, social confidence, and pride in appearance; instruments differ in their emphasis on these facets (Briggs & Cheek, 1986).

Personality measures are hard to validate, and a measure of inner feelings is especially troubling. Teacher ratings of self-concept, taken as one "criterion," yield correlations that range from 0.0 to 0.4. But a low correlation may show only that the teacher is unaware of the pupil's feelings or has a definition for the variable that does not match that of the inventory. We might become so specific as to check the child's statement

---

[1]Copyright © 1969, 1984 by Ellen V. Piers and Dale B. Harris. Reprinted by permission of the publisher, Western Psychological Services, 12031 Wilshire Boulevard, Los Angeles, CA 90025.

about his popularity against peer reports or against behavioral observations on the playground. But we can scarcely say that a medium-popular child who *says* "I am unpopular" is giving invalid information. His feeling may be genuine and painful. Another validity check: Clinic children can reasonably be expected to differ from nonclinic children. They do. But the clinic average is 52 desirable responses, in the study the PH manual reports, and the nonclinic average is 56 (out of 80 possible). The distributions overlap greatly.

In the end, the user of the PH scale has to judge validity mostly in terms of whether the content is sensible and whether she believes that the children in her group are taking the questions seriously. If so, a pileup of negative responses from any child is a cry for help.

The PH profile is based on six clusters of ten or more items each; short titles appear in Figure 14.1. The clusters all intercorrelate, but several correlations are as low as 0.2, indicating both a general factor and area-specific information. (Internal-consistency coefficients for subscales exceed 0.7.) Virtually nothing is known about the external correlates of the subscales. Nor do we know whether profile peaks and valleys would be stable on a 1-month retest, or highly unstable.

The developers did a poor job of norming the PH; see page 130. This shortcoming would not be important if interpretative emphasis were on the count of responses indicating distress; however, the publisher's profile form is norm-referenced. Figures 14.1 and 14.2 present a girl's profile in raw-score and percentile forms. The two give quite different impressions. (Note that my raw-score display carries the percentile information, and vice versa.)

The PH manual and report have commendable features. Jargon from psychiatry and personality theory is absent, and appropriate cautions against overinterpretation are given. This paragraph from the manual (p.

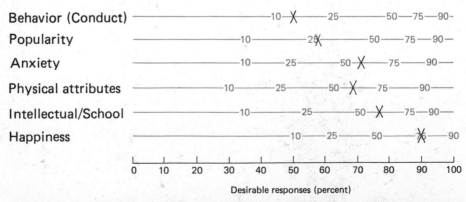

Figure 14.1. **Area self-esteem scores of a 16-year-old girl on a percentage scale.** Numbers within the diagram are percentile equivalents. (*Source*: The scores plotted were supplied by Western Psychological Services.)

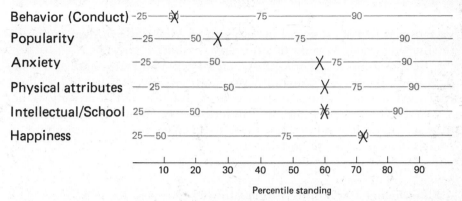

Figure 14.2. **The same scores on a percentile scale.** The scores plotted are the same as in Figure 14.1. Numbers within the diagram are percentages.

3) is noteworthy; something similar could be said about many other instruments and is not.[2]

> Because of doubts about the stability of self-concept in younger children below 7 or 8 years, the Piers-Harris has been standardized for use only above the third-grade level. Although the scale has been used experimentally with younger age groups . . ., there have not been any systematic attempts to validate . . . in earlier grades or with a preschool population. Individuals who use the scale with these younger age groups do so at their own risk [theirs? or the child's?] and should not assume comparability between their population and the samples from which the normative and other psychometric data presented in this manual were obtained.

A State-Trait Inventory   The State-Trait Anxiety Inventory (called "Self-Evaluation Questionnaire" on the page the examinee sees) has been widely used, especially in a flood of research on anxiety among high-school and college students. A bibliography lists over 2000 research reports that used the scale. STAI (C. D. Spielberger) is for ages 14 and up. A form for Grades 4–6 (CSTAI; C. D. Spielberger, C. D. Edwards, J. Montuori, R. Luschene) has much in common with the PH.

The trait scale of each form has 20 items. The novel feature of STAI (and CSTAI) is the roughly parallel second section in which the respondent indicates how he feels *at this moment*. The "state" section can be administered by itself. In some psychological experiments—on problem solving, frustration, and the like—as few as four "state" items may be given at key points in the experimental session. This monitors stress while interfering little with the intellectual task; the short scale is ade-

---

[2]Copyright © 1969 by Ellen V. Piers and Dale B. Harris. Reprinted by permission of the publisher, Western Psychological Services, 12031 Wilshire Boulevard, Los Angeles, CA 90025.

quate to check the average response to experimental conditions. Another variation is to ask for recall of one's state: How did you feel generally during this exam? During this therapy session?

Research on causal links between anxiety and learning or social behavior can reasonably concentrate on state anxiety. It is hard to see how trait anxiety could affect response to a situation if the anxiety is not aroused in that place and time. Indeed, stress conditions do not change trait scores greatly but do increase state anxiety. In one experiment four successive measures were taken:

Upon arrival for the session.

Following 10 minutes of relaxation exercises.

Following 10 minutes of work on a difficult test that subjects had been told was an "easy IQ test."

Following viewing of a film depicting unpleasant accidents in a workshop.

The average scores were 37, 31, 43, and 55. (This kind of evidence was originally used to select responsive items for the state scale; any tryout item whose average did not change between "relax" and "exam" conditions was discarded.)

Whereas trait anxiety has repeat correlations near 0.7 over 2 months or more, the correlations for state scores are typically about 0.3.

An Instrument for Screening Abnormality   The Psychological Screening Inventory (PSI; R. I. Lanyon) is intended for ministers and social service workers to use in judging whether a client's difficulties are serious enough to require referral for psychological help. Though descriptive interpretation is possible, the instrument has been validated chiefly as a screening device. The intercorrelations of the four scores are low, as they bear on different types of disturbance.

The author began by locating items that had shown promising validity in older instruments, put them through statistical trials and revisions, then added items to improve the balance. There are 130 true-false items; no item enters two keys. Two scales have discriminant keys and two sample broad content categories.

Negative emotional tone is the theme running through the 30-item Discomfort (Di) scale. Items call for reports on diverse content (headaches, confidence, appetite, . . .), half the items being worded positively. The items are said to have adequate intercorrelations despite their variety of specific content; such mixed items have been part of many older scales labeled "neurotic tendency" or the like. (Factor IV of the Big Five (p. 505.)

The Expression (Ex) scale (30 items) reports on vigor and activity of style (Factor I). This scale evidently was included less because it is required for screening than because the activity-potency theme has been prominent in other instruments.

Alienation (Al) consists of 25 items to which hospitalized psychiatric patients (mostly schizophrenic) responded differently from normal individuals. The latter were approached in shopping malls and bus depots and asked to take home the inventory, complete it, and mail it back. After the sample was edited to improve its distribution on age and education, 200 papers remained. The abnormal sample totaled only 140 cases and would by itself be inadequate for criterion keying. Fortunately, most items had previously shown some validity in other research, and the author discarded items whose correlations did not "make sense." The content touches on emotional distress, odd thoughts, feeling ill-treated, and lacking control of one's life.

Social Nonconformity (Sn) has 25 items that discriminated the normal group from persons in a reformatory. Topics include recklessness, blaming others, having been at odds with parents, and disregard for rules and conventions (Factor III).

The instrument is not trying to "predict" mental breakdown or incarceration; rather, the criterion keys signal present disturbance or deviation. The unfavorable self-report indicates that the person is likely to have bad relations with others and with institutions; still, altering his life situation or his coping mechanisms could alter the prognosis. Figure 14.3 illustrates one of the ways a professional might think about a PSI profile. The 50 ± 10 standard-score scale is for an approximate cross section of normal adults; scores above 70 are quite rare, and it is even more remarkable for a person to have extreme scores on two of the scales.

It appears that in a general population the two criterion keys have reliabilities no better than 0.60. This result is not surprising; the scales are short and markedly skewed. That is proper in a screening instrument, which is not intended to assess differences among adequately adjusted persons. The two homogeneous scales have reliabilities of 0.8 or a little less; again, skewness is partly responsible. Needed are reports on standard errors of the high scores—the ones that send important signals.

1. *What explanation can you offer for the great overlap of clinic and nonclinic distributions on the PH total score? Does the overlap imply poor validity?*

2. *How serious do you think are the difficulties of the girl whose PH scores are charted in Figures 14.1 and 14.2? Which picture do you think is most suitable for reporting to a teacher who has little technical background? (In answering, disregard the inadequacy of the norm sample.)*

3. *A reviewer (Dreger, in Buros, 1978, p. 683) regards STAI as a superior measure of anxiety but expresses the "major reservation" that it is open to faking. That is clearly true; the items are transparent. Would this fakability interfere with any appropriate use of the scale? For what uses would it not be very damaging?*

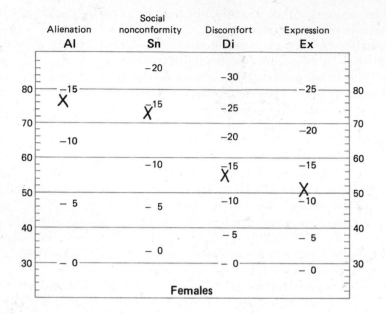

The 18-year-old adolescent girl whose PSI profile is shown sought help at community mental health clinic because of continual angry verbal battles with her mother. She reported that these fights had recently escalated to physical aggression, including scratching and hair-pulling. The client declared that her mother had become so violent that she feared for her own safety; in addition, her mother had ordered her to move out of the house. The client's composed demeanor, together with the obvious practical plight in which the circumstances appeared to have placed her, led the intake interviewer to give her a sympathetic hearing and to contact the school psychologist for further details. The PSI profile, however, indicated the possibility of a serious psychiatric disturbance (very high AI) plus a great deal of adolescent rebellion (high Sn). The information obtained from the school psychologist confirmed the likelihood of a formal thought disorder with paranoid elements, and this plus further case history information indicated with high probability that the story told to the intake inter-viewer was in large part delusional (including the acting-out aspects). The client, incidentally, showed no visible signs of having been involved in the kind of fighting she described.

Figure 14.3. **PSI profile of a rebellious adolescent girl.** (*Source*: The score information and the case description are quoted from the PSI manual (1978, pp. 10–11). The profile form is copyright © 1968 by Richard I. Lanyon and is reproduced by permission. It has been simplified and altered in its proportions for display here.)

4. *Suppose we could arrange for a student to fill out STAI on ten randomly scheduled occasions (different hours, different settings, over 4 months). Would you expect the average state score to coincide with the average trait score?*

5. *Would you prefer a state or a trait measure of anxiety to investigate each of the following questions? (The measure may be limited in its situational domain.)*
   a. *Is level of stomach acidity higher in anxious persons?*
   b. *Do children from different home backgrounds differ in the anxiety they experience in school?*
   c. *How well is counseling overcoming a shy person's anxiety in social situations?*

6. *In view of the cost to society of care for persons who have neglected their bodies and the cost of institutional care for mental patients, what would you think of a proposal that everyone have an annual medical checkup, one part of which would be a questionnaire more or less like PSI?*

7. *What kind of analysis would estimate a standard error of measurement for high scores on one of Lanyon's scales?*

Multiscore Descriptions

The Jackson Personality Inventory   Many counselors and investigators exploring individual differences would like a multiscore profile, describing variations within the normal range on scales with nonthreatening labels. They would like low intercorrelations between scores; repeating information under several names is inefficient and confusing. The dimensions of the Jackson Personality Inventory (D. N. Jackson; JPI) do not overlap much, and have a commonsense quality, as can be seen in Table 14.1 Although many scales resemble those of older instruments, few are tied closely to personality theory. JPI has been praised for painstaking construction that takes advantage of the computer and of the substantial critical literature on self-report methodology.

Table 14.1   CONVERGENT CORRELATIONS FOR JPI SCORES

	Self-report on short adjective checklist	Self-rating[a]	Peer rating
Anxiety	0.7	0.65	0.4
Breadth of interest	0.4	0.3	0.2
Complexity	0.65	0.4	0.35
Conformity	0.55	0.55	0.4
Energy level	0.7	0.55	0.45
Innovation	0.8	0.75	0.35
Interpersonal affect	0.65	0.6	0.3
Organization	0.8	0.6	0.35
Responsibility	0.45	0.15	0.35
Risk taking	0.75	0.7	0.5
Self-esteem	0.75	0.7	0.65
Social adroitness	0.15	0.1	0
Social participation	0.7	0.55	0.45
Tolerance	0.45	0.25	0.35
Value orthodoxy	0.7	0.55	0.55

[a]Average of two samples.

Source: JPI manual, 1976, p. 28.

For each scale, the manual provides a description such as this one for Risk Taking:

High scorer: Enjoys gambling and taking a chance; willingly exposes self to situations with uncertain outcomes; .... Called reckless, bold, impetuous, intrepid, enterprising, ...

Low scorer: Cautious about unpredictable situations; unlikely to bet; avoids situations of personal risk, even those with great rewards; .... Called cautious, hesitant, careful, wary, prudent, conservative. ...

Note that one could place a positive value on either end of the scale. Jackson sought to minimize the good/bad factor, and succeeded. Self-Esteem correlates less than 0.4 with most JPI scales. All items are in true-false form; 10 of the Risk Taking items describe rashness, and 10 describe caution, hence yea-saying cannot produce an extreme score.

Figure 14.4 displays the profile of one risk taker. The peaks are Risk Taking, Complexity, Energy Level, Self-Esteem, and Social Participa-

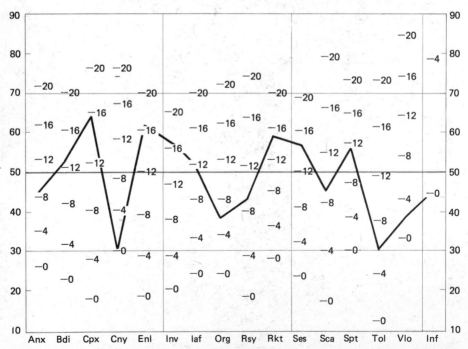

Figure 14.4. JPI profile of a 22-year-old male student. For interpretation of score abbreviations, see Table 14.1; Inf is a verification key that counts unusual responses. Norms are expressed on a 50 ± 10 standard-score scale. (*Source:* From the JPI manual, 1976, p. 21. Profile form copyright © 1976 by Research Psychologists Press. Adapted and reproduced by permission.)

tion; the deep valleys are Conformity and Tolerance. We are told that this young man was a leader of a peaceful demonstration on an academic freedom issue. The low Tolerance raises a question about his liberalism: "He shows a pervasive rejection of discrepant ideas and people who disagree with him."

The steps in instrument construction included the following:

1. Deciding what dimensions to measure and defining each, much as in the description of Risk Taking.
2. Having college students write 100 or more items for each dimension.
3. Editing items and assembling several promising sets for each dimension.
4. Tryout; items were retained that had variance and that correlated with their own dimension but not (in general) with social desirability or other dimensions.
5. Assembly of two parallel forms.
6. Further tryout, leading to some substitution or revision of items.

Jackson collected ratings from campus acquaintances to produce the correlations in Table 14.1. It is not astonishing that correlations with peer ratings are modest. (See the discussion of Table 14.3 on p. 544.) Homogeneity and match to supposedly relevant adjectives run low for some scales (Responsibility, Tolerance, Social Adroitness). Jackson has given rather weak answers to the critics' question, "Why *these* traits?" Lykken (in Buros, 1978, p. 872) makes a plea for greater logical consistency, for tough-minded editing of items. For example, "Einstein himself might have endorsed item 103 [scored for low Complexity], 'I try to make everything as simple and easy as I can.'"

The MMPI   In clinical practice and research, the Minnesota Multiphasic Personality Inventory (S. Hathaway and J. C. McKinley) is used far more than any other inventory, although the Minnesota group responsible for it long ago recognized many faults. It was long and inefficient, and a number of items showed their age. The dimensions used in summarizing responses are—to put it kindly—relics of an antiquated psychiatry. The MMPI was not revised for several decades, and score reports continued to rely on inadequate norms compiled in the 1950s. Interpreters made various stopgap repairs (Koss, in Newmark, 1979).

At long last, a revision is appearing. For MMPI-2, released in 1989, the psychologists responsible prepared new booklets, with inappropriate items dropped or rephrased. To get norms, they have administered these to samples from scattered communities, and also to patient samples. They are retaining the ten principal scales, adjusting keys to reflect changes in the item set and changes in the response distributions of normals and patient groups. The only step toward more fundamental revision is that about 100 fresh items have replaced old ones. As statistical analysis confirms hypotheses built into those items, they can be counted into scores on the old scales. Also, items may be regrouped to form new scales. MMPI-2 looks much like the original, but it is tuned to contemporary diagnoses and current population characteristics and has some new verification keys.

Although one can deplore that MMPI was out of date for so long, the story regarding other inventories is considerably sadder. Whereas the trail of Binet's instrument extends from a 1905 publication to a 1986 revision, and the Strong, the Wechsler, and several group tests of general ability were repeatedly revised, the MMPI is, to the best of my recollection, the only personality inventory to be substantially revised after the retirement of the original developer(s). There is a moral here, probably one about ever-changing fashions in the personality field.

MMPI was constructed 50 years ago, at a time when a primary task of clinical psychologists was to advise psychiatrists (or courts and other institutions) on the severity of a patient's disorder and on a label to describe his disorder. MMPI was an immediate success; it became available just when World War II was producing a great number of casualties requiring neuropsychiatric evaluation. After the war, civilian clinical psychology expanded rapidly and became steadily more independent of psychiatry, but the psychiatry-based MMPI was the instrument the psychologists knew best. Both psychologists and psychiatrists became increasingly dissatisfied with the traditional diagnostic categories to which scales were pointed, and with the very idea that the persons assigned to a category are homogeneous in the sense that patients with measles are. Descriptive interpretations were wanted. Partly for this reason hundreds of supplementary MMPI keys—covering ego strength, introversion, prejudice and other traits—appeared. Some of these served in isolated research, and a few enter the usual clinical workup; one reviewer dismisses all but a handful as useless to clinicians (Graham, 1987, p. 158). Meanwhile, the original discriminant keys acquired fresh connotations.

MMPI thrives not because of any excellence in design but because of the experience compiled. There are thousands of published research reports and case reports. Beyond that, many clinicians are "at home" with the instrument; each fresh record calls up memories of cases seen over the years. The various interpretative approaches currently in use are summarized by Butcher and Keller (in Goldstein & Hersen, 1984) and by Graham (1987).

At the start of MMPI development, discriminant keys (p. 483) were formed. The authors adopted criterion keying because they disdained available theories about abnormal personalities. Utterly miscellaneous items were assembled; for example:

I very much like hunting.
I believe in the second coming of Christ.
I am entirely self-confident.
I am seldom troubled by constipation.

The response scale is YES, NO, CANNOT SAY. (The "second coming" item is one of those dropped during the revision.)

MMPI criterion groups were patients whom professionals in a mental hospital had assigned to particular categories of disorder. Thus, MMPI scale 4, analogous to Lanyon's Social Nonconformity, was keyed not on miscellaneous prisoners but on persons classed as "psychopathic deviate" by the psychiatric staff. ("Antisocial personality," in a later jargon.) Responses in each patient group were compared with those of persons coming to visit patients in a city hospital. Items that showed a difference were counted in the key. Eight scales were constructed in this manner. Scales related to masculinity and introversion are also routinely scored as "clinical scales." Scores are converted to produce a normal distribution with a 50 ± 10 scale.

Although a full set of the major scores is usually printed out and perhaps charted, attention centers on the peaks. A code such as 49'83 . . . indicates the order of scores (4 most elevated), the prime indicating that both 4 and 9 ("manic") are above 70. The 49' profile hints at impulsiveness, self-indulgence, and possible delinquency. It is wrong to make a diagnosis out of context. We might find that an incoming patient and a successful actor have similar 49' profiles; but they are living in different worlds and the meanings of the profiles differ.

Students of MMPI created a vast lore characterizing persons with particular score patterns. Scattered investigations of persons with high scores on scale 4, for example, could be cumulated into this story (supplied by Meehl, in Cronbach & Meehl, 1955):

> Patients diagnosed "Psychopathic personality, asocial and amoral type" tended to score high.
> Delinquents (broadly defined) scored in a higher range than normals.
> Men who had shot a hunting companion had higher scores than other hunters.
> High school students judged by their peers not to be "responsible" scored higher than those judged responsible.
> Professional actors tend to score above average.
> Nurses with comparatively high scores are more often rated by supervisors as "not afraid of mental patients."

A high score on 4 thus implies a certain style, in most cases not pathological.

MMPI experience has been encoded in handbooks, "atlases," and programs for computer interpretation. The clinician interpreting the 49'83 . . . profile can turn to the 49 page of a source and read a summary culled from the literature and from clinic files. The interpretation of a 49' pattern is not a mere blending of what is said about 4' and 9'; it is an attempt at configural interpretation (p. 441). (Only combinations that occur fairly often are treated in that way.)

A description like that in Table 14.2 would be a starting point for considering anyone whose profile peaks are 4 and 9. It is most likely to

Table 14.2   PHRASES USED IN DESCRIBING PERSONS HIGH ON MMPI SCALES 4
             AND 9

marked disregard for social standards and values

frequently in trouble with authorities because of antisocial behavior

poorly developed conscience, easy morals, and fluctuating ethical values

narcissistic, selfish, and self-indulgent

quite impulsive, unable to delay gratification

not willing to accept responsibility for own behavior, rationalizing shortcomings and failures and
   blaming difficulties on other people

low tolerance for frustration

often appear moody, irritable, and caustic; intense feelings of anger and hostility

ambitious, energetic, restless, overactive

in social situations tend to be uninhibited, extroverted, talkative

create good first impression

seem to be incapable of deep emotional ties and keep others at an emotional distance

immature, insecure, and dependent; trying to deny those feelings.

Note: These phrases are extracted from continuous paragraphs in Graham (1987, pp. 109–110).

fit the person if both these scores reach 70. Golden (1979) warns clinicians not to equate the 49′ pattern with "antisocial personality" unless there is a history of deviant behavior. More generally, much reinterpretation in the light of background facts is needed to move from the prepackaged, high-contrast report on a type to a properly shaded picture of a real individual the clinician has seen. (Statements in Table 14.2 are from the guide Graham compiled from a dozen other summaries. In chopping words out of Graham's full sentences, I have not removed words that soften or qualify phrases.)

It is particularly important to recognize that the profile describes the person as he is at this time in his life. There is no finality about the MMPI "type." Typical retest correlations of scores are about 0.8 over a period of a week or so, and this drops to 0.4 (0.5–0.6 in psychiatric samples) over an interval of 1 year or more. We can only speculate about why the scale stabilities are so much worse than those Costa and McCrae summarized (p. 512). Possibly the MMPI samples were different in kind. Or possibly the heterogeneous criterion-keyed MMPI scales give less stable results than more transparent scales of conventional inventories. Two-point codes such as 49 are reproduced on a 1-week retest in only a third of the persons in a college sample (Graham, 1987, pp. 74–75). Naturally, a configuration is less stable than its components considered separately.

Within MMPI and other inventories, clinicians have identified lists of "critical items" that in themselves deserve special attention, just as they would if made in an interview. ("I hate my mother" might be so flagged.) To attend to such remarkable responses makes good sense, but so does Graham's warning (1987, p. 157):

> The reliability of each item is considerably less than that of the standard MMPI scales. Thus, the responses should not be overinterpreted. In a valid protocol, endorsement of critical items should lead the clinician to inquire further in the areas assessed by the items. No conclusions should be reached on the basis of critical item endorsements alone.

The eight scales keyed on patient responses were intended to signal cases of serious abnormality, and originally any standard score of 70 or over was considered to hint strongly at pathology. However, when MMPI was applied to students seeking counseling, to soldiers under temporary stress, and to employees, it became obvious that many persons who function well have some high scores. This lesson has not been well learned. Kunce and Anderson (in McReynolds & Chelune, 1984, p. 68) make this comment about a 1977 doctoral dissertation: Its author

> inferred from an MMPI study on graduate students in psychology that students in clinical psychology are more pathological than counseling or educational psychology students. Yet the same results could also have been interpreted to indicate that the clinical students showed a divergent, imaginative, cognitive personality style and were more theoretically oriented and less pragmatically oriented than the counseling or educational psychology students.

From the earliest years, evidence accumulated that the adolescent average is much above the adult average on each MMPI clinical scale, and the frequency of scores over 70 is correspondingly excessive (Archer, 1987). The MMPI developers of that day insisted that the same norms be used in preparing all profiles, a practice that led to a high rate of false-alarm signals among adolescents. As one part of the current renorming project, those now in charge intend to produce a separate booklet for adolescents including items appropriate to teenagers and having its own keys and norms.

The relation of MMPI scores in a normal population to personality as perceived by others is indicated in Table 14.3. Black (1953) asked women at Stanford to describe themselves and their dormitory acquaintances on an adjective checklist. The table shows some adjectives applied comparatively frequently (or—where "not" appears—infrequently) to women with particular MMPI high-point codes. The descriptions by peers are strikingly different from one category to the next and basically consistent with the usual clinical interpretations. Some contrasts appear between self-reports and reputations. We would expect self-reports to be comparatively favorable, but it is surprising that the "energetic" 9's see themselves as popular when others call them

Table 14.3 REPUTATIONS AND SELF-DESCRIPTIONS ASSOCIATED WITH
MMPI PEAKS OF COLLEGE WOMEN

Highest score	Description by dormitory mates	Self-description
2	Shy, not energetic, not kind, not relaxed	Shy, moody, not decisive, not energetic, not relaxed
3	Many physical complaints, flattering, not partial	Trustful, friendly, not emotional, not boastful
4	Incoherent, moody, sociable, frivolous, not self-controlled	Dishonest, lively, clever, not adaptable, not friendly, not practical
5	Unrealistic, natural, not dreamy	Shiftless, unemotional, not having wide interests, not popular
5 low	Worldly, not energetic, not rough, not shy	Self-destructing, self-dissatisfied, sensitive, shy, unrealistic
6	Shrewd, hard-hearted	Arrogant, shy, naïve, sociable
7	Dependent, kind, not self-centered	Indecisive, many physical complaints, soft-hearted, depressed, irritable
9	Shows off, boastful, selfish, energetic, not loyal, not peaceable, not popular	Enterprising, jealous, courageous, energetic, popular, peaceable, self-confident

Source: Black, 1953.

unpopular. The self-description of low 5's is almost the opposite of the peer description. (Scale 5 has somewhat different keys for men and women; a high score indicates marked departure from the traditional sex role.)

It is illuminating to compare the descriptions of these young women with the categories originally used in criterion keying. The mercurial quality of the 4's could, if much intensified, look like "psychopathic" personality. I leave comparisons of the other scales to the reader. Scales 1 (Hypochondriasis), 2 (Depression), and 3 (Hysteria) are based on subtypes of neurotic patients. Scales 6, 7, and 9 respectively are identified with Paranoia, Psychasthenia, and Hypomania. (Scale 8, based on schizophrenics, was not often a high point in Black's sample.)

MCMI-II The Millon Clinical Multiaxial Inventory (Theodore Millon) has a 1987 edition MCMI-II. The inventory is designed primarily for diagnosis of patients. Millon is critical of the use of MMPI as an all-purpose instrument, and urges that his instrument be applied only in agencies engaged in therapeutic or other case work. He includes marriage counseling, the correctional process, and social agencies; there is a separate Millon inventory for adolescents. Millon shaped his score report to correspond closely to the category system recommended by the American Psychiatric Association in its *Diagnostic and Statistical Manual for Mental Disorders.* Because Millon was part of their working group, he was able to align the profile with the 1987 modification of that system (called DSM-III-R). The underlying conceptualization, however, comes from Millon's own theory of psychopathology. Only a small fraction of the items strike a positive note ("make friends easily," for example). The following items are more typical:

> Lately, I've been sweating a great deal and feel very tense.
> I am often cross and grouchy.
> I think I'm a special person who deserves special attention from others.

MCMI presents 175 items—many fewer than MMPI. The item pool was suggested by the theory, and many rounds of statistical screening reduced the original pool (more than 1000 items) to the current 175. Trial scoring keys were based on constructs, but the final allocation of items to keys and the heavier weighting now given some items rested on criterion keying. Whereas MMPI keyed items that distinguished patients of a given type from normals, Millon required that the item differentiate patients with the relevant diagnosis from *other patients.* Millon's manual, particularly the first 50 pages, is worth reading as a thoughtful account of the problems in creating an instrument to diagnose pathology.

Before looking at the substance, notice in Figure 14.5 the unusual scale to which raw scores are converted. Millon rejected the normalized standard scores that most profiles employ, because distributions in patient populations are skewed. Moreover, he wished to recognize that 30 per cent in a patient population are likely to have anxiety, whereas the rate for manic disorder is more like 4 per cent. He therefore invented a BR (for "base rate") scale that follows rules approximately like this (the rules varying a bit with the scale):

85   Lower cutoff for regarding the characteristic as salient. The percentage of patients at and above 85 equals the estimated proportion having this as the salient diagnosis.

75   Lower cutoff for presence of the characteristic. The percentage of patients at and above 75 equals the estimated proportion in the clinical population who have the characteristic.

60   Median for a clinical norm group.

40   30th percentile among patients.

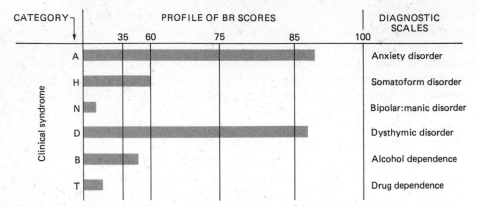

Figure 14.5. **The "Clinical syndrome" profile of Case 168252.** (*Source*: This is part of the profile on MCMI-II of a 40-year-old woman, discussed in the test manual (pp. 221–226). Copyright © 1977, 1822, 1983, 1987 by Theodore Millon.)

This conversion dramatizes scores that sum up many unfavorable self-reports, and compresses the adequate-or-better end of the range where MCMI does not purport to discriminate.

The report in Figure 14.5 highlights the woman's anxiety and dysthymia (depression, negative emotion). These current intense symptoms are consistent with the dependent and self-defeating style described in Figure 14.6. This woman's problems include family conflict and lack of

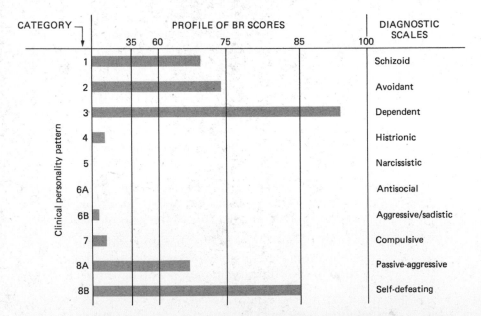

Figure 14.6. **The "Clinical personality pattern" of Case 168252.** (*Source*: This is part of the profile on MCMI-II of a 40-year-old woman, discussed in the test manual (pp. 221–226). Copyright © 1977, 1822, 1983, 1987 by Theodore Millon.)

confidence; the clinical reading of the profile sees her as excessively compliant, which places her in humiliating situations and heightens her sense of unworthiness. The computerized report ends with suggested treatment approaches that include anxiety-suppressing drugs, supportive therapy, changes in her environment that would bring her more occasions to take pride in herself, and other approaches.

Some Further Inventories   A brief account of inventories prominent in the current psychological literature is given here for reference. I do not include the inventories already discussed.

- Adjective Checklist (ACL); H. G. Gough and A. B. Heilbrun, Jr.: High school and adult. Adjectives ("arrogant," "calm," "defensive," . . .) to be checked. An objective means of securing reports from acquaintances; used also for rating oneself and other family members. Psychologists explore the meaning of other personality measures by seeing what adjectives those scores correlate with, as in Table 14.3. Summary scores describe various styles and "needs." An ACL self-report score rarely correlates higher than 0.4 with a related score on a conventional inventory.

- California Psychological Inventory (CPI); H. G. Gough. High school and adult. A lengthy criterion-keyed inventory with 20 principal scores including Sociability, Tolerance, and Intellectual Efficiency. The instrument has been used in an extraordinary amount of research, and Hough (1988) finds it more related to employment criteria than other inventories. A 1987 revision provides a scoring structure with three major dimensions and other features, including computerized interpretation (see p. 576).

- Edwards Personal Preference Schedule; A. L. Edwards. College. To reduce opportunity to show a "good" pattern, the respondent has to choose between paired statements of equal overall desirability. Scored in terms of "needs" for achievement, affiliation, and so on. Avoidance of psychiatric constructs and of subtle keying reduces misconceptions. Note the comment (p. 506) that measures of motives by questionnaire and by thematic tests do not represent the same variables.

- Eysenck Personality Questionnaire; H. J. and S. B. G. Eysenck. Forms for age 7 through adulthood. One of several inventories identified with the names of Eysenck or Maudsley [Hospital] that have been studied extensively, especially in England. The three score dimensions—psychoticism, extroversion, and neuroticism— play a central role in Eysenck's neo-Pavlovian theory of normal as well as abnormal personality. Scales are short (20–25 items per scale) and the YES/NO items transparent. Could serve as a preliminary screen; not a basis for final decisions about individuals.

- NEO Personality Inventory; P. T. Costa, Jr., and R. R. McCrae. Adults. Intended primarily to describe personalities in the normal range. Presents 181 items in two formats, one for self-report and one for obtaining a description from an acquaintance. The same scoring key is applied to both forms; the forms may be used independently or interpreted together. Generated by factor analysis, the scales measure the Big Five dimensions (p. 505). Subscores are charted within N, E, and O. Two of the six components of Neuroticism, for example, are Impulsiveness and Hostility. These correlate 0.35 and have alpha coefficients near 0.7, so the subdivision is meaningful.

- Personality Research Form (PRF); D. N. Jackson. Forms for ages 13 through college. Constructed in a manner like that for JPI, but covers different content. Scales resemble those of the Edwards inventory and the comments made about it apply. Jackson relies on balance of positive and negative endorsement items to control response bias. Correlations with ratings from acquaintances in the manual (p. 45) are at least as high as those for JPI (Table 14.1).

- Sixteen Personality Factor Questionnaire (16 PF); R. B. Cattell and associates. Age 16 through adult, with a special form for poor readers. Measures central factors in Cattell's system (see Table 13.3), on which he and his followers have conducted varied and extensive research. Unusual supplements include profiles for occupational groups, a handbook for clinical interpretation, and even a computerized evaluation for responses collected by marital counselors from couples. Reliability is sacrificed to bandwidth; even combining two forms yields scores with reliabilities ranging around 0.6. The other chief limitation is the claim that 16 PF meets the needs of almost any user; only a highly sophisticated reader can sort out the mass of background material and the comments of reviewers to decide for or against a particular application.

8. *The manual summarizes JPI Responsibility in such terms as "strong obligation to be honest," "sense of duty to others," "inflexible conscience." In Table 14.1, JPI Responsibility was correlated with ratings on "Trustworthy/Untrustworthy." Do the low correlations for this score in the table seem plausible?*

9. *The JPI profile arranges scores alphabetically. A computer printout can display scores in order from extreme to middling. For the student activist, the topmost rows would be Low Conformity, Low Tolerance, and Complexity. How suitable is this format?*

10. *Is it likely that the higher rate of adolescent MMPI responses indicating emotional tension and maladjustment represents a valid difference between adolescents and adults? Should persons of different ages who give similar responses be evaluated similarly?*

11. *Table 14.1 lists the JPI dimensions. Table 5.7 lists many of the dimensions ("needs") for which the PRF is scored. Which description appears to be most suitable where an inventory is a starting point for college counseling in-*

tended to promote self-understanding? Would much be gained by giving both inventories?

12. *For a multiscore instrument summarizing a 10-year-old's self-description, what is to be said for and against each of these methods of reporting to his parents and teacher?*

    a. *Profile displaying per cent of possible responses in a keyed direction (e.g., Dominance). The average profile for his sex-grade group is printed over it.*

    b. *Profile displaying percentile rank (within sex and grade) on each key. The average profile is represented by a flat line at 50.*

13. *Millon counts items that differentiate antisocial personalities from patients with other diagnoses. The MMPI counts items that differentiate those persons from normals. How are the two keys likely to differ? Which strategy seems preferable?*

14. *Here are additional facts (for males) about the subscales within NEO Neuroticism.*

    Anxiety and Depression correlate 0.7; internal consistencies 0.8 and 0.75.

    Anxiety and Impulsiveness correlate 0.3; internal consistencies 0.8 and 0.7.

    Anxiety and Vulnerability correlate 0.6; internal consistencies 0.8 and 0.75.

    Depression and Vulnerability correlate 0.65; internal consisten-cies 0.75 and 0.75.

    Impulsiveness and Vulnerability correlate 0.2; internal consistencies 0.7 and 0.75.

    Are these four variables distinct enough to be worth reporting? (Refer to Figure 8.1.)

VALIDITY FOR EVALUATING DISORDERS

Screening

Persons who displayed symptoms in the past are more likely than others to display symptoms in the future. Lasky et al. (1959) found that the thickness of a mental patient's file folder correlates 0.6 with his chances of being hospitalized again after release. Self-reports are considerably less potent as predictors of deviant behavior than are records of past deviant behavior. Prediction may be enhanced by the "Give-a-dog-a-bad-name" effect. Moreover, conflict with one's environment breeds future conflict unless someone helps resolve the initial conflict. These findings are precisely like the findings in the intellectual field: the best way to predict who will do well in schooling is to find out who has been doing well in school.

This argues for rather than against the importance of direct measurement. To predict from life history is a conservative strategy: good is expected of those good in the past, and the worst is expected of those with bad past records. The proper function of psychological methods is to locate the seemingly adjusted people for whom the risk of disturbance is high and the ones with histories of maladjustment who should respond to suitable treatment. This implies a need to measure not level of adjustment but probability of responding favorably to one or another treatment.

The screening instrument is not intended to analyze the person but to direct scarce professional time to cases meriting deeper study. The investigator validating a screening instrument needs criterion data to assess how well scores identify persons from the relevant population. The criterion for a screening instrument is often crude.

A somewhat representative validity report is that for PSI. I compress details given in the manual by combining psychiatric subgroups and by discussing just one cut score, for males only. The criterion for the Alienation (Al) key is patient/nonpatient status. As explained on page 535, the key was originally formed by contrasting community members with patients. The distributions for those two groups were studied to identify reasonable cut scores. Table 14.4 assumes that persons with standard scores of 60 or above on Al were flagged as possibly disturbed. The figures (for males in the keying sample) in the upper half of the table show that 75 per cent of the disturbed were detected at a price of 11 per cent errors on normals. The cross-validation (lower half of table) contrasted further normal males with mental hospital inpatients classed as having "functional psychosis." The percentages shifted, but the error rate remained about the same.

How adequate is this level of validity? Assume that the population has 1000 normals of whom 11 per cent have scores of 60 and over; that means 110 false alarms. Assume also that 75 per cent of disturbed persons reach a score of 60. If 200 disturbed persons were added to the

Table 14.4   SUCCESS OF A CUT SCORE IN DISTINGUISHING MENTAL PATIENTS

Group	N	Number exceeding cut score	Error rate (per cent)
Keying samples			
Patients	71	53	25
Normals	195	22	11
Cross-validation			
Patients	48	40	17
Normals	305	43	14

Source: Data from PSI manual, 1978, p. 20.

basic 1000 cases, the base rate would be 200/1200 or 17 per cent; and 260 (= 110 + 150) members of the population would score 60 or over. The fourfold table is:

	Disturbed	Normal	Total
High	150 hits	110 false positives	260
Low	50 misses	890	940
	200	1000	1200

Reviewing 260 persons could be a good investment, as the warning is confirmed in more than half the cases (150/260). But the warning is only preliminary; nearly half the warnings are false alarms.

Lower base rates would alter the picture.

Disturbed persons (*N*)	Base rate (%)	Interviews required (*N*)	Interviews confirming disturbance (%)
0	0	110	0
10	1	117	6
20	2	125	12
50	5	147	25
100	9	185	41
200	17	260	58

In a general community, the base rate is probably small and most of the "flags" are false alarms. The base rate will be higher among persons referred to a clinic, and the fraction of interviews "wasted" may be acceptable.

Short, undisguised questionnaires have been of distinct value in military screening. One questionnaire given 2081 recruits successfully called 525 persons suspect; 281 of them were later judged to present neuropsychiatric conditions (Harris, 1945). The test permitted psychiatrists to omit individual interviews with 1540 men—not a trifling saving. The screen missed 16 neuropsychiatric cases who got into difficulty while on duty.

In this kind of study, some apparent false positives may be unrecognized hits. Nonpatient status is no guarantee of mental health; many persons in the community have weaknesses that remain latent only so long as they are exposed to no exceptional stress. Much could be learned in a follow-up study if the analysis took into account family circumstances, pressures at work, and other events in the person's life that intervened between test and criterion evaluation.

Certain studies of surgical patients have a bit of this flavor. MMPI scores have been reasonably accurate at forecasting which patients will have psychological difficulties during the often-stressful postoperative period (Graham, 1987, p. 91). Pursuant to such a warning, preoperative or postoperative intervention can perhaps reduce the difficulty. Research evaluating the intervention, rather than a demonstration of predictive success, is needed to validate such a suggestion.

Inadequate or improper analysis often overestimates the success of a screening procedure. The following points are to be kept in mind:

- Validating a key or formula on the cases used in item selection and keying proves nothing. Cross-validation (p. 443) is essential to avoid placing trust in a screening rule that fits only the sample on which it was developed.
- To demonstrate "significant" differences (e.g., between a disturbed group and normals) is beside the point; with large samples, inaccurate predictions reach statistical significance.
- Comparing extreme groups can show that a relationship exists, but we ought to be told how strong the relation is over the entire population. A correlation calculated from extreme groups is exaggerated.
- A correlation, or a report of the percentage of correct decisions, should be augmented with a consideration of base rates.

Controls for past history would often reduce the apparent validity of screening. Few studies ask which tests can predict adjustment *within* a sample of persons with bad records, or within a sample with good case histories. The prediction formula ought also to be checked out on groups of uniform ability. The incompetent student or recruit will have problems of adjustment, and it is no brilliant achievement for an inventory to predict this. Within the incompetent group, some will develop emotional symptoms and some will not; the characteristics associated with breakdown in this group might well differ from the characteristics associated with breakdowns in the high-ability group.

15. *Callan (1972) identified MMPI items that "deviant" soldiers marked more often than others. (Deviancy included going AWOL and being punished for misconduct.) In a cross-validation, the key and cutoff rule picked 825 out of 3328 trainees as prospective deviants. The trainees who actually got in trouble (236) included 96 of those the instrument had picked. How satisfactory is the screening instrument?*

16. *Assume that 20 per cent of normals and 90 per cent of disturbed persons exceed a certain cut score. Evaluate the effectiveness of this screening, assuming a base rate of 5 per cent; of 20 per cent.*

Classification

Clinicians are often asked to distinguish one type of psychopathology from another. Classification is sometimes required for institutional bookkeeping. It is helpful in forming homogeneous groups for research (evaluation of drugs, for example), and it is used in laying initial treatment plans. By and large, attempts to classify on the basis of personality measures have worked out poorly. No more than two-thirds of the patients the interpreter assigns to a certain category will be assigned the same label on the basis of more extended clinical analysis. Tests of *intellectual* impairment are useful for differential diagnosis where schizophrenia or brain dysfunction is suspected (Filskov & Boll, 1982; Newmark et al., 1980; Phillips et al., 1980).

The Millon inventory is primarily designed to predict what label or labels the clinician working with a patient will apply, although Millon also makes treatment suggestions. Millon's manual has compiled hit/ miss statistics for all the scales. The report in Table 14.5 takes as criterion a clinician's judgment (made without knowing the inventory scores) as to whether serious anxiety is present. The percentages in the right-most column change markedly from scale to scale; for "thought disorder," with a 4 per cent base rate, the percentages are 55 (Highs) and 98 (Lows). Millon calculates an "overall diagnostic power" for thought disorder at 96 per cent; that half-truth is best ignored.

Interest in diagnostic categorization is much less today than it was when MMPI was constructed. The psychologist's aim has become one of improving the quality of life for the person and those around him. Often the intervention takes the form of a new institutional arrangement or a change in community services rather than an attempt to change the person's behavior directly. Even in the therapeutic setting, medical and psychoanalytic models have given way to a behavioral emphasis. One psychologist (Peterson, 1968, pp. 4–5, 32) with a strong background in MMPI diagnosis expressed more than two decades ago a view that is now almost universal:

> The main difficulty with the typological, disease-oriented approach [to] human problems is simply that we are not dealing with disease types in the assessment and modification of disordered behavior. A child who strangles kittens or spits at his mother does not have a disease. He *does* have something somebody defines as a problem. . . . The therapeutic need is to get the client to change his behavior, not to cure his illness, and the vital diagnostic need is for information contributory to the behavior changing enterprise.

Table 14.5   ACCURACY WITH WHICH A RECOMMENDED CUT
SCORE IDENTIFIES PATIENTS WITH SEVERE
ANXIETY

Anxiety score above 74?	Anxiety absent	Anxiety present	Total	Per cent correct
Yes	43	*219*	262	84%
No	*386*	55	441	88%
All patients	429	274	703	
Correctly identified	90%	80%		

Source: Estimated from Table 3-16 of the MCMI-II manual, 1987.

17. *Millon's overall figure for anxiety, 86 per cent, is not a bad summary. Why is the same technique misleading when applied to thought disorders?*

Forecasting Response to Psychological Intervention

In diagnosis, a reasonable surface question is whether the person is likely to benefit from therapy. The indication that persons with the 49' pattern change little in response to psychotherapy has a message for administrators of agencies. Apart from cases with such hard-shell resistance, it is difficult to believe that the person's response does not depend on which kind of treatment is undertaken.

Studying not psychopathology but participation in a weight-loss clinic, Janis (1978, 1982) and his co-workers found that, in general, it was persons with low self-esteem who stuck to the regimen through the treatment and follow-up period. When, however, Riskind (in Janis, 1982) encouraged clients with *high* self-esteem to take day-to-day responsibility for their own conduct, they adopted sound eating practices. Riskind's method did not work with clients reporting low self-esteem. Janis offers a tentative theory regarding the role of personality in responses to counseling.

Evaluations of therapy have typically divided a panel into experimental and control groups and given members of the experimental group an essentially uniform treatment—medication, behavior modification, group discussion, or whatever. Outcome means of the two groups are compared. The comparison may be made separately for those who score high and low on some personality scale; MMPI studies of this nature were reviewed by Widom (1979).

In clinical applications, assessment methods should be judged not by the truth of their descriptions or even their predictions about a fixed treatment, according to Hayes et al. (1987). These authors call for evidence that the data are useful in *directing* treatment. Hayes et al. reviewed research approaches for this utility-oriented validation. Essentially, one wants validated interpretative rules that choose a treatment or living environment for the individual—a classification decision (p. 168). In this vein, Moos (1987) reported several studies that demonstrate differential response to treatment settings and took a few steps toward explaining the processes operating.

The situational influence on behavior was turned to advantage in a prison. From MMPI profiles it was judged that certain prisoners were especially likely to assault others and that certain others were likely to be victims of assault. The "predatory" prisoners were assigned to one dormitory; the potential victims, to a second; and intermediate cases, to a third. Prior to the reassignment, 22 assaults had been reported in 9 months. Supervision was reduced in the third dormitory to permit more intensive supervision in the first two. In the subsequent 9 months there were nine reports of assault from the first dormitory, four from the second, and none from that with "intermediate" cases. (The study, by Bohn, was reported by Megargee & Bohn, 1979.) In studies that ignore situational influences, MMPI profiles do not predict "adjustment to prison" (Megargee & Carbonell, 1985).

18. *As originally conceived, the MMPI scales were to discriminate several kinds of patients from normals. Yet the traditional classification problem is to categorize a person who already is known to have social or emotional difficulty. What contrast groups will lead to relevant discriminant keys for this purpose? (For an effort in this direction, see Rosen, 1966.)*

19. *Is the original keying of MMPI more like the criterion keying of Strong or that of Kuder? Which procedure would you favor if a new instrument serving the wide-ranging purposes of MMPI is to have criterion keying?*

20. *If an "ideal" predictive study of operators in nuclear power plants were carried out, as outlined in Table 5.1, what would be a suitable criterion? (Note that, in sound plant operation, cross-checks are installed to prevent an operator error from having a large effect.)*

PREDICTIONS IN THE GENERAL POPULATION

Countless studies have pursued the attractive hypothesis that data on motivation, emotional stability, and so on will predict academic and vocational success. Apart from selection and guidance, understanding of styles and moods can be important in a teacher's or supervisor's planning. Also, findings that fall short of practical usefulness raise stimulating questions for theory.

Occupational Predictions

The profession's view of the value of personality inventories as predictors on the job was generally pessimistic from the 1960s until quite recently. Influential earlier summaries by Guion and Gottier (1965) and Ghiselli (1973) reported weak and inconsistent correlations of job success with trait measures. Recent surveys of civilian and military data (Hough, 1986, 1987, 1988) do find average correlations of 0.3 or better with some criteria. The better predictions were not for job performance but for delinquency and substance abuse—criteria of the "typical behavior" type. Hough (1986) criticizes earlier research for its shotgun character. Typically, all scales of an instrument were correlated against any available criterion, rather than matching up variables that had a plausible connection.

   Some solid positive findings are part of a resurgent interest today. From his lifetime of personnel research for the Sears organization, Bentz (in Bernardin & Bownas, 1985) concludes that personality appraisals are useful indicators of probable performance of executives. Still, few of his validity coefficients against managerial criteria were above 0.3. Table

14.6, coming from a study of female buyers, includes the most positive of his results. The criterion was a careful judgment of "potentiality"— the executive level to which each woman might ultimately be promoted. (Job performance was rated also, but rated potentiality was much better predicted.) The traits with sizable correlations in Table 14.6 are all suggestive of "the judicious executive." Combining personality and ability scores did not improve prediction—probably because dominance (and other traits) correlated with tested ability in this sample. (Incidentally, "Dominance" was labeled "Masculinity" when, long ago, Guilford developed the inventory used in this study.)

Two of the new, optimistic studies come from PDRI, the first a study of some 8000 soldiers in Project A. In 1987, Hough and associates designed new inventories, mostly for Big Five subtraits, and correlated scores with four carefully collected criteria (Figure 14.7). The first two criteria came mostly from tests; the other two are based on supervisor and peer ratings and on personnel files. The large, wide-range sample and the care given to criterion development warrant considerable trust in the findings.

Abilities did a fine job of predicting the two proficiency criteria. A weighted sum of temperament variables predicted the other two criteria at least as well as ability does. The two together would predict these important criteria with validity above 0.4. This recalls the finding (p. 416) that including information on personality was necessary to predict a combat criterion. (It is puzzling that the composite temperament score predicts proficiency criteria with validity near 0.25 when the component scores were invalid. Apparently, some prediction came from a count of haphazard responses and some from a report on physical activity.)

Maintenance workers in the electric power industry ($N > 2000$) were the subject of another PDRI study (Bosshardt et al., 1984). Great effort went into collecting criterion ratings on both abilities and typical behav-

Table 14.6 CORRELATIONS OF JUDGED POTENTIAL OF
WOMEN BUYERS WITH AN ABILITY
MEASURE AND 13 SELF-REPORT SCORES

Correlation	Scales
.50–.59	Dominance, Mental Ability
.40–.49	
.30–.39	Composure, Emotional Control, Objectiveness, Self-Confidence, Tolerance
.20–.29	Optimism, Sociability, Social Leadership
.10–.19	Reflectiveness, Seriousness
.00–.09	Activity, Agreeableness

Source: Bentz, in Bernardin & Bownas, 1985, p. 104. With 72 cases, the standard error of each correlation is 0.1 or more.

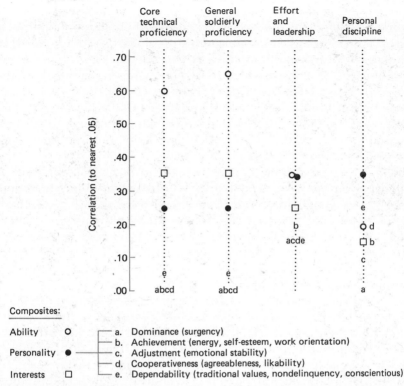

Figure 14.7. **Prediction of military criteria from personality and ability.** (*Source*: Data from Hough, 1988.)

ior. These two aspects were given roughly equal weight in the final criterion. The noncognitive predictors came from self-report on background, interests, and traits similar to those measured in JPI and CPI. A first analysis threw 17 of these into a regression computation, using a shrinkage formula (p. 443) to get a validity of 0.28. This result slightly exceeded the validity for 12 cognitive tests. The two sets combined had a shrunken validity of 0.34. More to the point, a fairly short battery chosen judgmentally in advance worked just as well. The short battery that gave the best result counted mechanical comprehension and use of mathematical formulas, and also scores for persistence, "work ethic," conscientiousness—and (low) artistic and (high) realistic interests (Bosshardt et al., 1984, pp. 88–92).

The validity coefficients in these two studies are not high. Why, then, the authors' enthusiastic presentations? The foremost reason, perhaps, is attentiveness to the message of utility analysis (p. 430)—a validity of 0.3 or a rise from 0.25 to 0.35 can be worth a lot of money to the employing firm—and, for the army, far more teams ready to carry out missions properly (see Butler, in Gifford, 1989b). Second, personality measures rarely have adverse impact on male minority applicants, so including them reduces the likelihood of a court challenge to the selection plan. Third, the validities are turning up in comparatively low-level jobs where abilities have limited predictive power.

The new results are somewhat stronger than results in the older literature, mostly because of the criteria. The criteria paid systematic, separate attention to typical behavior. Criteria were collected after workers or soldiers had time to settle into their work styles. Probably the fact that the instruments were designed for this population, and not for college students or for patients, improved results.

The most surprising fact is that a small set of measures chosen by psychologists on the basis of a job analysis did just as well as an empirically weighted composite of the 17 noncognitive dimensions originally chosen as potentially relevant. Neither personality theory nor daring is needed, of course, to recognize that conscientiousness is desired in maintenance workers. But we should note that, in the U.S. Army study, responsibility scores (e in Figure 14.7) were not dramatically more relevant than the other dimensions.

All in all, I would not advise entering personality scores directly in a selection rule until substantial validation on workers of the same type has shown positive results. That advice is underscored by still another PDRI study where the noncognitive predictors failed, a study of clerical workers and such specialists as claims processors in the insurance industry. There was a large sample, careful job analysis that did highlight responsibility and other traits, and other earmarks of PDRI work. The noncognitive scores had little relation to the criteria and did not contribute in a combining formula. Ability tests had enough predictive power to be useful (Peterson et al., 1982).

There is a case, in some settings, for basing decisions on inventory scores without direct validation. Great responsibilities are placed on operators of nuclear equipment, yet officials of power plants were able to list over 150 specific incidents of operators' disturbing behavior. Specialists in the psychometric approach to personality advised giving inventories to applicants, and retesting periodically after hiring to guard against emerging pathology (Dunnette et al., 1981). They recommended giving MMPI *and* CPI. Among other indicators they proposed to use, the 49' pattern was said to signify the possibility of argumentative hostility and impulsive action. Principal reliance should be placed on two clinicians' independent examination of the information, it was said, and the reviewers should be continually mindful that statistically abnormal responses are given by some emotionally stable persons. The case report would clear many workers. The others would be studied further by means of a personal history, the Loevinger Sentence Completion Test (on ego development and self-control), and a clinical interview (its topics to include leisure pursuits, history of reactions to stress, and present life stresses). A rejected worker would have the right to appeal; this could lead to several stages of reassessment—or the worker could at any time accept the "screen out" decision. Given the unwisdom of waiting to screen workers holding these jobs until behavior turns erratic, such cautious use of inventories would probably be endorsed by most psychologists. Some would prefer performance tests or projective tests to the questionnaires.

The relation of work success to personality is illuminated by many other studies. One is an analysis of practicing architects whose judged record of creativeness (*not* success!) was compared with concurrent scores on seven inventories (Hall & MacKinnon, 1969). A multiple correlation of around 0.4 (cross-validated) was found with most instruments. The MMPI proved worthless in this application whereas the Strong blank ran well ahead of the pack ($R = 0.55$). Among the single scales with comparatively large positive correlations are these: Strong Artist and Author; and desires for Change, Exhibition, and Autonomy on Gough's Adjective Checklist (ACL). The large negative correlations are equally illuminating; they include Strong Banker and Policeman; and ACL Self-Control and Personal Adjustment. Other inventories tended to confirm the picture of creativity implied by these correlations.

One would expect the rigid, conservative, nationalistic authoritarian to be the worst of candidates for the Peace Corps. Smith (1965) validated preinduction questionnaire measures of this trait against adaptation as a schoolteacher in Ghana, with the hunch that high scorers would make poor cultural ambassadors. The tests did not predict performance in the field. Smith tried to account for the near-zero correlations, noting first that the true authoritarian does not volunteer for the Peace Corps. Very likely the extreme Lows are too unruly and impulsive to adapt as the moderates (who within this select population rank as Highs) do. Then he notes that the Ghanaian school system is organized rigidly. Success on the job means fitting the demands of the system, even if one never gets around to making friends with the populace. As one reads Smith's postmortem on the once-lively hypothesis, the only wonder is that authoritarianism failed to correlate *positively* with success in that place and time.

A person adapts to role requirements. He becomes forceful as a parent, submissive in reporting to a commanding officer, boisterous at a party, decorous in church. Personality, as commonly measured, probably has much to do with the sort of work and personal relations a person *seeks*, including the way he defines a flexible role such as that of parent (Diener et al., 1984; Spokane, 1987). But it has comparatively little to do with his competence when thrust into a structured role. The adjusted person responds to the demands of the assignment.

Many times I have spoken of the potential importance of identifying types of situations in which a person will prosper. Such predictions on the basis of aptitude tests have been scattered and generally unimpressive; in contrast, personality inventories have produced a substantial array of interactive relationships (Patsfall & Feimer, in Bernardin & Bownas, 1985). The suggestive findings (p. 168) on individuals' responses to more and less rigid organizational styles are one example. Fiedler (in Magnusson & Endler, 1977) has amassed evidence that whether persons who have a given style of relating to others succeed or fail as leaders depends on characteristics of the work situation. Information on personality should help in fitting work assignments to individuals.

Some situations place strenuous demands on the individual, and then having a suitable personality is an *aptitude* requirement. Navy scientists volunteered to spend a 6-month winter in the Antarctic. The ones who described themselves as sociable sensation-seekers did comparatively badly; those who said they were introverted and not easily bored did well. A peer-rating criterion was predicted with validity around 0.4 (Busch et al., 1982).

21. *Suggest reasons why, in the Antarctic assignment, self-report scores did not correlate much more than 0.4 with peer ratings of performance.*

22. *In some decades the Army attracts so many recruits that it can reject a sizable fraction. Figure 14.7 indicates that ability strongly predicts proficiency and that a balanced ability-personality composite predicts effort and conduct. What would be a reasonable selection rule if 5 per cent of volunteers can be rejected? 25 per cent?*

Educational Predictions

In the academic realm, there have been many failures of prediction from inventories, along with positive reports that never get replicated. Even self-esteem or anxiety has only minimal correlation with achievement when ability is held constant (Bachman & O'Malley, 1977; Heinrich & Spielberger, 1982; Wylie, 1974, 1979). A replicated correlation for the Gordon Personal Profile (L. V. Gordon, 1978) perhaps illustrates the best that can be hoped for. Three of the four subscores (Ascendancy, Emotional Stability, and Sociability) have correlations with grade average that differ negligibly from zero. The fourth, Responsibility (= thorough, steady, and reliable), does not correlate appreciably with ability tests and does correlate with academic success. Three studies reported correlations close to 0.2; a fourth, largest study produced a correlation of 0.1. If $r = 0.2$, adding the Responsibility score to an ability score would improve the multiple correlation by 0.04 or less. After reflection on the published literature and after sponsoring studies of its own, the College Entrance Examination Board (1963) made a noteworthy official statement warning member colleges "of very serious risks that would certainly attend the actual use of [any existing personality] tests in making admissions decisions." The problems mentioned include possible misunderstanding by the public, faking and coaching, absence of parallel forms, overemphasis on scales that correlate only slightly with marks, and inability to allow for the fact that adolescent personalities are changing.

Institutions express recurrent interest in the possible contribution of "noncognitive" measures to selection, and some may yet prove to be of practical use. Attempting to measure "strength of motivation" by questionnaire seems hopeless, but preferred styles may help in classification. The biographical inventory may be turned to advantage on the assumption that a person who previously has persisted in tasks and enterprises is a good bet; questions of this character should refer to verifiable events and not invite generalized self-advertising. Inventories might be used not to "predict success" but to increase diversity. Thus, a medical school might distribute offers of admission in some specified proportion over qualified applicants whose preferences center on administrative or scientific or personal service activities.

Cronbach and Snow (1977) reviewed many studies on the response to instruction of different personalities. There were few studies of any one trait save anxiety, and rarely did investigators studying the same trait use the same measure of it. The summary grouped anxiety, dependency, and other indicators of inhibition under the label "defensive motivation" and confident, assertive, self-directing qualities as "constructive motivation." The broad conclusion was that students with constructive motivation benefited most from challenging instruction where there was comparatively little direction from the teacher and much opportunity for the learner to shape his activities. There were several reports that more defensive students were at their best when given orderly, firmly structured lessons. Results were inconsistent, and the outcome is expected to depend on other factors (subject matter, grade level, class ability, etc.)

One of the research programs entering the summary is that of Domino (1968, 1971). He investigated students at the high and low extremes on two CPI scores, Achievement-through-Conformity (Ac) and Achievement-through-Independence (Ai). Both traits imply positive self-reports. The high Ac speaks of himself as efficient, organized, responsible, and sincere. The high Ai calls himself mature, foresighted, demanding, and self-reliant. Domino interviewed the students' instructors about their teaching styles. Some courses, highly structured, left students with little freedom or independent responsibility. Some encouraged initiative and self-direction. Domino calculated each student's grade average over all the courses of each type that he had taken. The results showed an interaction effect for Ai, low Ai's doing better in more structured instruction. High Ac also was associated with superior grades, but it did not interact with instructor style.

In the second study (a formal experiment), four sections of introductory psychology were formed, each with students of one type. The instructor encouraged student initiative in two sections and pressed for conformity in two others. Figure 14.8 shows that a match between in-

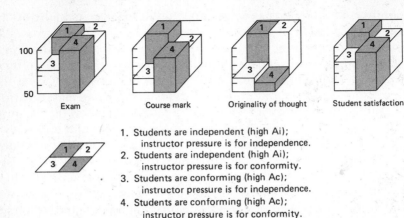

1. Students are independent (high Ai);
   instructor pressure is for independence.
2. Students are independent (high Ai);
   instructor pressure is for conformity.
3. Students are conforming (high Ac);
   instructor pressure is for independence.
4. Students are conforming (high Ac);
   instructor pressure is for conformity.

Figure 14.8. **Joint influence of teacher style and student personality.** Shading identifies classes where student self-report matched instructor's adopted style. For each variable, the group average is expressed as a percentage of the average in whichever group ranked highest. (*Source*: Data from Domino, 1971.)

structor style and student style worked out best, according to most criteria. With regard to originality, however, only the students' styles mattered. Also, the independent students were able to meet fairly well a demand that they conform. Several other findings reviewed by Cronbach and Snow are roughly in accord with those of Domino.

Research such as this contributes to understanding rather than to practice. Domino was comparing extremes, and relations would be weaker if the full range of student and teacher styles entered the analysis. Moreover, dozens of interest, ability, and personality variables affect response, so it would not be sensible to sort students into sections on the basis of Ai or any other such score. The finding does imply, however, that teaching different sections in different ways—and telling students in advance what style they can expect—would enable the student to sort himself into a section that he expects will suit him. Moreover, an adept teacher can provide for a variety of work styles within a single class.

The potential of personality measures for research is particularly well illustrated in the research program of Atkinson and his associates (Atkinson, 1981; Atkinson & Raynor, 1978). ("Need for achievement" [nAch] was measured by thematic tests [p. 631] rather than by self-report in this work and in the earlier studies directed by McClelland, but Atkinson did use a questionnaire to measure anxiety.) The argument can be sketched in a few sentences.

Anxiety expresses motivation to avoid psychological failure.

nAch expresses motivation to seek success, particularly in tasks where personal skill and effort make a difference.

> The combination of low anxiety and high nAch defines a resultant tendency to approach a challenge (to accept a gamble, to invest effort in a problem).

> The perceived difficulty of a task (or the odds against a gamble) acts as an intensifier. If probability of success is near 0.5, the tendency to approach (or to avoid) is strong; if the probability is near zero or one, there is no personal challenge.

In plain words, the person with strong net constructive motivation is attracted to activities where success appears highly uncertain and makes his greatest effort on such tasks. The defensive person will prefer easy tasks—or tasks where success is so unlikely that failure implies no personal shortcoming. Predictions cannot be made simply, however; additional motivations are aroused (e.g., affiliation, prestige, fear of rejection by peers for "showing off"); and alternative activities compete for time and attention with the task about which a prediction is made. States are of more immediate significance than traits; a state can be temporarily satiated or heightened by recent deprivation. Furthermore, learned roles seem to produce differences between the sexes in many of the laboratory and classroom situations where the theory has been tested (Farmer & Fyans, 1980).

Among the many offshoots of the theory is deCharms's (1976, 1980) educational experiment in which the motivation of inner-city youngsters was heightened by deliberately altering the self-concept. The students were taught (in Grades 6 and 7) to take responsibility for initiating activities, setting goals, and monitoring their progress. Scores on a thematic test of motivation increased sharply over those of a control group, and so did school achievement; the effect could be traced down to the end of high school.

23. *What role, if any, should personality inventories play in vocational counseling?*

24. *Research such as Domino's suggests how to teach conformers so that they will tend to earn better grades. Would some other policy contribute more to their long-run educational development?*

25. *What advantages does a biographical inventory have over a personality questionnaire in employee selection?*

26. *How might lack of confidence help one student to attain high marks, yet be a drawback to another?*

27. *A leadership score identifies pupils whose responses resemble those of other pupils who have become leaders. What characteristics other than leadership ability and interest are likely to distinguish student leaders in high school from the students who take little part in student affairs?*

28. *If school officials encourage pupils with high leadership scores to take leadership responsibilities, will this tend to increase or decrease the correlation between the original scores and leadership record by the end of high school?*

29. *Scores on certain instruments purport to identify students likely to be trou-*
    blemakers and potential delinquents. Assuming that such a score has very
    high stability and validity, could any legitimate use be made of such a test
    by high schools? If, as is the case, the validity coefficients are quite low,
    what undesirable effects may follow if such scores are collected by prin-
    cipals?

STRUCTURE OF THE INDIVIDUAL

No psychologist seriously believes that a person can be adequately characterized in 3 or 5 or 16 dimensions. Investigators try, however, to bring
a multitude of individuals into a single conceptual scheme. The attempt
to map dissimilar individuals onto a few dimensions is an effort to
achieve what the chemist does with a limited number of concepts such
as molecular weight and acidity. This search for dimensions that can be
woven into lawlike, universally applicable statements is referred to as
"nomothetic," in contrast to the "idiographic" portrayal of each person
as unique, as in a novel. (The words come from the Greek: *nomos* for
"law," *idios* for "one's own." Allport [1937], who gave the words their
place in psychology, emphasized that the approaches are supplementary, not antagonistic.)

The score on a trait is a statistical summary of behavior over many
situations. The person at either extreme of the scale is well characterized. He exhibits the trait (or its absence) in unusual degree and in a
large number of situations. If a man is perfectly honest, the adjective
really tells us how he acts, whereas a middling score on an honesty scale
tells little.

A middling score implies no lack of individuality. Rather, the person's behavior is not organized along the dimension we chose to score.
The description "50 per cent honest" inevitably is inadequate; *when* is
the person honest? (Burton, 1963). One man acts from need; he takes
money to feed his family, but will not cheat or lie. Another, prudent
rather than honest, acts honestly when he might be caught. Another
would never steal, but thinks it right to operate a business on the principle of "buyer beware." These men are all honest to an intermediate degree. A personalized description would replace the general trait dimension with dimensions that describe situations the person sees as calling
for an honest act (and the opposite). The person has his own way of slic-
ing up his world; situations one person perceives as similar are not similar for another.

Psychoanalysts—and those psychologists who probe the person's
perceptual world—have written idiographic characterizations, but their
work has been to a large degree artistic. How well an individual can be
"characterized" through reproducible methods remains an open
question.

A Semantic Differential Case Study   A provocative example of the possibilities is the study of Eve. The psychiatrists Thigpen and Cleckley (1953, 1957) vividly described her "split personality," and the film *Three Faces of Eve* portrayed it artistically. Osgood and Luria (1954) characterized each of Eve's personalities objectively.

They employed the Semantic Differential method, which measures connotations of words or phrases. The stimulus is rated on a scale, scales and stimuli being mixed in random order. Successive items might appear as follows:

MY FATHER	soft	___:___:___:___:___:___:___	hard
FRAUD	rich	___:___:___:___:___:___:___	poor
CONFUSION	fair	___:___:___:___:___:___:___	unfair
MY FATHER	deep	___:___:___:___:___:___:___	shallow

The scale is to be checked rapidly to capture first impressions. The method has varied uses. Items like those just listed could elicit the concepts of a patient. A study of political views could use names of nations as stimuli (keeping the scales the same).

One method of scoring assigns the scales to "good-bad," "strong-weak," and "active-passive" keys; for example, "soft" can be equated with "weak" and "passive." Checkmarks are converted to numbers running from $+3$ to -3, and, for each stimulus, scales within a key are averaged. Thus, we could say that a respondent has indirectly described his father at $+1$ on good, $+2.4$ on strong, and -0.4 on active.

Eve White had three identities who "took possession" of her at various times, and her therapists were able to administer the Semantic Differential to each persona in turn. Figure 14.9 presents two of the configurations. The black ball represents the midpoint on all scales. "Good" is at the top, "active" at the left, and "weak" toward the viewer. The heavy line connecting the black ball with "doctor" (who is always good, strong, very active) helps to orient the figure.

Two psychologists interpreted these structures with no further knowledge of the case. In Eve White's record they pointed out the separation of love and sex, the meaninglessness of the spouse, the weakness of "me." Eve Black seems to place hatred and fraud in a favorable cluster with "me" and rejects spouse, love, job, and child. (The third self, Jane, is normal; love and sex are closely linked and favorable.) An impressionistic "guess" led to this summary of the first two personalities (Osgood & Luria, 1954):

Eve White is the woman who is simultaneously most in contact with social reality and under the greatest emotional stress. She is aware of both the demands of society and her own inadequacies in meeting them. She sees herself as a passive weakling and is also consciously aware of the discord in her sexual life, drawing increasingly sharp distinctions between love as an idealized notion and sex as a crude reality. She maintains the greatest diver-

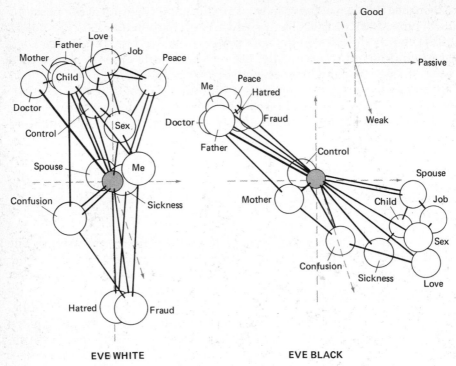

EVE WHITE   EVE BLACK

Figure 14.9. **Meaning systems of the two Eves.** (*Source*: Osgood & Luria, 1954.)

sity among the meanings of various concepts. She is concerned and ambivalent about her child, but apparently is *not* aware of her own ambivalent
attitudes toward her mother. . . . Eve White [is] accepting the mores or values of others (particularly her mother) but continuously criticizing and pun-
ishing herself. . . .

Eve Black is clearly the most out of contact with social reality and simultaneously the most self-assured. To rhapsodize, Eve Black finds Peace of
mind through close identification with a God-like therapist (My Doctor,
probably a father symbol for her), accepting her Hatred and Fraud as perfectly legitimate aspects of the Godlike role. Naturally, she sees herself as a
dominant, active wonder-woman and is in no way self-critical. She is probably unaware of her family situation. . . . Like a completely selfish infant, this
personality is entirely oriented around the assumption of its own perfection.

The pattern corresponds well with the therapists' picture. They described the same personalities in these phrases, among others:

EVE WHITE: demure, almost saintly, seldom lively; tries not to blame her
husband for marital troubles; every act demonstrates sacrifice for her little
girl; meek, fragile, doomed to be overcome.

EVE BLACK: a party girl, shrewd, egocentric; rowdy wit; all attitudes whim-
like; ready for any little irresponsible adventure; provocative; strangely secure from inner aspect of grief and tragedy.

With respect to common dimensions, Eve White has low self-esteem and is perfectionistic and unwilling to express emotion. The Semantic Differential points to specific sources of conflict: lack of acceptance of spouse and sex and also her child's weakness and need for protection. (Mrs. White's feeling that she could not give her child adequate protection was a precipitating cause of her illness.) Eve Black is shallow, uncontrolled, self-centered—extrovert on any questionnaire and on MMPI surely a 49' or 94'. She identifies strongly with men and rejects child and spouse. One can begin to guess what persons and treatments are likely to win her respect and cooperation and what rewards she is likely to work for. Such information goes far beyond what one can get from even the most valid description of her general style. The rewards that a therapist might ordinarily hold out as hopes—opportunity to hold a job, restoration of marriage—were spurned by Eve Black. The cooperation that eventually permitted some success in therapy came only when the therapist appealed to Eve Black's fear of sickness. (In a new book, Eve now tells her own story of disorder and recovery; Sizemore, 1989).

The Osgood-Luria method of studying personality has unfortunately not been pursued in the decades since their report, but the "personal construct" approach that the late George Kelly (1955) introduced at the same time does have followers.

Kelly's Phenomenological Approach   Kelly's "personal construct" theory is cognitive and phenomenological. Behavior is the result not of habit or impulse so much as it is a response to the situation—as the person construes it. The data and interpretations are concerned with the individual's perceptions and the system of meanings they derive from. Kelly's approach, therefore, contrasts with the behaviorist and trait approaches that ask about typical behavior in a class of situations *the tester* considers to be similar.

Whereas most inventories ask about response to people in general or to a broad class such as persons in authority, the Kelly procedure asks about particular persons in the respondent's life. The Role Concept Repertory Test ("Rep test") can begin with a standard list of roles, for example: "Your wife or present girlfriend" and "The person you feel most sorry for." Alternatively, it can be completely individualized, starting with persons the subject names. The heart of the technique is to ask (for any three roles or persons), "In what important way are two of these alike and different from the third?" Kelly thus elicits dimensions from the person himself, making the technique far more idiographic than Osgood's.

Mischel (a student of Kelly), in his introductory text on personality theory, uses a 25-year-old unmarried graduate student as a running example of the application of many measurement techniques, including the Rep test. Gary was selected as representative of "ordinary" people, yet, of course, was unique. The Rep test dialog went as follows, in part (Mischel, 1981, p. 288):

> List the three most important people in your life.
> —*Me, my brother, my father.*
>
> How are any two of these alike and different from the third?
> —*My brother and I both know how to be tough and succeed, no matter what—my father is soft, knocked out, defeated by life.*
>
> Think of yourself now, five years ago, and five years from now. How are any two of those alike and different from the other?
> —*Five years ago I was warmer, more open and responsive to others than I am now. Now I'm mostly a scheming brain. Five years from now I hope to have recaptured some of that feeling and to be more like I was five years ago.*

From this pair of responses we see that Gary is strongly aware of two dimensions: success and deliberate toughness. From other responses Mischel picks up two other dimensions central to Gary: security versus liberty (Gary wants both but believes they are hard to achieve within a single pattern of living) and rationality versus emotionality (Gary attaches a strong positive value to being rational). The test responses provide obvious leads for further conversation, and Mischel's two pages of summary include many sentences of this personalized character: "He generally prefers women who are stimulating and challenging though he fears all forms of domination through either authority or emotional ties."

The technique of eliciting the person's own dimensions can be applied to any kind of stimulus. Most important, it can be used to find out how the person thinks of the tasks or social situations he commonly encounters (or avoids). Such a phenomenological inquiry is a usual part of nonbehaviorist counseling, and it almost always takes the form of an informal interview. An adaptation of Kelly's structured method would extend the studies of situational variance such as Domino's that have used nomothetic (i.e., universal) categories for situations.

Kelly approached psychotherapy by trying to modify the person's construct system. His followers, extending this style of therapy, use the basic technique of eliciting constructs in an informal manner (Landfield & Leitner, 1980). For their purposes, the standardized approach of the Rep test is cumbersome and concentrates too narrowly on constructs of persons.

Those of Kelly's followers interested in measurement and research on personality seem never to have found a convenient method of compiling individualized responses into "data." They back off to measures of *style* of construing; Fransella and Bannister (1977, esp. pp. 111ff.), after describing those techniques and some useful research based on them, warn that the summary variables lose the essence of the personal constructs. Typical nomothetic measures report the complexity of the construct system and the extent to which the person differentiates (separates) himself from others. The conflict between the technically minded, person-centered followers of Kelly, and those more interested in construal itself, together with the isolation of both from mainstream psychology, is traced instructively by Neimeyer (1985, Chap. 8).

30. *Fishbein and Azjen (see p. 501) showed that people differ reliably in the trait "tendency to act in a religious manner," but that standing on this trait did not predict behavior in particular situations.*
    a. *The actions in the list could be grouped into subsets. What subsets, if any, might account for much of the variation in behavior?*
    b. *Would it be possible to describe more of a person's religious behavior idiographically by grouping situations with respect to dimensions he considers significant? If so, illustrate.*

31. *Is idiographic analysis appropriate only to self-reports, or could it be applied to behavioral observations?*

32. *Gary's MMPI profile (Mischel, 1981, p. 147) has a 28' . . . pattern, with score 2 (originally keyed on depressed patients) reaching 80. Mischel notes traits commonly associated with that profile in patients: Avoids close relations with other people; high-strung; tends to be resentful; lacking in ambition. How does this trait description differ* in character *from the description based on the Rep test?*

33. *Is the Semantic Differential fakable? Can it obtain information the person is not consciously aware of?*

HUMAN JUDGES AS TEST INTERPRETERS

I have delayed comparison of interpretations by humans and by computers to this point, in part because many of the issues originated in experiences with the MMPI. The topic is relevant to ability tests as well as personality inventories, and to personnel practice as well as to clinical practice. The main question in this section is: Are human decisions as good as those made by the computer? That question is too broad to be answered, and it is typically reduced to a simpler one: When predicting a definite criterion on the basis of a file of information, does the human reviewer do better than a statistical formula applied to all or part of that information?

A computer cannot set policy. Only humans can weigh values and decide what risk to take. Once the policy is explicit, the computer can carry it out. The computer can weigh up any number of facts, including exceptional ones ("lived for 2 years in Thailand") if the policy is clearly stated. It can easily execute the following rule intended to increase diversity: "Among those whose predicted grade average is between 2.5 and 3.5, select 70 per cent at random for admission." Another option: ". . . divide passable applicants into groups on the basis of interests, and pick at random—with higher acceptance rates at higher ability levels."

The machine applies the rule impartially and with perfect consistency. Another obvious advantage: the computer processes standardized information cheaply—25 cents per case versus $40 for the human report writer, as estimated for one situation by Vale et al. (1986). What the computer cannot do is process information the rule does not say how to use. The human looking at a file or interviewing a candidate applies judgment to unusual facts that the computer has to ignore.

Nonpsychologists and a great many psychologists have reservations about mechanical decision making. Colleges and universities, for example, are advised not to select applicants according to their rank order on predicted grade average. Rejecting lower-ranking applicants without individual consideration has been repeatedly condemned because supplementary facts can alter the apparent significance of a score. The counterargument is that human judgments are erratic, often giving weight to facts whose relevance is slight or unverified.

To compare human and computer, it is necessary to compare error rates when they both judge one person after another, judgments that can be checked against a criterion. In these "horse race" trials, bets on the computer pay off. Paul Meehl (1986, p. 374) refers to the history of

> 90 investigations, predicting everything from the outcome of football games to the diagnosis of liver disease [where] you can hardly come up with a half dozen studies showing even a weak tendency in favor of the clinician.

From another summary (Nisbett & Ross, 1980, p. 141):

> Human judges are not merely worse than *optimal* regression equations; they are worse than almost any regression equation. Even if the weights in the equation are *arbitrary,* as long as they are nonzero, positive, and linear, the equation generally will outperform human judges. . . . [I]n many of the studies, the judges have had not merely expertise in the particular judgmental domain, but also formal training in the statistical procedures necessary for prediction.

For the evidence see Meehl's classic analysis (1954); Dawes (1979); Dawes & Corrigan (1974); and Slovic & Lichtenstein (1971). But the answer given by this literature is overemphatic. Many of the horse races were unfair because the computer was allowed to fit its formula to the sample and was not subjected to cross-validation. The humans were relying on *past* experience and the trial was a cross-validation for them.

In these studies, the computer usually constructs its own rule by processing data formally—for example, by calculating a regression equation to predict the diagnosis actually given patients. This is actuarial interpretation in a strict sense: the statement printed out is *completely* determined by prior evidence linking that statement to the variables being interpreted. Although the horse race comparisons stressed actuarial methods, we shall see that many computer interpretations rest on rules supplied by a human expert—or a programming whiz masquerading as expert (see below).

The formula derived from tabulated experience with a recurring criterion makes efficient use of that information. In particular, a statistical combining rule makes cautious predictions when the data available for prediction have modest validity (Einhorn, 1986). It "regresses toward the mean," rarely predicting a very good or very bad outcome. Human judges, in contrast, are likely to predict some A grades and some D-minuses; they cover the whole range of the criterion distribution instead of playing it safe. When these far-out predictions miss, they can miss by a lot. Also, humans have biases. Clinicians tend to predict trouble or breakdown too often, whereas the sophisticated analyst programming a computer will make sure that (if breakdowns are few) the rule predicts no more breakdowns than were found in past tabulations. (That honors both the base rate and the fallibility of close calls.)

Meehl (1986) illustrates some of the decisions for which it is appropriate to use a formula, if one exists: parole prediction, predicting law-school success, response to Elavil, continuance in group therapy. Where a formula has been provided to answer a question, the judge can beat the formula only by bringing in additional facts *and weighing them correctly*. Typically, judges relying on professional lore and common sense are not aware of the weights they are using. "Policy capturing" research uses various techniques to find out what weights human decision makers actually give to facts and value considerations. Their decisions often do not correspond to the policies they say they are following (Edwards et al., 1975).

Figure 14.10 gives a simple example. Two interviewers rated job

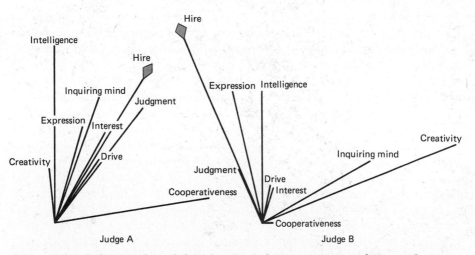

Figure 14.10. **Relation of candidates' traits to hiring recommendations of two interviewers.** The length of the ray indicates the s.d. of ratings on the variable (ignoring any portion unrelated to intelligence and cooperativeness). The angle between two rays is small if the correlation of the variables is high. (*Source*: This figure is adapted from Cronbach, 1958, p. 364; the data are from J. Sternberg, 1950.)

applicants and recommended (separately) for or against hiring. I correlated the recommendation with the ratings and arrived at the configurations by factor analysis. Each diagram locates "Intelligence" as a vertical axis and "Cooperativeness" as a second dimension. These two ratings were uncorrelated for Judge B and very slightly correlated for Judge A. The lengths of the arrows for Cooperativeness indicate that A perceived large differences in this trait whereas the ratings B gave were nearly uniform. In hiring, Judge A gave nearly equal weight to intelligence and cooperation. Judge B cared about intelligence, but gave no preference to those he saw as being creative and inquiring as well. These raters, trying to serve the same firm, were playing the game by entirely different rules, rules of which they were only half aware. Of course, they disagreed in many of their recommendations. Necessarily, one or both disagreed with whatever formula experience would have justified. (A recent study had appreciable success in retraining interviewers to avoid such idiosyncrasies; see Dougherty et al., 1986.)

The implication of the research on judgment is that a formula should be preferred when it truly fits the decision in hand. But in certain cases a question extends beyond the setting, population, and criterion to which the experience table applies (Cronbach, 1982). Then judgment *must* be brought in—if no more than a judgment to let the computer apply a rule developed for a *different* situation. Facing nonstandard situations, the individual judge will find it advisable to be cautious in the "allowances" she makes for unvalidated factors. The institution will find it advisable to call upon more than one judge and to conduct research on the policies of the judges and their validity.

Humans are at their best in thinking about questions for which no formula exists (Should *this* child be left in *this* home?), and in monitoring an evolving situation where new information trickles in and new questions are to be recognized.

To bring into focus the contrast between decisions suited to the actuary and to the clinician, I remind you of two Wechsler interpretations by Matarazzo. In one case (p. 247), tabulated data called the shot. A large V/P difference had been found many times in cases of brain damage and not in schizophrenics. When the medical evidence called for a choice between those diagnoses, the observed V/P difference implied brain damage. In another case (p. 306), responses of an executive implied, to the clinician, marked disturbance of function. It is hard to see how a table or cookbook could include a rule for interpreting all such unusual protocols. More to the point, the clinician had to judge on the spot how to handle this man's breakdown. (Business as usual? Reassurance? Push toward therapy?) The clinician's choice was guided by experience that he probably could not recall specifically. A statistical experience table to guide these decisions might be collected with enormous effort. ("Among N examinees who showed these signs of distress and were pushed toward therapy, outcomes were positive in x per cent; . . . .") But a usable tabulation based on many persons whose resources and stresses resemble this man's will never be available. Psychological histories of similar cases accumulate slowly, and old records may be a poor basis for judgments about persons who are tested after prevailing social attitudes have changed.

34. *Gough (1967) found that medical school interviewers tended to favor appli-cants described (independently) as healthy, masculine, robust, cheerful, or-ganized, and relaxed and not as individualistic, frank, unconventional, and complicated. Should a medical faculty prefer this kind of student?*

THE COMPUTER AS TEST INTERPRETER

Reports at Three Levels

Computer-based test interpretations (CBTI) range from mere score re-ports to elaborate characterizations. Some systems (sold or leased) per-mit immediate interpretation on the psychologist's or school's micro-computer, whereas others are available only as a mail-in service. Telephone hookups and electronic mail are beginning to provide ex-tremely rapid feedback from a distance. The important differences have to do with the character of the interpretation rather than the delivery mechanism. To present that topic I shall speak of Levels I, II, and III; there is no standard terminology, and other writers make similar distinc-tions a bit differently.

Level I The least elaborate reports add almost nothing to the numerical information in the scores.

- The CogAT printout for Patrick Blanch (p. 261) translated score names and the numbers into everyday English. Prediction and ex-planation were minimal.
- The Piers-Harris CBTI, intended for teachers, likewise sticks close to facts. It goes beyond the scores to list whichever of the pupil's responses an "at risk" sample gave oftener than an unselected group. We could fuss about the instability of single responses; but (save for adding in item norms) the report is only providing what the teacher could have seen had *she* given and scored the test. Her unaided judgment about which responses to take as warning signs would be untrustworthy. Also, the computer's highlighting saves her time. On the other hand, the CBTI may overdramatize when it prints a page of "bad signs" observed.

Level II The second level moves toward prediction, classification, or characterization, but it avoids thin and slippery ice. At their strongest, Level II inferences rest directly on rock-solid data.

Experience relating ability tests to success in training was displayed in Table 5.1 and Figures 5.1 and 11.3. This kind of information is easily translated into a printout of "your most likely grade." The actuarial statement has to be taken pretty much at face value, and it does not tell the whole story. For example, even a professional reader of such tables cannot be certain whether voluntary dropouts were counted as failures or ignored. Also, a professional probably will recognize the limitations of a partial criterion, but the client will not.

Experience tables rarely differentiate finely. "Chances of succeeding in college" is much too broad. Another number would be needed to describe "chances of succeeding in a 4-year college where the freshman SAT average is in the 800–1000 range." Colleges in that range are not equally demanding, and neither are courses of study within any college. The experience table goes as far as the recorded facts allow; however, as with all score reports, it serves best as a starting point for thought.

- The report for the Strong blank (Hansen, in Butcher, 1987) has both Level I and Level II features. It includes the full display of the material in my Figures 12.4 and 12.5. The prose describes in lay language the general and basic scales on which the person scored high. Instead of interpreting separately the individual's high scores, the CBTI lists occupations consistent with both a favored general theme and any high basic scores within it. These associations come from accumulated Strong data. The CBTI does not attempt to integrate information across themes, but the counselor is encouraged to take that creative, speculative step.

A conservative interpreter of personality measures wants to avoid intuitive or impressionistic statements, and would like to tie all statements to tabulated data. The CBTI might state only the probability of some outcome. Automated interpretation that assigns a diagnosis or a treatment recommendation has been discouragingly errorful, and such a verdict has too much the tone of final truth. Most current reports therefore have a descriptive style, leaving choice of action to the user.

- About as actuarial as any current CBTI is the publisher's service for the Personality Inventory for Children (PIC) (p. 597). PIC is like the inventories of this chapter, particularly MMPI, except that PIC items are marked by the mother or other caregiver to describe the child.

    In the research that produced the system (Lachar & Gdowski, 1979), PICs were filled out for 431 children and adolescents referred to one clinic. A total of 332 "external criteria" of three types were collected: (1) the parent's statements at intake about developmental history and current problems; (2) a list of behavioral problems checked by a clinician after working with the case; (3) teachers' reports on conduct and achievement. The data, mostly in checkmark form, came ready for statistical treatment. (Note that the criteria were not fully independent of the PIC responses, because the clinician dealt with the parents and perhaps the teacher did.)

Some of the findings about cases who had DLQ scores in the top 15 per cent of the clinic intake appear in Table 14.7. These items and many others were compressed into the following paragraph, which goes into the automated report whenever DLQ exceeds 109 (Lachar, in Butcher, 1987).

> Law-enforcement agencies may be aware of delinquent child behavior such as truancy, running away from home, or alcohol/drug abuse. Mental health professionals are likely to be pessimistic about remediation of current problems, and may feel that institutional treatment is indicated. (From Lachar & Gdowski, 1979, p. 95.)

Note that almost nothing has been added to the statements the raters checked, and that the language is hedged with "may" and the like. Paragraphs describing less extreme behavior are prepared in the same way for cut scores at 99, 90, and 80. Thus, at 80, one statement is: "A hostile, unsocialized orientation may be suggested by argumentativeness, lying, and stealing."

• A characterization of normal personalities that is formally data-based is offered in the printout for Gough's California Personality

Table 14.7 CRITERION STATEMENTS ASSOCIATED WITH HIGH DLQ SCORES

			Incidence	
Statement	Informant[a]	r	High DLQ	All others
Often skips school	P	.55	79	16
Uses drugs	P	.4	43	7
Poor class attendance	T	.2	48	20
Truancy	C	.45	73	17
History of problematic substance (alcohol) abuse	C	.4	50[b]	8[b]
Precocious sexual behavior or promiscuity	C		62[c]	5[c]
Involved with police	C	.45	61	9
Poor prognosis for remediation of current problems	C	.25	73	48

[a]P, parent; T, teacher; C, clinician.
[b]Male adolescents only.
[c]Female adolescents only. Correlation not reported.

Source: Lachar & Gdowski, 1979, pages 41–42, 59–60, 77–79.

Inventory. Hundreds of adults who had taken CPI were observed by psychologists during several days of "house party" assessment (p. 637) that included tests, interviews, and social interactions. Each observer recorded her final impressions via Q sort (p. 592). Gough correlated the average judgment on each Q statement with each CPI scale. He found Responsibility, for example, strongly associated with these descriptors:

> Genuinely values intellectual and cognitive matters
> Has high aspiration level for self
> *Low on* Is self-indulgent
> *Low on* Characteristically pushes and . . . sees what he or she can get away with
> *Low on* Is unpredictable and changeable

The computer, considering the person's high scores together, lists the six statements most associated and the six least associated with his pattern. Permuting 100 statements creates an endless variety of "clinical impressions."

One can imagine a Level II report having virtually no element of judgment behind it—a report, for instance, of the rate at which drivers with certain scores have been involved in reportable accidents. But most CBTI at Level II do not rest on a criterion of recorded behavior; they rest on judgment—on grades assigned by instructors, for example, or descriptions filtered through the head of a clinician or assessor. The computer is systematically matching the person to judgments made in the past about persons similar to him in some respects.

Because of its consistency, the automated application of these judgmental norms is likely to be more strongly correlated with a criterion than the report one clinician would make after seeing the person in the flesh (Goldberg, 1970). Dougherty et al. (1986) played the following game with three interviewers. Each interviewer rated candidates on eight attributes *(X)* and also rated suitability for the job *(A)*. The investigators calculated weights for predicting the interviewer's *A* from his or her own *X*'s; the result was a separate policy-capturing formula *(B)* for each interviewer. The three *B*'s correlated 0.23, 0.19, and 0.26 with an independent job-performance criterion. The corresponding *A*'s had validities 0.15, 0.02, and 0.26. So the formula won in two of the three instances, even though it was merely a reproducible distillation of the interviewer's judgment.

Level III   The most elaborate programs, at Level III, direct the computer to "think like a clinician." Whatever lore has accumulated, whether on a statistical or impressionistic base, is considered. Usually an "If . . ., then . . . " rule calls up particular sentences or passages from this base. Here is a tiny segment from the rules used in one MMPI program:

If (a) Scale 4 exceeds 69 and (b) Scale 9 exceeds 69 and (c) if both are higher than scales 1, 2, 3, 6, 7, and 8; *then* use paragraph 59. (From Lachar, 1974, p. 130; paraphrased.)

Paragraph 59 resembles Graham's description of the 49' type (p. 542).

- The publisher of MMPI sponsors several versions of The Minnesota Report (J. N. Butcher; service operated by National Computer Systems). Here are excerpts from the 1000-word CBTI of a 28-year-old patient whose scores 2 and 6 were very high (Butcher, 1987, pp. 171–172).

> A pattern of chronic psychological maladjustment characterizes individuals with this MMPI profile. The client is overwhelmed by anxiety, tension, and depression. He feels helpless and alone, inadequate and insecure, and believes that life is hopeless and that nothing is working out right. He attempts to control his worries through intellectualization and unproductive self-analyses, but he has difficulty concentrating and making decisions.

The report goes on to mention feelings of guilt, a wish to escape family domination, the possibility of suicide, a possible neurological disorder—and adds a positive sentence or two.

- For employers requesting an evaluation of a job candidate or employee Butcher's Minnesota Personnel Interpretive Report avoids the language of clinicians. (There is also a succinct Personnel Screening Report.) The CBTI on a man applying to an airline as a pilot (Butcher, 1987, pp. 187–188) includes many positive statements. The most negative remarks are triggered chiefly by a score of 71 on scale 4:

> Because this applicant tends to become bored easily and seeks thrills, he may have problems keeping a steady pace in life and is likely to be considered unreliable at times. He may have difficulties with authority and may resist convention and rules, which might cause interpersonal problems at work.

This kind of blind interpretation has its best use in steering the employer to check back with pointed questions to previous employers or other informants.

Essentially, a Level III CBTI like the ones illustrated tries to capture the strategy of a single clinician, presumably a knowledgeable one. During development the trial program can be checked by asking independent clinicians to compare the computer's interpretation with their own, but developers do not tell the profession much about their checking processes. Karson and O'Dell (in Butcher, 1987) say more than most developers about programming to mimic the psychologist. Programs are trade secrets, Lachar's open publication being a rare exception. Also, isolated rules such as the one I have given do not convey much sense of the flow of the whole. For these reasons, subscribers to CBTI at Level III have to judge them mostly by their output.

Hazards and Safeguards

Computer interpretation is an entrepreneurial business, at this time far more in the stage of "Buyer beware!" than other aspects of testing. A preliminary statement on appropriate practices of developers and purchasers has been adopted as a supplement to the *Testing standards.* I shall refer to it as the Guidelines (American Psychological Association, 1986; published in Butcher, 1987). The Guidelines are not forceful, which is understandable when there is no professional consensus.

Contributors to Butcher's volume make a generally favorable evaluation of systems coming from prominent publishers, reserving their complaints for systems marketed by firms with lesser reputations. On the other hand, Matarazzo (1986a, 1986b; see also correspondence in *American Psychologist,* 1987, *41*, 94–96, 191–193) has commented scathingly on most present practices. Moreland (1987), having watched the field at close range, provides another constructively critical source. I shall mix ideas from these sources, with few direct attributions.

Who Should See the Report? Computer reports at Levels II and III should be regarded as a consultation with a fellow professional by the psychologist, counselor, or other qualified user of the instrument. What the consultant says is to be considered alongside other information. The Guidelines say that CBTI "should be used only in connection with professional judgment." The professional—whether a personnel specialist, physician, or psychologist—should be one qualified to give and interpret the test for herself.

Placing responsibility (including liability for malpractice!) on the professional who receives the report is a major safeguard. The computer is attempting the difficult feat of blind interpretation. It will be told the person's sex, age, and perhaps education; but it has no good way to fine-tune reports in the light of even those few facts. Marital, criminal, and clinical histories are unlikely to be supplied, and the computer would not know what to do with them. It is the clinical receiver of the CBTI who has to put it into context.

Present CBTI, with a few exceptions, interpret one test at a time. But many psychological assessments involve several tests plus other sources of information. It is unreasonable to expect a person with limited psychological training to pull together all this material.

Some printouts are intended for the person evaluated or for a parent, teacher, employer, or other nonpsychologist. In time, experience and discussion will clarify which reports can safely be supplied without a professional intermediary. "Self-interpretation" is far from dependable (p. 469), and we also know that general criticisms ("You are not considerate of others") may be threatening and/or ineffectual. A personnel report such as Butcher's should be interpreted to the employer by someone who knows the limitations of the test and of CBTI.

Critical Evaluation   Matarazzo (1986a, 1986b) believes that promoters of computer services are encouraging incautious behavior of inadequately trained psychologists and physicians to whom they sell:

> . . . undisguised hucksterism of the crassest kind. . . . neatly typed, valid-sounding narrative interpretations that are the products, for the most part, of secretly developed disks of software that have not even been offered for scientific evaluation (as has clinical judgment), let alone met even the most rudimentary tests of science (Matarazzo, 1986b, p. 15; here compressed).

Matarazzo tells us that physicians accept CBTI from firms "picked out of the yellow pages"; in medical matters, they would accept only consultants whose credentials they know.

The first task of the clinician receiving the CBTI is to reject or amend it in the light of her extra facts and her judgment. To be sure, she must remain mindful of the fallibility demonstrated in horse races, but not to second-guess is to assume that the half-informed computer can do no wrong. Many skeptics fear that typical CBTI purchasers are insufficiently aware of the limitations of the software and will accept the reports unquestioningly. This risk is of course even greater when CBTI at Level II or III are placed in the hands of persons with limited training in test interpretation.

The shoddy character of many commercial packages concerns Butcher, Moreland, and their associates. Butcher spoke memorably (in Buros, 1978) about "misstatements of staggering proportions." Some programs are apparently being written by computer wizards who know nothing about test interpretation. Some reports provide more gloss than substance. They may "ring true" to the reader because they are loaded with "Barnum" sentences—the fortune-teller generalities like these (from Forer, 1949) that apply to anyone:

You have a tendency to worry at times, but not to excess.

You have found it unwise to be frank in revealing yourself to others.

Your sexual adjustment has presented problems to you.

Even when the CBTI characterization is sharp—apart from muting qualifiers ("may" and "seems to")—it is just one possible story. A live clinician would often suggest competing integrations; these encourage deeper study of the case. (Matarazzo remarks that there could easily be four sensible blind interpretations of the same MMPI profile.)

The psychologist considering competing services can try to judge them for herself. A company will usually supply one or more specimen reports, and some will supply a "free sample" by interpreting a test protocol the potential customer sends in. Not many consumers are sufficiently expert to make a close evaluation of such samples. Some systems have been reviewed in the *MMY;* and reviews also appear in *Computers in Human Behavior.* Dissatisfaction is a frequent note in these reviews, even when the service comes from an old-line firm (see Buros, 1978, pp. 616–624; and Mitchell, 1985, pp. 1003–1011). Reviews cannot keep up with the flood of new releases, and they do not provide an adequate forum to develop a community opinion.

CBTI are on the record and therefore are more accessible to criticism than judgments made in a practitioner's office. No clinician's description has been subjected to the line-by-line critique Matarazzo (1986a) brings to bear on one CBTI. With the reports down in black and white, tough-minded validation is not logically impossible—but evaluating even one system would require a large effort.

Validation Methods A kind of validation reported in some manuals, though superficial, is better than nothing. A clinician who has worked with a case is asked to check paragraphs as valid descriptions of the person, invalid, or uncertain. This design contains no safeguard against the rater's leniency and can give a high score to a report in Barnum style.

Perhaps the most practical approach is illustrated in Graham (1977). He sent a number of MMPI protocols to several services, and compared the reports they delivered. If this could be arranged as a regular procedure, with the evaluation being made by a team of experts rather than one reviewer, consumers would be able to choose the system that best fits their proposed use. Consumer reports would help small firms that supply good software and penalize firms whose software authors showed poor judgment.

A particularly sophisticated validation was carried out by Moreland and Godfrey (1987). They started with the MMPI protocol of a client the judge had seen and selected another protocol for which the profile had the same high-point code. The Minnesota Report CBTI were printed out for each examinee. The judge—an experienced user of these CBTI—was asked to rate how well each description fitted the client, as judged from interview and other information. To disguise the task, the judge was told that one of the two reports represented a system undergoing tryout. In all, 86 pairs of reports were rated, section by section, each pair by one of eight clinicians. Accuracy scores (number of sections, out of seven, judged "mostly accurate") had a median of 4 for the real reports and 3 for the bogus ones.[3] The range of ratings was wide and the distri-

---

[3]This performance is somewhat better than it seems at first glance, in that there were three other response options: mostly inaccurate, report unclear, and I don't know (i.e., clinician's information insufficient).

bution irregular. Strikingly, the most common rating of real reports was 6 and that of falsely matched reports was 2.

35. *Actuarial statements such as the percentages reported in the Piers-Harris CBTI and in Table 14.7 are generally based on convenience samples. Is it appropriate to ask, as with norms, that statistics on which CBTI is based be representative of a well-defined and relevant population?*

36. *In one system, the computer program "branches" on marital status. When identical answer sheets from a married person and a divorced person are interpreted, about 20 per cent of the statements in the printouts differ. Recognizing that the married person may be considering divorce and that the divorced person may have achieved a stable readjustment, can such branching be justified?*

37. *In the absence of substantial validation reports, consumers have to fall back on other indicators. Moreland (1987) suggests the following considerations. How satisfactory is each as a basis for selecting a system?*
   a. *Is the system author recognized as an expert user of the instrument?*
   b. *Has the developer published extensive material on the instrument?*
   c. *Is the program based on the orthodox lore for the instrument?*

38. *How does the Moreland-Godfrey design guard against each of the following?*
   a. *The bias of a rater to give good marks to a report that is written in a familiar style.*
   b. *The tendency of raters to credit a report that makes nondifferentiating Barnum-type statements.*
   c. *The possibility that a report is accurate in recognizing degree of pathology but not in describing the patient as an individual.*

Chapter
15

Judgments and Systematic Observations

15A. What characteristics of a rating or reporting form improve the quality of the information obtained?

15B. Reports from informants reflect the psychology of the informant as well as the events the informants saw. Illustrate.

15C. What can be learned from peer reports that cannot be learned more validly from direct observation?

15D. What are the features of a superior sampling plan for making observations on typical everyday behavior?

15E. Typical behavior reflects the person's life setting as well as characteristics internal to the person. Illustrate.

Abbreviation in this chapter: PDRI for Personnel Decisions Research Institute.

ORIENTATION

We have reached a mopping-up stage. The four sections of this chapter are not closely related and can be studied as four separate minichapters, each acquainting you with valuable techniques. The first section draws attention to uses of ratings in personnel research, patient management, screening schoolchildren for maladjustment, and collecting research data. What is said about ratings for one purpose carries over to the others. Become aware of likely sources of error and of what can be done about them.

In a sense reports from acquaintances are also ratings. The techniques are usually different, however, and the data tend to be more elaborate. Much that was said about problems of self-report in Chapters 13 and 14 applies to reports from informants; look on this section as a set of further examples (hence a review).

In evaluation, in casework, and in organizational or community psychology, assessing situational demands and supports can be as important as assessing persons. Few investigators have developed psychometric methods for studying situations, and I merely offer one example. (Do not overlook the powerful, simple idea of matrix sampling, which is tucked in here.)

For many purposes, observation yields the most valid information on typical response. As in the section on ratings, concentrate on possible shortcomings and the ways in which quality of data can be improved.

RATINGS BY SUPERVISORS AND PROFESSIONAL OBSERVERS

Reputation counts. A person who has impressed earlier teachers as imaginative is favored by a college admissions committee. Supervisors' opinions determine who gets promoted in an organization. Teachers find out what children think of each other in order to understand relationships in the classroom and to identify social misfits. Ratings provide criteria of job performance, of patients' progress in mental hospitals, and of children's development. This chapter considers techniques for eliciting impressions, based on past experience, from informants and then turns to systematic observations. Information has to be put in standard form to permit systematic analysis. Free-form descriptions by industrial supervisors, teachers, interviewers, or superior officers are hard to compare because their emphases and language vary. Therefore, raters are usually asked to check applicable phrases or appropriate points on scales.

Sources of Error

One gets bad information on typical behavior if the informant has not had good opportunities to observe. Even with good opportunities, rating is a complex and error-prone cognitive process. It is found, for example, that run-of-the-plant supervisor's ratings reflect the worker's job knowledge more than his typical behavior (Hunter, in Landy et al., 1983). Persistent and systematic attention is needed to assess whether the worker works at his best level, whereas gaps in knowledge force themselves on the supervisor's attention.

The variables to be rated may be ill defined. Left to supply their own meanings, raters define leadership (for example) in many ways. To one judge, "leadership" suggests conscious wielding of authority, crisp decisions, and general dominance. A person rated high by this judge would receive a lower rating from a judge who looks for a leader to encourage subordinates, bring out cooperative decisions, and subordinate his own views to the views of the group.

The response alternatives too may be ambiguous (p. 515). Some older scales asked for ratings of, for example, "friendliness" on a scale from 0 to 100. A particular number is used by different raters to indicate quite different behavior. *Average, excellent*, and the like, are equally indefinite.

Among errors introduced by the judge, the most serious is leniency or generosity. Company commanders rate 98 per cent of their junior officers in the top two categories (out of five) on efficiency reports. Such ratings provide little information. There are several reasons for generosity: the rater may feel that she is admitting poor leadership if she says that subordinates are not performing well; she tends to feel kindly toward associates; she thinks she may have to justify any implied criticism; and she finds it easier to speak well of everyone than to discriminate. Whereas ratings by laypersons err on the generous side, social workers, counselors, and others in the helping professions have somewhat the opposite tendency. Even rating a standard stimulus on videotape, they rate the target persons as less able and less adjusted than lay observers do (Garner & Smith, 1976; Wills, 1978).

The observer's overall evaluation strongly influences ratings on more specific traits. The tendency to give uniform ratings across the board is called a "halo effect." Rater-to-rater agreement on a trait does not often exceed the *within*-rater correlation for traits that supposedly are distinct. Because halo blurs specifics, profiles for the same worker provided by independent raters rarely agree about the worker's particular strengths and weaknesses. Note how modest are the correlations in the diagonal of Table 15.1. The table, from the PDRI study (p. 427) represents especially careful data collection. After averaging the reports of two or three raters per worker it was possible to separate two subsets of scales, related to emotional stability and problem-solving ability. These two composites correlated 0.6, which was low enough to imply some divergence. Indeed, the dimensions were predicted by somewhat different tests—making the research on selection twice as rich as most studies with ratings as criteria.

Table 15.1 INTERCORRELATIONS OF RATINGS ON POWER PLANT OPERATORS

	(1)	(2)	(3)	(4)	(5)	(6)
(1) Maintaining standard operations	**0.55**	0.6	0.6	0.5	0.65	0.8
(2) Relationship with co-workers	0.6	**0.5**	0.4	0.35	0.65	0.65
(3) Problem-solving ability	0.6	0.4	**0.6**	0.65	0.55	0.7
(4) Mechanical understanding	0.5	0.35	0.65	**0.6**	0.45	0.6
(5) Overall emotional stability	0.65	0.65	0.55	0.45	**0.6**	0.7
(6) Overall job performance	0.8	0.6	0.7	0.6	0.7	**0.7**

Source: Dunnette et al., 1982, p. 128 and Appendix S.

Note: Correlations are based on average ratings given by two supervisors and the interrater correlations in the diagonal describe the reliability of such averages.

In ratings collected routinely, it is rare to have more than one reliable dimension, and that dimension may not validly represent performance. When department heads rated lower-level supervisors in one study, the rating correlated only 0.2 with an objective record of the work performance of each crew. These were supposedly ratings on productivity, but the rating correlated 0.6 with how long the department head had known the foreman, and 0.65 with her liking for the foreman (Stockford & Bissell, 1949).

Particularly discouraging is a report from the Korean War. When effectiveness of bombing teams was rated, officers and men generally agreed about which teams were most effective. But an observational study demonstrated that bombing accuracy was entirely inconsistent from day to day and so could not truly be judged. Evidently legends were built up as a consequence of random incidents; the raters could report reliably on the teams' reputations, but not on effectiveness (Hemphill & Sechrest, 1952). Likewise, ratings on job knowledge correlate only about 0.35 with the knowledge measured by a formal test. Such findings are particularly distressing in view of the prominence of ratings as criteria.

Clinical ratings suffer from the same faults. Ratings on depression and anxiety are dominated by a global impression of the person's position in the range from health to sickness. Speaking particularly of ratings collected to evaluate the benefit mental patients receive from drugs, Gleser (1968) urged that trait and state labels be replaced by reports on specific symptoms. Psychiatrists, she says, assign their own meanings to traits. "Thus, one doctor might think of bound anxiety and consider certain somatic symptoms as evidence of anxiety. Another might pay attention only to anxiety manifested in the interview in the form of restlessness, tremor, perspiration, etc."

"Policy-capturing" studies (p. 571) can identify what raters are taking into account and can be a basis for retraining raters or clarifying instructions. A somewhat less ambitious step is to estimate and allow for a judge's constant error. Thus, a college learns to allow for the fact that one high school has a "tough" grading or rating policy whereas another school is lenient. It is rarely practical to make statistical corrections for differences among individual raters.

1. *Why might "integrity" and "kindness" be especially hard to rate reliably?*
2. *Which of the following traits would probably be hardest to rate reliably after observations: "skill in self-expression," "freedom from tension," "leadership"?*
3. *Ratings on leadership made at Officer Candidate School correlated only 0.15 with ratings on combat leadership made by superior officers observing the men in combat (Jenkins, 1947). Why is the correlation so low?*
4. *School marks may be regarded as ratings. Which sources of error discussed in this section affect marks?*

Improvement of Ratings

Efforts to improve ratings encounter the same obstacles as efforts to improve self-reports. Again, the tester must assume that the respondent will give false information if that will bring psychological rewards. Whereas the information affects the ratee's future rather than the rater's, the rater's motives are engaged. I have mentioned the rater's inclination to interpret the reports she gives as a reflection on her own teaching or supervision or therapeutic skill. Sometimes a rater gives a middling rating because she wishes to retain an employee who might otherwise be promoted. Seeking to be helpful, a teacher rating a scholarship applicant may enlarge upon his merits nearly to the point of perjury.

For research it may be desirable to collect special reports rather than to rely on reports filed for some operational purpose. Supervisors could tell the investigator seeking criterion data far more than they are willing to put into company files, especially if the policy is to let workers see the operational ratings.

Another motivational problem is that raters and observers may not be fully attentive and self-critical. Reid (1970) asked observers to code videotapes (of children) under two conditions. The observer thought that she was the only coder for certain tapes. For other tapes she understood that there would be additional coders against whom her reliability would be judged. Errors were twice as great in the ratings she did not expect to be checked. Coders should know that a random sample of their analyses will be cross-checked, wherever that is feasible.

I mentioned ambiguity earlier. Gleser (1968) recounts an instance where two psychiatrists differed radically in rating the current degree of illness of schizophrenic patients. One psychiatrist was reporting typical behavior, whereas the other was rating the most extreme deviant behavior shown by the patient.

The question to raters, then, must be carefully posed. Although it is sometimes necessary to word scales succinctly, one can usually get a respondent to take rather lengthy instructions seriously when she will be reporting on many ratees. It is profitable to train raters not only in research but in management applications. When the training occurs prior to the observations, raters are likely to focus their observations better.

Attempts to train raters have had mixed success. What appears most likely to work is a clear exposition of what the rater is to attend to and how to use the rating form, combined with practice and feedback. See, for example, Athey and McIntyre (1987).

Averaging across judges allows many of their errors to balance out. Where the interjudge correlation is about 0.45, two *pairs* of independent judges will correlate 0.6, and in accord with the Spearman-Brown formula, averages of five judges correlate 0.8. The bias of one judge tends to cancel the bias of another, and each adds information the other had no opportunity to observe. It is not helpful, however, to add in an uninformed rater. An elementary precaution, often overlooked, is to ask the rater how well she knows the ratee and in what kinds of situation she has observed him. With respect to each trait rated, there should be a place to indicate "insufficient opportunity to observe." Conrad (1932) directed raters to star traits that they regarded as especially important in each child's personality. Interjudge correlations on all traits ranged from 0.7 to 0.8. But for the traits three judges agreed in starring, the ratings correlated as high as 0.96.

Many reporting formats and scoring systems for ratings have been tried. On the whole, it appears that the knowledge and motivation of the informant affect validity more than do features of the scale. Still, carefully designed forms elicit better communication than amateurish ones. Bernardin and Beatty (1984, Chaps. 4, 6) give extensive references on the techniques to be introduced here and to the evaluative research. They emphasize that the choice of format should depend on the function to be served. In general, they say, the most valid methods are those that place the greatest demands on the raters—and on the persons who develop and update the systems.

Scale Formats   A descriptive rating form similar to Figure 15.1 is generally suitable for a routine collection of information. At each scale point a recognizable behavior pattern is described. In general, 5- to 7-point scales serve adequately.

The form shown has a "graphic" feature. The rater is allowed to mark at intermediate points if she does not find any one of the descriptions entirely apt. Numbering the descriptions—so that decimals can represent intermediate ratings—is an alternative device.

Marks based on observation of a student's work or review of products may be improved by defining standards clearly. It can be advantageous to separate aspects of good performance and prepare a rating scale for each one. A weighted combination provides an overall mark. The marks

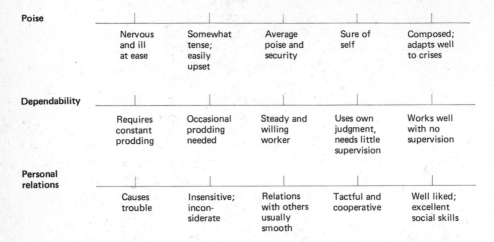

Poise

| Nervous and ill at ease | Somewhat tense; easily upset | Average poise and security | Sure of self | Composed; adapts well to crises |

Dependability

| Requires constant prodding | Occasional prodding needed | Steady and willing worker | Uses own judgment, needs little supervision | Works well with no supervision |

Personal relations

| Causes trouble | Insensitive; inconsiderate | Relations with others usually smooth | Tactful and cooperative | Well liked; excellent social skills |

Figure 15.1. **Descriptive graphic rating scales.** These scales for rating applicants or workers are adapted from the following sources: A General Foods Corporation form (National Industrial Conference Board, 1942), a Mutual Life Insurance Company of New York form (Marting, 1967), and a form from the National Retail Merchants Association (1968).

so generated often differ from the instructor's direct overall rating. Oaks et al. (1969) demonstrate this with data from a clinical course for medical students and discuss some of the errors that the piecemeal rating process overcomes.

The "behaviorally anchored rating scale" (BARS) is well regarded for situations where raters are willing to give the attention it demands. The basic idea is derived from the critical-incidents technique (p. 410); descriptions of acts communicate better than generalized phrases do (Bernardin & Smith, 1981). Various formats have appeared. Sometimes incidents reflecting high, medium, or low degrees of a characteristic are arranged along a scale. The rater is asked to recall incidents of the person's actual behavior and to pinpoint a scale position that best sums them up.

In the BARS scales illustrated in Figure 15.2 the rater is first to decide which of the three levels best represents her impression of the target and then to shade the meaning downward or upward, if that gives a better fit. Thus, a rater who identifies a worker as superior (rating of 8) is told to shade that to 7 if she recalls occasions when the person has performed less well. The scale in Figure 15.2 was developed as part of the power plant study discussed in Chapter 11; the agreement between two raters is represented by a correlation of 0.4 or better.

The graphic format in Figure 15.3 assigns a precise point on the scale to each behavioral description. In development of such a scale, judges are asked to assign a scale value to each sentence. Sentences on whose placement judges tend to agree are spaced along the scale accord-

MAINTAINING STANDARD OPERATIONS: MONITORING, INSPECTING, TESTING AND ADJUSTING EQUIPMENT

Inspects condition of equipment routinely, systematically, and thoroughly. Monitors equipment to confirm proper operating conditions and detects *valid* indicators of non-standard operating conditions. Recognizes situations likely to develop into problems and corrects conditions to prevent problems from occurring.

1 2 3 BELOW STANDARD	4 5 6 FULLY ADEQUATE	7 8 9 SUPERIOR
• Carries out standard inspections irregularly.	• Systematically follows all standard inspection and monitoring procedures.	• Alert at all times to indications of equipment condition and operations.
• Shows periods of inattention during monitoring	• Shows good knowledge of most likely non-standard conditions.	• Shows unusual facility for detecting non-standard situations during routine inspections and continuing surveillance.
• Misses detection of nonstandard conditions,	• Shows good awareness of indicators of non-standard situations and what to do about them.	• Shows superior knowledge of what to do about non-standard conditions.
• Actions intended to bring operations back to standard are delayed or incorrect.		

Examples Illustrating BELOW STANDARD Maintenance of Standard Operations	Examples Illustrating FULLY ADEQUATE Maintenance of Standard Operations	Examples Illustrating SUPERIOR Maintenance of Standard Operations
• Operator fell asleep while monitoring a boiler feed pump. Unit tripped when operator did not hear low pressure and drum level alarms as load was increased.	• On routine check, operator detected leaky weld on supply line to boiler feed pump and scheduled repair during low load demand period.	• Although not a part of regular inspection, operator opened a tell-tale valve and discovered water in main turbine oil tank (due to a tube leak in one of turbine lube oil coolers). He switched to alternate oil cooler, drained the water, and set up centrifuge on contaminated tank.
• Operator did not make assigned round due to poor weather and did not detect vibration of deep well pump shaft bearing which had lost its oil seal. Shaft was bent and bearing destroyed.	• Operator noted that water level showed no decrease in unit from which condensate make-up water was being transferred. Inspection showed level float had been hung. Transfer of water was stopped preventing loss of unit vacuum.	• Operator investigated a slight noise by opening access doors to boiler and discovered a superheat leak which he then arranged to have repaired.
• During start-up testing, operator silenced an oil alarm without noting its cause. A few hours later, the high head charging pump failed.	• Operator noted and corrected fan outlet temperature which had drifted to 275°F on unit designed to carry 265°F.	• Operator noticed that a truck presumably delivering nitrogen scheduled for unloading had a flammable sticker on it. Upon checking, truck was found to be carrying hydrogen instead.

Figure 15.2. An employee-rating scale anchored in behavior. (*Source:* From Job Performance Appraisal Booklet for Power Plant Operators. Copyright © 1980 by Edison Electric Institute and reproduced by permission, with some modification.)

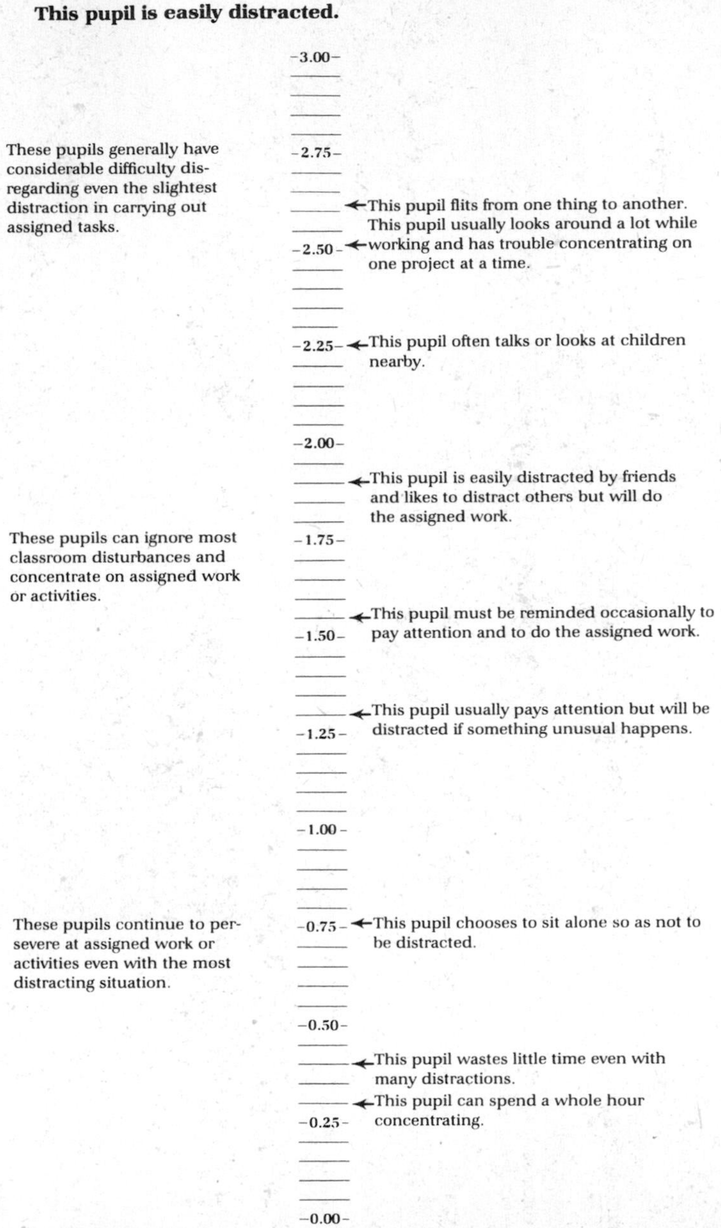

This pupil is easily distracted.

-3.00-

These pupils generally have   -2.75-
considerable difficulty disregarding even the slightest
distraction in carrying out   ◄This pupil flits from one thing to another.
assigned tasks.   This pupil usually looks around a lot while
                                   -2.50- ◄working and has trouble concentrating on
                                            one project at a time.

                                   -2.25- ◄This pupil often talks or looks at children
                                            nearby.

                                   -2.00-
                                           ◄This pupil is easily distracted by friends
                                            and likes to distract others but will do
                                            the assigned work.
These pupils can ignore most   -1.75-
classroom disturbances and
concentrate on assigned work
or activities.
                                           ◄This pupil must be reminded occasionally to
                                   -1.50- pay attention and to do the assigned work.

                                           ◄This pupil usually pays attention but will be
                                   -1.25- distracted if something unusual happens.

                                   -1.00-

These pupils continue to per-   -0.75- ◄This pupil chooses to sit alone so as not to
severe at assigned work or   be distracted.
activities even with the most
distracting situation.

                                   -0.50-
                                           ◄This pupil wastes little time even with
                                            many distractions.
                                           ◄This pupil can spend a whole hour
                                   -0.25- concentrating.

                                   -0.00-

Figure 15.3. **A pupil-rating scale anchored in behavior.** (*Source*: From Pupil Behavior Rating Scale by N. M. Lambert, E. M. Bower, and C. S. Hartsough. Reproduced by permission of the publisher, CTB/McGraw-Hill, Del Monte Research
Park, Monterey CA 93940. Copyright © 1979 by McGraw-Hill, Inc. All Rights
Reserved. Printed in the U.S.A.)

ing to the average of the judgments. The rater is to think about the sentences, not the numerical equivalents. Stability coefficients over 4 months are near 0.75 for pupil ratings in this format. Several scales can be combined as an overall evaluation of adjustment to school.

The BARS is troublesome to develop and use, and in comparative tests against other formats it does not consistently give better data. A simple numerical scale often works just as well; but each procedure is superior for some jobs and some traits (see Borman, in Berk, 1986). Bernardin and Smith (1981) argue that only a few varieties of BARS take advantage of some key virtues. In particular, they hope that raters in an institution who know that they will be called on to use such scales will form the habit of recording relevant incidents as these occur. Then the report comes from active observation, not dim memory.

Scorable Report Forms   Inventories like those for self-reports can be filled out by informants. Items referring to related acts or characteristics are accumulated into scores, hence the name "summative scales." Several recommendations are worth consideration in preparing such devices (Lorr et al., 1963):

- Limit each rating to a single variable. Too often, labels entangle two traits or kinds of behavior.
- Provide several items touching on the same aspect of behavior. This plan improves reliability just as lengthening a test does.
- Scales should describe the strength of a trait (as in the excitement examples that follow) and not present "opposite" traits as a bipolar scale. Bipolar descriptions are treacherous because logical opposites may not be psychological opposites; the opposite of "excitement" could be boredom or it could be self-control.
- Keep items as free as possible of theoretical preconceptions. Avoid words such as "regression," "mannerisms," and "acting out"; stick to everyday language.
- The span of the scale should not extend beyond the range of cases. On each item, some persons should receive ratings at the highest and lowest extremes.

Extreme statements that are never checked take up space and time. However, strongly worded end-of-scale options have value as buffers. In collecting student opinions for purposes of improving college instruction, my associates and I wanted each student's response to a standard list of positive and negative comments. The page of critical remarks that might apply to a course offered these response options:

YES, A SERIOUS FAULT   YES, A MINOR FAULT   NOT TRUE OF THIS COURSE

The "serious" response was almost never given, but its presence enabled students to express discontent at the next level without seeming to condemn the instructor as a simple YES would. Likewise, for positive comments, the following scale worked well:

YES!   YES   NOT MUCH   NOT AT ALL

This gave students a gentle way to tell where there was room for improvement; instructors worried a bit about statements that drew YES rather than YES! responses.

The Inpatient Multidimensional Rating Scale (M. Lorr and C. J. Klett) records the psychiatric interviewer's impressions. Each of the 75 items belongs to one of ten subsets—for example, Excitement, Hostile Belligerence, Paranoid Projection, Grandiose Expansiveness. The interviewer records impressions from the interview, ignoring other data in the record, in response to questions such as these:

COMPARED TO THE NORMAL PERSON TO WHAT DEGREE DOES HE . . .

  7. Express or exhibit feeling and emotions openly, impulsively, or without apparent restraint or control?
    Cues: Shows temper outbursts; weeps . . .
  9. Manifest speech that is hurried, accelerated, or pushed?
  40. Try to dominate, control, or direct the conduct of the interview?
    Cues: Number of times he interrupts, . . .

These items all count in the Excitement score. Responses are made on a 9-point scale:

NOT AT ALL   VERY SLIGHTLY   A LITTLE . . . MARKEDLY   EXTREMELY

The excitement items are scattered among items on other qualities, and thus the rater is not conscious of the summary dimension. Although the use of multiple items has a clear advantage, one must not increase the rater's task to the point where she responds hastily or fails to return the rating form.

The authors' studies indicate that persons observing the same interview agree well ($r = 0.9$ for Excitement). Also, internal-consistency analysis is favorable; the coefficient for Excitement is 0.9—remarkable for a 9-item scale. What is lacking is evidence of consistency over interviews and of stability (in the absence of radical or extended treatment).

Q Sorts   Interviewers and observers form complex impressions. Much of this information is lost if one collects only a few numerical ratings. A written description often includes vague remarks applicable to almost anyone and fails to touch on some important characteristics. Moreover, descriptions in essay form are hard to compare.

The Q sort is an excellent way to capture such impressions (Block, 1961). Standard phrases, on cards, cover the aspects of personality or performance important to those who will use the report. For examples, see pp. 493, 576, and 594. The California Q-Sort Deck and the California Child Q-Set are intended for research on persons in the normal range. The sensitivity of the technique makes it especially useful in studying short-term changes.

The informant is directed to sort the cards into, say, 9 piles, distributing the 100 statements in this manner:

	Most descriptive						Least descriptive		
Pile	1	2	3	4	5	6	7	8	9
Number of cards	5	8	12	16	18	16	12	8	5

The number of statements, piles, and sorting rules may, of course, be different from this. Standardizing the shape of distribution makes the report on one item dependent on the response made to other items, but no great harm results.

The sorting procedure has the advantage that the sorter can shift items back and forth as she proceeds. The boundaries of a category such as DEFINITELY TRUE may shift while one is working down a list, but in a Q sort we may expect the items in the same final pile to be equally descriptive of the person as the rater sees him.

Once finished, the sort may be examined impressionistically or processed formally. The median position (pile number) of statements on a theme provides a score for anxiety or dominance or the like. Another approach is to treat the item placements as a column of scores and correlate one description with another. Thus, a correlation could describe the similarity of a particular wife and husband, or of the wife's self-description to the husband's description of her. This and other elaborate analyses of Q sorts can distort the data (Cronbach, 1958).

Table 15.2 illustrates research with the Q sort. Women outstanding in mathematical research were interviewed and tested by psychologists who used the Q sort to record their impressions. Independently, qualified mathematicians indicated the degree to which these women were original and creative (not merely competent and productive). Each Q statement was correlated with this criterion. The correlations in Table 15.2 are remarkably high, especially for single items given to a select sample.

To obtain self-reports on work styles another deck of statements was prepared. These items (among others) were commonly rated as self-descriptive by the creative group:

Subordinates other things to research goals.
Is thorough and patient in approach to research issues.
Solution to a problem often comes from an unexpected direction.

Table 15.2   CHARACTERISTICS ASSOCIATED WITH CREATIVITY IN WOMEN
MATHEMATICIANS

Correlation with criterion	Q-sort statement
+0.6	Thinks and associates ideas in unusual ways; has unconventional thought processes.
+0.55	Is an interesting, arresting person.
+0.5	Tends to be rebellious and nonconforming.
+0.5	Genuinely values intellectual and cognitive matters.
+0.4	Is self-dramatizing; histrionic.
	. . .
−0.4	Is moralistic.
−0.4	Favors conservative values in a variety of areas.
−0.4	Behaves in a sympathetic or considerate manner.
−0.45	Is a genuinely dependable and responsible person.
−0.6	Judges self and others in conventional terms like "popularity," "the correct thing to do," social pressures, etc.

Source: Helson, 1971. The items appear in the California Q-set (see p. 593).

The following items figured in the self-characterizations of the less-creative group:

Enjoys instructing and working with students.
Grasps other people's ideas quickly.
Desire for a salary increase is an important motivating factor.
Has an active, efficient, well-organized mind.

Criterion Keying   A combination of choice response with criterion keying has sometimes been applied to get personnel evaluations. A superior identifies one or more good and poor workers; then each person is described by marking a checklist of descriptive phrases. Data from many raters and ratees are compiled. Phrases applied more often to the superior workers than to the others are considered relevant. All phrases are also rated on social desirability. Then pairs are made up; a criterion-related statement is paired with an equally favorable statement that did not correlate with the criterion. Thus "Wins confidence of co-workers" might be paired with "Punctual in completing reports." In one operational use of the scale, a superior is instructed to pick, in each pair, whichever phrase best describes her subordinate. The number of criterion-relevant phrases marked is the score. Sets of four phrases may be used instead of pairs; also, phrases negatively correlated with the criterion can be counted in with negative weights.

Because the supervisor does not know the scoring key, her opportunity to give too favorable a report is greatly reduced. The possibly greater validity of the ratings is offset by the resistance of informants. They resent being asked to supply information whose implications they cannot foresee. Moreover, ratings in organizations usually should be fed back, to encourage self-improvement; concealed scoring rules make feedback useless (P. C. Smith, in Dunnette, 1976, p. 761).

5. *Describe a suitable rating technique for each of these purposes.*
    a. *Obtaining ratings from principals to be used in deciding which teachers should receive salary increases for special merit.*
    b. *Obtaining ratings from principals to be used solely as a criterion for validating a teacher certification procedure.*
    c. *Obtaining information regarding parents' impressions of their children's personalities, to be filed at school and referred to by teachers and others facing decisions about the child.*
    d. *Maintaining weekly records of ward behavior of patients as seen by attendants, to be considered in periodic evaluation of the treatment plan.*
    e. *Obtaining reports from supervisors of student teachers, to be used by campus instructors in helping the student to improve.*
6. *To what extent does the California Q-Set appear to go beyond the good-active-strong scheme?*
7. *Every example in this section called for responses to many items or scales (although sometimes only one of several companion dimensions was displayed). The simplest technique, where each supervisor knows many employees, is to ask for ranking on a single global dimension. Compared with more complex reports, what are the weaknesses of a single ranking?*

INFORMATION FROM ACQUAINTANCES AND ASSOCIATES

How members of a family or working group perceive each other and how students perceive their teachers can provide important data for social psychology. Such facts can be used in altering the group process and in individual casework. Information from associates is also used in making assignments (of military officers, for example).

Mothers' Reports on Children

The "adaptive behavior" questionnaires discussed in Chapter 7 obtain information from parents of children who encounter difficulty in schools. Among procedures that develop more elaborate descriptions are the Child Behavior Checklist (CBCL) and the Personality Inventory for Children (PIC). The former adopts conservative psychometric techniques—the questions are face valid and interpretations stick close to the data. The data are organized into homogeneous keys intended to facilitate classification of problem children. The PIC relies on criterion keying to score miscellaneous variables.

The Child Behavior Checklist   The CBCL system provides three companion instruments with essentially similar content: CBCL proper for obtaining the parent's report, TRF for eliciting reports from teachers, and DOF for tallying what is seen during scheduled observations. The parent is asked whether during the previous 6 months the child showed a particular kind of behavior often, sometimes, or never. The wording is kept simple, and the four-page form can be filled out quickly. Note especially that the items (illustrated in the third column of Table 15.3) are in everyday language, even though the scales (second column) refer to pathology. In clinical settings the informants' reports would be studied in combination with interviews, medical information, and ability tests.

In the report form, the same questions are used for ages 4 to 14, but the profile is based on within-sex norms for an age band (4–5, 6–11, 12–16). All items describe problems or difficulties. There is another version for ages 2–3.

CBCL is essentially a multidimensional screening instrument, in-

Table 15.3   HIERARCHICAL MAPPING OF PROBLEM BEHAVIOR IN CHILDREN

Broad factors	Scales within factors	Topics within scales (illustrative)
Internalizing	Schizoid	Auditory hallucinations Fears school
	Depressed	Feels worthless Needs to be perfect
	Uncommunicative	Secretive Shy, timid
	Obsessive-Compulsive	Strange ideas Can't sleep
	Somatic complaints	Stomach problems Headaches
(Mixed)	Social withdrawal	Unliked Likes to be alone
Externalizing	Hyperactive	Can't concentrate Acts too young
	Aggressive	Argues Cruel to others
	Delinquent	Steals outside home Vandalism

Source: Patterning varies slightly across sex and age groups (Achenbach & McConaughy, 1987, p. 30). This pattern applies to boys aged 6 to 11. Wording of actual items is less terse than in this compilation.

tended to detect markedly deviant behavior of any kind. As is appropriate, score distributions are severely skewed. In the Aggressive category, the maximum score for a boy (age 6–11) is 46, but the median is only 5. For a child below about the 70th percentile in a category, the precise magnitude of the score is unimportant; the report places him in the normal range. The instrument spreads out those children for whom many problems of much the same kind are checked.

Table 15.3 illustrates the hierarchical system used in the profile. The authors hope that grouping profiles into types will enable clinicians and research workers in various places to describe children in standard terms so that their experience can be cumulated (Edelbrock & Achenbach, 1980). They provide formulas to sort most members of an age-sex group into the likely categories.

"No informant . . . can provide a totally comprehensive and veridical picture. . . . Each type of informant embodies unique perspectives, qualifications, and biases" (Edelbrock & Achenbach, 1984, p. 207). A mother's report reflects her relations with the child and her sense of the level of behavior that can properly be described as "too neat," "loud," and so on. The profile, then, is a statement about the mother-child dyad. Achenbach and McConaughy (1987) presented several cases in which disagreement between observers shed light on the child's life circumstances. Agreement of father and mother ($r = 0.6$) and stability of scores over time are rather satisfactory. Informants of different kinds (parent and teacher, teacher and observer) correlate only 0.3 (Achenbach, McConaughy, & Howell, 1987).

The main use of the instrument will be to suggest how a particular child should be handled—at home, at school, or in a treatment center. The research program will collect experience showing how children with different characteristics respond to particular interventions.

The Personality Inventory for Children   A unique inventory has been constructed to capture impressions of a child from the mother (or other informant) in scorable form. The scores form a profile as ambitious as that for the MMPI, accompanied, if desired, by a page of descriptive and evaluative prose from the computer. The PIC (R. D. Wirt, D. Lachar, J. K. Klinedinst, and P. D. Seat) was developed over a 20-year period by investigators at the University of Minnesota with an adaptation of the original MMPI techniques. The 600 (!) descriptive sentences are combined into nearly three dozen (!) scales, of three kinds: control, actuarial, and content. The control scales alert the psychologist to any extreme response bias (e.g., the mother's wish to present the child in a favorable light). There are four summary scales, which have to do with self-control, social competence, internalization, and cognitive development. One version of PIC allows administering just enough items to obtain these summary scores, and another omits 180 items entering scales currently considered "experimental."

The instrument is applied mostly at ages 6–16. Norms for the profile summarize reports apparently collected around 1960 in Minneapolis, on about 100 boys and girls spread evenly over those ages.

Criterion keying produced the following scales, among others:[1]

- Adjustment (ADJ). Counts responses given especially often by mothers describing emotionally disturbed boys.
- Ego Strength (ES). The criterion groups consisted of elementary school children described by teachers as good-active-sociable.
- Achievement (ACH). Counts items marked—more often than by other mothers—by mothers of second- and third-graders classed as "learning disabled" (and not "retarded").
- Intellectual Screening (IS). Similar, but based on retarded children. Standing within an age group is interpreted, the age groups being 3–5, 6, 7, 9, and 10–16. (For other scales, ages 6 to 16 enter the same distribution.)
- Delinquency (DLQ). Responses used by mothers to characterize 12- to 16-year-olds (most of them boys) who had been judged delinquent by a legal process. It is specifically noted that the score is a sign of "concurrent" delinquency.
- Delinquency Prediction (DP). The criterion group consisted of 191 boys tested at ages 10–12 and later split to distinguish the 30 who acquired police or traffic records from the remainder.

Keys formed on boys only or on cases from a limited age range are applied to both sexes and all ages.

"Content" scales were generated chiefly by having professional judges pick out items on a certain theme, then discarding any that did not show reasonable consistency with that set as a whole. Scales are not homogeneous in the usual sense. Thus, one scale Development (DVL) consists of items that judges picked as indicating poor intellectual or physical development (apparently making no differentiation with respect to age or sex). Here are three responses keyed in this scale:[2]

> My child can [not] cut things with scissors as well as others of his (her) age.
> My child has no special talents.
> My child could [not] print his (her) first name by age six years.

The inserted "[not]" indicates that the response FALSE to the original item is counted. I name, by way of illustration, a few other content scales: Depression, Anxiety, Family Relations (i.e., cohesion), and Social Skills.

PIC offers an impressive report on many aspects of a child, but one

---

[1]The ES and DP scales are called "experimental."
[2]Reproduced by permission of Western Psychological Services.

in which clinicians and school personnel may place too much trust.[3] The developers evidently hoped that the history of MMPI would be repeated, with a large volume of research by interested psychologists building a base for interpretations that would go beyond what the keying process alone could justify. Although the PIC booklet became available in 1958, the 1987 manual can cite only about 170 references to data-based studies. This number is appreciable but far below the MMPI pace of some 100 studies per year.

Many of the studies are in dissertations or other sources not readily available, and the 70-page text of the manual is not an adequate review. The manual lays out reasons for the proposed interpretations, but we badly need an outsider's careful appraisal of the validity arguments for the 17 main scales. A large book could barely do justice to the numerous concerns that arise about validity of the separate scales and the computerized case report (p. 575). Because of the subtleties of each argument, the small samples in much of the research, the range of ages and presenting problems considered, and the variety of possible decisions, to review even one scale would be a tough job. And that review is sure to end with a call for more research!

Users are encouraged to think of PIC as measuring the child. In fact, it is summarizing the mother's perception of the child or, more precisely, the perception the mother wants the clinician to *think* she has. How family members perceive each other has been a fruitful field of research just because it is found that perceptions do not coincide with facts. The information can be of value to the clinician *if* given a phenomenological interpretation.

Table 15.4, based on a parent questionnaire simpler than PIC, demonstrates that the score reflects the parent at least as much as the child. Five-year-olds had been referred to a clinic because of uncooperative behavior. Their mothers filled out a self-report on depression and an inventory describing the child. Observers, visiting each home four times, tallied whether the child did or did not obey each of the mother's commands or requests. The mothers' reports showed some agreement with this criterion, but the descriptions of children given by depressed mothers were substantially more negative than those from the nondepressed.

As one sample of the validation research for PIC itself, consider the IS scale. At the time of intake, a clinician may wish not to give a mental test unless there is reason to suspect intellectual inadequacy. The IS

---

[3]Reviews of PIC have been severely critical because it claims to do so much (Achenbach, 1981; Reynolds and Tuma, in Mitchell, 1985). Those reviews did not take into account a 1982 modification, and additions to the manuals since that date. For a rejoinder to Achenbach by two of the test's authors see Lachar and Wirt, 1981. A review by Knoff in the 1989 *MMY* goes more fully into virtues and faults of PIC.

Table 15.4 AVERAGE MALADJUSTMENT SCORES OF
CHILDREN, FROM MOTHERS' REPORTS

Compliance observed in home	Mothers classified by self-report		
	Nondepressed	Depressed	All mothers
Above median	60	68	64
Below median	64	81	72
All children	62	74	68

Source: Brody & Forehand (1986).

Note: Higher scores indicate more signs of child maladjustment in the mother's report.

scoring of the mother's impressions (the "first name" and "scissors" items are both counted) is intended to flag cases of retardation. A cross-validation sample of 75 children in one clinic was given an individual mental test, with the results in Table 15.5. (The IQ,IS correlation was 0.55 for this sample.) High IS scores seem to be raising relevant questions about the group flagged. The errors may be acceptable, especially as the clinician can use other facts along with the IS score in deciding whether to give a test.

PIC scales tend to have mixed content, and IS is particularly heterogeneous. The key counts the mother's statements that the child lacks average intelligence and has been put in a class for slow learners. One scarcely needs elaborate scoring to obtain that basis for decisions. But the key also counts as indicators of retardation the mother's statements that the child is popular and believes in God; one wonders how that information can be pertinent. The authors' justification is that such tangential items help to narrow the screened group; the item about the belief in God is said to distinguish retarded from psychotic children.

8. *Chapter 13 discussed factors that make the self-report untrustworthy as a description of typical behavior. Which of those factors might influence a*

Table 15.5 NUMBER OF CHILDREN WITH EACH
COMBINATION OF IS AND IQ SCORES

IS standard score	IQ<70	IQ 70–84	IQ>84	Total
Above 89	8	7	3	18
80–89		1	3	4
70–79	2	4	8	14
60–69	2	7	10	19
Below 60	___	3	17	20
Total	12	22	41	75

Source: Data from PIC manual, 1984, p. 50.

mother's response to CBCL when her child has been referred for the atten-tion of a mental-health treatment center?

9. *What conclusions are suggested by the following facts from 55 "normal" cases (sexes mixed, 6-year age range)?*

	Adj	Ach	Dvl	DP
Correlation of scores based on responses of father and mother	0.57	0.68	0.59	0.43
Correlation of scores based on two testings of mother (2-week interval)	0.93	0.90	0.93	0.86

10. *An advertising leaflet for PIC and its computer interpretation carries this headline: "Provides objective measures of General adjustment, Cognitive development, Academic achievement, Emotional adjustment, Behavioral di-mensions, Family function." What changes can you suggest to reduce possi-ble misconceptions?*

11. *A second-grader is referred to the clinic after persistent unruly behavior at home and school. He has not been placed in a special class by the school. What IS score would lead you, as a clinician, to decide to give a mental test?*

12. *Adolescents referred to a clinic were rated on several dimensions by the resident who conducted the intake interview. One dimension, "antisocial behavior," is a composite of ratings on truancy, drug and alcohol use, trou-ble with police, and dislike for school. This rating correlated 0.5 with the DLQ score of PIC (Lachar et al., 1984). What influences hold down the cor-relation?*

13. *In an attempt to widen the usefulness of PIC, a profile form for ages 3–5 was made available. The norms for these ages are based on about 100 boys and 100 girls. The criterion keys apparently were based on older groups that only occasionally included children as young as 5. And, as the manual says, few validity studies have included young children. Should the instrument be made available at this time for use at preschool ages?*

14. *For the Anxiety key of PIC, standard scores 50 and 70 for females (ages 6 to 16) are equivalent to 6 and 14 raw-score points, respectively. At ages 3 to 5, the equivalent scores are 3.5 and 7.5 points. What does this suggest regard-ing the wisdom of using the same profile form at all ages above 5?*

Peer Ratings

To obtain "peer ratings" or "sociometric ratings," group members are asked to rate each other. Peers can report not only on social attributes but on any readily observed aspect of style. Black's study (p. 543) in which students rated others living in the same dormitory is one example. Whereas only one or two teachers know a student well, 10 to 30 raters give reports in a class or dormitory. As a consequence, each average rat-ing is highly reliable. Moreover, the informants are knowledgeable and are accustomed to judging peers (Lindzey & Byrne, 1968). The same is to be said of adults who work together.

Social acceptance is a major influence on happiness and mental health. Popularity is about as stable from year to year as intellectual achievement, which adds to its significance. Peers and superiors have different perceptions. A child who impresses his peers as being a leader may not be so regarded by the teacher; the peers, for example, may consider amiability, whereas the teacher notices energy and initiative. The two reports gain in meaning when considered together. It is, for example, the student rated unfavorably by *both* teachers and peers who is most likely to drop out of school (Barclay, 1966).

The peer rating is an objective statement about reputation. Reputation is based to some extent on behavior, but social relationships color what peer observers notice. Among adolescents, correlations of reputations with observations of corresponding behavior vary with the trait (0.45 to 0.7 in the study of Newman & Jones, 1946). Leadership ratings by fellow soldiers in one squad correlated 0.8 with ratings given to the same persons after all had been shuffled into new squads and new barracks and had worked with their new companions for 4 weeks (L. V. Gordon & F. F. Medland, 1965). This compares well with the correlation of 0.9 between ratings 4 weeks apart in squads kept intact.

We desire each peer rater to describe many individuals. An adjective checklist such as Black's can be marked quickly, can cover many aspects of behavior, and is scorable.

Nomination Techniques   An alternative is to ask for nominations. Each member of the group is asked to name persons outstanding in a particular respect, such as leadership. This reduces the respondent's labor without much loss of significant information. Names of persons lacking in leadership may also be solicited, but this practice arouses anxiety. Group members know that they are being considered for unfavorable nominations, and, as raters, they are reluctant to speak unfavorably of associates. In general, anyone collecting peer ratings ought to think through the legitimacy of the undertaking and ought to avoid deception.

An important distinction is to be made between unsigned and signed responses. Signed responses (more intrusive) offer information on group structure (Gronlund, 1985, Chap. 15; Lindzey & Byrne, 1968). Practitioners have used such information to form congenial work groups and living units, and to study (and reduce) ethnic cleavage in a student body. Affiliations within the peer group are significant also in research on the development of motivation, values, and group morale.

Peer reports are among the most valid predictors of work criteria (Kane & Lawler, 1978). Among officer candidates, peer reports correlate about 0.5 with ratings by superiors in later duty assignments—extremely impressive when the criterion reliability is about 0.5. The traits that predict criteria tend to be in the good-strong-active sector, but "agreeableness" and "sociability" do not predict (Kraut, 1975; Tupes, 1957). Peer judgments of colonels predict who will become generals, and ratings of management trainees forecast promotion within a corporation (Downey et al., 1976; Harrell, 1972; Roadman, 1964). Moreover, patients in a ward are as good as the professional staff at predicting which of them will be rehospitalized (Lasky et al., 1959).

A variant of the nomination technique was worked out by Hartshorne and May (1929) to compare children's reputations for honesty with their response to experimental temptations (p. 618). Their "Guess Who" format survives today in research on social acceptance (e.g., of retarded children who are mainstreamed). It is sometimes used in screening school populations for children whose maladjustment might otherwise be overlooked. One screening procedure uses in combination a teacher rating (Figure 15.3), self-rating, and peer rating. In Grades 3 to 7, the peer report form is The School Play (N. M. Lambert and E. M. Bower). Eleven roles such as these are described:

> Someone who is liked by everybody and who tries to help everybody. A bully— someone who picks on smaller boys and girls.

The respondent is to name the class member who could best play the part.

The argument for using such an intrusive instrument in mass screening is not persuasive. The validity study (Lambert, 1963) had as its criterion an excellent clinical evaluation of adjustment. The criterion was predicted (around 0.5; good enough for screening) by the summary of *teacher* responses on several scales like Figure 15.3. Maladjusted girls in Grade 5 tended to receive few mentions from peers; maladjusted boys in Grades 2 and 5 tended to pick up negative mentions; neither score related to the criterion among second-grade girls. It appears that no formal rule applied to the peer information improved the hit rate appreciably.

15. *Surgency (energetic, talkative, enthusiastic) correlates very little with leadership behavior as rated by observers, but correlates substantially with frequency of election as leader. Explain his finding. What does it imply regarding the use of peer ratings as criteria?*

16. *In squadrons of fliers on combat duty, the "administratively designated leaders" were often not the ones named as preferred work leaders by the men (Kelly, 1947, p. 133). What practical suggestions follow from this finding?*

17. *Love (1981) obtained peer judgments of police officers in three forms: ranking, nomination, and rating scale (BARS). The rating technique was less reliable (over sets of raters) than the other two, and less correlated with supervisors' judgments. Suggest an explanation.*

PARTICIPANTS' REPORTS ON SETTINGS

When trying to understand why a certain type of student persists in one college and tends to drop out of another, one wants to know how the colleges differ and, more particularly, how students *think* they differ. To investigate successful and unsuccessful teachers, one wants to know how they differ in their style and emphasis. One could send a trained observer, but it is easier to have the students or other participants record their impressions.

The usual report form is a descriptive questionnaire rather like the personality questionnaire in format. A count of TRUE responses for any item, over the sample of participants, gives a reliable report. Instruments have been prepared for several levels of schooling, for hospital wards, for work settings, and so on; a published series is the Social Climate Scales (R. H. Moos and others).

In a conventional test, every examinee confronts the same items. To collect data on groups, matrix sampling is an economical substitute. A basic item pool is divided at random into several subsets, and each group member fills out one of these short test forms. Thus, 200 questions on college environment can be divided into 5 subsets, and each respondent answers 40 questions. This saves time without serious loss in the quality of information about the situation. A far larger variety of items can be administered in a given time; hence the data are richer.

Moos (1979) finds subscales of roughly the same character applicable in the several settings:

Relationship (involvement, affiliation or cohesion, support)

Personal growth (competition or pressure, autonomy, cultural orientation, etc.)

System maintenance and change (order, clarity, innovation)

Insofar as a theory has developed around instruments of this type, it is that the personality can be described in terms of "needs"—for change, achievement, affiliation, and so on—and the situation can be described in terms of "presses" to behave in certain ways. A "press" might include formal demands from the figures in authority, subtle demands contained in the expectations of the group, and opportunities to receive reward and attention for acts of a certain kind.

Like peer ratings and self-reports, the reports on climate are reports of perceptions rather than strictly factual reports on events, as illustrated in Figure 15.4. Each of 295 classes was judged by its student members and by the class teacher. It is not too surprising that the teacher speaks a bit more favorably than the students, but an important message comes across when students conspicuously disagree with the teacher's self-rating on clarity and emotional support, while averaging only a point lower elsewhere. For the same reason, Moos suggests that the counselor of adolescents and adults may find it useful to collect impressions of the home climate from each family member along with their descriptions, on the same inventory, of the ideal home climate.

18. *Student behavior (e.g., absenteeism) and accomplishment correlate, across classrooms, with the description the classes gave of the classroom climate (Moos, 1979). Evaluate the plausibility of the following hypotheses.*

   a. *When a class is doing well, this produces desirable behavior and a favorable report on the climate.*

   b. *Certain kinds of climate stimulate cooperation and effective work.*

19. *Evaluators seek to determine whether it is beneficial to use parents as volunteer aides in fourth-grade classrooms having many minority students. Explain how climate descriptions could provide one measure of the success of the change. Also, could climate descriptions clarify why the change improves learning in some classrooms and not others?*

20. *For which of these applications would you expect inventories collecting impressions of participants to be reasonably valid?*

   a. *To examine whether students from minority groups perceive the social environment of an integrated college as students of majority background do.*

   b. *To determine which prisoners have adjusted adequately to the social environment of a corrective institution.*

   c. *To collect information for a top-level administrative review of the correctional institutions of a state system.*

   d. *To distinguish elementary schools that use formal and informal methods, in a study intended to assess educational outcomes under each approach.*

21. *Figure 15.4 plots average raw scores. The manual for the scale provides norms for students and teachers, essentially consistent with the facts in Figure 15.4. Should the profile for responses of a single class and its teacher be plotted in terms of raw ratings or standard scores?*

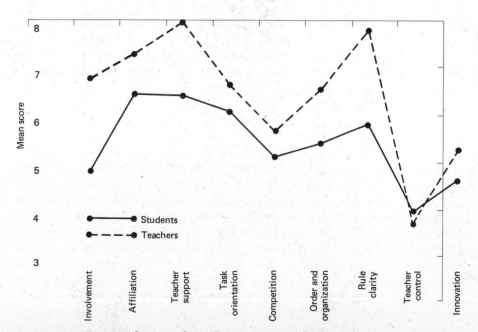

Figure 15.4. **How students and teachers perceive classrooms.** Responses are recorded on a range from 0 to 10. (*Source*: Moos, 1979, p. 148.)

DIRECT OBSERVATION

Choice of the Situations

Self-reports and reports of informants are haphazard composites. The rater did not see the individual in all situations, and selective recall operates. Systematic observations in an ecologically representative sample of times and places can come closer to typical behavior.

Comparison is inexact because one does not observe two individuals in the same situation. Even when the situation is externally constant, previous conditions affect behavior. When Jimmy fidgets more than Johnny in the classroom, one could infer that Jimmy is "restless," "nervous," or "jumpy." If the impression is confirmed on other observations, this difference seems fundamental. But if Jimmy usually comes to school without breakfast, if he expects to be criticized by the teacher for poor work, or if he is too large for the chairs provided, the difference in activity may tell nothing about restlessness per se. In fact, if conditions were reversed, Johnny might be more restless than Jimmy is now. Observations show how people typically act under their present conditions.

Some records of behavior can be nearly complete. Production of individual workers may be recorded routinely. A mechanical device on a commercial airplane records its motion together with conversations in the cockpit. Some investigators have persuaded subjects to wear microphones and transmitters that allow all their conversations to be recorded (except when the subject throws a switch for privacy). Weight watchers may keep a diary in which they record what they eat, when, and under what circumstances. To cut back the volume of information, one has three options. Attention can focus on "significant" incidents identified by a quick scan of the record (or, in the case of the flight recorder, by external evidence that an episode was unusual). Representative samples can be extracted for coding and tabulation, or a simple numerical summary (number of eating incidents per week) can be taken off. Weick (1985) discusses at length the decisions needed in planning for observation.

Ordinarily, one wants observations under conditions typical of the person. The fact that observations are being made may or may not make the situation and response atypical. The production record and the flight record are parts of the natural environment. Students are quick to accept observers in the classroom or in the schoolyard and can be expected to go about their affairs normally unless the observer conspicuously takes notes on them. What has gone onto White House tapes illustrates that a person can become habituated to a recording procedure to the point where it does not constrain him or her. The weight watcher is a different case entirely; although the diary provides data, its main function is to heighten self-consciousness and influence eating behavior. In intermediate cases—teachers, counselors, or ward attendants—it is reasonable to expect a tendency to "put on a good show." Some brief studies comparing observations made with and without the targets' awareness are summarized by Foster and Cone (in Ciminero et al., 1986). Because awareness of the observer may lead to atypical response, these authors recommend various precautions—in particular, use of covert observation when that is ethically justifiable, and habituating the subjects to observers before data are recorded "for keeps."

The Schedule for Sampling

Extreme variation in performance is illustrated by a study of navigators. The student on a mission was to compute his air speed by dead reckoning on each leg of a flight. The accuracy score had a split-half reliability of 0.77; this is an indication of leg-to-leg consistency under unchanging conditions with the same equipment. A day-to-day correlation was also computed; it was 0.00! (Carter & Dudek, 1947). Scores were determined almost entirely by transient conditions (e.g., wind) rather than by the individual's ability.

Observing on many days in many circumstances gives a score that is likely to agree with a score collected on another series of days. Systematic scheduling improves representativeness. To study social contacts of preschool children, for example, a schedule may be drawn up. The observer watches a child for 1 minute, noting social interactions and checking a form to record what occurred. Children are watched in a predetermined order, different from day to day. Each child is observed during the first 5 minutes of the free-play hour, during the second 5 minutes on another day, and so on. The cumulative picture is likely to be far more typical than an equal amount of evidence obtained in a few longer observations. Moreover, errors of memory are few when the observer can make full notes during or just after observing. Observers are usually asked to record salient facts about the situation as well as the actions of the target, so that similar situations can be grouped for analysis.

Other controls are used when observing is incidental to other activities, for example, in tracking the behavior of persons undergoing behavior modification. Time sampling may be accomplished by having the person carry a signal device that goes off at irregular intervals, at which time she records that she has or has not just been engaged in the target behavior (nail biting, for example) and what the circumstances are (Hormuth, 1986). Note that this is more constructive than asking the person to record each incident of nail biting. Unscheduled recording is inaccurate and loses the opportunity to encourage the person by noting the times when she is not biting her nails. One timing device is the spring-driven parking meter reminder; each time it goes off and a record is made, the respondent can ask an acquaintance to reset it for an arbitrary time lapse. You will also recall the contribution of a radio-controlled beeper to the Experience Sampling study (p. 43).

Time samples are especially suitable for facts that can be expressed numerically (e.g., number of social contacts), but the data can also sustain judgmental interpretations. Observer-to-observer correlations, following extended sampling of children's behavior in a day camp, were near 0.9 for the following attributes, among others: instigation of physical aggression, parallel play with peers, withdrawal from the social environment, affection-seeking, attempts to master gross motor tasks (Crandall, 1966).

Applying Generalizability Theory The larger the sample, the better. The theory of Chapter 6 applies: When single observations correlate only 0.1, observations in ten situations ought to correlate 0.5 with a second set of ten observations; 30 observations bring the correlation to 0.75. Short observations are generally advisable. Five-minute observations on each of six children—repeated on 12 days—use the observer's time much better than observing each child for 30 consecutive minutes on each of 2 days.

Having two or more observers look at the same target irons out biases, but the behavior sample is narrowed if they make their records at the same time. Simultaneous observation does make sense for training observers and for getting evidence of their agreement. When error is disturbingly large, the investigator has several options. One is to sample more thoroughly—more occasions or more observers or both. Another is to reduce observer error by giving clearer instructions and more training. If scores depend heavily on the situation, breaking the domain into subdomains and sampling from each is appropriate. Generalizability studies play an important role in pilot work. They can assess the magnitude of multiple sources of error and so suggest how to adjust the observing schedule.

A suitably simple example comes from observations of the eating behavior of adolescents (Coates & Thoresen, 1978). The counselor was trying to modify behavior that contributed to obesity; the observations provided initial baseline data and later checked on effectiveness. It was recognized that behavior might vary from day to day, that systematic differences among observers might occur, and that some "residual" unsystematic variation was inevitable. To assess error, two observers collected data together, observing each counselee several times and making their records independently. Chiefly, they watched the adolescents at the family dinner table.

One variable was the number of helpings the youngster took. The information from this kind of study is best reported in the form of variances. Recall that a variance is a squared s.d.; variances can be added to describe the cumulative effect of several sources. For number of helpings, these are the key variances:

Client variation over occasions	0.00
Observer constant error	0.00
Observer-client interaction	0.00
Residual	3.5

The zeros tell important stories. The adolescents were highly consistent from day to day; they either did or did not take seconds. Observers did not vary systematically either in the average score over all clients or in the average they would assign any one person in the long run. The residual suggests some wild random errors, however, as if one observer were recording three helpings when her companion was recording one. Faced with such a strange result, I would first check the arithmetic! Then I would look for possible causes. Debriefing the observers shortly after they turned in discrepant reports would perhaps pinpoint the trouble. If the random disagreements continue, the only salvation is to average many observations.

Time spent in eating produced these variances:

Clients	Occasions	Observers	Client-observer interaction	Residual
7.7	4.2	0.0	0.0	2.5

The observer and interaction variances of zero say that it doesn't matter which observer collects these data. Being able to regard observers as interchangeable makes it far easier to schedule data collection. The adolescents differed considerably in eating time. The residual error (haphazard variation of observers) can be reduced either by averaging two or more observers on each occasion or by observing on more days. If typical behavior during (say) the baseline period is of interest, one ought to observe on several days, so as to average out occasion-to-occasion fluctuations.

Note that my interpretation did not look at a reliability (generalizability) coefficient. The purpose of measurement here was to study systematic changes in individuals, not individual differences.

22. *Why might an unfair picture of a child's behavior be obtained if he were always observed during the first 5 minutes of the play period and never during the second 5 minutes?*

23. *As a criterion in selection research, would it be better to test every flier with repeated landings on the same day or with a similar number of landings spread over several days?*

24. *A child performed each of several tasks while raters scored the mother's behavior on a scale of 1 to 9 (Leler, 1970; summarized in Cronbach et al., 1972). Here are some of the variances calculated:*

	Task-to-task	Rater-to-rater	Subject-rater interaction	Residual
M reasons with child	0.7	1.2	0.6	1.1
M discourages C's talking	1.1	0.2	1.0	1.6

Note: Subject refers to the mother-child pair.

What interpretations or recommendations can you suggest?

Observer Error and Its Reduction

An observer notices some happenings and ignores others. Especially in social situations, the complexity of events prevents exhaustive reporting. Observers overemphasize some types of events and fail to report others.

The following reports were written by observers after seeing a filmed preschool scene of about 10 minutes' duration. The film was shown twice without sound. The observers were directed to note everything they could about one boy, Robert, and were told to use parentheses to set apart inferences or interpretations. Numbers in these accounts, referring to scenes in the film, have been inserted to aid comparison.

Observer A: (2) Robert reads word by word, using finger to follow place. (4) Observes girl in box with much preoccupation. (5) During singing, he in general doesn't participate too actively. Interest is part of time centered elsewhere. Appears to respond most actively to sections of song involving action. Has tendency for seemingly meaningless movement. Twitching of fingers, aimless thrusts with arms.

Observer B: (1) Looked at camera upon entering (seemed perplexed and interested). Smiled at camera. (2) Reads (with apparent interest and with a fair degree of facility). (3) Active in roughhouse play with girls. (4) Upon being kicked (unintentionally) by one girl he responded (angrily). (5) Talked with girl sitting next to him between singing periods. Participated in singing. (At times appeared enthusiastic.) Didn't always sing with others. (6) Participated in a dispute in a game with others (appeared to stand up for his own rights). Aggressive behavior toward another boy. Turned pockets inside out while talking to teacher and other students. (7) Put on overshoes without assistance. Climbed to top of ladder rungs. Tried to get rung which was occupied by a girl but since she didn't give in, contented himself with another place.

Observer C: (1) Smiles into camera (curious). When group breaks up, he makes nervous gestures, throws arm out into air. (2) Attention to reading lesson. Reads with serious look on his face, has to use line marker. (3) Chases girls, teases. (4) Girl kicks when he puts hand on her leg. Robert makes face at her. (5) Singing. Sits with mouth open, knocks knees together, scratches leg, puts fingers in mouth (seems to have several nervous habits, though not emotionally overwrought or self-conscious). (6) In a dispute over Parcheesi, he stands up for his rights. (7) Short dispute because he wants rung on jungle gym.

Observer D: (2) Uses guide to follow words, reads slowly, fairly forced and with careful formation of sounds (perhaps unsure of self and fearful of mistakes). (3) Perhaps slightly aggressive as evidenced by pushing younger child to side when moving from a position to another. Plays with other children with obvious enjoyment, smiles, runs, seems especially associated with girls. This is noticeable in games and in seating in singing. (5) Takes little interest in singing, fidgets, moves hands and legs (perhaps shy and nervous). Seems in song to be unfamiliar with words of main part, and shows disinterest by fidgeting and twisting around. Not until chorus is reached does he pick up interest. His especial friend seems to be a particular girl, as he is always seated by her.

To reduce errors, recording should be separated from judging, to the extent practicable. The cost and inconvenience of videotaping or other automatic recording is often warranted by the opportunity it affords for scoring by several viewers and for rescoring if, as an investigation proceeds, a new code is considered desirable. Also, recordings can be judged in scrambled order, removing the risk of biases arising from increased experience of raters or increased boredom, or from expectation of change as treatment progresses. Even where videotaping is impractical in collecting final data in the field, it is a major resource for pretraining of observers.

Should field notes be a free description? or an attempt to code, act by act, what is going on? No general recommendation can be made. As with other procedures, structure focuses attention and makes sure that the same variables are examined for everyone. Where the information summary will be highly structured—a statistical summary perhaps— then the original record will ordinarily employ a predetermined code. The more narrowly the observer is allowed to concentrate, the more closely observers are likely to agree. But relevant information that does not fit the pigeonholes is lost.

Making sure that observers know what to look for is an obvious step. But observers should be left ignorant of the hypotheses the observations are to check. Observers are subtly motivated to support the conclusions they believe the investigator expects. (Also, their data tend to conform to their own expectations; Wildman & Erickson, in Cone & Hawkins, 1977.) Insofar as possible, neither observers nor judges should know who is in an experimental group, who has received therapy and who has not, who comes from "a good home," or who has been diagnosed as "hyperactive."

Objectivity has its virtues, but there is much to be said for seeing through the eyes of participants. One can play back a classroom recording to a teacher, for example, stopping it periodically for the teacher's interpretation of what was happening or what she was trying to do. Some of the statements may be defensive rationalizations, but they add a dimension to the data. Anthropologists have developed a variety of techniques for understanding a culture through the eyes of its members, working on the assumption that a social group gives meanings to behavior that an outsider is unlikely to perceive (Goodenough, in Triandis & Berry, 1980).

25. *What do you think really happened in scene 4 of the film? Which observer came closest to adequate reporting of it?*

26. *Which of the numbered scenes appears to give the most significant information about Robert? How many of the observers reported that information?*

Chapter
16

Inferences from Performance

16A. A performance test of a trait like persistence tends to have lower form-to-form reliability than an inventory or an ability test. Why?

16B. In what ways do psychologists keep examinees from knowing what kind of information a performance test or projective test is collecting? What is to be said for and against such concealment?

16C. Responses to stylistic tests such as the Bender are interpreted as signs of forces within the person. How can inferences about unobservable characteristics be validated?

16D. In assessing the stress created under temporary experimental conditions of various types, what advantage does a short TAT-like test have over a questionnaire on emotional states? (Assume that groups are assigned randomly to conditions.)

16E. Why have validations of modern assessment centers yielded more favorable reports than earlier validations of assessment of professionals?

Abbreviations in this chapter: LGD for Leaderless Group Discussion; MCT for Mechanical Comprehension Test; TAT for Thematic Apperception Test.

ORIENTATION

This final chapter surveys methods of observing in a standardized situation. Some are single-score measurements of narrow aspects of behavior, but the chapter ends with assessments that consider ability and personality as an indivisible whole.

Much of the chapter is descriptive, introducing a variety of techniques. You should identify purposes that might lead a tester to choose each approach, and the advantages and disadvantages of each one. The chapter provides a form of review, as the critical questions to be raised about its tests were all prominent somewhere in earlier chapters.

Psychologists are sharply divided about the merits of stylistic tests (and some who favor one of them will disapprove of the next). My brief account cannot give you a basis for a firm opinion, but you should try to understand why these tests draw both strong positive and strong negative evaluations.

The integrative approach to assessment, in its old and new versions, is a fitting ending for the book, as it illustrates how testing evolves. Figure 16.6 is worth unpacking; it catalogs difficulties testers face (and, to some extent, overcome). Use it in particular to see why the first wave of assessment encountered difficulty, and why present practice is more successful.

PERFORMANCE TESTS

Procedures

A performance test is an observation of response to a standard task, usually one designed to bring out evidence on a specific characteristic. The control and expression of aggression, for example, is hard to observe systematically in daily life because provocations occur at unpredictable moments. To observe aggression, two psychologists placed classes of boys, during their sports period, in an inadequate room; about half the boys could play at any one time. The experimental arrangement doubled the amount of aggression displayed, generating plenty of data (Winder & Wiggins, 1964). Another provocative tactic is to challenge the opinions expressed in an interview. Such stress techniques have to be handled sensitively, of course.

Performance tests differ. The test may measure numerically one narrow construct such as persistence in routine work. It may yield scores on persistence and caution and tempo simultaneously. It may try to appraise the person's whole life-style. Tasks may be natural (perhaps sampled from a prospective assignment) or highly artificial.

The tests range from highly structured to almost totally unstructured. A situation is structured if it has a definite meaning. In a structured situation, the respondent knows what he is expected to do and how he is expected to do it. Well-structured tasks are excellent for measuring ability just because they set the same target for everyone. An unstructured situation has so little pattern that it can be given almost any meaning. The strange sound in the night is unstructured. Is it the wind? A burglar? A cat? In the unstructured situation, one must guide oneself. The greater the ambiguity, the greater the opportunity for the individual to set his own goal. Structure is minimal when, for example, the psychologist turns the test taker loose in a studio equipped with varied art media and materials, saying no more than, "You may do anything you like with these."

So-called "projective" techniques, in particular, provide little structure. The test taker is free to project unconscious thoughts, wishes, and fears into the situation. The householder who interprets the creak in the dark as a burglar may be more anxious than one who interprets the same stimulus as a natural phenomenon and goes back to sleep.

Galton compared testing to the geologist's "sinking shafts at critical points." Ratings return surface impressions. The time sample sinks its shaft at random. The performance test bores in at supposedly critical points. Most performance tests in the psychometric tradition have many or all these features:

- Standardization. The stimulus situation is controlled, reproducible, applicable in a nearly uniform manner to everyone.
- Specificity. The investigator is interested in a sharply defined trait. The report refers to a narrower construct than the good-strong-active dimensions of self-ratings.
- Quantification. Performance is reduced to scores, the scoring rules locating everyone on the same scale or scales.
- Disguise. The test taker is led to believe that one characteristic is being tested when the observer is looking at another. For example, "Pick the funniest jokes in this collection." In research on the individual's sense of humor, this inquiry may be disguised as a study of the jokes. The score could be based on the type of joke the person picks (e.g., hostile), not on whether he picks the ones most people consider funny.
- Attention to process. The style of performance is given more attention than the amount or quality of response.

Standardized Settings for Observation   The simplest procedures in this category are no more than standardized observations. In research on parent-child interaction and its effects, the observer visits the home. She records, as systematically as she chooses, such variables as amount of encouragement, how closely the child clings to the mother, and so on. The observer's acts may follow standard instructions but the situation is uncontrolled. The data are not comparable from home to home or occasion to occasion because the ongoing activities are not comparable. Changing to a more standard situation promotes comparability. A task may be taken into the home, introduced into the everyday setting for care, or set up in a laboratory. Standardized procedures can carry the same operations into different cultures,

An international team set out to study whether certain child-rearing practices of Japanese and U.S. mothers reflect the social status and other characteristics of the family and affect the child's readiness for school similarly. The team designed situations considered to fit both cultures and developed scoring rules that can be applied in either language.

When mother and child first come to the testing center, they are taken to the test room, where pegboard materials are laid out (and a remote-controlled video camera is mounted). "Let Tommy become accustomed to the room before the day's work begins," says the experimenter; the mother is encouraged to play with the child, using the games if she wishes. The experimenter then absents herself for 10 minutes. The trays with colored pegs and pegboard are open, and the lid showing the patterns (in four colors) is in plain view (Figure 16.1). The mother can occupy herself or interact, can lead the child or leave him free. Sound tapes are made and later transcribed for rating by as many raters as needed to obtain reliability. Additional ratings are made from the videotape.

The second procedure was structured by the requirement that the mother teach the child. With the child absent, the experimenter taught the mother a sorting game. Scripted instruction led the mother to infer and explain a system of the form "Tall blocks marked with X go together" (color and shape being ignored). When the mother had succeeded, she was told to teach the game however she liked. The examiner said that after 20 minutes he would return and test the child's understanding (by means of additional blocks the mother had not seen). Interest, of course, centered on the mother's teaching style and the child's responsiveness, not primarily on the child's success.

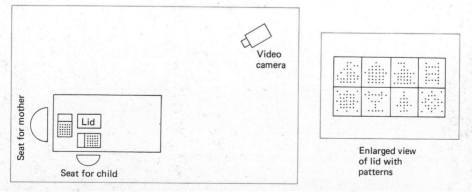

Figure 16.1. **Standardized arrangement for observing mother and child.** (*Source*: Adapted from Hess and Azuma, 1973.)

Standardized social situations have been used also at older ages, more for research in social psychology than for assessment (Carlsmith et al., 1976). Behavioral assessors find controlled situations a useful supplement to self-report, particularly where research data are wanted (Ciminero et al., 1986, esp. Chap. 8, 10; Cone & Hawkins, 1977). In studying phobias and treatments for them, for example, they may wire the person to apparatus that records physiological changes and then expose him to a series of pictures or objects, some neutral and some related to the phobia. Before-and-after measures on physiological response to snakes, for example, probably give more trustworthy data on the depth and breadth of change in fear than does self-report. Observed role-playing (p. 492) has advantages over self-report or everyday observation; these procedures offer rich descriptive information and are ordinarily not reduced to summary scores. On the other hand, a single role enactment—a one-item test—may be a poor sample.

Scores from Ability Tests   Many ability tests have been called objective tests of personality. Self-regulation, planfulness, and similar stylistic variables can properly be regarded as information on personality.

A good example is Porteus's measure of style in maze performance. He developed an objective Q score "intended to reveal any haphazard, impulsive, or overconfident habits of action." Two contrasting styles are displayed in Figure 16.2. Both girls solve the problem, but one proceeds painstakingly down the middle of the road through the center of every gap. The other swoops along, cutting corners and boundaries. Porteus's complete reports on these girls are convincing evidence that the styles

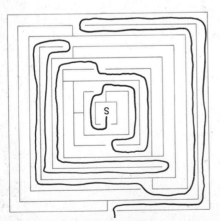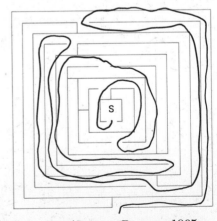

Figure 16.2. Stylistic differences in maze performance. (*Source*: Porteus, 1965, p. 234. Reproduced by permission of Pacific Books and The Psychological Corporation. New Series from "The Maze Test and mental differences," copyright 1933 by S. D. Porteus; and "The Porteus Maze Test and intelligence," copyright 1950 by S. D. Porteus, copyright renewed 1978 by D. Hebden Porteus and John R. Porteus. Published by The Psychological Corporation. All rights reserved.)

are as personalized and stable as a signature. Porteus developed his scoring scheme especially to identify delinquents; the more reckless girl in Figure 16.2 is a delinquent. Q scores for delinquents run much higher than those of nondelinquents (Riddle & Roberts, 1977). Even within the narrow range of a group of criminals, the style of Porteus performance distinguishes the more psychopathic from the less psychopathic, as judged by prison psychiatrists (Schalling & Rosén, 1968). All of this supports the validity of stylistic evidence, but of course does not warrant reliance on the Q score in deciding which adolescents to suspect of misconduct.

Some ability tests have been specially designed to stretch adaptive powers to the limit. June Downey, for example, in one of her "will-temperament tests" of the 1920s, asked subjects to copy a sentence backward (last letter first . . .) without interruption, *as slowly as possible.* In an "operational stress test" tried with military fliers, the candidate was to throw levers as called for by signal lights while being bombarded with oral commands to work faster and to stop making errors. There are thousands of measures of adaptive abilities or preferred tempos that one or another investigator has proposed. The laboratory of R. B. Cattell alone derived more than 2000 scores from several hundred procedures, grouping them under 21 factors (Cattell & Warburton, 1967). A kit of measures of ten factors (Extroversion, Depression, Anxiety, Ego strength, . . .) is available (Objective-Analytic Batteries; R. B. Cattell and J. M. Schuerger).

The attempt to capture information on personality by the methods of objective psychometrics has borne little fruit, despite effort by giants such as Thurstone and Cattell. There are several difficulties. First, effort has not been cumulative; with few exceptions, a technique is studied only by its inventor and those he or she has trained. Second, considering one score at a time and trying to assess what is in the person's makeup without regard to the situation within which he acts is a feeble way to account for behavior. Third, although measures such as the Operational Stress Test correlate with important criteria, the relationship usually washes out when ability (as measured by ordinary tests) is held constant.

Observations of style are important in modern theory of information processing (Chapter 8), but at this time no one is reducing such measures to standard form or interpreting them as measures of a stable temperament. Later in the chapter we shall see how complex observations of style in intellectual tasks are used by clinicians; this effort is essentially independent of theory of information processing. Structured observations of social behavior and of reactions to threatening situations do play a variety of roles in current practice and research.

Testing Response to Temptation   A fixed situation appeals to specific motivations and may not have the same significance for every examinee. To lead up to discussion of this and other aspects of validity, I describe procedures that expose a person to temptation. In such situations, society defines one response as right and another as wrong. Few violations would be observed in many hours of ordinary time sampling, and few would be acknowledged in self-report. "Entrapment" procedures could violate the rights of those tested, but the risks are comparatively small when the only intention is to analyze group data for research purposes. The most elaborate and inventive effort in this direction was the Character Education Inquiry of Hartshorne and May (1928, 1929, 1930).

To appraise honesty in test taking, children in a class were asked to place marks in small circles while keeping their eyes closed. It was impossible to do well. Many children turned in "successes" they could have obtained only by peeking.

Honesty with money was tested by arranging an arithmetic lesson in which each pupil handled a boxful of coins. Each box was secretly identified. At the end of the lesson the pupil carried his own box to a pile in front of the room. Unaware that boxes could be identified, many pupils took advantage of the opportunity to keep some money.

The Hartshorne-May findings on character led one national agency working with youth to revise its program completely because the study showed that those who had received most recognition in the agency's character-building activities were on the average *most* likely to cheat (Maller, 1944). Striving for recognition in competition and pushing for high scores may stem from the same basic feeling of inadequacy. McClelland (in Rabin, 1981) demonstrates the continuing fascination of these data by offering just the opposite interpretation: More mature children, entering adolescence, may act less morally because they are pushing to show their autonomy.

Motivation to put forth effort has been of particular interest because it is obviously a link between aptitude and achievement. To test children's persistence in the face of obstacles, Hartshorne and May had them read a story that builds to a climax: "Again the terrible piercing shriek of the whistle screamed at them. Charles could see the frightened face of the engineer. . . ." To learn the ending they must read the difficult printed material that follows:

CHARLESLIFTEDLUCILLETOHISBACK"PUTYOURARMSTIGHTA-ROUNDMYNECKANDHOLDON.

. . . .

NoWho   WTogETBaCkoNthETREStle.HoWTOBRingTHaTTErrIFIEDB-URDeNOFACHiLDuPtO

. . . .

fiN ALly tAp-taPC AME ARHYTH Month e BriD GeruNNing fee Tfee TcomING

The pupil separates each word with a vertical mark as he deciphers it; the amount deciphered is the index of persistence (Hartshorne & May,

1928, vol. 1, p. 292). The ambiguity of single tests is nicely illustrated by this task. Does it measure interest in adventure stories? Compulsiveness in following directions? Tolerance for annoyance? Enjoyment of an intellectual challenge? Or mostly reading skill and fluid ability?

Derivatives of the Hartshorne-May procedures are used, for example, in research concerned with the influence of models and of persuasion. Thus, Bandura and Whalen (1966) arranged for children to win coins in a game and gave them the option of depositing some of their winnings in a box as a contribution to orphans. When child models, coached to drop in some of their winnings, were used, their action stimulated other children to do the same. (For the tester, this is a reminder that test performance will be altered if the examinee can observe what others are doing. These influences are probably especially strong in character tests.)

How a person thinks about moral dilemmas is an important aspect of character, especially for educators. Tests of moral judgment (p. 101) are intellectual tests, many of them being influenced by the research of Piaget. They correlate modestly with measures of behavior, but they do not purport to predict. Some tests for children (e.g., Selman & Lieberman, 1975) are much like Wechsler Comprehension items, with higher scores being given for responses that show full appreciation of the dilemma. Another approach (Kohlberg, 1973) is to tell a story about a painful dilemma to adolescents and adults and by Socratic questioning trace the depth of their reasoning. In the same vein, Rest (1976) produced an experimental objective test in which respondents rate the importance of various value considerations in resolving a dilemma. For a critical review of thought and research procedure related to moral development, see Burton and Casey (1980).

1. *In each of the following enterprises, would it be preferable to employ observations in natural conditions or standardized observations where conditions are fixed in advance and identical for all examinees?*
   a. *A telephone company wishes to rate its operators on courtesy and clarity of speech. It is able to tap conversations and make recordings.*
   b. *Navy personnel are to be screened for tendency to panic under conditions of extreme noise, as in amphibious landings.*
   c. *An investigator wishes to study the habitual recklessness of 7-year-old boys in climbing and jumping.*

2. *To what extent may each of the following be considered an unstructured stimulus?*
   a. *A teacher, during an examination, glances up from her desk and barely observes a hasty movement of one boy who is pulling his hand into his lap from the aisle.*
   b. *In duplicate bridge, the same set of hands is played at every table.*
   c. *A questionnaire is designed to obtain information about age, income, education, and so on. All logical alternative answers are anticipated and presented on the blank in multiple-choice form.*

3. *To what extent could the respondent "fake good" in each of the following procedures if he knew what the tester was looking for?*
   a. *The tendency of a person to "repress" certain threatening ideas is measured by exposing words in a tachistoscope. Any one word is exposed very briefly and then again at increasing exposures until the person reads it. Into a list of neutral words are mixed a number of words related to sex, aggression, or some other possibly threatening topic. The score is the extra exposure required for loaded words.*
   b. *Persistence is measured by determining how long a person remains at work on a college final examination when he may leave as early as he chooses.*
   c. *An "in-basket" test presents a person with an array of information about a job he is supposed to fill: the community, the organization he works for, his associates, his responsibilities, and so on. Then (under some time pressure) he is to work through the correspondence and memos in his basket, disposing of each by a referral, by a direct reply or instruction to his staff, or by disregarding it. His performance is judged in terms of the soundness of his judgment, what priorities he assigns, and what style (e.g., buck-passing, tendency to "call a meeting," etc.) he displays.*
   d. *A preschool child is asked to learn to assemble a wooden gasoline station. The teacher shows him what to do, but does a number of things not included in the oral directions and not essential to the task—for example, storing the box under the table before proceeding, laying all the pumps side by side in parallel at the outset, and so on. The number of these incidental acts that the child copies when his turn comes is taken as a measure of dependency.*

4. *Children from homes with low socioeconomic status cheated more on achievement tests than other children $r = 0.5$ (Hartshorne & May, 1928). How safe is it to conclude that these children were more likely to violate other standards of good conduct?*

Problems of Design and Validity

With the example of character tests before us, we can discuss the evaluation of performance measures. The ultimate contribution of a procedure depends primarily on whether a theoretical explanation for the performance can be worked out, but that takes a long time. A theoretical advance suggests ways to refine the test, and an improvement in the test gets data that suggest ways to refine the theory. Examining a new procedure in its primitive form, one cannot say whether it will ultimately make a contribution.

Certain types of statistical research enter into the evaluation and improvement of nearly all performance tests. An ideal performance test of personality would satisfy the standards implied by this list of questions (though how close a test should come to the ideal depends on the use intended).

- Does the test obtain an accurate measure of usual behavior, one that represents the universe of tasks like this and all occasions within this period of the subject's life?
- Are the scores stable over a reasonable period of time?
- Is there convergence between this evidence and evidence of other kinds that is thought to reflect the same trait?
- Can the scores be largely explained by well-established constructs? In particular, does ability greatly influence the score? If so, the procedure is not giving an adequate measure of a "new" variable.

Consistency over Forms and Trials   A performance test is likely to be less accurate than other procedures. The test is often brief. The entire box-of-coins test of honesty consists of a single item that the child passes or fails. The cheating-on-circles test has many "items" in the sense that we could count how many circles have been dotted, but the decision to open one's eyes and cheat is a single decision. One critical act determines the score. This probably accounts for the low magnitude of most correlations between performance tests. Some of the tests may be highly valid, within the limits imposed by inadequate sampling.

Scores on one trial reflect temporary motivation and factors in the immediate situation. Moreover, whereas the person observed in his daily life is in a "steady state," a person tested in a strange situation is working out a fresh adaptation. Whether the person would respond similarly on further trials of the procedure is an open question. For instance, some children who did not steal coins on the one-trial test might do so if retested after some classmate says that he took coins. A conformity test puts the subject in a small group in which everyone else has been coached by the experimenter to give a bad answer. (At the simplest, everyone may be estimating the lengths of lines; when a 12-inch line is displayed, the confederates give answers close to 18 inches before the question comes round to the subject. Does he say "12" or "18"?) Not only did subjects conform less on a second test trial given a week after the first, but those who bowed to group pressure on both occasions had markedly different personalities from those who conformed on the first exposure only (Steiner & Vannoy, 1966).

To estimate the level of consistency requires a generalizability study with, as a minimum, two forms of the test given on separate days by different examiners. For cheating tests there were retest correlations of 0.75 over 6 months and 0.4 between early adolescence and adulthood (Hartshorne & May, vol. 2, pp. 88–89; Jones, 1946). We expect character to change; hence these results are satisfactory. Moreover, they suggest that the cheating test is reasonably accurate.

Generalization over Tasks   Test interpretation ordinarily refers to a broad trait: to "cheating" rather than to "cheating in a test of two-digit multiplication." To sustain the broad interpretation, one must have reasonable consistency across measures of cheating in various school subjects and cheating in tasks not related to school. To sustain a still broader interpretation in terms of "good character," cheating must correlate with honesty in handling money and so on.

A general measure could be built up by combining several tasks, each containing the same common element along with different specifics, but this is almost never practicable. A study evaluating character development might reduce the weight of specific content, however, by applying different tests to different subsamples. A genuine change in the desired direction should show up on all the tests.

Hartshorne and May (1930) established that a general trait cannot be measured by one or two specific behavior samples. Although each deception test was generalizable over forms and time, tasks correlated little with each other. The correlation between cheating on a classroom test and on the Circles test was only 0.5 even after correction for sampling errors. Although the positive correlations indicate a weak general-honesty factor (Burton, 1963), they contradict the notion that honesty is unified. Furthermore, honesty, cooperation, and so on intercorrelated only about 0.25, making untenable the view that a generalized "good character" accounts for desirable actions. Whatever "general factor" there may be in character has small influence on any one type of behavior.

Control for Ability   One tends to think of a personality trait as independent of ability, but the two interpenetrate in perplexing ways. The child who can do his schoolwork does not need to cheat; does his not cheating imply honesty? One should always be aware of the possibility that ability accounts for differences in style, and sometimes it makes sense to adjust scores so as to remove the ability effect.

Thus one might pretest children on arithmetic, sort them into five ability strata, and provide for each stratum a test that causes its members considerable difficulty. Then all children are given some incentive to cheat. A separate analysis at each ability level is advisable. Cheating by a student with a good school record has a different and probably more pathological significance than cheating by an inept student. The same is to be said about anxiety, drive to excel, and so on. Separate analyses of personality data by ability levels might explain many presently conflicting results.

When a personality test confounds a trait with other variables—and this is nearly inevitable—one wants to be sure that the *independent portion* is accurately measured and stable. How much of the 6-month stability of cheating scores results because low achievement is stable, so that the same children have an incentive to cheat? Such questions are rarely examined.

5. *What types of error in character tests do split-half correlations on a single trial ignore?*

6. *It has been suggested that the general factor running through honesty tests may be an indication, not of honesty, but of willingness to accept risk of detection and punishment. Is it possible to design unambiguous tests so as to settle this issue?*

7. *If 9-year-old boys are sorted out on general ability and moral judgment by dividing at the medians, what personalities would you expect in the High-High, Low-Low, High-Low, and Low-High groups?*

TWO STYLISTIC TESTS

Tests of perception borrowed from the laboratory have great value for professionals dealing with cases of possible brain damage. Behavior disorders and learning disabilities may have organic as well as emotional roots; measures of perceptual abilities help in evaluating both the severity and locus of organic impairment. Perceptual tests are useful also with mental patients and in the studying of effects of stress on normals, because perceptual distortions hint at emotional disturbances and disorders of thought processes. I shall discuss here two wide-band tests that have been especially prominent in psychological practice.

The Bender Gestalt and the Rorschach originated in different traditions. (For the respective histories, see Hutt, 1985, and Rabin, 1981.) The former, in which simple patterns are to be copied, grew out of theories of Gestalt psychologists about how the brain processes information; pattern perception was thought to be a sensitive indicator of disturbed functioning. Rorschach, working in the tradition of Freud and Jung, wanted to penetrate to an assumed inner personality. The inkblots have little patterning; there is no "right" answer to "What do you see here?" Rorschach interpreters assume that when external structure is lacking, the response reflects mostly the person's intellectual resources, emotional state, and coping style. Although both techniques can be scored and interpreted as objectively as the Wechsler, their interpretation is usually more elaborate and impressionistic, as we shall see.

In the Bender and the Rorschach, attention centers on the style of response. Such *stylistic* tests may be contrasted with *thematic* tests, in which the interpreter is especially concerned with the content of thoughts and fantasies. The stylistic and thematic categories are not mutually exclusive. Obsessions are sometimes revealed in the Rorschach protocol, and one can observe intellectual style in the Thematic Apperception Test (which the following section of this chapter will take up).

The Bender Gestalt

The Bender Visual Motor Gestalt Test (L. Bender; adapted by Hutt) displays a page of figures (Figure 16.3), which the subject is to copy. Responses may differ in a hundred ways; the performance may be scored

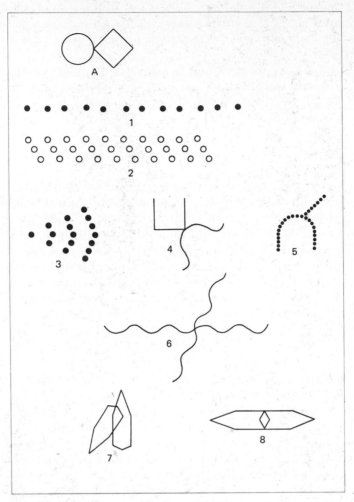

Figure 16.3. **Bender Gestalt patterns to be copied.** These figures are from the Hutt adaptation. In the original Bender version, the figures are arranged differently, and the lines are heavier. (*Source*: Permission has been granted from Lauretta Bender, M.D., and the American Orthopsychiatric Association to reproduce plate 1, Page 4 from the Visual Motor Gestalt Test and Its Clinical Use, published by the American Orthopsychiatric Association in 1938.)

by rules, or the tester's observations may be interpreted clinically. Mercer included the Bender (scored by the rules of Koppitz, 1975) in SOMPA (p. 248) as a screening device, along with physical coordination tests. Disturbance of simple sensorimotor processes is seen by many psychologists as a sign of possible neurological impairment and emotional difficulties. At school entrance, however, scores on the Bender are unstable (as with most pencil-and-paper tests). Moreover, first- and second-graders find drawing so difficult that the Koppitz score is in part a measure of general problem-solving ability. Poor Bender performance at any age above 8 should lead to closer study of a case.

The Bender was seen originally as a near-objective method of identifying pathology, particularly of the nervous system. Some keys count features often seen in records of persons with brain damage. The hit rate is too low to separate these patients from normals and neurotics. Bigler and Ehrfurth (1981), though not denying that poor Bender performance can be a significant signal, demonstrate that some persons with unmistakable brain damage do well on the Bender. Such misses are costly. These authors consider other techniques (including X-ray scanning) much more dependable, and they warn especially against relying on Bender scores alone. For an extensive summary of studies on the Bender, see Buckley (1978, on children) and Tolor and Brannigan (1980).

One bit of evidence for construct validity is particularly neat. In open-heart surgery, the external heart-lung machine creates microemboli (floating particles) that can damage nerve tissues. To test experimentally a filter designed to remove microemboli, the Bender was given before and after the surgical operation to patients in four conditions. Ob-

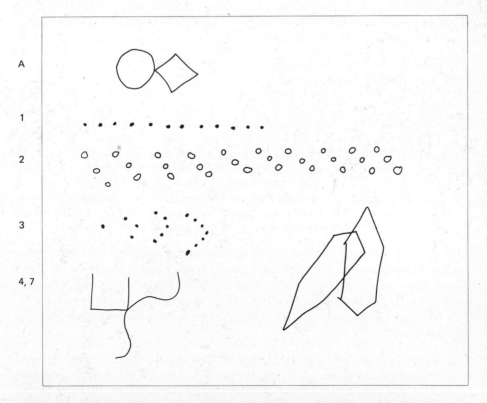

Figure 16.4. **David's Bender reproductions.** (*Source*: Reproduced by permission from Hutt, 1985, p. 192. In this illustration three figures have been omitted.)

jective scoring of the Bender showed which patients' performance deteriorated (perhaps only temporarily). The conditions and findings were as follows (Landis et al., 1974):

1. Bubble oxygenator, no filter   (18,000 emboli/min.)   57%   deteriorated
2. Bubble oxygenator, with filter   (1,800 emboli/min.)   21.5%   deteriorated
3. Membrane oxygenator, no filter   (1,500 emboli/min.)   21.5%   deteriorated
4. Membrane oxygenator, with filter   (100 emboli/min.)   0%   deteriorated

In Chapters 2 and 13, I discussed briefly the impressionistic, dynamic interpretation that derives hypotheses about inner forces from test performance. A report based on the Bender (Hutt, 1985, pp. 191–197) provides a good example of a full-blown clinical interpretation (though a clinician would, of course, prefer to combine information from several sources). The interpreter was given the test record that is partly reproduced in Figure 16.4, along with the minimal information that the patient David is 25 years old, single, with a high school education. My extract will cover only a fraction of the analysis, and I have edited slightly for ease of reading.

David's drawings are basically good. Hutt first notes that the reproduced figures are arranged in the same sequence as in the original, the first six being aligned with the left margin, but that the last two drawings are fitted into the right half of the page.

> Our first hunches then are: this individual has strong orderly, i.e., compulsive needs, tending towards a sort of compulsive ritual, but tries to deny them [the first drawing being displaced away from the margin and the examiner having noted that David draws fast and unhesitatingly] . . ., and he is oppressed with some (probably) generalized feelings of anxiety and (more specifically) personal inadequacy (clings to the left margin and is "constrained" to use all of the space available on this one sheet). We raise at once the question, "How strong and from what source is this anxiety and what is his defense?" We can speculate, from his use of space, that he attempts in some way to "bind" his anxiety, i.e., he cannot tolerate it for long or in large amounts, and that one of the features of this young adult's functioning is the need of control. . . . The super-ego is very strict.

Here Hutt looked at the style of performance, and then tried to infer what inner tensions and defenses could generate such a style. As Hutt said, these are initial hunches to be checked against other evidence in the protocol and against all other information about David.

Among his more detailed analyses, Hutt remarks on the reproduction of pattern 2.

> Further evidence of marked variability. The examiner notes, "Checks number of columns about two-thirds through." The angles of the columns of dots differ, becoming more slanted, with a correction towards the end. The whole figure is exaggerated in the lateral plane. Together, these findings suggest a strong need to relate to people, but difficulty in establishing such

relationships. . . . We have evidence for the presence of considerable internal tension with an attempt at denial of its existence. How can we explain the apparent contradiction of the need for order and control with the speed and variability of performance? His compulsive defenses do not function effectively enough.

As Hutt goes through the remaining drawings, the following traits are mentioned (along with reminders that the interpretation, based on limited information, is tentative): suppressing conscious hostile feelings. . . deferential, conforming. . . depressive reactions. . . feelings of sexual inadequacy. . . high aspiration. . . masochistic needs. . . acting out, impulsivity. . . .

There are more startling things to come. Hutt turns to thematic interpretation, following certain Freudian ideas about "masculine" and "feminine" designs:

> In figure 4, David has increased the vertical sides of the open square. . . .
> His reaction to authority figures can now be inferred more completely: he
> is hostile to such figures, unable to express this hostility directly, and reacts
> either symbolically or impulsively. In line with the "acting out" hypothesis,
> the former is more likely. The curved portion is enlarged, flattened out in
> the middle and reveals an impulsive flourish at the upper end. Now we may
> speculate that David's major identification is with a female figure, but she
> is perceived as more masculine (i.e., dominant, aggressive) than feminine
> and is reacted to openly with antagonism. It is interesting that the upper
> portion of the curved figure extends well above its position on the stimulus
> card, and is at least as high up as the vertical lines. Here we may conjecture
> that David's mother (or surrogate) was stronger psychologically than his fa-
> ther, or at least seemed so and that David would like to use his mother (or
> women) to defy his father (or men).

Hutt is able to give a detailed rationale for each of his inferences. More important, Hutt's description agrees well with the therapist's notes. Here is what the therapist (quoted by Shneidman, 1951, pp. 268–269) said about David:

> He seemed suspicious, indecisive and unable to relax. . . . There seems to
> be considerable guilt in relation to his own hostility. He has established
> some defenses against this through obsession but these defenses are crack-
> ing and he fears that his hostile impulses might become so great that he
> would be unable to control them. . . . The patient seemed obsessed with
> thoughts about death, homicide, and suicide.

Word for word, there is confirmation of hostile impulses David fears to express, ineffectual defense through obsession, and so on. Other remarks of the therapist support some of Hutt's most hazardous-seeming guesses: "The father seems to be a hazy person in the patient's life." "He talked of wishing to strangle his mother." "Had difficulty with authority figures." Hutt learned far more about the depths of personality than one might expect from a little task suitable for a child's drawing exercise.

Hutt's technique has not been favored by clinical psychologists who value objectivity over "insight" and who regard situational variables as more significant than inner dynamics. Even in 1970 Mosher called Hutt's work an anachronism:[1]

> The unusually sensitive clinician, and Hutt is undoubtedly a good example, may well be able to keep these [situationist] assumptions in mind . . .; but the neophyte, the hack, and perhaps even the average clinician, may be more likely to look up a test factor in Hutt's book and conclude that the increase in curvature on figure 4 reveals overactive emotionality. While Hutt cautions against such usage, I doubt that such warnings are sufficient to prevent simplistic "dream book" interpretation.

The Rorschach

Hermann Rorschach, a Swiss psychiatrist, showed that patients of different types respond to inkblots differently. His method, published in 1921, was altered and extended over the years (Beck, 1961–1978; Exner, 1986; Klopfer et al., 1970; Rorschach, 1921/1942). The respondent is to tell what he sees in ten inkblots, blots whose form is so irregular as to permit innumerable interpretations. The blots are calculated to arouse emotional response with their bloody reds, ominous blacks, and luminous grays and with their forms suggestive of nursery animals, overbearing giants, and sex organs. Some patients become agitated while responding to the cards, and impulsiveness or anxiety damages some responses of seemingly normal individuals.

Mischel (1981, p. 192) points out that projective techniques were seen as a "situationless situation," providing so few cues that the responses would have to be generated by forces and associations within the person. It was hoped that responses would reveal motives (guilt, hostility, etc.) the person was unwilling to admit (to others and perhaps to himself). Today it is recognized that the response is a sample of problem-solving behavior in the specific setting of the test, a self-regulated performance. "Hidden" motives may operate, but much else determines the response.

Scoring and Interpretation   Rorschach interpretation begins with rather objective scoring. The major scores are concerned with number of responses, location, determinants, and content. Location scores count how many responses use the whole blot (W), obvious subdivisions (D), or details (Dd). The determinant scores consider how form, color, movement, and shading influence responses. "Movement" (M), for example, is scored when the response describes humans in motion. CF is scored when the response depends on form and color, with color more signifi-

---

cant. Form is scored + or −, according to the fit between the response and the stimulus. Finally, responses are assigned to content categories.

The scoring of four responses will illustrate the procedure. Card X is a mixture of brightly colored forms. Consider these four responses:

1. A big splashy print design for a summer dress.
2. Enlarged photograph of a snowflake [refers to a large irregularly shaped area].
3. Two little boys blowing bubbles. You just see them from the waist up.
4. Head of a rabbit.

Follow-up questions provide part of the basis for this scoring:

Response	Location	Determinant and form level	Content
1	W	CF +	Art, Clothing
2	D	F −	Nature
3	D	M +	Part of human
4	D	F +	Part of animal

The quality of responses indicates something about intellectual level and carefulness. Much is made of evidence on control over impulses and emotions. Movement responses are thought to represent imagination and creative impulses arising from within. Color responses are thought to represent emotional reactions to external stimuli. Responses true to the forms in the blot imply attentiveness to reality. A person who harmonizes form and movement is said to use constructively his inner impulses; a person who rarely reports a movement response is regarded as lacking in imagination or as repressing it.

The flavor of Rorschach interpretation is illustrated in the following fragment from a case report by Palmer (1983, p. 379); the interpretation is part of a larger story based on TAT plus interviews with Larry and his parents. Larry, a 15-year-old from a "good" family, had been arrested twice for possession of marijuana; he felt oppressed by his father (even adding "sir" when he swore at him), forged a report card to appease his father, and consequently was expelled from school.

> Although Larry gave 33 responses to the Rorschach inkblots, many of which were quite detailed and imaginative, only 2 could be scored as containing the human figures in action, 1 of which was the popular response to Card III. In contrast, 9 of his responses were primarily based on the color of the cards and 5 were scored CF. This experience balance indicated that Larry remained chiefly dependent on cues from his environment and that little had been internalized. . . .
>
> [C]onsiderable feelings of tension and anxiety [were] evidenced by responses such as the one to Card IX, which he described as a volcanic explosion, the dark colors showing fire and lava and the pastel shading indicating gas and clouds. . . . Other responses also suggested a considerable underly-

ing depression and overt anxiety, such as those to Card IV, which he saw as the kind of stove used in military barracks, bulging out a cloud of black smoke.

In 8 different responses he was fascinated by the white space; the most significant of these appeared on Card VII (often the card that is associated with feelings about maternal figures), which Larry saw as "a gaping canyon surrounding such high cliffs that no one can possibly descend into it." The psychologist interpreted Larry's attention to the empty space as indicating not only negativism and resistance but also feelings of emptiness and depression.

Validation of Hypotheses There has been considerable formal research on the hypotheses that enter such interpretations, but the complexity of the technique has made comprehensive research exceedingly difficult (Zubin et al., 1965, pp. 193–239). Sometimes the evidence is strikingly favorable, sometimes not.

Rorschach (1942, p. 7) said that movement responses are indicative of personalities that "function more in the intellectual sphere, whose interests gravitate more towards their intrapsychic living rather than towards the world outside themselves." Support is seen in ratings made by clinical assessors using other data (Barron, 1955). Persons with strong M tendencies were described by the independent observers as inventive, having wide interests, introspective, concerned with self as object, valuing cognitive pursuits. Those giving few M responses were described as practical, stubborn, preferring action to contemplation, and inflexible in thought and action.

Hundreds of additional studies could be cited, each dealing with one bit of Rorschach lore. About half of the experimental tests of Rorschach hypotheses give results consistent with clinical theory. The interpretation certainly has "validity greater than chance." On the other hand, relationships of Rorschach indicators with particular traits are not strong. Many personality factors and abilities influence any one score, and no direct interpretation can be made with confidence.

Composites of scores have been proposed as trait measures or as predictors of criteria (of presence of organic brain damage, for example). Generally, these formulas prove valueless on cross-validation, having no validity or too many false positives. The responses do provide a basis for judging the adequacy of thought processes. Exner (1986, pp. 434ff.) discusses how this information along with facts about the person's life situation and feelings can be the starting point for a therapeutic plan.

8. *Why might a "perfect" Rorschach accuracy score, 100 per cent F +, suggest a personality pattern that is undesirable for many situations?*

9. *Do the Rorschach scores related to quality of output reveal maximum ability or typical behavior? How does the Rorschach compare with the Binet test in that respect?*

THEMATIC TESTS

Thematic tests elicit open or disguised statements of beliefs, attitudes, and motives. Within that definition, nearly all self-report tests are thematic. Among unstructured thematic techniques we might count the Rep test and a request that the person write (or tell) his life story. A handful of projective tests, including sentence completion and story completion, are primarily thematic. It is hoped that the person will produce responses whose psychological significance he does not fully realize. The pictorial Thematic Apperception Test has been most used and has had the greatest influence on research.

The TAT and Its Meaning

The Thematic Apperception Test (TAT; C. Morgan and H. A. Murray) asks the test taker to interpret a picture by telling a story—what is happening, what led up to the scene, what will be the outcome. It is presumed that the person projects himself into the scene, identifying with a character just as he vicariously takes the place of the actor when he sees a film. TAT consists of 20 pictures, some of the pictures being different for men and women. Since two 1-hour sessions are required for the full test, testers ordinarily use selected cards.

TAT, designed to cover the whole range of ideas and behavior, cannot cover any topic thoroughly. Although a person obsessed with independence conflicts may bring them into story after story, most people reveal feelings about authority only on one or two cards. Any single picture is indefinite enough to bring out different types of information from different persons. Flexibility that permits the respondent to reveal almost any trait or theme prominent in his personality structure is an advantage in a free-ranging exploration of personality. It is a serious disadvantage when one wishes to answer a specific question.

Focused tests are designed to elicit thematic responses that bear on a single question. For example, Murphy and Likert (1938) carried out research on labor-management conflict with pictures of, for example, strikers in conflict with police. A focused test for fliers was based on the hypothesis that outwardly directed aggression would be associated with tolerance for high centrifugal forces. The criterion was a measure of the force required to produce blackout in a human centrifuge. In the best-designed of several validation studies, the score from the thematic test classified 18 of 25 subjects correctly as having high or low tolerance (Silverman et al., 1957).

Formal Scores   For a synoptic test like TAT, it is possible to develop scoring rules for dozens of variables: reaction to difficult tasks, originality, reliance on luck and magical intervention, the percentage of stories

with unhappy outcomes, the number of female characters seen as predatory, and so on. Formal TAT scoring most often emphasizes "needs"
—concerns for achievement, affiliation, power, and the like. Two-month
stability coefficients are in the range from 0.6 to 0.9 for such scores as
abasement themes, giving stories with positive outcomes, and presence
of words referring to relief of tension. When one recognizes the variety
of scores obtained from an hour or two of testing, this quality of information is impressive.

The TAT tradition, however, is oriented to impressionistic interpretation and not formal scoring. For most users, the scores are a preliminary memorandum. One user after another developed her own pet scoring system to the point where "there would seem to be as many thematic
scoring systems as there were hairs in the beard of Rasputin" (Murstein,
1963, p. 23).

Impressionistic Interpretation The stories may indicate a defeatist attitude, concern about overbearing authority figures, preoccupation with
sex, and so on. The interpreter also considers such stylistic matters as
fluency and concern with accuracy in fitting the story to the picture.

The interpreter looks at each story in turn, deriving hypotheses from
the plot, the symbolism, and the style. The hypothesis from one story
(e.g., "This man represses hostile feelings") is checked against subsequent stories. The interpreter must weigh conflicting indications and
must integrate information on intellectual powers, emotional conflicts,
and defense mechanisms.

A few illustrations of the impressionistic analysis can be given. Card
I of TAT shows a boy, perhaps 10 years old, looking at a violin lying on
a flat surface. A girl, age 14, told this story (Henry, 1956, p. 111):

> Right now the boy is looking at the violin. It looks like he might be kind of
> sad or mad because he has to play. Before he might have played ball with
> the other boys and his mother wouldn't let him. He had to go in and play.
> Looks like he might practice for a little while and then sneak out.

Henry commented on how clearly the story "takes into account the basic
stimulus demands of the picture" and goes on to "entirely relevant elab-
orations of good quality . . . [which] attribute motive and action to the
characters." Henry correctly placed the girl's general ability at or above
the 95th percentile.

The response of a 42-year-old clerk is interpreted thematically (p.
145):

> The story behind this is that this is the son of a very well-known, a very
> good musician and the father has probably died. The only thing the son has
> left is this violin which is undoubtedly a very good one and to the son, the
> violin is the father and the son sits there daydreaming of the time that he
> will understand the music and interpret it on the violin that his father had
> played.

The first sentence shows preoccupation with excellence, Henry says, and a conviction that to match the example is impossible. The man dreams of things within himself, and takes no action to carry out his ambition.

A third story, told by a 29-year-old male recently come to the United States, is interpreted metaphorically (Henry, p. 178):

> A young boy sitting in front of a violin spread out on white table, or white linen. It is not clear in the expression of the face if he thinks in glorification and admiration of what the violin and music could hold for him or if he is bored and in disgust with the lesson he has to take and doesn't want.

Note, says Henry, the emphasis on conflicting alternatives: glorification or disgust, has to take and doesn't want. This personality "may well be marked by its attraction to opposites." The core of conflict appears to be sexual, the basic issue being whether woman can be

> both the Madonna and the sexual object. . . . This is an instance of the use of the violin as a sexual symbol. The man is basically preoccupied with some strong emotional issue; hence he utilizes form details in a distorting manner [e.g., "violin spread out"]. . . . He feels impelled to make a formal heterosexual adjustment as well as a conventional social adjustment, even though both are somewhat forced and against his will.

These excerpts by no means represent the intricacy of a full interpretation in which stories are compared with each other and with background information. For examples of full interpretations see Henry (1956). Interpretations are extremely tentative if the psychologist is properly trained. They are discarded unless supporting evidence shows up elsewhere in the test or the person's history. These illustrations do indicate the individuality of TAT responses and the variation in the interpreter's attack.

Correlates of Responses

Relation to Other Behavior   It is too simple to say that the stories describe what the person does or would like to do. Yet if there were no correspondence with behavior, the information from fantasy would seem irrelevant. Nonchance correspondence turns up with some frequency, but relations are often puzzling (Varble, in McReynolds, 1971).

Frequency of behavioral aggression correlated with aggression themes in stories given by problem boys. Fear of punishment judged from overt behavior correlated with frequency of mention of punishment in stories. The trait configuration matters. Every one of the seven boys with high TAT aggression and *low* fear of punishment behaved very aggressively; only two out of nine with high TAT aggression and *high* fear of punishment acted aggressively (Mussen & Naylor, 1954). In another study, a score representing *inhibition* of aggression and denial of aggressive impulses correlated as strongly with aggressive action as did presence of aggressive TAT plots (Skolnick, 1966). Olweus (1969) made a careful theoretical elaboration and obtained strong evidence for it. Among boys whose tests showed little inhibition, strength of aggressive themes correlated around 0.5 with rated overt aggression; among inhibitors, the correlation was about −0.5. A comparable result emerged when aggressive behavior of patients in a neuropsychiatric hospital was rated by attendants (Pittluck, 1950). Aggressive behavior went with aggressive TAT stories; but the patient whose stories muffled the aggression (by introducing a plot justification or some other mechanism) was much more likely to control his aggression in the ward. To summarize: A "dimension" of response (e.g., large number of aggressive themes) cannot be interpreted except in the context of a theory that considers other variables in person and situation.

Transient Situational Influences Situational factors influence TAT performance, as was neatly demonstrated by Clark (1952). He gave TAT to college men after having presented a series of slides of nude females on the pretext that rating their sexual attractiveness had something to do with studying relations of body type to personality in a psychology course. The control group, meanwhile, had been kept busy rating landscapes. On TAT, 66 per cent of the controls gave responses high in sex imagery, compared to 27 per cent among experimentals. One might well conclude that taking sexual drives out for exercise reduces their intensity. But Clark destroys that interpretation by another experiment, essentially repeating the first one but in the context of a fraternity beer party. Sexual content was higher than in the classroom experiment, but a score that cut off the highest 26 per cent of the controls cut off 60 (!) per cent of the experimentals. Clark's interpretation is that guilt over sexual arousal in the classroom served to inhibit sexual responses on TAT. We do not know how many sexual responses came to the subjects' minds in the first experiment and were suppressed.

The way the TAT is administered has a substantial effect on validity, according to Lundy (1988). Part of his evidence comes from an experiment with testing technique (in which high school classes gave written responses). Criteria reflected affiliation, achievement, and power motives seen in the students' life activities. Validities were about 0.3 with one set of directions, and tended to be tiny or negative with others (for example, those giving cues that TAT was "a personality test"). The directions that produced validity were neutral, intended to induce a relaxed, self-expressive mind set.

The sensitivity of thematic tests enhances their validity as experimental measures of motivational states. Among the most interesting of the studies is one on parachutists. Fenz and Epstein (1962) prepared pictures having high, low, or no relevance to parachuting. (See Figure 16.5.) Members of a sport parachuting club were tested on the day when

Figure 16.5. **Thematic pictures to measure reactions of parachutists.** (*Source*: Fenz & Epstein, 1962. Reprinted with permission from *Journal of Personality*, vol. 30, no. 3. Copyright © 1962 by Duke University Press.)

they were scheduled to jump and also either 2 weeks before or 2 weeks after the jump (with a parallel set of pictures). The parachutists were much more aroused on the day of the jump. The skin conductance measure of Table 16.1 is a "sweaty palm" reaction; just showing a picture related to parachuting on the day of the jump produced a flash of tension. Whereas stories produced on the day of the jump carry a positive message about parachuting (more so than on the nonjump day), many of these stories are so exaggerated that they suggested deliberate denial of

Table 16.1   PHYSIOLOGICAL RESPONSE OF PARACHUTISTS
TO THEMATIC PICTURES

Relevance of picture to parachuting	Mean response of nonparachutist controls	Mean response of parachutists	
		2 weeks from jump	On day of jump
None	1.0	0.7	1.1
Low	0.8	0.8	1.3
High	0.9	1.0	2.2

Source: Fenz & Epstein, 1962; see also Fenz, 1964.

fear; e.g., "He is not afraid at all, just looks that way because of the wind that is blowing in his face. He will have a wonderful jump. It will be great, just great!"

10. *Harrison (1965, p. 590) says that negative evidence on TAT should be given much less credence than positive evidence:*

    Negative validity results ... do not necessarily constitute damaging evidence, for the researchers may have employed improper methods of analysis in confounded designs against unreliable or otherwise inadequate criteria. ... Positive results do demonstrate something, assuming that the work has been done honestly and that grievous errors have not been introduced into the design.

    What are the merits and demerits of this position? Is it pertinent only to projective tests?

11. *How many traits are mentioned in Henry's three interpretations?*

12. *Can one regard the frequency of punishment by authority in TAT stories as an indication of how often the respondent has been punished in life?*

INTEGRATIVE ASSESSMENT

As we have seen, a psychologist studying the nuances of performance on a single test such as the Wechsler or Bender, in the light of the person's background, can reach broad conclusions. Typically, however, the study of an individual calls upon a variety of information.

In clinical practice with adults and children, diverse information—medical and neurological; from family members, teachers, or work associates; from interviewing the subject; possibly from observation in classroom or ward—is brought together with whatever tests seem relevant. A staff conference is commonly the means of integration, as staff members have seen the person in different settings and apply different expertise. Comprehensive assessment is wanted to evaluate the seriousness of difficulties and lay out remedial plans (environmental or therapeutic). A comparison of initial and later assessments guides further stages of case management and provides data for program evaluation. The extent and formality of analysis will differ with the problem, the resources available, and the professional theories favored by the staff. I shall not describe clinical decision making, turning instead to efforts at comprehensive assessment of persons who are functioning adequately. The issues and general conclusions to be developed are relevant to clinical practice.

History of Assessment Programs

In the United States, thinking about normal personalities during the last 50 years has evolved particularly from the base laid at the Harvard Psychological Clinic, where Henry A. Murray led or taught many who became eminent contributors. R. W. White's account (in Rabin, 1981) of the origins of the influential *Explorations in Personality* (Murray et al., 1938) reminds us that Murray's was a team approach. Orientations of team members ranged widely: Freudian, Jungian, medical, anthropological, experimental. A diverse set of investigations and novel observing procedures were put in place, each under one staff member. Approximately 50 students were enlisted to serve as subjects for *all* the investigations. The staff tried to arrive at a shared understanding of the students and worked out a framework for thinking about personality.

Situational forces were given almost as much weight as internal motives. Motives (conscious and unconscious), perceptions, and world views were considered more fundamental than patterns of overt action; this phenomenological emphasis is evident in the TAT, which emerged from the project. The person was viewed as an active problem solver, interpreting new social demands in the light of his needs and applying a preferred coping strategy.

The thinking was turned to practical use when the wartime Office of Strategic Services (OSS, a predecessor of the CIA) needed a thorough psychological screening of prospective employees, some of whom would be assigned to covert operations and some to unglamorous desk work. Part of the assessment staff came from the Harvard team. The assessment methods included situational tests that had been pioneered by German military assessors and extended by British officer selection boards (Wiggins, 1973, Chap. 11). Because the assignments of most of the recruits were unforeseeable and because of the great variety of assignments, job analysis was impossible, and the secrecy of the work precluded the usual cycles of tryout and feedback. The assessors, therefore, had to appraise adaptability, vigor, and reaction to stress on the basis of unvalidated indicators.

"House party" assessments of 2 or 3 days permitted the team to observe candidates in off hours as well as in structured discussions and tasks. As many as 35 separate procedures were used to collect data, including conventional tests, peer ratings, interviews, role playing, and projective and performance tests. Some tasks were assigned to groups to permit observations of social interaction. Among several procedures designed to observe response to stress and frustration, the candidate was asked to direct two men in building a wooden structure; the helpers had been coached to be clumsy and sluggish or disrespectful. As at Harvard, the assessors came together to agree on a final report. They rejected some applicants and, for those accepted, pointed out qualities to be considered in making assignments.

Validity information from the OSS experience was necessarily sketchy, and the main report made only modest claims to success (OSS Assessment Staff, 1948). Wiggins (1973, p. 536) reworked the data considering base rate and selection ratio; he figured that the assessors judged 77 per cent of the cases correctly and that this was enough above the chance hit rate of 63 per cent to provide worthwhile payoff.

In the ensuing decade, various assessment projects were carried out, partly for practical purposes, partly to validate and improve assessment methods. Included were studies of students entering training in clinical psychology (Kelly & Fiske, 1951; Kelly & Goldberg, 1959) and psychiatry (Holt & Luborsky, 1958), of British civil servants (P. E. Vernon, 1950), of American officer candidates (Holtzman & Sells, 1954; Holmen et al., 1956); and Peace Corps volunteers (see Wiggins, 1973). Particularly notable was the extended work of a diverse staff at the Institute for Personality Assessment and Research (IPAR) at Berkeley; I have referred earlier to fragments of their work on architects (p. 559) and mathematicians (p. 593). The validation reports from these several studies were not wholly negative, as we shall see; but it was discouraging to find that an expensive and elaborate technique produced validities comparable to those achieved with a few structured predictors. The impressionistic, dynamic interpretations seemed to make no contribution.

Today the principal residue of this line of effort is in assessments of executives (Finkle, in Dunnette, 1976; Thornton & Byham, 1982). A program to select executive trainees for telephone companies (Bray & Grant, 1966) is regarded as a particular success, and 1000 other firms choose trainees in a similar manner. The method is also used in selecting police and military officers. These activities are far more conservative than the earlier waves of assessments, with greater reliance on face-valid work samples and little explicit attention to personality (Bray, 1982). Whereas the earlier assessments were made by assessment professionals, psychologists and managers usually serve together as assessors of executives. As we shall see, the evidence on validity is favorable.

Specialized Tests for Organizational Behavior

Before reviewing the reports on validity, I describe two further standardized test procedures; they or their close cousins play a part in most current executive assessment. The first, the in-basket technique, requires the person to play the role of manager. (It is a simplified version of the Island Story test from British house-party assessment, in which the candidate was to imagine himself appointed chief administrator of a remote island, to digest a large file of information, and then to resolve problems.) The second, the Leaderless Group Discussion, also descends from a house-party technique.

The In-Basket Test   An in-basket used by the Sears firm is described as follows (Lopez, 1966):

> The candidate for appointment or promotion is told to assume that he has just been assigned to replace a store manager in Exville, who is out of action

with a heart attack. It is Sunday; he must go to the store today and in three hours cope with problems on the manager's desk. He cannot reach other employees on Sunday, and, because he has a trip to make, anything postponed must await his return on Thursday. He receives a chart of the store organization and a personnel list. The basket contains 37 "items"—letters, memos, policy papers for review, forms to sign, etc.—realistically done up on Sears forms. (But familiarity with company practice gives no real advantage.) Having disposed of as many items as he can by decision, referral, or whatever, the man writes down his reason for each action.

Various scores are obtained, including productivity (number of items dealt with), depth or thoughtfulness of response, and sensitivity to human relations. Scorers may also write descriptive reports on the style displayed. Frederiksen et al. (1972) describe several other in-baskets and reproduce 50 pages from one of them. Although our concern here is with assessment of individuals, it should be noted that in-baskets are also used for training and for checking on the effects of training. Moreover, Frederiksen et al. showed that, for purposes of research on organizational characteristics, the baskets could be designed to simulate alternative styles of organization (e.g., rule-bound).

Although the in-basket has appealing face validity, it is limited as a measuring device. The person's many responses are interrelated because the person is playing a consistent role. Scores on one basket generally correlate around 0.3 with scores on the same variable from another basket; thus each basket is acting like a one-item test. Reliability rises to 0.5 for a few important stylistic variables such as courtesy shown in communications (Frederiksen et al., 1972, pp. 66, 154–157). Distributions on many variables are strongly skewed; that is, few respondents exhibit the characteristic often. (For example, the average score on "goal setting" was approximately 1 per cent of the maximum possible.) Skewness reduces correlations with criteria. For the two least skewed variables in one study, the in-basket score correlated about 0.3 with supervisor ratings (Brass & Oldham, 1976). The in-basket may gain some of its validity by duplicating information obtainable more cheaply by a conventional ability test, and it gives peers and assessors less basis for forming impressions than does observed performance in a group situation.

As with other complex assessments, the required value judgments are hard to make. Courtesy is to be appreciated, but does it contribute greatly to effectiveness? When the respondent prefers face-to-face communication to resolving a problem by a memo, is that to be regarded as a good or bad sign? In the absence of research on the job in a particular institution, the interpreter has to rely on some stereotyped theory of good management.

Group Discussions   In the Leaderless Group Discussion (LGD) a group of persons are told to discuss, for example, how to increase movie attendance. The LGD is unstructured: no rules of procedure are established, the topic is left largely undefined, and the group (whose members first met at the assessment center) have no established friendships or dominance relations. Social patterns build up quickly, and the role the person plays is presumably similar to the role he is prone to adopt elsewhere.

The variables observers commonly are asked to rate have to do with prominence, goal facilitation (efficiency, suggesting useful ideas), and sociability. The LGD also provides part of the acquaintance needed to make peer ratings, which are typically part of the assessment.

The effectiveness of LGD can be evaluated in several ways. Stability over trials is fairly high; with a week between tests, the correlations range from 0.75 to 0.9. Over longer time intervals or with radical changes in the type of problem, correlations drop to about 0.5. The test is measuring some consistent and general aspect of personality. Behavior in practical situations is no doubt determined by many forces other than personality (seniority, relative prestige, specifically relevant knowledge, etc.), but LGD scores nonetheless have predictive value. Bass and Coates (1952) compared LGD scores with ratings by superiors given as much as 9 months later and found correlations of 0.4. Arbous (1955) found a validity of 0.6 for LGD against rated promise of executives in training. Suitability for the British foreign service as rated after 2 years on duty was predicted (validity 0.3) by LGD at the time of selection (P. E. Vernon, 1950).

LGD illustrates the advantage that can be obtained from systematic observations. Social relations are important in personnel assignment, yet difficult to judge validly from questionnaires, letters of recommendation, or interviews. LGD is an economical "work sample" of group behavior. It avoids much of the bias inherent in summary impressions. Army colonels' ratings of cadet potential were much poorer predictors of later merit ratings than were total scores recorded by these same colonels acting as observers for an LGD session (Bass, 1954).

No doubt LGD is "fakable." The applicant who wants to make an impression surely will say more and try to lead. But this only increases the validity of the technique. If he lacks social skills, his ineptness will be clear to the observer. If he "puts on a good show," he is likely to put on an equally good show on a job, where he is motivated to display the same skills.

Validity, Past and Present

My review of the many reports on validity—some rudimentary and some exhaustively detailed—will be synoptic and selective; for fuller summaries, see Dunnette (in McReynolds, 1971), Finkle (in Dunnette, 1976), Gaugler et al. (1987), and Wiggins (1973).

The First Wave One finding noted early and confirmed often was that assessors obtain their best results when predicting toward a known criterion, applicable to all persons accepted. P. E. Vernon (1950), reporting on house-party assessment of executive-level civil servants, emphasizes the contribution job analysis made to the positive results. (Also, training the observers brought considerable improvement; Vernon & Parry, 1949.) The final assessment predicted grades in a training course with validity 0.8. (That, in a group with restricted range! Is it possible that the criterion raters were acquainted with the assessment ratings?) Ratings on the job were predicted with r's of 0.5 and above. Judges who observed the work sample performance provided particularly valid impressions; peer ratings were somewhat valid; written tests were next to useless.

The most noteworthy finding from the study of clinical psychologists (Kelly & Fiske, 1951, p. 169) was that clinical competence (as rated by whoever supervised a trainee's internship) was predicted with validity 0.37 on the basis of only the credentials file plus ability tests and inventories. That is not bad, considering the weakness of the criterion. More important, validity did not rise above 0.42 when the case conference also took into account reports from interviews and projective tests. Judgments based on all these data *plus* performance tests produced a validity of 0.37. Another blow to projective tests came in a study where entering aviation cadets took a group inkblot test, a sentence-completion test, a psychosomatic inventory, and so on. Authorities on projective methods could not do better than chance in identifying trainees who had to be eliminated when they developed overt personality disturbances (Holtzman & Sells, 1954).

Criterion inadequacy had sad consequences for a validation on U.S. Air Force captains (Wiggins, 1973, pp. 539–543, based on unpublished technical reports by D. W. MacKinnon and others.) The several criteria of officer effectiveness supplied by the Air Force intercorrelated only 0.3. The assessors could predict these criteria with validities around 0.1 to 0.2—disappointing, but how can one hope to predict inconsistent criteria? Impressions formed by observation seemed to have some validity, whereas neither objective nor projective test scores predicted better than chance.

The difficulties of assessment on the basis of inferred personality structure reflect the inadequacies of human judgment that appear even in well-structured predictions (p. 569). Beyond that, the attempt to use information of many kinds, related to many aspects of the person, presented a task beyond the reach of personality theory in this generation. Luborsky's (1954) poignant remarks about the study of psychiatrists no doubt apply to many other dynamic assessments: "Reviewing some predictions on which we erred, we were impressed with our correct assessment of many specific qualities and our inability to cast these up into proper balance so as to judge ability to develop skill as a psychiatrist."

Figure 16.6 makes evident how difficult a task the assessors undertook. Along each path from top to bottom, the chart identifies some

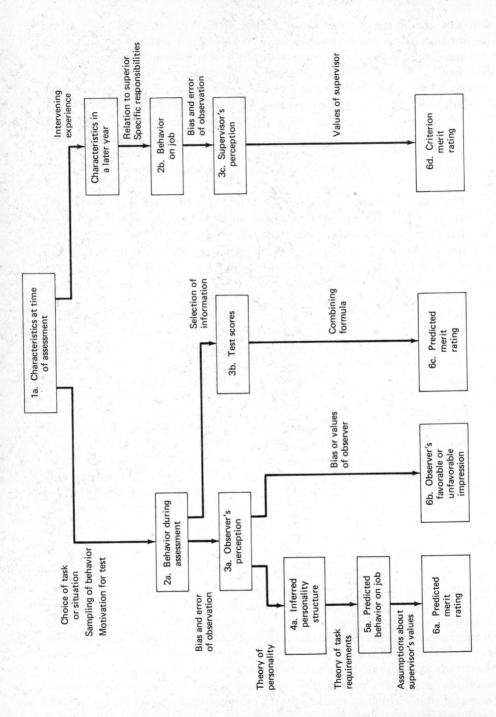

Figure 16.6. Stages in assessment and in criterion development.

sources of change in behavior and some limitations on inference. At the upper left, attention is drawn to the fact that the observer collects fragmentary samples of performance. Below box 2a, the left-hand branch represents impressionistic assessment, and the branch leading to the center of the chart refers to statistical-actuarial prediction. Obviously, the adequacy of prediction by formula depends on the relevance of the scores and the data from which the formula was derived, but subjectivity is not a source of error. The simplest assessment, leading to box 6b, stands or falls with the judgment of the assessor. Some of this error can be ironed out by combining observers, but invalid shared stereotypes (e.g., of what a psychiatrist should be) survive in the average.

Complex dynamic assessment (at the far left) is more vulnerable. There is, first of all, a mapping of perceptions onto a theory of personality, from which conclusions are drawn about the person's inner motives, conflicts, and constructs. Then the assessor must draw, from observation of persons in the occupation or from her imaginings, a conception of the roles the jobholder should perform and combine this with the image of the personality in order to judge whether the person will fit into the role. Even that is not the end, for prediction of a criterion rating has to go beyond job performance to what the supervisor will think of that performance. As indicated on the right side of the chart, behavior on the job (2b) is not the criterion; the criterion is attenuated or biased by the same processes of observation and judgment that impair predictive assessments. The attempts at generalized assessments for the wide range of duties in the OSS and the wide range of roles clinical psychologists and psychiatrists play could at best point toward generalized stereotypes of job requirements. One of the clearest messages from personnel research is the contribution job analysis makes to silhouetting the predictor's target.

Assessment of Executives   Not surprisingly, current assessment projects have taken a conservative turn. They make predictions essentially of type 6b, and they place much of the burden of judgment not on psychologists coming from a distance but on managers and supervisors who know the work demands and standards of the employing firm. The behavior sampled is largely matched to the characteristics overtly to be observed on the job—social interaction, for example. Even when projective techniques are used, the evaluation concentrates on indications of ambition and other qualities desired in executives. The company has constructed an image of the kind of person it wants as executive, so the assessors have a good chance to recognize who will please the company. If the company template is not a sound one, "valid" prediction of judgments made on the job may not be picking the executives who would do the company the most good.

Validity coefficients with global criteria of managerial performance or with rate of advancement in rank or salary as criteria have often exceeded 0.4. On the other hand, the average validity over 47 reports was only 0.3 (Gaugler et al., 1987). Cascio and Silbey (1979) review such experience and argue that the cost of an assessment technique should not deter its use for positions where a firm gains many thousands of dollars by assigning the responsibility to a better-qualified person.

Telephone company assessors made an explicit prediction as to who would or would not reach a middle-management post within 10 years. Among college graduates, the percentage who reached middle management 6 to 8 years later was 50 for those judged favorably and 11 for those judged doubtful; for the noncollege group, the corresponding proportions were 37 and 5 (Bray & Grant, 1966; for later histories, see Bray, 1982). In this study and the one to be described next, assessments were not reported to the company, and the criteria could not have been contaminated. (That is not the case in the majority of validations of assessments.)

In Table 16.2 we see that criterion rankings 2 years after an assessment tended to confirm what was originally said about strengths and weaknesses, as well as about overall merit. Although the literature taken all together suggests validity "greater than chance," I judge that the relationship of assessment profiles to criterion profiles is weak and inconsistent. Still, firms want advice about what assignment to consider for each individual.

Many attempts have been made to determine which procedures contribute most to the assessment, but studies are too small to produce clear evidence. Every technique is supported as making an independent contribution by one research report or another. The following turn up repeatedly as showing direct validity against the criterion, influence on assessors' final ratings, and some degree of independence from the other predictors:

Straightforward measures of academic ability.

Interview to assess energy and motivation.

Table 16.2   CORRELATION OF CRITERION RANKINGS WITH ASSESSMENTS OF MARKETING MANAGERS

Predictions of success by assessors	Judgments made on the job		
	Forecasting-budgeting	Sales	Interpersonal relationships
Forecasting-budgeting	**0.5**	0.15	0.35
Sales	0.0	**0.6**	0.4
Interpersonal relationships	0.0	0.25	**0.45**

Source: Albrecht et al., 1964, p. 356.

Note: The intercorrelations of the three predictions ranged from 0.45 to 0.7; N = 31. Rankings from several informants were pooled in the criterion.

Business simulations.

LGD.

Peer ratings of likability or social effectiveness.

No one can say whether objective scoring of the performance tests would have an advantage over the usual practice of rating the performances, but subjective evaluation seems natural to managers and adds to the appeal of the recommendations. Another open question is whether the integrative conference produces a final rating of overall merit that is more valid than the unweighted sum of scores or ratings from four or five procedures.

The good reputation of assessment centers illustrates the general qualities that have been associated with nearly all the more successful applications of testing. The approach is empirical, does not depend on psychological theory, and is intellectually and socially conservative.

By empiricism, I refer to the checking of test scores against other sources of evidence to determine what interpretative concepts or predictions are valid. The leaders in the development of assessment centers kept appraisals of early trials locked in files for years while they amassed case histories to determine which clues to rely on and how adequate the assessment was. The move away from assessment of personality "in depth" was dictated by follow-up findings; the state of the art in this generation clearly did not justify basing personnel decisions on dynamic interpretation. The empirical tradition goes back to Binet, who, you will recall, tried an almost endless variety of tests in order to find the ones most reflective of intellectual functioning.

Little or no theory enters into the interpretation of peer ratings or MCT or a self-report of clerical interests. Knowledge has developed around particular instruments such as the Wechsler, the MMPI, and the Strong. If any such body of interpreted experience constitutes "theory," it has not shaped or been much shaped by the remainder of psychological theory. Binet snatched up instruments from any source and let his own results rather than the existing theory determine his scale. Murray was equally eclectic, demonstrating his distrust of any theory by calling on all the theories simultaneously. Content-valid tests and the actuarial approach get little help from theory. One reason for the distance between the study of test data and the larger body of psychological ideas is the traditional emphasis of experimental psychology on elementary stimuli, processes, and reactions; it is hard to connect the findings with complex processes. It is perplexing that Piaget's elaborate theory, which dealt with complex processes from the outset, left so little trace on practical psychological testing. Piagetian constructs did shed light on test performance, and mental tests predicted Piagetian performances, but only with respect to moral judgment did Piaget's ideas inspire collection of information not available from conventional tests.

Empirical medicine was practiced with only modest success in the centuries before the germ theory of disease and modern pharmacology revolutionized medicine. The day will surely come when new theory revolutionizes thought about individuality and the procedures by which people are characterized. Perhaps the emergent theory of information processing will lead to a revolution in testing; if not, it will nonetheless amplify and amend test interpretations.

Current assessment is conservative. The assessors try to find out who will fit into the firm as it now operates. They take peer ratings seriously, having established that those who impress associates in one situation are likely to make a good impression on similar persons in other situations. The assessment is manifestly designed to find out who will fit into the system as it stands. So is setting up an actuarial table to indicate which candidates for parole are most likely to commit new crimes if released.

TOWARD AN ECOLOGICAL VIEW

A social scientist or philosopher taking a detached view of the systems where tests are applied would raise questions about the standard ways of operating. Might it be possible to modify the firm or its conception of effective management? To modify the college and its conception of success? To provide supports for the parolee that would make recidivism less likely? One can scarcely criticize those asked to provide predictions for doing that as well as possible, but someone should be scrutinizing the criterion and all the aspects of training, supervision, and the institutional organization that lead up to the criterion. Such questions are raised at times, as in studies of the difference between rule-bound and flexible organizations (p. 168) and in efforts of colleges to assist individuals who would be unlikely to survive if admitted on a sink-or-swim basis. The contributions of psychological testing to the redesign of services, however, have been much less conspicuous than its contributions to organizational continuity.

Social science, including psychology, is quite good at assessing the current state of affairs, at building up experience tables, at making short inferences. Forecasts are necessarily imperfect. No problem has been studied more exhaustively than the prediction of college marks, and the predictions still contain a considerable measure of error. That is inherent in the richness of the choices available to the student (not all of them academic), the variety of accomplishments and shortcomings that are averaged into the grade record, and, of course, the unforeseeable intrusions of illness and family problems and luck-of-the-draw in roommates and teachers. The point to emphasize is not the limits of prediction—which, in this essentially static institution, have very nearly been reached—but the excellence of a conservative technology.

The central problem for testers is that long-reach inferences have to be made. They will be made with or without the aid of tests, with or without the aid of social science knowledge and social technology. Someone has to decide whether this youngster will be held in an institution or placed in a foster home or returned to a parent. Someone (or some bureau) must decide who shall be eligible for expensive forms of therapy covered by third-party payments such as Medicare. The government of Venezuela committed itself to raise the educability and productivity of its next generation by dedicating the proceeds of a temporary oil bonanza to a massive effort to improve "intelligence." Results from various trials can describe only the skills developed by children within a year or two, whereas the decision to make a continuing investment hinges on benefits envisioned over the whole of these citizens' working lives. Long-reach inferences are required whenever a treatment or policy that worked for one set of cases is considered for use under other circumstances (Cronbach, 1982).

As earlier chapters have said, large amounts of judgment, based on the best current understanding, are required to arrive at and defend a policy or practice. Everyone, including the tough-minded empiricist who distrusts judgment and urges reliance on formulas, confronts problems for which there is no experience table. When empiricists do have an experience table, they must judge which cases and situations the table applies to. No one can defend mechanical rules that refuse to consider the facts about individual backgrounds and life situations. To help the individual chart his own course, the professional should do more than present odds derived from a faceless statistical aggregate. Psychology has gone far beyond folk wisdom by observing individuals over years and even decades and by closely observing persons in work settings and classrooms and during retraining intended to modify conduct and feelings. The resulting concepts suggest facts to collect in investigating particular families, schools, and factories or in identifying assets, limitations, and undeveloped strengths of an individual. The soundness of interpretations has been steadily improved by the very process of exposing oversimple and incorrect interpretations.

Perhaps the most important extension in recent years is the increased awareness that a psychology of individual organisms is inadequate. Bronfenbrenner (1979) introduced a profound book with these words: "Human abilities and their realization depend in significant degree on the larger social and institutional context of individual activity." Around each person there is an immediate social ecology created by the persons he interacts with, and these persons are part of a larger system of institutions embedded in a community embedded in a culture. Messages are transmitted all up and down the line—messages of demand, messages of reward, and subtler signals that also shape behavior. These transactions support development along some lines while neglecting or restricting abilities to play other roles.

Psychologists will have to learn from sociology and anthropology if they are to understand individuality in its context. Experimental investigations of educational, therapeutic, and other efforts designed to promote the welfare and functioning of community members have too often characterized treatments by simple labels. To try to generalize about "special education" is as senseless an act of labeling as is a generalization about "the retarded child." The identification, analysis, and objective assessment of situational differences has barely begun—but a beginning has been made in measures of group climate and in studies of situational influences on expression of personality, for example. For advancing understanding and for improving the quality of individual lives, the greatest hope lies in an intensified study of the interconnections between characteristics of persons and characteristics of settings.

Appendix
A

Selected Publishers and Test Distributors

American College Testing Program, P. O. Box 168, Iowa City, IA 52240. (*ACT*)

American Guidance Service, Publishers' Building, Circle Pines, MN 93940. (*AGS*)

Buros Institute of Mental Measurements, 136 Bancroft Hall, Lincoln, NE 68588. (*BI*)

Consulting Psychologists Press, 577 College Avenue, Palo Alto, CA 94306. (*CPP*)

CTB/McGraw-Hill, 2500 Garden Road, Monterey, CA 93940. (*CTB*)

DLM Teaching Resources, P. O. Box 4000, Allen, TX 75002. (*DLM*)

Educational and Industrial Testing Service, P. O. Box 7234, San Diego, CA 92107. (*EdITS*)

Educational Testing Service, Princeton, NJ 08541. (*ETS*)

Hadassah-Wizo-Canada Research Institute, P. O. Box 3160, Jerusalem, Israel. (*HWC*)

Institute for Personality and Ability Testing, P. O. Box 188, Champaign, IL 61820-0188. (*IPAT*)

National Computer Systems, P. O. Box 1416, Minneapolis, MN 55440. (*NCS*)

NFER-Nelson Publishing Co., Ltd., 2 Oxford Road East, Windsor, Berks SL 1DF, England. (*NFER*)

Pro-Ed, 5341 Industrial Oaks Boulevard, Austin, TX 78735.

Psychological Assessment Resources, Inc., P. O. Box 998, Odessa, FL 33556. (*PAR*)

Psychological Corporation, 555 Academic Court, San Antonio, TX 78204. (*PC*)

Publishers Test Service, 2500 Garden Road, Monterey, CA 93940. (*PTS*)

Reitan Neuropsychology Laboratories, 1338 East Edison Street, Tucson, AZ 85719.

Research Psychologists Press, P. O. Box 610984, Port Huron, MI 48061. (*RPP*)

Riverside Publishing Co., 8420 Bryn Mawr Avenue, Chicago, IL 60631. (*Riv*)

Scholastic Testing Service, Inc., P. O. Box 1056, Bensenville, IL 60106.

Science Research Associates, 155 North Wacker Drive, Chicago, IL 60606. (*SRA*)

Test Corporation of America, 4050 Pennsylvania Avenue, Kansas City, MO 64111. (*TCA*)

Touchstone Applied Science Associates, P. O. Box 382, Brewster, NY 10509. (*TASA*)

University of Illinois Press, 54 East Gregory Drive Champaign, IL 61820. (*UIP*)

Western Psychological Services, 12031 Wilshire Boulevard, Los Angeles, CA 90025. (*WPS*)

Appendix
B

Classified List of Tests and Inventories

For techniques and testing programs mentioned in this book, this appendix lists the main proprietary versions; it also lists a few other prominent tests. Mention of a test does not constitute a recommendation. Subtests such as Block Design and generic techniques such as the in-basket appear in the subject index. If a test does not fit neatly into one category, its placement is partly arbitrary.

A notation of the form *Riv* or *WPS* identifies a publisher or distributor whose full name and address appear in Appendix A. (Many tests have additional distributors not identified here.) An occasional entry identifies both distributor and developer or sponsor—for example, *ETS* for the College Board. Brackets indicate a secure testing program; addresses are not provided for some of these sources. The entry *O/C* means "out of catalog."

INDIVIDUALLY ADMINISTERED TESTS OF GENERAL MENTAL ABILITY OR DEVELOPMENT

Bayley Scales of Infant Development; *PC*, 271–273, 285, 287

British Ability Scales; *NFER*, (American version, entitled Differential Ability Scales; *PC*), 100–102, 137, 142

Infant Psychological Development Scales; *UIP*, 271–272

Kaufman Adolescent and Adult Intelligence Test (KAIT); *AGS*, 257

Kaufman Assessment Battery for Children (KABC); *AGS*, 118, 253–257, 281, 336, 378–379

Peabody Picture Vocabulary Test; *AGS*

Porteus Mazes; *PC*, 38–39, 616–617

Stanford-Binet Intelligence Scale (SB); *Riv*, 69, 233, 242, 261–264, 281, 285, 300, 336

Wechsler scales; *PC*, 135, 243–247, 336

Wechsler Adult Intelligence Scale (WAIS), 79, 116, 277, 283, 306–307, 381

Wechsler Intelligence Scale for Children (WISC), 57, 71, 133, 241, 243–247, 276, 278, 281, 285, 294–295, 335

Wechsler Preschool and Primary Scale of Intelligence (WPPSI), 285, 287

GROUP-ADMINISTERED TESTS OF GENERAL MENTAL ABILITY OR DEVELOPMENT

American College Testing Assessment (ACT); *[ACT]*, 264–269, 437

Army Examination Alpha; *O/C*, 233–235

Cognitive Abilities Test (CogAT), also primary-grade version; *Riv*, 258–261, 299, 307, 375–377

Embedded Figures Test (EFT), also children's version; *CPP*, 16–18, 183

Law School Admission Test (LSAT); [Law School Admission Council], 121, 166, 186, 194

Metropolitan Readiness Tests; *PC*, 125

Multidimensional Aptitude Battery (MAB); *RPP*, 248

PMA Readiness Level; *SRA*, 383

Raven's Progressive Matrices; *PC*, 277, 381

Scholastic Aptitude Test (SAT); [*ETS* for the College Board], 7, 11, 13, 63, 66, 67, 83–85, 91, 92, 118, 134, 174, 176, 194, 264–269

ACHIEVEMENT BATTERIES

California Achievement Tests; *CTB*, 127

Comprehensive Tests of Basic Skills; *CTB*

Iowa Tests of Basic Skills (ITBS); *Riv*, 119, 299

Metropolitan Achievement Tests; *PC*, 68, 135

ACHIEVEMENT TESTS IN PARTICULAR SCHOOL SUBJECTS

Advanced Placement Test in European History; [*ETS* for the College Board], 363, 365–368

Degrees of Reading Power (DRP); *TASA*, 106

Reading Yardsticks; *Riv*, 364

INSTRUMENTS USED IN ASSESSING HANDICAPS AND EDUCATIONAL RISKS IN CHILDREN AND/OR ADULTS

AAMD Adaptive Behavior Scale; *CTB, PAR*, 251

Adaptive Behavior Inventory for Children (ABIC); *PC*, 251

Arthur Point Scale of Performance Tests; *PC*

Halstead-Reitan Neuropsychological Test Battery; *Reitan*

Healy Completion; see Arthur Point Scale, 306

Kaufman Test of Educational Achievement; *AGS*

Learning Potential Assessment Device (LPAD); *HWC*, 343–346

Luria-Nebraska Neuropsychological Battery; *WPS*

McDermott Multidimensional Assessment of Children (M-MAC); *PC*, 355–356

Porch Index of Communicative Ability, also children's version; *CPP*, 404

System of Multicultural Pluralistic Assessment (SOMPA); *PC*, 133, 248–253

Vineland Adaptive Behavior Scales; *AGS*, 251

Woodcock-Johnson Psycho-educational Battery; *DLM*

MULTIPLE APTITUDE BATTERIES

Armed Services Vocational Aptitude Battery (ASVAB); *[Military Enlistment Processing Command]*, 47, 82–83, 146, 152, 393–394, 398

Differential Aptitude Tests (DAT)*; *PC*, 59–60, 113, 122–123, 127–128, 131, 390–393, 400–401

Computerized Adaptive Edition, 61–62, 141

Flanagan Aptitude Classification Tests; *SRA*, 425

General Aptitude Test Battery (GATB); [*(NCS)* for United States Employment Service], 118, 394–397, 399, 403, 453–455

Schaie-Thurstone Adult Mental Abilities Test; *CPP*, 383

TESTS OF SPECIALIZED ABILITIES

Ayres Scale for the Measurement of Handwriting; *O/C*, 99

Bennett Test of Mechanical Comprehension (MCT)*; *PC*, 59–61, 113, 135, 158, 176–177, 180–182, 197, 220

Christensen-Guilford Fluency Tests; *CPP*

*See also *Mechanical comprehension* in index.

INTEREST INVENTORIES

PERSONALITY INVENTORIES FOR GENERAL USE

PERSONALITY INVENTORIES PRIMARILY FOR CLINICAL OR SCREENING USE

Basic Personality Inventory; *RPP*

Millon Adolescent Personality Inventory; *NCS*

Millon Clinical Multiaxial Inventory (MCMI); *NCS,* 544–547, 553

Minnesota Multiphasic Personality Inventory (MMPI); *NCS* for University of Minnesota Press, 539–544, 553–555, 576–577, 580

Psychological Screening Inventory (PSI); *RPP,* 534–536

Woodworth Personal Data Sheet; *O/C,* 529

RATING SCALES AND INVENTORIES FOR OBTAINING EVALUATIONS

California Q-Sort Deck, also children's version; *CPP,* 592–594

Child Behavior Checklist (CBCL); *PC,* 595–597

Inpatient Multidimensional Rating Scale; *CPP,* 592

Personality Inventory for Children (PIC); *WPS,* 574–575, 597–601

Pupil Behavior Rating Scale; *PTS,* 590

School Play; *PTS,* 603

Social Climate Scales; *CPP,* 604–605

PERFORMANCE TESTS OF PERSONALITY

Bender Visual Motor Gestalt Test; *AGS, WPS,* 623–628

Downey Will-Temperament Tests; *O/C,* 617

Objective-Analytic Batteries; *IPAT,* 617

PROJECTIVE TECHNIQUES

Children's Apperception Test; *PC, WPS*

Rorschach Psychodiagnostic Test; *PAR,* 628–630

Rosenzweig Picture-Frustration Study; *PAR*

Thematic Apperception Test (TAT); *PAR, PC,* 20, 631–636

References

Achenbach, T. M. (1981). A junior MMPI? *Journal of Personality Assessment, 45,* 332–333.

Achenbach, T. M., & McConaughy, S. H. (1987). *Empirically based assessment of child and adolescent psychopathology: Practical applications.* Beverly Hills: Sage.

Achenbach, T. M., McConaughy, S. H., & Howell, C. T. (1987). Child/adolescent behavioral and emotional problems: Implications of cross-informant correlations for situational specificity. *Psychological Bulletin, 101,* 213–232.

Ackerman, P. L. (1987). Individual differences in skill learning: An integration of psychometric and information processing perspectives. *Psychological Bulletin, 102,* 3–27.

Adorno, T. W., et al. (1950). *The authoritarian personality.* New York: Harper & Row.

Albrecht, P. A., Glaser, E. M., & Marks, J. (1964). Validation of a multiple assessment procedure for managerial personnel. *Journal of Applied Psychology, 48,* 351–360.

Allport, G. W. (1937). *Personality: A psychological interpretation.* New York: Holt, Rinehart and Winston.

American Educational Research Association, American Psychological Association, and National Council on Measurement in Education. (1985). *Standards for educational and psychological testing.* Washington, DC: American Psychological Association.

American Personnel and Guidance Association. (1978, October 5). Responsibilities of users of standardized tests. *Guidepost,* pp. 5–8.

American Psychological Association. (1973). *Ethical principles in the conduct of research with human participants.* Washington, DC: Author.

American Psychological Association. (1981). Ethical principles of psychologists. *American Psychologist, 36,* 633–638.

American Psychological Association. (1986). *Guidelines for computer-based tests and interpretations.* Washington, DC: Author.

Amrine, M. (Ed.). (1965). [Special issue.] *American Psychologist, 20*(11).

Anastasi, A. (1988). *Psychological testing* (6th ed.). New York: Macmillan.

Anastasi, A., & Drake, J. D. (1954). An empirical comparison of certain techniques for estimating the reliability of speeded tests. *Educational and Psychological Measurement, 14,* 529–540.

Andrews, B. J., & Hecht, J. T. (1976). A preliminary investigation of two procedures for setting examination standards. *Educational and Psychological Measurement, 36,* 45–50.

Andrews, J. D. W. (1967). The achievement motive and advancement in two types of organizations. *Journal of Personality and Social Psychology, 6,* 163–168.

Angleitner, A., & Wiggins, J. (Eds.). (1986). *Personality assessment via questionnaire.* Berlin: Springer.

Appell, M. J., Williams, C. M., & Fishell, K. N. (1962). Significant factors in placing mental retardates from a workshop situation. *Personnel and Guidance Journal, 41,* 260–265.

Appleby, A. N., Langer, J. A., & Mullis, I. V. S. (1989). *Crossroads in American education.* Princeton, NJ: Educational Testing Service.

Arbous, A. G. (1955). *Selection for industrial leadership.* London: Oxford University Press.

Archer, R. P. (1987). *Using the MMPI with adolescents.* Hillsdale, NJ: Erlbaum.

Arvey, R. D. (1979). Unfair discrimination in the employment interview. *Psychological Bulletin, 86,* 736–765.

Asher, J. J., & Sciarrino, J. A. (1974). Realistic work sample tests: A review. *Personnel Psychology, 27,* 519–533.

Astin, A. W., Green, K. C., Korn, W. S., & Schalit, M. (1987). *The American freshman: Norms for Fall 1987.* Los Angeles: Higher Education Research Institute, University of California.

Athey, T. R., & McIntyre, R. M. (1987). Effect of rater training on rater accuracy: Levels-of-processing theory and social facilitation theory perspectives. *Journal of Applied Psychology, 72,* 567–572.

Atkinson, J. W. (1981). Studying personality in the context of an advanced motivational psychology. *American Psychologist, 36,* 117–128.

Atkinson, J. W., & Raynor, J. O. (Eds.). (1978). *Personality, motivation, and achievement.* Washigton, DC: Hemisphere.

Ayres, L. P. (1912). *A scale for measuring the quality of handwriting of school children.* New York: Russell Sage Foundation.

Bachman, J. G., & O'Malley, P. M. (1977). Self-esteem in young men: A longitudinal analysis of the impact of educational and occupational attainment. *Journal of Personality and Social Psychology, 35,* 365–380.

Baller, W. R., Charles, D. C., & Miller, E. L. (1967). Mid-life attainment of the mentally retarded: A longitudinal study. *Genetic Psychology Monographs*, 75, 235–329.

Baltes, P. B., & Nesselroade, J. R. (1979). History and rationale of longitudinal research. In J. R. Nesselroade & P. B. Baltes (Eds.), *Longitudinal research in the study of behavior and development*. New York: Academic Press.

Bandura, A., & Whalen, C. K. (1966). The influence of antecedent reinforcement and divergent modeling cues on patterns of self-regard. *Journal of Personality and Social Psychology*, 3, 373–382.

Bannatyne, A. (1974). Diagnosis: A note on recategorization of the WISC scaled scores. *Journal of Learning Disabilities*, 7, 272–274.

Barclay, J. R. (1966). Sociometric choices and teacher ratings as predictors of school dropout. *Journal of School Psychology*, 4, 40–44.

Barnette, W. L. (1951). An occupational aptitude pattern for engineers. *Educational and Psychological Measurement*, 11, 52–66.

Barr, P. M., & Samuels, M. T. (1988). Dynamic assessment of cognitive and affective factors contributing to learning difficulties in adults: A case study approach. *Professional Psychology*, 19, 6–13.

Barrett, G. V., Phillips, J. S., & Alexander, R. A. (1981). Concurrent and predictive validity designs: A critical reanalysis, *Journal of Applied Psychology*, 66, 1–6.

Barron, F. (1955). Threshold for the perception of human movement in inkblots. *Journal of Consulting Psychology*, 19, 33–38.

Barron, F., & Harrington, D. M. (1981). Creativity, intelligence, and personality. *Annual Review of Psychology*, 32, 439–476.

Bartholomeo, D. (1980). The study of error. *College Composition and Communication*, 31, 253–269.

Bartling, H. C., & Hood, A. B. (1981). An 11-year follow-up of measured interest and vocational choice. *Journal of Counseling Psychology*, 28, 27–35.

Bartram, D. (1987). The development of an automated testing system for pilot selection: The MICROPAT project. *Applied Psychology: An International Review*, 36, 279–298.

Bartram, D., Banerji, N., Rothwell, D., & Smith, P. (1985). Task parameters affecting individual differences in pursuit and compensatory tracking performance. *Ergonomics*, 28, 1633–1652.

Barzun, J. (1959). *The House of Intellect*. New York: Harper & Row.

Bass, B. M. (1954). The leaderless group discussion. *Psychological Bulletin*, 51, 465–492.

Bass, B. M., & Coates, C. H. (1952). Forecasting officer potential using the leaderless group discussion. *Journal of Abnormal and Social Psychology*, 47, 321–325.

Baughman, E. E., & Dahlstrom, W. G. (1968). *Negro and white children*. New York: Academic Press.

Baumrind, D. (1978). Nature and definition of informed consent in research involving deception. *The Belmont Report: Ethical principles and guidelines for the protection of human subjects in research. Appendix*, Sec, 23. (Vol. 2). (DHEW Pub. No. (OS) 78-0014). Washington, DC: Government Printing Office.

Beck, S. J. (1961–1978). *Rorschach's test* (3 vols.). New York: Grune & Stratton.

Becker, W. C., & Krug, R. S. (1964). A circumplex model for social behavior in children. *Child Development, 35*, 371–396.

Bem, D. J., & Allen, A. (1974). On predicting some of the people some of the time: The search for cross-situational consistencies in behavior. *Psychological Review, 81*, 506–520.

Benjamin, M., et al. (1981). Test anxiety: Deficits in information processing. *Journal of Experimental Psychology, 73*, 816–824.

Berk, R. A. (Ed.). (1982). *Handbook of methods for detecting test bias*. Baltimore: Johns Hopkins University Press.

Berk, R. A. (Ed.). (1984). *A guide to criterion-referenced test construction*. Baltimore: Johns Hopkins University Press.

Berk, R. A. (Ed.). (1986). *Performance assessment: Methods and applications*. Baltimore: Johns Hopkins University Press.

Berland, J. C. (1981). Untitled remarks at Conference on human assessment and cultural factors, Queens University, Kingston, Ont.

Berland, J. C. (1982). *No five fingers are alike*. Cambridge, MA: Harvard University Press.

Bernardin, H. J., & Beatty, R. W. (1984). *Performance appraisal: Assessing human behavior at work*. Boston: Kent.

Bernardin, H. J., & Bownas, D. A. (Eds.). (1985). *Personality assessment in organizations*. New York: Praeger.

Bernardin, H. J., & Smith, P. C. (1981). A clarification of some issues regarding the development and use of Behaviorally Anchored Rating Scales (BARS). *Journal of Applied Psychology, 66*, 458–463.

Bersoff, D. N. (1988). Should subjective employment devices be scrutinized? *American Psychologist, 43*, 1016–1018.

Bethell-Fox, C. E., Lohman, D. F., & Snow, R. E. (1984). Adaptive reasoning: Componential and eye-movement analysis of geometric analogy performance. *Intelligence, 8*, 205–238.

Betz, N. E. (1975). Prospects: New types of information. . . . In D. J. Weiss (Ed.), *Computerized adaptive trait measurement*. Minneapolis: University of Minnesota, Psychometric Methods Program.

Betz, N. E., & Weiss, D. J. (1976a). *Effects of immediate knowledge of results and adaptive testing on ability test performance* (Research Report 76-3). Minneapolis: University of Minnesota. Psychometric Methods Program.

Betz, N. E., & Weiss, D. J. (1976b). *Psychological effects of immediate knowledge of results and adaptive ability testing* (Research Report 76-4). Minneapolis: University of Minnesota, Psychometric Methods Program.

Biber, B., et al. (1952). *Life and ways of the seven to eight year old*. New York: Basic Books.

Bigler, E. D., & Ehrfurth, J. W. (1981). The continued inappropriate single use of the Bender Visual Motor Gestalt Test. *Professional Psychology, 12,* 562–569.

Binet, A. (1909). *Les idées modernes sur l'enfant.* Paris: Flammarion.

Black, J. D. (1953). *The interpretation of MMPI profiles of college women.* Doctoral dissertation, University of Minnesota, Minneapolis.

Block, J. (1961). *The Q-sort method in personality assessment and psychiatric research.* Springfield, IL: Thomas.

Block, J. (1981). Some enduring and consequential structures of personality. In A. I. Rabin et al. (Eds.), *Further explorations in personality.* New York: Wiley.

Block, J., Weiss, D. S., & Thorne, A. (1979). How relevant is a semantic similarity interpretation of personality ratings? *Journal of Personality and Social Psychology, 37,* 1053–1074.

Bloom, B. S. (1976). *Human characteristics and school learning.* New York: McGraw-Hill.

Borgen, F. H., & Seling, M. J. (1978). Expressed and inventoried interests revisited: Perspicacity in the person. *Journal of Counseling Psychology, 25,* 536–543.

Borkenau, P., & Amelang, M. (1985). The control of social desirability in personality inventories: A study using the principal-factor deletion technique. *Journal for Research in Personality, 19,* 44–53.

Borkowski, J. G., & Cavanaugh, J. C. (1979). Maintenance and generalization of skills and strategies by the retarded. In N. R. Ellis (Ed.), *Handbook of mental deficiency* (2d ed.). Hillsdale, NJ: Erlbaum.

Bornstein, M. H., & Sigman, M. D. (1986). Continuity of mental development from infancy. *Child Development, 57,* 251–274.

Boruch, R. F., & Cecil, J. S. (1979). *Assuring confidentiality of social research data.* Philadelphia: University of Pennsylvania Press.

Bosshardt, M. J., Rosse, R. L., & Peterson, N. G. (1984). *Development and validation of an industry-wide electric power plant maintenance selection system* (Technical Report No. 94). Minneapolis: Personnel Decisions Research Institute.

Botwinick, J., & Siegler, I. C. (1980). Intellectual ability among the elderly: Simultaneous cross-sectional and longitudinal comparisons. *Developmental Psychology, 16,* 49–53.

Bower, G. L., & Lewis, J. R. (1975). *ASVAB expectancy tables* (Technical note). Randolph Air Force Base, TX: Armed Forces Vocational Testing Group.

Boyer, E. L. (1987). *College: The undergraduate experience in America.* New York: Harper & Row.

Brace, C. L. [and others]. (1980). Multiple review of A. R. Jensen's *Bias in mental testing. Behavioral and Brain Sciences, 3,* 325–372.

Bracken, B. A. (1986). Review of the McDermott Multidimensional Assessment of Children. *Computers in Human Behavior, 2,* 309–316.

Bradburn, N. M., Sudman, S., et al. (1979). *Improving interview method and questionnaire design.* San Francisco: Jossey-Bass.

Bradshaw, J. L., & Nettleton, N. C. (1981). The nature of hemisphere specialization in man. [With commentary by P. Bertelson and others.] *Behavioral and Brain Sciences, 4,* 51–91.

Brass, D. J., & Oldham, G. R. (1976). Validating an in-basket test using an alternative set of leadership scoring dimensions. *Journal of Applied Psychology, 61,* 652–657.

Bray, D. W. (1982). The assessment center and the study of lives. *American Psychologist, 37,* 180–189.

Bray, D. W., & Grant, D. L. (1966). The assessment center in the measurement of potential for business management. *Psychological Monographs, 80* (17).

Brieman, L., et al. (1984). *Classification and regression trees.* Belmont, CA: Wadsworth.

Breland, H. M. (1979a). *Can multiple-choice tests measure writing skills?* New York: College Entrance Examination Board.

Breland, H. M. (1979b). *Population validity and college entrance measures.* New York: College Entrance Examination Board.

Brennan, R. L. (1983). *Elements of generalizability theory.* Iowa City: ACT Publications.

Briggs, S. R., & Cheek, J. M. (1986). The role of factor analysis in the development and evaluation of personality scales. *Journal of Personality, 54,* 106–148.

Brislin, R. W., Lonner, W. J., & Thorndike, R. M. (Eds.). (1974). *Cross-cultural research methods.* New York: Wiley.

Brody, G. H., & Forehand, R. (1986). Maternal perceptions of child maladjustment as a function of the combined influence of child behavior and maternal depression. *Journal of Clinical and Consulting Psychology, 54,* 237–240.

Brogden, H. E. (1949). A new coefficient: Application to biserial correlation and to estimation of selective efficiency. *Psychometrika, 14,* 169–182.

Brogden, H. E. (1951). Increased efficiency of selection resulting from replacement of a single predictor with several differential predictors. *Educational and Psychological Measurement, 11,* 173–196.

Bronfenbrenner, U. (1979). *The ecology of human development.* Cambridge: Harvard University Press.

Bronson, W. C. (1966). Central orientations: A study of behavior organization from childhood to adolescence. *Child Development, 37,* 125–155.

Brown, A. L., & De Loache, J. S. (1978). Skills, plans, and self-regulation. In R. S. Siegler (Ed.), *Children's thinking: What develops.* Hillsdale, NJ: Erlbaum.

Brown, S. H. (1981). Validity generalization and situational moderators in the life insurance industry. *Journal of Applied Psychology, 66,* 664–667.

Brown, S. H., Stout, J. D., Dalessio, A. Y., & Crosby, M. M. (1988). Stability of validity indices through test score ranges. *Journal of Applied Psychology, 73,* 736–742.

Bryk, A. S., & Raudenbush, S. (1986). A hierarchical model for studying school effects. *Sociology of Education, 59,* 1–17.

Buckley, P. D. (1978). The Bender Gestalt Test: A review of reported research with school age subjects. *Psychology in the Schools, 15,* 327–338.

Burisch, M. (1978). Construction strategies for multivariate personality inventories. *Applied Psychological Measurement, 2,* 97–111.

Burkhart, B. R., Christian, W. L., & Gynther, M. D. (1978). Item subtlety and faking on the MMPI: A paradoxical relationship. *Journal of Personality Assessment, 42,* 76–80.

Buros, O. K. (Ed.). (1941–1978). *The mental measurements yearbooks.* Highland Park, NJ: Gryphon Press.

Burton, R. V. (1963). Generality of honesty reconsidered. *Psychological Review, 70,* 481–499.

Burton, R. V., & Casey, W. M. (1980). Moral development. In R. H. Woody (Ed.), *Encyclopedia of clinical assessment.* San Francisco: Jossey-Bass.

Busch, C. M., Schroeder, D. H., & Biersner, R. J. (1982). *Personality attributes associated with personal and social adjustment in small, isolated groups.* Paper presented at the meeting of the Eastern Psychological Association.

Buss, D. M., & Craik, K. H. (1984). Acts, dispositions, and personality. In B. A. Maher & W. B. Maher (Eds.), *Progress in experimental personality research* (Vol. 13). Orlando, FL: Academic Press.

Butcher, J. N. (Ed.). (1972). *Objective personality assessment: Changing perspectives.* New York: Academic Press.

Butcher, J. N. (Ed.). (1987). *Computerized psychological assessment.* New York: Basic.

Callan, J. P. (1972). An attempt to use the MMPI as a predictor of failure in military training. *British Journal of Psychiatry, 121,* 553–557.

Callaway, E. (1975). *Brain electrical potentials and individual psychological differences.* New York: Grune & Stratton.

Campbell, D. P. (1965). The vocational interests of APA presidents. *American Psychologist, 20,* 636–644.

Campbell, D. P. (1971). *Handbook for the Strong Vocational Interest Blank.* Stanford, CA: Stanford University Press.

Campbell, D. T., & Fiske, D. W. (1959). Convergent and discriminant validation by the multitrait-multimethod matrix. *Psychological Bulletin, 56,* 81–105.

Campbell, J. P. (1974). *A Monte Carlo approach to some problems in multivariate prediction, with special reference to multiple regression.* Minneapolis, MN: Psychology Department, University of Minnesota. (NTIS No. AD 783091)

Campbell, J. P. (Ed.). (1986). *Improving the selection, classification, and utilization of Army enlisted personnel: Annual report, 1986 fiscal year* (ARI Technical Report 813101). Alexandria, VA: U.S. Army Research Institute for the Behavioral and Social Sciences.

Cannell, J. J. (1988). Nationally normed elementary school testing in America's public schools: How all 50 states are testing above the national average [with commentaries]. *Educational Measurement: Issues and Practice, 7*(2), 3–24.

Cantoni, L. J. (1954). Guidance: 4 students 10 years later. *Clearing House, 28,* 474–478.

Cantoni, L. J. (1955). High school tests and measurements as predictors of occupational status. *Journal of Applied Psychology, 39,* 253–255.

Carlsmith, M., Ellsworth, P. B., & Aronson, E. (1976). *Methods of research in social psychology.* Reading, MA: Addison-Wesley.

Carnegie Council on Policy Studies in Higher Education. (1977). *Selective admissions in higher education.* San Francisco: Jossey-Bass.

Carroll, J. B. (1980). *Individual differences in psychometric and experimental cognitive tasks* (Report No. 163). Chapel Hill: University of North Carolina, The L. L. Thurstone Psychometric Laboratory.

Carroll, J. B., Kohlberg, L., & DeVries, R. (1984). Psychometric and Piagetian intelligences: Toward resolution of controversy. *Intelligence, 8,* 67–91.

Carter, L. F., & Dudek, F. J. (1947). The use of psychological techniques in measuring and critically analyzing navigators' flight performance. *Psychometrika, 12,* 31–42.

Cascio, W. F. (1987). *Costing human resources: The financial impact of behavior in organizations* (2d ed.). Boston: Kent.

Cascio, W. F., Alexander, R. A., & Barrett, G. V. (1988). Setting cutoff scores: Legal, psychometric, and professional issues and guidelines. *Personnel Psychology, 41,* 1–24.

Cascio, W. F., & Silbey, V. (1979). Utility of the assessment center as a selection device. *Journal of Applied Psychology, 64,* 107–118.

Cattell, R. B. (1971). *Abilities: Their structure, growth, and action.* Boston: Houghton Mifflin.

Cattell, R. B., Eber, H. W., & Tatsuoka, M. M. (1970). *Handbook for the Sixteen Personality Factor Questionnaire (16 PF).* Champaign, IL: Institute for Personality and Ability Testing.

Cattell, R. B., & Warburton, F. W. (1967). *Objective personality and motivation tests.* Urbana: University of Illinois Press.

Chapman, P. (1988). *Schools as sorters: Lewis M. Terman, applied psychology, and the intelligence testing movement, 1890–1930.* New York: New York University Press.

Charters, W. W., Jr. (1963). Social class and intelligence tests. In W. W. Charters, Jr. & N. L. Gage (Eds.), *Readings in the social psychology of education.* Boston: Allyn & Bacon.

Chase, W. G., & Simon, H. A. (1973). The mind's eye in chess. In W. G. Chase (Ed.), *Visual information processing.* New York: Academic Press.

Chi, M. T. H., Glaser, R., & Farr, M. J. (1988). (Eds.). *The nature of expertise.* Hillsdale, NJ: Erlbaum.

Chipman, S. F., Segel, J. W., & Glaser, R. (Eds.). (1985). *Thinking and learning skills* (Vol. 2). Hillsdale, NJ: Erlbaum.

Ciminero, A. R., Calhoun, K. S., & Adams, H. E. (Eds.). (1986). *Handbook of behavioral assessment* (2d ed.). New York: Wiley.

Clark, R. A. (1952). The projective measurement of experimentally induced levels of sexual motivation. *Journal of Experimental Psychology, 44,* 391–399.

Coates, T. J., & Thoresen, C. E. (1978). Using generalizability theory in behavior observation. *Behavior Therapy, 9,* 605–613.

Code of Fair Testing Practices in Education. (1988). Washington, DC: Joint Committee on Testing Practices.

Coffman, W. E. (1966). *A factor analysis of the Verbal section of the Scholastic Aptitude Test* (Research Bulletin 66–30). Princeton, NJ: Educational Testing Service.

Cole, M., Gay, J., & Glick, J. (1968). Some experimental studies of Kpelle quantitative behavior. *Psychonomic Monograph Supplements, 2*(10), 173–190.

Cole, M., Hood, L., & McDermott, R. (1978). *Ecological niche-picking: Ecological invalidity as an axiom of experimental cognitive psychology.* New York: Rockefeller University, Laboratory of Comparative Human Cognition.

Cole, M., et al. (1971). *The cultural basis of learning and thinking.* New York: Basic Books.

College Entrance Examination Board. (1963). A statement on personality testing. *College Board Review, 51,* 11–13.

College Entrance Examination Board. (1977). *On further examination: Report of the Advisory Panel on the Scholastic Aptitude Test score decline.* New York: Author.

Committee on Psychological Tests and Assessment. (1988). *Implications for test fairness of the "Golden Rule" Company settlement.* Washington, DC: American Psychological Association.

Cone, J. D., & Hawkins, R. P. (Eds.). (1977). *Behavioral assessment: New directions in clinical psychology.* New York: Brunner/Mazel.

Conrad, H. S. (1932). The validity of personality ratings of nursery-school children. *Journal of Educational Psychology, 23,* 671–680.

Conrad, H. S. (1944). *Statistical analysis for the Mechanical Knowledge Test.* Princeton, NJ: College Entrance Examination Board.

Cooil, B., Winer, R. S., & Rados, D. L. (1987). Cross-validation for prediction. *Journal of Marketing Research, 24,* 271–279.

Cook, T. D., et al. (1975). *"Sesame Street" revisited: A case study in evaluation research.* New York: Russell Sage Foundation.

Cooper, G. D., et al. (1967). The Porteus maze test and various measures of intelligence with southern Negro adolescents. *American Journal of Mental Deficiency, 71,* 787–792.

Cooper, W. H. (1981). Ubiquitous halo. *Psychological Bulletin, 90,* 218–244.

Corno, L., & Snow, R. E. (1986). Adapting teaching to individual differences among learners. In M. C. Wittrock (Ed.), *Handbook of research on teaching* (3d ed.). New York: Macmillan.

Costa, P. T., Jr., & McCrae, R. R. (1988). Personality in adulthood: A six-year longitudinal study of self-reports and spouse ratings on the NEO Personality Inventory. *Journal of Personality and Social Psychology, 54,* 853–863.

Coulter, W. A., & Morrow, H. W. (Eds.). (1978). *Adaptive behavior: Concepts and measurements*. New York: Grune & Stratton.

Counseling from profiles: A casebook for the Differential Aptitude Tests. (1977). New York: Psychological Corporation.

Cox, C. M. (1926). *Genetic studies of genius: II. The early mental traits of three hundred geniuses*. Stanford, CA: Stanford University Press.

Craik, K. (1986). Personality research methods: An historical perspective. *Journal of Personality, 54*, 18–51.

Crandall, V. C. (1966). Personality characteristics and social and achievement behaviors associated with children's social desirability response tendencies. *Journal of Personality and Social Psychology, 4*, 477–486.

Crocker, L., & Algina, J. (1986). *Introduction to classical and modern test theory*. New York: Holt, Rinehart and Winston.

Cronbach, L. J. (1958). Proposals leading to analytic treatment of social perception scores. In R. Tagiuri & L. Petrullo (Eds.), *Person perception and interpersonal behavior*. Stanford, CA: Stanford University Press.

Cronbach, L. J. (1970). *Essentials of psychological testing* (3d ed.). New York: Harper & Row.

Cronbach, L. J. (1975). Five decades of public controversy over mental testing. *American Psychologist, 30*, 1–13.

Cronbach, L. J. (1977a). *Educational psychology* (3d ed.). New York: Harcourt Brace Jovanovich.

Cronbach, L. J. (1977b, September 7). Review of ASVAB Armed Services Vocational Aptitude Battery. *Congressional Record, 123*, 28041–28042.

Cronbach, L. J. (1979). The Armed Services Vocational Aptitude Battery—A test battery in transition. *Personnel and Guidance Journal, 58*, 232–237.

Cronbach, L. J. (1980). Validity on parole: How can we go straight? *New Directions for Testing and Measurement, 5*, 99–108.

Cronbach, L. J. (1982). *Designing evaluations of educational and social programs*. San Francisco: Jossey-Bass.

Cronbach, L. J. (1984). *Essentials of psychological testing* (4th ed.). New York: Harper & Row.

Cronbach, L. J. (1988). Internal-consistency of tests: Analyses old and new. *Psychometrika, 53*, 63–70.

Cronbach, L. J., & Drenth, P. J. D. (Eds.). (1972). *Mental tests and cultural adaptation*. The Hague: Mouton.

Cronbach, L. J., & Gleser, G. C. (1965). *Psychological tests and personnel decisions* (2d ed.). Urbana: University of Illinois Press.

Cronbach, L. J., Gleser, G. C., Rajaratnam, N., & Nanda, H. (1972). *The dependability of behavioral measurements*. New York: Wiley.

Cronbach, L. J., & Meehl, P. E. (1955). Construct validity in psychological tests. *Psychological Bulletin, 52*, 281–302.

Cronbach, L. J., & Schaeffer, G. A. (1981). *Extensions of personnel selection theory to aspects of minority hiring* (Report 81-A2). Stanford, CA: Stanford University, Institute for Educational Finance and Governance.

Cronbach, L. J., & Snow, R. E. (1977). *Aptitudes and instructional methods.* New York: Irvington. Paperback edition, 1981.

Cronbach, L. J., et al. (1980). *Toward reform of program evaluation.* San Francisco: Jossey-Bass.

Crosby, R. C., & Winsor, A. L. (1941). The validity of students' estimates of their own interests. *Journal of Applied Psychology, 25,* 408–414.

Crouse, J., & Trusheim, D. (1988). *The case against the SAT.* Chicago: University of Chicago Press.

Crowley, A. O. (1983). Predicting occupational entry: Measured versus expressed interests. *Journal of Occupational Psychology, 56,* 57–61.

Crowne, D. P., & Marlowe, D. (1964). *The approval motive.* New York: Wiley.

Crumbaugh, J. C. (1980). Graphoanalytic cues. In R. H. Woody (Ed.), *Encyclopaedia of clinical assessment.* (Vol. 2). San Francisco: Jossey-Bass.

Crumbaugh, J. C., & Stockholm, E. (1977). Validation of graphoanalysis by "global" or "holistic" method. *Perceptual and Motor Skills, 44,* 403–410.

Czikszentmihalyi, M., & Larson, R. (1984). *Being adolescent: Conflict and growth in the teenage years.* New York: Basic Books.

Dahlstrom, W. G. (1980). Screening for emotional fitness: The New Jersey case. In W. G. Dahlstrom & L. E. Dahlstrom (Eds.), *Basic readings on the MMPI.* Minneapolis: University of Minnesota Press.

Damrin, D. E. (1959). The Russell Sage Social Relations Test: A technique for measuring group problem solving skills in elementary school children. *Journal of Experimental Education, 28,* 85–99.

Dance, K. A., & Neufeld, R. W. J. (1988). Aptitude treatment-interaction research in the clinical setting: A review of attempts to dispel the "patient uniformity" myth. *Psychological Bulletin, 104,* 192–213.

Darley, J. G., & Hagenah, T. (1955). *Vocational interest measurement: Theory and practice.* Minneapolis: University of Minnesota Press.

Darlington, R. B. (1978). Reduced-variance regression. *Psychological Bulletin, 85,* 1238–1255.

Dauterman, W. L., & Suinn, R. M. (1966). *Stanford-Ohwaki-Kohs Tactile Block Design Intelligence Test for the Blind; Final report.* Washington, DC: Vocational Rehabilitation Administration.

Davis, B. D., & Flaherty, P. (Eds.). (1976). *Human diversity: Its causes and social significance.* Cambridge, MA: Ballinger.

Davis, W. A. (1951). Socio-economic influences upon children's learning. *Understanding the Child, 20,* 10–16.

Dawes, R. M. (1979). The robust beauty of improper linear models in decision making. *American Psychologist, 34,* 571–582.

Dawes, R. M., & Corrigan, B. (1974). Linear models in decision making. *Psychological Bulletin, 81,* 95–106.

Dawis, R. V., & Lofquist, L. H. (1984). *A psychological theory of work adjustment.* Minneapolis: University of Minnesota Press.

Dean, R. S. (1984). Functional lateralization of the brain. *Journal of Special Education, 18,* 239–256.

deCharms, R. (1976). *Enhancing motivation: Change in the classroom.* New York: Irvington.

deCharms, R. (1980). The origins of competence and achievement motivation in personal causation. In L. J. Fyans Jr. (Ed.), *Achievement motivation.* New York: Plenum.

deGroot, A. D. (1966). Perception and memory versus thought. In B. Kleinmuntz (Ed.), *Problem solving research, methods, and theory.* New York: Wiley.

Delclos, V. R., Burns, M. S., & Kulewicz, S. J. (1987). Effects of dynamic assessment on teachers' expectations of handicapped children. *American Educational Research Journal, 24,* 325–336.

Diamond, E. E. (Ed.). (1975). *Issues of sex bias and sex fairness in career interest measurement.* Washington, DC: National Institute of Education.

Diener, E., Larsen, R. J., & Emmons, R. A. (1984). Person × situation interactions: Choice of situations and congruence response models. *Journal of Personality and Social Psychology, 47,* 380–392.

Digman, J. M., & Inouye, J. (1986). Further specification of the five robust factors of personality. *Journal of Personality and Social Psychology, 50,* 116–123.

Dobzhansky, T. (1973). *Genetic diversity and human equality.* New York: Basic Books.

Dolliver, R. H., & Hansen, R. N. (1977). [Review of the Self-Directed Search.] *Measurement and Evaluation in Guidance, 10,* 120–123.

Domino, G. (1968). Differential predictions of academic achievement in conforming and independent settings. *Journal of Educational Psychology, 59,* 256–260.

Domino, G. (1971). Interactive effects of achievement motivation and teaching style on academic achievement. *Journal of Educational Psychology, 62,* 427–431.

Donlon, T. F. (Ed.). (1984). *The College Board technical handbook for the Scholastic Aptitude Test and achievement tests.* New York: College Board.

Dougherty, T. W., Ebert, R. J., & Callender, J. C. (1986). Policy capturing in the employment interview. *Journal of Applied Psychology, 71,* 9–15.

Downey, R. G., Medland, F. F., & Yates, L. G. (1976). Evaluation of a peer rating system for predicting subsequent promotion of senior military officers. *Journal of Applied Psychology, 61,* 206–209.

Dreyer, G. F., & Sackett, P. R. (1981). Some problems with applying content validity to assessment center procedures. *Academy of Management Review, 6,* 551–560, 567–568.

DuBois, P. H. (Ed.). (1947). *The classification program.* Washington, DC: Government Printing Office.

Duncan, A. K. (1947). Some comments on the Army General Classification Test. *Journal of Applied Psychology, 31,* 143–149.

Dunnette, M. D. (1957). Vocational interest differences among engineers employed in different functions. *Journal of Applied Psychology, 41,* 273–278.

Dunnette, M. D. (1971). The assessment of managerial talent. In P. McReynolds (Ed.), *Advances in psychological assessment* (Vol. 2). Palo Alto, CA: Science and Behavior Books.

Dunnette, M. D. (1974). Personnel selection and job placement of disadvantaged and minority persons: Problems, issues, and suggestions. In H. L. Fromkin & J. J. Sherwood (Eds.), *Integrating the organization.* New York: Free Press.

Dunnette, M. D. (Ed.). (1976). *Handbook of industrial and organizational psychology.* Chicago: Rand McNally.

Dunnette, M. D., & Borman, W. C. (1979). Personnel selection and classification systems. *Annual Review of Psychology, 30,* 477–525.

Dunnette, M. D., Bownas, D. A., & Bosshardt, M. J. (1981). Prediction of inappropriate, unreliable, or aberrant job behavior in nuclear power plant settings. Minneapolis: Personnel Decisions Research Institute.

Dunnette, M. D., et al. (1962). A study of faking behavior on a forced-choice self-description checklist. *Personnel Psychology, 15,* 13–24.

Dunnette, M. D., et al. (1982). *Development and validation of an industry-wide electric power plant operator selection system.* Minneapolis: Personnel Decisions Research Institute.

Eckland, B. K. (1980). Competent teachers and competent students. *Behavioral and Brain Sciences, 3,* 341–342.

Edelbrock, C. S., & Achenbach, T. M. (1980). A typology of Child Behavior Profile patterns: Distribution and correlates for disturbed children aged 6–16. *Journal of Abnormal Child Psychology, 8,* 441–470.

Edelbrock, C., & Achenbach, T. M. (1984). The teacher version of the Child Behavior Profile: I. Boys aged 6–11. *Journal of Consulting and Clinical Psychology, 52,* 207–217.

Educational Testing Service. (1980). *An approach for identifying and minimizing bias in standard tests: A set of guidelines.* Princeton, NJ: ETS, Office of Minority Education.

Edwards, W., Guttentag, M., & Snapper, K. (1975). A decision-theoretic approach to evaluation research. In E. L. Streuning & M. Guttentag (Eds.), *Handbook of evaluation research* (Vol. 1). Beverly Hills: Sage.

Eells, K., et al. (1951). *Intelligence and cultural differences.* Chicago: University of Chicago Press.

EEOC et al. (1978). Adoption by four agencies of Uniform Federal Guidelines on Employee Selection Procedures. *Federal Register, 43,* 38290–38315.

EEOC et al. (1979). Adoption of questions and answers. . . . *Federal Register, 44,* 11996–12009.

Efron, B. (1983). Estimating the error rate of a prediction rule: Improvement on cross-validation. *Journal of the American Statistical Association, 78,* 316–331.

Efron, B., & Diaconis, P. (1983). Computer intensive methods in statistics. *Scientific American, 248*(5), 116–130.

Einhorn, H. J. (1986). Accepting error to make less error. *Journal of Personality Assessment, 50,* 387–395.

Ekstrom, R. B., French, J. W., & Harman, H. H. (1976). *Kit of factor-referenced cognitive tests.* Princeton, NJ: Educational Testing Service.

Ekstrom, R. B., French, J. W., & Harman, H. H. (1979). Cognitive factors: Their identification and replication. *Multivariate Behavioral Research Monographs, 79*(2).

Elliott, C. D., Murray, D. J., & Pearson, L. S. (1978). *British Ability Scales. Manual 3: Directions for administering and scoring.* Windsor, England: NFER Publishing Company.

Elliott, R. (1987). *Litigating intelligence: IQ tests, special education, and social science in the courtroom.* Dover, MA: Auburn House.

Embretson, S. (Ed.). (1985). *Test design: Developments in psychology and psychometrics.* Orlando, FL: Academic Press.

Epstein, S. (1979). The stability of behavior: On predicting most of the people much of the time. *Journal of Personality and Social Psychology, 37,* 1097–1126.

Ericsson, K. A. (1987). Theoretical implications from protocol analysis on testing and measurement. In R. R. Ronning et al. (Eds.), *The influence of cognitive psychology on testing.* Hillsdale, NJ: Erlbaum.

Evans, F. R., & Pike, L. W. (1973). The effects of instruction for three mathematics item formats. *Journal of Educational Measurement, 10,* 257–272.

Exner, J. E., Jr. (1986). *The Rorschach: A comprehensive system. Vol. 1. Basic foundations* (2nd ed.). New York: Wiley.

Eyde, L. D., Moreland, K. L., Robertson, G. J., Primoff, E. S., & Most, R. B. (1988). Test user qualifications: A data-based approach to promoting good test use. *Issues in scientific psychology.* Report of the Test User Qualifications Working Group of the Joint Committee on Testing Practices. Washington, DC: American Psychological Association.

Eyde, L. D., & Quaintance, M. K. (1988). Ethical issues and cases in the practice of personnel psychology. *Professional Psychology: Research and Practice, 19,* 148–154.

Eysenck, H. J. (Ed.). (1973). *The measurement of intelligence.* Lancaster, England: Medical and Technical Publishing Co.

Eysenck, H. J. (1979). *The structure and measurement of intelligence.* New York: Springer.

Eysenck, H. J. (Ed.). (1982). *A model for intelligence.* Berlin: Springer.

Fagan, J. F., III. (1985). A new look at infant intelligence. In D. K. Detterman (Ed.), *Current topics in human intelligence: Vol. 1. Research methodology.* Norwood, NJ: Ablex.

Fahmy, M. (1954). *Initial exploring of the Shilluk intelligence.* Cairo: Dar Misr Printing Co.

Fancher, R. (1985). *The intelligence men: Makers of the IQ controversy.* New York: Norton.

Farmer, H. S., & Fyans, L. J., Jr. (1980). Women's achievement and career motivation: Their risk taking patterns, home-career conflict, sex role orientation, fear of success, and self-concept. In L. J. Fyans, Jr. (Ed.), *Achievement motivation.* New York: Plenum.

Farr, S. P., Greene, R. L., & Fisher-White, S. P. (1986). Disease process, onset, and course and their relationship to neuropsychological performance. In S.

B. Filskov & T. J. Boll (Eds.), *Handbook of clinical neuropsychology* (Vol. 2). New York: Wiley.

Feather, N. T. (1961). The relationship of persistence at a task to expectation of success and achievement related stories. *Journal of Abnormal and Social Psychology, 63,* 552–561.

Feldt, L. S., Steffen, M., & Gupta, N. C. (1985). A comparison of five methods for estimating the standard error of measurement at specific score levels. *Applied Psychological Measurement, 9,* 351–361.

Fenz, W. D. (1964). Conflict and stress as related to physiological activation and sensory, perceptual, and cognitive functioning. *Psychological Monographs, 78*(8).

Fenz, W. D., & Epstein, S. (1962). Measurement of approach-avoidance conflict along a stimulus dimension by a thematic apperception test. *Journal of Personality, 30,* 613–632.

Ferrera, R. A., Brown, A. L., & Campione, J. C. (1986). Children's learning and transfer of inductive reasoning rules: Studies of proximal development. *Child Development, 57,* 1087–1099.

Feuerstein, R. (1979). *The dynamic assessment of retarded performers.* Baltimore: University Park Press.

Feuerstein, R. (1980). *Instrumental enrichment.* Baltimore: University Park Press.

Feuerstein, R., Haywood, [H.] C., & Rand, Y. (1982). *Examiner manuals for the Learning Potential Assessment Device.* Jerusalem: Hadassah-Wizo-Canada Research Institute. [Preliminary version]

Filskov, S. B., & Boll, T. J. (1982). *Handbook of clinical neuropsychology* (Vol. 1). New York: Wiley.

Fink, A. M., & Butcher, J. N. (1972). Reducing objections to personality inventories with special instructions. *Educational and Psychological Measurement, 32,* 631–639.

Fishbein, M., & Azjen, I. (1974). Attitudes toward objects as predictors of single and multiple behavioral criteria. *Psychological Review, 81,* 59–74.

Fivars, G. (1980). *The critical incident technique: A bibliography* (2d ed.). Palo Alto, CA: American Institutes for Research.

Flanagan, J. C. (1954). The critical incidents technique. *Psychological Bulletin, 51,* 327–358.

Flanagan, J. C., et al. (1973). *The career data book: Results from Project TALENT's five-year follow-up study.* Palo Alto, CA: American Institutes for Research.

Flaugher, R. (1978). The many definitions of test bias. *American Psychologist, 33,* 671–679.

Fleishman, E. A., & Quaintance, M. K. (1984). *Taxonomies of human performance: The description of human tasks.* Orlando, FL: Academic Press.

Flynn, J. R. (1984). The mean IQ of Americans: Massive gains 1932 to 1978. *Psychological Bulletin, 95,* 29–51.

Flynn, J. R. (1987). Massive IQ gains in 14 nations: What IQ tests really measure. *Psychological Bulletin, 101*, 171–191.

Ford, A., et al. (1944). *The sonar pitch-memory test: A report on design standards.* San Diego, University of California Division of War Research.

Ford, J. B. (1957). Some more on the Samoans. *American Psychologist, 12,* 151.

Forehand, G. A. (1968). On the interaction of persons and organizations. In R. Tagiuri & G. H. Litwin (Eds.), *Organizational climate: Explorations of a concept.* Boston: Harvard University, Graduate School of Business Administration.

Forer, B. R. (1949). The fallacy of personal validation: A classroom demonstration of gullibility. *Journal of Abnormal and Social Psychology, 44,* 118–123.

Fransella, F., & Bannister, D. (1977). *A manual for repertory grid technique.* London: Academic Press.

Frederiksen, N. R. (1984). The real test bias: Influences of testing on teaching and learning. *American Psychologist, 39,* 193–202.

Frederiksen, N. R. (1986). Toward a broader conception of human intelligence. *American Psychologist, 41,* 445–452.

Frederiksen, N. R., et al. (1972). *Prediction of organizational behavior.* New York: Pergamon.

Freedman, D. G. (1958). Constitutional and environmental interactions in rearing of four breeds of dogs. *Science, 127,* 585–586.

Fuchs, D., & Fuchs, L. S. (1986). Test procedure bias: A meta-analysis of examiner familiarity effects. *Review of Educational Research, 56,* 243–262.

Fulero, S. M. (1988). Tarasoff: 10 years later. *Professional Psychology: Research and Practice, 19,* 184–190.

Gardner, H. (1983). *Frames of mind.* New York: Basic Books.

Gardner, J. (1961). *Excellence: Can we be equal and excellent too?* New York: Harper & Row.

Gardner, R. C. (1960). Motivational variables in second-language acquisition. Unpublished doctoral dissertation, McGill University, Montreal.

Garner, A. M., & Smith, G. M. (1976). An experimental videotape technique for evaluating trainee approaches to clinical judging. *Journal of Consulting and Clinical Psychology, 44,* 945–950.

Gaugler, B. B., Rosenthal, D. B., Thornton, G. G., III, & Bentson, C. (1987). Meta-analysis of assessment center validity. *Journal of Applied Psychology, 72,* 493–511.

Getzels, J. W., & Jackson, P. W. (1962). *Creativity and intelligence.* New York: Wiley.

Ghiselli, E. E. (1973). The validity of aptitude tests in personnel selection. *Personnel Psychology, 26,* 461–477.

Gifford, B. R. (Ed.). (1989a). *Testing policy and testing performance: Education, language, and culture.* Boston: Kluwer Academic Publishers.

Gifford, B. R. (Ed.). (1989b). *Test policy and the politics of opportunity allocation: The workplace and the law.* Boston: Kluwer Academic Publishers.

Glaser, R. (1977). *Adaptive education: Individual diversity and learning*. New York: Holt, Rinehart and Winston.

Glaser, R., & Bassok, M. (1989). Learning theory and the study of instruction. *Annual Review of Psychology, 40*, 631–666.

Glaser, R., & Bond, L. (Eds.). (1981). Testing: Concepts, policy, practice, and research [Special issue]. *American Psychologist, 36*(10).

Gleser, G. C. (1968). Psychometric contributions to the assessment of patients. In D. H. Efron et al. (Eds.), *Psychopharmacology: Review of progress, 1957–1967*. Washington, DC: Government Printing Office.

Glutting, J. J. (1986). The McDermott Multidimensional Assessment of Children: Contribution to the development of individualized educational programs. *Journal of Special Education, 20*, 431–445.

Goldberg, L. R. (1970). Man versus model of man: A rationale, plus some evidence, for a method of improving on clinical inferences. *Psychological Bulletin, 73*, 422–432.

Goldberg, L. R. (1972). Parameters of personality inventory construction and utilization: A comparison of predictive strategies and tactics. *Multivariate Behavioral Research Monographs, 72*(2).

Goldberg, L. R. (1986). Some informal explorations and ruminations about graphology. In B. Nevo (Ed.), *Scientific aspects of graphology: The Handbook*. Springfield, IL: Thomas.

Goldberg, L. R., & Rorer, L. G. (1966). Use of two different response modes and repeated testings to predict social conformity. *Journal of Personality and Social Psychology, 3*, 28–37.

Golden, C. J. (1979). *Clinical interpretation of objective psychological tests*. New York: Grune & Stratton.

Goldstein, G., & Hersen, M. (Eds.). (1984). *Handbook of personality assessment*. New York: Pergamon.

Gordon, L. V. (1978). *Gordon Personal Profile Inventory* manual. New York: Psychological Corporation.

Gordon, L. V., & Medland, F. F. (1965). The cross-group stability of peer ratings of leadership. *Personnel Psychology, 18*, 173–177.

Gottfredson, L. S. (Ed.). (1986). The *g* factor in employment. [Special issue.] *Journal of Vocational Behavior, 29*, 293–450.

Gottfredson, L. S., & Sharf, J. C. (Eds.). (1988). Fairness in employment testing [Special issue.] *Journal of Vocational Behavior, 33*(3).

Gough, H. G. (1954). Some common misconceptions about neuroticism. *Journal of Consulting Psychology, 18*, 287–292.

Gough, H. G. (1967). Nonintellectual factors in the selection and evaluation of medical students. *Journal of Medical Education, 42*, 642–650.

Graham, J. R. (1977). *The MMPI: A practical guide*. New York: Oxford University Press.

Graham, J. R. (1987). *The MMPI* (2nd ed.). New York: Oxford University Press.

Green, G. L., & Cascio, W. F. (1987). Is cost accounting the answer? Comparison of two behaviorally based methods of estimating the s.d. of job performance in dollars with a cost-accounting-based approach. *Journal of Applied Psychology, 72,* 588–595.

Gronland, N. (1985). *Measurement and evaluation in teaching* (5th ed.). New York: Macmillan.

Gross, A., & Fleischman, L. (1983). Restriction of range corrections when both distribution and selection assumptions are violated. *Applied Psychological Measurement, 7,* 227–237.

Guilford, J. P. (1965). Intellectual factors in productive thinking. In M. J. Aschner & C. E. Bish (Eds.), *Productive thinking in education.* Washington, DC: National Education Association.

Guilford, J. P. (1988). Some changes in the structure-of-intellect model. *Educational and Psychological Measurement, 48,* 1–4.

Guion, R. M. (1980). On trinitarian doctrines of validity. *Professional Psychology, 11,* 385–398.

Guion, R. M., & Gottier, R. F. (1965). Validity of personality measures in personnel selection. *Personnel Psychology, 18,* 135–164.

Gustafsson, J.-E. (1976). *Verbal and figural aptitudes in relation to instructional methods.* Gothenburg: Acta Universitatis Gothoburgensis.

Gynther, M. D., & Burkhart, B. R. (1983). Are subtle MMPI items expendable? In J. N. Butcher & C. D. Spielberger (Eds.), *Advances in personality assessment* (Vol. 2). Hillsdale, NJ: Erlbaum.

Haan, N. (1981). Common dimensions of personality development: Early adolescence to middle life. In D. H. Eichhorn et al. (Eds.), *Present and past in middle life.* New York: Academic Press.

Haier, R. J., et al. (1988). Cortical glucose metabolic rate correlates of abstract reasoning and attention studied with positron emission tomography. *Intelligence, 12,* 199–217.

Hall, W. B., & MacKinnon, D. W. (1969). Personality inventory correlates among architects. *Journal of Applied Psychology, 53,* 322–326.

Hammond, S. M. (1984). An investigation into the factor structure of the General Aptitude Test Battery. *Journal of Occupational Psychology, 57,* 43–48.

Haney, W. M. (1984). Testing reasoning and reasoning about testing. *Review of Educational Research, 54,* 597–654.

Haney, W., & Madaus, G. (1988). The evolution of ethical and technical standards of testing. In R. K. Hambleton & J. Zaal (Eds.), *Handbook of testing.* Amsterdam: North-Holland.

Haney, W. M., & Reidy, E. F. (Eds.). (1987). Golden rule or ruse? [Special issue]. *Educational Measurement: Issues and Practice, 6(2).*

Hansen, J.-I. C. (1988). Changing interests of women: Myth or reality? *Applied Psychology: An International Review, 37,* 133–150.

Harrell, T. W. (1972). High earning MBA's. *Personnel Psychology, 25,* 523–530.

Harris, D. H. (1945). Questionnaire and interview in neuropsychiatric screening. *Journal of Applied Psychology, 30,* 644–648.

Harrison, R. (1965). Thematic apperception methods. In B. B. Wolman (Ed.), *Handbook of clinical psychology.* New York: McGraw-Hill.

Hartigan, J. A., & Wigdor, A. K. (Eds.). (1989). *Fairness in employment testing: Validity generalization, minority issues, and the General Aptitude Test Battery.* Washington, DC: National Academy Press.

Hartshorne, H., & May, M. A. (1928). *Studies in deceit* (2 vols.). New York: Macmillan.

Hartshorne, H., & May, M. A. (1929). *Studies in service and self-control.* New York: Macmillan.

Hartshorne, H., & May, M. A. (1930). *Studies in the organization of character.* New York: Macmillan.

Hayes, S. C., Nelson, R. O., & Jarrett, R. B. (1987). The treatment utility of assessment: A functional approach to evaluating assessment quality. *American Psychologist, 42,* 963–974.

Haywood, H. C., et al. (1975). Behavioral assessment in mental retardation. In P. McReynolds (Ed.), *Advances in psychological assessment* (Vol. 3). San Francisco: Jossey-Bass.

Heaton, R. K., & Pendleton, M. G. (1981). Use of neuropsychological tests to predict adult patients' everyday functioning. *Journal of Abnormal Psychology, 49,* 807–821.

Hebb, D. O., & Williams, K. A. (1946). A method of rating animal intelligence. *Journal of Genetic Psychology, 34,* 59–65.

Heinrich, D. L. & Spielberger, C. D. (1982). Anxiety and complex learning. In H. W. Krohne & L. Laux (Eds.), *Achievement, stress, and anxiety.* Washington, DC: Hemisphere.

Heller, K. A., Holtzman, W. H., & Messick, S. (Eds.). (1982). *Placing children in special education: A strategy for equity.* Washington, DC: National Academy Press.

Helme, W. H., Gibson, W. A., & Brogden, H. E. (1957). *An empirical test of shrinkage problems in personnel classification research* (Technical Research Note 84). Washington, DC: Adjutant-General's Office, Personnel Research Branch

Helmreich, R. L., Sawin, L. L., & Carsrud, A. L. (1986). The Honeymoon Effect in job performance: Temporal increases in the predictive power of achievement motivation. *Journal of Applied Psychology, 71,* 185–188.

Helson, R. (1971). Women mathematicians and the creative personality. *Journal of Consulting and Clinical Psychology, 36,* 210–220.

Helson, R., & Moane, G. (1987). Personality change in women from college to midlife. *Journal of Personality and Social Psychology, 53,* 176–186.

Hemphill, J. K., & Sechrest, L. B. (1952). A comparison of three criteria of air crew effectiveness in combat over Korea. *Journal of Applied Psychology, 36,* 323–327.

Heneman, R. L. (1986). The relationship between supervisory ratings and results-oriented measures of performance: A meta-analysis. *Personnel Psychology, 39,* 811–926.

Henry, W. E. (1956). *The analysis of fantasy.* New York: Wiley.

Herrnstein, R. J. (1982, August). IQ testing and the media. *Atlantic, 250,* 68–84.

Hess, R. D., & Azuma, H. (1973). Unpublished manual. School of Education, Stanford University.

Hickman, J. A., & Reynolds, C. R. (1986). Are race differences in mental test scores an artifact of psychometric methods? A test of Harrington's experimental model. *Journal of Special Education, 20,* 409–430.

Higher Education Research Institute. (1982). *Final report of the Commission on the Higher Education of Minorities.* Los Angeles: Author.

Hilton, T. L. (1980). *Annotated bibliography of Growth Study papers* (Research Report 80-2). Princeton, NJ: Educational Testing Service.

Hilton, T. L., Beaton, A. E., & Bower, C. P. (1971). *Stability and instability in academic growth—A compilation of longitudinal data* (Research Report 0-0140). Princeton, NJ: Educational Testing Service.

Hofstadter, R. (1944). *Social Darwinism in American thought.* Philadelphia: University of Pennsylvania Press.

Hogan, T. P., & Mishler, C. (1980). Relationships between essay tests and objective tests of language skills for elementary school students. *Journal of Educational Measurement, 17,* 219–227.

Holden, C. (Oct. 28, 1977). Health records and privacy: What would Hippocrates say? *Science, 198,* 382.

Holland, J. L. (1985). *Self-Directed Search: Professional manual, 1985 edition.* Odessa, FL: Psychological Assessment Resources.

Holmen, M. G., & Docter, R. (1972). *Educational and psychological testing.* New York: Russell Sage Foundation.

Holmen, M. G., et al. (1956). *An assessment program for OCS applicants* (HumRRO Technical Report No. 26). Washington, DC: George Washington Univ.

Holt, R. R., & Luborsky, L. (1958). *Personality patterns of psychiatrists.* New York: Basic Books.

Holtzman, W. H., Diaz-Guerrero, R., & Swartz, J. (1975). *Personality development in two cultures: A cross-cultural longitudinal study of school children in Mexico and the United States.* Austin: University of Texas Press.

Holtzman, W. H., & Sells, S. B. (1954). Prediction of flying success by clinical analysis of test protocols. *Journal of Abnormal and Social Psychology, 49,* 485–490.

Honzik, M. P., Macfarlane, J. W., & Allen, L. (1948). The stability of mental test performance between two and eighteen years. *Journal of Experimental Education, 17,* 309–324.

Hook, C. M., & Rosenshine, B. V. (1979). Accuracy of teacher reports of their classroom behavior. *Review of Educational Research, 49,* 1–12.

Hormuth, S. E. (1986). The sampling of experiences *in situ. Journal of Personality, 54,* 262–293.

Horn, J. L., & Cattell, R. B. (1966). Refinement and test of the theory of fluid and crystallized intelligence. *Journal of Educational Psychology, 57,* 253–276.

Horn, J., Donaldson, E., & Engstrom, R. (1981). Apprehension, memory and fluid intelligence decline in adulthood. *Research on Aging, 3,* 33–84.

Horne, L. V., & Garty, M. K. (1981). *What the test score really reflects: Observations of teacher behavior during standardized test administration.* Paper presented to the American Educational Research Association.

Hough, L. (1984). Development and evaluation of the "accomplishment record" method of selecting and promoting professionals. *Journal of Applied Psychology, 69,* 135–146.

Hough, L. M. (Ed.). (1986). *Utility of temperament, biodata, and interest assessment for predicting job performance: A review and integration of the literature.* Minneapolis: Personnel Decisions Research Institute.

Hough, L. (1987). *Overcoming objections to the use of temperament variables in selection.* Paper presented at the meeting of the American Psychological Association.

Hough, L. (1988). *Personality assessment for selection and placement decisions.* Paper presented at the meeting of the Society for Industrial and Organizational Psychology.

Houts, P. L. (Ed.). (1977). *The myth of measurability.* New York: Hart.

Humphreys, L. G. (1981). The primary mental ability. In M. P. Friedman et al. (Eds.), *Intelligence and learning.* New York: Plenum.

Humphreys, L. G., & Taber, T. (1973). Postdiction study of the Graduate Record Examination and eight semesters of college grades. *Journal of Educational Measurement, 10,* 179–184.

Hunt, E. B. (1974). Quote the Raven? Nevermore! In L. W. Gregg (Ed.), *Knowledge and cognition.* Potomac, MD: Erlbaum.

Hunt, E. B., Pellegrino, J. W., Frick, R. W., Farr, S. A., & Alderton, A. (1988). The ability to reason about movement in the visual field. *Intelligence, 12,* 77–100.

Hunter, J. E., & Hunter, R. F. (1984). Validity and utility of alternative predictors of job performance. *Psychological Bulletin, 96,* 72–98.

Hunter, J. E., & Schmidt, F. L. (1981). Fitting people to jobs: The impact of personnel selection on national productivity. In E. A. Fleishman (Ed.), *Human performance and productivity.* Hillsdale, NJ: Erlbaum.

Hunter, J. E., Schmidt, F. L., & Hunter, R. (1979). Differential validity of employment tests by race: A comprehensive review and analysis. *Psychological Bulletin, 86,* 721–735.

Hunter, J. E., Schmidt, F. L., & Rauschenberger, J. M. (1977). Fairness of psychological tests: Implications of four definitions for selection utility and minority hiring. *Journal of Applied Psychology, 62,* 245–260.

Hutt, M. L. (1985). *The Hunt Adaptation of the Bender-Gestalt Test* (4th ed.). New York: Grune & Stratton,

Jack, L. M. (1934). An experimental study of ascendant behavior in preschool children. *University of Iowa Studies on Child Welfare, 9*(3).

Jackson, D. N. (1975). The relative validity of scales prepared by naive item writers and those prepared by empirical methods of personality scale construction. *Educational and Psychological Measurement, 35,* 361–370.

Jaeger, R. M. (1973). The national test-equating study in reading (The Anchor Test Study). *Journal of Educational Measurement, 4*(4), 1–8.

Jäger, A. O. (1982). Mehrmodale Klassifikation von Intelligenzleistungen. Experimentelle kontrollierte Weiterentwicklung eines deskriptiven Intelligenzstrukturmodell. *Diagnostica, 28,* 195–226.

Jäger, A. O. (1984). Intelligenzstrukturforschung, konkurrierende Modelle, neue Entwicklungen, Perspektiven. *Psychologische Rundschau, 35,* 21–25.

Janis, I. L. (1978). Personality differences in decision making under stress. In K. R. Blankstein et al. (Eds.), *Advances in the study of communication and affect* (Vol. 6). New York: Plenum.

Janis, I. L. (Ed.). (1982). *Counseling on personal decisions: Theory and research on short-term helping relationships.* New Haven: Yale University Press.

Jenkins, W. O. (1947). A review of leadership studies with particular reference to military problems. *Psychological Bulletin, 44,* 54–79.

Jensen, A. R. (1973). *Educability and group differences.* New York: Harper & Row.

Jensen, A. R. (1980). *Bias in mental testing.* New York: Free Press.

Jensen, A. R. (1981). *Straight talk about mental tests.* New York: Free Press.

Jensen, A. R. (1985). The nature of the black-white difference on various psychometric tests: Spearman's hypothesis. [With commentary by P. D. Pardis and others.] *Behavioral and Brain Sciences, 8,* 193–263.

Johnson, E. S., & Baker, R. F. (1972). *Some effects of computerizing an experiment in human problem solving* (Report 105). Chapel Hill: University of North Carolina, L. L. Thurstone Psychometric Laboratory.

Jones, L. V. (1984). White-black achievement differences: The narrowing gap. *American Psychologist, 39,* 1207–1213.

Jones, V. (1946). A comparison of measures of honesty at early adolescence with honesty in adulthood—A follow-up study. *American Psychologist, 1,* 261.

Jöreskog, K. G., & Sörbom, D. (1979). *Advances in factor analysis and structural equation models.* Cambridge, MA: Abt Books.

Kamphaus, R., & Reynolds, C. R. (1987). *Clinical and research applications of the K-ABC.* Circle Pines, MN: American Guidance Services.

Kane, J. S., & Lawler, E. E., III. (1978). Methods of peer assessment. *Psychological Bulletin, 85,* 555–586.

Kanfer, R., Ackerman, P. L., & Cudeck, R. (Eds.). (1989). *Abilities, motivation and methodology: The Minnesota symposium on learning and individual differences.* Hillsdale, NJ: Erlbaum.

Kaplan, R. M. (1982). Nader's raid on the testing industry. *American Psychologist, 37,* 15–23.

Kaufman, A. S. (1979). *Intelligent testing with the WISC-R.* New York: Wiley.

Kaufman, A. S., & McLean, J. E. (1987). Joint factor analysis of the K-ABC and WISC-R with normal children. *Journal of School Psychology, 25,* 105–118.

Keith, T. Z., Fehrmann, P. G., Harrison, P. L., & Pottebaum, S. M. (1987). The relation between adaptive behavior and intelligence: Testing alternative explanations. *Journal of School Psychology, 25,* 31–43.

Kelly, E. L., & Fiske, D. W. (1951). *The prediction of performance in clinical psychology.* Ann Arbor: University of Michigan Press.

Kelly, E. L., & Goldberg, L. R. (1959). Correlates of later performance and specialization in psychology. *Psychological Monographs, 73*(12).

Kelly, G. A. (Ed.). (1947). *New methods in applied psychology.* College Park: University of Maryland.

Kelly, G. A. (1955). *The psychology of personal constructs* (2 vols). New York: Norton.

Kelman, H. C. (1967). Human use of human subjects: The problem of deception in social psychological experiments. *Psychological Bulletin, 67,* 1–11.

Kendall, P. C., & Butcher, J. N. (Eds.). (1982). *Handbook of research methods in clinical psychology.* New York: Wiley.

Kiesler, D. N. (1983). The 1982 Interpersonal Circle: A taxonomy for complementarity in human reactions. *Psychological Review, 90,* 185–214.

Kirk, B. A. (1952). Test versus academic performance in malfunctioning students. *Journal of Consulting Psychology, 16,* 213–216.

Klass, E. T. (1978). Psychological effects of immoral actions: The experimental evidence. *Psychological Bulletin, 85,* 756–771.

Klopfer, B., et al. (1970). *Developments in the Rorschach technique* (3 vols.). New York: Harcourt Brace Jovanovich.

Knauft, E. G. (1955). Test validity over a seventeen-year period. *Journal of Applied Psychology, 39,* 382–383.

Kohlberg, L. (Ed.). (1973). *Collected papers on moral development and moral education.* Cambridge, MA: Harvard University Press.

Kohs, S. C. (1923). *Intelligence measurement.* New York: Macmillan.

Koppitz, E. M. (1975). *The Bender Gestalt test for young children* (2d ed.). New York: Grune & Stratton.

Koretzky, M. B., Kohn, M., & Jeger, A. M. (1978). Cross-situational consistency among problem adolescents: An application of the two-factor model. *Journal of Personality and Social Psychology, 36,* 1054–1059.

Kraiger, K., & Ford, J. E. (1985). A meta-analysis of ratee race effects in performance ratings. *Journal of Applied Psychology, 70,* 56–65.

Kraut, A. I. (1975). Prediction of managerial success by peer and training staff ratings. *Journal of Applied Psychology, 60,* 14–19.

Kroonenberg, P. M., & ten Berge, J. M. F. (1987). Cross-validation of the WISC-R factorial structure using three-mode principal components analysis and perfect congruence analysis. *Applied Psychological Measurement, 11,* 195–210.

Kuder, G. F. (1977). *Activity, interests, and occupational choice.* Chicago: Science Research Associates.

Kulik, J. A., Bangert-Drowns, R. L., & Kulik, C.-L. C. (1984). Effectiveness of coaching for aptitude tests. *Psychological Bulletin, 95,* 179–188.

Kunce, J. R., & Reeder, C. W. (1974). SVIB scores and accident proneness. *Measurement and Evaluation in Guidance, 7,* 118–121.

Labov, W. (1970). The logic of nonstandard English. In F. Williams (Ed.), *Language and poverty.* Chicago: Markham.

Lachar, D. (1974). *The MMPI: Clinical assessment and automated interpretation.* Los Angeles: Western Psychological Services.

Lachar, D., & Gdowski, C. (1979). *Actuarial assessment of child and adolescent personality.* Los Angeles: Western Psychological Services.

Lachar, D., Gdowski, C., & Snyder, D. (1984). External validity of the Personality Inventory for Children (PIC) profile and factor scales: Parent, teacher, and classroom ratings. *Journal of Consulting and Clinical Psychology, 52,* 155–164.

Lachar, D., & Wirt, R. D. (1981). A data-based analysis of the psychometric performance of the Personality Inventory for Children (PIC): An alternative to the Achenbach review. *Journal of Personality Assessment, 45,* 614–616.

Lambert, N. M. (1963). *The development and validation of a process for screening emotionally disturbed children in school.* Sacramento: California State Department of Education.

Landfield, A. W., & Leitner, L. M. (Eds.). (1980). *Personal construct psychology: Psychotherapy and personality.* New York: Wiley.

Landis, B., et al. (1974). Bender-Gestalt evaluation of brain dysfunction following open heart surgery. *Journal of Personality Assessment, 38,* 556–562.

Landy, F. J. (in press). *The test validity yearbook: Organizational.* Hillsdale, NJ: Erlbaum.

Landy, F., Zedeck, S., & Cleveland, J. (Eds.). (1983). *Performance measurement and theory.* Hillsdale, NJ: Erlbaum.

Larson, A., & Larson, L. K. (1987). *Employment discrimination.* New York: Matthew Bender.

Lasky, J. J., et al. (1959). Post-hospital adjustment as predicted by psychiatric patients and by their staffs. *Journal of Consulting Psychology, 23, 213–218.*

Latona, J. R., Harmon, L. W., & Hastings, C. N. (1987). Criterion-related validity of the UNIACT with special emphasis on the World of Work Map. *Journal of Vocational Behavior, 30,* 49–60.

Law School Admission Council. (1977). *Reports of LSAC sponsored research: Vol. 3: 1975–1977.* Princeton NJ: Author.

Learning Disabilities: A report to the U.S. Congress. (1987). Prepared by the Interagency Committee on Learning Disabilities. Available from NICHD Office of Research Reporting, P.O. Box 29111, Washington, DC 20040.

Leinhardt, G., & Seewald, A. M. (1981). Overlap: What's tested, what's taught. *Journal of Educational Measurement, 18,* 85–96.

Leler, H. O. (1970). *Mother-child interaction and language performance in young disadvantaged Negro children.* Doctoral dissertation, Standard University, Stanford, CA.

Lerner, B. (1977). *Washington v. Davis:* Quantity, quality and equality in employment testing. In P. Kurland (Ed.), *Supreme Court Review, 1976.* Chicago: University of Chicago Press.

Lerner, B. (1979). Employment discrimination: Adverse impact, validity, equality. In P. B. Kurland & G. Casper (Eds.), *Supreme Court Review, 1979.* Chicago: University of Chicago Press.

Levin, H. M. (1989). Ability testing for job selection: Are the economic claims justified? In B. R. Gifford (Ed.), *Test policy and the politics of opportunity allocation*. Boston: Kluwer Academic Press.

Levine, E., Ash, R. A., & Bennett, N. (1980). Exploratory comparative study of four job analysis methods. *Journal of Applied Psychology, 65*, 524–525.

Levine, G., Preddy, D., & Thorndike, R. L. (1987). Speed of information processing ability and level of cognitive ability. *Personality and Individual Differences, 8*, 599–607.

Lewis, M. (Ed.). (1976). *Origins of intelligence: Infancy and early childhood*. New York: Plenum.

Lewis, M. (1983). *Origins of intelligence: Infancy and early childhood* (2nd ed.). New York: Plenum.

Lidz, C. S. (1987). *Dynamic assessment: An interactional approach to evaluating learning potential*. New York: Guilford.

Lindzey, G., & Byrne, D. (1968). Measurement of social choice and interpersonal attraction. In G. Lindzey & E. Aronson (Eds.), *The handbook of social psychology* (2d ed.). (Vol. 2). Reading, MA: Addison-Wesley.

Linn, R. L. (1978). Single-group validity, differential validity, and differential prediction. *Journal of Applied Psychology, 63*, 507–512.

Linn, R. L. (1982). Admissions testing on trial. *American Psychologist, 37*, 279–291.

Linn, R. L. (1983). Predictive bias as an artifact of selection procedures. In H. Wainer & S. Messick (Eds.), *Principals of modern psychological measurement*. Hillsdale, NJ: Erlbaum.

Linn, R. L. (Ed.). (1989a). *Educational measurement*. New York: American Council on Education Macmillan.

Linn, R. L. (Ed.). (1989b). *Intelligence: Measurement, theory, and public policy*. Urbana: University of Illinois Press.

Linn, R. L., Harnisch, D. L., & Dunbar, S. B. (1981). Validity generalization and situational specificity: An analysis of the prediction of first-year grades in law school. *Applied Psychological Measurement, 5*, 281–289.

Lippmann, W. (1923, January 3). The great confusion. *New Republic, 33*, 145–146.

Lipsett, L., & Wilson, J. W. (1954). Do "suitable" interests and mental ability lead to job satisfaction? *Educational and Psychological Measurement, 14*, 373–380.

Loehlin, J. C., Lindzey, G., & Spuhler, J. N. (1975). *Race differences in intelligence*. San Francisco: Freeman.

Loehlin, J. C., Willerman, L., & Horn, J. M. (1988). Human behavior genetics. *Annual Review of Psychology, 39*, 101–123.

Lofquist, L. H., & Dawis, R. V. (1969). *Adjustment to work*. New York: Appleton.

London, M., & Bray, D. W. (1980). Ethical issues in testing and evaluation for personnel decisions. *American Psychologist, 35*, 890–901.

Lopez, E. C., & Yoshida, R. K. (1987). The efficacy of discrepancy models in identifying learning disabled students: A two strike count? In J. W. Gottlieb

& B. W. Gottlieb (Eds.), *Advances in special education* (Vol. 6). Greenwich, CT: JAI Press.

Lopez, F. M., Jr. (1966). *Evaluating executive decision making.* New York: American Management Association.

Lord, F. M. (1974). Estimation of latent ability and item parameters when there are omitted responses. *Psychometrika, 39,* 247–264.

Lord, F. M. (1980). *Applications of item response theory to practical testing problems.* Hillsdale, NJ: Erlbaum.

Lord, F. M., & Novick, M. R. (1968). *Statistical theories of mental test scores.* Reading, MA: Addison-Wesley.

Loret, P. G., et al. (1974). *Anchor Test Study: Equivalence and norms tables for selected reading achievement tests.* Washington, DC: Government Printing Office, 1974.

Lorr, M., Klett, C. J., & McNair, D. M. (1963). *Syndromes of psychosis.* New York: Pergamon.

Lorr, M., & McNair, D. M. (1965). Expansion of the interpersonal behavior circle. *Journal of Personality and Social Psychology, 2,* 823–830.

Love, K. G. (1981). Comparison of peer assessment methods: Reliability, validity, friendship bias, and user reaction. *Journal of Applied Psychology, 66,* 451–457.

Lowell, F. E. (1941). A study of the variability of IQ's in retest. *Journal of Applied Psychology, 25,* 341–356.

Luborsky, L. (1954). Selecting psychiatric residents: survey of the Topeka research. *Bulletin of the Menninger Clinic, 18,* 252–259.

Lundy, A. (1988). Instructional set and Thematic Apperception Test validity. *Journal of Personality Assessment, 52,* 309–320.

Macfarlane, J. W., Allen, L., & Honzik, M. P. (1954). *A developmental study of the behavior problems of normal children between twenty-one months and fourteen years.* Berkeley: University of California Press.

Madaus, G. F. (Ed.). (1983). *The courts, validity, and minimum competency testing.* Boston: Kluwer-Nijhoff.

Magnusson, D., & Backteman, G. (1978). Longitudinal stability of person characteristics: Intelligence and creativity. *Applied Psychological Measurement, 2,* 481–490.

Magnusson, D., & Endler, N. S. (Eds.). (1977). *Personality at the crossroads: Current issues in interactional psychology.* Hillsdale, NJ: Erlbaum.

Maller, J. B. (1944). Personality tests. In J. McV. Hunt (Ed.), *Personality and the behavior disorders.* New York: Ronald.

Marshalek, B. (1981). Trait and process aspects of vocabulary knowledge and verbal ability. Unpublished doctoral dissertation, Stanford University, Stanford, CA.

Marshalek, B., Lohman, D. F., & Snow, R. E. (1983). The complexity continuum in the radex and hierarchical models of intelligence. *Intelligence, 7,* 107–128.

Marshall, T. W., & Klimoski, R. J. (1986). Estimating the validity of cross-validity estimation. *Journal of Applied Psychology, 71,* 311–317.

Marting, E. (Ed.). (1967). *AMA book of employment forms.* New York: American Management Association.

Maslow, A. P., et al. (Eds.). (1980). *Construct validity in psychological measurement.* Princeton, NJ: Educational Testing Service.

Matarazzo, J. D. (1972). *Wechsler's Measurement and appraisal of adult intelligence* (5th ed.). New York: Oxford University Press.

Matarazzo, J. D. (1986a). Clinical psychological test interpretations by computer: Hardware outpaces software. *Computers in Human Behavior, 1,* 235–253.

Matarazzo, J. D. (1986b). Computerized clinical psychological test interpretations: Unvalidated plus all mean and no sigma. *American Psychologist, 41,* 14–24.

Matarazzo, J. D., & Herman, D. O. (1984). Base rate data for the WAIS-R: Test-retest reliability and VIQ-PIQ differences. *Journal of Clinical Neuropsychology, 6,* 351–366.

McBride, J. R., Corpe, V. A., & Wing, H. (1987). *Equating the Computerized Adaptive Edition of the Differential Ability Tests.* Paper presented at the meeting of the American Psychological Association.

McCall, R. B., Hogarty, P. S., & Hurlburt, N. (1972). Transitions in infant sensorimotor development and the prediction of childhood IQ. *American Psychologist, 27,* 728–748.

McClelland, D. C. (1973). Testing for competence rather than "intelligence." *American Psychologist, 28,* 1–14.

McClelland, D. C. (1979). *Power: The inner experience.* New York: Irvington.

McCormick, E. J. (1979). *Job analysis: Methods and applications.* New York: Amacom.

McCormick, E. J., Denisi, A. S., & Shaw, J. B. (1979). Use of the Position Analysis Questionnaire for establishing the job component validity of tests. *Journal of Applied Psychology, 64,* 51–56.

McCrae, R. R. (1987). Creativity, divergent thinking, and openness to experience. *Journal of Personality and Social Psychology, 52,* 1258–1265.

McCrae, R. R., & Costa, P. T., Jr. (1983). Social desirability scales: More substance than style. *Journal of Consulting and Clinical Psychology, 51,* 882–888.

McCrae, R. R., & Costa, P. T., Jr. (1984). *Emerging lives, enduring dispositions: Personality in adulthood.* Boston: Little, Brown.

McCrae, R. R., & Costa, P. T., Jr. (1987). Validation of the five-factor model of personality across instruments and observers. *Journal of Personality and Social Psychology, 52,* 81–90.

McFall, R. M., & Marston, A. R. (1970). An experimental investigation of behavior rehearsal in assertive training. *Journal of Abnormal Psychology, 76,* 295–303.

McGauch, J. L., Jennings, R. D., & Thomson, C. V. (1962). Effect of distribution of practice on the maze learning of descendants of the Tryon maze bright and maze dull strains. *Psychological Reports, 10,* 147–150.

McGee, M. G. (1979). *Human spatial abilities: Sources of sex differences.* New York: Praeger.

McHenry, J. J., et al. (1987). *Project A validity results: The relationship between predictor and criterion domains.* Paper presented to the meeting of the Society of Industrial-Organizational Psychology.

McReynolds, P. (Ed.). (1971). *Advances in personality assessment* (Vol. 2). Palo Alto, CA: Science and Behavior Books.

McReynolds, P. (Ed.). (1975). *Advances in personality assessment* (Vol. 3). San Francisco: Jossey-Bass.

McReynolds, P. (Ed.). (1977). *Advances in personality assessment* (Vol. 4). San Francisco: Jossey-Bass.

McReynolds, P., & Chelune, G. J. (Eds.). (1984). *Advances in psychological assessment* (Vol. 6). San Francisco: Jossey-Bass.

McReynolds, P., et al. (1976). *Manual for the Impro-I.* Mimeographed. Reno: University of Nevada, Department of Psychology.

Mecham, R. C. (1985, August). *Comparative effectiveness of situational, generalized, and job component validation methods.* Paper presented at the meeting of the American Psychological Association.

Mecham, R. C., Jeanneret, P. R., & McCormick, E. J. (1983). The applicability of job component validity based on the PAQ to the Uniform Guidelines' validation requirements: a reply to Trattner. Unpublished.

Meehl, P. E. (1954). *Clinical versus statistical prediction.* Minneapolis: University of Minnesota Press.

Meehl, P. E. (1978). Theoretical risks and tabular asterisks. Sir Karl, Sir Ronald, and the slow progress of soft psychology. *Journal of Consulting and Clinical Psychology, 46,* 806–834.

Meehl, P. E. (1979). A funny thing happened on the way to the latent entities. *Journal of Personality Assessment, 43,* 564–577.

Meehl, P. E. (1986). Causes and effects of my disturbing little book. *Journal of Personality Assessment, 50,* 370–375.

Meehl, P. E., & Rosen, A. (1955). Antecedent probability and the efficiency of psychometric signs, patterns or cutting scores. *Psychological Bulletin, 52,* 194–216.

Megargee, E. I., & Bohn, M. J., Jr. (1979). *Classifying criminal offenders.* Beverly Hills: Sage.

Megargee, E. I., & Carbonell, J. L. (1985). Predicting prison adjustment with MMPI correctional scales. *Journal of Consulting and Clinical Psychology, 53,* 874–883.

Melnick, D. E. (1988). *Computer-based testing in medical education and evaluation.* Philadelphia: National Board of Medical Examiners.

Melnick, D. E., & Clyman, S. G. (1988). Computer-based simulations in the evaluation of physicians' clinical competence. *Machine-mediated Learning, 2,* 257–269.

Mercer, J. R. (1979). *Technical manual, System of Multicultural Pluralistic Assessment.* New York: Psychological Corporation.

Mercer, J. R., & Lewis, J. E. (1977). *Parent interview manual, System of Multicultural Pluralistic Assessment.* New York: Psychological Corporation.

Messick, S. (Ed.). (1976). *Individuality and learning.* San Francisco: Jossey-Bass.

Messick, S. (1980a). *The effectiveness of coaching for the SAT: Review and reanalysis of research from the fifties to the FTC.* Princeton, NJ: Educational Testing Service, 1980.

Messick, S. (1980b). Test validity and the ethics of assessment. *American Psychologist, 35,* 1012–1027.

Messick, S., & Jungeblut, A. (1981). Time and method in coaching for the SAT. *Psychological Bulletin, 89,* 191–216.

Meyer, H. H. (1987). Predicting supervisory ratings versus promotional progress in test validation studies. *Journal of Applied Psychology, 72,* 696–697.

Mill, J. S. (1977). *Collected works.* (J. M. Robson, Ed.). Toronto: University of Toronto Press. (Original work published 1859.)

Miller, T. L. (Ed.). (1984). Kaufman Ability Battery for Children [Special issue.] *Journal of School Psychology, 18*(3).

Millman, J., Bishop, C. H., & Ebel, R. (1965). An analysis of test-wiseness. *Educational and Psychological Measurement,* 1965, *25,* 707–726.

Mills, C. N., & Melican, G. J. (1988). Estimating and adjusting cutoff scores: Features of selected methods. *Applied Measurement in Education, 1,* 261–275.

Mischel, W. (1965). Predicting the success of Peace Corps volunteers in Nigeria. *Journal of Personality and Social Psychology, 1,* 510–517.

Mischel, W. (1968). *Personality and assessment.* New York: Wiley.

Mischel, W. (1977). On the future of personality measurement. *American Psychologist, 32,* 246–254.

Mischel, W. (1981). *Introduction to personality* (3d ed.). New York: Holt, Rinehart and Winston.

Mischel, W. (1984). Convergences and challenges in the search for consistency. *American Psychologist, 39,* 351–364.

Mischel, W., & Peake, P. (1982). Beyond deja vu in the search for cross-situational consistency. *Psychological Review, 89,* 730–755.

Mitchell, J. V., Jr. (Ed.). (1985). *The ninth mental measurements yearbook.* Lincoln: University of Nebraska.

Moos, R. (1979). *Evaluating educational environments.* San Francisco: Jossey-Bass.

Moos, R. (1987). Person-environment congruence in work, school, and health care settings. *Journal of Vocational Behavior, 31,* 231–247.

Moreland, K. J. (1987). Computer-based test interpretations: Advice to the consumer. *Applied Psychology: An International Review, 36,* 385–399.

Moreland, K. J., & Godfrey, J. O. (1987). A controlled study of The Minnesota

Report: Adult clinical system. *News Network, 1*(1), 1–11. (Available from *NCS*.)

Moriarty, A. E. (1966). *Constancy and IQ change: A clinical view of relationships between tested intelligence and personality.* Springfield, IL: Thomas.

Mosher, D. L. (1970). Optimist and pessimist. *Contemporary Psychology, 15,* 373–374.

Mosier, C. I. (1947). A critical examination of the concepts of face validity. *Educational and Psychological Measurement, 7,* 191–205.

Mossholder, K. W., & Arvey, R. D. (1984). Synthetic validity: A conceptual and comparative review. *Journal of Applied Psychology, 69,* 322–333.

Mosteller, F., & Tukey, J. W. (1977). *Data analysis and regression.* Reading, MA: Addison-Wesley.

Murphy, G., & Likert, R. (1938). *Public opinion and the individual.* New York: Harper & Row.

Murphy, K. R., & Davidshofer, C. O. (1988). *Psychological testing: Principles and applications.* Englewood Cliffs, NJ: Prentice-Hall.

Murray, H. A., et al. (1938). *Explorations in personality.* Cambridge, MA.: Harvard University Press.

Murstein, B. I. (1963). *Theory and research in projective techniques (emphasizing the TAT).* New York: Wiley.

Mussen, P. H., & Naylor, H. K. (1954). The relationships between overt and fantasy aggression. *Journal of Abnormal and Social Psychology, 49,* 235–240.

Naglieri, J. A., & Jensen, A. R. (1987). Comparison of black-white differences on the WISC-R and the K-ABC: Spearman's hypothesis. *Intelligence, 11,* 21–43.

Nanda, H. (1967). *Factor analytic techniques for interbattery comparison and their application to some psychometric problems.* Doctoral dissertation, Stanford University, Stanford, CA.

National Industrial Conference Board. (1942). Employee rating. *Studies in Personnel Policy,* No. 39. New York: Author.

National Retail Merchants Association. (1968). *Appraising retail executive and employee performance.* New York: Author.

Neimeyer, R. A. (1985). *The development of personal construct psychology.* Lincoln: University of Nebraska Press.

Newman, F. B., & Jones, H. E. (1946). The adolescent in social groups. *Applied Psychological Monographs,* No. 9.

Newmark, C. S. (Ed.). (1979). *MMPI: Clinical and research trends.* New York: Praeger, 1979.

Newmark, C. S., et al. (1980). Using discriminant function analysis with clinical, demographic and historical variables to diagnose schizophrenia. *British Journal of Medical Psychology, 53,* 365–373.

Nietzel, M., & Bernstein, D. (1976). Effects of instructionally mediated demand on the behavioral assessment of assertiveness. *Journal of Consulting and Clinical Psychology, 44,* 500.

Nisbett, R. E., & Ross, L. (1980). *Human inference: Strategies and shortcomings of human judgment.* Englewood Cliffs, NJ: Prentice-Hall.

Norton, S. D. (1981). The assessment center process and content validity: A reply to Dreyer and Sackett. *Academy of Management Review, 6,* 561–566.

Oaks, W. W., Scheink, P. A., & Husted, F. L. (1969). Objective evaluation of a method of assessing student performance in a clinical clerkship. *Journal of Medical Education, 44,* 207–213.

Oden, M. H. (1968). The fulfillment of promise: 40-year follow-up of the Terman gifted group. *Genetic Psychology Monographs,* 1968, 77(1), 3–93.

O'Leary, K. D., & Wilson, G. T. (1975). *Behavior therapy: Application and outcome.* Englewood Cliffs, NJ: Prentice-Hall.

Olson, C. A., & Becker, B. E. (1983). A proposed technique for the treatment of restriction of range in selection validation. *Psychological Bulletin, 93,* 137–148.

Olweus, D. (1969). *Prediction of aggression.* Stockholm: Scandinavian Test Corporation.

Olweus, D. (1979). Stability of aggressive reaction patterns in males: a review. *Psychological Bulletin, 86,* 852–875.

Ombredane, A., Robaye, F., & Plumail, H. (1956). Résultats d'une application répétée du matrix-couleur à une population de Noirs Congolais. *Bulletin, Centre d'Études et Recherches Psychotechniques, 6,* 129–147.

Ord, I. G. (1971). *Mental tests for pre-literates.* London: Ginn.

Osgood, C. E., & Luria, Z. (1954). A blind analysis of a case of multiple personality using the Semantic Differential. *Journal of Abnormal and Social Psychology, 49,* 579–591.

Osofsky, J. D. (Ed.). (1979). *Handbook of infant development.* New York: Wiley. 1979.

OSS Assessment Staff. (1948). *Assessment of men.* New York: Holt, Rinehart and Winston.

Osterlund, B. L., & Cheney, K. (1978). A holistic essay-reading composite as criterion for the validity of the Test of Standard Written English. *Measurement and Evaluation in Guidance, 11,* 155–158.

Owen, D. (1985). *None of the above.* Boston: Houghton Mifflin.

Pace, C. R., & Friedlander, J. (1981). *The meaning of response categories: How often is "Occasionally," "Often," and "Very often"?* Paper presented to American Educational Research Association.

Pace, L. A., & Schoenfeldt, L. F. (1977). Legal concerns in the use of weighted applications. *Personnel Psychology, 30,* 159–166.

Palmer, J. O. (1983). *The psychological assessment of children* (2d ed.). New York: Wiley.

Parker, J. C., et al. (1983). Mental status outcomes following carotid endarterectomy: A six-month analysis. *Journal of Clinical Neuropsychology, 5,* 345–353.

Parry, M. E. (1968). Ability of psychologists to estimate validity of personnel tests. *Personnel Psychology, 21,* 139–147. ·

Paunonen, S. V., & Jackson, D. N. (1985). The validity of formal and informal personality assessments. *Journal of Research on Personality, 19*, 331–342.

Peabody, D., & Goldberg, L. R. (in press). Some determinants of factor structures from personality–trait descriptions. *Journal of Personality and Social Psychology.*

Pearlman, K. (1980). Job families: A review and discussion of their implications for personnel selection. *Psychological Bulletin, 87*, 1–28.

Pearlman, K., Schmidt, F. L., & Hunter, J. E. (1980). Validity generalization results for tests used to predict job proficiency and training success in clerical occupations. *Journal of Applied Psychology, 65*, 373–406.

Personnel classification tests. (1946). (*War Department Technical Manual 12–260*). Washington, DC: War Department.

Pervin, L. A., & Lewis, M. (Eds.). (1978). *Perspectives in interactional psychology.* New York: Plenum.

Petersen, N. S., & Novick, M. R. (1976). An evaluation of some models for culture-fair selection. *Journal of Educational Measurement, 13*, 3–29.

Petersen, S. E., Fox, P. T., Posner, M. I., Mintun, M., & Raichle, M. E. (1988). Positron emission tomographic studies of the cortical anatomy of single-word processing. *Nature, 331*, 585–589.

Peterson, D. R. (1968). *The clinical study of social behavior.* New York: Appleton.

Peterson, N. G., Rosse, R. L., & Houston, J. S. (1982). *The job effectiveness prediction system. Technical report No. 4. Validity analysis.* Minneapolis: Personnel Decisions Research Institute.

Phillips, W. M., Phillips, A. M., & Shearn, C. R. (1980). Objective assessment of schizophrenic thought. *Journal of Clinical Psychology, 36*, 79–89.

Piaget, J., & Inhelder, B. (1956). *The child's conception of space.* London: Routledge & Kegan Paul.

Pittluck, P. (1950). *The relation between aggressive fantasy and overt behavior.* Doctoral dissertation, Yale University, New Haven.

Plake, B. S. (Ed.). (1984). *Social and technical issues in testing.* Hillsdale, NJ: Erlbaum.

Plake, B. S., & Witt, J. C. (Eds.). (1986). *The future of testing.* Hillsdale, NJ: Erlbaum.

Porteus, S. D. (1965). *Porteus maze test—fifty years' application.* Palo Alto, CA.: Pacific Books.

Powers, D. E. (1986). Relations of test item characteristics to test preparation/test practice effects: A quantitative summary. *Psychological Bulletin, 100*, 67–77.

Prediger, D. J. (1976). A world-of-work map for career exploration. *Vocational Guidance Quarterly, 24*, 198–208.

Prediger, D. J. (1981a). Getting "ideas" out of the DOT and into vocational guidance. *Vocational Guidance Quarterly, 29*, 293–305.

Prediger, D. J. (1981b). A note on Self-Directed Search validity for females. *Vocational Guidance Quarterly, 30*, 117–129.

Prediger, D. J. (1989). Ability differences across occupations: More than g. *Journal of Vocational Behavior, 34*, 1–27.

Preston, C. E. (1964). Psychological testing with Northwest Coast Alaskan Eskimos. *Genetic Psychology Monographs, 69*, 323–419.

Preston, H. O. (1948). *The development of a procedure for evaluating officers in the United States Air Force:* Pittsburgh: American Institute for Research.

Prestwood, J. S., & Weiss, D. J. (1978). *The effects of knowledge of results and test difficulty on ability test performance and psychological reactions to testing* (Research Report 78-2). Minneapolis: University of Minnesota, Psychometric Research Program.

Psychological Corporation. (1982). The use of separate-sex norms in counseling (*Bulletin from the Test People,* No. 6). [Available from *PC.*]

Pursell, E. D., Dossett, D. L., & Latham, G. P. (1980). Obtaining valid predictors by minimizing rating errors in the criterion. *Personnel Psychology, 33*, 91–96.

Quay, L. C. (1974). Language dialect, age, and intelligence-test performance in disadvantaged black children. *Child Development, 45*, 463–468.

Rabbitt, P. M. A. (1985). Oh g, Dr. Jensen! or, g-ing up cognitive psychology. *Behavioral and Brain Sciences, 8*, 238–239.

Rabin, A. I. (Ed.). (1981). *Assessment with projective techniques: A concise introduction.* New York: Springer.

Raudenbush, S. W. (1984). Magnitude of teacher expectancy effects on pupil IQ as a function of the credibility of expectancy induction: A synthesis of findings from 18 experiments. *Journal of Educational Psychology, 76*, 85–97.

Reid, J. B. (1970). Reliability assessment of observational data: A possible methodological problem. *Child Development, 41*, 1143–1150.

Reilly, R. R., & Chao, G. T. (1982). Validity and fairness of some alternate employee selection procedures. *Personnel Psychology, 35*, 1–67.

Reitan, R. M. (1985). Relationship between measures of brain functions and general intelligence. *Journal of Clinical Psychology, 41*, 245–253.

Resnick, L. B. (Ed.). (1976). *The nature of intelligence.* Hillsdale, NJ: Erlbaum.

Rest, J. (1976). New approaches to the assessment of moral judgment. In T. Lickona (Ed.), *Moral development and behavior.* New York: Holt, Rinehart and Winston.

Reynolds, C. R. (1984). Critical measurement issues in learning diabilities. *Journal of Special Education, 18*, 451–475.

Reynolds, C. R., & Brown, R. T. (Eds.). (1984). *Perspectives on bias in mental testing.* New York: Plenum.

Reynolds, C. R., Chastain, R. L., Kaufman, A. S., & McLean, J. E. (1987). Demographic characteristics and IQ among adults: Analysis of the WAIS-R standardization sample as a function of the stratification variables. *Journal of School Psychology, 25*, 323–342.

Reynolds, C. R., & Gutkin, T. B. (Eds.). (1982). *The handbook of school psychology.* New York: Wiley.

Reynolds, C. R., & Willson, V. L. (Eds.). (1985). *Methodological and statistical advances in the study of individual differences.* New York: Plenum.

Riddle, M., & Roberts, A. H. (1977). Delinquency, delay of gratification, recidivism, and Porteus Maze Tests. *Psychological Bulletin, 84*, 417–425.

Rist, R. C. (1970). Student social class and teacher expectations: The self-fulfilling prophecy in ghetto education. *Harvard Educational Review, 40*, 411–451.

Roadman, H. C. (1964). An industrial use of peer ratings. *Journal of Applied Psychology, 48*, 211–214.

Robertson, G. (1988). *A new Test Purchaser Qualification Form for educational tests: The final product*. Paper presented at the meeting of the American Psychological Association.

Robinson, D. D. (1972). Prediction of clerical turnover in banks by means of a weighted application blank. *Journal of Applied Psychology*, 1972, 56, 282.

Roe, A. (1963). *An adaptive decision structure for educational systems* (Report 63-63). Los Angeles: University of Southern California, Department of Engineering.

Rorschach, H. (1942). *Psychodiagnostics: A diagnostic test based on perception* (2nd ed.) (P. Lemkau & B. Kronenberg, Trans.). Bern: Huber. (First German edition published 1921.)

Rosen, A. (1966). Development of MMPI scales based on a reference group of psychiatric patients. *Psychological Monographs, 70*(8).

Rosenthal, R. (1966). *Experimenter effects in behavioral research*. New York: Appleton.

Roskind, W. L. (1980). *Detroit Edison Co. v. N.L.R.B.*, and the consequences of open testing in industry. *Personnel Psychology, 33*, 3–9.

Royer, F. L., & Weitzel, K. E. (1977). Effect of perceptual cohesiveness on pattern recording in the block design task. *Perception and Psychophysics, 21*, 39–46.

Rubin, D. B., & Stroud, T. W. F. (1977). Comparing high schools with respect to student performance in university. *Journal of Educational Statistics, 2*, 139–155.

Rundquist, E. A. (1966). Item and response characteristics in attitude and personality measurement. *Psychological Bulletin, 66*, 166–177.

Sackett, P. R., Zedeck, S., & Fogli, L. (1988). Relations between measures of typical and maximum job performance. *Journal of Applied Psychology, 73*, 482–486.

Salmon-Cox, L. (1981). Teachers and standardized achievement tests: What's really happening. *Phi Delta Kappan, 62*, 631–634.

Sarason, I. G. (Ed.). (1980). *Test anxiety: Theory, research, and applications*. Hillsdale, N.J.: Erlbaum.

Sarason, S. B., Mandler, G., & Craighill, P. G. (1952). The effect of differential instructions on anxiety and learning. *Journal of Abnormal and Social Psychology, 47*, 561–565.

Sarnacki, R. E. (1979). An examination of test-wiseness in the cognitive test domain. *Review of Educational Research, 49*, 252–279.

Sattler, J. M. (1974). *Assessment of children's intelligence*. Philadelphia: Saunders.

Sattler, J. M. (1981). *Assessment of children's intelligence and special abilities* (2d ed.). Boston: Allyn & Bacon.

Sattler, J. M. (1988). *Assessment of children's intelligence and special abilities* (3d ed.). San Diego: Author.

Sattler, J. M., & Gwynne, J. (1987). White examiners generally do not impede the intelligence test performance of black children. *Journal of Consulting and Clinical Psychology, 50,* 196–208.

Savell, J. M., Twohig, P. T., & Rachford, D. L. (1986). Empirical status of Feuerstein's "Instrumental Enrichment" (FIE) technique as a method of teaching thinking skills. *Review of Educational Research, 56,* 381–409.

Sawyer, R., & Maxey, E. J. (1979). *The validity over time of college freshman grade prediction equations* (Research Report 80). Iowa City: American College Testing Program.

Sawyer, R., & Maxey, E. J. (1982). *The relationship between college freshman class size and other institutional characteristics and the accuracy of freshman grade predictions* (Research Report 82). Iowa City: American College Testing Program.

Scarr, S. (1981). *IQ: Race, social class and individual differences, new studies of old problems.* Hillsdale, NJ: Erlbaum.

Schafer, R. (1954). *Psychoanalytic interpretation in Rorschach testing.* New York: Grune & Stratton,

Schafer, R. (1978). Psychological test responses manifesting the struggle against decompensation. *Journal of Personality Assessment, 42,* 562–571.

Schaie, K. W. (1983). The Seattle longitudinal study: A 21-year old exploration of psychometric intelligence in adulthood. In K. W. Schaie (Ed.), *Longitudinal studies of adult psychological development.* New York: Guilford.

Schalling, D., & Rosén, A.-S. (1968). Porteus maze differences between psychopathic and non-psychopathic criminals. *British Journal of Social and Clinical Psychology, 7,* 224–228.

Schlei, B. L., & Grossman, P. (1983). *Employment discrimination law* (2d ed.). Washington, DC: Bureau of National Affairs.

Schletzer, V. M. (1963). *A study of the predictive effectiveness of the Strong Vocational Interest Blank for job satisfaction.* Doctoral dissertation, University of Minnesota, Minneapolis.

Schletzer, V. M. (1966). SVIB as a predictor of job satisfaction. *Journal of Applied Psychology, 50,* 5–8.

Schmidt, F. L., & Hunter, J. E. (1977). Development of a general solution to the problem of validity generalization. *Journal of Applied Psychology, 62,* 529–540.

Schmidt, F. L., Pearlman, K., & Hunter, J. E. (1980). The validity and fairness of employment and educational tests for Hispanic Americans. *Personnel Psychology, 33,* 705–724.

Schmidt, F. L., Hunter, J. E., & Pearlman, K. (1981). Task differences and validity of aptitude tests in selection: A red herring. *Journal of Applied Psychology, 66,* 166–185.

Schmidt, F. L., Pearlman, K., Hunter, J. E., & Hirsh, H. R. (1985). Forty questions about validity generalization and meta-analysis. [With commentary by P. R. Sackett, M. L. Tenopyr, N. Schmitt, & J. Kehoe.] *Personnel Psychology, 38*, 697–798.

Schmidt, F. L., et al. (1979). The impact of valid selection procedures on workforce productivity. *Journal of Applied Psychology, 64*, 609–626.

Schmitt, N., Gooding, R. Z., Moe, R. A., & Kirsh, M. (1984). Meta-analyses of validity studies published between 1964 and 1982 and the investigation of study characteristics. *Personnel Psychology, 37*, 407–422.

Schneider, B. (1978). Person-situation selection: A review of some ability-situation interaction research. *Personnel Psychology, 31*, 281–297.

Schorr, D., Bower, G. N., & Kiernan, R. (1982). Stimulus variables in the block design task. *Journal of Clinical and Consulting Psychology, 50*, 479–488.

Schrader, W. B., & Pitcher, B. (1969). *Relation of mean and standard deviation of LSAT scores to validity coefficients.* Unpublished report to Law School Admission Council. Princeton, NJ: Educational Testing Service.

Schwartz, P. A., & Krug, R. E. (1972). *Ability testing in developing countries: A handbook of principles and techniques.* Palo Alto, CA: American Institutes for Research.

Scribner, S., & Cole, M. (1973). Cognitive consequences of formal and informal schooling. *Science, 182*, 553–559.

Searle, L. V. (1949). The organization of hereditary maze-brightness and maze-dullness. *Genetic Psychology Monographs, 39*, 279–325.

Sears, P. S., & Barbee, A. H. (1977). Career and life satisfaction among Terman's gifted women. In J. Stanley et al. (Eds.), *The gifted and the creative: Fifty-year perspective.* Baltimore: Johns Hopkins University Press.

Sears, R. R. (1977). Sources of life satisfactions of the Terman gifted men. *American Psychologist, 32*, 119–128.

Seashore, H. G., & Ricks, J. H., Jr. (1950). *Norms must be relevant* (Test Service Bulletin 39). New York: Psychological Corporation.

Selman, R. L., & Lieberman, M. (1975). Moral education in the primary grades: An evaluation of a developmental curriculum. *Journal of Educational Psychology, 67*, 131–142.

Sessions, F. Q. (1955). An analysis of the predictive value of the Pre-Engineering Ability Test. *Journal of Applied Psychology, 39*, 119–122.

Shannon, C., & Weaver, W. (1949). *The mathematical theory of communication.* Urbana: University of Illinois Press.

Shapiro, M. B. (1957). Experimental method in the psychological description of the individual psychiatric patient. *International Journal of Social Psychiatry, 3*, 89–103.

Sharp, D., Cole, M., & Lave, C. (1979). Education and cognitive development: The evidence from experimental research. *Monographs of the Society for Research in Child Development, 44*(1–2).

Sherman, S. W., & Robinson, N. M. (Eds.). (1982). *Ability testing of handicapped people: Dilemma for government, science, and the public.* Washington, DC: National Academy Press.

Shneidman, E. S. (Ed.). (1951). *Thematic test analysis.* New York: Grune & Stratton.

Shweder, R. A., & d'Andrade, R. G. (1979). Accurate reflection or systematic distortion? A reply to Block, Weiss, and Thorne. *Journal of Personality and Social Psychology, 37,* 1075–1084.

Silverman, A. J., et al. (1957). Prediction of physiological stress tolerance from projective tests. *Journal of Projective Techniques, 21,* 189–193.

Sizemore, C. C. (1989). *A mind of my own.* New York: Morrow.

Skaggs, G., & Lissitz, R. W. (1986). Test equating: Recent issues and a review of recent research. *Review of Educational Research, 56,* 495–529.

Skolnick, A. (1966). Motivational imagery and behavior. *Journal of Consulting Psychology, 30,* 463–478.

Slack, W. V., & Porter, D. (1980). The Scholastic Aptitude Test: A critical appraisal. *Harvard Educational Review, 50,* 154–175.

Slovic, P., & Lichtenstein, S. (1971). Comparison of Bayesian and regression approaches to the study of information processing in judgment. *Organizational Behavior and Human Performance, 6,* 649–744.

Smedslund, J. (1961). The acquisition of conservation of substance and weight in children. *Scandinavian Journal of Psychology, 2,* 1–10, 71–84, 85–87, 153–160, 203–210.

Smith, E. R., & Tyler, R. W. (1942). *Appraising and recording student progress.* New York: Harper.

Smith, M. B. (1965). An analysis of two measures of "authoritarianism" among Peace Corps teachers. *Journal of Personality, 33,* 513–535.

Snow, R. E. (1989). Aptitude-treatment interaction as a framework for research on individual differences in learning. In Ackerman, P. L., Sternberg, R. J., & Glaser, R. (Eds.), *Learning and individual differences: Advances in theory and research.* New York: Freeman.

Snow, R. E., Bethell-Fox, C. E., & Seibert, W. F. (1985). *Studies in cine-psychometry.* (Technical report). Stanford, CA: Stanford University, Aptitude Research Project, School of Education.

Snow, R. E., & Farr, M. J. (Eds.). (1987). *Aptitude, learning, and instruction. Vol. 3. Cognitive and affective processes.* Hillsdale, NJ: Erlbaum.

Snow, R. E., Federico, P.-A., & Montague, W. E. (Eds.). (1980). *Aptitude, learning, and instruction.* (2 vols.). Hillsdale, NJ: Erlbaum.

Snow, R. E., Kyllonen, P. C., & Marshalek, B. (1984). The topography of ability and learning correlations. In R. J. Sternberg (Ed.), *Advances in the psychology of human intelligence* (Vol. 2). Hillsdale, NJ: Erlbaum.

Society for Industrial and Organizational Psychology. (1987). *Principles for the validation and use of personnel selection procedures.* College Park, MD: Author.

Sokal, M. M. (Ed.). (1987). *Psychological testing and American society, 1890–1930.* New Brunswick, NJ: Rutgers University Press.

Spielberger, C. D., Anton, W. D., & Bedell, J. (1976). The nature and treatment of test anxiety. In M. Zuckerman & C. D. Spielberger (Eds.), *Emotion and anxiety: New concepts, methods and applications.* Hillsdale, NJ: Erlbaum.

Spielberger, C. D., et al. (1978). Examination stress and test anxiety. In C. D. Spielberger & I. G. Sarason (Eds.), *Stress and anxiety* (Vol. 5). Washington, DC: Hemisphere.

Spitz, H. H. (1986). *The raising of intelligence.* Hillsdale, NJ: Erlbaum.

Spokane, A. R. (Ed.). (1987). Conceptual and methodological issues in person-environment fit research [Special issue.] *Journal of Vocational Behavior, 31*, 217–361.

Staats, A. W., & Burns, G. L. (1981). Intelligence and child development: What intelligence is and how it is learned and functions. *Genetic Psychology Monographs, 104*, 237–301.

Standards, see American Educational Research Association.

Starch, D., & Elliott, E. C. (1912). Reliability of grading high school work in English. *School Review, 20*, 442–457.

Starch, D. & Elliott, E. C. (1913). Reliability of grading high school work in mathematics. *School Review, 21*, 254–259.

Steiner, I. D., & Vannoy, J. S. (1966). Personality correlates of two types of conformity behavior. *Journal of Personality and Social Psychology, 4*, 307–315.

Sternberg, J. (1950). *An analytical study of a selection interview procedure.* Master's thesis. Syracuse University, Syracuse, NY.

Sternberg, R. J. (1977). *Intelligence, information processing, and analogical reasoning.* Hillsdale, NJ: Erlbaum.

Sternberg, R. J. (Ed.). (1982). *Handbook of human intelligence.* New York: Cambridge University Press.

Sternberg, R. J. (Ed.). (1985). *Human abilities: An information-processing approach.* New York: Freeman.

Sternberg, R. J. (Ed.). (1986). *Advances in the psychology of human intelligence* (Vol. 3). Hillsdale, NJ: Erlbaum.

Sternberg, R. J. (Ed.). (1988). *Advances in the psychology of human intelligence* (Vol. 4). Hillsdale, NJ: Erlbaum.

Sternberg, R. J., & Powell, J. S. (1983). The development of intelligence. In P. H. Mussen (Ed.), *Handbook of child psychology, Vol. 3. Cognitive development.* New York: Wiley.

Sternberg, R. J., & Rifkin, B. (1979). The development of analogical reasoning processes. *Journal of Experimental Child Psychology, 27*, 195–232.

Stewart, K. J., & Moely, B. E. (1983). The WISC-R third factor: What does it mean? *Journal of Consulting and Clinical Psychology, 51*, 940-941.

Stockford, L., & Bissell, H. W. (1949). Factors involved in establishing a merit rating scale. *Personnel, 26*, 94–116.

Stricker, L. J. (1984). Test disclosure and retest performance on the SAT. *Applied Psychological Measurement, 8*, 81–87.

Strong, E. K., Jr. (1943). *Vocational interests of men and women.* Stanford, CA: Stanford University Press.

Strong, E. K., Jr. (1955). *Vocational interests 18 years after college.* Minneapolis: University of Minnesota Press.

Stuit, D. B. (Ed.). (1947). *Personnel research and test development in the Bureau of Naval Personnel.* Princeton, NJ: Princeton University Press.

Super, D. E., & Crites, J. O. (1962). *Appraising vocational fitness* (2d ed.). New York: Harper & Row.

Tenopyr, M. L. (1988). Artifactual reliability of forced-choice scales. *Journal of Applied Psychology, 73,* 749–751.

Tenopyr, M. L., & Oeltjen, P. D. (1982). Personnel selection and classification. *Annual Review of Psychology, 33,* 581–618.

Terman, L. M. (1916). *The measurement of intelligence.* Boston: Houghton Mifflin.

Terman, L. M. (1954). The discovery and encouragement of exceptional talent. *American Psychologist, 9,* 221–230.

Terwilliger, J. S. (1960). *Representation of vocational interests on an absolute scale.* Master's thesis, University of Illinois, Urbana, IL.

Thayer, P. W. (1977). Somethings old, somethings new. *Personnel Psychology, 30,* 523–524.

Thigpen, C. H., & Cleckley, H. (1953). A case of multiple personality. *Journal of Abnormal and Social Psychology, 49,* 135–151.

Thigpen, C. H. & Cleckley, H. A. (1957). *The three faces of Eve.* New York: McGraw-Hill.

Thorndike, R. L. (1963). *The concepts of over- and under-achievement.* New York: Columbia University, Teachers College.

Thorndike, R. L. (Ed.). (1971). *Educational measurement.* Washington, DC: American Council on Education.

Thorndike, R. L. (1982). *Applied psychometrics.* Boston: Houghton Mifflin.

Thorndike, R. L., Hagen, E., & Sattler, J. (1986). *The Stanford-Binet Intelligence Scale: Fourth edition, Technical manual.* Chicago: Riverside.

Thornton, G. G., III, & Byham, W. C. (1982). *Assessment centers and managerial performance.* Orlando, FL: Academic Press.

Tittle, C. K., & Zytowski, D. G. (Eds.). (1978). *Sex-fair interest measurement: Research and implications.* Washington, DC: National Institute of Education.

Tolor, A., & Brannigan, G. G. (1980). *Research and clinical applications of the Bender-Gestalt Test.* Springfield, IL: Thomas.

Topman, R. M., & Jansen, T. (1984). "I really can't do it, anyway": The treatment of test anxiety. In H. M. van der Ploeg, R. Schwarzer, & C. D. Spielberger (Eds.), *Advances in test anxiety research* (Vol. 3). Lisse: Swets and Zeitlinger.

Trattner, M. H. (1979). Task analysis in the design of three concurrent validity studies of the Professional and Administrative Career Examination. *Personnel Psychology, 32,* 109–119.

Travers, J. R., & Light, R. L. (1982). *Learning from experience: Evaluating early childhood demonstration programs.* Washington, DC: National Academy Press.

Triandis, H. C., & Berry, J. (1980). *Handbook of cross-cultural psychology. Vol. 2. Methodology.* Boston: Allyn & Bacon.

Trickett, E. J., & Moos, R. H. (1970). Generality and specificity of student reactions in high school classrooms. *Adolescence, 5,* 373–390.

Tryon, G. S. (1980). The measurement and treatment of test anxiety. *Review of Educational Research, 50,* 343–372.

Tryon, R. C. (1940). Genetic differences in learning ability in rats. *Yearbook of the National Society for the Study of Education, 39,* 111–119.

Tryon, R. C. (1957). Reliability and behavior domain validity: Reformulation and historical critique. *Psychological Bulletin, 54,* 229–249.

Tucker, J. A. (1977). Operationalizing the diagnostic-intervention process. In T. Oakland (Ed.), *Psychological and educational assessment of minority children.* New York: Brunner/Mazel.

Tupes, E. C. (1957). Relationships between behavior trait ratings by peers and later officer performance of USAF Officer Candidate School graduates. *(AF-PTRC Research Bulletin 57–125).* Randolph Air Force Base, TX: Air Force Personnel Research and Training Command.

Turkat, I. D. (Ed.). (1985). *Behavioral case formulation.* New York: Plenum.

Tyler, R. W. (1950). *Basic principles of curriculum and instruction.* Chicago: University of Chicago Press.

Undheim, J. O. (1981). On intelligence IV: Toward a restoration of general intelligence. *Scandinavian Journal of Psychology, 22,* 251–266.

United States Employment Service. (1983a). *The dimensionality of the General Aptitude Test Battery (GATB) and the dominance of general factors over specific factors in the prediction of job performance for the U.S. Employment Service* (USES Test Research Report No. 44). Washington, DC: Author.

United States Employment Service. (1983b). *Overview of validity generalization for the U.S. Employment Service* (USES Test Research Report No. 43). Washington, DC: Author.

United States Employment Service. (1983c). *Test validation for 12,000 jobs: An application of job classification and validity generalization analysis to the General Aptitude Test Battery* (USES Test Research Report No. 45). Washington, DC: Author.

Urry, V. W. (1977). Tailored testing: A successful application of latent trait theory. *Journal of Educational Measurement, 14,* 181–196.

Uzgiris, I. C., & Hunt, J. McV. (Eds.). (1987). *Infant performance and experience.* Urbana: University of Illinois Press.

Vale, C. D., Keller, L. S., & Bentz, V. J. (1986). Development and validation of a computerized system for personnel tests. *Personnel Psychology, 39,* 525–542.

Vanderplas, J. H., & Vanderplas, J. M. (1981). Effects of legibility on verbal test performance of older adults. *Perceptual and Motor Skills, 53,* 183–186.

Vernon, P. A. (1983). Recent findings on the nature of *g. Journal of Special Education, 17,* 389–400.

Vernon, P. A. (Ed.). (1987). *Speed of information processing and intelligence.* Norwood, NJ: Ablex.

Vernon, P. E. (1950). The validation of civil service selection board procedures. *Occupational Psychology, 24,* 75–95.

Vernon, P. E. (1965). Ability factors and environmental influences. *American Psychologist, 20,* 723–733.

Vernon, P. E. (1969). *Intelligence and cultural environment.* London: Methuen.

Vernon, P. E. (1979). *Intelligence: Heredity and environment.* San Francisco: Freeman.

Vernon, P. E., & Parry, J. B. (1949). *Personnel selection in the British forces.* London: University of London Press.

Vygotsky, L. S. (1986/1934). Thinking and speech. In L. S. Vygotsky, *Collected works: Problems of general psychology* (Vol. 1), (N. Minick, trans.). New York: Plenum.

Wainer, H. W. (1978). On the sensitivity of regression and regressors. *Psychological Bulletin, 85,* 267–273.

Wainer, H. W. (1986). Five pitfalls encountered while trying to compare states on their SAT scores. *Journal of Educational Measurement, 23,* 69–81.

Wainer, H. W., & Braun, H. (Eds.). (1988). *Test validity.* Hillsdale, NJ: Erlbaum.

Wallach, M. A., & Kogan, N. (1965). *Modes of thinking in young children.* New York: Holt, Rinehart and Winston.

Wallach, M. A., et al. (1962). Contradiction between overt and projective personality indicators as a function of defensiveness. *Psychological Monographs,* 1962, 76(1).

Waller, N. G., & Ben-Porath, Y. S. (1987). Is it time for clinical psychology to embrace the five-factor model of personality? *American Psychologist, 42,* 887–889.

Ward, W. C., Frederiksen, N., & Carlson, S. B. (1980). Construct validity of free-response and machine-scorable forms of a test. *Journal of Educational Measurement, 17,* 11–30.

Webb, E. J., et al. (1981). *Nonreactive measures in the social sciences* (2d ed.). Boston: Houghton Mifflin.

Wechsler, D. (1974). *Manual for the Wechsler Intelligence Scale for Children— Revised.* New York: Psychological Corporation.

Weick, K. E. (1985). Systematic observational methods. In G. Lindzey & E. Aronson (Eds.), *Handbook of social psychology* (3d ed.). (Vol. 1.) New York: Random House.

Weikart, D. P., Bond, J. T., & McNeil, J. (1978). *Ypsilanti preschool project: Preschool years and longitudinal results through fourth grade* (Monograph No. 3.) Ypsilanti, MI: High/Scope Research Foundation.

Weiss, J. (1987). *Truth-in-testing and the Golden Rule principle: Two practical reforms.* Paper presented to the meeting of the National Council on Measurement in Education.

Weisz, J. R., & Yeates, K. O. (1981). Cognitive development in retarded and non-retarded persons. *Psychological Bulletin, 90,* 153–178.

Wepman, J., et al. (1976). Learning disabilities. In N. Hobbs (Ed.), *Issues in the classification of children* (Vol. 1). San Francisco: Jossey-Bass.

Werner, P. D., Rose, T. L., & Yesavage, J. A. (1983). Reliability, accuracy, and decision-making strategy in clinical predictions of imminent dangerousness. *Journal of Consulting and Clinical Psychology, 51,* 815–825.

Wernimont, P. F., & Campbell, J. P. (1968). Signs, samples, and criteria. *Journal of Applied Psychology, 52,* 372–376.

Wesman, A. G. (1952). Faking personality test scores in a simulated employment situation. *Journal of Applied Psychology, 36,* 112–113.

West, S. G. (Ed.). (1983). Personality and prediction: Nomothetic and idiographic approaches [Special issue]. *Journal of Personality, 51,* 275–604.

White, M., & Miller, S. R. (1983). Dyslexia: A term in search of definition. *Journal of Special Education, 17,* 5–10.

Wick, J. W. (1983). Reducing the proportion of chance scores in innercity standardized testing results: Impact on average scores. *American Educational Research Journal, 20,* 461–463.

Widaman, K. F. (1985). Hierarchically nested covariance structure models for multitrait-multimethod data. *Applied Psychological Measurement, 9,* 1–26.

Widaman, K. F., & Carlson, J. S. (1989). Procedural effects on performance on the Hick paradigm: Bias in reaction time and movement time parameters. *Intelligence, 13,* 63–85.

Widom, C. S. (1979). MMPI profiles and the longitudinal prediction of adult social outcome. In C. S. Newmark (Ed.), *MMPI: Clinical and research trends.* New York: Praeger.

Wiener, G. (1957). The effect of distrust on some aspects of intelligence test behavior. *Journal of Consulting Psychology, 21,* 127–130.

Wigdor, A. K., & Garner, W. R. (Eds.). (1982). *Ability testing: Uses, consequences, and controversies* (2 vols.). Washington, DC: National Academy Press.

Wigdor, A. K., & Hartigan, J. A. (Eds.). (1988). *Interim report: Within-group scoring of the General Aptitude Test Battery.* Washington, DC: National Academy Press.

Wiggins, J. S. (1973). *Personality and prediction: Principles of personality assessment.* Reading, MA: Addison-Wesley.

Willemin, L. P., Mellinger, J. J., & Karcher, E. K., Jr. (1958). *Identifying fighters for combat.* Technical Research Report 1112, Personnel Research Branch. Washington, DC: Adjutant-General's Office.

Willerman, L. (1978). *The psychology of individual and group differences.* San Francisco: Freeman.

Willingham, W. W., & Breland, H. M. (1982). *Personal qualities and college admissions.* New York: College Entrance Examination Board.

Willingham, W. W., et al. (1988). *Testing handicapped people.* Boston: Allyn & Bacon.

Wills, T. A. (1978). Perception of clients by professional helpers. *Psychological Bulletin, 85,* 968–1000.

Wilson, D. P. (1951). *My six convicts*. New York: Holt, Rinehart and Winston.

Wilson, J. W., & Carpenter, K. E. (1948). The need for restandardizing altered tests. *American Psychologist, 3*, 172f.

Wilson, R. S. (1983). The Louisville Twin Study: Developmental synchronies in behavior. *Child Development, 54*, 298–316.

Wimsatt, W. C. (1981). Robustness, reliability and overdetermination. In M. B. Brewer & B. E. Collins (Eds.), *Scientific inquiry and the social sciences*. San Francisco: Jossey-Bass.

Winder, C. L., & Wiggins, J. S. (1964). Social reputation and social behavior: A further validation of the peer nomination theory. *Journal of Abnormal and Social Psychology, 68*, 441–448.

Winkler, R. C., & Mathews, T. S. (1967). How employees feel about personality tests. *Personnel Journal, 46*, 490–492.

Wise, L. L., Campbell, J. P., & Peterson, N. G. (1987). *Identifying optimal predictor components and testing for generalizability across jobs and performance composites*. Paper presented to the meeting of the Society of Industrial-Organizational Psychology.

Wissler, C. (1901). *The correlation of mental and physical tests*. New York: Columbia University,

Witkin, H. A., & Goodenough, D. R. (1981). *Cognitive styles: Essence and origins*. Psychological Issues Monograph 51. New York: International Universities Press.

Wober, M. (1972). Culture and the concept of intelligence: A case in Uganda. *Journal of Cross-cultural Psychology, 3*, 327–328.

Wolf, T. H. (1973). *Alfred Binet*. Chicago: University of Chicago Press.

Wolman, B. B. (Ed.). (1985). *Handbook of intelligence: Theories, measurements, and applications*. New York: Wiley.

Wood, R. L. (1979). The relationship of brain damage . . . to quantitative intellectual impairment. In D. J. Oborne et al. (Eds.), *Research in psychology and medicine* (Vol. 1). London: Academic Press.

Woodruffe, C. (1984). The consistency of presented personality: Additional evidence from aggregation. *Journal of Personality, 52*, 307–317.

Wylie, R. C. (1974, 1979). *The self-concept: Theory and research on selected topics* (2 vols.). Lincoln: University of Nebraska Press.

Yeh, J. (1978). *Test use in the schools*. Los Angeles: University of Calfornia, Center for the Study of Evaluation.

Yen, W. M., Green, D. R., & Burket, G. R. (1987). Valid normative information from customized achievement tests. *Educational Measurement: Issues and Practice, 6*(1), 7–13.

Yerkes, R. M. (Ed.). (1921). Psychological examining in the United States Army. *Memoirs of the National Academy of Sciences*, No. 15.

Yoakum, C. S., & Yerkes, R. M. (1920). *Army mental tests*. New York: Holt.

Zubin, J., Eron, L. D., & Schumer, F. (1965). *An experimental approach to projective techniques*. New York: Wiley.

Zuckerman, M. (1976). General and situation-specific traits and states: New approaches to assessment of anxiety and other constructs. In M. Zuckerman & C. D. Spielberger (Eds.), *Emotions and anxiety*. Hillsdale, NJ: Erlbaum.

Zytowski, D. G. (1968). Relationship of equivalent scales on three interest inventories. *Personnel and Guidance Journal, 47,* 44–49.

Zytowski, D. G. (Ed.). (1973). *Contemporary approaches to interest measurement*. Minneapolis: University of Minnesota Press.

Zytowski, D. G. (1974). Predictive validity of the Kuder Preference Record, Form B, over a 25-year span. *Measurement and Evaluation in Guidance, 1,* 122–129.

Zytowski, D. G. (1976). Predictive validity of the Kuder Occupational Interest Survey: A 12- to 19-year follow-up. *Journal of Counseling Psychology, 22,* 221–223.

Zytowski, D. G., & Borgen, F. H. (1983). Assessment. In W. B. Walsh & S. H. Osipow (Eds.), *Handbook of vocational psychology* (Vol. 2). Hillsdale, NJ: Erlbaum.

Glossary

Ordinarily, an important term is omitted from this list if it appears at only one place in the book and is explained there. Also, minor uses of a term are usually omitted from the statement here.

ability What the person can do when striving toward some goal; or, a concept used to explain that result. Includes knowledge, physical strength and coordination, reasoning, sensory acuity, and social skills.

achievement test A measure of knowledge or proficiency. The term is usually applied to an examination on outcomes of school instruction.

actuarial A method of making decisions. A rule based on tabulated experience is applied to new cases to predict likely outcomes. The term implies that psychological judgment does not enter into the prediction.

adaptive testing A procedure in which later questions are chosen in the light of earlier performance. Most often, the later questions are ones the examinee's previous responses indicate will be neither easy nor very difficult for him.

aptitude test A measure intended to predict success in a job, educational program, or other practical activity. Usually, a test of ability.

assessment Broadly, any procedure that measures or describes. Most often refers to integration of several pieces of information, in order to reach a judgment about an individual's mental health or fitness for an assignment. Sometimes, a study of a group or a situation.

attenuation The correlation between scores on two variables is reduced by errors of measurement. This reduction is called attenuation. Formulas to correct for attenuation estimate how closely the measures would agree if errors could be eliminated from one or both of them.

base rate The proportion of cases of a certain type found in a particular population. (Example: the proportion of this clinic's intake who have severe anxiety.)

bias An item can be called unbiased, with respect to groups A and B, if members of the groups matched on the ability the whole test measures are equally likely to pass the item. A selection test can be called unbiased if subsets of A and B having the same test score have, on average, equal criterion scores.

biodata Responses to questions about life history, including interests, hobbies, and work experiences.

choice response Refers to tests that offer fixed response options (multiple-choice, true-false, like-dislike, . . .).

classification Broadly, any decision in which alternative descriptive labels or courses of action are available, and one of them is chosen for the individual. In personnel psychology, the term usually refers to assignment to one of *several* jobs or military specialties.

construct A concept referring to a class of responses (e.g., aggressive) or of situations (e.g., stressful) that enters a theoretical explanation. Sometimes, a more abstract explanatory concept (e.g., ego strength, g).

construct validity The theory surrounding construct C indicates how persons high and low in C are expected to differ in various characteristics or responses. The more of these expectations that are confirmed when score X is used to appraise C, the greater the support for the claim that X measures C. Construct validity is judged from the strength, consistency, and completeness of such evidence.

constructed response Contrasts with *choice response*. Examples of constructed (or "free") response: defining a word, naming a word when given its definition, writing a paragraph, assembling blocks to match a pattern.

content reference See *domain reference*.

content validity Content validity of an ability test is investigated by judging the extent to which the items or situations presented are appropriate to its purpose, suitably balanced over topics or subskills, and free from irrelevant sources of difficulty. The term also applies where an interest inventory or an observation plan is intended to represent an aspect of typical response.

convergence of indicators A finding that two ways of measuring a certain construct give similar results.

correlation A statistic that describes, on a scale from -1.00 to $+1.00$, the strength and direction of the relationship between two sets of scores for the same persons.

criterion A standard against which the success of predictions is judged. When a test is used to predict job performance or other future outcome, observation of outcomes in a set of cases provides a criterion. For a diagnosis, the criterion is usually an independent diagnosis considered to be rather trustworthy but impractical for routine use.

criterion key For a test intended to predict a criterion, this type of key counts items that, in a tryout group, correlated with the criterion.

criterion reference Strictly speaking, an interpretation, based on an experience table, that translates a person's observed score into the probability of his reaching a satisfactory level on a specified criterion measure. (Example: Has a 90 percent chance of passing calculus.) The term is sometimes used loosely as a synonym for *domain reference*.

cross-validation When a scoring key or a prediction formula has been "fitted to" the data of a first sample, a cross-validation examines its success in predicting for an independent sample.

crystallized ability When superior performance depends less on adaptive response than on simple recall or practiced skill, a test may be said to measure a crystallized ability. (Examples: vocabulary, calculation.)

cut score In selection on the basis of a test or composite measure, the score level below which applicants are rejected. In screening for adjustment, the level above (or below) which persons are flagged as at risk.

diagnosis Narrowly, choosing one of a set of labels that best fits an individual's disorder or disability. Broadly, developing an understanding of the individual's difficulties and (insofar as possible) their origins.

divergence of indicators See *multitrait-multimethod*.

divergent thinking Intellectual fluency. Finding a variety of possible solutions to a problem.

domain reference A domain-referenced interpretation translates a score into an estimate of level or amount of ability. (Example: can recognize the meanings of about 500 Spanish words.) The term is applicable also to frequency or strength of typical responses (time spent in social interaction, for example).

dynamic assessment The examinee finding a task troublesome is given hints. Interpretation centers on his ability to profit from such guidance, on this task and similar ones subsequently given without prompting.

dynamic interpretation Explanation of a personality in terms of motives, beliefs, and emotional forces.

error of measurement Scores from independent applications of the same procedure are likely to differ. Such discrepancies are attributed to error of measurement (unless the intent is to measure a transient state).

evaluation, program Collection and interpretation of evidence on the functioning and consequences of a social, therapeutic, or educational service.

experience table A listing based on past cases. Shows the proportion of persons, at each level of test score, who reached one or another standard on the criterion measure. Close synonym: *expectancy table*.

face validity A test has face validity if, to test takers and other nonprofessionals, its tasks or questions *appear* relevant to the intended decision. Contrasts with *content validity;* genuine validation asks penetrating, sophisticated questions about the content.

factor A test score can be described as a weighted sum of reference variables plus error. The reference variables, called factors, may be used as theoretical constructs. The factors of greatest interest are "common" factors that appear in several scores. Usually, a few common factors can sum up most of the information in a large number of scores.

faking Giving a self-description intended to create a particular impression, instead of striving to give an honest report.

fluid ability Ability to analyze an unfamiliar problem mentally and respond successfully. (Expertise that helps only with problems in a particular area is supplementary.)

generalizability Similar to *reliability*. A generalizability analysis identifies how much various influences (e.g., occasion-to-occasion differences) contribute to score variance.

general mental ability When intercorrelations among ability measures are consistently positive, one interpretation is that an underlying general ability contributes to all the performances. Intellectual tasks typically have consistent positive correlations.

guessing, correction for In a multiple-choice test, chance successes enable a person who answers more questions to earn a higher score than others having the same ability. A correction formula offsets this, reducing the count of right answers by a fraction of the count of wrong answers.

homogeneity See *internal consistency.*

homogeneous key Counts up responses that correlate positively with each other. Usually, these responses appear to reflect a common ability or attitude.

interaction The regression of outcome onto predictor P can be calculated for a group whose level on variable V is high, and for a group whose level is low. If the strength or direction of the relation changes from one group to the other, it is said that the outcome depends on the interaction of V and P. A similar statement applies when groups given different treatments are analyzed and the predictor-outcome relationship changes from one treatment to the other.

internal consistency The stronger the intercorrelations among a test's items, the greater its homogeneity. An internal-consistency index ordinarily reflects both homogeneity and test length. Formulas of this type, applied to scores from items, estimate the correlation (reliability coefficient) to be expected if two independent, more or less equivalent forms of a test are applied on the same occasion.

inventory A questionnaire, typically one that presents many questions about each aspect of personality that is under investigation. Directions may ask for a self-description or a description of an acquaintance who is being assessed.

item bank A file of test items classified by content and difficulty level.

item response theory An "item response curve" relates the probability of success on a test item to whatever dimension dominates the corresponding item pool. Item response theory assumes that the curve has a particular shape. This makes it possible to estimate, from a person's responses to several items, his position on the underlying dimension.

job analysis Determination, by observation and interview, of the array of knowledge, skills, attitudes, and other characteristics used in successful performance of a particular job.

maximum performance How well a person can do some type of task when making his best effort. Close synonym: *ability.*

mean The average of a set of scores.

median The middle score in a set of scores; or, a statistical estimate of the point on the score scale that divides a population exactly into halves.

minimum competency The label commonly given to a state-mandated test of basic skills that a student must pass in order to be certified as a high school graduate.

multitrait-multimethod Refers to a type of validation study. At least two methods (such as rating and self-report) are used to measure at least two variables A, B,.... The intercorrelations from a *multitrait-multimethod* matrix. If two measures of A correlate positively, this "convergence" supports the claim that they reflect the same variable. Between same-method measures of distinct traits, a comparatively low correlation is usually desired. Low r_{AB} ("divergence") encourages the attempt to interpret A and B as separate constructs.

norm(s) A report, usually in tabular form, of the distribution of test scores found in some reference group; or, statistics that summarize such a distribution.

normal distribution The hump-shaped frequency distribution approximated in a long series of chance events (for example, each person tosses 100 coins and the number of heads is taken as his score). Most test-score distributions have a shape roughly like the normal distribution.

norm reference An interpretation based on the position of a person's score in the distribution of his own local group or of a broader reference group.

objectivity The less scores are affected by judgment in observing or scoring responses, the greater the objectivity of the procedure. Choice-response tests scored by a fixed key are called "objective" tests.

peer rating A classmate, fellow soldier, or other acquaintance marks a rating scale or inventory to describe the target person. Usually, the average of several such reports is taken as the target's peer rating.

percentile Person P's percentile score tells what percentage of cases in a reference group have scores lower than P's—after allowing for ties. (The simplest allowance is to count half the persons at P's level as "below" him.)

performance test Among ability tests, the term is usually applied to those where the respondent is to execute an appropriate physical action—tracing a maze path, for example. (Wechsler's Performance section, however, includes pictorial tests where the response is verbal.) Among personality measures, the term is applied to observations of response in a standardized situation, usually a situation that arouses strong motives.

profile A chart reporting several scores for a person on presumably comparable scales. Or, a string of scores that could be so charted.

projective technique Any of several methods asking for interpretation of an ambiguous stimulus such as a hazy picture. In supplying a meaning, the person is thought to "project" his own beliefs, concerns, and motives.

psychomotor Refers to abilities that require coordinated adaptation of muscular actions. (Example: aiming at a target that moves irregularly.)

range The highest and lowest scores in a set, or their difference. ("The range is from 8 to 22" or "The range is 14.")

range, restriction of For many reasons, a group of persons being studied may have a smaller spread of scores than the population about which a conclusion is desired. This is particularly a problem in validating an employment test on a sample of workers, already on the job, whose ability range is ordinarily less than that of unscreened applicants. Reducing the range lowers the correlation of predictor with criterion. A correction formula estimates what the correlation would be if the whole population provided data.

raw score The measure of performance that is given directly by the scoring rule for a test, before conversion on the basis of a reference group or a judgmental recoding.

regression The Y-on-X regression line describes the trend of Y scores, on average, with changes in the level of X. There is a corresponding X-on-Y regression equation. Best-fitting straight lines serve for most purposes, but curved lines are fitted at times.

reliability The more reliable a measuring procedure is, the greater the agreement between scores obtained when the procedure is applied twice.

response set or style A person who predominantly gives one type of response to items where he is uncertain has a "set" to give that response. (E.g.: Says

"No"; or, omits.) The set may be a temporary state; if it appears consistently on many occasions, it can be called a "style."

scatter diagram A plot of two variables in which one point stands for the score-pair of each person.

scholastic aptitude A mixture of abilities to comprehend and reason, helpful in learning from academic courses.

screening The procedure, early in a multistage decision process, that rules some persons out of consideration for some opportunity, or that "clears" some persons while flagging for further study those who show indications of maladjustment or other difficulty.

selection A decision in which a candidate for a job or for training is or is not accepted.

self-report Information supplied by the person being assessed, usually in the form of responses to a questionnaire.

sign An observation from which it is inferred that the person has a certain characteristic not yet observed.

spatial Refers to a problem where success depends mostly on imagining how objects or diagrams will appear after rotation, combination, or other transformation.

stability To the extent that individual standings fluctuate, or there is systematic change in standings over time, the scores lack stability. Correlating a test with a later retest gives a kind of reliability coefficient in which true changes are counted as "errors of measurement."

standard deviation (s.d.) The most common statistical description for the spread of a set of measurements. As a rule of thumb, two-thirds of the scores are likely to fall within 1 s.d. of the mean.

standard error of measurement A standard deviation describing how much repeated measures on the same person are expected to vary.

standardization Fixing materials, directions, and scoring rules so that a test can be given in the same way by different examiners. (In some writings, *standardization* refers to establishing norms for a test.)

standard score States how many standard deviations above or below the mean a person's raw score is. May be expressed on various scales. A 50 ± 10 scale locates the mean at 50 and counts 1 s.d. as 10 points.

style When it is possible to perform a kind of task in various ways, a person usually has a preferred style: painstaking, or careless; global, or analytic; expansive, or restrained;. . . . See also *response set*.

test A systematic procedure for observing behavior and describing it on a numerical scale, or in terms of categories.

trait A tendency to act—or to react emotionally—in a certain way (e.g., punctuality, fear of large dogs). In psychology, usually thought of as a matter of degree, not as an all-or-none attribute.

true score The hypothetical score a person would earn if there were no error of measurement. Best visualized as the average of many independent applications of the measuring procedure, during a period in which the characteristic that is of interest does not change.

typical response How, on average, a person reacts to situations of a certain kind. Includes thoughts and feelings, as well as overt acts.

validation Investigation into the soundness of a test interpretation, or of a rule for interpretation. Although a single study can provide some validation, the ideal is a process that accumulates and integrates evidence on appropriateness of content, correlations with external variables, and hypotheses about constructs.

validity generalization The hypothesis that a positive test-criterion relationship established in one job in one firm implies a similar positive relationship for that job in other firms, or in other jobs from the same broad family.

variance The squared standard deviation.

Name Index

Subject Index[1]

Abilities, multiple, 236–239, 272, 390–405, 436
Ability, 38–41. *See also* Clerical abilities; General mental ability
  crystallized, 296–300, 381, 382
  fluid, 296–299, 355, 380
  improvement of, 305, 340–347, 355
Ability grouping. *See* Instruction
Ability to learn, 52, 303–304, 342–343. *See also* Educational success; Instruction; Maze task; Memory
Ability-personality complex, 38, 238, 322–324, 328, 332–333, 346, 388–389, 478–480, 552, 616–617, 622
Absolute zero, 102
Achieve, motivation to, 506–507, 561–563
Achievement tests, 40–41, 171–172, 358–367, 652. *See also* Content validation; Evaluation; Mathematics; Quantitative ability; Reading, tests of
  as administrative controls, 7, 78, 127
  overlap with general ability, 298–300, 402–403
  scores and norms, 118–119, 126–127
Acquiescence, 175, 470, 516–517
Actuarial interpretation, 153, 497, 510–512, 643. *See also* Clinical interpretation versus statistical; Criterion keying; Experience table
Adaptive behavior, 249, 251–253
Adaptive testing, 49, 61–62, 140–141, 213. *See also* Dynamic assessment
Adjustment. *See* Anxiety; Screening, for emotional disorder; Self-esteem
Administering tests, 47–50, 55–95, 329–331, 634
Advanced placement tests, 365–368
Adverse impact, 448. *See also* Fairness

Age changes in ability, 241, 283–284. *See also* Development; Stability
Age scales, 118–119
Aggression, 499, 509, 554–555, 613, 631, 633–634
Air Force. *See* Aviators; Military personnel
Alpha coefficients, 202–205
American Psychological Association, 13–14, 148, 339, 578
Analogies task, 231, 265, 316–317, 337. *See also* Matrix task
Analytic research, 293, 307–308
Anchor test, 135
Antisocial personality. *See* Responsibility (and related) scores
Anxiety
  effect on performance, 79–82, 306, 367, 560–563, 625–626
  measurement of, 80, 530–533, 585
  situational factors, 502, 534, 635
Aptitude, 40, 298–300, 390–405. *See also* Clerical abilities
Arithmetic. *See* Mathematics; Quantitative ability
Army. *See* Military personnel
Assertive behavior, 491–492, 494. *See also* Aggression
Assessment, 32
  behavioral, 53–54, 502, 519, 616
  dynamic, 87–88, 342–347
  integrative, 636–646
  state and national, 5, 78, 362–363
Associations, professional, 13
Attenuation, 213–214, 280, 433
Attentional tests in infancy, 272–273
Attitude measures, evidence from, 29, 501, 517, 559
Auditory abilities, 47, 142–143, 210–211, 236, 332, 382, 442–443

---

use in selection, 463, 510–511. *See also* Screening for emotional disorder
Self-understanding, 26–27, 403–404, 463, 480–482
Semantic differential, 565–567
Sentence completion technique, 94
Sex differences
  in ability scores, 114, 131–133, 300, 450–451
  in interest measurement, 463, 485–486
Sign versus sample, 51–52, 105, 497, 508–512
Situation. *See also* Sampling of behavior
  description of, by participants, 603–605, 611
  as influence on behavior, 42, 53–54, 499–503, 607, 634–636, 647–648
Situational test, 491–492, 523, 637–640
Skewed distribution, 120, 535
Social class. *See* Culture; Disadvantaged children; Home background
Social interactions, observations of, 196, 334, 607, 639–640. *See also* Peer ratings
Sociometric data. *See* Peer ratings
Spatial ability, 382, 392, 396
  processes underlying, 308–311
  relation to educational criteria, 357
  relation to occupational criteria, 397–398
Spearman-Brown formula, 203, 207–208
Special education, 5, 248–249, 348–352. *See also* Retarded persons
Spectrum of general ability tests, 296–298
Speech performance, 75, 404–405
Speed of response, 228, 301–303, 328. *See also* Perception, speed and accuracy
Speeded tests, reliability, 205. *See also* Time limits
Split-half procedure, 203–205
Stability, 198, 621–622. *See also* Age changes in ability
  of general mental ability, 277, 284–288, 402
  of interests, 476–478
  of reputation, 602
  of specialized abilities, 389, 402–404
  of trait measures, 499, 512–513, 531, 533, 535, 542
Standard deviation, 114–115
Standard error, 192–194, 202, 207, 210, 213, 278–279
Standardization of procedure, 9, 11–13, 33–36, 41–43, 66, 329, 491, 499, 614. *See also* Directions; Norms
Standard score, 116–118, 241
Standards for tests and testing, 14–15, 21, 578
  origins and purposes, 148–150, 178–179
  practices recommended, 90–91, 95
Standards of performance, 107–109
Stanine, 118
State of person
  during a test, 79–82, 634
  as object of measurement, 52, 404, 508–509, 533–534, 634–636
Strategy of test taker, 83, 308–311. *See also* Style of test taker
Structure in situations and tasks, 35, 613–614
Style of test taker, 16–18, 305–307, 328, 333, 344–346, 616–617. *See also* Personality; Response sets
Stylistic tests, 623–630
Subtle items, 472, 520
Synthetic validity, 435

Tailored tests. *See* Adaptive testing
Teachers
  judgments by, 88, 99, 229, 353–359, 493, 531, 590, 596–597, 603
  judgments or observations regarding, 88, 158, 518, 591–592, 604–605
  tests given to, 559
Tester
  interaction with test taker, 69–76, 89, 306, 329–330, 332–333, 345, 525
  motives, 74–78
  personal characteristics and qualifications, 18–23
Testing industry, 10–12, 16, 21
Tests. *See* Analogies; Maze; Standardized; etc.; *for particular tests see Appendix B*
  choosing, general principles, 15–20, 145–146, 214–222
  choosing, in personnel selection, 18–20, 411–415
  classification of, 32–44
  criticism and review, 16, 145–148, 217–222, 234–235, 522–526
  definition, 4, 32
  functions, 4, 24–29, 462–463, 488–490
  sources of information on, 16, 147–148
Test User Qualification Working Group, 21
Test-wiseness, 82–83
Thematic test, 623, 631–636
Time limits, 70, 258, 302, 329
Trade and technical work. *See* Occupational choice and success
Trait
  conceptualization, 52–53, 497–510, 564, 584, 621–622
  versus state, 52, 533–534
Trends in ability over time, 118, 130–131, 283, 335
True score, 192–194, 280
Typical response, 37–38
  in criterion situations, 416
  measures of, 41–45, 461–640

Underachievement, 298–299, 349
Unidimensional scaling, 136–143
Uniform Federal Guidelines, 447, 453
U.S. Employment Service, 394–397, 453–455
Universe score, 195
Unusual uses task, 340, 388
Utility, 26–27, 422, 428–431, 479, 511, 557–558, 644

Validation, 150–189, 580–581, 620–622. *See also* Content validation; Construct validation; Criterion-oriented validation; Educational success; Fairness; Occupational choice and success; Screening for emotional disorder
  time considerations, 154–156, 412–413, 415–416, 485
Validity coefficient, 161–167, 213–214, 428–431. *See also* Correlation
Validity generalization, 433–437
Variance, 115. *See also* Factor analysis
  of errors, 192, 193
  sources of, 195–196, 199–201, 608–609
Verbal ability, 281–282, 295, 307, 379, 383. *See also* General mental ability